HAND BOOK
OF
COMMERCIAL INFRMATION
FOR
INDIA

HAND BOOK
OF
COMMERCIAL INFRMATION
FOR
INDIA

C.W.E COTTON

GYAN

Published by

Gyan Publishing House
5, Ansari Road
Daryaganj, New Delhi-110002
Phone: 011-47034999, 9811692060
E-mail: books@gyanbooks.com

Distribution Network
gyanbooks.com
India, USA, Canada, UK, Australia

ISBN: 978-93-7133-781-6 (PB)

First Published, 1937

2nd Impression 2025

Printed at: Gyan Press, Delhi.

HAND BOOK OF COMMERCIAL INFRMATION FOR INDIA

Author C.W.E Cotton

HAND BOOK

OF

COMMERCIAL INFORMATION

FOR

INDIA

THIRD EDITION

Issued with the authority of the Central Government

HAND BOOK

OF

COMMERCIAL INFORMATION

FOR

INDIA

THIRD EDITION

Issued with the authority of the Central Government

PUBLISHED BY THE MANAGER OF PUBLICATIONS, DELHI
PRINTED BY THE MANAGER, GOVERNMENT OF INDIA PRESS, NEW DELHI
1937

List of Agents in India from whom Government of India Publications are available.

(a) PROVINCIAL GOVERNMENT BOOK DEPOTS.

MADRAS:—Superintendent, Government Press, Mount Road, Madras.

BOMBAY:—Superintendent, Government Printing and Stationery, Queen's Road, Bombay.

SIND:—Manager, Sind Government Book Depot and Record Office, Karachi (Sadar).

UNITED PROVINCES:—Superintendent, Government Press, Allahabad.

PUNJAB:—Superintendent, Government Printing, Punjab, Lahore.

CENTRAL PROVINCES:—Superintendent, Government Printing, Central Provinces, Nagpur.

ASSAM:—Superintendent, Assam Secretariat Press, Shillong.

BIHAR:—Superintendent, Government Printing, P. O. Gulzarbagh, Patna.

NORTH-WEST FRONTIER PROVINCE:—Manager, Government Printing and Stationery, Peshawar.

ORISSA:—Press Officer, Secretariat, Cuttack.

PRIVATE BOOK-SELLERS.

Advani Brothers, P. O. Box 100, Cawnpore.
Aero Stores, Karachi.*
Banthiya & Co., Ltd., Station Road, Ajmer.
Bengal Flying Club, Dum Dum Cantt.*
Bhatia Book Depot, Saddar Bazar, Ranikhet.
Bhawnani & Sons, New Delhi.
Book Company, Calcutta.
Booklover's Resort, Taikad, Trivandrum, South India.
Burma Book Club, Ltd., Rangoon.
Butterworth & Co. (India), Ltd., Calcutta.
Careers, Mohini Road, Lahore.
Chatterjee & Co., 3, Bacharam Chatterjee Lane, Calcutta.
Chukervertty, Chatterjee & Co., Ltd., 13, College Square, Calcutta.
Das Gupta & Co., 54/3, College Street, Calcutta.
Delhi and U. P. Flying Club, Ltd., Delhi.*
English Book Depot, Ferozepore.
English Book Depot, Taj Road, Agra.
English Bookstall, Karachi.
Faqir Chand Marwah, Peshawar Cantt.
Fono Book Agency, Simla.
Gautama Brothers & Co., Ltd., Meston Road, Cawnpore.
Higginbothams, Madras.
Hindu Library, 137-F., Balaram De Street, Calcutta.
Hyderabad Book Depot, Chaderghat, Hyderabad (Deccan).
Imperial Book Depot and Press, near Jama Masjid (Machhliwalan), Delhi.
Indian Army Book Depot, Dayalbagh, Agra.
Indian Army Book Depot, Daryaganj, Delhi.
Indian Book Shop, Benares City.
Indian School Supply Depot, Central Avenue, South, P. O. Dharamtala, Calcutta.
Insurance Publicity Co., Ltd., Lahore.
International Book Service, Poona 4.
Jacques & Co., Kamptee Road, Nagpur, Messrs. Neston.
Jaina & Bros., Mori Gate, Delhi and Connaught Place, New Delhi, Messrs. J. M.
Kamala Book Depot, 15, College Square, Calcutta.
Karnataka Publishing House, Bangalore City.
Keale & Co., Karachi.
Kitabistan, 17-A, City Road, Allahabad.
Krishnaswami & Co., Teppakulam P. O., Trichinopoly Fort, Messrs. S.
Lahiri & Co., Calcutta, Messrs. S. K.
Local Self-Govt. Institute, Bombay.
London Book Co. (India), Arbab Road, Peshawar, Murree, Nowshera, Rawalpindi.
London Book House, 17, Rajpur Road, Dehra Dun.
Malik & Sons, Sialkot City.
Messrs. U. P. Malhotra & Co., Post Box No. 94, Lahore.
Minerva Book Shop, Anarkali Street, Lahore.
Modern Book Depot, Bazar Road, Sialkot Cantt.
Modern Book Depot, Napier Road, Jullundur Cantt.
Mohanlal Dossabhai Shah, Rajkot.
Nandkishore & Bros., Chowk, Benares City.
New Book Co., "Kitab Mahal", 192, Hornby Road, Bombay.
Newman & Co., Ltd., Calcutta, Messrs. W.
Oxford Book and Stationery Company, Delhi, Lahore Simla, Meerut and Calcutta.
Parikh & Co., Baroda, Messrs. B.
Pioneer Book Supply Co., 20, Shib Narayan Das Lane, Calcutta and 219, Cloth Market, Delhi.
Popular Book Depot, Grant Road, Bombay.
Punjab Religious Book Society, Lahore.
Raghunath Prasad & Sons, Patna City.
Rama Krishna & Sons, Booksellers, Anarkali, Lahore.
Ram Krishna Bros., Opposite Bishrambag, Poona City.
Ram Narain Lal, Katra, Allahabad.
Ramesh Book Depot and Stationery Mart, Kashmere Gate, Delhi.
Ray & Sons, 43, K. & L. Edwardes Road, Rawalpindi, Murree and Peshawar, Messrs. J.
Roy Chowdhury & Co., 72, Harrison Road, Calcutta, Messrs. N. M.
Saraswati, Book Depot, 25, Lady Hardinge Road, New Delhi.
Sarcar & Sons, 15, College Square, Calcutta, Messrs M. C.
Sarkar & Co., Ltd., 18, Shama Charan De Street, and 6, Hastings Street, Calcutta Messrs. P. C.
Sharada Mandir Ltd., Nai Sarak, Delhi.
Standard Bookstall, Karachi.
Standard Bookstall, Quetta.
Standard Book Depot, Lahore, Dalhousie and Delhi.
Standard Law Book Society, 69, Harrison Road, Calcutta.
Tara & Sons, Razmak, (India), Messrs. B. S.
Taraporevala Sons & Co., Bombay, Messrs. D. B.
Thacker & Co., Ltd., Bombay.
Thacker, Spink & Co., Ltd., Calcutta and Simla.
Tripathi & Co., Booksellers, Princes Street, Kalbadevi Road, Bombay, Messrs. N. M.
University Book Agency, Kacheri Road, Lahore.
Upper India Publishing House, Ltd., Literature Palace, Ammuddaula Park, Lucknow.
Varadachary & Co., Madras, Messrs. P.
Venkatasubban, A., Law Bookseller, Vellore.
Wheeler & Co., Allahabad, Calcutta and Bombay Messrs. A. H.
Young Man & Co., (Regd.), Egerton Road, Delhi.

* Agent for publications on Aviation only.

CONTENTS.

PART I.

PART II.

PART III

PART IV.

PART IV—*contd.*

B. Provincial and Local—

PART IV—*concld.*

B. Provincial and Local—*contd.*

PART V

Principal Ports and Trade Centres

PART V—*contd.*

Principal Ports and Trade Centres—*contd.*

PART VI

PART VII

PART VIII

PART VIII—*contd.*

Principal Exports—*contd.*

PART VIII—*concld.*

PART IX

APPENDICES.

PREFACE TO THE FIRST EDITION.

The object of this Handbook is to give readers in other parts of the world a bird's-eye view of the foreign trade of British India. The undertaking was suggested by Mr. Chadwick, Indian Trade Commissioner in London, who pointed out that though Sir George Watt's Dictionary of the Economic Products of India and the abridgment of that work entitled "The Commercial Products of India' furnish much valuable information, they are not compiled on lines directly helpful to business men and omit many details which foreign traders want to know. A handbook with many of the features suggested by Mr. Chadwick, but dealing with the trade of the Madras Presidency only, which appeared in 1916, and the consular report compiled by Mr. Baker, American Consul at Bombay, and published in Washington in 1915, contain much of the necessary material, but as the latter was written chiefly with the object of interesting American exporters in India's import trade, the information to be found in it regarding exports is generally not sufficiently detailed. From the point of view from which the present book is written the import trade is of secondary importance, and general economic conditions and the difficulties of currency and finance which have hampered commercial development in India from time to time have only been briefly alluded to. In the case of every article of present or potential importance figuring in the statistics of exports, however, an attempt has been made to specify the areas in which it is obtainable, the port or ports from which it is shipped, the method of marketing and the unit of sale and shipment. India is so vast and so remote that there is no doubt that on the Continent and in America, if not in the United Kingdom, abundant ignorance prevails with regard to the commercial geography of the country and her trade potentialities. The earlier chapters in the Handbook deal with the principal ports and the facilities for trade at each, while the chief commercial organisations are enumerated and their activities described. Elsewhere will be found a conspectus of the various weights and measures in use in the chief trade centres, while the appendices contain the tonnage schedules in force at the five principal ports and a glossary of the vernacular terms which occur in the book. It is hoped that this varied material will enable all who are anxious to purchase India's manufactures or raw materials to make larger use of the opportunities which undoubtedly exist for increased trade.

I take this opportunity of expressing my grateful acknowledgments to the numerous friends, official and non-official, who have scrutinised my draft articles and assisted me with material. Among the numerous books consulted in addition to those referred to earlier in this preface, the 'Quinquennial Review of Mineral Production in India' (1909-1913) and the 'Munitions Board Handbook' (1919) have been found particularly helpful. My clerk, M. A. Krishnan, who has seen the book through the press and is responsible for the statistical tables and the index, deserves special mention.

C. W. E. COTTON.

CALCUTTA :

26th September, 1919

PREFACE TO THE SECOND EDITION.

The opportunity offered for a wider circulation of this Handbook by the British Empire Exhibition at Wembley, coinciding with the practical exhaustion of the first edition, has prompted the Government of India to ask me to prepare a new edition this year. No new features have been introduced, but the statistics have been brought up to date and the letter-press generally revised. My special thanks are due to those who have helped me to make Parts III A, IV, and V more complete, and to the Commercial Intelligence Department which recruited and supervised the work of the tabulating staff, who have worked hard and well.

C. W. E. COTTON.

MADRAS STATES AGENCY:
Trivandrum, April, 1924.

PREFACE TO THE THIRD EDITION.

The book was last revised by the late Mr. Cotton in 1924. It was felt that on account of the many changes which had since taken place in the course of trade and commerce of India the publication had lost much of its value as a book of reference. The Government of India, therefore, decided to have a new edition prepared and the work was entrusted to me in May 1935. No radical alterations in the general structure of the book have been attempted. The only new features which have been introduced are the addition of a bibliography, the indication in the map of India of the names of some of the ports which have lately come into prominence and a somewhat greater elaboration of the details in certain chapters of the Handbook, *e.g.*, tea, rubber, etc. The tables have been abridged to show figures under each head for the pre-war, post-war and the last four years and the information given in the letter-press has been brought up to date. My thanks are due to the Heads of Departments and the Collectors of Customs who so readily responded to my requests for information. The staff worked with enthusiasm.

R. R. SAKSENA.

NEW DELHI:

November 15, 1936.

NOTE.—In this volume all the sterling figures prior to 1st April 1927 have been calculated on the basis of 1 Rupee = 1s. 4d. and the later figures on the basis of 1 Rupee = 1s. 6d.

HANDBOOK

OF

COMMERCIAL INFORMATION

PART I

INTRODUCTORY.

India is the largest of the three peninsulas which mark the sourthern configuration of the continent of Asia This peninsula falls into four well marked divisions. Firstly, the Himalayan range which forms a great natural frontier including the valley of Kashmir and the kingdom of Nepal with Bhutan abutting on the great table-land of Tibet Secondly, the Indo-Gangetic plain lying between the mountain range to the north and a line drawn from Karachi to Delhi and Delhi to Calcutta. South again of this line is the peninsula proper with an elevated plateau in the centre buttressed towards its sourthern extremities by two ranges of hills known respectively as the Eastern and Western ghats, the former being much more distinctive and considerable The fourth division Burma, which properly belongs to the Malayan peninsula, lies to the east.

Area.

The total area of the Indian Empire is 1,808,679 sq miles, with a population (according to the Census of 1931) of 352 837,778 people It is perhaps not generally appreciated what a large portion of this is not directly under British administration. The area of British India is 1,096,171 sq. miles, with a population of 272 millions, while the Indian States comprise 712,508 sq miles, with a population of 81 millions.

British India.

The territory under the control of the Governor-General in Council is divided into ten major provinces and five lesser charges, each with its separate Local Government or Administration. The Local Governments are the three presidencies of Madras, Bombay and Bengal, the United Provinces of Agra and Oudh, the Punjab, Burma, Bihar and Orissa, the Central Provinces, Assam, and North West Frontier Province. The minor administrations include Delhi, British Baluchistan, Coorg, Ajmer-Merwara, and the Andaman Islands. The following statement shows the administrative divisions of British India, and the present form of Government.

TABLE NO. 1.—*The administrative divisions of British India with their area and population.*

Divisions.	Form of Government.	Head-quarters.	Hill Station.	Area (sq. miles)	Population (1931 Census.)
Presidencies—					
Madras . .	Governor-in-Council.	Madras .	Ootacamund	142,277	46,740,107
*Bombay .	,,	Bombay	Mahableshwar. Poona.	123,679	21,930,601
Bengal . .	,,	Calcutta	Darjeeling.	77,521	50,114,002
Provinces—					
United Provinces.	,,	Allahabad. Lucknow	Naini Tal .	106,248	48,408,763
Punjab . .	,,	Lahore	Simla .	99,200	23,580,852
Burma . .	,,	Rangoon.	Maymyo .	233,492	14,667,146
Bihar & Orissa	,,	Patna	Ranchi	83,054	37,677,576
†Central Provinces.	,,	Nagpur	Pachmarhi	99,920	15,507,723
Assam .	,,	Shillong.	Shillong .	55,014	8,622,251
North-West Frontier Province.	,,	Peshawar	Nathiagali	13,518	2,425,076
Administrations—					
Baluchistan .	Agent to the Governor General and Chief Commissioner	Quetta	Quetta .	54,228	463,508
Ajmer-Merwara	Agent to the Governor General Rajputana and Chief Commissioner	Ajmer .	Mount Abu	2,711	560,292
Coorg . .	‡Chief Commissioner	Mercara.	Mercara .	1,593	163,327
Delhi . .	,,	Delhi	Delhi .	573	636,246
Andaman and Nicobar Islands.	,,	Port Blair	Port Blair	3,143	29,463

*Including Sind. †Including Berar ‡Held as a collateral appointment by the Resident in Mysore.

Indian States.

The map shews that, while a considerable portion of the interior is comprised of Indian States, the coast line is held mainly by the Provinces. The Chief exceptions lie on the west coast from the Gulf of Cambay to Cutch and in Travancore and Cochin The Indian States possess few ports of importance, but developments in the port of Cochin (which is partly situated in the Madras Presidency) will make that harbour growingly important, and the port of Bhavnagar for its size deals with a considerable share of the west coast trade. The consequence of lack of ports in Indian States is that the contribution of

Indian States to the volume of exports, though undoubtedly considerable, is almost completely obscured in the statistical tables, as shipment is necessarily effected in most instances from British Indian ports. The premier State of India is Hyderabad, though Kashmir is the largest in area. Other of the most important States from a commercial aspect are Mysore and Travancore in South India, Baroda in Western India, and Gwalior and Indore in Central India. These States all possess considerable economic resources, which are now being developed. Development is also expected owing to mineral resources in the Eastern States bordering on Bihar and Orissa.

The following table shews the principal Indian States with their area and population:—

TABLE No. 2—*The principal Indian States with their area and population.*

Name of the State.	Area.	Population.
	(Sq. miles.)	(1931 Census.)
Kashmir and Jammu	85,885	3,646,243
Hyderabad	82,698	14,436,148
Federated Shan States	57,816	1,506,337
Jodhpur	35,016	2,125,922
Mysore	29,475	6,557,871
Orissa Feudatory States	28,648	4,652,007
Gwalior	26,367	3,523,070
Bikaner	23,317	936,218
Western India States Agency	35,442	3,999,250
Bhutan	18,000	300,000
Jaipur	15,579	2,631,775
Bahawalpur	16,434	984,612
Rewa	13,000	1,587,445
Udaipur	12,694	1,566,910
Indore	9,902	1,325,089
Manipur	8,638	445,606
Baroda	8,164	2,443,007
Travancore	7,625	5,095,973
Cutch	7,616	514,307
Bhopal	6,924	729,955
Patiala	5,942	1,625,520
Kolhapur	3,217	957,137
Alwar	3,158	749,751
Cochin	1,417	1,205,016
Cooch Behar	1,318	590,866
Pudukkottai	1,179	400,694
Rampur	893	464,919
Kapurthala	599	316,757

Since 1858 the Supreme Authority in India is vested in the Crown acting through a Secretary of State assisted by a Council. In 1920 a High Commissioner for India in London was appointed under the provisions of Section 29-A of the Government of India Act, 1919, who discharges functions in England similar to those of the High Commissioner representing the self-governing Dominions except that he exercises no diplomatic functions. The administration of the Government of India is vested in a Governor General who is also Viceroy, assisted by an Executive Council and the Commander-in-Chief who is also a member of the Council. The six Members of the Executive Council hold separate

Administration.

portfolios, the present distribution being Home, Education and Health and Lands, Commerce and Railways, Industries and Labour, Finance, and Law and Legislation. Under the control of the Education, Health and Lands Department are Agriculture and Forests, while railway affairs are controlled by a Railway Board under a Chief Commissioner who has the right of direct access to the Viceroy. Posts and Telegraphs, Civil Aviation, Broadcasting and the Indian Stores Department are among the departments controlled by the Department of Industries and Labour. Under the Finance there is the Central Board of Revenue in charge of Customs, Excise, Income-tax, Opium, Salt and Stamps. The Commander-in-Chief holds charge of the Army Department, Foreign affairs are the special portfolio of the Viceroy. More detailed information of the work of the principal departments which have commercial or quasi-commercial interests is given in Part III.

Under the Government of India Act, 1919, the development of industries has become a provincial transferred subject. The policy to be pursued in the matter of granting assistance to industries, the development of technical and industrial education and to a large extent the research work necessary to establish the value of raw materials, is now determined by the Ministers in charge of the provincial departments of industries The proposal of the Indian Industrial Commission, which sat from 1916 to 1918 under the Chairmanship of Sir Thomas Holland, to create an Imperial Industrial Service has in consequence of these changes not materialized but the constitution permits the Central Government to retain control over industrial subjects when it considers such a course to be necessary

When the new Government of India Act, which has recently been put on the Statute Book, comes into operation, there will be several changes in the character of administration, of which the most noteworthy are the introduction of Provincial Autonomy, the inauguration of a Federation for India, the creation of two more Governor's provinces, *viz* , Sind and Orissa, and the separation of Burma from India It has been arranged, however, between the Governments of India and Burma that there will be no dislocation of trade and commerce consequent on this separation, and the position will come under review at the end of three years. At the centre, with the inauguration of the Federation, Indian States will have the option to associate for the first time with British India in dealing with problems which are the common concern of India as a whole. With the exception of Defence, Foreign affairs and Ecclesiastics, all the subjects will be under the charge of Ministers responsible to the Federal Legislature. In order, however, to ensure the smooth working of the new form of Government, special powers will be vested in the Governors of the provinces and the Governor General to meet emergencies.

PART II

THE INDIAN RAILWAY SYSTEM.

Length of Indian Railway System.

The total length of railways opened in British India and Indian States on 31st March 1934 amounted to 42,953 miles of which 21,132 miles were of the standard gauge (5′ 6″) 17,644 miles of the metre gauge (3′ 3-3/8″) and 4,177 of other gauges (2½′ and 2′). These figures include the West of India Portuguese Railway (51 miles) running for all but two miles of its length in Portuguese territory and the Pondicherry and Peralam-Karaikal lines (22½ miles) which are partly in French India The total mileage under construction or sanctioned for construction on the same date aggregated 462 miles

Government of India's Control.

The Government of India exercises under the Indian Railways Act, 1890, certain general powers in respect of all the railways in India and has a preponderating financial interest in nearly all of them Up to 1922 all railway administrations for which the Government of India has to provide funds had to submit an annual programme to the Railway Board, which prepared a general programme of capital expenditure for the ensuing year for the sanction of the Secretary of State, and the Government of India and made budget provision for the needs of each railway according to the programme finally sanctioned. In the year 1924, the Railway Finances were separated from the General Finances of the Government of India, and in 1926, the powers of the Governor General in Council were greatly enhanced by the Secretary of State for India in Council in railway matters, the most important of these enhanced powers being the power to sanction capital expenditure on New and Open Lines, up to £1,125,000. A very extensive programme of improvements and developments was taken up but it had to be curtailed, though steadily, in later years on account of financial stringency. The funds for capital expenditure on railways were obtainable only at rates of interest substantially higher than those procurable in earlier years. On account of this rise in the rate of interest some projects, either for extension to the railway system or for improvements to the existing system, became unremunerative and had to be abandoned During this period some of the company managed Railways, such as Burma, E. I., G. I P., and Southern Punjab etc., were taken under State-management. The programme which up to 1929-30 was on the basis of five years and later, on the basis of three years, is being prepared annually at present.

The capital expenditure budgetted for during the eleven years ending 1933-34 is tabulated below.

Railway Expenditure.

TABLE No 3.—*Capital expenditure incurred between 1923-24 and 1933-34 for railways (including Provincial lines.)*

Year.	Capital expenditure.
	£
1923-24	13,137,000
1924-25	8,977,067
1925-26	12,832,133
1926-27	18,116,933
1927-28	16,862,925
1928-29	19,018,200
1929-30	22,637,550
1930-31	9,906,525
1931-32	5,017,500
1932-33	53,550
1933-34	1,540,875

Chief Railway Systems.

The diversity of conditions governing the relation of the State to the railways in India is due chiefly to the variations of policy adopted from time to time towards railway construction Broadly speaking, the principal railways fall under three categories—firstly, five railways owned and worked by the State, *viz*, the North Western, the East Bengal, the East Indian, the Great Indian Peninsula and the Burma Railways, secondly, those owned by the State but worked on its behalf by companies enjoying a guarantee of interest from Government, five in number, *viz*, Bombay, Baroda and Central India, Madras and Southern Mahratta, Assam-Bengal, Bengal-Nagpur and South Indian, Railways; and thirdly, lines the property of private companies and worked some by the owning companies and some by the State or by companies working State-owned system, the principal being the Bengal and North-Western and Rohilkund and Kumaon Railway system Besides there are a number of lines which are the property of Indian States or District Boards or constructed under a guarantee of minimum interest given by such Boards Of the total mileage, open on 31st March, 1934, of 42,953 miles, 31,696 miles or about 74 per cent were State-owned, and 19,125 miles, or 45 per cent directly managed by Government

Railway Surpluses.

Under the Separation Convention the railways are required to pay to the General Revenues of the Government of India 1 per cent on the capital at charge of commercial lines (excluding the capital contributed by railway companies and Indian States) at the end of the penultimate financial year plus 1/5th of any surplus profits remaining after payment of this fixed return If any surplus remaining after this payment to general revenues exceeded in any year £2½ millions, one third of the excess over £2½ millions is also required to be paid to the general revenues, and the balance is to be credited to the reserve fund to meet deficits in the years of adversity. Under this Convention, the railways made this payment from current surpluses in the first five years, *i e*, from 1924-25 to 1928-29, in the 6th year partly from the year's surplus and partly from previously accumulated reserves; and in the 7th wholly from the latter source. In the last three years they have been unable to make any contribution.

Though the last 4 years of the decade were years of severe economic depression, the result of working of State-owned railways during the decade may be summarised as a surplus of £15 millions and an accumulated balance in Depreciation Fund of £24 millions or £39 millions in all, of which about £31 5 millions was paid to general revenues. The payment of £31·5 millions made to general revenues during the first seven years of the period under the Separation Convention of 1924, converted the surplus of £15 millions in working to a deficit of £16 5 millions in all. It was ultimately to meet these deficits that temporary loans amounting to over £16·5 millions had to be obtained from the Depreciation Fund from 1931-32 onwards.

TABLE No 4.—*Profits and losses earned by State railways (including Provincial railways) from 1923-24*

Year.	Gross.	Net.	Contribution to General Revenues (Central)
	£	£	£
1923-24	22,406,533	4,308,533	.
1924-25	25,566,667	8,794,933	4,522,800
1925-26	23,522,200	6,203,600	3,660,267
1926-27	23,095,600	5,005,600	4,007,533
1927-28	29,221,100	8,167,575	4,708,725
1928-29	28,134,675	5,873,400	3,923,925
1929-30	25,892,700	3,044,700	4,588,950
1930-31	20,731,425	—3,878,550	4,301,775
1931-32	17,890,275	—6,892,725	
1932-33	17,074,875	—7,662,600	
1933-34	18 568,650	—5,964,825	

The corresponding figures for railways other than State lines were as shown in the table below —

TABLE No 5 —*Profits and losses earned by railways other than State lines from 1923-24 onwards.*

Year.	Gross profit (In thousand.)
	£
1923-24	3,949
1924-25	4,524
1925-26	4,343
1926-27	4,283
1927-28	4,908
1928-29	5,108
1929-30	4,778
1930-31	3,877
1931-32	3,412
1932-33	3,454
1933-34	3,716

The first line opened in India was from Bombay to Kalyan, a distance of 33 miles (one of three experimental railways sanctioned in 1849), but railway construction on an ambitious scale really dates from the acceptance by the Court of Directors of the East India Company of the policy laid down in Lord Dalhousie's famous minute of 1853 advocating the construction by guaranteed companies of a series of trunk lines uniting the various provinces together and connecting the trade centres upcountry with the principal ports By the end of 1859 eight companies with a contemplated mileage of 5,000 and an aggregate guaranteed capital of £52 millions had been floated in England, *viz.*, (i) East Indian, (ii) Great Indian Peninsula, (iii) Madras, now merged partly in the Madras and Southern Mahratta and partly in the South Indian, (iv) Bombay, Baroda and Central

History of Construction.

India, (v) Eastern Bengal, (vi) Calcutta and South Eastern, now merged in the Eastern Bengal Railway, (vii) Scinde Punjab and Delhi, now merged in the North Western and (viii) Great Southern of India (now South Indian) railways.

Each of these companies contracted with the East India Company (or Secretary of State for India) to construct and manage a specified line in return for the provision of land and the guarantee of interest varying, according to the market rate prevailing when the various contracts were made, from 4½ to 5 per cent on the capital outlay Half of any surplus profit earned in any half-year was to be retained by Government to be applied to repay advances made under its guarantee, and while the railways were held on 99-year leases, the State reserved the right to take over any line after 25 or 50 years upon terms calculated to represent the Company's interest therein, against a corresponding right of the latter to surrender and receive payment of its capital at par Very close control was instituted by Government over the management and working of the railways constructed on these terms, which, though of great political and military value, imposed in some cases a considerable burden upon Indian revenues, as the expectations in regard to profits were not in all instances realised owing to heavy initial outlay incurred in the construction of lines on the standard gauge, uneconomical alignment and alteration of routes and more transitory causes such as the Mutiny of 1857 and the Orissa famine of 1865-67 The original policy was modified in 1862 in favour of construction under subsidy but without guarantee and with a minimum of Government interference but this attempt to attract capital was a complete failure, and in 1869 it was decided to raise the capital required for railway construction in India by direct State agency and to make working expenditure a charge on current revenues Simultaneously the right of pre-emption at the end of 25 years was in the case of several of the more important guaranteed lines surrendered by Government in exchange for the absolute right to half the surplus profits in any half-year By the end of 1879 though 6,128 miles had been opened by companies and 2,175 miles by Government at an approximate cost, respectively, of £97,872,000 and £23,695,226 the Famine Commissioners appointed after the great famine of 1877-78 pointed out that construction was still 5,000 miles short of the mileage needed to secure protection of the country from the consequences of the seasonal failure and that the limit put upon the borrowing powers of the Government for railway purposes hampered progress It was consequently decided once more to try and attract private capital under guarantee, and although the contract terms offered under the modified guarantee system were less favourable than previously, several companies were formed which have since contributed materially to the development of the Indian railway system. To this period belongs the application of the same principles to railway construction in Indian States of which the pioneers were Baroda and Hyderabad In dealing with the guaranteed Companies formed before 1869 and with those formed since 1881, it has been the general practice to use in someway or other at the earliest possible date the right reserved by the Government, of terminating the contracts existing with the companies. In some cases the railways were purchased and transferred to State management in conjunction with other lines. In some other cases, the lines were allowed to be worked by companies after being purchased. In the case of South Indian, Bombay, Baroda and Central India, Southern Mahratta, and Bengal Nagpur the original company (or a new company closely related to the old one) has been allowed to function but under more favourable terms to the State. This method was adopted also in regard to the East Indian, and Great Indian Peninsula Railways, but the contracts under which they were being worked having terminated the management of these lines was taken over by the State with effect from the 31st December 1924 and 30th January 1925 respectively Similarly the Burma Railways were taken over on 31st December 1928 The Government has the preponderating financial interest in the lines worked by the two classes of guaranteed companies, those formed before 1869 and retained as working agencies with reduced capital after purchase, and those formed on terms more favourable to the State. After 1880, it has exceedingly wide control over the methods of working, and it has the right of taking possession of the lines at specified terms on repayment at par of the capital of the companies.

Indian States Railways.

The rulers of Indian States have grown more appreciative in recent years of the advantages of the improved railway communications within their territories, and as examples of recent construction, the Mysore-Arsikere and Bangalore-Chik-Ballapur Railways in Mysore State (the latter financed by an Indian Company under a guarantee from the Mysore Darbar), and the Quilon-Trivandrum line in Travancore, which were opened in 1917-18, may be cited Some of these railways *e g.*, the Cochin-Shoranur Railway, have been constructed out of accumulated State balances Following the announcement of the Government of India in December 1923 of their policy in the matter of construction and maintenance of railways in Indian States, great progress has been made by Indian States in respect of providing railway communications within their territories The Kazipet-Balharshah section of H E H the Nizam's State Railway was completely opened for traffic by the end of 1928 and now forms an important link, facilitating communication between the Madras Presidency and the Central Provinces and reducing the distance between Madras and Delhi by 200 miles. Some of the other important lines constructed by or at the cost of Indian States during the last decade are the Hanumangarh-Sadulpur Chord of the Bikaner State Railway, the Shimoga-Arasalu-Anantapuram section of the Mysore State Railway, the Samdari-Bhiumal section of the Jodhpur Railway, the Bidar-Purli section of H E H the Nizam's State Railway, the Fort Abbas-Baghad (Hotwala) section which was financed by the Bahawalpur Durbar and is worked by the North-Western Railway, and the conversion to broad gauge of the Shoranur-Cochin Railway originally built on the metre gauge

The mileage on the 31st March 1934, under the various gauges in Indian States is shown in the subjoined table

TABLE NO. 6.—*Mileage under various gauges in Indian States in March 1934.*

Gauges.	Miles.
5′ 6″	1,495
3′ 3-3/8″	4,221
2′ 6″ } 2′ 0″ }	1,031

The importance of branch and feeder lines as contributory to the growth of traffic in the main lines has been fully recognised. These lines are constructed under an agreement by which the State guarantees a minimum return on the capital or alternatively undertakes that the line shall receive, out of the earnings of the main line from traffic contributed by the branch, such a sum known as a rebate, as will make up the total earnings of the branch company to a specified sum. Further the branch lines also participate in the profits exceeding the guaranteed minimum of the main line. As the Government was unable to furnish the necessary capital, this scheme originated about forty years ago. Under this system and some other special concessions, certain branch lines were constructed, but in 1925 the Government of India, in pursuance of the recommendation of the Acworth Committee decided that the Branch line policy should be abandoned and that endeavour should be made to reduce the number. The financing of the District Board railways is secured by a special cess levied by the District Board throughout the district. The Tanjore District Board constructed a railway on capital raised by a levy of a special cess and in 1917-18 the Salem-Suramangalam line was built by the South Indian Railway with funds provided by the Salem District Board. These railways have since been acquired by the Government—the Tanjore line on 1st April 1928 and the Salem Suramangalam line on 1st April 1929. The Tinnevelly-Tiruchendur Railway financed by the Tinnevelly District Board and sanctioned for construction in 1915 was completed in 1923.

District Board Railways.

The construction and management of State railways was under the control of the Public Works Department of the Government of India until 1905, when, as the result of Mr Robertson's report, a Railway Board consisting of a Chairman and two members and secretariat establishment was created to secure expert consideration of the larger problems of railway administration and finance and a more settled and continuous policy in railway construction. With effect from the 1st April, 1924 the Railway Board has been re-constituted and consists of a Chief Commissioner as President, a Financial Commissioner, and two members. The appointment of Chief Commissioner was sanctioned in November, 1922, and he is solely responsible under the Government of India for arriving at decisions on technical questions and advising the Government on matters of Railway policy. With effect from 1st April 1929, an additional post of Member was created to deal with staff and Labour questions which were increasing in number and complexity. In 1931-32, in view of the decline in traffic earnings and in the number and magnitude of Engineering works, owing to financial stringency, it was decided to keep two posts of Members in abeyance. The Railway Board as at present existing, consists of a Chief Commissioner, a Financial Commissioner and one Member. The appointment of Financial Commissioner was made in April, 1923. The reorganised constitution has been framed on the recommendations of the Chief Commissioner, which were based on the main principles underlying the report of the Railway Committee of 1921 presided over by Sir William Acworth. Briefly these principles are that the Railway

The Railway Board

Department (Railway Board) should be given such independence in carrying out its work as is compatible with its position as a Department of the Government of India, and such freedom in shaping and carrying out railway policy as will enable it to treat the railways of India as a property to be developed on commercial lines In addition to the preparation of the railway programme, the Railway Board decides all general questions of policy and economy and settles disputes between competing interests while its administrative functions include the construction of new lines by State agency, the approval of rates for passengers and goods, the settlement of train services and through traffic arrangements, the control and promotion of the staffs of State railways and general supervision of the expenditure and working of lines in which the Government of India is principally interested The offices of the Railway Board are in Simla from April to October and at Delhi from November to March. The companies working most of the Indian railways are sterling companies with Boards of Directors in London, who communicate with the Railway Board through the Agents of the lines in India On these Boards a representative of the India Office holds a watching brief as Government Director. Under the Government of India Act, 1935, the executive authority of the Federation in respect of the regulation and the construction, maintenance and operation of railways shall be exercised by a Federal Railway Authority. The appointment of the President of this Authority will be made by the Governor-General who is further empowered to appoint not less than three-sevenths of the members of this body Apart from its other functions, the Federal Railway Authority shall maintain and control a "Railway Fund" to which all moneys received for railway purposes shall be credited and out of which all expenditure, whether on revenue or capital account, shall be defrayed The Governor-General may also from time to time appoint a Railway Rates Committee to give advice to the Railway Federal Authority in connection with any disputes between persons using a railway and the Authority as to rates or traffic facilities which the Governor-General may require the Authority to refer to the Committee The Act also provides for the establishment of a Railway Tribunal consisting of a President who will be one of the Judges of the Federal Court and two other persons to be selected by the Governor-General in his discretion being persons with railway administrative or business experience It shall be the duty of the Railway Tribunal to make orders varying or discharging a direction or order of the Railway Federal Authority, orders for the payment of compensation or damages and of costs and orders for the production of documents and the attendance of witnesses as the circumstances of the case may require The Railway Federal Authority, every Federated State and every other person or authority affected by the decision of the Railway Tribunal shall be bound to give effect to the orders of the Tribunal An appeal shall lie to the Federal Court from any decision of the Railway Tribunal on a question of law, but no appeal shall lie from the decision of the Federal Court on any such appeal. The jurisdiction of the judicial courts in India with respect to any matter with respect to which the Railway Tribunal has jurisdiction has been ousted under the Act.

Table No. 7.—*Main Results of working of all Class I Indian Railways treated as one system.*

Particulars.	1923-24	1924-25.	1925-26.	1926-27.	1927-28.	1928-29.	1929-30.	1930-31.	1931-32.	1932-33.	1933-34
Total capital outlay (in millions of £).	464	473	487	505	594	599	617	627	631	638	635
Gross earnings outlay (in millions of £)	70	74	73	72	86	86	84	77	71	70	72
Working expenses (in millions of £) .	44	45	46	45	52	53	55	54	49	48	48
Percentage of working expenses to gross earnings . . .	63 42	60·35	62·66	61·88	61 07	61·98	65·83	70·01	69·08	68·27	66·74
Net earnings (in millions of £) . .	26	29	27	28	33	33	29	23	22	22	24
Percentage of net earnings to total capital outlay . . .	5·49	6·21	5·61	5·47	5·63	5·47	4·66	3·69	3·46	3·48	3·78
Unit mileage of passengers (in millions)	18,688	19,102	19,513	19,603	20,908	21,248	22,194	19,709	17,340	16,891	16,385
Freight ton-mileage of goods (in millions)	18,638	21,064	19,662	20,103	21,620	21,645	21,625	20,146	18,107	16,978	18,460
Average rate (in pies) charged for carrying a ton of goods one mile .	6 06	5·91	6·13	6·05	6 00	6·15	6·11	5·96	6·05	6·25	6·22
Average rate (in pies) charged per passenger per mile—											
First Class . . .	23·2	21·8	20·6	18·9	16·8	16·9	16·1	16·3	17·2	18·2	18·0
Second Class . . .	10·5	9·93	9·45	8·53	7·74	7·84	7·64	7·53	8·22	8·77	8·71
Intermediate Class . . .	5·09	4·92	4·91	4·56	4·25	4·16	4·00	4·08	4·20	4·24	4·20
Third Class	3·44	3·45	3 45	3·33	3·22	3·07	2·99	2·99	3·10	3·18	3·13

In the foregoing table the main results of the working of all Indian railways treated as one system during the eleven years ending 1933-34 are set forth, while in Appendix III will be found the principal railways with mileage open or in course of construction on the 31st March 1934, and the area and trade centres served by them.

India-Ceylon Route.

A new route for traffic between India and Ceylon was opened in 1914 *via* Adam's Bridge, where the extension of the South Indian railway across the island of Rameswaram to Dhanuskodi is connected by a service of turbine steamers with the Ceylon railway terminus at Talaimanaar across a 22-mile strait. The old steamship route from Colombo to Tuticorin has thus, so far as passenger traffic is concerned, been practically superseded.

Gauges

The standard gauge on Indian railways is 5′ 6″, but in 1870, chiefly for reasons of economy, the metre gauge of 3′ 3-3/8″ was adopted provisionally for certain new lines, and has since been a permanent feature of the railway system. An important development in the trunk system has been made by the construction of the Kazipet-Balharshah section of H E. H the Nizam's State Railway, which, as mentioned before, has provided a direct connection from Delhi to Madras, while the completion of the line between Raipur and Vizianagram has brought the Central Provinces into direct touch with the new harbour at Vizagaptam Among existing services, those from Peshawar to Calcutta and from Peshawar to Bombay may be mentioned as of special importance on account of the great length covered by a single run

PART III.

A.—DEPARTMENTS CONNECTED WITH TRADE.

Department of Commercial Intelligence and Statistics.

The Commercial Intelligence Department located at Calcutta was created in 1905 and with it was incorporated the Department of Statistics which ceased to exist as a separate Department since December, 1922. This Department forms a convenient link between the Commercial public and the Government of India and is responsible for the collection and dissemination of commercial information with a view to the promotion of Indian trade, especially on the export side. It answers trade enquiries, effects trade introductions, disseminates information regarding trade openings in other countries to firms in India and circulates information regarding Indian produce and manufactures to merchants abroad who are likely to be interested in such information It advises the Government of India in regard to the fixation of tariff valuations for the purpose of customs duties levied in India. It also publishes a periodically revised Directory of Exporters of Indian Produce and Manufactures, the Indian Customs Tariff, and a weekly Journal styled 'The Indian Trade Journal' which gives publicity to all changes in the Customs tariffs of the United Kingdom and other countries likely to affect Indian interests, Government orders affecting trade, tender notices issued by Government Departments and local bodies, information relating to prices and trade movements and also information of commercial value on various other subjects. The Department is also responsible for the compilation and publication of the Annual Review of Trade and all the statistical volumes issued by the Government of India, covering not only commercial but also judicial, administrative and agricultural subjects. Among the important statistical publications for which the Director General of Commercial Intelligence and Statistics is responsible are (1) Annual Review of the Trade of India, Statement of the Foreign Sea-borne Trade and Navigation of British India, Statistical Abstract for British India, Agricultural Statistics of India, Estimates of Area and Yield of Principal Crops in India, (2) Index Numbers of Indian Prices (Quinquennial), and Wholesale Prices of Certain Staple Articles of Trade at selected Stations in India (quarterly) and (3) Monthly Statistics of the Production of Certain selected Industries of India, Monthly Statistics of Cotton Spinning and Weaving in Indian Mills, Monthly Survey of Business Conditions in India, Monthly Accounts relating to the Sea-borne Trade and Navigation of British India, Accounts relating to the Coasting Trade and Navigation of British da, Kathiawar and Travancore Trade Statistics, Indian Customs Revenue Statement. Trade at Stations Adjacent to Land Frontier Routes. Raw Cotton Trade Statistics, the Monthly Accounts relating to the Inland (Rail and River-borne) Trade of India and the Sea-borne Trade accounts for the calendar years.

A new Section known as the Statistical Research Branch has recently been established under the Director General of Commercial Intelligence and Statistics. The main function of this new Branch is to do research work on economic problems in which the Government of India are interested and to carry out a continuous analysis and interpretation of economic and statistical facts and phenomena for a proper appreciation of the economic situation in the country and this Branch is also responsible for the issue of the Monthly Survey of Business Conditions in the country. As the Statistical Research Branch has been created mainly to advise Government on economic questions, it has been located at the headquarters of the Government of India and the headquarters of the Director General of Commercial Intelligence and Statistics are also now with those of the Government of India. He is assisted by a Deputy Director of Commercial Intelligence and a Deputy Director of Statistics at Calcutta and by a Deputy Director of Statistical Research at the headquarters office.

The Department is, through the medium of the Indian Trade Commissioners in London, Hamburg and Milan, in close touch with the trade developments of interest to India, in the United Kingdom and on the Continent, and it arranges for the collection of representative samples of Indian produce and manufactures for display at the various fairs and exhibitions in the United Kingdom and on the Continent in which the Indian Trade Commissioners participate. Further, by arrangement with the Board of Trade, His Majesty's Trade Commissioners in the Dominions and Colonies and His Majesty's Consular Officers in other parts of the world correspond with the Director General of Commercial Intelligence and Statistics in Indian trade interests, report to him openings for Indian exports and reply to local enquiries for Indian goods and in this way much has been done to stimulate the overseas demand for Indian produce and manufactures Sample consignments are arranged for by the Department when required Steps have also been taken to push Indian trade with Egypt, Palestine, Iraq, Iran and the Far East with the assistance of Consular and other British Officers

Commercial Library.

In the same building, and controlled by the Commerical Intelligence Deaprtment is a Commercial Library and Reading Room which is open daily on working days free of charge, to the public. It contains up-to-date books of reference on technical and scientific subjects, periodicals and reports, official and unofficial. Arrangements have also been made to make the books in the Library, subject to certain exceptions, available on loan throughout India upon deposit of the value as security. The Library contains over 17,000 volumes on different subjects of commercial and industrial interest as well as Indian and Foreign statistical publications and over 350 technical and commercial journals and market reports.

Indian Trade Journal.

The Indian Trade Journal publishes the annual Indian Customs Tariff and as stated above gives publicity to all alterations in the Customs tariffs of the United Kingdom and other countries likely to affect Indian interests. It also publishes notices of tenders called for and contracts placed by Government Departments and other public bodies, crop reports and seasonal crop forecasts, analysis of India's trade statistics, quarterly and annual reports of the Indian Trade Commissioners, annual review of the Sugar industry of India, market reports, prices and trade movements of the staple exports and imports, graphs showing the trend of wholesale prices, index numbers of wholesale prices in Calcutta by groups of articles, trade enquiries for the purpose of securing trade introductions, Government orders, communiqués and other notifications affecting trade.

The Department specialises on overseas trade subjects and welcomes enquiries relating to Indian trade, which should be addressed to the Director General of Commercial Intelligence and Statistics. India, 1, Council House Street, Calcutta.

The Geological Survey Department.

The Geological Survey Department has been in existence for nearly 85 years. It was organised by Dr. Thomas Oldham, who arrived in India for the purpose in 1851. At that time there was only one other geologist on the staff, but in the course of the next 12 years, the total strength of the Department was raised to 12. Thirty years later it was 13, and in 1901, 50 years after it had been founded, that, with the addition of two mining specialists, was still the sanctioned cadre. In 1906 the total staff was increased to 20, and at the end of 1922 the sanctioned cadre was increased to 30, which was actually filled by 1930, when with 6 Class II posts the total strength was 36 In 1932, as a result of retrenchment, the sanctioned cadre was drastically reduced from 30 to 14, and the Class II officers increased from 6 to 10, giving a total strength of 24 in the gazetted rank In 1935 the cadre was increased again to 17, the total actual strength remaining at 24, whilst the total sanctioned strength was increased to 27.

Activities.

The activities of the department are directed mainly to the completion of a geological map of India, and to the collection and dissemination of information regarding the mineral resources of the country. The director gives expert advice with regard to the administration of the rules for the grant of prospecting licenses and mining leases and is consulted on all questions regarding the mineral policy of India; investigations are also carried out on behalf of Provincial Governments, the Army Department, and local bodies, concerning water supply, the location of dam-sites, earthquakes, landslips, hydro-electric sites, road-metal, building materials and other problems; the Department is responsible for the upkeep and administration of the geological section of the Indian Museum; it issues annual statistics of the output of Indian minerals and it furnishes professors and lecturers in geology for various educational institutions in India.

The sanctioned cadre of the Department is at present: 1 Director, 3 Superintendents and 13 Assistant Superintendents. Its headquarters are in Calcutta, but its activities extend to the whole Indian Empire and frequently beyond. The survey parties usually leave for the field in October returning to headquarters for recess in

May. Owing to the large number of applications for advice and assistance both from Government officials and from the general public a small proportion of the staff is retained in Calcutta throughout the year; this includes the Curator of the Museum and Laboratory and the Palaeontologist. Geological specimens are determined free of charge; many hundreds of such determinations, involving numerous qualitative chemical analyses, are made every year. Fire assays and quantitative work are not, as a rule, undertaken for the public, applicants being usually referred either to the Government Test House or to one or other of the numerous professional analysts in India. Information with regard to the mineral resources of the country is given freely, and the greater part of the time of the clerical staff at headquarters is occupied with replies to enquiries of this nature.

Publications.

The Geological Survey of India issues various publications including—

(1) *Records*, which are published at the rate of approximately one volume of four parts per annum. The *Records* contain the Annual Report of the Department, the Annual Review of Mineral Production, and papers dealing with both scientific and economic matters Every fifth year, one volume of the *Records* is devoted to a review of the mineral production of India during the preceding quinquennial period. Volumes LXIX, LXX are in course of publication (1935);

(2) *Memoirs*, which are issued from time to time as material is available; they are chiefly descriptive, and relate to the geology and mineral resources of areas which constitute more or less well-defined stratigraphical or geographical units. They also contain papers in the nature of monographs which are not suitable for publication in the *Records*. Volumes LXVIII and LXIX are now in course of publication (1935).

(3) *Palaeontologia Indica*, published also as material accumulates, and consisting of descriptions of fossils collected during the course of the operations of the Department. Some 50 volumes have been published;

(4) Miscellaneous publications, such as manuals, bibliographies guides, special works, etc., issued from time to time.

Geological galleries.

The geological collections, most of which are housed in the geological section of the Indian Museum comprise some 45,000 specimens of rocks, 14,000 of minerals, and 49,000 of fossils, of which over 16,000 are types. There are four geological galleries in the Museum—

(a) the Mineral gallery containing a large collection of both Indian and foreign minerals, a complete collection of Indian minerals of economic value, and a representative collection of Indian rocks and building stones;

b) Meteorite gallery in which is housed one of the finest collections of meteorites in the world, comprising representatives of 297 stony and 175 iron meteorites.

(c) the Siwalik gallery containing a collection of Tertiary mammals; and

(d) the Palaeontological gallery, in which are invertebrate fossils and Gondwana plants.

The galleries are open to the public free of charge daily from 10 A.M. to 5 P.M. except the first Monday of each month on which they are reserved for Indian ladies, and Friday, on which day a fee of four annas is charged. A member of the staff of the Geological Survey is placed at the disposal of visitors on Mondays and Fridays, with the exception of the first Monday in each month, to act as a guide to the collections. Arrangements are also made for students to have ready access to them.

Library.

The library of the Geological Survey of India is probably the finest scientific library in the East; it contains more than 60,000 volumes, including a very complete set of scientific serials, most of the latter being obtained by exchange of publications with learned societies and other scientific institutions throughout the world. Free access to the library is allowed during office hours, and every facility is given to persons wishing to consult geological literature.

The Department of Mines.

Activities.

The Department of Mines in India came into existence in 1902. It is mainly responsible for the administration of the Indian Mines Act (Act IV of 1923) and the Regulations, Rules and Bye-laws made thereunder. It is also responsible for the administration of the Land Acquisition (Mines) Act (Act XVIII of 1885). Under the Indian Mines Act, 1923, Regulations, Rules and Bye-laws have been made to provide for the safety and effective management of all mines. The Inspectors have powers to call upon mineowners to remedy dangers and to enforce compliance with the provisions of the regulations, rules and bye-laws The cause and circumstances of nearly all the fatal accidents and serious accidents of importance and all complaints of breaches of regulations and rules are investigated Under the Land Acquisition (Mines) Act, the working of which is confined to Bengal and Bihar and Orissa, the officers of the Department act as mining advisers to the Local Government with reference to the support which should be left under railways or to the protective works which should be carried out if such support is not given. For this purpose a surveying staff is employed. In provinces to which the Land Acquisition (Mines) Act does not apply and where the coal under railways is reserved by Government as landlords, the services of the Department are from time to time enlisted.

Staff.

The cadre consists of one Chief Inspector, three Inspectors, one electric Inspector, four Junior Inspectors and two Assistant Inspectors. As more than three quarters of the work refers to the coalfields of Bengal and Bihar and Orissa the headquarters of the Department have been, since 1909, at Dhanbad, in the district of Manbhum, in Bihar and Orissa, on the edge of the Jharia Coalfield. For purposes of administration, British India and Burma are divided into two circles with one of the Inspectors in charge of each. The Inspector in charge of No. 1 Circle, which includes the Jharia Coalfield, is stationed at Dhanbad, and the Inspector in charge of No. 2 Circle, which includes the Raniganj Coalfield, is stationed at Sitarampur in Bengal. The remaining mines in Bihar and Orissa, all the mines in the Punjab, Baluchistan, North-West Frontier Province, Rajputana and the United Provinces are in No. 1 Circle, while those in Assam, Bombay, the Central Provinces, Madras and Burma are in No. 2 Circle. The third Inspector is usually stationed at headquarters. Each Inspector has two junior Inspectors and one Assistant Inspector to assist him.

Statements are prepared annually of figures of output, labour, etc.. from all the mines and an annual report is issued. Lists of mines, both coal and other than coal, being worked, are also prepared and kept up to date by the Department.

Arrangements have been made by the Rewa and Korea Durbars with the Government of India for officers of the Department to inspect mines in these States twice a year.

The department is closely associated with mining education. The Chief Inspector is a member of the Governing Body of the Bengal Engineering College, a member of the Governing Body of the Indian School of Mines, Dhanbad, and President of the Mining Education Advisory Board under which part times mining instruction is given in the coalfields of Bengal and Bihar and Orissa. The two Circle Inspectors are members of this Board and each is the Chairman of sub-Committees on the coalfields. The Chief Inspector is also a member of the Jharia and Asansol Mines Boards of Health and the Jharia Water Board

The Indian School of Mines.

The Indian School of Mines, Dhanbad, was established in 1926 for the purpose of providing facilities for training men for the coal mining industry and for other mineral industries throughout India The situation of the School is near the Jharia Coalfield—the most important in India—and within easy reach of the Raniganj, Giridih and Bokaro coalfields, which, together with the Jharia coalfield, are responsible for about 90 per cent of the output of coal in British India. The School provides high grade instruction in Mining Engineering and Geology. It contains fully equipped laboratories and workshops, and the instruction given is on a plane comparable with that of similar institutions in Great Britain. The following courses are offered.—Three years' Certificate Courses in Coal Mining, in Metalliferous Mining and in Geology; four years' Associateship Courses in Mining Engineering and in Geology. The School is open to students from any part of India and Burma. The standard of education required for admission to the School is a pass in the Intermediate Examination in Arts or Science of an Indian University or its equivalent The School is managed by a Governing Body presided over by the Director, Geological Survey of India, and having about fifteen members representative of mining and educational interests from various parts of India.

The staff consists of a Principal, who is also a senior Professor in Mining, four Professors and two lecturers with a full staff of assistants. Scholarships tenable at the School are awarded annually by the Government of India and by certain Local Governments.

The course at the School commences on the 1st November of every year and terminates on the 31st July of the following year. There is a long vacation of three months during which the students are expected to work in mines or carry out geological field work for a period of about two months. Tuition fees are payable by each student in two equal instalments in November and April as follows.—First and second years, two instalments of Rs. 60; Third and fourth years, two instalments of Rs. 90. A hostel is provided for the accommodation of students attending the School and arrangements have been made for messing, medical attendance, recreation, etc.

The Patent Office.

The law and procedure in India for the protection of inventions and registration of designs closely follows that in the United Kingdom, the only difference of importance being that in the absence of any legal provision for the registration of Trade Marks, India cannot become a party to the International Convention for the protection of industrial property, under which certain rights of priority are obtainable in other countries. The reciprocal arrangement with the United Kingdom and other parts of His Majesty's Dominions affords, however, a partial substitute.

The Patent Office does not undertake to give opinions on the India only (*i e.*, not in Indian States) and patents granted under it are not valid in the United Kingdom or any of the British Possessions; nor does this Act permit the registration of trade and property marks or names.

The officer who administers this Act is designated the Controller of Patents and Designs His office is at 1, Council House Street, Calcutta, and all communications relating to applications for patents and the registration of designs should be addressed to him The Patent Office Handbook contains current regulations governing the grant of patents and also instructions for the guidance of inventors and others and may be purchased at annas eight or ten pence per copy excluding postage.

The Patent Office does not undertake to give opinions on the interpretation of patent law or on the advisability of protecting inventions and designs or on their infringement or to recommend any particular agent or assist in the disposal of inventions. Trade and property marks are not registered.

The Customs Department.

The Customs Department is controlled by the Central Board of Revenue which is attached to the Finance Department of the Government of India. The Collectors of the five principal ports, Calcutta, Bombay, Madras, Rangoon and Karachi, and the Assistant Collectors at these ports and at Chittagong are members of the Imperial Customs Service. Two posts of Collectors are reserved for members of the Indian Civil Service temporarily attached to the Imperial Customs Service and three for members of the Imperial Customs Service proper The subordinate staff of all Custom Houses is appointed locally For customs purposes Aden is not a part of British India.

The minor ports in the Madras Presidency, some of which are of considerable importance, are under the general control of the Collector of Customs, Madras. The littoral is divided into circles each of which is in charge of an Inspector of Customs. In the Madras and Bombay Presidencies the staff of the Customs Department, except at the chief ports, is united with the staff of the Salt Department and the collectors of Customs are also *ex-officio* Collectors of Salt Revenue. The four ports in Sind which are open to foreign trade are under the jurisdiction of the Collector of Customs, Karachi, and the minor ports in Burma are similarly under the jurisdiction of the Collector of Customs, Rangoon. The ports in Orissa, whose foreign trade is negligible, are staffed by provincial officers and controlled by the Government of Bihar and Orissa.

The Customs revenue in India is derived mainly from import duties. The duties levied by the East India Company varied from 3½ per cent. to 5 per cent for British goods, double rates being charged on foreign goods. In 1859 the differential duties were abolished, and the general rate was raised to 10 per cent. It was reduced to 7½ per cent. in 1864 and to 5 per cent. in 1875. General customs duties were abolished in 1882, and from that year till 1894 no import duties were levied except those on arms and ammunition (which were retained for administrative purposes) and on liquors, opium and salt (which were complementary to the excise policy) and a duty of ½ anna per gallon on petroleum which was imposed for revenue purposes in 1888

History of the Indian Tariff.

In 1894 it was considered necessary, owing to the fall in the sterling value of the rupee, to re-impose import duties at a general rate of 5 per cent. Railway materials and machinery were, however, left free, and the duty on iron and steel was fixed at 1 per cent. Later in the same year cotton piece-goods and yarn, which had remained free, were subjected to a duty of 5 per cent. accompanied by an excise duty of 5 per cent on Indian yarn of counts above 20s In 1896 the duty on cotton piece-goods was lowered to 3½ per cent.; an excise duty at the same rate was placed on all Indian mill-woven cloth, cotton yarn being admitted free. In 1910-11, the duty on silver was raised from 5 per cent to 4 annas (4*d*) per ounce and the duties on tobacco, wine and beer were also increased. With these exceptions, the tariff as re-imposed in 1894 remained unaltered until 1916

In 1916 the tariff was completely recast in order to provide additional revenue to meet the financial disturbances set up by the war. The general rate was raised from 5 to 7½ per cent., machinery (except for cotton spinning and weaving) and railway materials were made liable to duty at 2½ per cent., and the duty on iron and steel was raised from 1 to 2½ per cent ; increases were also made in the special duties for salt, liquors, cigars and cigarettes, arms and ammunition and petroleum. The following articles were subjected to special duties, namely, sugar (10 per cent.) silver manufactures (15 per cent.), coal (8 annas per ton) and manufactured tobacco (50 per cent.) The cotton duty and cotton excise remained at 3½ per cent.; but the former was raised to 7½ per cent. in 1917. Books, gold, living animals, raw cotton, raw wool, cotton spinning and weaving machinery, quinine, and certain agricultural instruments continued to be admitted free. In 1917 an import duty on petrol of six annas per gallon with an equivalent excise duty was imposed for the first time.

In 1921 the general rate was raised to 11 per cent., the excise duty on cotton piece-goods remaining at 3½ per cent.; the duties on liquors, sugar and tobacco (other than unmanufactured tobacco) were enhanced; a specific duty (12 annas per gross) was placed on matches; and a special category of articles in the nature of luxuries such as confectionery, motor cars, silk piece-goods and watches was brought into a 20 per cent. schedule. Cotton machinery was brought under the 2½ per cent rate and metallic ores of all sorts were made free.

In 1922 the general rate was raised to 15 per cent. (the duties on cotton goods remaining unchanged); the luxury rate was raised to 30 per cent ; a duty of 5 per cent. was imposed on cotton yarn which had been free since 1896; the duty on iron and steel and railway materials was raised from 2½ to 10 per cent ; and increases were made in the duties on matches, sugar, kerosene and liquors.

The general outline of the tariff remained unchanged until 1931, but, apart from various minor adjustments certain important changes in respect of individual items took place in the intervening period The principal change was the introduction from time to time of special protective duties. Iron and steel were protected in 1924, paper in 1925, matches in 1928 and cotton piece-goods in 1930. Other changes of importance were the imposition of a specific duty on saccharine in 1923; the fixing of uniform import and excise duties on motor spirit in 1925; the substitution of specific duties for *ad valorem* duties on sugar and cigarettes in 1925; the introduction of an intermediate duty on silk mixtures in 1925; the placing of machinery, mill stores and printing and lithographic materials on the free list in 1927; the addition of a two anna tax on motor spirit for the Road Fund in 1929; and the introduction of a duty on silver at 4 annas per ounce in 1930. The excise duty on cotton goods was removed in 1925.

In March 1931 the duties on liquors were enhanced by approximately one third; the duty on sugar, which had been increased in 1930, was further enhanced; and spices and betel-nuts were transferred to the 30 per cent, schedule In addition to this, goods on the 10 per cent. list were subjected to an additional duty of 2½ per cent., those on the 15 per cent. list, to an additional duty of 5 per cent.; and those on the 30 per cent. list, to an additional duty of 10 per cent., with corresponding enhancements of the non-protective special duties. In 1931, also, duties of a protective character were imposed on foreign salt, wheat, heavy chemicals and silver thread and wire. In the autumn of that year a surcharge of 25 per cent. was added to all existing duties.

In 1932, a protective duty was imposed on sugar and wire and wire nails and a specific duty was also imposed for protective purpose on wood pulp which had previously been free.

In January 1933, in order to give effect to the Trade Agreement made at Ottawa in August 1932, preferential duties were introduced in the tariff for certain selected Empire goods, the difference between the standard and the preferential rates of duties being, with a few exceptions, 10 per cent. In 1933 a minimum specific duty was imposed on uppers for boots and shoes not entirely made of leather and minimum specific duties were also imposed on artificial silk goods and artificial silk manufactures for administrative reasons.

In 1933 and 1934, certain minimum specific duties were prescribed for textiles generally and for certain classes of heavy chemicals, paints and colours, earthenware and enamelled ironware, and the tariff entries relating to all these articles were reclassified. A Trade Agreement was also made with Japan under which the extent of imports of cotton piece-goods from that country into India has been fixed on the basis of the amount of raw cotton imported by her from India. Other changes made in the Tariff were the introduction of a uniform duty on cigarettes, the enhancement of the duty on unmanufactured tobacco and the reduction of the duty on silver to five annas per ounce which has since been further reduced to annas 2 per ounce. In 1935 a protective duty of 12 annas per maund was imposed on imported broken rice.

Export Duties and Cesses.

Until 1860 there was a general export duty of 3 per cent *ad valorem*, but by 1875 it was only applicable to oil, rice, indigo and lac. The duty on wheat was abolished in 1873, and the duties on indigo and lac were remitted in 1880, but the duty of 3 annas per maund on rice continued till 1930 when it was reduced to 2¼ annas per maund. Duties on jute, tea and raw hides and skins were imposed in 1916, 1916 and 1919, respectively. The duty on hides and skins was imposed as a measure of protection for the Indian tanning industry, a rebate of two-thirds of the duty being allowed on exports to the Empire and there tanned. The rebate system was abolished in 1923. The duty remained unchanged at 5 per cent. from 1923 to 1934 when the duty on raw hides was abolished. Raw skins were made free in 1935. The duty on tea was removed in 1927. The duties on jute have remained unchanged since 1917. Cesses are levied on Indian tea, coffee, jute, soft coke, lac and cotton.

Salt.

The taxation of salt is a legacy from the Mughals Excise duty is levied on salt manufactured in the country, whether by solar evaporation of sea water, lake water or pit brine, or by extraction from the salt mines in the Punjab or the quarries in the North-West Frontier Province This excise duty, together with the import duty on foreign salt which follows the rate of excise duty prevailing from time to time, has always furnished a considerable revenue. From 1888 to 1903 the rate of excise duty was Rs. 2-8-0 (3*s* 4*d*) per maund of 82 2/7 lbs., except in Burma which enjoyed a privileged rate Between 1903 and 1907 it was gradually reduced to Re. 1 (1*s*. 4*d*.) per maund. In 1916 the rate was raised to Rs. 1-4-0 (1*s*. 8*d*) and from the 1st of March 1923 it was further raised to Rs. 2-8-0 (3*s*. 4*d*). Since the 1st of March 1924 the standard rate has been Rs. 1-4-0 (1*s*. 10½*d*) at the present rate of exchange, but a surcharge of 25 per cent. was added with effect from the 30th of September 1931 under the Indian Finance (Supplementary and Extending) Act of that year and this surcharge is still in force. An additional import duty of 4 annas 6 pies per maund was imposed with effect from the 18th of March 1931 on all foreign salt other than Aden salt imported into British India. This additional duty was reduced to 2 annas 6 pies at the beginning of the financial year 1933-34. In 1936 the additional duty was further reduced to 1 anna 6 pies and is to remain in force for two years. Salt manufactured in Goa and imported into British India is also subject to the additional duty.

A little less than half of the indigenous salt is manufactured or mined by Government and the balance is produced under licence and excise. The imports (including imports from Aden) represent a little less than one-fourth of the total annual consumption which is approximately 52,000,000 maunds. The import duty is collected through the various Custom Houses but is credited to a separate head from the ordinary customs revenue.

Excise Duties.

Apart from the salt tax, excise duties are now levied on petroleum, silver, sugar, matches, mechanical lighters and steel ingots.

The excise duty on petroleum was imposed by the Motor Spirit Duties Act, 1917, in order to restrict the consumption of petrol in India. The original rate was 6 annas per gallon, the corresponding import duty being 7½ annas per gallon. The duty was continued as a revenue measure by the Motor Spirit Duties Act, 1919. The excise and import duties were equalised at 4 annas per gallon in 1925 but were again raised to 6 annas in 1929 and to 8 annas in 1931. The proceeds of the additional excise duty of 2 annas imposed in 1931 are used for road development. The Indian Finance (Supplementary and Extending) Act imposed a surcharge of 25 per cent. and the present rate is therefore 10 annas per gallon.

With effect from the 1st of March, 1922, the provisions of the Motor Spirit Duties Act, 1917, were applied to kerosene. The original rate of excise duty was one anna per gallon, the import duty being 2½ annas per gallon. In 1930 the excise duty was raised to 1½ annas per gallon and the import duty was reduced to 2¼ annas per gallon. In 1931 both of these rates were increased by 9 pies per gallon, and a surcharge of 25 per cent. was added by the Indian Finance (Supplementary and Extending) Act, 1931. Thus the excise duty is now 2 annas 9¾ pies per gallon and the import duty 3¾ annas per gallon.

Silver was made subject to an excise duty of 4 annas per ounce by the Silver (Excise Duty) Act, 1930, and a corresponding import duty was imposed at the same time. These duties were raised to 6 annas per ounce in the following years and the surcharge of 25 per cent. raised them to 7½ annas per ounce. The rates were, however, reduced to 5 annas per ounce in 1932 and to 2 annas per ounce in 1935.

The excise duties on sugar, matches, mechanical lighters and steel ingots were first imposed in 1934.

Customs Revenue.

The Customs revenue collected at the six principal ports and the all-India totals for the years 1931-32 to 1935-36 are given in the table below. The totals for 1913-14 for all ports were £6,246,348 (imports) and £858,432 (exports). The corresponding figures for 1918-19 were £8,395,767 (imports) and £2,460,995 (exports).

TABLE No. 8.—*Customs revenue collected at the six principal ports and totals for British India from 1931-32 to 1935-36. (excluding salt).*

Ports.	1931-32.		1932-33.		1933-34.		1934-35.		1935-36.	
	Import duty.	Export duty.	Import duty.	Export duty.	Import duty.	Export duty.	Import duty.	Export duty.	Import duty.	Export duty.
	£	£	£	£	£	£	£	£	£	£
Calcutta . . .	7,789,000	2,379,000	8,282,000	2,372,000	6,852,000	2,635,000	7,391,000	2,691,000	7,583,000	2,821,000
Bombay . . .	9,222,000	41,000	11,801,000	26,000	10,465,000	34,000	11,529,000	21,000	11,803,000	10,000
Madras . . .	2,395,000	8,000	2,668,000	5,000	2,406,000	6,000	2,515,000	3,000	2,352,000	500
Rangoon . . .	2,122,000	525,000	2,650,000	416,000	2,174,000	378,000	2,314,000	353,000	2,510,000	313,000
Karachi . . .	4,192,000	42,000	4,665,000	30,000	3,603,000	35,000	4,018,000	21,000	3,747,000	9,000
Chittagong . . .	122,000	59,000	103.000	32.000	90,000	73,000	103,000	64,000	115,000	39,000
Total for all India .	27,060,000	3,191,000	31,428,000	2,979,000	26,764,000	3,261,000	29,132,000	3,242,000	29,257,000	3,264,000

The Indian Stores Department.

The Indian Stores Department is the outcome of the recommendations of the Stores Purchase Committee, and was constituted in January, 1922. Its main function is to purchase in India and abroad in accordance with the Stores Purchase Rules, stores of all descriptions, except lethal munitions, foodstuffs, medical stores, stationery and a few other classes of articles, for the Departments of the Central Government and the minor Local Administrations, and to inspect stores purchased by the Department or by the consuming departments direct. Its services are also available to such major Local Governments, Indian States, public bodies, etc., as may desire to avail themselves of those services.

The Department consists of the office of the Chief Controller of Stores, which is located at the headquarters of the Government of India, Purchase Circles at Calcutta, Bombay and Karachi, a Test House at Calcutta, and inspection agencies at Calcutta, Jamshedpur. Bombay, Madras, Cawnpore, Lahore and Karachi. The Headquarters office, which is under the direct charge of the Chief Controller of Stores, comprises an Administration and Intelligence Branch, a Purchase Branch and an Inspection Branch. The Administration and Intelligence Branch is in charge of the general administration and market intelligence. The Purchase Branch deals with indents for purchase of stores and the Inspection Branch is responsible for all technical work of the Department, namely, drawing up of specifications, giving technical advice to Purchase officers, indenting departments and manufacturers, standardisation of stores, etc. The Provincial Purchase Circles are intended to deal with indents of comparatively small value, which can be most efficiently handled locally by officers stationed at important market centres. The Inspection Circles undertake the inspection not only of finished articles but also of stores throughout the process of manufacture in cases where manufacture is carried out. For this purpose an expert staff of Inspectors and Examiners is employed in each Circle. At the Government Test House are undertaken physical and chemical tests and also analyses of various description of stores. The organisation is fully equipped with an expert staff with up-to-date machinery and appliances. The organisation at Jamshedpur is known as the Metallurgical Inspectorate, and is in charge of an officer designated as the Metallurgical Inspector who is assisted by a staff of expert metallurgists. Its function is to inspect throughout the process of manufacture mainly the products of the Tata Iron and Steel Company Limited, but it also carries out such other tests and inspection of metals as fall within its scope

All requests for purchase are made by means of indents drawn up on special forms prescribed by the Department and are submitted to the Chief Controller of Stores or to the appropriate Controller of Purchase in the case of demands which the Provincial Controllers are competent to handle. For all orders of Rs. 5,000 and upwards, tenders are usually invited by means of advertisements. For orders below Rs. 5,000, tenders are ordinarily invited only from known and reliable firms who are on the approved list of contractors. A statement of all orders placed by the Department, of the value of Rs 100 and above is published every week in the Indian Trade Journal. Purchases made by the Department are not completed until the articles have been subjected to a very rigid and thorough inspection unless the indenting Department prefers to obtain uninspected supplies.

The Department is also prepared to undertake inspection in cases where purchases are made by another authority. Calls for inspection in such cases are submitted to the head of the Inspectorate in whose area the inspection is to be carried out. For its services a departmental charge of 2 per cent. of the value of the articles purchased is made in cases in which the Department undertakes both purchase and inspection. In cases where the Department carries out purchase or inspection only, the charge is limited to 1 per cent. of the value of the articles purchased or inspected.

In connection with the purchasing arrangements, the Intelligence Branch of the Department maintains up-to-date and reliable information regarding sources of supply, markets, prices, etc. It also scrutinizes indents placed by departments on the Director-General, India Store Department, London, and places whenever possible consumers in touch with Indian sources of supply.

The purchasing activities of the Department are not confined to the Indian markets Orders for stores not obtainable in India are placed abroad in accordance with the Stores Purchase Rules. The Indian Stores Department and the India Store Department, London, are at present entirely distinct organisations and function independently of each other, but the services of the London Stores Department are freely utilized by the Indian Stores Department for the inspection of stores purchased from abroad

A new organisation known as the Industrial Intelligence and Research Bureau has been attached to the Department recently, as an experimental measure. The principal functions of the Bureau are —

(1) The Collection and dissemination of industrial intelligence.

(2) Collaboration with Provincial Directors of Industries and Industrialists in all matters relating to industrial research

(3) The publication at intervals of bulletins relating to industrial research and other matters connected with industrial development.

(4) Assistance to industrialists in India by giving advice and making suggestions as to the directions in which research should be undertaken.

(5) To collaborate with the various organisations of the Central and Local Governments with a view to ensuring that specifications prepared or issued by them provide as far as possible for industrial standardisation.

(6) To assist in the organisation of industrial exhibitions in India.

The Bureau is in charge of an officer designated as the Director and has been attached to the Head Office of the Indian Stores Department in order that it may benefit from all the available resources of the Department in the form of information regarding industries, accumulated technical knowledge and experience and the facilities for research work which the Department possesses.

B.—MISCELLANEOUS ITEMS OF LAW AND PRACTICE AFFECTING TRADE.

Merchandise Marks.

Importers into India, especially from countries other than the United Kingdom, would do well to make themselves acquainted with the law and regulations relating to merchandise marks. In Appendix II will be found the principal provisions of the Indian Merchandise Marks Act, 1889, and connected Acts and the notifications issued thereunder. The following summary of the regulations in force does not claim to be exhaustive. For those seeking more complete information a reference is suggested to the Merchandise Marks Manual which is published under the authority of the Government of India and is obtainable of all agents for the sale of Indian Government publications.

Infringements or offences may be classified conveniently under four heads—

(1) Counterfeit trade marks,

(2) Trade descriptions that are false in respect of the country of origin,

(3) Trade descriptions that are false in other respects, and

(4) Lengths not properly stamped on piecegoods.

(1) Counterfeit trade marks.

The provisions regarding counterfeit trade marks do not cover general get up but do extend to other marks or combination of marks, the imitation of which is reasonably calculated to lead persons to believe that the goods are the manufacture of some persons other than they really are. *e g*, piece-goods are identified in the bazaar by their coloured labels or by the manufacturer's or importer's number impressed upon them or the merchandise of a particular firm may be known by the firm's name or initials which form no part of the trade mark These provisions are intended not only to protect manufacturers against piracy, but the general public from being supplied with goods of inferior or unknown quality under cover of a well known brand. If notice of such infringement is given beforehand by the aggrieved party to the Customs authorities, the goods on arrival are detained, if there is reasonable justification, pending (1) execution of an indemnity bond within 24 hours or deposit of security in cash or currency notes to the amount of 10 per cent. on the estimated value of the goods and (2) institution of proper legal proceedings within a month. *Bona fide* applications made in the absence of definite information for a watch of possible infringements are usually granted for a period of 3 months renewable on reasonable grounds. But formal registration of marks, etc , by Customs officers is prohibited. If in the course of the ordinary Customs examination an infringement is discovered, intimation is sent to the person whose mark is infringed to enable him to proceed as indicated above, but the goods are released if he fails to take preliminary action within a period of 4 days.

It is not necessary to mark the country of origin on any goods imported into India, except where the goods made or produced beyond the limits of the United Kingdom or British India have applied thereto any name or trade mark being or purporting to be, the name or trade mark of any person who is a manufacturer, dealer or trader in the United Kingdom or in British India or where the goods bear some other mark or indication which is held under the regulations to constitute a false trade description with regard to origin, in the absence of any counter-indication of the real country of origin, *e.g.*, Scotch whisky or Jamaica rum, if the produce of Holland. Similarly cognac and sherry require respectively the specific counter-indications 'Not made in France', 'Not made in Spain', if not the produce of those countries. The commonest class of cases falling under this description is where the goods bear a mark or label with English words (most frequently the words 'trade mark'), the use of the English language being taken to indicate that the goods are the product of the United Kingdom or British India, and therefore to constitute a false trade description unless corrected by a definite indication of the country of origin (such as 'Made in France') or an indication negativing the implication to be drawn from the use of the English language, such as 'Made Abroad', 'Not made in the United Kingdom or British India', 'Foreign Made' or 'Foreign Produce' When the name used is the name of a place in the United Kingdom or British India a counter-indication is required, *e g*, the word 'Beston' requires, in the case of American goods, the counter-indication U S. A., but 'Made in New York or Philadelphia' does not The use of the English language on foreign made goods is admissible as part of the goods themselves, *e g.*, the word "Stamps" or 'Photographs' on albums but not expressions such as 'A present for a good boy' or 'Superior quality'. A consignment of spelter bearing the words 'Extra pure' on the top of the slabs without counter-indication of country of origin, *viz.*, Japan, which was stamped on the reverse with a rubber stamp, was held liable to penalty.

(2) Trade description false in respect of country of origin.

In the case of goods made or produced in a foreign country, the trade description indicative of origin in the United Kingdom or British India which has been corrected by the use of such an expression as 'Made Abroad' may still be false, if it also suggests that the goods were manufactured in a foreign country other than the actual country of origin (*e.g.*, scents made in Japan bearing the word 'parfumerie'). The counter-indication, which should be such as to negative both these implications, must either specify the actual country of origin or must run 'Not made in United Kingdom or British India or X' (X being the other foreign country in which the goods might wrongly be supposed to have been manufactured) Similarly the use in a trade description of the language of one foreign country on goods produced in another requires counter-indication of the latter. English manufacturers using French expressions on their goods were ordered to attach a prominent and permanent label 'Made in England' on the offending goods.

When the misleading words or marks consist of what is or purports to be the name or trade mark of a manufacturer, dealer or trader in the United Kingdom or British India, a specific and distinct counter-indication of the country of origin is necessary, *e.g.*, pen-holders of German manufacture bearing the name of a British Indian trader without the country of origin were ordered to be reshipped. Initials are not however treated as names requiring a counter-indication unless they are likely to suggest the name of a British manufacturer; and an exception is made in the case of coverings or labels made in a foreign country but bearing the name of a British Indian manufacturer or dealer who has imported the coverings or labels for his own goods. Goods made or produced in a foreign country but bearing the name or trade mark of a British Indian dealer or a trade description consisting of Indian vernaculars or numerals or pictorial representations such as Indian deities or emblems must bear a counter-indication which is however waived in the case of goods manufactured in the United Kingdom unless in the latter case there is good ground for considering that the marking conveys the impression of Indian origin. A penalty was imposed in lieu of correct stamping on safety matches made in Sweden bearing the word *Om* in Bengali but without any indication of the country of origin.

Dhooties of English manufacture with the words *Bande Mataram* in Bengali woven along the whole borders with the words 'Manchester' stamped in Bengali only in one place were confiscated subject to redemption and reshipment on payment of a penalty and this decision was upheld in appeal.

It is important to note that whenever an indication of the country of origin is required under the regulations, such indication should be (1) in the same language and character as the name or trade mark or trade description, (2) sufficiently conspicuous and indelible and (3) should be repeated for each application of the mark or description in such a manner that it cannot be removed afterwards.

Other false trade descriptions are frequently found on goods in respect of (*a*) their number, quantity, measure, gauge or weight, or (*b*) the material of which they are composed.

(3) Other false trade descriptions.

The cases under (*a*) usually affect (1) woollen and cotton goods in respect of their measure, size or weight, and (2) packages, boxes or cartons bearing incorrect indications in respect of the quantities contained in them.

Paper wrappers of cotton braid each containing twelve skeins were marked '6 grs. yards' implying that each skein was 72 yards long whereas the actual length of the braids varied from 44 to 51 yards. Deletion of the misleading marking was ordered under penalty

Offences under (*b*) are held to be committed when the trade description suggests that the article is made of a material superior in quality and value than it really is and as such is likely to deceive the buyer. Iron nails described as 'brass nails' were passed on penalty and deletion of the word "brass".

A large number of cases under this head occur in connexion with consignments of white zinc, white and red lead, linseed oil and turpentine which are very frequently imported adulterated. The general rule is that when the percentage of impurity exceeds 5 per cent. (10 per cent. in the case of turpentine) but not 50 per cent., a qualifying description such as 'adulterated' or 'reduced' is held to be sufficient, but if it exceeds 50 per cent. the actual percentage should also be stated. Similarly it has been ruled that condensed milk containing less than 8 per cent. of butter fat contravenes the regulations unless marked 'prepared from skimmed milk'.

(4) Lengths not properly stamped on piecegoods.

As a general rule the Merchandise Marks Act does not require goods to be stamped or marked, though it insists that any stamps or marks affixed should be correct, but by a special provision piece-goods which are ordinarily sold by length or by the piece must be correctly and properly stamped with the lengths in standard yards. The stamping must be in English numerals accompanied by the word 'yards', (abbreviation 'yds.'), though marking in inches may be permitted on cloths of small dimensions and delicate make in accordance with the custom of the trade but in all cases it should be placed conspicuously on the fabric itself so as not to be ordinarily removable. Cotton and woollen piece-goods imported for the personal use of individuals or private associations of individuals and not for trade purposes need not be stamped. The Collector has also the discretion not to detain unstamped piece-goods which are of such a nature that they would be liable to serious depreciation in value, if stamped. For the purpose of this regulation, piece-goods are defined as including cotton and woollen piece-goods excepting certain specified descriptions; the provisions however do not apply to any fabric which comes within the scope of the above definition but is ordinarily sold by the unit or with reference to the number. Pieces of mosquito netting imported without the lengths stamped on them were directed to be stamped under penalty or in the alternative with an enhanced penalty in lieu of stamping.

Registration of Trade Marks.

There is no recognised registration of trade marks in India, but in view of the growing demand from the commercial public the question of initiating legislation for the registration of Trade Marks is receiving the consideration of the Government of India. Registration of new trade marks on payment of a fee is made by the Madras and South Indian Chambers of Commerce and as evidence of the date on which the mark or ticket was registered, may be useful in subsequent litigation, though it conveys no legal rights. The Bombay Millowners' Association keeps a register of all trade marks in use by members and has a special set of rules governing their registration to which all members upon election agree to conform, in view of the protection afforded by the Association to the trade marks and tickets used by them.

Registration of Partnerships and Business names.

The question whether the registration of business partnerships and business names should be made compulsory by legislation has been frequently considered by the Government of India in the past. As a result of the recommendations of the Civil Justice Committee, which reported in the year 1925, an Act to define and amend the law relating to partnerships, entitled the Indian Partnership Act, 1932 (IX of 1932) was passed, which repealed Chapter XI of the Indian Contract Act, 1872, and also the whole of the Burma Registration of Business Names Act, 1920. The Act provides for the registration of firms and explains the rights and liabilities of partners.

PART IV

COMMERCIAL ORGANISATIONS.

The principal non-official organisations connected with trade are the Chambers of Commerce at Calcutta, Bombay, Madras, Rangoon, and Karachi and other important centres with a membership, except in Bombay, preponderatingly European, though open to Indians also. Closely connected with these and not infrequently employing the same secretariat staff are the associations representing particular branches of trade such as jute mills, cotton mills, etc. The Trades Associations represent the retail traders in the principal cities, and latterly, other associations representing general interests have grown up with an exclusively Indian membership. The Associated Chambers of Commerce of India represent mainly the European interests, while the Federation of Indian Chambers of Commerce and Industry perform the same functions in respect of Indians. These chambers and associations though they differ from time to time on questions of policy, are in no sense antagonistic to the older associations The membership of most of these bodies is confined to the province or city where their headquarters are situated; but they maintain close touch with similar organisations at other trade centres. In the case of jute which is grown chiefly in Bengal, the associations connected with it are representative of the entire industry.

These Associations and the leading Chambers of Commerce in particular keep the Government apprised from time to time of the problems affecting commercial development in India and, undoubtedly, perform important functions in focussing non-official opinion and representing commercial sentiment the value of which is reflected in the recognition, varying according to their status and traditions, which they enjoy at the hands of Government. The Bengal and Bombay Chambers of Commerce have the privilege of electing a representative each to the Council of State and 6 and 2 representatives respectively to the Legislative Councils of the respective Presidencies. The Madras Indian Commerce and the Indian Merchants' Chamber and Bureau (Bombay) elect a representative each to the Legislative Assembly while the Millowners' Associations at Bombay and Ahmedabad; and the Bengal National Chamber of Commerce, the Marwari Association (Bengal) and the Bengal Mahajan Sabha enjoy the privilege in rotation of electing a representative in the Assembly. The Rangoon Chamber elects one representative to the Council of State and two to the local Legislative Council. The representation of other commercial and industrial bodies on the local legislative Councils is shown below:—

Name of constituency	No. of seats.
Madras—	
Madras Chamber of Commerce	2
Madras Trades Association	1
Southern India Chamber of Commerce	1
Nuttu Kottai Nagarthers Association	1
Madras Planters' Association	1
Bombay—	
Karachi Chamber of Commerce	1
Bombay Trades Association	1
Ahmedabad Millowners' Association	1
Indian Merchants' Chamber and Bureau	1
Bombay Millowners Association	1
Bengal—	
Indian Jute Mills Association	2
Indian Tea Association	1
Indian Mining Association	1
Calcutta Trades Association	1
Bengal National Chamber of Commerce	2
Bengal Marwari Association	1
Bengal Mahajan Sabha	1
United Provinces—	
Upper India Chamber of Commerce	2
United Provinces Chamber of Commerce	1
The Punjab—	
Punjab Chamber of Commerce and Trades Association	1
Punjab Industries	1
Bihar and Orissa—	
Bihar Planters	1
Indian Mining Association	1
Indian Mining Federation	1
Burma—	
Burma Indian Chamber of Commerce	1
Burmese Chamber of Commerce	1
Rangoon Trades Association	1
Chinese Chamber of Commerce	1
Central Provinces—	
Central Provinces and Berar Mining Association	1
Central Provinces Commerce and Industries	1
Assam—	
Assam Valley Planting	3
Surma Valley Planting	2
Commerce and Industry	1

These representatives being non-officials enjoy complete freedom of attitude with regard to any legislation or subject of debate which may come before the councils. The Chambers are also represented in quasi-Government institutions such as Port Commissions while seats are reserved for them on the Improvement Trusts of Calcutta and Bombay and on Municipal Corporations. It is usual for both the Imperial and Provincial Governments to obtain the views of the leading Chambers and commercial associations before embarking upon measures which, however, remotely, are likely to affect trade, and every consideration is given to any advice tendered.

The London Chamber of Commerce opened in 1912 an East India Section specially charged with the advocacy in the United Kingdom of questions of commercial interest in India.

London Chamber of Commerce.

An Indian Chamber of Commerce was established in 1927 in London with a view to further the Indian commercial interests represented in Great Britain and located in London.

The constitution and aims of some of the principal commercial bodies are separately treated in the following paragraphs.

A.—General.

The Associated Chambers of Commerce of India.

The organisation styled the Associated Chambers of Commerce of India and Ceylon (now the Associated Chambers of Commerce of India) was established at a conference of representatives of the Chambers which was held in Calcutta on the 8th and 9th January 1920. The first attempt at concerted action by the Chambers was made in 1905 when a conference was held at Calcutta. No further step in the same direction was, however, taken until 1917, when a second conference was held at Delhi to consider the question of Indian trade after the war. But meanwhile the need for an organisation had made itself felt from time to time and after the war it was considered that the time had come when European commercial interests throughout India ought to be more closely organised. It was accordingly decided, at the conference on the 8th and 9th January 1920, to constitute an Association having for its main objects the promotion and protection of the trade, commerce, industries and manufactures of India and Ceylon. The Association at the present time consists of the following fifteen Chambers namely:—Bengal, Bombay, Burma, Calicut, Chittagong, Cocanada, Cochin, Coimbatore, Karachi, Madras, Narayanganj, Northern India, Punjab, Upper India and Tuticorin.

The Ceylon Chamber of Commerce seceded from the Association in 1932 and the name of the Association was then altered to the Associated Chambers of Commerce of India.

The Association was incorporated in 1920 under the provisions of Article 26 of the Indian Companies Act. Among its activities is the organising of an annual meeting of its members at which commercial and industrial questions are discussed and suitable resolutions adopted. The conference of January 1920, to which reference has already been made, was the first of these gatherings. Since then meetings have been held—at the headquarters of the Association for the time being—at Calcutta in January 1921, 1922 and 1923; at Bombay in December 1923; at Calcutta in December 1924 and 1925; at Cawnpore in December 1926; at Calcutta in December 1927 and 1928 and at Bombay in December 1929 From 1930 onwards the annual conferences have taken place at Calcutta The Articles of Association provide for the election of a Chamber by whom a president for the year is nominated and also of two Chambers each of whom nominates a Vice-President for the year. A Secretary is also appointed yearly at the annual meeting. There is no Managing Committee, the executive work of the Association being conducted by the President and Secretary. Since the year 1930 the President of the Bengal Chamber has been the President of the Association and the Secretary of the Bengal Chamber the Secretary.

The conferences at Calcutta have usually been opened by H. E. the Viceroy or H. E. the Governor of Bengal and they have in the past been attended by members of the Central and Local Governments, other Government officials and delegates from all the constituents Chambers. Resolutions relating to Constitutional matters, Law and Legislation, Currency and Finance, Railways, Posts and Telegraphs, Customs Duties and Tariffs, Shipping, and general questions are put forward for discussion; and such resolutions as are adopted unanimously are forwarded to the Government Department concerned for consideration and appropriate action.

The Association is represented in the Indian Legislative Assembly by a member nominated by H. E. the Governor-General in Council, on the recommendation of the constituent Chambers.

The Association is also represented on the Central Advisory Committee for Lighthouses and the Imperial Council of Agricultural Research and is a member of the Federation of Chambers of Commerce of the British Empire, on the Council of which it has two representatives, one of whom is a Vice-President of the Federation.

Federation of Indian Chambers of Commerce and Industry.

The Federation of Indian Chambers of Commerce and Industry, founded in 1926, is a central organisation representating Indian commercial and industrial interests in India. The main objects of the Federation are to promote Indian business in matters of inland and foreign trade transport, industry and manufactures and finance, to collect and desseminate statistical and commercial information, to support or oppose legislative or other measures affecting the commercial interests of the country, as the case may be, to provide for arbitration when occasion arises, to promote unanimity and uniformity of practice amongst the members of the commercial or industrial community and to do all such lawful acts as may be beneficial or conducive to the attainments of the objects or any of them. There are three classes of members--ordinary, foreign Indian Chambers eligible for corresponding membership and eminent Indians eligible for Honorary membership. The Federation is represented on various bodies, notably, in the several committees of the Imperial Council of Agricultural Research, and the Governing Body of the International Labour Organisation.

A representative's office is maintained in Berlin to encourage and develop trade relations between the two countries.

The membership of the Federation is 48.

All-India Organisation of Industrial Employers, Cawnpore.

The All-India Organisation of Industrial Employers was established on 12th December 1932 and is a body allied to the Federation of Indian Chambers of Commerce and Industry. Its objects are to promote the industrial development, to nominate delegates and advisers to represent the employers at the International Labour Conference, League of Nations, International Chamber of Commerce, etc., to encourage or discourage legislative or other measures likely to affect industrial interests, to take necessary steps in regard to the recommendations or convention of the International Labour Conference, to regulate conditions of employment of industrial labour, etc.

The membership of the organisation is open to any individual firm, joint-stock company or corporation engaged in any industry in India and also to industrial associations.

The organisation is represented on the Governing Body of the International Labour Organisation and its office is located in Kamla Tower, Cawnpore.

Indian National Committee of the International Chamber of Commerce, Cawnpore.

The Indian National Committee was established to further the objects of the International Chamber of Commerce, Paris, which are, briefly, to facilitate the commercial intercourse of countries, to secure harmony of action on all international questions affecting finance, industry and commerce and to encourage cordial relations between businessmen and commercial organisations.

It has 36 organisation Members and 87 Associate Members. It is allied to the Federation of Indian Chambers of Commerce and Industry and its office is at Kamla Tower, Cawnpore.

Indian Chamber of Commerce, Calcutta.

The Indian Chamber of Commerce was established in 1926. Its objects are to promote and protect the trade, commerce and industries financed or managed by Indians, to encourage or discourage legislative measures likely to affect trade and commerce, to collect and disseminate commercial information and to provide for arbitration The Chamber issues certificates of origin and survey certificates in respects of foreign exports.

The Chamber is represented on various bodies such as, the Calcutta Port Trust, local advisory committees of the principal Railways, etc.

Membership is open to any trading concern or joint-stock company financed or managed mainly by Indians. Members are of two classes—local and mofussil, and number 218.

Some important commercial associations are affiliated to the Chamber, namely, Indian Sugar Mills' Association, Indian Colliery Owners' Association and Jute Balers' Association, etc.

The affairs of the Chamber are administered by a committee of 21 members consisting of a President, two vice-Presidents, and 18 ordinary members, and a paid Secretary.

The office is at 135 Canning Street, Calcutta.

Indian Colliery Owners' Association, Calcutta.

The Association was started in 1933 to promote mainly the coal mining industry, trade and commerce of India. Any person or firm or joint-stock company engaged in coal mining industries or by-products thereof, is eligible for membership. The Head Office of the Association is at Jharia and a branch office at 135, Canning Street. Calcutta.

Indian Chamber of Commerce, Lahore.

The Indian Chamber of Commerce was established in 1912, and was registered under the Indian Companies Act, 1882 in 1913. Its objects are mainly to promote the trade, commerce and manufactures in the Punjab, to collect and circulate statistics and other commercial information and to arbitrate in the settlement of disputes. The Chamber is a member of the Federation of Indian Chambers of Commerce and Industry, and of the International Chamber of Commerce, Paris. There are three classes of members, Honorary, Ordinary and Additional The Chamber is represented on the Joint Development Board Punjab, Local Board of Economic Enquiry, Indian Central Cotton Committee, etc.

The affairs of the Chamber are managed by an executive committee, consisting of a President, two vice-Presidents, 12 members, an Honorary Secretary and a joint Honorary Secretary.

The Head office is at 7 A, Nisbet Road, Lahore with a branch at Amritsar.

Indian Jute Mills Association, Calcutta.

The Indian Jute manufacturers' Association was constituted in 1884, the name being altered at a special general meeting in July 1902 to the "Indian Jute Mills Association" when a complete set of rules and regulations was adopted. They were extensively revised in 1930, and, in 1931 the Association was registered under the Indian Trades Union Act, (XVI of 1926).

The Association started with a membership of 19 which has risen to 54. The objects of the Association are to encourage and secure united feeling and action, to collect and classify facts and statistics, to open out new markets, if practicable, to fix points of custom, to standardize contracts, to obtain the removal of grievances, to arbitrate on matters of dispute, to communicate with public authorities or kindred associations, to impose restrictive conditions on the conduct of the trade and to adjust the production of the mills in the Association to the demand in the world market, to encourage and finance technical developments in plant and machinery for the manufacture of jute and its products and scientific exploration of new uses to which jute can be applied, and the discovery of by-products; generally to promote and to protect the interests of those engaged in the jute industry in all matters relating to it, especially in those touching the interests of the members of the Association, and to do all such other lawful acts as are incidental or conducive to the attainment of the above objects or any of them.

The Association returns two representatives to the Bengal Legislative Council.

The affairs and funds of the Association are managed by a Committee consisting of a Chairman and 6 members who are appointed annually at a general meeting. The Secretary and Assistant Secretary of the Bengal Chamber of Commerce are ex-officio Secretary and Assistant Secretary of the Association. The Office of the Association is at the Royal Exchange, 2, Clive Street, Calcutta.

East India Cotton Association, Limited, Bombay.

The East Indian Cotton Association, Limited, Bombay, was founded in 1921 to provide, regulate and maintain suitable buildings or rooms for a Cotton Exchange in the City of Bombay and elsewhere in India, to provide forms of contracts and regulate the carrying out and enforcement or cancellation of contracts, to adjust controversies between persons engaged in the cotton trade, to establish just and equitable principles in the said trade, to maintain uniformity in rules; regulations and usages of the said trade; to fix or adopt standards of classification in the same, to acquire, preserve and disseminate useful information connected with the cotton interest throughout all markets, to decrease the local risk attendant upon business, and generally to promote the cotton trade throughout India, and augment the facilities with which it may be conducted to establish, regulate and maintain a clearing house for the purpose of dealing with cotton and transactions therein; to prescribe the principle of framing of contracts with a view to eliminate the temptation and possibility of speculative manipulation; and to make from time to time bye-laws, rules and regulations respecting the cotton trade, etc.

The affairs of the Association are managed by a Board of Directors, a Clearing House Manager and a Secretary.

Upon the establishment of the East Indian Cotton Association, the Bombay Cotton Trade Association was wound up voluntarily.

Indian Tea Association.

The Indian Tea Association, Calcutta, was formed at a meeting of Calcutta tea agency firms in 1881, the objects and duty of the Association being to promote the common interest of all persons concerned in the cultivation of tea in India.

The Association started with a membership of companies and estate owners representing a planted area of over 103,000 acres, which had increased at the end of 1934 to 424,295½ acres. Proprietors and managers of, and agents for, tea estates (including limited companies) are eligible for election as members, all applications being dealt with by the General Committee.

The business and funds of the Association are controlled by a General Committee consisting of 12 firms who are elected annually by the members of the Association. Each of the 12 firms elected nominates a gentleman to represent them on the General Committee, and the General Committee elect their own Chairman and Vice-Chairman. The Secretary and Assistant Secretary of the Bengal Chamber of Commerce are ex-officio Secretary and Assistant Secretary of the Association which was affiliated to the Chamber in May 1885.

The Association has since 1900 maintained a scientific department dealing with many and varied questions affecting tea cultivation and undertaking the investigation of problems relating to the manufacture of tea. The European staff of this department consists of a Chief Scientific Officer, two Chemists, a Mycologist, a Bacteriologist and a Botanist, and the results of their investigations are published from time to time in the form of bulletins, monographs and annual reports.

The Association nominates one representative to the Bengal Legislative Council.

The Headquarters of the Indian Tea Association are at the Royal Exchange, 2, Clive Street, Calcutta.

Indian Central Cotton Committee.

This Committee was constituted by the Government of India on the 31st March 1921, to secure co-operation and co-ordination in all matters relating to cotton, to act as an advisory body to Government and the trade, to promote the improvement of cotton growing and marketing in India and to act as a centre for the dissemination of information on these subjects. The Vice-Chairman, Imperial Council of Agricultural Research, is President and the membership consists of the representatives of the various Provincial Departments of Agriculture, of Chambers of Commerce, of the Empire Cotton Growing Corporation, of Commercial Associations connected with the cotton industry, of cotton growers and of cotton-growing Indian States, with the Expert Adviser to the Imperial Council of Agricultural Research in agricultural matters, the Director General of Commercial Intelligence and Statistics and the Commercial nominees of the Governments of Bombay, Madras, the Punjab, Bengal, the United Provinces and the Central Provinces. The Indian Cotton Cess Act of 1923 has given the Committee incorporation as a permanent body and prescribed its constitution. All sections of the trade including spinners and manufacturers, merchants, brokers and ginners are represented on it, and it is therefore in a position to offer authoritative advice to the Government of India and Local Governments on all problems affecting the industry.

Indian Mining Association.

The Indian Mining Association (founded in 1892) was the outcome of the activities of a Mining Sub-Committee of the Bengal Chamber of Commerce. The objects of the Association are to protect, by every legitimate means, the interests of those engaged in developing the mining industries of India, to foster those industries, to provide a ready means of arbitration for the settlement of disputes between mining proprietors and to take part in discussions affecting or having a bearing upon mines, their development or working, and for this purpose to enter into communication with the Government and other public bodies.

All persons or companies engaged in conducting mining enterprises are eligible to be members of the Association. The Committee are empowered by the rules to appoint honorary members but such members have no voting privileges.

The Association originated with a membership of 13 which had increased to 146 in 1924 but subsequently declined, owing to the trade depression, to 90 in 1934. Members of the Association were responsible for approximately 65 per cent. of the coal raised in India in 1934. Practically all the European and a number of Indian coal concerns in Bengal and Bihar and Orissa are members. The Association enjoys the privilege of electing a representative to each of the Legislative Councils of Bengal and Bihar and Orissa.

The Headquarters of the Association are at the Royal Exchange, 2, Clive Street, Calcutta, and its business is conducted by a Committee of seven members who appoint their own Chairman.

Indian Mining Federation.

This Association founded in March 1913 represents mainly Indian capital in the Coal mining industry of Bengal, Bihar and Orissa and the Central Provinces. Almost all the Indian colliery owners are members of the Federation.

The Federation is widely represented on various public bodies and institutions both of Bengal and Bihar and Orissa, and elects a member to the Legislative Council of the latter province.

The registered office of the Federation is at 15, Clive Street, Calcutta which has a branch on the Jharia coalfield. Its affairs are administered by an Executive Committee of fifteen members assisted by a paid Secretary.

It frequently issues circulars summarising the activities of the Committee supplemented by statistics relevant to the coal trade and the traffic position. It maintains a free reading room for its members.

Mining and Geological Institute of India.

This Institute was founded in 1906, "to promote the study of all branches of mining, geology, metallurgy and engineering in India, with a view to disseminate the information obtained for facilitating the scientific and economic development of the mineral industries of India." Its ordinary membership is open to persons possessing a degree or first class diploma in geology, mining, metallurgy or engineering from a recognised University or School of Science, or a first class certificate of competency as a manager of mine, or experience in mines, or works, or practical field work extending over certain specified periods and under certain conditions of responsibility.

Meetings for the reading and discussion of papers and excursions to mines or engineering works of interest are held at frequent intervals. The Institute publishes an annual volume of Transactions. A technical library which is accommodated in the Indian School of Mines, Dhanbad, is maintained for the benefit of members in the coalfields of Raniganj and Jharia. Special investigations are made from time to time.

The affairs of the Institute are administered by a President and a Council of 20 members elected annually from the general body. At the end of October, 1934, the membership consisted of 235 ordinary members. The headuqarters of the Institute are in Calcutta.

Wine, Spirit, and Beer Association of India.

The Wine, Spirit and Beer Association of India was founded in 1892 with headquarters at the Royal Exchange Buildings, Calcutta, to encourage and secure united feeling and action amongst shippers and importers, to decide points of custom, to arbitrate in matters of dispute, to communicate with public bodies, authorities and kindered associations, to watch the operation of the Excise and Customs laws as they may affect the trade, and generally to promote and protect the interests of persons engaged in the wine, spirit and beer trade of India. The business and affairs of the Association are managed by a General Committee consisting of not more than 12 firms, of which six are resident in Calcutta and are appointed annually at the general meeting held during the month of March in each year.

B.—Provincial and Local

(i) Chambers of Commerce.

The Bengal Chamber of Commerce was founded in 1834, when Lord William Bentinck was Governor-General. Little is known of its early history. There are no records prior to 1851, when it was more or less reconstituted. For very many years it was housed in the Bengal Bonded Warehouse in Clive Street. But in 1893 the then President, Sir James Mackay (the late Viscount Inchcape of Strathnaver) acquired on its behalf the premises of the New Oriental Bank Corporation in liquidation. These premises stood at the corner of Clive Street and what was known then as Old China Bazar Street, on what is reputed to have been the site of Clive's Government House, and later of the house in which Sir Philip Francis lived.

Bengal Chamber of Commerce.

The Bank premises were utilised by the Chamber and the Royal Exchange until 1915, when they were demolished and the present Royal Exchange was erected. The establishment of a Commercial Exchange was mooted in Calcutta as far back as 1857; and in 1881 the organisation of a mercantile exchange was contemplated. But it was not until 1893, when the Oriental Bank premises were acquired, that the idea took practical shape. A mercantile exchange, which by special permission of Queen Victoria was styled the Royal Exchange, was then established as part of the Chamber. The Exchange now consists of upwards 660 members and the Exchange Hall which is a prominent feature of the present building is used by them daily as a place of meeting for the transaction of business.

The Chamber itself was incorporated in 1893 as a public company under section 26 of the Indian Companies Act. Prior to that time it had been an unregistered association of merchants, bankers, shopowners, insurance companies, brokers and others engaged in commerce and industry. It now consists of 221 members and may fairly claim to be thoroughly representative of the European trade, commerce and manufacturers of the city. It is managed by a President, a Vice-President, and a committee of seven who are elected annually by the members and who conduct its business in accordance with the provisions of the articles of Association. In addition to the work of the Chamber proper, as represented by this Committee, there are no fewer than 26 Commercial associations and organisations recognised by and affiliated to the Chamber whose business is transacted by the secretariat staff of the Chamber, subject to the direction of Committees and Sub-Committees.

An important branch of the work of the Chamber is the measuring and weighing of most of the principal commodities exported from Calcutta. For this work the Chamber has a special Department—the Licensed Measurers' Department—which has been in existence for fifty years. It maintains a staff of about 100 measuring officers who measure and weigh goods chiefly in course of shipment. The measurements so recorded are used by the steamship companies as the basis upon which to calculate freights charged to exporters, and the weights are required chiefly by exporters for contract purposes. The volume of business transacted by the Department has naturally been affected by the recent trade depression, but the number of packages measured during the year ended 30th June 1934 amounted to as much as 6,869,670 and the number of packages weighed was 6,230,355.

There is also in existence in connection with the Chamber a Tribunal of Arbitration for the settlement and adjustment of disputes and differences relating to trade, business, manufactures, etc. (Arbitrators are drawn from among the members of the Chamber, and the arbitrations are conducted in accordance with the provisions of the Indian Arbitration Act, 1889. Its awards may be filed by either party to any particular dispute in the Calcutta High Court and be made a decree of the Court. The tribunal transacts a considerable volume of business which, however, has been adversely affected by the depression as in the case of the Chamber's Licensed Measurers' Department.

Bengal National Chamber of Commerce, Calcutta.

This Chamber, which is the premier institution of the Indian commercial community in Bengal and the oldest Indian chamber of commerce in India, was founded in 1887. The principal objects of the Chamber are to aid and stimulate the development of commercial and industrial enterprise in Bengal, and to protect the interests of all persons trading therein, to promote unanimity and uniformity of practice amongst the members of the trading community and to represent their views and requirements to the authorities, and to arbitrate, when occasion arises, between parties willing to submit their differences to the decision of the Chamber.

Under the revised constitution of the Chamber, facilities of Associate and Honorary membership have been extended to the entire trading community in Bengal. The number of members on the roll is over 300. Almost all the leading Indian commercial and industrial firms and persons in every branch of the inland and foreign trade in Bengal are members of the Chamber. A considerable portion of the joint stock capital invested in Bengal in banking, insurance, steamer services, cotton mills, etc., is also represented. The constitution of the chamber provides for a close association as between the chamber and various sectional organisations of trades and industries in Bengal.

The Chamber enjoys the privilege of electing representatives to the Legislative Assembly, the Bengal Legislative Council, the Calcutta Port Trust, the Calcutta Improvement Trust, Bengal Industries Board, Economic Enquiry Board Bengal, and other important bodies.

The headquarters of the Chamber are at Calcutta and its affairs are administered by a committee of 32 members in addition to the President, two vice-Presidents, and the Honorary Treasurer, with the help of the Secretary and a number of Departmental committees.

Marwari Chamber of Commerce, Calcutta.

This Chamber was established in 1900 with a view to developing and protecting the trade, commerce and manufacture of India, and in particular that of Calcutta, to consider all questions relating thereto and to oppose or promote any legislative enactments relating to commerce in general. The Chamber is generally consulted by Government on matters of public concern as well as on all commercial matters. It is not affiliated to any other public or commercial body but undertakes arbitration work between parties willing to abide by its decision, which under its rules, is not necessarily confined to business disputes.

The number of members on the roll is 1,500.

Muslim Chamber of Commerce, Calcutta.

The Muslim Chamber of Commerce was established in 1932. The objects are mainly to promote and protect the trade, commerce, agriculture and industries of India, particularly those in which Muslims are interested, to urge or oppose legislative or other measures affecting such trade, commerce, etc., to collect and disseminate statistics and other information consistent with the objects of the Chamber, to arbitrate in the settlement of disputes, when so desired, to maintain uniformity in rules, regulations, and usages in the various branches of trade, etc.

The Chamber is represented on certain important bodies, namely, Calcutta Port Trust, Board of Economic Enquiry for Bengal, Indian Accountancy Board, Paris International Congress of Exchange, etc. Membership is open to any firm, joint-stock company, or other trading corporation.

The affairs of the Chamber are administered by a committee consisting of a President, four vice-Presidents, 15 ordinary members and a Secretary.

The office is located at 22. Canning Street, Calcutta.

Muslim Chamber of Commerce, Bihar and Orissa.

The Muslim Chamber of Commerce of Patna was established in 1932 with the object of promoting the commercial well-being of the Muslim community in India in general and that of Bihar and Orissa in particular. It has objects similar to those of other Chambers. The Chamber is administered by a committee not exceeding 15 members including a President, 3 vice-Presidents, 1 Secretary, 1 Assistant Secretary, 1 Treasurer and 1 Legal Adviser. The office of the Chamber is at Patna.

Bombay Chamber of Commerce.

The Bombay Chamber of Commerce, Bombay, was founded in 1836. Its affairs are controlled by a President, Vice-President and Committee of seven. This Chamber has given particular attention to the publication of statistical returns and enjoys special facilities from the Custom House for their preparation. The daily issues include an arrival return and trade return, details of all import and export manifests are published twice a week and current quotations weekly, while the figures of exports and imports (principal articles) by sea are issued monthly, in addition to special returns of imports of piecegoods and yarns and exports of cotton. A Measurement Department is responsible for the measurement of exports in the docks prior to loading and as elsewhere one of the most important functions performed by the Chamber is that of arbitration in commercial disputes.

The Chamber elects a representative to the Council of State and two to the Bombay Legislative Council. It has one seat on the Bombay Municipal Corporation and five on the Port Trust. The number of members is unlimited. Every person, firm or company engaged or interested in mercantile pursuits is eligible for election as a member

On the 30th June 1935 the total membership of the Bombay Chamber of Commerce amounted to 192. Of these fourteen represent banking institutions; ten shipping agencies and companies; three firms of solicitors; three railway companies; ten engineers and contractors and the remainder, firms engaged in general mercantile business.

The Indian Merchants' Chamber, Bombay.

The Indian Merchants' Chamber, Bombay, was established in 1907 to promote and protect the trade, manufactures and commerce of India, and to secure organised action on all subjects relating to the interests of the Indian business community directly and indirectly. Thirty leading Commercial Associations of Bombay are affiliated to the Chamber, which is thus thoroughly representative of Indian Commercial interests. The Chamber elects a representative each to the Indian Legislative Assembly and the Bombay Legislative Council. It also elects five representatives to the Bombay Port Trust; one to the Bombay Municipality; one to the Indian Central Cotton Committee; one to the Senate of the Bombay University; one to the Governing Body of the I. M. M. T. S. "Dufferin"; etc. It publishes quarterly an Anglo-Gujarati journal giving commercial and statistical information. It has inaugurated a Commercial Examination scheme and issues Diplomas to successful students in specialised Commercial Subjects. It also issues Certificates of Origin for goods exported from the country. It has about 600 members on its Register.

Maharashtra Chamber of Commerce.

The chamber was established to encourage friendly relations and intercourse among the merchants and manufacturers of Maharashtra. Its objects are similar to those of other sister organisations. Membership is open to any individual or firm or joint stock company engaged in trade, commerce and industry within its jurisdiction. There are three classes of members, Patrons, Life members and Ordinary The Committee of the Chamber is composed of the President, three Vice-Presidents and fourteen members, plus one member apiece for each district having more than five members on the roll. In addition there are certain co-opted members. The office of the Chamber is located in Phoenix Building, Ballard Estate, Bombay.

Madras Chamber of Commerce.

The Madras Chamber of Commerce was founded in 1836 with a view to watch and protect the interest of trade; to receive and collect information on all matters of mercantile interest bearing upon the removal of grievances and the promotion of common good; to communicate with authorities and with individual parties thereupon; to receive references on matters of custom or usage in doubt or dispute, deciding on the same and recording the decision made for future reference; and to form by that and other means a code of practice whereby the transactions of business by all engaged in it may be simplified and facilitated.

The number of members on the roll at present is 56, including the leading firms in Madras, the principal banks and the two railways serving the Presidency. The Cochin, Calicut and Cocanada Chambers of Commerce are affiliated to the Madras Chamber, which is itself affiliated to the British Imperial Council of Commerce, London, and is also an original member of the Associated Chambers of Commerce of India. The Madras Trades Association and the United Planters' Association of Southern India are represented on the Chamber by Honorary members, and Government officials interested in trade and commerce are also invited to join the Chamber from time to time in a similar capacity.

The Chamber has two seats on the Madras Legislative Council, and has in addition three seats on the Corporation of Madras and four seats on the Madras Port Trust Board. The Chamber is also represented on the Advisory Committees of the South Indian and Madras and Southern Mahratta Railways, the Madras provincial Cotton Committee, the provincial State Aid to Industries Board and the Indian Tea Cess Committee.

The Chamber undertakes arbitrations and surveys with reference to matters relating to piecegoods and yarns and general disputes. It publishes fortnightly a price current and market report, also tonnage schedules, etc., and an annual volume which contains its Proceedings for the previous year. Trade marks and tickets are registered on application and payment of a fee which differentiates against non-members, provided that no objection is raised when the proposal is circulated. No application is favourably entertained from an Indian firm trading under a European name. Though registration conveys no right which the party registering does not already possess at law, it dates in a way the use of a particular ticket or mark by an individual firm which may have evidential value in the event of subsequent litigation.

The affairs of the Chamber are conducted by a Chairman, a Vice-Chairman and a Committee of five members, with the aid of a Secretary. The representatives of the Chamber on the Madras Legislative Council are also *ex-officio* members of the Committee during their term of office. In addition to these there are special sub-committees, for Exports, Imports, and Skins and Hides.

Bihar and Orissa Chamber of Commerce.

The Chamber was formed with the object of promoting the commercial and industrial interests of the province. The membership is open to all commercial and industrial concerns as well as to individuals interested in the economic uplift of the province. It is represented on certain important public bodies, *viz.*, Local Legislative Council, Advisory Committees of railways, the University, the Board of Industries, etc. Its affairs are administered by a President, two Vice-Presidents, one Honorary Secretary, and one Joint Honorary Secretary. The registered office of the Chamber is at Patna.

Orissa Chamber of Commerce.

The Chamber was founded with objects similar to those of other kindred organisations. The membership is open to any Indian gentleman, firm or association engaged in trade and industry. There are five classes of members. Patrons, Resident members, Moffusil members, Association, and Honorary members. The business of the chamber is conducted through an executive committee consisting of a President, Vice-President, and seven members. The office is located in Cuttack.

The Southern India Chamber of Commerce (founded in 1909) claims to represent Indian commerce, trade, industries and banking in the City of Madras and the up-country districts of the Presidency. The objects of the Chamber are identical with those of similar bodies and its affairs are managed by an Executive Committee of twenty-four members and a President and two Vice-Presidents. Two Honorary Secretaries are elected from among the members of the Executive Committee every year and there is also a paid Assistant Secretary. There are about 500 members, resident and non-resident, on the rolls of the Chamber including several Associations and Chambers of Commerce in the districts. The Chamber has been recognised in several statutes and it enjoys the right of sending one representative to the Madras Legislative Council, two to the Madras Port Trust, two to the Madras Corporation, two to the Madras University and one to the Madras Board of Industries. The Chamber registers trade marks, surveys goods and undertakes arbitration of disputes.

Southern India Chamber of Commerce.

The Cocanada Chamber of Commerce, established in 1868, has no branches, but more or less represents the European mercantile community of the north-east coast of the Madras Presidency carrying on business in Cocanada and in other parts of the districts of Godavari, Kistna, Vizagapatam and Ganjam. It is managed by a Committee consisting of a Chairman and two members, appoints arbitrators and conducts surveys and publishes annually a report of the proceedings of the Chamber and statistical information regarding the trade of Cocanada port.

Cocanada Chamber of Commerce.

This Chamber, formerly called the Native Chamber of Commerce was founded in 1885. All Indian merchants engaged or interested in mercantile pursuits and disposed to aid in carrying into effect the objects of the Chamber are eligible for membership. The Chamber undertakes the survey of goods and publishes a fortnightly price current.

Godavari Chamber of Commerce, Cocanada.

The Chamber enjoys the privilege of electing three members to the Cocanada Port Conservancy Board.

The Tuticorin Chamber of Commerce, founded in 1906, has no branches, but represents the European mercantile community of Tuticorin and neighbourhood. The affairs of the Chamber are managed by a Committee of three members, one of whom is the Chairman the executive work being in the hands of the Honorary Secretary. The Chamber appoints arbitrators, and collects and classifies, for inclusion in an annual report, statistical and commercial information bearing on the trade interests of the port.

Tuticorin Chamber of Commerce.

The Cochin Chamber of Commerce (founded in 1857) has no Branches, but is a member of the Associated Chambers of Commerce of India. It represents the British European mercantile community of Cochin. It is managed by a Chairman, an Honorary Secretary, and a Committee, appoints arbitrators and

Cochin Chamber of Commerce.

publishes annually a report containing statistical information regarding the trade of Cochin in particular and of Malabar Coast ports in general.

Calicut Chamber of Commerce.

This chamber was founded in 1923 to promote, foster and protect the commerce of the port of Calicut and the mercantile interests of the Malabar coast. Its affairs are managed by an executive committee consisting of a Chairman, two members and an Honorary Secretary.

Tellicherry Chamber of Commerce.

All European firms or individuals engaged in mercantile pursuits in Tellicherry are eligible for membership of the local Chamber of Commerce. Its affairs are managed by an Honorary Secretary under the general supervision of the members.

The Negapatam Chamber of Commerce, Negapatam.

The Negapatam Chamber of Commerce was established in 1931 to promote harmony and union among the members of the commercial community and to protect the interests of trade, commerce and industry of India in general and of Negapatam in particular. The Chamber conducts arbitrations and surveys in all disputes arising out of commercial transactions, registers trade marks and issues licenses to brokers and convasing agents. The certificates of the country of origin issued by the Chamber have recently been recognised by the Governments of Straits Settlements and Federated Malay States.

The office bearers of the Chamber consist of a President, Vice-President, two Joint Secretaries and a Treasurer.

Coimbatore Chamber of Commerce, Coimbatore.

This Chamber was established in 1922 with a view to promote, foster and protect the commerce and the mercantile interests of the Coimbatore town and districts by collecting and classifying all relevant information and forming a court of reconciliation and of arbitration to parties willing to abide by its decision. Members are of two classes—ordinary and honorary. There are 11 members. Its affairs are managed by a committee consisting of a chairman, an honorary secretary and three other chamber members.

Mysore Chamber of Commerce, Bangalore.

The Mysore Chamber of Commerce was established in 1915 to promote and protect the commercial interests in the State of Mysore by means of activities similar to other Chambers. The Chamber has been recognised by the Government of India as competent to issue certificates of origin. Individuals, firms, joint-stock companies, corporations and Associations engaged or interested in trade, commerce, industry, transport, finance and other mercantile pursuits are eligible for membership. Members are of two classes: honorary and ordinary. The Chamber is represented on important public bodies like the Legislative Council, Representative Assembly, City Municipal Council. etc.

The management of the Chamber is vested in a committee consisting of not less than fourteen and not more than eighteen ordinary members including a President, vice-President and a Secretary.

The Chamber was registered in March 1933 under the Indian Companies Act, 1913 The object of the Chamber is to promote trade and commerce. Every person firm or company residing at or carrying on business at Nagpur is eligible for membership. The number of members is 60. The Chamber is represented on the local Municipal Committee. Its affairs are administered by a Managing Board consisting of a President, two Vice-Presidents, one Secretary and nine members.

Nagpur Chamber of Commerce.

The Karachi Chamber of Commerce, founded in 1860 on lines similar to those of Bombay, has for its objects the promotion and protection of the general mercantile interest of the province of Sind, to communicate with the public authorities with similar associations, in other places and with individuals on all subjects of general mercantile interest, to collect and classify commercial information and to receive and decide references on matters of usage and custom in dispute. Its affairs are managed by a Chairman, a Vice-Chairman, and a Committee of eight elected annually The Chamber elects a representative to the Bombay Legislative Council and four representatives on the Karachi Port Trust. The number of members on the roll is 59 and there are five honorary members.

Karachi Chamber of Commerce.

The Chamber undertakes to nominate European arbitrators for the settlement of disputes as to the quality or condition of merchandise and appointment a public measurer to measure pressed bales of cotton, wool, hemp, hides and other merchandise at the port. It also publishes weekly a price current and market report and monthly statements of imports and exports of various commodities.

The Chamber was founded in 1916 and incorporated in 1925 under the Indian Companies Act, VII of 1913. Its objects are mainly to safeguard and promote common commercial interests of the Indian Maritime Traders in particular, to nominate delegates and advisers, etc., to represent the employers of India at the Annual International Labour Conferences of the League of Nations, to take all steps necessary in regard to the recommendations or conventions of the International Labour Conferences, etc. The Chamber has the right of representation in the following bodies among others, *viz.*, Karachi Municipal Corporation and Bombay Board of Communications (jointly with the Karachi Indian Merchants' Association), Karachi Port Trust, etc. In co-operation with the Karachi Indian Merchants' Association, it compiles and publishes trade returns, and railway statistics. The number of members is 294. The business of the Chamber is managed by a committee composed of one Chairman, two Vice-Chairmen, one Honorary Secretary, one Joint Honorary Secretary and 21 members.

The Buyers' and Shippers' Chamber, Karachi.

The Chittagong Chamber of Commerce was founded in 1906 to represent the commercial interests of the European and Indian communities in Eastern Bengal. Its membership includes also the Surma Valley and Assam branches of the Indian Tea Association. The Chamber elects three members to the Chittagong Port Trust and is represented on the local Municipality.

Chittagong Chamber of Commerce.

When requested by the parties, the Chamber appoints arbitrators for the settlement of commercial disputes.

The objects of the Chamber are to promote and protect trade, commerce and manufactures of Eastern Bengal in particular. The Chamber is composed of sixteen members including the President, Vice-President and Honorary Secretary. The office of the Chamber is at Narayanganj, Bengal.

Narayanganj Chamber of Commerce.

The Berar Chamber of Commerce was established in 1933 with objects similar to those of other Chambers. The membership is open to any Indian firm, company or association, engaged in trade in Berar. There are three classes of members—ordinary, patrons and honorary. The Chamber is administered by a committee consisting of the President, Vice-President, Secretary, and fourteen other members. The office is at Rajasthan Building, Akola, Berar.

Berar Chamber of Commerce, Akola.

The Upper India Chamber of Commerce, Cawnpore, was inaugurated in September 1888 and the first general meeting took place in January 1889.

Upper India Chamber of Commerce, Cawnpore.

The chief aims and duties of the Chamber are to promote and protect the general commercial and industrial interests of the United Provinces of Agra and Oudh, to encourage friendly feelings and unanimity among manufacturers and merchants on all subjects involving their common good, to act as a medium of communication with Government and to receive references from and to arbitrate between parties willing to abide by the decision of the Chamber.

The Chamber began with a membership of 22 which has now increased to 61. Among the members are included all the railways serving these provinces the principal banks, and, save for a few small ginning and flour and similar mills, all the power-driven industries of the United Provinces and some in the adjoining provinces. The major portion of the joint stock capital invested in Agra and Oudh is represented on the Chamber and in addition there is a considerable individual membership.

Officers of Government in the Departments of Commerce and Industry, of Agriculture, and of Posts and Telegraphs are annually elected Affiliated Members of the Chamber.

The Chamber is affiliated to the Federation of Chambers of Commerce of the British Empire, London; the London Chamber of Commerce (Incorporated). London and to the International Federation of Master Cotton Spinners' and Manufacturers' Associations. Manchester, and is a member of the Associated Chambers of Commerce of India, Calcutta, and the Employers' Federation of India, Bombay.

It returns two members to the United Provinces Legislative Council and is also represented on the Provincial Board of Industries; the Provincial Board of Agriculture; the Board of Economic Enquiry, United Provinces; the Cawnpore Municipal Board; the Indian Central Cotton Committee; the Provincial Board of Loan Commissioners; and the Advisory Committees of the various Railways of the Province.

The Chamber maintains a tribunal of arbitration and a commercial survey which are freely availed of.

The headquarters of the Chamber are at Cawnpore and its affairs are administered by a Committee of ten, including a President and a Vice-President

United Provinces Chamber of Commerce, Cawnpore.

The United Provinces Chamber of Commerce, Civil Lines, Cawnpore, founded in 1914, is the oldest and the only recognised Indian Chamber in the Province. It is a member of the International Chamber of Commerce, Paris and enjoys the right of representation in the Local Legislative Council, Cawnpore Municipal Board. and the Provincial Boards of Industries, Agriculture, Education and Economic Enquiry. Most of the Mofussil trade bodies in the province are affiliated to the Chamber.

Merchants Chamber of United Provinces, Cawnpore.

The Chamber was founded in 1932 with the object of safeguarding and promoting the interests of the mercantile community in the United Provinces. It collects and disseminates statistical and other commercial information, and issues an English and a Hindi bulletin monthly. The executive committee of the Chamber consists of one President, two Vice-Presidents, eighteen ordinary members and a Secretary.

Punjab Chamber of Commerce, Delhi.

The Punjab Chamber of Commerce, Delhi (founded in 1905) with local committees at Amritsar and Lahore, is concerned with the trade and manufactures of the North-West Frontier Province and Kashmir as well as of the Punjab. The Chamber shares with the Punjab Trades Association the seat allotted to the representation of Commerce in the Punjab Legislative Council.

Northern India Chamber of Commerce, Lahore.

The Northern India Chamber of Commerce founded in 1923, aims at the promotion and protection of commercial interests in Northern India by fostering friendly feelings and disseminating statistical and other necessary information. It has the right of representation on the Punjab Board of Economic Enquiry, the Communications Board, Punjab, and other bodies. The Chamber is administered by a committee of twelve members including the office-bearers.

Burma Chamber of Commerce.

The Burma Chamber of Commerce is an association of merchants, bankers, and shipping concerns, banded together to protect their several interests. It was first established in 1853, but its activities were somewhat desultory until 1877 when trade was confronted with so many difficulties with regard to trade with Upper Burma and various export and import problems that a public meeting was held to secure a greater measure of general support. The progress of the Chamber has been continuous ever since. Its membership now comprises all the leading banks and firms in Rangoon; and to it are affiliated the Burma Planters' Association, the Burma Fire Insurance Association, the Burma Marine Insurance Agents' Association and the Burma Motor Insurance Agents' Association. It also has a court of expert surveyors and arbitrators whose duty it is to settle commercial disputes and obviate recourse to legal proceedings.

The Chamber is directly represented on the Council of State, the Burma Legislative Council, the Rangoon Port Trust, the Rangoon Corporation and the Rangoon Development Trust.

The Headquarters of the Chamber are at 581, Merchant Street, Rangoon, and its affairs are administered by a Committee of eleven, including a Chairman and a Vice-Chairman.

Burma Indian Chamber of Commerce, Rangoon.

The Chamber was formed in 1926 to safeguard particularly the interests of the commercial community. It is represented on the local Legislative Council, Port Trust, the Railway Advisory Board, etc. The affairs of the Chamber are managed by a managing committee

The Burmese Chamber of Commerce, Rangoon.

The Burmese Chamber of Commerce was established in 1919 to foster, develop and protect Burmese commerce, manufactures, trade and all mercantile interests of Burmans, and to provide for arbitrations between parties willing to abide by the judgment of arbitrators appointed by the Chamber.

The membership of the Chamber is open to all Burmese corporations, companies, firms or persons engaged or interested in mercantile pursuits.

The address of the Chamber is 237, Phayre Street, Rangoon.

(ii) COMMERCIAL ASSOCIATIONS.

Marwari Association, Calcutta.

The Marwari Association of Calcutta is a non-political organisation, founded in 1898, with the object of promoting the social, moral and intellectual as well as the commercial well-being of the Marwari community.

The membership of the Association, numbering about 300, consists of the principal Marwari business firms in Calcutta and other prominent men of the same community. Its membership covers all the various branches of trade, both inland and foreign, in which the Marwaris are interested, and its representative character is recognised by Government, its opinion being frequently sought on matters of general public interest and on questions affecting the Marwari community in particular.

The Association elects a representative to the Bengal Legislative Council and one to the Legislative Assembly alternately with two other commercial bodies.

The office-bearers of the Association, who are annually elected, consist of a President, four Vice-Presidents, an Honorary Secretary, a Joint Honorary Secretary, a Treasurer, an auditor and thirty-two committee members.

The address of the Association is 134, Machuabazar Street, Calcutta.

Blanket and Shawl Traders Association, Calcutta.

This Association was started in 1938 with the object, among others of promoting the trade in textiles generally and Blankets, Shawls and Rugs, etc., particularly, and safeguarding the interests of dealers in these commodities. It is affiliated to the Marwari Chamber of Commerce. There are about 200 members.

Calcutta Grain, Oilseed and Rice Association.

The Calcutta Wheat and Seed Trade Association was formed in 1884 for the regulation of the Calcutta wheat and seed trade, to adjust disputes, and generally to promote and protect the interests of the trade in Calcutta. In 1930, in order to provide for widening the scope of the Association's activities, the title was altered to the Calcutta Grain, Oilseed and Rice Association. The affairs and funds of the Association are managed by a Committee of five members consisting of a Chairman and four members who are elected annually at the general meeting of the Association. The offices are in the Royal Exchange Buildings, Calcutta.

Calcutta Hides and Skins Shippers' Association.

The Association was founded early in 1919 with the object of promoting and protecting the interests of those engaged in the hide and skin trade and of developing the trade in raw hides with the British Empire and the Allies. It also includes in its purview an examination of the best methods of flaying, preserving and curing of raw hides. Its membership includes all leading shippers in Calcutta and people upcountry shipping through Calcutta agency firms. It is affiliated to the Bengal Chamber of Commerce and its affairs are administered by a Committee consisting of a Chairman and four members, the Secretary and Assistant Secretary of the Chamber being *ex-officio* Secretary and Assistant Secretary of the Association. The offices of the Association are in the Royal Exchange Buildings.

Indian Engineering Association, Calcutta.

The Association, then known as the "Engineering and Iron Trades Association", resumed its activities in 1909 after a period of several years of dormancy. In 1912, the title was altered to the "Indian Engineering Association".

The objects of the Association, as set out in the Rules, are "the protection of the various industries engaged in the working or manufacturing of metals and machinery in India; the development of such trades and industries, and the furtherance of the common interests of those engaged therein.

The Association works as an Association connected with the Bengal Chamber of Commerce; it represents the views of its members to all public bodies concerned, and to the various Governments in India, and attempts to further the expansion of the trades and manufactures in which its members engage. All firms engaged in the manufacturing of metals or machinery, in their own workshops in India, are eligible as candidates for membership.

The business and funds of the Association are managed by a Committee of seven members, elected annually, and the Secretarial work is carried out by the staff of the Bengal Chamber of Commerce.

Indian Sugar Mills Association, Calcutta.

The Indian Sugar Mills Association was founded in 1932 to promote and protect the sugar industry in India in all its aspects. It encourages research work and uniformity of practice, provides for a tribunal of arbitration for the settlement of commercial disputes, collects and disseminates statistical information, etc. In 1935 the Indian Sugar Marketing Board was created to co-ordinate the sale of sugar at various places. The Association has a membership of 102 mills.

Its affairs are administered by a committee of 16 members, including a President and two Vice-Presidents. The office is at 135, Canning Street, Calcutta.

Calcutta Jute Fabrics Shippers' Association, Calcutta.

The Association was founded in 1898; its objects are to encourage and secure united feeling and action amongst shippers; to collect and classify facts, statistics, to fix points of custom, adopt uniform forms of contract, to obtain the removal of grievances, to arbitrate in matters in dispute other than those provided for under the rules of the Chamber of Commerce, to communicate with public bodies and authorities, or kindred Associations, and generally to promote and protect the interests of those engaged in the jute fabrics export trade of the port of Calcutta, and especially in matters touching the interest of members of this Association.

All persons and firms directly connected with the export of jute fabrics from Calcutta are eligible for election. The affairs of the Association are managed by a Committee of five members, appointed annually, and the secretarial work is carried on by the staff of the Bengal Chamber of Commerce.

Indian Tea Cess Committee, Calcutta.

The Indian Tea Cess Committee was constituted under the provisions of Act IX of 1903. The object of the Act was to provide for the creation of a fund to be expended for promoting the sale and increasing the consumption of Indian tea in India and elsewhere. The fund is constituted from the cess collected on the exports of tea. The propaganda work is carried on in India, United States of America and the United Kingdom.

The administrative committee consists of twenty members representing the tea growers and the general commercial community. The representatives of the latter are four in number: three of them are nominated by the Bengal Chamber of Commerce and one by the Madras Chamber of Commerce. The representatives of the tea growers are nominated by the following Associations:—

Indian Tea Association (Calcutta)	Seven.
Assam Branch Indian Tea Association	Two.
Surma Valley Branch, Indian Tea Association	Two.
Darjeeling Planters' Association and Terai Planter's Association (jointly)	One.
Duars Planters' Association	Two.
Indian Tea Planters' Association, Jalpaiguri	One.
United Planters' Association of Southern India	One.

The office of the committee is at the Royal Exchange, Calcutta.

The name of the committee has recently been changed to "Indian Tea Market Expansion Board".

Bombay Millowners' Association.

The Bombay Millowners' Association (established in 1875) was founded with the object of protecting the interests of Millowners and users of steam, water and electric power in India, and the promotion of good relations between the persons and bodies using such power.

The membership is preponderatingly Indian and the affairs of the Association are managed by a Committee of twenty including a Chairman and Deputy Chairman.

The Millowners Association elects a representative to the Legislative Assembly alternately with the Ahmedabad Millowners' Association. It is also entitled to representation on the Local Legislative Council, Bombay Port Trust Board, Bombay Municipal Corporation, the Indian Central Cotton Committee, the University of Bombay and elsewhere. The Association keeps registers of all trade marks, trade numbers and trade names used by members and has framed a special set of rules governing such registration. All disputes between members in connection with the registration of any trade mark, trade number or trade name have to be submitted to arbitration.

There were on the 1st of January 1935, 100 members, of which 91 were cotton mills, 4 woollen mills, 2 silk mills, 1 ginning and pressing factory and 2 combined cotton, woollen and silk establishments.

The Association prepares annually a statement showing the names of all cotton spinning and weaving mills working or in course of erection in India, their capital, the total number of spindles and looms in each, the average number of hands employed and the approximate quantity of cotton consumed, and various other monthly statistical returns showing the exports and imports of piecegoods and yarn from and into Bombay and British India. Particular mention may be made of the Fortnightly Quotations issued in respect of the chief lines of yarn and piecegoods manufactured by member mills, the weekly price records of the principal lines of yarn and piecegoods imported into the various ports in India, the regular reports on market conditions in Bombay and other upcountry consuming centres.

Bombay Piece-Goods Native Merchants' Association.

This Association, which was founded in the year 1881, has for its objects the promotion of friendly relationship and unity among merchants in the city of Bombay dealing in piecegoods, with a view to facilitate and protect this particular line of trade. It corresponds with public bodies on matters affecting piecegoods trade. and also hears and decides disputes referred to it for arbitration.

The affairs of the Association are vested in a Committee composed of 15 members. The office bearers are a Chairman, a Vice-Chairman, Honorary Secretary, and a Treasurer.

Grain Merchants' Association, Bombay.

This Association was founded in 1899 'to promote and protect the interests of merchants, to put the grain and seeds trade on a sound footing' and to receive and decide references on matters of usage and customs and form a code of practice for simplifying and facilitating business in the grain and seeds trade and to arbitrate between parties willing to refer to and abide by the judgment of the Association. It is an influential body possessing a large membership, and its affairs are administered by a Chairman, Vice-Chairman and two Secretaries and a Managing Committee of 30 members.

Ahmedabad Millowers' Association.

The Ahmedabad Millowners' Association was started about 1891 with the object of protecting the interests of millowners and users of motive power of any description in Gujarat and Kathiawar and those connected with them and the promotion of good relations between the persons and bodies using such power. The Association represents the chief industrial interests in Gujarat, *viz.*, cotton spinning and weaving, power-generating, the manufacture of chemicals and drugs, foundries and iron works

The affairs of the Association are managed by a Committee of ten members, including a President, Vice-President and the Secretary. It elects a representative to serve on the Indian Legislative Assembly alternately with the Bombay Millowners' Association and also elects a representative to the Bombay Legislative Council.

The Native Share and Stocks Brokers' Association, Bombay.

The Association was formed to support and protect the character and status of brokers and to further the interests of both brokers and the public dealing in stocks, share and like securities and in exchange. The office of the Association is at Bombay.

Bombay Shareholders Association, Bombay.

The Bombay Shareholders' Association was established in 1928, mainly to promote and safeguard the rights and interests of shareholders and the investing public by collecting and publishing relevant information, conducive to the attainment of its objects. Membership is open to any major person who is a registered holder of shares of a company established in India or a company registered abroad but operating in India.

The affairs are conducted by a managing Committee consisting of not less than 20 and not more than 40 members. The office of the Association is at Agha Khan Building, Dalal Street, Fort, Bombay.

Seed Traders' Association, Bombay.

The Seed Traders' Association was formed to promote the trade in Indian Produce. It aims at the regulation of contracts and provides a Board of arbitration for settlement of disputes. There are two classes of members—merchants and brokers. The managing Committee consists of a President, a Vice-President and 18 members.

Bombay Shroff Association, Bombay.

The Association was established in 1910. Its objects are to foster harmony among shroffs and commission agents, to make rules and regulations for *hundis* to promote indigenous banking and to decide matters referred for arbitration. It maintains a commercial library and supplies forms with a view to encourage a standard *hundi* form for the country. Its office is at 233, Shroff Bazar, Bombay

The Exchange was established in 1923 to regulate the bullion trade in the city. All matters connected with the bullion trade are attended to by a Board consisting of a President, a Vice-President, and eight members assisted by a merchants' committee of 9 members. Its office is at Shroff Bazar, Bombay.

Bombay Bullion Exchange Limited, Bombay.

The Indian Sugar Producers' Association was established at Cawnpore in 1912, the first Annual General Meeting of the Members being held on the 9th March 1912. The aims and objects of the Association, broadly speaking, are to ensure, as far as possible, a common policy and concerted action whenever such is called for in the interests of the sugar industry. Problems affecting the sugar industry are naturally of a special character and while, in general matters, Chambers of Commerce serve this as other industries adequately, where the interests of the grower, the manufacturer, the refiner and to some extent, of the dealer, coincide the problem is best dealt with by an independent organisation. Government has recognised this and the Association can claim to have done useful work during the twenty-three years of its existence.

Indian Sugar Producers' Association, Cawnpore.

Beginning with the enrolment of 13 members, it now represents a substantial proportion of the established White Sugar Manufacturers of India.

The Committee of management consists of a Chairman, Vice-Chairman and five members The office of the Secretary is situated at Cawnpore.

The Association aims at the protection and promotion of skins and hide trade. The membership is open to all merchants, bankers, shipowners, tradesmen, representatives of commercial companies, brokers, persons and firms engaged in skins and hide trade Its affairs are managed by a committee consisting of a President, two to seven Vice-Presidents, two to four Secretaries, a Treasurer and not more than forty Members (excluding the President and Vice-Presidents). Its office is located at 33, Errabalu Chetty Street, George Town, Madras.

Southern India Skins and Hide Merchants' Association, Madras.

The Association was founded in 1902 and registered in 1925 under the Indian Companies Act, 1913. The obejcts are, briefly, to safeguard and promote the trade, commerce and industry of Indians in Karachi and elsewhere, to urge or oppose legislative and other measures likely to affect trade, to collect and disseminate statistical and other relevant information, to settle commercial disputes referred to for arbitration, etc. A produce Exchange Department and a Clearing House are maintained to regulate the trade in grain and seeds It has a membership of 211. The Association is represented on the Karachi Municipal Corporation (jointly with the Buyers and Shippers' Chamber, Karachi), Karachi Port Trust, Indian Central Cotton Committee, Lloyd Barrage Advisory Committee, etc. The office is located in Bunder Road, Karachi.

Karachi Indian Merchants' Association, Karachi.

The Association was founded in 1900 to protect and promote the interests of the landholders of Bengal and tenants. It also aims at securing the agricultural trading, commercial, sanitary and educational improvements in the Presidency. The membership is limited to the class of landholders of Bengal. Its affairs are administered by a President, 8 Vice-Presidents, 2 Honorary Secretaries, 1 Honorary Joint Secretary, 1 Honorary Assistant Secretary and an executive committee consisting of 32 members. The office is at 10, Old Post Office Street, Calcutta.

Bengal Landholders' Association, Calcutta.

The Employers' Federation of Southern India was founded in the year 1920, its aims and intentions being to promote better feelings between employer and employee, encourage the payment of fair rates of wages, collect and classify facts and statistics, fix points of customs, standardize forms of contract, arbitrate on matters of dispute, promote and protect the mutual interests of employers and employees and particularly to safeguard employers against misguided and unfair action by employees.

The Employers' Federation of Southern India.

All persons employing upwards of 100 employees are eligible to join the Federation.

The number of members of the Federation is 36 which includes the principal employers of labour in the Madras Presidency, representing approximately 42,164 employees.

The affairs of the Federation are managed by a Committee of a Chairman and 5 members, who are elected annually, the Secretary of the Madras Chamber of Commerce being *ex-officio* Secretary of the Federation.

The Federation is recognised by the Local Government, and consulted on all important matters relating to labour.

(iii) PLANTERS' ASSOCIATIONS.

So far back as 1801 the indigo planters of Bihar formed themselves into an association to facilitate correspondence with Government in the interests of the community, to safeguard those interests and to deal with applications for the settlement of differences between one member and another or between members and the local zamindars and ryots. The objects of the Association have remained much the same throughout, though the rules were remodelled in 1837 at the instance of Government and altered in 1877 and 1905.

Bihar Planters' Association.

When the successful exploitation of synthetic indigo had driven many of the planters to cultivate sugar cane, oats and other crops, it was decided in 1905 to change the name of the Association to the Bihar Planters' Association, Limited. Its membership now comprises about 46 factories, practically all of which cultivate sugarcane and some manufacture sugar. It is managed by a Board of Directors, a Chairman, Vice-Chairman and a General Secretary, who are appointed yearly

United Planters' Association of Southern India, Coonoor.

The United Planters' Association of Southern India (Incorporated) was formed as the result of a conference of different District Planters' Associations held in 1893. The first General Meeting took place in 1894 at Bangalore where the Head Office was situated until 1919. The registered office of the Association has always been in Madras. The Headquarters of the Association and the Secretary's Office are now situated at "Glenview", Coonoor.

The chief objects for which the Association was established were, to promote and protect in all parts of the world the interests of the various planting industries carried on in Southern India, the collection and dissemination of statistics and information relating to such industries, and the settlement by arbitration of disputes among its members.

The present organisation of the Association admits to membership the various District Planters' Associations, which are incorporated in Southern India, and any company, firm or person who is interested in the planting industry. In addition to a number of individual firms and companies, the membership includes thirteen District Associations. The control is in the hands of a General Committee of 26 members who work through an Executive Committee of five.

The activities of the Association include a Labour Department with four divisional officers and numerous agents throughout Southern India, and a Scientific Department of three European scientific agricultural experts, four Indian Scientific Officers, and a large subordinate Indian staff. It maintains two experimental stations. It elects an additional member to the Madras Legislative Council, and is represented on the Indian Tea Association, the Indian Tea Cess Committee; and by an Honorary Member on the Chamber of Commerce, Madras.

At the headquarters of the Association at Coonoor, the "Planters Chronicle", the official organ of the United Planters' Association of Southern India, is edited. This paper is published fortnightly and is distributed free of charge to all members of the Association and to various scientific bodies all over the world.

The Association is represented in London by the South Indian Association, 21, Mincing Lane, London, E. C.-3.

Bengal and Assam.

There are no provincial organisations in Bengal and Assam to represent the tea-planting community outside the Indian Tea Association, but there are five district associations, namely, the Assam and Surma Valley branches of the Indian Tea Association, the Darjeeling Planters' Association, affiliated to the Indian Tea Association, the Duars and Terai Planters' Association, Indian Tea Planters' Association, Jalpaiguri, India Tea Growers' Association, Assam, Bengal Planters' Association, Surma Valley Indian Tea Planters' Association, Terai Indian Planters' Association, and Tripura Tea Association.

(iv) TRADES ASSOCIATIONS.

Calcutta Trades Association.

The chief objects of the Calcutta Trades Association which was founded in 1830 and incorporated under the Indian Companies Act, 1882, are to encourage friendly communication amongst persons engaged in business in Calcutta, especially on subjects involving their common interests, to collect and circulate statistics and other information relating to retail trade, to consider all questions connected with the trade of Calcutta, and to promote or oppose any legislative or other measures affecting such trade: and further to arbitrate in disputes between parties where the assistance of the Association in that manner is sought for.

The membership of the Association is confined to firms engaged in retail trade in Calcutta, whether the proprietorship of such firms be vested in an individual, a partnership, or a joint-stock company. There are two classes of members—Permanent, enjoying all the privileges of the Association and. Associate, having full political rights but without the power to vote at the General Meetings.

The administration of the affairs of the Association is vested in the Master, Deputy Master, the immediate Past Master, the Treasurer and a Committee consisting of six members elected at the annual General Meeting and six appointed by the Master. All Past Masters are also—*ex-officio* members of the Committee, so long as they are members of, or are connected with subscribing firms. The Secretary is the executive officer of the Association.

The principal officer of the Association, formerly styled President has, since 1831 been designated Master.

In 1834 the Governor-General, Lord William Bentinck, acceded to a request contained in a memorial addressed to him that the Association should be recognised as a public body, with authority to address Government when they desired, and had sufficient and reasonable cause for so doing, and under subsequent administrations, the status of the Association has continued to be recognised. The Local Government has not only done the Association the honour of submitting various matters of public importance for its consideration. but has also conferred upon the members the right of nominating a representative to the Legislative Council of the province and another to the Calcutta Port Trust.

The registered office of the Association is situated at 34, Dalhousie Square, South.

The Calcutta Import Trade Association.

The Calcutta Import Trade Association, which was formed in 1890, seeks to encourage and secure united feeling and action amongst importers, and generally to promote and protect the interests of those engaged in the import trade of the Port of Calcutta, especially in matters touching the interests of its members. Among the main objects for which it was established are the collection and classification of facts and statistics, the fixation of points of customs, and the adoption of uniform forms of contract. The Association endeavours to obtain the removal of grievances and hardships, it arbitrates in matters of dispute other than those provided for under the Piecegoods Arbitration Rules of the Bengal Chamber of Commerce and it communicates with Government, with public bodies and authorities and with kindred Associations, on many matters of importance to its members.

The affairs of the Association are conducted by a Committee of seven members appointed at a general meeting held each year, the Secretary and Assistant Secretary of the Bengal Chamber of Commerce being *ex-officio* Secretary and Assistant Secretary of the Association. The offices of the Association are situated in the Royal Exchange, 2, Clive Street, Calcutta. More than fifty of the leading firms in Calcutta connected with the import trade comprise the membership of the Association.

Bombay Presidency Trades Association.

This Association was founded in 1902 with the object of promoting and safeguarding the interests, general or particular of the trading community in the Bombay Presidency and also of collecting and distributing such information as may protect members of the Association from loss or damage likely to arise in whatever manner. It undertakes arbitration when called upon to do so, collects debts due to members and acts as trustees on their behalf for liquidation, by persons indebted, of debts due to them. It keeps a watch over legislative or other measures affecting trade and, when found necessary, addresses Government in that regard. The Association sends a representative to the Bombay Legislative Council and, jointly with the Bombay Chamber of Commerce, to the Legislative Assembly. Other functions of the Association are the collection and circulation of statistical information relating to trade and the fixing of holidays to be observed by members.

The affairs of the Association are administered by the Master, the immediate Past Master, the Treasurer and Secretary, together with a Committee of five persons (exclusive of the *ex-officio* members of the Committee) subject to the control of the Association in general meeting. The Past Masters are *ex-officio* members of the Committee so long as they are members of, or are connected with members of the Association. The present membership amounts to 39

The offices are situated at Budri Mahal, 217-219, Hornby Road, Fort, Bombay.

Madras Trades Association.

The Madras Trades Association, established in 1856 and subsequently incorporated under the Indian Companies Act, was founded with the object of promoting the interests of the trading community of Madras, of furthering the adoption of a more healthy system of trade with reference to credit, and of obtaining, as far as possible, accurate information of the position and movements of those dealing with or indebted to its members. It undertakes arbitration when necessary, collects debts due to the members and generally acts as trustee for the liquidation, by persons indebted, of debts due to them. All questions relating to hours of business and the fixing of holidays are dealt with by the Association, and in addition it promotes or opposes legislative or other measures affecting trade. The present membership of the Association is 19 consisting of both European and Indian firms engaged in trade. The administration of affairs is vested in the members and is controlled by the members in General Meeting, the principal officers being the Chairman, the Vice-Chairman, and the Treasurer and Secretary.

The Association has the right of electing a representative to the Madras Legislative Council, 2 Trustees to the Madras Port Trust, and 3 Councillors to the Municipal Corporation.

The registered office of the Association is situated at Spencer Buildings, Mount Road, Madras.

Rangoon Trades Association.

The Rangoon Trades Association was founded in the year 1898 with the object of promoting the interests of the trading community of Rangoon and for the general adoption of healthier system of retail trade with reference to credit. It acts as arbitrator in disputes, collects debts due to Members and acts as trustee for the liquidation, by persons indebted, of debts due to Members of the Association. It arranges hours of business and holidays, promotes or opposes any legislative or other measures affecting trade, and collects and circulates trade statistics. Its Membership, at present numbering 36, consists of firms engaged in trade in Rangoon whether the proprietorship of such firms be vested in an individual, a partnership, or a joint-stock company. The administration of affairs vests in a President, a Vice-President and Treasurer, and a Committee consisting of six members elected at the annual General Meeting. Past Presidents are *ex-officio* Members of the Committee so long as they are Members of, or are connected with, subscribing firms. The Association has the right of electing a representative to the Burma Legislative Council, to the Rangoon Corporation, to the Port Trust, to the Development Trust and to the Railway Advisory Committee.

The Registered office of the Association is situated at 33, Randeria Building, 62, Phayre Street, Rangoon.

PART V.

PRINCIPAL PORTS AND TRADE CENTRES.

Though the geographical position of India is favourable for international commerce, the littoral of the peninsula is remarkably deficient in harbours to accommodate vessels of the draught now employed in the carrying trade. The west coast ports from Baluchistan to Cape Comorin, with the exception of Karachi, Gulf of Cutch ports, Gulf of Cambay ports, Bombay, Mormugao and Cochin, are practically closed to traffic from the end of May to the beginning of September by the violence of the monsoon, and the east coast is surfbound and without any natural harbours, though Madras and Vizagapatam are artificial harbours which offer a safe berth to vessels in all weathers. Calcutta, admirably situated for trade in the rich Gangetic delta, is handicapped not by its distance from the sea but by the bars which tend to form in the Hooghly, and Chittagong, though nearer the sea, suffers in an accentuated form from a similar handicap. Burma is very similarly conditioned, Rangoon, Moulmein, Bassein and Tavoy being all on estuaries at some distance from the Bay of Bengal, and the three last-named suffer also from indifferent internal communications. As a result of these physical characteristics practically six-sevenths of India's foreign trade is concentrated in seven ports, Calcutta, Bombay, Rangoon, Karachi, Madras, Cochin and Vizagapatam, to name them in order of their importance, of which Bombay, Karachi and Cochin alone are natural harbours.

The major ports of Calcutta, Bombay, Rangoon, Karachi, Madras and Chittagong are for administrative purposes placed under the control of bodies styled Port Trusts or Port Commissioners. These bodies are composed of Trustees or Commissioners partly nominated and partly elected, who, subject to the control of the Local or Imperial Government, have certain wide powers vested in them by law to levy dues and taxes in connection with the landing and shipping of goods and to utilize the amounts so realised for the betterment of the amenities of the port

In the following pages are reviewed the principal features of the different ports beginning with Aden, and after crossing to Karachi following the coastline right round the peninsula to the southermost confines of Tenasserim.

Aden.

Aden is situated on a volcanic peninsula at the junction of the gulf of the same name with the Red Sea and the Indian Ocean. Though the Civil Administration is under the jurisdiction of the Government of India, the Indian Sea Customs Act does not apply and imports therefrom into British India with the exception of Salt are regarded as foreign imports.

The Settlement, including the island of Perim in the Red Sea, has an area of about 80 sq. miles and a population of 46,638 (Census of 1931). The Port known as Steamer Point has an outer harbour giving a safe anchorage to a number of vessels, while the inner harbour is dredged to a minimum depth of 32′-6″ with 4 berths dredged to 35 feet and affording safe accommodation for vessels upto 33 feet in draught (vessels of deeper draught can be handled by working the tides). There are 4 oil berths connected to the land installation by submarine pipe lines, 2 of which have been dredged to a minimum depth of 35 feet at L. W., there are 2 other berths dredged to a similar depth available for the supply of bunker Coal and general purposes. There are no deep water wharves and cargo is therefore loaded and discharged by lighters of which there are a large number available.

Considerable quantities of cargo intended for the adjacent Italian and French Colonies, Abyssinia, Arabia, the Soudan, the Persian Gulf and Mombasa, are unloaded here for transhipment and similarly, produce from these places is reconsigned at Aden to destinations in Europe, Asia and the United States of America. When the Government of India Act of 1935 comes into force on April 1, 1937 Aden will cease to be under the jurisdiction of the Government of India.

Karachi.

The port of Karachi in the Province of Sind is situated in latitude 24° 47′ North, longtitude 68° 58′ East, and is the nearest port in India to Europe. For about a hundred and fifty years, Karachi has been the gate of foreign commerce not only for Sind but also for a great part of North-West India, Baluchistan and Afghanistan; but the value of its trade at the time of the conquest of Sind in 1843, amounted to no more than £80,000 annually. In 1863, the value rose to £4,440,000 but this was due to a temporary cause, *viz.*, the effect of the American war on the Indian cotton market, and it was not until after direct rail communication had been established with the Punjab in 1878 that this level was again touched. Though Karachi possesses large railway workshops, well equipped modern flour mills, an optical factory and a carbon and ribbon manufacturing factory, it cannot be regarded as an industrial centre, but it is of importance as the principal market and port of shipment for the surplus produce of North-Western India and as a storage depot for the manufactures and foreign produce which the hinterland requires in exchange for the raw products sent down. The principal exports are wheat, cotton, barley, rice, gram, oil seeds, wool, hides and skins and animal bones (bone meal, bone dust, etc.), and the principal imports, cotton and woollen piece-goods, sugar, machinery, iron and steel, mineral oils, coal and coke (largely on Government account for the North-Western Railway) This port now ranks as the third maritime port of importance in India

Situation and History

With the introduction of the air mail services between India and foreign countries in the year 1929, Karachi has become the leading air port of India. It is now the headquarters of the Chief Aerodrome Officer, Civil Aviation Department.

The following regular air services operate between India and foreign countries :—

(1) Imperial Airways Limited (British)

(2) Air France (French).

(3) K. L. M. (Dutch).

The Imperial Airways Limited, operate bi-weekly services between England and India with terminal air ports at Croydon and Karachi respectively. In conjunction with the Indian Trans-Continental Airways, the Imperial Airways Limited, have extended the services to Calcutta and also to Singapore *via* Calcutta and Rangoon. From Singapore, the service has been further extended to Brisbane (Australia).

The Air France operate between France and French Cochin China with terminal air ports at Marseilles and Saigon.

The K L. M. operate bi-weekly services between Holland and Java with terminal air ports at Amsterdam and Batavia.

Besides the above mentioned services with foreign countries, there are also bi-weekly services between Karachi and Madras, and Karachi and Lahore, operated by Messrs. Tatas Limited and Indian National Airways, Limited, respectively. Both of these services connect with the Imperial Airways services.

Irrigation.

With the opening of the Lloyd Barrage and Canals system at Sukkur in January 1932, this port has the prospect of still further development in the future. Agriculture in Sind has entered upon a new and important phase. The assured and perennial irrigation water supply afforded by this great engineering project has relieved the cultivators from the uncertainty and hazard which dominated their agricultural practice in the past. Vast areas of waste land have now been brought under cultivation, and the productivity of much of the old cultivated area has also greatly increased. The economic utilisation of huge areas of land and the diversity of the crops which can be grown under the perennial water supply will make large quantities of surplus produce available for export in the course of time, and with such immense agricultural possibilities in store, the future welfare of the Province of Sind in general and of the port of Karachi in particular seems to be assured.

Railway Connections.

The present population of Karachi is 2,60,000. The only railway line directly serving Karachi is the North Western Railway (Broad Gauge) which runs on the right bank of the Indus to Sukkur and Quetta, and on the left bank to Lahore *via* Hyderabad (Sind) and Rohri. At Hyderabad, the narrow gauge Jodhpur-Bikaner Railway connects with the North Western Railway. The interior of Sind is tapped by a few small feeder railways on the narrow gauge constructed and managed by Messrs Forbes Forbes Campbell & Company, of Karachi.

Facilities of the Port.

The facilities of the port now include a continuous line of Wharfage 8,600 feet in length on the east side of the harbour and on the west side four new berths of modern construction of a total length of 1,300 feet.

These wharves can accommodate ten steamers of 550 feet, two of 500 feet, three of 450 feet, one of 400 feet, and one of 350 feet, with 26 to 29 feet of water alongside, and one of 325 feet, with 18 feet draft, and three of 575 feet and one of 600 feet with 32 feet draft. There are ten electric cranes of 2 tons, eighty-six hydraulic cranes of 35 cwt., seven of 30 cwt., one of 30 tons and one of 14 tons on the wharves; and one 30 ton floating crane. The Boat Basin at the south end of the wharves contains the Commissariat Wharf, the Passenger Landing Pier and the Railway Wharf. There is also a Bulk Oil Pier which lies south of the Boat Basin. Pipes are laid down from the pier to the oil installations which are in the immediate neighbourhood. Liquid fuel pipes and connections are available from berths 2 to 6 of the Keamari Wharves, and are connected to the oil installations permitting two ships to be bunkered with oil fuel simultaneously or one ship being bunkered and one tanker discharging simultaneously in addition to the service from the oil pier. At the north-east end of the harbour are the Native Jetty and the Napier Mole Boat Wharf. Six lightering piers for landing and shipping stores and the heavy lift pier north of ship wharves accommodates barges There are in addition 5 swinging and 13 fixed moorings.

Dry Dock: Length on blocks 238 feet, breadth at entrance 50 feet, depth on sill at H. W O. S. T. 12¾ feet.

Depth of water: High tide 36½ feet, Low tide 27 feet.

Port Trust.

The affairs of the port are managed by a Port Trust Board of fifteen members of whom the Chairman is appointed by Government. Four of the members are elected by the Karachi Chamber of Commerce, two by the Karachi Indian Merchants' Association, two by the Buyers' and Shippers' Chamber, one by the Karachi Municipal Corporation and five are nominated by Government, including a representative of labour.

Since 1907, Karachi has been recognised as a first class port and is the headquarters of a Collector of the Imperial Customs Service, with three Assistant Collectors.

Trade of the Port.

The value of the foreign and coasting trade of the port in private and Government merchandise and the revenue and expenditure of the Port Trust during the twelve years ending 1934-35 are given in the table below:—

TABLE No. 9.—*Value of the trade of the port of Karachi and the revenue and expenditure of the Port Trust over a series of years.*

Years.	Import.	Export.	Total.	Revenue.	Expenditure.
	£	£	£	£	£
1923-24 . .	25,615,237	34,261,255	59,876,492	459,930	410,266
1924-25 . .	30,364,640	42,811,673	73,176,313	581,118	476,610
1925-26 . .	26,931,043	29,096,454	56,027,497	430,081	428,644
1926-27 . .	28,464,907	21,822,520	50,287,427	415,516	395,122
1927-28 . .	31,252,326	26,109,315	57,361,641	511,011	456,172
1928-29 . .	32,971,312	25,343,802	58,315,114	525,579	523,141
1929-30 . .	29,632,150	23,007,750	52,639,900	525,188	530,298
1930-31 . .	25,977,312	17,450,473	43,427,785	559,000	544,985
1931-32 . .	32,154,320	14,703,654	36,857,974	477,501	533,167
1932-33 . .	19,975,062	13,524,487	33,499,549	444,139	472,322
1933-34 . .	16,634,442	15,155,730	31,790,172	464,537	492,790
1934-35 . .	18,783,054	18,309,946	37,093,000	522,001	496,733

The deficits in the years 1931-32, 1932-33 and 1933-34, were due to slump in trade caused by the world economic depression. The years 1934-35 showed a welcome improvement.

The number of vessels (exclusive of fishing boats) entering the port in 1934-35 was 3,713 with an aggregate tonnage of 25,60,715 as compared with 3,116 with an aggregate tonnage of 23,78,403 in the previous year. Of 924 steamers entering in 1934-35, no less than 715 were British.

The debt of the Port Trust Board on the 31st March 1935 amounted in round figures to £3,180,675 against which may be set immensely valuable property in land and material and reserve funds exceeding £7,002,150 in value.

Improvement Scheme.

The Karachi Port Improvement scheme sanctioned in 1921 was considerably modified owing to trade depression in recent years. Only four of the six new berths proposed to be constructed on the West side of the harbour have been completed and only two of these have so far been equipped with electric cranes and transit sheds. These two berths each 550 feet long are dredged to 32 feet below low water. The transit sheds measure 530 feet × 130 feet and the berths are well served with railway sidings. Both export and import cargo is dealt with expeditiously at these new berths.

Minor Ports in Sind.

There are two other ports in Sind open to foreign trade, Keti Bandar and Sirganda, under the jurisdiction of the Principal Collector of Customs, Sind, but neither of them is of sufficient importance to deserve detailed mention. South of Sirganda is Mandvi the chief port of Cutch.

Bedi.

The principal port in the State of Nawanagar is Bedi Bandar, situated a few miles from the city of Jamnagar, at the head of a tidal creek some eight miles long, near the mouth of which is the roadstead called Rozi, in which ocean-going vessels lie at anchor. For steamers of any size Bedi offers no port facilities in the generally accepted sense of the term Such vessels do, and always must, cast anchor miles from Bedi itself in the uncertain waters of the Gulf of Cutch—uncertain because of siltation and the constantly shifting sandbanks.

The tidal creek connecting the Gulf with Bedi contains but little water at low tide, and no dredging could compete with the siltation to which the creek is subject. There is at the head of the creek a spacious basin equipped with warehousing accommodation and railway connection offering facilities to merchants for the effective conduct of extensive trade. Goods are transhipped between this basin and steamers lying in the Gulf by means of lighters of modern type, which are towed up and down the creek by well equipped tugs as the state of the tide permits. These lighters and tugs are so constructed as to lie without damage or inconvenience on the bottom of the basin when the tide runs out.

In 1930-31 [illegible] vessels called at the port including coasting

connections at other places in Kathiawar and beyond, have an [illegible] in developing a very large and important traffic. The figures are given below:—

	Value of imports.	Value of exports.
	£	£
1926-27	1,628,000	244,600
1927-28	1,614,000	521,250
1928-29	1,926,750	1,074,000
1929-30	2,089,500	720,500
1930-31	1,812,750	534,750
1931-32	630,750	169,500
1932-33	539,250	135,000
1933-34	447,000	335,250

No merchandise is handled at Rozi. Its landing stage, connected by road and rail to Jamnagar, is used exclusively for mails and passenger traffic to and from Cutch.

Okha.

Port Okha, situated in a detached portion of Baroda State far distant from Gaekwar's main territories in Gujarat is wholly dissimilar from all other Kathiawar ports. It is an entirely modern conception, begun and completed with great enterprise for the express purpose of dealing with ocean-going traffic and commodities unconnected with the trifling requirements of the scanty population of Okha Mandal. It lies in a strategic position at the extreme north-east point of the Kathiawar peninsula readily accessible to all steamers trading along that coast. The Harbour scheme has been well designed: there is an excellent ferro concrete jetty. served by railway lines and trains, alongside which two large vessels can lie at all states of the tide and there are also swinging moorings for other vessels in a protective position. The harbour is well lighted; the warehouse accommodation and railway connections are all excellent and the lay out of the administrative buildings and the residential quarters is well conceived and executed. The port is available even to the large ships at all states of tides and at all seasons of the year. The disadvantages are that the approach channel from the sea is circuitous and not devoid of risk, and that Okha is far removed from the large centres of population being 231 miles from Wadhwan Junction through which railway centre its traffic must pass In 1930-31, 34 ocean-going steamers and 214 coasting steamers visited the port. The following are the figures of imports and exports.

	Value of imports.	Value of exports.
	£	£
1926-27	198,600	533
1927-28	562,656	137,175
1928-29	704,550	219,225
1929-30	694,800	88,830
1930-31	451,875	90,900
1931-32	417,975	21,390
1932-33	440,100	50,325
1933-34	366,600	166,725

The principal items of imports are China clay, dyes, textile machinery, iron and steel, railway plant, motor cars, starch and sugar; of export, seeds and cotton. Sugar is responsible for more than 1/3rd of the customs duty realised.

Just below is Dwarka a famous place of pilgrimage and a port of call on the Bombay Karachi route. Steamers lie off at some distance from the shore and the traffic is chiefly local.

Porbandar.

The foreign trade of Porbandar was at one time prosperous but it is now chiefly coastwise.

The Portuguese port Diu on the island of that name on the southernmost extremity of the same peninsula boasts an excellent harbour but its exchanges, once considerable with Mozambique, are now completely stagnant.

Bhavnagar.

Half way up the Gulf of Cambay on its western side lie the port and town of Bhavnagar, the capital of the State of that name. The Gulf is defined by low lying banks of alluvial origin and is characterised by a very great range of tide, attaining as much as 40 feet at Bhavnagar, which is situated on a creek several miles from the open waters of the Gulf. The port facilities comprise an anchorage 8 miles or more from the port proper, between which and large vessels at the anchorage goods are moved in lighters while the port itself can accommodate small coasting steamers which lie on the mud at low tide. There is ample warehouse accommodation and good direct railway communication with the whole of India The volume of trade at all Bhavnagar ports is as shown below :—

	Value of imports.	Value of Exports.
	£	£
1926-27	1,602,400	1,344,067
1927-28	2,256,225	2,166,450
1928-29	2,621,625	2,245,425
1929-30	1,623,525	1,502,750
1930-31	1,799,925	1,107,075
1931-32	568,875	145,650
1932-33	1,749,525	549,675
1933-34	1,724,625	816,150

Surat.

Situated 14 miles from the sea with which it is connected by a river negotiable only by small country craft, Surat was one of the earliest and most important of the East India Company's factories and its trade was very considerable in agricultural produce and cotton, the value of which was estimated in 1801 at over £1 million. A hundred years later this total had contracted to £200,000 and in the last fifteen years the decrease has been even more marked, most of the trade being now transferred to Bombay owing to the linking up of the two ports by the Bombay, Baroda and Central India Railway. South of Surat is Daman, the capital of the Portuguese Settlement of that name, which has an area of 82 sq. miles and a population of 47,000. Even after the decline of the Portuguese power in India the volume of shipments of cotton goods made in Gujarat to East Africa was considerable and between 1817 and 1837 there was also a flourishing opium traffic with Macao, but since then the foreign trade of Surat has dwindled to nothing.

Mormugao.

On the Konkan coast south of Bombay there is no port of any size until one reaches Mormugao, though Janjira, Malwan and Vengurla have between September and May a considerable coasting trade with Bombay and Malabar coast ports. Mormugao situated on the eastern extremity of the peninsula of that name in Portuguese India about 5 miles south of Panjim or Nova Goa, the capital, is the terminus of the west of India Portuguese Railway. This line was built by an English Company under the guarantee of the Portuguese Government and worked since 1903 by the Madras and Southern Mahratta Railway. The port is also worked by the Railway but quay and tonnage dues are collected by the Government of Portuguese India and handed over to the Railway The Portuguese Government also appoint the Port Officer, the Port Health Officer and customs establishment.

Mormugao has developed considerably during the past 4 years. The harbour consists of a breakwater 1713½ feet long constructed in 1916 with a good lighthouse with a range of 12 miles at the end of the breakwater, which runs practically north and south. At the end of the breakwater a mole 885 feet long has been built at right angles (east and west), thus enclosing the harbour, which provides good protection against the south west monsoon The port is open all the year round. There are at present 5 berths alongside the quay wall, capable of taking ships from 22 feet to 30 feet draught. A new deep water quay in continuation is under construction and a large sea area is being reclaimed There are 12 steam travelling cranes on the quay of 1 and 1½ tons capacity one of 30 tons and 4 electric cranes of 3 tons. It is proposed to substitute electric cranes in the near future. The loading and unloading of all ships is done by stevedores, railway wagons coming alongside the quay. The harbour is dredged by a steam dredger. The harbour and sheds are lit with electric light. Ample shed accommodation is provided there being 9 sheds belonging to the Railway and 3 sheds to private firms. There is a Railway Telegraph office which receives and despatches all classes of telegrams, cables and wireless messages. The British Consulate and the Railway and Harbour offices are at Mormugao Harbour. At Vasco-da-Gama 2 miles away the Burmah-Shell and Standard Vacuum have large installations for the storage of oil.

Mormugao is a distributing port and her foreign exports consist chiefly of the produce of the Bombay-Deccan, Hyderabad and Mysore, particularly manganese, groundnuts and cotton, coconuts and occasionally manganese ore. The value of the imports and exports by sea excluding re-exports during the 12 years ending 1934 is shown in the following table:—

	Imports.	Exports.
	£	£
1923	535,120	79,537
1924	554,147	99,537
1925	434,541	80,106
1926	456,566	80,507
1927	484,714	85,540
1928	473,075	104,036
1929	517,610	115,369
1930	590,467	100,890
1931	583,522	91,646
1932	558,531	69,321
1933	510,648	72,780
1934	496,860	55,716

Bombay.

Situation and History.

The port of Bombay which is situated on an island of the same name in latitude 18° 55′ N, longitude 72° 54′ E, owes its importance to its geographical position and to its magnificient natural harbour. As is well known, the island was part of the dowry of Catherine of Braganza, Queen of Charles II, who conferred it for an annual rent of £10 upon the East India Company in 1668 After the conquest of the Deccan 150 years later Bombay became a provincial capital but until the middle of the 19th century it continued little more than a collecting centre for the smaller ports of the west coast and for the relatively small strip of land between the western Ghats and the sea. A period of progress was initiated by the establishment in 1838 of a regular monthly mail service to England by the overland route across Egypt and twelve years later commenced the work of linking up Bombay by railway with the cotton growing tracts above the Ghats and the wheat fields of the Punjab and the United Provinces. The American Civil War gave Bombay cotton an unparalleled opportunity and, if the reckless speculation which ensued swallowed up many private fortunes, the port itself emerged with its wharves and accommodation greatly increased and improved and its commercial potentialities unimpaired.

In the following table the total value of the trade of the port during the thirty-seven years ending 1934-35 is recorded.

TABLE No. 10.—*Total value of the trade of the port of Bombay (foreign and coasting) in private and Government merchandise from 1897-98.*

Year.	Value of imports.	Value of exports.	Total.
	£	£	£
1897-98	34,850,330	28,889,260	63,739,590
1902-03	38,562,000	39,104,460	77,666,460
1907-08	60,852,330	46,791,000	107,643,330
1912-13	85,471,660	56,922,660	142,394,320
1917-18	79,642,660	70,921,600	150,564,260
1922-23	123,445,332	93,571,311	217,016,643
1927-28	110,127,670	77,701,823	187,829,493
1932-33	57,308,415	84,202,931	141,511,346
1933-34	51,003,802	82,376,665	133,380,467
1934-35	59,362,458	85,236,719	144,599,177

In spite of the disorganisation caused by plague since 1896 not only to the facilities of the port but also to the local industrial position, the trade of Bombay, as the above table indicates, has until recently continued uninterruptedly to expand, and owing to a variety of causes it suffered to a smaller extent than any other port in India from the adverse conditions created by the war. A setback noticeable in recent years is apparently a reflection of general adverse trade conditions. The recovery made in the year 1934-35, however, suggests that the trade is likely to reach the pre-depression level in the near future.

Railway and Sea Connections.

Bombay is connected with Gujarat and Northern India by the Bombay, Baroda and Central India Railway, and with the Deccan, Central India, the Gangetic plain, Calcutta and Madras by the Great Indian Peninsula Railway. Of the raw materials brought down to the port for export, by far the most important is cotton, the other principal items being coal, hides, twist and yarn, grain and seeds, and manganese ore, while bullion, cotton manufactures, hardware, metals, machinery, kerosene oil, sugar and timber are the chief imports. Bombay has not the advantages possessed by Calcutta in having rich coal fields within two hundred miles or a system of navigable rivers to bring produce down to the port, but on the other hand she boasts a natural harbour directly upon the sea, which, thanks to its situation, is open at all times of the year.

The principal shipping lines calling at Bombay are the same as those of Calcutta. There is also a large pilgrim traffic to the Hedjaz and trade with the Persian Gulf ports in which Indian merchants take a preponderating part. The coasting trade with Karachi, Kathiawar, the Malabar coast and Goa is of considerable importance. The number of vessels which entered and cleared in the foreign trade in the year 1913-14 was 1,536 with an aggregate tonnage of 3,837,111. In 1934-35, the corresponding figures were 1,282 and 5,960,555.

The affairs of the Port of Bombay are under the supervision and control of the Bombay Port Trust, a corporate body created by an Act of Legislature, consisting of a whole-time Chairman appointed by Government and twenty-one members of whom eight are nominated by Government including one representative of Labour, five by the Bombay Chamber of Commerce, five by the Indian Merchants' Chamber, two by the Municipal Corporation of the City of Bombay and one by the Bombay Millowners' Association. The whole of the administration of the harbour, lighting, pilotage, docks, bunders, railway, and landed estate is carried out under this Board.

Administration.

The Board had its origin in 1862 in a private concern called the Elphinstone Land and Press Company; this Company entered into a contract with Government to provide a hundred acres for the terminus of the Great Indian Peninsula Railway, receiving in return the right to reclaim from the sea for its own advantage two hundred and fifty acres fronting its own properties. Developments of the port immediately followed, but Government, seeing the inadvisability of vesting such a monopoly of the harbour front in a private Company, decided to buy it out and transfer its properties to the charge of a public trust In 1869, therefore, the rights of the Company were taken over by Government and finally vested in a newly created Port Trust in June 1873. In 1879 the Trust was reconstituted by fresh Act of Legislature on a basis which has remained practically unchanged to the present date.

The Harbour.

The Port of Bombay, a deep arm of the sea between the Island of Bombay and the mainland, owes its importance to its geographical position and to its magnificient natural deep water harbour. Its central position and accessibility by sea and land have made Bombay the main gateway and distributing entrepot for the overseas trade of Western and Central India.

The harbour, which is one of the safest and most spacious in the world, covers some 74 square miles and provides secure and ample shelter for shipping at all seasons of the year, being about 14 miles long, 4 to 6 miles wide, with a general depth varying from 22 to 40 feet The entrance to the harbour is from the south-west; and the Colaba peninsula, the narrow strip of land which constitutes the Southern extremity of Bombay Island, forms a natural breakwater affording protection from the violence of the monsoon. The extreme range of tide is 18 feet 7 inches and the range between low and high spring tides is 12 feet.

The port and its approaches are excellently lighted. The three principal entrance lights are Prongs Lighthouse to the north, Kennery Lighthouse to the south and the unattended floating Light Vessel. Kennery Lighthouse is situated on the island of that name, which is about 11 miles south of Bombay and is about 154 feet above sea level and visible for 18 miles. Prongs Lighthouse which marks a reef running south from Colaba Vessel exhibits the white group flashing light from a masthead 32 feet above the water and is visible for 11 miles Prongs and Kennery Lighthouses are connected by wireless telephone with the Pilot Vessel and the Port Signal Station situated on the tower of Ballard Pier.

As a further aid to vessels making the port there is a fixed Wireless Beacon at Kennery Island which has a maximum range of 100 miles, and there is also the Direction Finding Station at Juhu some sixteen miles on the coast north of Bombay, from which accurate bearings may be obtained.

On the Port Signal Station storm warnings received from the Meteorological Office at Poona by telegraph are hoisted by day and night immediately on their receipt.

Pilotage is compulsory in Bombay for vessels exceeding 100 tons.

There are three enclosed Wet Docks and two Dry Docks particulars of which are as follows:—

The Wet and Dry Docks.

Name and date of completion.	Width of entrance.	Depth on sill at H W. O. S. T	Water area	Lineal feet quayage.	Number of births (including Harbour walls.)
			acres.	feet.	
Prince's Dock (1880) . .	66′	28′	30	6,910	14
Victora Dock (1888) . .	80′	30′	25	7,805	16
Alexandra Dock (1914)	100′	41′ (on outer sill) 37′ (on inner sill)	49¼″	16,055	20 (*plus* 3 berth for ferry steamers)

Name and date of completion	Width	Length.	Depth.
	Feet	Feet	
Merewether (1891) . .	65	525	26′ 6″ on sill at M H. W.
Hughes (1914) . .	100	1,000	34′ 6″ on sill at M H W.

Hughes Dry Dock is divided in the centre so that it can be used, if required, as two docks.

Between four and five million tons of cargo are handled annually over the dock quays. Every berth in the docks, except two which are reserved as open berths for certain classes of bulk cargo, has its own enclosed transit shed, fully equipped with hydraulic cranes and hoists, shoots for discharge of bag cargo, lock-up pinjras for valuable goods, etc. The total floor area of the sheds is approximately 2,500,000 square feet.

All the sheds in Alexandra Dock have rail sidings both on the quay front and at the rear, with large sorting yards on each side of the dock; the majority of the berths in the older Docks are also rail-served. The total number of moveable hydraulic cranes of various capacities in all three Docks is two hundred and nine, the two older docks being equipped with 30-cwt. cranes and Alexandra Dock with 35-cwt. of the luffing type with a 38-feet rake from the quay wall. There are also a number of five and six ton quay cranes, two fixed cranes of 30 tons and 100 tons and a 60-ton floating crane, in addition to several portable runabout cranes of varying capacity.

All berths in Alexandra Dock are provided with oil bunkering service pipes connecting with the liquid fuel installations and special berths are set aside at the Harbour Walls for the discharge of bulk fuel oil, kerosene, and lubricating oils. **Bunkering and discharge can be carried out simultaneously as the service pipes have been duplicated.** A specially equipped barge is provided for the reception of oil waste and bilge refuse.

In addition to the transit sheds each dock has an extensive range of warehouses fronting on the main roads behind the docks and being also rail-served, goods can be loaded direct into railway wagons. The total floor area is approximately one million square feet. The largest type are three-storied and a certain number known as 'protected' are reserved for the storage of special classes of cargo, chiefly piece-goods.

The Bunders.

Besides the enclosed docks, there are situated along the harbour front a number of "Bunders" or open wharves and basins where the traffic carried by coasting and country craft and "overside" cargo from the docks and the stream is handled These bunders which comprise an aggregate quayage of 30.000 lineal feet, are equipped with cranes, sheds and other facilities for loading, unloading and storing cargo.

The Railway.

The port Trust Railway handles nearly 50 per cent of the railborne goods traffic of Bombay Though only 7½ miles in actual length, it comprises nearly 120 miles of main lines and sidings which are divided into five sections, all directly linked with the docks and wharves—(1) the receiving and despatching yard at Wadala where the link with the trunk railways is formed, (2) the bulk oil Depots, (3) the Mazagon-Sewri Reclamation with its depots for cotton, grain. etc , (4) the Prince's and Victoria Docks and (5) the Alexandra Dock and Ballard Pier

The Storage Depots.

Bulk Oil Installations—The great bulk oil installations, some 83 acres in extent, are divided into three groups (*a*) the liquid fuel and lubricating oil depots at Malet Bunder immediately north of the docks, (*b*) the kerosene Oil Installations at Sewri and (*c*) the Petrol Installations still further to the north on the Wadala Reclamation The total capacity of all the various oil depots is about 56 million gallons. The installations, which are all on land leased from the Port Trust, are served by the Bombay Port Trust Railway and have pipe line connections aggregating 20 miles in length to the several loading and discharging berths at the Docks and at Pir Pao. Petrol and high grade kerosene are handled at the special berth at Pir Pao at the north end of the Harbour, a distance of 5½ miles from the storage tanks at Sewri and Wadala

The Cotton Depot, which covers an area of 127 acres and is one of the largest in the world, was constructed in 1923 at a cost of £1,000,000. Situated on the western side of the Mazagon-Sewri Reclamation, the Depot comprises 178 ferro-concrete godowns of a total capacity of one million bales, and 230 jethas or raised plints (of which a few have covered monsoon protection) accommodating a like number On each side of the Depot are 20 receiving and despatching stations in echelon and a railway yard with 8 miles of track. All the godowns are equipped with Grinnell Sprinklers and the depot has its own Fire Brigade, Salvage Corps Station, dispensaries, etc.

The Grain Depot.—To the east of Cotton Depot, on the opposite side of the Port Trust Railway, lies the Grain Depot which, as regards layout and communications, is a model of its kind. Over 80 acres in extent, it provides more than one million square feet of covered accommodation arranged in parallel rows of sheds 500 and 1,000 feet long by 110 feet wide, equipped with excellent roads, water supply and electric lighting and power. Between each row of sheds are feeder lines off which run echelon sidings—import on one side and export on the other. Opened in 1914 for the reception, storage and shipment of grain and seeds, it has since been considerably extended to meet the increasing demand of other trades. An area of 7 83 acres of covered and open accommodation is now leased to General Motors (India), Limited for their Assembly Factory.

Besides the above depots, there are several other storage depots for trades such as manganese ore, coal, building materials, hay and straw, etc.

Industrial sites, an area of close on 26 acres laid out in conveniently sized plots admirably situated as regards road and rail facilities, have been set aside on one of the Trust's newest reclamations at Wadala.

Practically the whole of the Port Trust Docks and estates are on land reclaimed from the harbour. The reclamation carried to completion by the Trust during the first thrity years of its existence comprised 167 acres of foreshore land from Sewri Bunder on the north to Apollo Reclamation and the Colaba Bunders on the south. In 1908 the Trust embarked on the Mazagon-Sewri Reclamation scheme which was completed in 1912 and added 583 acres to the area of Bombay Subsequently reclamations at Wadala, Tank Bunder and Colaba provided a further 310 acres The total area of the Port Trust estates is 1880 acres or approximately one-eighth of the Bombay City and Island.

The following table gives a comparison between the years 1913-14 and 1934-35 of the principal items of import and export trade dealt with at the port of Bombay.

Trade of the Port.

TABLE NO 11 —*Quantities of the principal items of import and export at the port of Bombay in 1913-14 and 1934-35*

IMPORTS.

Quantity 1913-14.	Particulars of the principal items of trade.	Unit.	Quantity. 1934-35.
326,000	Bricks, Tiles, Chunam and sand	Tons	211,000
656,000	Coal	,,	197,000
522,000	Cotton	Bales	741,000
96,000	Firewood	Tons	34,000
298,000	Grain	,,	406,000
125,000	Hardware	Packages	22,000
12,000	Do.	Tons	20,000
238,000	Iron and Steel	,,	80,000
139 000	Machinery Boilers and Railway Materials.	,,	91,000
	Oil, fuel	Gallons	49,800,000
42,649,000	Oil, Kerosene	,,	46,379,000
452,000	Piecegoods	Bales and cases.	326,000
225,000	Sugar	Tons	83,000
102,000	Timber	,,	77,000
49,000	Twist and yarn	Bales	101,000

EXPORTS

Quantity. 1913-14.	Particulars of the principal items of trade.	Unit.	Quantity 1934-35.
2,195,000	Cotton	Bales	1,924,000
451,000	Grain	Tons	167,000
51,000	Groundnuts	,,	80,000
(404,000 *Nos*)	Hides	,,	2,000
31,000	Iron	,,	35,000
612,000	Manganese ore.	,,	54,000
31,000	Myrobalans	,,	31,000
5,267,000	Oil, Kerosene	Gallons	633,,000
237,000	Piecegoods	Bales and cases.	364,000
822,000	Seeds	Tons	254,000
46,000	Sugar	,,	14,000
529,000	Twist and yarn	Bales	105,000

In some articles, the trade at the port of Bombay, though comparatively unimportant in the pre-war period, is now considerable volume of trade in these articles in 1934-35 was as shown below:—

IMPORTS.

Particulars of the articles.	Unit.	Quantity, 1934 35.
Glassware	Packages	119,000
Motor cars and Lorries	,,	18,000
Petrol	Gallons	22,000,000
Paper and stationery	Packages	243,000
Tea	,,	216,000
Wine, Spirit and Beer	Gallons	1,479,000

EXPORTS.

Oil, fuel (including bunkers)	Gallons	13,597,000

In the following table are shown the revenue and expenditure of the Port Trust during thirty-seven years ending 1934-35. In that period the income of the Commissioners has steadily increased and is now nearly six times what it was in 1897-98.

TABLE NO. 12.—*Revenue and Expenditure of Bombay Port Trust from 1897-98.*

Year.	Receipts.	Expenditure.
	£	£
1897-98	306,590	319,730
1902-03	394,000	366,600
1907-08	518,400	436,460
1912-13	592,530	515,130
1917-18	1,166,930	1,041,330
1922-23	1,730,823	1,718,310
1927-28	2,108,025	2,051,475
1932-33	1,730,850	1,845,225
1933-34	1,840,275	1,840,125
1934-35	1,879,085	1,850,700

The total capital expenditure as at 31st March 1935 amounted to Rs. 24·16 crores (£18,120,000). The total debt of the Trust is Rs. 20·30 crores (£15,225,000), repayment of which is provided for by annual equated payments or sinking fund contributions from revenue; the accumulation of the sinking fund as at 31st March 1935 was over Rs. 5 crores (£3,750,000). In addition to this, apart from property appreciation, the Port possesses Reserve and other funds totalling Rs. 84 lakhs (£630,000).

Mangalore.

To the South of Goa lies the Bombay district of North Kanara with the ports only open to the coasting trade of Karwar, Honavar and Bhatkal, the last named being close to the Frontier of the Madras District of South Kanara. Passing Coondapoor which is a port of call only for steamers on the Bombay-Mangalore run, Mangalore, the district headquarters with a population of 66,000 is reached at the junction of the Gorpur and Netravati rivers, about 130 miles south of Mormugao. It is a tidal port served chiefly by backwater communication with the hinterland. There is a Port Officer and Customs Collector There is also a Port Conservancy Board. Mangalore is the North-western terminus of the South Indian Railway. Vessels up to 200 tons can anchor inside the backwater; larger vessels lie about two miles from the shore. There is a small light-house. The chief exports to Europe are pepper, tea and cashew kernels from neighbouring areas, coffee and sandal-wood from Mysore, rubber to Ceylon and tiles, rice, salt fish, dried fruits and fish manures to Ceylon, Goa and the Persian Gulf, Cashew kernals are exported to the United States of America also.

The foreign import trade is steadily increasing Mangalore is the favourite port on the coast for the Laccadive and Amindivi Islanders, who bring their coir and other cocoanut produce there for sale Sugar is also imported from Java. 114 steamers aggregating 213.420 tons cleared the Port in 1913-14. 121 steamers aggregating 178,962 tons in 1922-23 and 170 steamers aggregating 287,443 tons in 1932-33.

Tellicherry.

Tellicherry with a population of about 30,349 is situated on the Calicut-Mangalore extension of the South Indian Railway, about 94 miles South of Mangalore and 14 miles South of Cannanore. a town of about the same size with much smaller foreign trade. Steamers which anchor about two miles off the shore, can work at Tellicherry even during the monsoon when all the other ports on the coast are closed, owing to the natural backwater provided by the rocky approaches to the Port. There is a small light-house. A sea wall of laterite in cement, 1,195 feet in length, has been built to afford protection against erosion and a pier, 560 feet in length, provided with six 1-ton and one 5-ton fixed cranes, with iron girders runs into the sea. There is a Port Conservator and a Customs Collector at this port The principal exports are coffee and pepper, which come down by road from estates in Mysore and Coorg, copra, sandal-wood, tea, ginger, cardamom and rose-wood. The foreign trade is steadily increasing. The chief imports are sugar from Java, wet dates, rice and provisions and machinery for estates 128 steamers aggregating 381,146 tons cleared the port in 1913-14, 101 steamers aggregating 319,748 tons in 1922-23 and 234 steamers aggregating 501,425 tons in 1933-34.

Mahe.

About five miles South of Tellicherry one enters the small French Settlement of Mahe with an area of about five square miles and a population of about 11,000 in charge of an administrateur. The town itself is picturesquely situated on the slopes of a hill on the southern bank of the Mahe River where it enters the Arabian Sea. There has been no foreign trade for several years except through the adjoining port of Tellicherry.

Calicut.

Calicut, the capital of the Malabar District, is some 42 miles south of Tellicherry and about 90 miles north of Cochin. It is 413 miles by rail from Madras, and the Headquarters of a Port Officer and Customs Collector and also of an Inspector of Customs, subordinate to the Collector of Customs and Salt Revenue, Madras. A Chamber of Commerce was opened here in 1923 and a Port Conservancy Board in 1935 The population is 99,273. The Port is practically closed during the south-west monsoon from the end of May until the latter half of August. The sea is very shallow and steamers anchor about three miles from the shore, connection being maintained by lighters and small boats. Native craft of 150 tons and below lie about 800 yards off the shore

Port Facilities.

There are two piers about 1,200 yards apart, each 775 feet long called the North and South pier They are fitted with eight and seven cranes respectively—(two cranes on the North pier and one on the South pier being of five ton capacity, two steam cranes of 3 ton capacity, one on each pier and the remaining five on each pier being of one-ton capacity)—to facilitate shipment into lighters. The northern pier is opposite to the Custom House, and the Southern abuts on the native bazaar. Beypore, seven miles to the south at the mouth of the river of that name, is regarded as a wharf of Calicut Port. It has ten wharves along the river bank and native craft of 150 tons burthen are able to anchor half a mile from the mouth. The light-house at Calicut is visible 12 miles out at sea

The number of steamers clearing the port in 1913-14 was 187, the figures of total tonnage being 567,620. The corresponding figures for 1922-23 were 212 and 564,193 and for 1933-34, 564 and 1,155,618 The principal exports are coir, coir fibre, copra, coffee, tea, pepper, ginger, rubber, groundnut, raw cotton and fish-manure The foreign import trade, which is insignificant, consists chiefly of metals, machinery and provisions, sugar, cotton piece-goods, cement, pepper, wet dates and kerosene oil

Cochin.

Cochin, situated about 90 miles south of Calicut, and recently declared a major port, is the most important port between Bombay and Colombo, and in the Madras Presidency the value of its trade is only exceeded by that of Madras. The system of back-waters running parallel with the coast affords cheap transport and excellent waterways connecting several places of importance in the Cochin and Travancore States and when the natural situation of the port has been fully developed, its position should ensure a very great increase in its trade. Cochin is nearly 300 miles nearer to Aden than Bombay and over 300 miles nearer to Durban. It is 242 miles nearer Aden than is Colombo. A vessel sailing from Aden to Fremantle adds only 39 miles to her voyage by touching at Cochin instead of at Colombo, and thereby serves the whole of South India. About a mile to the south-east of the entrance to the Harbour is the town of Mattancherry, a flourishing centre of trade in the Cochin State. The coast line for about 200 miles further south belongs to the Indian State of Travancore.

New Harbour Scheme.

The Cochin Harbour scheme commenced with the cutting open of a channel across the bar at the mouth of the backwater to provide access to ocean going steamers at all tides and in all weather conditions into the inner harbour where anchorage accommodation is provided for such vessels. As part of the scheme. over 400 acres of land has been reclaimed adjoining the Venduruthi Island for port purposes, where it is proposed to locate the offices, godowns, and buildings required for the harbour authority and some buildings have already been constructed and are in occupation. Further 400 acres is to be reclaimed. The success of the scheme depended on the possibility of dredging the bar to a depth of 30 feet, and keeping it open at all seasons of the year at a cost within the financial capacity of the port. Accordingly an experimental channel about 150′ wide was cut across the bar and completed in May 1923 at a cost of about £60,000. The harbour Engineer's report on the result of the experiment was considered by the Government and the experiment declared a success and the next scheme, *viz.*, the dredging of the permanent channel and the provision of mooring for vessels was completed. A dry dock at a cost of 4 lakhs of Rupees (£50,000) has also been completed. An approach channel 3 miles long and 450′ wide was dredged to a depth of 37 feet, at low water and by March 1930 the inner harbour had been made practicable for any ship which can pass through Suez Canal As a part of the scheme to improve the facilities of this harbour, it is proposed to connect the reclaimed area called 'Willingdon Island' with the mainland of Ernakulam and British Cochin by means of bridges The railway will then run on the reclamation area along the wharves and transit sheds which will be constructed there The offices of the Harbour Engineer-in-Chief to the Government of Madras have been constructed. Though the present port of Cochin lies in British territory, it is impossible to carry out any large developments without including in it areas of the Cochin State and ultimately of the Travancore State also. An agreement has therefore been entered into by the British Government with the Cochin and Tranvancore Durbars under which, subject to certain conditions, the three Governments jointly finance the development of the harbour and divide equally among themselves the Customs collections of the port from the time it became the regular practice for ocean-going steamers to come inside and discharge at moorings; the existing arrangements under the Interportal Convention of 1865 being superseded. It is hoped to introduce a Port Trust Bill at a very early date and constitute a Trust for the Port on the lines of those at Bombay and other major ports. As a result of the new harbour scheme, Ernakulam has been linked with the Podanur-Mangalore broad-gauge section of the South Indian Railway by a broad-gauge line to Shoranur, so that no break of gauge may check the traffic of the port with the fertile hinterland, it is designed to serve. The broad-gauge was opened on the 22nd October 1934. There are through trains to Madras, Bangalore and Trichinopoly which are reached in just over a night's journey. Ootacamund and Nilgiris are nearer still and can be reached like Calicut, Coimbatore and the planting Districts of the Anamalais in a few hours by road or rail.

There is a flashing light with an optical range of 16·3 miles in normal weather conditions, and a flag staff close by for signalling. The approach channel has recently been lit with flashing lights. The largest steamers using eastern waters can now enter at any time of day or night in seasons and moor in the calm waters of the inner harbour and take in supplies of good Alwaye water which is preferred to even Colombo water by the vessels. At present there are 9 large and 2 small berths in the harbour for mooring steamers. Steamers now anchor inside the harbour just opposite to the various godowns, thus making discharge easy and less expensive: Launches tow the cargo boats to and from the steamers. The new Custom House has a wharf with a crane line consisting of 1 (5 ton) and four (2 ton) cranes for landing and shipping heavy packages. There is an out agency of the South Indian Railway Company at Mattancherry (Cochin State) about 3 furlongs to the east of the Custom House, managed by Messrs Madura Co., Ltd., where goods and passengers are booked. The Customs and Port Offices and principal business houses occupy the foreshore of British Cochin, while the railway serving the port has its terminus at Ernakulam, the capital of the Indian State of Cochin, on the eastern side of the backwater about three miles away. There is a very powerful tug 'Cochin' for towing steamers into and out of the harbour. There is also the specially designed suction dredger 'Lord Willingdon' which is ceaselessly working to keep the channel always at the required depth.

Present Port Facilities.

By the Interportal Convention of 1865, the Cochin Durbar agreed to abolish the tobacco monopoly and inland transit duties at its ports and to equalize the rates of Customs duties at its ports with those in force at British Indian ports as well as to sell salt within its limits at prices ruling in the adjoining district of Malabar. In return for these concessions, the British Government guaranteed a minimum Customs and Tobacco revenue of £7,360. As there are no ports in the State open to foreign trade and as the Customs revenue has increased very considerably at Cochin in recent years, this subsidy has lately been increased. The exports from Cochin consist chiefly of coir, yarn, coir mats and mattings, lemon grass oil, cashew kernels, copra, coconut oil, tea and rubber and the groundnut trade has great potentialities especially now that the railway communications have improved and the area under this crop in the adjoining districts is steadily increasing. The port is the headquarters of a Port Officer and an Inspector of Customs. The population of British Cochin is 21,000 and of Ernakulam 23,000.

Customs Arrangement

Recently the Cochin Government has appointed;

(i) The Collector of Customs and Salt Revenue, Madras, as the chief Customs Officer, for the Port of Cochin to hear and dispose of all appeals;

(ii) The Deputy Commissioner of Salt and Customs Revenue, Madras, and the Assistant Commissioner of Salt and Customs Revenue, Central Division, Madras, to be Customs Collectors; and

(iii) The Inspector of Customs, British Cochin, to be Customs Collector and all officers subordinate to him to be officers of Customs under their respective designations and the Central Board of Revenue as the Chief Customs Authority.

There has been a steady increase in the number of steamers entering and clearing the port. The number of steamers clearing the port in 1913-14 was 225, their aggregate tonnage being 715,313. The corresponding figures from 1922-23 to 1933-34 are as follows —

Year.	No. of vessels.	Tonnage.
1922-23	223	730,588
1923-24	257	753,352
1924-25	273	792,874
1925-26	276	801,088
1926-27	306	817,724
1927-28	366	968,675
1928-29	470	1,147,043
1929-30	505	1,190,064
1930-31	600	1,418,142
1931-32	602	1,427,870
1932 33	619	1,432,337
1933-34	675	1,679,347

The imports and exports of this port have increased from about 500,000 tons in the official year 1930-31 to about 800,000 tons in 1934-35. Its unique advantages as a passenger port are only just beginning to be realised. Since the beginning of this year passenger steamers of the most prominent lines in the East, *viz*, P & O and B I S N. Line, Bibby Line and Ellerman and City Lines have been regularly calling at this port.

Alleppey.

Alleppey, the premier port and commercial centre in Tranvancore with a population of 43,800 is situated about 50 miles North of Quilon and 35 miles south of Cochin. A canal connects the port with the interior backwaters. It is a convenient depot for the storage and disposal of all fresh produce and possesses a roadstead affording safe anchorage during the greater part of the year. A mud bank in the roadstead acts as a natural breakwater against the force of the roughest seas. The aggregate tonnage of vessels touching at the port is about 300,000

The chief exports are copra, coconuts, coir fibre and matting, cardamoms, ginger and pepper. The port possesses a lighthouse and pier, and tramway worked by coolies conveys goods from the latter to the warehouses.

Shipping facilities at the port have been considerably reduced on account of the sand accretion at the pier in 1933. To restore these facilities, the Tranvancore Government are extending the pier by 209 feet. The construction of a boat basin is also under their consideration.

Quilon.

Quilon, the Coilum of Marco Polo, has been a trading centre from very early times It is connected with Alleppey by backwater and is on the Shencottah-Quilon-Trivandrum branch of the South Indian Railway. The chief industries are cotton spinning and tile manufacture Vessels anchor about ¾ mile from the shore and a railway siding runs up to the landing place. The chief exports are coconut oil coir mats, timber and fish, but the foreign trade is insignificant.

Tuticorin.

After rounding Cape Comorin, the southern most point of the Peninsula, one enters again the Madras Presidency and reaches Tuticorin. This port which is open all the year round with a population of 60,092, has next to Madras and Cochin the largest trade in Southern India It is the headquarters of a Sub-Collector a Port Officer and of an Inspector of Customs and is the south-eastern terminus of the South Indian Railway The Port is in exclusive charge of an Inspector of Customs and constitutes a Circle by itself, the minor ports of Kavalapatnam and Kulasekarapatnam which were formerly under his control having been transferred to the Jurisdiction of the Inspector of Salt and Customs, Tuticorin Circle, Tuticorin

The harbour is so shallow that steamers anchor about 5 miles from the shore and continuous dredging is necessary to keep the channel open between the shore and the roadstead

Port Facilities.

At the same time Hare Island upon which the Light House is situated, affords considerable protection to the lighters and other craft used for landing and shipping, and the work is seldom interrupted by bad weather The port is equipped with 6 piers The South Indian Railway runs alongside the landing and shipping wharves from which passengers and goods can be transhipped to launches and lighters About £15,600 have been spent since 1911-12 in affording increased facilities for the landing, shipping, storing and clearing of goods. These improvements include four new piers, four goods sheds, new trolly lines, sheds for storing combustibles and reclamations along the foreshore for stacking goods

New Harbour Scheme.

A scheme for the construction of a deep water harbour at Tuticorin was prepared in 1923 in which it was contemplated to dredge a narrow land-locked canal through the coral reef and Hare Island with two sidings each 700 feet long at the western extremity of the canal for vessels to lie in and to excavate a turning basin beyond the western extremity with banks of the north and south sides to accommodate two other vessels. The cost of the scheme was estimated at about £294,667. A sum of about £40,000 was spent during the year 1923-24 and estimates for £80,000 were sanctioned for 1924-25. In 1926, the Harbour Engineer-in-Chief to Government reported that the dredger in use was unable to cope with the work and wished to purchase one for £98,388. This with other expenses brought the total cost of building the harbour to £380,000. In 1928 a Committee of Harbour Engineers was appointed. This Committee was not in favour of a partial scheme of about £450,000 as it would not bring sufficient benefit to the traders and thereupon recommended 2 schemes. One to cost £1,200,000 to provide a dock near the town and not at Hare Island and the other to cost £900,000 with dock at Hare Island. The Port Trust expressed their inability to meet any expenditure in excess of £450,000 and approached the Government of India for a free grant from Central Revenues. The scheme was held in abeyance in the year 1929 for want of finance. In May 1930 the Government of India declined to make any grant for the purpose and the Trust abandoned the whole of the works so far constructed at a cost of nearly £210,000 which includes the cost of the stores, dredgers, plant, etc.

A bill for the constitution of a Port Trust was passed by the Madras Legislative Council in the year 1924 and a Trust was formed in the same year.

Passenger traffic to and from Ceylon has been largely diverted consequent on the opening of the Dhanushkodi route and the volume of goods traffic has not yet recovered to pre-war levels

There is a very considerable trade with Ceylon in rice, pulses, onions, chillies and livestock for consumption in that island Other chief articles of export are raw cotton (to Japan and United Kingdom), tea, senna leaves, palmyra fibre and cardamoms The number of steamers that cleared from the Port and their total tonnage from 1913-14 to 1933-34 and the value of the foreign trade from 1913-14 to 1933-34 are shown in the following tables.

TABLE No. 13.—*Volume of foreign trade of Tuticorin port in 1913-14, 1918-19 and from 1930-31 onwards.*

Year.	Foreign trade.		Total.
	Imports.	Exports.	
	£	£	£
1913-14	832,066	4,472,152	5,304,218
1918-19	705,175	2,981,855	3,687,030
1930-31	1,252,053	2,402,373	3,654,426
1931-32	1,045,092	1,698,425	2,743,517
1932-33	1,075,603	1,707,841	2,783,444
1933-34	814,555	1,687,243	2,501,799

TABLE No. 14.—*Number of Steamers that cleared from Tuticorin Port in 1913-14, 1918-19 and from 1930-31 onwards, and their total tonnage.*

Year.	No. of Steamers cleared.	Tonnage.
1913-14	526	1,183,736
1918-19	114	239,135
1930-31	418	1,160,676
1931-32	474	1,275,461
1932-33	504	1,751,272
1933-34	491	1,448,598

Dhanushkodi.

Dhanushkodi is the terminus of the South Indian Railway on the South-eastern extremity of the Island of Rameswaram at the junction of Palk Strait with the Gulf of Mannar and connected with Talaimannar in Ceylon 21 miles distant by a daily turbine steamer service, the journey being made in about two hours. The port is equipped with one pier. Cargo is loaded direct from the railway trucks on this pier into steamer hatches. The port was opened on the 1st March 1914 and so far has scarcely justified the expenditure incurred upon it. It is the headquarters of an Inspector of Customs. The chief exports are fish (dry and salted), rice, tea and cotton piecegoods. The population consists almost entirely of the employees of the Railway, Post Office and Customs. All business on behalf of shippers is transacted by the South Indian Railway. The number and tonnage of vessels cleared during twelve years ending 1934-35 with the value of the export trade are shown in the following table:—

TABLE No. 15.—*Number and tonnage of vessels cleared from Dhanushkodi and the value of export trade.*

Year.	No.	Tonnage.	Value of export trade.
			₹
1923-24	396	98,383	1,339,917
1924-25	396	99,029	1,359,435
1925-26	400	97,349	1,506,090
1926-27	416	104,056	1,781,039
1927-28	452	107,581	2,317,959
1928-29	438	102,787	2,052,500
1929-30	400	112,218	2,031,336
1930-31	382	138,492	1,781,588
1931-32	408	137,032	1,190,682
1932-33	398	139,275½	1,071,788
1933-34	407	139,316	1,042,053
1934-35	399	138,753½	930,270

Negapatam.

The Chief Port in the Tanjore District is Negapatam about 13 miles South of Karikal, with a population of 55,000. The harbour is equipped with wharves and other facilities for the landing and shipment of goods and the considerable foreshore to the north is utilised for the storage of timber. Nagore is the eastern terminus of a branch of the South Indian Railway and a siding runs into the harbour premises at the Negapatam Beach station. The port is further connected by river and canal with the tobacco growing areas to the south.

A safe anchorage for steamers is found within two miles of the shore and there is a plentiful supply of boats of from 5 to 12 tons which serve as lighters. The numerous sailing craft which trade between this port and Ceylon anchor about half a mile away Negapatam is the headquarters of a Port Officer and Customs Collector as well as of an Inspector of Customs whose jurisdiction extends to the whole of Karikal Frontier (Land Customs), and the port of Negapatam only (Sea Customs) The harbour is situated at the junction of the Kaduvaiyar river with the sea and the bar at the mouth cannot be crossed by fully laden boats at low water. Nagore, 5 miles to the north, a great place of pilgrimage for Muhammadans, is a wharf of Negapatam There is a light house at the Port.

Port Facilities.

The European Mail for the Straits Settlements is railed from Bombay to Negapatam and thence taken to Penang and Singapore by a connecting steamer. The number and aggregate tonnage of the steamers clearing the port during 1933-34 was 140 and 498,631 tons respectively, as compared with 130 steamers, aggregating 419,859 tons in 1923-24 The principal exports from Negapatam are groundnuts for Europe (chiefly to Marseilles and Trieste prior to the war) and coloured cotton piecegoods, tobacco and fresh vegetables for Penang, Singapore and Colombo, the port being the chief provisioning centre, for the coolies who are constantly leaving by this route to work on rubber and tea estates in Ceylon and the Federated Malay States.

Foreign Trade.

Karikal.

The French settlement of Karikal, covering an area of 53 square miles and a sea board of 12 miles with about 57,500 inhabitants, is surrounded except to seaward by the Tanjore District. Karikal, the capital, is situated on the north bank of the river Arasalar about 1½ miles from its mouth The Administrateur is subordinate to the Governor of Pondicherry. The port boasts a light house, 142 feet high, and is connected by railway with Peralam. The port is an open roadstead and has no direct trade with France, but there is a considerable rice traffic by country boat with Ceylon and the Strait Settlement The Standard Oil Company has a large installation at Karikal, which is a free port, including several big storage tanks. In this way the bonding of large quantities of oil is avoided despatches being made into adjoining British territory and duty paid thereon only when requisitioned. In 1934, 2·7 million imperial gallons of oil were imported by sea.

The chief traffic is rice, betelnuts, matches, fire works and kerosene oil.

Cuddalore.

Cuddalore is situated about 15 miles south of Pondicherry with a population of 57,358 according to the recent census taken in 1931. Cuddalore Old Town is on the main line of the South Indian Railway from Madras to Dhanushkodi and is connected with the port by a siding which runs upto the wharves. Steamers anchor about a mile off-shore, and the harbour wharves are situated on the western bank of the Uppanar backwater and have been provided with a quay wall to facilitate the loading and unloading of cargo boats therefrom. There is a lighthouse on the eastern bank of the back-water. Cuddalore is the headquarters of the Port Officer and Customs Collector with an Inspector of Salt and Customs whose jurisdiction extends over the ports of Cuddalore, Porto Novo, Tirumalaivasal, Tranquebar and Velanganni and Salt Factories of Cuddalore, Manambadi, Neidavasal, Tranquebar and Negapatam. The export trade consists principally of groundnut kernels (chiefly to Marseilles) and coloured piecegoods (to the Straits Settlements) in small quantities. The coasting trade consists mainly of grain and pulse. The foreign import trade is chiefly of boiled betelnuts from the Straits.

The number and aggregate tonnage of steamers clearing the port in 1934-35 was 212 and 727,663 respectively.

Proceeding further north the coastline for fifteen miles is that of Pondicherry.

Pondicherry.

Pondicherry, the Capital of the French Settlements in India (Establishments Francais Dans l'Inde) and the residence, of the Governor, is situated on the Coromandel Coast, 104 miles South of Madras, by road through Chingleput, Tindivanam and Mahilam. The roadstead possesses as good an anchorage as is to be found in the Bay of Bengal and there is also a pier 300 yards long fitted with electric elevators and having a reinforced concrete flooring with two lines of rails to facilitate the landing and shipment of goods. The town, which has a population of 43,500 enjoys a good water supply and is lighted by electricity. Steamers can anchor within two or three hundred yards of the pier but loading and unloading is done mostly from the shore in country boats.

Situation.

Pondicherry is the centre of the export trade in groundnuts from French territory and the adjoining British districts to Marseilles The town contains three spinning and weaving mills, of which the most important is under English management, these three mills have 1,691 looms and 71,752 spindles and find employemnt for 6,000 persons and their productions are shipped chiefly to the French Colonies. There is also a cottage industry for producing coloured cloth called *SAY-LASSE*, which is exported to Singapore, but this has become of very minor importance owing to trade slump and keen competition from the Japanese market. There is a factory where bonemeal manure is prepared for the planters in the Shevaroy Hills and in Ceylon and an ice manufactory. The Standard Oil and the Burma Oil Companies have small storage tanks near the railway station.

Trade and Industries.

Pondicherry is the headquarters of a British Consul General and there is a Chamber of Commerce founded in 1854 and reorganised in 1934. The French territory round Pondicherry has an area of approximately 115 square miles and a population in 1931 of about 183,500 and the frontier which has a perimeter of about 70 miles, is guarded by a cordon of land customs posts, the principal one being at Pondicherry station as the bulk of the traffic is rail-borne. Pondicherry is connected with the main line of the South Indian Railway by a branch which takes off at Villupuram and is also connected by motor services with Cuddalore, fifteen miles to the South with Tindivanam 29 miles to the North-west and with Markkanam 20 miles to the North-east. The principal exports are shelled groundnuts (arachides decortiquees), unbleached cloth, guinees (blue cloth manufactured locally, chiefly for French Colonies), ghee, onions, mangoes and bonemeal manure. The chief imports are raw cotton, arecanuts, foodstuffs, cement, wood and other building materials, wines, spirits, cotton piecegoods, silk piecegoods, silver, sugar, saccharine and gold lace, by sea, and by land coal, gunnies and motor spirit. Pondicherry is a free port but nominal import duties are levied on sugar, silver, gold thread, spirits, matches, saccharine and perfumes from 1934 onwards. There are special arrangements in force to regularise the free transport of articles that are dutiable in British India between one French village and another through intervening British villages The British Indian rupee is the usual unit of currency, though the only Bank in Pondicherry is a branch of the Banque de L'Indo Chine This Bank issues notes, which are legal tender only in French India, of one, ten and fifty rupees denomination The trade statistics are shown in francs. The combined value of the imports into and exports from Pondicherry and Karikal, in 1934, amounted to 307,858,882 francs, (imports 139,339,264 and exports 168,519,618) and the tonnage of vessels entering and clearing during 1934 was 104,748 tons and the number of ships 323

Madras.

The next port of importance as one proceeds northwards, (for *Sadras* and *Covelong* have degenerated into mere fishing villages) is Madras, the capital and chief port of the Presidency of that name, 1,032 miles South-west of Calcutta, which has a population exceeding half a million. Until an artificial harbour was constructed, Madras was an open roadstead with a surf-beaten coast line, communication between ship and shore being effected by *masula* boats and *catamarans*. The present harbour has been formed by two concrete walls projecting into the sea so as to enclose a space of about 200 acres with an entrance from the north-east, within which as many as 14 vessels drawing up to 31′-6″ can be accommodated.

Wharves and Quays.

There are seven wharves five of which are provided with all modern convenience for rapid discharge and loading, and alongside each one vessel can lie in 26 to 30 feet of water at low tide. There are also seven mooring berths inside the harbour, and one berth outside, protected by the north arm of the harbour Two tugs, one of 800 I. H. P and the other of 450 I. H. P. are available at all hours for assisting in the mooring and unmooring of vessels. Landing and shipping of cargo for vessels at moorings is effected by lighters of 20 to 100 tons capacity. These lighters are discharged and loaded at the wharves The western face of the harbour has been quayed so that the ships can now lie alongside and work cargo direct out of and into the sheds There are three other quays, connected up by rail with all parts of the harbour for the discharge of case oil and petrol, coal, horses and cattle Vessels can enter and leave the harbour at all times of the day and night Oil from bulk oil steamers is pumped ashore direct through the pipes into the merchants' installations

Cranes.

The West quay is provided with modern hydraulic and electric cranes, capable of working directly into, and out of, the holds of vessels lying alongside and there are several small one-ton hydraulic cranes between berths for loading or discharging lighters and barges In addition to these there are ten one-ton, and five two-ton, hydraulic cranes at the wharves for lighter working, and several steam cranes varying from two-ton to five-ton capacity The cranes for working heavy lifts consist of one 15-ton gantry crane, one 33-ton, and one 40-ton titan There is also a new 10-ton electric crane under erection

Other Facilities.

The warehouse accommodation covers over 16 acres and includes five transit sheds for the storage of goods in transit between ship and shore, three warehouses with flat roofs and three sheds with asbestos-cement corrugated sheet roofing, for the convenience of shippers dealing in groundnuts and other products which ordinarily need to be cleaned, dried and graded before shipment from Madras

There is a nine-acre boat basin which gives the necessary protection to all small craft in bad weather It is provided with 2,800 feet of shallow quay walling alongside, and about 1,250 feet of this quay walling is used by barges and cargo boats lying alongside for the landing and shipping of iron and stone and non-dutiable coastwise cargo This boat basin also contains a slipway for the repair of vessels up to 900 tons An area has also been reserved in which smaller boats and barges can be built

There is a two-acre timber pond provided with small jetties and cranes together with all facilities for handling timber for which there is a large storage area adjacent.

Railway Communications.

The harbour is connected with the broad gauge system of the Madras and Southern Mahratta Railway on one side and the metre gauge system of the South Indian Railway on the other All sheds and quays are adequately served by railway sidings so that cargo may be discharged into or out of railway wagons directly by steamers

Port Trust.

The affairs of the port are administered under the Madras Port Trust Act, 1905 (II of 1905) (as amended up to 1929) by the Madras Port Trust Board consisting of fourteen members, four nominated by Government, four elected by the Madras Chamber of Commerce, two by the Southern India Chamber of Commerce, one by the Madras Piecegoods Merchants' Association, one by the Southern India Skin and Hides Merchants' Association and two by the Madras Trades Association, and a Chairman. Normally the Government nominees include the Collector of Customs, the Presidency Port Officer, and the Agents of the Railways working into Madras The Board are also Conservators of the Port under the Indian Ports Act, with a permanent official as Deputy Port Conservator.

The value of the foreign and coasting trade of the port in private and Government merchandise, and the revenue and expenditure of the Port Trust are shown below.

TABLE No. 16.—*Value of the trade of the Port of Madras and the income and expenditure of the Port Trust over a series of years.*

Year.	Value of imports.	Value of exports.	Total.	Receipts.	Expenditure.
	£	£	£	£	£
1897-98	4,789,686	3,783,738	8,573,424	41,712	41,774
1902-03	5,105,249	3,622,794	8,638,043	49,224	38,237
1907-08	7,198,012	4,918,648	12,116,660	70,134	50,219
1912-13	8,438,056	6,004,815	14,442,871	83,025	56,567
1917-18	8,859,774	7,224,478	16,084,252	107,068	81,635
1922-23	15,420,770	9,152,826	24,573,596	186,950	148,904
1927-28	19,282,160	16,891,596	36,173,756	337,853	248,936
1932-33	12,721,454	8,370,126	21,091,580	223,980	240,938
1933-34	11,822,170	8,746,499	20,568,669	229,881	225,045
1934-35	13,498,566	8,576,409	22,074,975	254,547	227,380

The debt of the Port Trust Board to the Government on the 31st March 1935 amounted to £839,619 These loans are being paid off by equated monthly payments at a rate which will amortise part of the loans in 1952 and the rest in 1982

A sterling loan of £330,000 was raised in the London market in 1923 for providing a large increase in the shed space, modern electric portal cranes to work directly from ship's holds, and for the construction of an additional ships' quay, in addition to many other amenities Interest on this loan is paid half-yearly, on the 1st May and 1st November, at 5½ per cent. per annum A sum of £2,925 is contributed half-yearly to the Sinking Fund established for the amortisation of the loan in 1953 and the half-yearly contributions are invested in the Government of India 4½ per cent Sterling Loan 1950-55 The total amount of securities that stood to the credit of the Sinking Fund on the 31st March 1935 was £90,213-6-11.

Principal Imports and Exports.

The chief imports into Madras are rice and foodgrains, coal, oils, manures, paper and stationery, timber, sugar, dyeing and tanning substances, metal, glass and glassware, chemicals, hardware, machinery, motor vehicles, cycles and accessories, cotton manufactures, provisions, railway plant and rolling stock, building materials including cement, skins and hides, liquors, spices, fodder, bran and cattle food, cotton twist and yarn, tobacco, fruits and vegetables, gunnies, matches, raw cotton, soaps, apparel and the chief exports, groundnuts, skins and hides, onions, tobacco, raw cotton, ores, scrap iron, kerb stones, cotton manufactures, oil cakes, turmeric, manures, and coffee.

The number of vessels that entered and cleared the port in the foreign trade in 1913-14 was 511, with an aggregate tonnage of 1,182,944, the corresponding figures for 1934-35 being 784 and 2,609,138.

North of Madras is no port of importance open to foreign trade until one reaches Masulipatam.

Masulipatam.

Masulipatam, the principal port in the delta of the Kistna river, is now connected by a branch line from Bezwada with the main line from Madras to Calcutta The railway has a goods siding for traffic which runs along the wharves and facilitates shipment. A Port Conservator and a Customs Collector are stationed here The Port has few natural advantages Large vessels cannot anchor within five miles from the shore and the harbour wharves (six in number) are distant another three miles up a tortuous tidal creek, with a light-house near the entrance. Native craft up to about 150 tons can cross the bar at the south of this creek at high tides but in foul weather communication between ship and shore is practically suspended. Steamers touch here occasionally and foreign trade is chiefly by steam vessels with foreign ports, the principal exports being groundnuts, castor-seed and oil cake The prosperity of the port has never recovered from the cyclone of 1864, when a tidal wave caused a disastrous inundation involving the loss of 30,000 lives The present population is about 57,000

In 1934-35, 53 steam vessels and 34 sailing vessels cleared with an aggregate tonnage of 199,020 and 3,872 respectively.

Cocanada.

Cocanada is situated on the Cocanada bay just north of Godavari river, some 80 miles south of Vizagapatam and 270 miles north of Madras. In spite of several disabilities it ranks fifth in importance among the ports of the Madras Presidency Large steamers anchor about 6 to 7 miles from the shore and service is maintained with lighters ranging from 16 to 86 tons which land their cargo at the numerous small wharves and jetties constructed on the banks of the Cocanada canal The bar has to be constantly dredged to maintain 4 to 7 feet L. W. O S. T. There are 42 jetties and wharves from which goods may be shipped.

Cocanada with a population of 65,952 is the headquarters of a Port Officer and Customs Collector the latter being subordinate to the Inspector of Salt and Customs Revenue, Penuguduru Circle, Guruzanapalli. There are two Chambers of Commerce for Indian and European mercantile communities.

The principal shipments to Europe are raw cotton to the United Kingdom and groundnuts and castor-seeds to all continental ports. Rice and paddy used to go in large quantities to Ceylon and Mauritius. This trade is however affected by the advent of Siam rice. The import trade consists chiefly of kerosene from America, sugar from Java and metals from the United Kingdom, Germany and Belgium. Cocanada is connected by a branch railway line from Smalkot (10 miles distant) with the main line from Madras to

Calcutta. There is a station near the wharves with a large shed for the storage of goods awaiting shipment. In the year 1922-23, 159 steamers with an aggregate tonnage of 496,021 cleared the port. The corresponding figures for the year 1934-35 are 278 and 863,551.

Vizagapatam.

Vizagapatam with a population of 57,303 is now a major port with great potentialities situated at the headquarters of the district of that name, about 545 miles south of Calcutta and 105 miles north of Cocanada. Two miles from the port at Waltair is the junction of the Madras and Southern Mahratta with the Bengal Nagpur Railway.

New Harbour Scheme.

The scheme of development of a deep water harbour by dredging out the swamp about six sq miles in area and widening and deepening at the same time the tidal creek which connects it with the sea has practically been completed. The harbour has also been constructed and is worked as part of the Bengal Nagpur Railway undertaking. The opening of the Vizianagaram-Raipur line in 1932 has considerably reduced the distance to 'Central Provinces' markets and as a result of this, a vast area in the Central Provinces which is rich in manganese, cotton and oil seeds, will be served by this port. The harbour has a quay wall with accommodation for 3 vessels. Four more vessels can be berthed in the stream. Projects are also in progress to extend quay walls and sheds on the west side of the harbour for oil and manganese There are 4 electric cranes for loading and unloading cargo. Vizagapatam is the headquarters of the Traffic Manager who is the Port Officer and of the Customs Collector who is a subordinate of the Inspector of Salt and Customs Revenue, Penuguduru Circle, Guruzanapalli The principal exports are manganese (taken to London, Dundee, Dumkirk, Calais Antwerp, Stetting. Yingkow Workington. Naoyetsu, Fushiki and Kamaishi) myrobalams. niger and rape seeds and oil cakes and there is considerable cooly traffic at certain seasons with Rangoon All foreign imports are received direct from Foreign ports, but a few are transhipped at Madras, Calcutta and Rangoon. 159 steamers with a total tonnage of 419,607 cleared from the port in 1924-25 and 219 steamers with a total tonnage of 655,282, in 1933-34.

Bimlipatam.

The port of Bimlipatam is 22 miles north-west of Waltair. A good road connects it with Vizianagaram sixteen miles distant and another road with Vizagapatam. Public buses ply between Bimlipatam and the above places.

The foreign trade has revived to some extent. The imports are of little importance. There are considerable exports of Bimlipatam jute (hibiscus cannabinus), myrobalans, niger seeds, gingelly seeds and groundnut kernels.

Coastwise imports and exports are of little importance.

Passenger steamers from and to Rangoon are not now calling at this port, but proceed to Vizagapatam where there are better facilities.

There are many private godowns for storing produce awaiting shipment, but no wharves with cranes. The harbour is an open roadstead and ships lie about a mile off the shore and loading and unloading is effected by lighters.

The number of steamers clearing in 1934-35 was 26 with an aggregate tonnage of 96,341 which were engaged mostly in foreign trade.

Gopalpur.

In the Ganjam District, the only port deserving mention is Gopalpur, which is situated ten miles from Berhampur on the Bengal Nagpur Railway. The foreign trade at this port consists of mainly imports of dutiable cargo from foreign countries brought by transhipment from Madras and Rangoon Ports and from Ceylon direct by coasting steamers. There are also imports and exports of coastwise free cargo and foreign free cargo from and to the Straits Settlements. The steamers engaged in cooly traffic with Rangoon call regularly twice a week once to land and once to ship.

North of Gopalpur, the sea board for 250 miles is that of Orissa, the maritime trade of which is chiefly inter-Provincial and the only ports that deserve mention are Balasore, Chandbali, Cuttack, False point and Puri.

Balasore.

Until the opening up of the country after the great famine of 1866, Balasore situated on the right bank of the Burabalang river and the headquarters of the district of that name, was the only port of which Orissa could boast. It was frequented at that time by vessels with cargoes of rice from Madras and with cowries, then largely used for currency, from the Laccadives and Maldives The port is of historical interest as being one of the earliest European Settlements in India, factories having been established here in the 17th century by English, Dutch, French, Danish and Portuguese Merchants. The subsequent growth of Calcutta as the chief entrepot of commerce and the silting of the river together with the abandonment by Government of its monopoly of the salt trade and manufacture have all contributed to the decline of the port.

Balasore as a port is practically defunct. Foreign ships have ceased to visit since 1904 and coastal ships since 1910 An occasional country craft of negligible tonnage enters during the cold weather season for paddy but beyond that there is no sea-borne trade. There is no import trade

Chandbali.

Chandbali situated on the left bank of the Baitarani river is the only port of any importance on the Orissa Coast. It has a flourishing coasting trade with Calcutta but there is no direct foreign trade as in former days The exports consist mainly of rice and the imports are cotton twist, piecegoods, kerosene oil, salt and gunny bags. There is a growing passenger traffic with Calcutta served by two Steamship Companies, namely, The Chandbali Steamer Service Company Limited, and the Bengal and Orissa Steamship Company. Passenger traffic was badly hit by the opening of the

Bengal Nagpur Railway as prior to that line Chandbali was the entry for all passengers to Orissa, especially the pilgrims traffic to Puri. The value of the trade of Chandbali in 1934-35 was £91,430 the number of steamers then cleared being 87 with a tonnage of 13,545.

Cuttack and False Point.

Cuttack with a population of 65,000 is situated 253 miles from Calcutta at the apex of a triangle formed by the Mahanadi and Katjuri rivers It is on the main line of railway running between Madras and Calcutta and is connected by canal with Chandbali between which a small inland steamer trade exists and which links Cuttack with Calcutta.

The port of False Point has been closed since October 22, 1924 as the seaborne trade had entirely disappeared. The decline of the small ports is said to be due to a variety of reasons and usually the chief reason quoted is that the Ports have silted up but this is not actually the case. The Ports have declined for two main reasons namely the coastal Railway which has automatically cut out the sea trade since it cannot assist it and secondly that larger deep draft steamers have taken the place of the smaller coasting steamers and sailing ships of 30 years ago. The long and deeper draft steamers cannot enter such small ports as Balasore, Chandbali and False Point and hence the trade which at one time found its way by sea has now been caught by the railway and carried to the larger ports like Calcutta from where it is distributed elsewhere

Puri.

Puri is an open roadstead. It has a small Customs Office. There is an oscilliating light exhibited which is visible for 10 miles. Few steamers have visited the Port of late years chiefly owing to trade depression and the failure of the local crops There is no import trade.

In the year 1934-35 two ships only cleared with a tonnage of 6,614 and the value of the trade was £2,360. But in a good year this trade may show an increase of as much as ten or twelve times of the recorded trade in 1934-35.

Calcutta.

Calcutta, situated in latitude 22° 33′ N., longitude 38° 21′ E. on the river Hooghly with a population, including that of Howrah, of about 1,485,582 is the premier city in India and was until 1911, the Imperial Capital. The port serves the great jute, tea and coal industries, the wheat and seeds traffic of Bihar and the United Provinces and generally the agricultural areas tapped by the main lines of the East Indian, Bengal Nagpur and Eastern Bengal Railways and by the numerous waterways connecting the delta with the interior of Bengal and Assam. The total volume of the rail-borne traffic of Calcutta during the last pre-war year amounted to 10,389,000 tons of which 8,605,000 tons were inwards and 1,784,000 tons outwards, while river steamers and country boats brought into Calcutta during the same year an additional 1,126,000 tons. In 1921-22, the total volume for the year amounted to 7,979,000 tons, of which 6,253,000 tons were inwards and 1,726,000 tons outwards.

while river steamers and country boats brought in an additional 1,227,000 tons. Fgures for the years 1922-23 to 1932-33 are not available as the registration of inland trade statistics remained discontinued during that period. From 1933-34 the Accounts relating to the Inland (Rail and River-borne) trade of India have been revised in a modified form In 1933-34, the total value of rail and river borne traffic of Calcutta amounted roughly to 7,136,900 tons inwards and 1,212,500 tons outwards. The corresponding figures for 1934-35 are 6,619,700 tons inwards and 1,616,900 tons outwards.

The growth of the sea-brone trade of the port particularly in the ten years preceding the outbreak of war had been very remarkable and is shewn in the table below giving the volume and value of merchandise imported and exported. To this progress a set-back, which is reflected in the same table, was caused by the prolongation of hostilities as the situation of Calcutta precluded any military traffic as at Bombay and Karachi from being handled to any considerable extent in mitigation of the effects of the scarcity of private tonnage and of the restrictions imposed upon certain classes of exports and imports and upon shipment of goods to particular destinations The trade in the immediate aftermath of the war was marked by great variations, but from 1921-22 there was a steady improvement till 1928-29 Since then, due to economic depression, the trade suffered a decline, and as is indicated in the following table, in recent years it has been much below the pre-war level.

TABLE No 17 —*Total value of the trade of Calcutta in private and Government merchandise from 1897-98.*

Year.	Value of imports	Value of exports.	Total
	£	£	£
1897-98	24,194,556	34,115,694	58,310,250
1902-03	27,206,587	39,222,673	66,429,260
1907-08	44,745,939	52,770,448	97,516,387
1912-13	49,198,270	74,571,532	123,769,802
1913-14	56,548,746	75,000,913	131,549,659
1914-15	47,268,779	52,775,117	100,043,896
1915-16	43,575,434	63,671,836	107,247,270
1916-17	46,211,473	66,787,289	112,998,762
1917-18	47,552,767	62,141,170	109,693,937
1918-19	56,294,737	76,510,900	132,805,637
1919-20	60,167,054	93,850,336	154,017,390
1920-21	81,966,592	74,958,706	156,925,298
1921-22	70,635,859	60,955,127	131,590,986
1922-23	57,011,653	79,881,368	136,893,021
1923-24	54,580,173	83,131,409	137,711,582
1924-25	59,370,217	95,269,484	154,639,701
1925-26	55,209,512	98,105,648	153,315,160
1926-27	55,581,776	85,448,114	141,029,890
1927-28	65,214,730	104,766,368	169,981,098
1928-29	66,789,924	103,927,367	170,717,300
1929-30	63,104,338	95,954,560	159,058,898
1930-31	38,695,733	61,400,257	100,095,990
1931-32	25,998,514	44,197,224	70,195,739
1932-33	26,332,897	39,472,075	65,804,972
1933-34	24,439,470	44,170,625	68,610,095
1934-35	26,833,826	43,146,443	69,980,269

The gross registered tonnage of vessels entering the port has increased ten-fold in the last sixty years. The number of vessels that entered and cleared from the port with cargoes in the foreign trade in 1934-35 was 1,118 with a gross tonnage of 6,906,963, as compared with 999 of 3,077,199 tons burden in the last pre-war year. The principal items in the import and export trade and the volume of the traffic are shewn in the following tables. Shipments of coal which had increased from 7,600 tons in 1882-83 to over 3 million tons in 1913-14 (exclusive of bunker coal and Government stores) fell away thereafter and the total for 1922-23 was only 910,000 tons. There has been a steady improvement in recent years and in 1934-35, the shipments of coal amounted to 2,645,491 tons (including 565,384 tons of Bunker Coal). The movements of rice are entirely dependent on the character of the season and there are therefore large fluctuations as between different years especially on the import side, *e.g.*, over 417,000 tons were imported in 1919-20 as compared with only 66,000 tons in 1922-23, while in 1934-35, 572,280 tons were imported

TABLE NO. 18.—*Quantity and value of the principal items of import and export in the trade of Calcutta in 1913-14 and 1934-35.*

Imports.

1913-14.		Principal items of trade	1934-35.		
Quantity.	Value.			Quantity.	Value.
	£				£
1,610,874,392	18,470,083	Cotton piecegoods	Yds.	497,534,056	6,030,662
501,292	6,809,358	Metals and Ores .	Tons	175,702	3,149,447
102,114,362	29,022,631	Oils	Gals.	109,627,312	3,396,286
Not available.	2,190,238	Machinery and Millwork		..	3,306,562
Not available.	525,594	Instruments, apparatus, etc.		..	1,285,553
640,710	293,778	Chemical and chemical preparation.	Cwts	1,388,186	898,711
Not available.	1,044,175	Hardware .		..	758,111
301,518	496,353	Provision and Oilman's store.	Cwt.	327,591	654,943
349,009	357,603	Paper and Paste board	Cwt.	868,000	625,862
1,467	291,081	Motor Vehicles . .	Nos.	4,433	572,840
Not available.	598,739	Woollen goods .		..	555,844
1,833,526	458,647	Liquors	Gals	1,234,064	504,504
398,168	2,380,434	Rice.	Tons	572,280	2,705,843

Exports.

Quantity.	Value.	Principal items of trade		Quantity.	Value.
670,504	40,889,971	Jute manufactures .	Tons	798,863	18,089,720
697,846	18,691,152	Jute Raw . .	Tons	715,778	7,706,821
94,825	7,155,659	Tea	Tons	98,922	9,043,386
28,676	1,361,065	Cotton Raw . .	Tons	6,122	225,705
346,737	3,501,878	Rice	Tons	106,861	789,720
95,839	620,930	Pulses	Tons	41,956	293,158
55,415	5,663,115	Hides and skins Raw .	Tons	25,282	1,577,150
16,445	1,276,428	Lac	Tons	19,005	2,450,128
43,533	222,794	Manures . . .	Tons	30,918	139,080
3,045,516	1,920,108	Coal (excluding Bunker coal).	Tons	2,080,107	1,355,971
226,049	2,416,994	Seeds . . .	Tons	111,618	997,688
82,592	282,418	Pig Iron . . .	Tons	417,046	694,981
74,575	98,500	Manganese ore . .	Tons	208,493	267,635
2,066	236,765	Mica	Tons	4,686	458,037

The affairs of the port are administered by a Port Trust, founded in 1870, which is at present composed of a Chairman, a Deputy Chairman and seventeen Commissioners, of whom twelve are elected and five nominated by the Local Government, the twelve elected Commissioners being returned, six by the Bengal Chamber of Commerce, one by the Calcutta Trades Association, one by the Corporation of Calcutta and four by such body or bodies as the Local Government from time to time select as best representing the interests of the Indian Mercantile Community.

Administration.

The powers and duties of the Commissioners are prescribed by the Calcutta Port Act 1890 as amended by Bengal Act VI of 1926. Under Section 7 of the Indian Ports Act they are also appointed conservators of the Port of Calcutta, and, as such, have charge of the navigable channels of the river, though the Pilot service is not under their control.

The income of the Port Trust was £1,008,562 in 1913-14, £2,128,012 in 1930-31, £2,002,640 in 1931-32, £1,847,751 in 1932-33, £2,162,222 in 1933-34, and £2,296,486 in 1934-35.

TABLE NO. 19—*Income and expenditure of the Port Commissioners during the year 1923-24 to 1934-35.*

Year.	Income.	Expenditure.
	£	£
1923-24	1,739,268	1,747,062
1924-25	185,490	1,872,949
1925-26	2,141,850	2,102,940
1926-27	2,080,145	2,078,630
1927-28	2,541,159	254,737
1928-29	2,563,704	2,414,412
1929-30	2,579,858	2,740,680
1930-31	2,128,012	2,510,586
1931-32	2,002,640	2,350,826
1932-33	1,847,751	1,902,397
1933-34	2,162,222	2,230,634
1934-35	2,296,486	2,338,409

When the Port Trust came into being in 1870 they took over from Government four screw-pile Jetties fitted with steam cranes and sheds, a wharf for inland vessels, offices and some minor works of improvement of the river banks which formed the foundation of the present inland vessels' wharves They also leased from Government the Strand Bank.

Extent of the Port.

The Commissioners were debited with a capital sum of £66,666, repayable in ten triennial instalments and upon which interest at 4½ per cent. was payable under the provisions of the Act. For the £66,666 debited to them, they received from Government, on the 17th October 1870, the work specified and cash balances aggregating £14,293

In the sixty years that have elapsed extensive properties on both sides of the river have been acquired by and are now vested in the Port Commissioners At the end of the year 1934-35, the total value of the Commissioners' capital assets amounted to £23,514,050.

The limits of the port which originally extended only from Cossipore to Garden Reach, a distance of about 9 miles, were increased in 1886 to Budge Budge which is 16 miles below Calcutta in order to include the petroleum depot at that place, and in 1921 northwards 9 miles to Konnagar. The Port includes the Calcutta jetties which are situated immediately south of Howrah Bridge, all lands comprised in the area occupied by the King George's Dock and Kidderpore Docks, the petroleum depot at Budge Budge and a number of moorings in the stream where the greater portion of the coasting traffic is dealt with by steamers discharging into and loading direct from boats.

Port Facilities.

Vessels can discharge at the Jetties, in moorings or in the Docks. All the facilities commonly found in a first class Port are provided and communication between the various points in the Docks and Jetties including all the Commissioners' Warehouses is maintained by the Commissioners' Railway which has over 170 miles of permanent way and connects with all the main railway systems serving Calcutta. Goods can therefore be railed from any point on the Commissioners' premises to any part of India.

Principal Wharves.

Kidderpore Docks.—These consisting of Nos. 1 and 2 Docks and Tidal Basin were opened in 1892. There is a lock entrance 580 ft. long by 80 ft. wide from the river, which gives access to the Dock system.

Dock No. 1—This Dock is 2,700 feet in length by 600 feet wide, with a depth of 30 feet of water and has twelve berths serving single-storeyed cargo sheds, which are provided with hydraulic cranes to lift 35 cwts. and 5 tons

In addition there is one general berth in the tidal basin.

Dock No. 2.—This has a length of 4,500 feet by 400 feet and also provides a depth of 30 feet of water. It has five general produce berths serving double-storeyed sheds and eleven coal berths. Two of the latter are each fitted with five 8 ton special hydraulic coal loading cranes.

King George's Dock—was opened on the 29th December 1928 and comprises a Lock Entrance 700 feet long by 90 feet wide, two Graving Docks arranged in tandem, three import berths, one export berth, one lying-up berth, a berth for the discharge of non-dangerous petroleum and a special berth for inland steamers.

The import berths are served by three-storeyed sheds of the most modern type, each of which has a total floor area of 187,928 sq. feet, and the export berth by a two-storeyed shed having a floor area of 153,570 sq. feet. Each berth is 600 feet long and can accommodate vessels drawing up to 33 feet of water. Six quay cranes, four yard cranes, and ten lifts each of 2 ton capacity all electrically operated have been provided at each of these berths.

Garden Reach Jetties.

The Garden Reach Jetties, one of the latest additions to the Port and finished since the War, consists of a coaling jetty for ships up to 463 feet in length and four jetties for ships up to 600 feet, and they are built on the most modern lines. The transit sheds are double-storeyed, the largest having an area of 127,000 sq. feet on each floor and are fully equipped with electric cranes, lifts and trolley lines, while there are specially designed facilities for rail and lorry traffic.

The Calcutta Jetties.

The Jetties situated on the riverside below Howrah Bridge are the oldest part of the Port and as has been previously stated were taken over from Government by the Commissioners in 1870, when the Commission was first instituted. There are nine Jetties with a total length of 4,735 feet but only six of them are available for ocean-going steamers. One has been put out of commission as a measure of economy and the remaining two are reserved entirely for boat traffic.

Of the seven steamer jetties three are provided with two-storeyed and four with single-storeyed sheds, all of which are equipped with 35 cwt. cranes.

Heavy Lifts are dealt with by floating cranes of which there are three, with lifting capacities of 20, 30 and 60 tons. Heavy lifts are landed from boats at Mullick Ghat by means of a 30 ton Goliath crane. An auxiliary 10 ton crane is also provided. There is also a sheer legs in the Kidderpore Docks capable of lifting up to 100 tons

Petroleum Wharves.

The Petroleum Wharf at Budge Budge is situated some 14 miles below the entrances to the Docks Budge Budge is the oil depot for Calcutta where petrol and kerosene and other oils in bulk are discharged.

There are six pontoon jetties at which non-dangerous petroleum and its products are discharged, and one which is reserved for the discharge of dangerous petroleum.

The storage installations, which have a total capacity of over 50,000,000 gallons, are owned by various companies who rent sites on land owned by the Port Commissioners. The depot is served by the Eastern Bengal Railway but a considerable amount of oil in tins and drums is also sent away to Assam and East Bengal by river steamers.

There is also a new berth constructed in King George's Dock for the discharge of non-dangerous petroleum

Dry Docks.

Five dry docks, owned by the Port Commissioners, are available for the use of shipping, three in the Kidderpore Docks, and two in King George's Dock; they are able to take the largest vessels trading to the Port.

Special Purposes.

The Calcutta Jetties are used exclusively for the discharge of miscellaneous import cargoes. Some miscellaneous import cargoes, bag imports and all exports are dealt with in the Kidderpore Docks, in King George's Dock and at the Garden Reach Jetties.

Ships using the Commissioners' wharves also discharge into and load from lighters which are privately owned. Many ships do not make use of the wharves but do all their discharging and loading by means of lighters.

There is always an ample supply of lighters and in busy years more than 4,000,000 tons of imports and exports have been handled by this means

The principal imports are Cotton goods, Rice, Salt, Petroleum, Iron and machinery, while the chief exports are Jute, Gunnies, Tea. Hides, Oil Seeds, Rice, Manganese Ore, Pig Iron and Coal.

Imports and Exports.

The Commissioners provide extensive warehouse accommodation consisting of two Tea Warehouses having a storage area of 304,000 sq. feet, a Grain and Seeds Depot at Kantapukur having a storage area of about 1,000,000 sq. feet and consisting of 31 single-storeyed sheds, "A" and "B" sheds at Kidderpore, and the Fairlie, Clive, Canning and Strand Warehouses, situated close to the Calcutta Jetties with a total floor area of 93,000 sq. feet. Much of this accommodation is let out to firms, who then become entirely responsible for the custody and handling of goods while they remain in the warehouse.

Storage.

The remaining part is utilised as public sheds, and the liability as of a bailee remains with the Commissioners.

The River Hoogly is a difficult river to navigate and the conservancy of the hundred and twenty odd miles between Calcutta and the Sandheads forms an important part of the activities of the Port Commissioners, who maintain a large and expert staff of River Surveyors, etc., for the purpose.

Approach to the Port.

The approach to the Hooghly River is marked by light vessels—The Mutlah, the Eastern Channel and at times the Pilot's Ridge, the first and the last being about 40 miles apart. The Eastern Channel Light Vessel near which ships pick up their Pilot is 120 miles from Calcutta and the channels, bars and crossings are adequately marked by attended and unattended Light Vessels and Channel buoys. The Lighted channel extends from the Eastern Channel to Hospital Point a distance of 80 miles and from Ulubaria to Calcutta, a distance of 15 miles.

The Bars and Crossings in the River especially those within 40 miles of Calcutta are subject to seasonal changes Three suction dredgers are maintained and the Bars are dredged as necessary to allow ships up to 30 feet draught to use the Port.

Stevedoring is a private enterprise. The service is performed by old and well-equipped Companies who hold contracts with the principal steamship lines Efficient and plentiful labour is always available. Vessels are loaded and dischrged rapidly and efficiently. Continuous day and night, Sunday, and holiday service is always forthcoming

Stevedoring.

Pilotage is compulsory between Garden Reach and Sandheads and an extra fee is charged for night navigation. The charges vary with the draught of the vessel. The Commissioners' Harbour Masters take charge of vessels when they arrive at Garden Reach.

Pilotage.

Chittagong.

The port of Chittagong, with a population of 53,156, is situated in latitude 22°-14′ N. and longitude 90°-50′ E, about 10 miles from the mouth of the Karnafuli River in East Bengal. Though it has been a trading centre since the 16th century when the Portuguese frequented it, it was not until the Assam Bengal Railway was completed in 1895, that its claim to be regarded as a natural outlet for the trade of Assam and North-East Bengal was recognised. Jute, formerly the chief article of export, was brought down by water to Sea-going sailing vessels moored in the stream while the tea trade was non-existent and the import trade insignificant. At the present time the export trade consists chiefly of Tea, Jute, Wax, Cotton, Rice, Paddy, Oils, Provisions, Spices, Tobacco, Poultry and Livestock.

Jute arrives generally ready for shipment, by train from Chandpur after being baled there or in Narayanganj and is shipped either from the transit sheds at the Jetties or direct from the wagons, when convenient, while tea is conveyed from the estate to the nearest station on the Assam Bengal Railway which unloads it directly into the transit sheds at the Jetties.

The popularity of the port for shipment of tea, which is now the chief export, has developed enormously during recent years, the main reason being accessibility and light handling which ensures the arrival of consignments on the London markets in good condition. The foreign import trade which is slowly increasing consists chiefly of salt for which special storage accommodation to the extent of 18,735 tons is provided by Government, iron and steel materials, cotton piece-goods, tea chests, Machinery, Hardware and cutlery, Liquors, Chemicals and drugs and oils.

Port Facilities.

The present amenities of the port consist of four jetties 2,100 feet long built by and belonging to the Assam Bengal Railway, which are fitted with four 10 ton and seventeen 35-cwt. cranes. The Railway has also constructed seven sheds of which three are storage sheds and four transit sheds The storage sheds are mainly used for rice and miscellaneous cargo removed from the transit sheds. The space available in the stage sheds is 94,100 sq feet and they can accommodate 88,500 chests of tea, 37,400 bales of jute or 170,000 bags of rice. The four transit sheds can accommodate 181,000 chests of tea, 103,000 bales of Jute or 280,000 bags of rice.

All sheds have concrete cement flooring, corrugated iron roofing and are illuminated with electric lights They are also fitted throughout with upto date fire protection appliances. Grinnell's automatic sprinkler service is installed in all sheds.

Space is available for the construction of an additional jetty.

Vessels of any size with draft between 22 to 26 feet can proceed 9 miles up the Karnafuli to Chittagong at High Water Ordinary Spring Tides.

There are five berths for ocean-going vessels at the Assam Bengal Railway Jetties where the depth of the river is 26 feet and two sets of fixed moorings There are also two berths at Guptakhali for steamers in the oil trade.

Night pilotage is in force except during the South West Monsoon.

The port was formally declared a major Port on the 1st April 1928, and its administration transferred from the Government of Bengal to the Government of India. The Trust at present consists of 12 Commissioners—the Chairman and one Commissioner being appointed by the Governor-General in Council, the Collector of Chittagong District and the Collector of Customs, Chittagong, *ex-officio*, one Commissioner being appointed by the Administration of the Assam Bengal Railway three elected by the Chittagong Chamber of Commerce, three elected by the Indian Merchant's Association, Chittagong, or by such bodies or firms as the Governor-General in Council may, from time to time, select as best representing the interests of the Indian mercantile community at Chittagong, and one elected by the Municipal Commissioners at Chittagong. The Custom House is in charge of an officer of the rank of Assistant Collector in the Imperial Customs Service.

Port Trust.

The value of the trade of the port in 1934-35 was £4,692,176 in the foreign trade and £3,226,782 in the coasting trade and that in 1924-25 was £7,925,591 in the foreign trade and £2,631,545 in the coasting trade. The revenue of the Port Trust for the last 10 years has varied from £52,500 to £75,000. In 1934-35 it was £77,887 and in 1925-26 it was £54,305 The principal sources of revenue of the Port Trust are river dues at Re. 1 per ton plus a temporary surcharge of 12½ per cent, Port dues at 4 annas per registered ton plus a temporary surcharge of 12½ per cent. and a special duty on exports of raw jute at 2 annas per bale of 400 lbs and manufactured jute at 12 annas per ton. The revenue is subject to considerable fluctuations due to the imports of rice.

Trade of the Port.

In spite of the general trade depression the Commissioners have steadily pursued their policy of developing the port. Following the purchase of 2,000 ton hopper suction dredger "Patunga", placed in commission in 1928, the Commissioners in 1929 extended the Cutting Bend revetment by 2,000 feet at a cost of £11,250 to stabilise river conditions at Gupta Point (4¼ miles from the sea down the river). In 1930 the Patunga Revetment and Training Wall Scheme was commenced, a work extending over 12,000 feet along the right bank at the mouth of the river. This work has been virtually completed at a cost of £93,750 and the channel over the Outer Bar stabilised and deepened. In 1931, 5,200 feet of the left river bank at Kolagaon was revetted at a cost of £14,250 to safeguard the maintenance of deep water alongside the Assam Bengal Railway Jetties. In 1932, the Juldia half tide training wall estimated to cost £101,250 was commenced, and is due for completion in 1936. The object of this work is to close the Juldia Channel or south entrance to the river and to divert the discharge into the north entrance or Patunga Channel thereby eliminating the Inner Bar and improving the Outer Bar. A scheme for the development of this work into a full tide training wall at an additional cost of £22,500 is awaiting Government sanction. A scheme for the improvement of the Gupta Crossing Bar at a cost of approximately £60,000 is in course of preparation.

Improvements of the Port.

The installation of a new 65,000 candle power light at Norman's Point Lighthouse in 1927 was followed by the installation of a similar light in Kutabdia Lighthouse in 1932. In 1934 Government of India superseded the old Light-vessel "Sarsuti" stationed on the South Patches Shoal, by the modern type Light-vessel "Thibaw" equipped with diaphone fog signalling apparatus and a flashing light of 38,000 candle power operating on an Aga constant level table. In 1932 a river-lighting scheme was inaugurated whereby night pilotage was brought into being and shipping enabled to take advantage of the higher night tide during the fair weather season. The port has now the capacity of dealing with ships of draft ranging from 22 feet on neap tides to 26 feet on spring tides, throughout the year.

Pilotage rates were reduced by 10 per cent. in 1930 and have been maintained at this reduced level upto the present day.

FINANCES.

Since 1927, the Port Commissioners have expended £337,500 on the improvement of the port, of which £165,000 have been met from Government loan and the remainder either by contribution from Revenue or advances from Reserve Funds.

The Commissioners were compelled to levy a surcharge of 12½ per cent on River and Port dues in September, 1933, but it is hoped that circumstances will enable these to be remitted in the near future.

The value of the foreign and coasting trade of Chittagong in private merchandise in the year 1934-35 was as follows:—

TABLE NO 20.—*Value of the foreign and coasting trade of Chittagong in 1934-35.*

Items of trade.	Foreign trade.	Coasting trade.
	£	£
Imports	623,341	2,623,649
Exports	4,068,835	603,133
Total .	4,692,176	3,226,782

The corresponding figures for 1924-25 were £7,925,591 (foreign) and £2,631,545 (coasting).

The number of vessels that entered and cleared the port in the foreign trade in 1924-25 was 74 with an aggregate tonnage of 252 013. The corresponding figures for 1934-35 were 104 and 366,378.

There is at present no railway connecting India proper with Burma, one route *via* Chittagong through Chakaria, Maungdaw Buthidaung to Akyab, a length of 211·08 miles has been surveyed and estimated for in detail and in 1931 the first section of this project, a length of 29·19 miles, from Chittagong to Dohazuri was opened to traffic.

A reconnaissance survey of a route from Ledo in North Assam through the Hukon to join with the Mu Valley Branch of the Burma Railways was made in 1917-18. No further work has since been done.

The shortest sea route is between Chittagong and Akyab.

Meghna Bridge.

The construction of a bridge with a total length of 3,000 feet over the river Meghna between Ashuganj and Bhairab Bazar was sanctioned in February 1935 and it is expected to be completed in about 3 years. The completion of the bridge will give the populous districts of Dacca and Mymensingh direct and more rapid communication with the Chittagong Division and Assam. At present goods wagons are transported by a somewhat cumbrous wagon ferry and passengers have to detrain and cross the river by steamer. It is anticipated when the bridge is completed more business will be done by Chittagong and the Chittagong port with the Dacca and Mymensingh districts, the benefit to be derived from rapid and direct communication with the port without a break of gauge should be a great stimulus to the trade.

Akyab.

Akyab, the headquarters of the Arakan Division and the only port on the western seaboard of Burma of any commercial importance, has a population exceeding 38,000. There are six public and thirty-five private wharves, the former being fitted with one 5-ton and one 3-ton crane in addition to two hand cranes The port which is situated on the Cherogeah Creek is the headquarters of a Port Officer who is *ex-officio* Customs Collector. There is a jetty for deep-sea vessels which can accommodate ships with a draught of 18 feet, but the loading and unloading of cargo is usually carried out in the stream Akyab has no railway communications but the British India Steam Navigation Company and the Bengal Burma Steam Navigation Company run a bi-weekly steamer service from Rangoon to Chittagong *via* Akyab, and the ships of these two Companies alternatively call once a week at Kyaukpyu and between October and April at Sandoway A launch service owned by the Arakan Flotilla Company plies between Akyab and other Arakan coast ports, and a large sea-borne trade is carried on by native craft. The principal articles of import are hardware, liquor, machinery, provisions and textiles and the only exports of importance are rice and paddy.

Clearances from this port during the 3 years ending 1934-35 were as follows:—

	No. of steamers.	Tonnage.
1932-33	283	567,330
1933-34	299	612,813
1934-35	322	614,016

Bassein.

Bassein, the headquarters of the Irrawaddy Division, with a population of 45,662 is situated nearly seventy miles from the sea and is important only as a rice shipping centre. The Port Officer is *ex-officio* Customs Collector. The main branch of the Bassein river is navigable by vessels of a draught of 27 feet and large quantities of rice are loaded during the season by ocean-going steamers. The import trade is unimportant. There is direct railway communication with Rangoon and several river steamer services exist, the most important of which is that run by the Irrawaddy Flotilla Company. There are five public and twenty private wharves for the landing and shipping of goods, but the port at present lacks warehouses and cranes and loading is effected entirely in the stream.

Clearances from this port during the 3 years ending 1934-35 were as follows:—

	No. of steamers.	Tonnage.
1932-33	87	281,991
1933-34	97	314,893
1934-35	97	310,703

Rangoon.

Rangoon, the capital of Burma and the headquarters of the local Government, with a population of about 399,000 is the chief port of the province of Burma, and in the volume and value of its trade the third seaport of British India. It is situated on the Hlaing or Rangoon River about 24 miles from the sea and is served by the Burma Railways, a metre gauge system, which connects Rangoon with the most important towns of the Province and with the Shan States. The total mileage of Burma Railway is 2,050 miles.

Port Facilities.

The present facilities of the Port include a Wharf of a total length of 3,330 feet, comprising 7 berths with a depth of 25 feet below low water of spring tides, and equipped with six 3-ton electric cranes, ten 3-ton and thirteen 35-cwt. hydraulic cranes together with a pontoon jetty 500 feet in length, for ocean-going steamers. The wharf area is equipped with one 10-ton transporter crane and two 7-ton steam cranes. In addition there is one jetty 278 feet in length, with a depth of 25 feet below low water of spring tides, carrying a sheerleg for heavy lifts, the weight of which is now limited to 20 tons. Proposals for the reconstruction of this jetty to provide two deep-water berths for ocean-going steamers and a 40-ton crane are under consideration. To accommodate inland vessels 43 pontoon jetties and 29 fixed jetties are provided. There are 21 swinging moorings and 18 fixed moorings in the river for ocean-going steamers, 4 of the latter being reserved for oil tankers. The port lacks a dry dock suitable for ocean-going vessels, but in every other respect is well equipped with modern equipment for loading and unloading vessels and for the handling and storage of cargo.

The affairs of the Port are administered by a Trust consisting of 17 members, of whom 4 are nominated by Government, 3 are *ex-officio* members by virtue of the Government appointments which they hold, 8 are elected by the four Chambers of Commerce, 1 is elected by the Rangoon Trades Association and 1 by the Municipal Corporation.

Port Trust.

The following table shows the income and expenditure of the Port Commissioners. It will be remarked that in recent years of trade depression, in spite of some decline in income, there has been no substantial deficit. The two main sources of revenue, river dues on goods and port dues on vessels, have been reduced to 5 annas and 4½ annas per ton, respectively, compared with statutory maxima of 8 annas and 6 annas, and reduction of other scheduled charges range from 10 per cent. to 25 per cent (and up to 60 per cent. in the case of rents).

TABLE NO. 21 —*Income and expenditure of the Rangoon Port Trust.*

Year.	Income.	Expenditure.
	£	£
1890-91	70,566	86,104
1905-06	127,543	126,458
1922-23	512,949	439,525
1927-28	647,748	613,366
1928-29	613,297	643,609
1929-30	615,824	614,967
1930-31	605,433	607,156
1931-32	567,560	589,032
1932-33	516,192	530,707
1933-34	531,664	540,922
1934-35	565,123	505,036

The figures for expenditure exclude sums transferred to Reserve Funds.

The total liability in respect of borrowings on capital account by 31st March 1935 amounted to £3,782,150. Provision for paying off this liability is made by means of Sinking Funds. The amount standing at the credit of the Sinking Funds on 31st March 1935, taking the investments at market value, was £1 911,065 and at the credit of the Reserve Funds and accumulated Revenue Account £1,100,761.

The value of the foreign and coasting trade of the port in private and Government merchandise from 1924-25, to 1934-35 is given in the table below:—

Trade of the Port.

TABLE No. 22.—*Value of the trade of the port of Rangoon from 1924-25 to 1934-35.*

	Year.	Import.	Export.	Total.
		£	£	£
(a)	1924-25	26,719,482	40,254,649	66,974,131
(a)	1925-26	28,636,064	47,837,342	76,473,407
(a)	1926-27	28,492,635	40,325,479	68,818,115
(a)	1927-28	31,561,278	45,438,959	77,000,237
(a)	1928-29	26,470,375	40,933,009	67,403,385
(a)	1929-30	26,376,574	43,553,882	69,930,456
	1930-31	21,499,588	35,211,182	56,710,770
	1931-32	16,503,800	28,084,965	44,588,765
	1932-33	15,582,736	30,500,430	46,083,166
	1933-34	13,869,844	30,118,984	43,988,827
	1934-35	15,544,161	33,182,363	48,726,524

(a) Government Stores not included.

The foreign sea-borne trade westward is carried principally by vessels of the Bibby, Henderson, Ellerman's City and Hall, Swedish East Asiatic, Nourse, American-Indian, Hansa and British India lines, while traffic to the Far East is principally in the hands of the British India and Java Bengal lines, the Nippon Yusen Kaisha and Osaka Shosen Kaisha The British India Steam Navigation Company and the Scindia Steam Navigation Company enjoy the bulk of the coasting trade, and the Irrawaddy Flotilla Company operating from Rangoon has almost a monopoly of the very considerable river-borne traffic. The headquarters of the railway and of all other large concerns in Burma are in Rangoon, and about 90 per cent. of the foreign trade of the province passes through the port Of the coasting trade, about 86 per cent. of the trade with other provinces and about 47 per cent. of the inter-portal provincial trade goes through Rangoon. There is a large Chinese trading population in the city and considerable trade is done with the Far East. The principal imports from foreign countries are cotton manufactures, including twist and yarn, metals, provisions and oilman's stores, wines and spirits, silk, sugar, salt, woollen goods, leather goods, glass, cement, bricks and tiles, chemicals, instruments, apparatus, machinery and millwork, hardware, paper and paste board and oils, mineral and non-mineral. Rangoon's chief exports to foreign countries are rice, paddy, grain and pulse, paraffin wax, hides and skins, raw cotton, pig lead, zinc concentrates, copper mattee, wood and timber, rice bran, rubber, mineral oils, tobacco, cutch and lac.

The following table shows the number of steamers with tonnage that entered and cleared from this port during the 3 years ending 1934-35:—

TABLE No. 23.—*Number of steamers with tonnage that entered and cleared.*

Year.	Entry.		Clearance.	
	No.	Tonnage.	No.	Tonnage.
1932-33	1,436	4,105,392	1,439	4,120,115
1933-34	1,459	4,193,191	1,481	4,245,940
1934-35	1,472	4,295,573	1,459	4,271,046

Moulmein.

Moulmein, near the mouth of the Salween River is the largest of the Tenasserim ports and the headquarters of a Port Officer who is also the Customs Collector and has a population of 65,506 Two regular lines of steamers run fortnightly to Moulmein, one the British India Steam Navigation Company from Rangoon to Penang *via* Moulmein, Tavoy, Mergui and Victoria Point and back and the other the Straits Steamship Company from Penang to Moulmein *via* these ports and back. The railway from Rangoon has captured much of the sea-borne trade its terminus being at Martaban, on the bank of the Salween opposite to Moulmein and connected with Moulmein by a steamer ferry service. There are launch services from Moulmein up the Salween, Ataran and Gyaing rivers There are fourteen public and fifty private wharves for the landing and shipping of goods, but no cranes. Steamers use their own winches and donkey engines to lift cargo. Loading is usually done in the stream off Mupan, about three miles below Moulmein town. The principal imports into Moulmein are coconuts, coal and coke, iron and steel, sugar, provisions and oilman's stores, gunny bags, petroleum and kerosene, while the chief exports are rice and paddy, rice bran, rubber-raw, teak and jungle wood, chillies, tobacco, tin ore and betelnuts.

Clearances from this port during the 3 years ending 1934-35 were as follows:—

	No. of steamers.	Tonnage.
1932-33	160	390,600
1933-34	160	392,947
1934-35	148	346,372

Tavoy.

Tavoy, which is situated about 35 miles from the mouth of the Tavoy river, came into prominence owing to the hectic exploitation during the war, of the wolfram and tin mining industries. The population which exceeded 135,000 in 1919 has now fallen to 29,000. In addition to two public wharves there are fifteen private wharves for the landing and shipping of goods. The Deputy Commissioner is *ex-officio* Customs Collector. A weekly steamer service between Tavoy and Rangoon is maintained by British India Steam Navigation Company as far as the mouth of the Tavoy river which is unnavigable for ocean-going steamers and passengers and cargo is conveyed by launch to the town The fortnightly services run by the British India Steam Navigation Company and the Straits Steamship Company Limited, also call at Tavoy There is a daily motor service by road from Ye (90 miles south of Moulmein with which it has been connected by railway) to Tavoy.

Clearances from this port during the 3 years ending 1934-35 were as follows:—

	No. of steamers.	Tonnage.
1932-33	179	122,266
1933-34	215	133,307
1934-35	183	121,720

Mergui.

Mergui is the centre of the Burma rubber and pearl-fishing industry. The area of cultivation under rubber in the district has increased from 17,500 acres in 1922, to 39,302 acres in 1934-35 The port possesses two public and four private wharves for the landing and shipping of goods. The Deputy Commissioner is *ex-officio* Customs Collector. Exporters for the most part use their own jetties.

The import trade is not of much importance The principal exports are fish manure, tin ore and wolfram ore, shells and cowries, rubber and tin.

Clearances from this port during the 3 years ending 1934-35 were as follows:—

	No. of steamers.	Tonnage
1932-33	158	109,734
1933-34	178	108,374
1934-35	156	102,794

TONNAGE CLEARANCES WITH CARGOES.

The following table shows the tonnage of steamers and sailing vessels that cleared with cargoes from the Province of Burma distinguishing British and British Indian from foreign ships during the years 1924-25 to 1934-35.

Table No. 24.—*Tonnage of steamers and sailing vessels that cleared with cargoes from Burma ports from 1924-25 to 1934-35.*

Year.	Tonnage.		Total.
	British ships including British Indian.	Foreign ships.	
1924-25	4,078,132	1,008,845	5,086,977
1925-26	4,318,034	1,173,387	5,491,421
1926-27	3,987,724	1,124,482	5,112,206
1927-28	4,419,167	948,429	5,367,596
1928-29	4,977,158	795,252	5,772,410
1929-30	4,777,684	1,081,681	5,859,365
1930-31	4,688,768	1,191,357	5,880,125
1931-32	5,238,017	1,033,226	6,271,243
1932-33	4,651,256	906,264	5,557,520
1933-34	5,013,097	944,922	5,958,019
1934-35	5,161,950	945,394	6,107,344

The nationality of the vessels that cleared during the years 1930-31 to 1934-35 is shown in the following table —

Table 25.—*Nationality of vessels cleared with cargoes from 1930-31 to 1934-35.*

Nationality.	Number of vessels.				
	1930-31.	1931-32.	1932-33.	1933-34.	1934-35.
British	3,468	3,550	3,266	3,233	3,270
German	33	40	40	34	32
Japanese	170	124	125	109	101
Norwegian	94	80	53	79	105
Dutch	72	49	41	48	40
Italian	24	32	17	17	19
French	1	..	..	..	..
Greek	..	..	..	.	4
Swedish	9	10	14	13	15
American	2	..	..	..	..
Chinese	2	4	..	3	1
Jugo-Slav	2	2	..	..	..
Danish	2	10	3	5	4
Finish	4	..	..	..	1
Portuguese	..	..	1	1	..
Total	3,883	3,901	3,560	3,542	3,592

PRINCIPAL TRADE CENTRES.

India's foreign trade is to a great extent centred in the five principal ports but though the population is chiefly rural, there are a considerable number of towns in the interior which deserve mention either as distributing or industrial centres. CALCUTTA is of importance from the latter point of view as the centre of the jute manufacturing industry, all the jute mills in Bengal being situated within its boundaries or within a few miles of them on the banks of the Hooghly. There are several flour and paper mills, match factories, chemical works and rice mills, a large number of oil mills, iron foundries, tanneries, etc., and the great Tata Iron and Steel Works at Jamshedpur are only about 150 miles away. Though an examination of the share register of the jute mills and other company-owned trading concerns in Calcutta would probably disclose a preponderance of Indian holders, control with but few exceptions is in the hands of British firms acting as managing agents. Calcutta is also an important centre for the export of tea and is the home of many miscellaneous industries such as soap, perfumery and toilet goods, enamelled and porcelain ware, glassware, galvanised ware, celluloid and horn articles, cardboard boxes and tin cans, hats, waterproof cloth, etc. Coal also forms an important commodity in its trade. Calcutta exports the bulk of the raw hides and skins. The outstanding industrial features of BOMBAY and its environs are its cotton spinning and weaving mills, 73 in number, dyeing and bleaching works and metal stamping factories and the Hydro-electric works at Lonavla and in the Andhra valley. It is at the same time the chief distributing centre in western India for very large imports of cotton manufactures. A preponderating share of the trade of Bombay is in Indian hands and the majority of the mills are under Indian management. Bombay is one of the most important markets of oilseeds and has a valuable crushing and oil refining industry. There is considerable trade in oil cake with the United Kingdom. MADRAS industrially is of no great importance, though it possesses the two most up-to-date cotton textile mills in India It is not a terminal port and therefore, whenever tonnage is scarce, it is liable to suffer from infrequency of steamers calling. Madras is an exporting centre for groundnuts, flue-cured and other types of tobacco and tanned hides and skins The chief industry of RANGOON is rice milling, but there is also a large export trade in timber, oil, pig lead and paraffin wax, and the city is developing rapidly in commercial importance. Though European capital and control predominate, there is a considerable Indian and Chinese element participating in the trade of Rangoon In KARACHI the wheat trade is largely financed by European firms, though Parsees if to a much smaller extent than at Bombay, have important commercial interests. Karachi is an important distributing centre for Punjab and Sind wheat.

Cawnpore.

Of the trade centres in the interior, Cawnpore in the United Provinces with a population of 244,000, is industrially and commercially of great and growing importance. It is an important railway Junction and its situation about 870 miles from Bombay and 630 from Calcutta has made it a convenient distributing centre for the imports of Manchester piecegoods, hardware and machinery from both these ports, while its factories produce very large quantities of leather goods, woollens, cotton textiles and tents. The city also boasts of flour mills, oil mills, bristle factories and chemical works and there are a number of flourishing minor industries.

Delhi.

Delhi, with a population of 447,000, is now the capital of the Indian Empire. It is the junction for nine railway lines and an important clearing house for the Punjab and the western districts of the United Provinces particularly in cotton, silk and woollen piecegoods. There are cotton spinning and weaving mills, a biscuit factory, and several flour mills. It is noted also for its art industries, such as ivory carving, jewellery, lace work, silversmiths' work, pottery and gold and silver embroidery. Delhi is famous for Jaridar (embroidered) shoes and slippers and for its lamb-skin and fur trade. It is also known as a buying centre for milch cattle and buffaloes.

Ahmedabad.

Ahmedabad, with a population of 314,000, is, next to Bombay, the most important industrial centre in that Presidency. It contains 99 cotton mills.

Amritsar.

Amritsar, about 30 miles east of Lahore with a population of 265,000, is also of considerable importance commercially. Apart from its entrepôt trade in piecegoods, a large business in skins and hides is done here and its carpet industry is well-known. Amritsar is an important storehouse for grains and possesses two active "Option" or "Futures" markets for wheat.

Agra.

Agra, with a population of 230,000, is, of course, chiefly famous for the architectural monuments of the Moghuls though its manufactures of carpets and daris, embroideries, and stone work are considerable. It is also a collecting centre for better qualities of hides.

Asansol.

Asansol which has a population of 31,000 is an important rail way junction and one of the chief centres of the coal industry in India.

Bangalore.

Bangalore in the Mysore State has a population of 306,000. It is 219 miles by rail from Madras. Its chief manufactures are carpets, cotton textiles and woollen goods and leather. The Civil and Military Station, which adjoins the city, is an assigned tract under the administration of the British Resident. Bangalore has many miscellaneous industries both private and State-aided such as soap, porcelain, shellac, furniture, gasmantles, white lead and cigarettes.

Lahore.

Lahore, with a population of 430,000, is the capital of the Punjab and though of small importance industrially, apart from the large workshops of the North Western Railway, it is the chief trading centre for the agricultural produce of the province. It tends relatively to lose its place as a trading centre for agricultural produce owing to the development of canal colonies as in other districts of the Punjab.

Sialkot.

Sialkot which has a population of 101,000 is the centre of the sports goods industry in the Punjab.

Benares. Benares, (population 205,000), situated on the Ganges about 400 miles north-west of Calcutta, is the holy city of the Hindus. Commercially it is chiefly of interest on account of the very considerable silk weaving industry established there.

Lucknow. Lucknow, with a population of 275,000, is the cold weather capital of the United Provinces. Its industries are of small moment but commercially it is of interest as a distributing and collecting centre for the rich agricultural produce of Oudh.

Nagpur. Nagpur, (population 215,000), on the line between Calcutta and Bombay at the junction of the Great Indian Peninsula and Bengal Nagpur Railways, is the capital of the Central Provinces. Its commercial importance is due to its prosperous weaving mills, cotton ginning and pressing factories and the extensive manganese deposits in the neighbourhood. Nagpur is famous for its loose-skinned *sangtara* oranges.

Jubbulpore. Jubbulpore, (population 124,000), an important railway junction linking the East Indian with the Great Indian Peninsula Railway contains a central gun carriage factory, a spinning and weaving mill, a number of pottery works, and railway workshops

Mirzapur. Mirzapur, in the United Provinces (population 61,000), boasts a considerable brass industry for the manufacture of domestic utensils, but it is mainly important commercially on account of its shellac and carpet factories.

Madura. Madura, with a population of 182,000, is the centre of considerable silk and cotton weaving and dyeing industries and is the second town of importance in the Madras Presidency.

Vizagapatam. Vizagapatam which has a population of 57,000 has recently been declared a major port Manganese ore, myrabolam and groundnuts are the chief exports from the port. "*Lanka*" and "*pothi*" tobaccoes are alsc exported.

Lashkar (Gwalior). Lashkar, the Capital of the Gwalior State, (population 87,000), contains a number of State-owned factories and is the centre of an important stone quarrying and carving industry. Lashkar is gaining importance in tobacco cultivation and manufacture of *deshi* cigarettes.

Dacca. Dacca, with a population of 138,000, is the most important city in Eastern Bengal, in the heart of the jute growing districts. Its muslins were formerly famous in Europe and there are still a number of handlooms working in the district. It is a large collecting centre for hides and skins.

Mandalay, the chief city of Upper Burma, with a population of 148,000, is located about 400 miles north of Rangoon on the Irrawaddy river. In the days of the Burma kings it thrived, but now its trade is declining, though the silk manufacturing industry is still of some importance.

Mandalay.

Srinagar, the capital of Kashmir, with a population of over 174,000, is situated on the Jhelum river. It is famous for its embroideries and carved wood work, and the largest silk filature in India.

Srinagar.

Sholapur and Amraoti are the centres respectively of the cotton industries of the Bombay, Deccan and Berar, and other important cities not separately noted are. Hyderabad, the capital of the Nizam's Dominions with a population of 467,000, the centre of a considerable cotton trade. Allahabad (population 184,000) is an important railway cetre, Jaipur (population 144,000) in the Indian State of the same name, the chief commercial city in Rajputana and famous for its artistic pottery and brassware, and Baroda, the capital of the Gaekwar's territory about 245 miles north-east of Bombay. Mysore the garden city of Southern India with a population of 107,000 is famous for the manufacture of sandal-wood oil, silk, ivory and sandal-wood carving and incense sticks.

Other Cities.

PART VI.

THE FINANCING OF TRADE.

The bulk of India's external trade is financed by branches of the large British, Colonial and foreign exchange banks The principal exchange banks transacting business in India are (1) *The Chartered Bank of India, Australia and China*, with branches in Calcutta, Bombay, Madras, Rangoon, Cawnpore, Delhi, Amritsar and Karachi: (2) *The National Bank of India* with branches in Calcutta, Bombay, Madras, Rangoon, Karachi, Lahore, Armitsar, Delhi, Cawnpore, Chittagong, Mandalay, Tuticorin, Cochin and Aden; (3) *The Mercantile Bank of India* with branches in Calcutta, Howrah, Madras, Rangoon, Karachi, Simla and Delhi, (4) *the Eastern Bank* with branches in Calcutta, Bombay, Madras and Karachi, and also in Baghdad. (5) *the P & O Banking Corporation* with branches at Bombay, Calcutta and Madras, (6) *the Lloyds Bank* with branches at Bombay, Calcutta, Karachi, Rangoon, Delhi, New Delhi, Simla, Lahore Amritsar, Rawalpindi, Murree, Srinagar and Gulmarg; the head offices of these six banks being in London; (7) *the Hong Kong and Shanghai Banking Corporation* with its head office at Hong Kong, and branches in Bombay, Calcutta and Rangoon; (8) *the Yokohama Specie Bank*, with its head office at Yokohama, and branches in Calcutta, Bombay, Karachi and Rangoon and (9) *the National City Bank of New York*, with branches at Calcutta, Bombay and Rangoon.

Exchange Banks.

It is to the Indian branches of these and other similar banking institutions that bills drawn on Indian importers of foreign merchandise will ordinarily come for collection on maturity, being sent to them either direct by the foreign drawer, or by head office or other branch of the bank which has purchased the bills from him or with which he has arranged a credit, and both in this way and in supplying local knowledge of the reliability and standing of purchasing firms, the Indian branches play a part of considerable importance in the import trade of the country But it is with the export trade that their operations are chiefly concerned, and the methods which they adopt for financing it deserve explanation in rather more detail

Except in the occasional years of famine or severe scarcity, the balance of trade is ordinarily, and often very largely, in favour of India; that is to say, the value of exported produce and merchandise appreciably exceeds the value of imported goods, and consequently the proceeds of import bills received by the Indian branches of the exchange banks for collection are in most years, even when supplemented by the considerable deposits that they obtain, insufficient to provide funds for the purchase of all the exporters' bills offered to them. The banks place themselves in funds by rediscounting their bills with the Imperial Bank of India and the Reserve Bank of India; by selling sterling drafts on London to the Reserve Bank of India; and by importing sovereigns and gold and silver bullion.

Balance of Trade.

Purchase of Sterling.

Prior to May 1923, and to a certain extent until March 1925, the obligations of the Government of India in England used to be met by the sale by the Secretary of State for India of rupee bills of exchange (usually called Council bills) and telegraphic transfers payable at the treasuries in India. This system of sale of council bills in England was replaced by that of purchase of sterling in India—to a certain extent since May 1923 and entirely from May 1925, the Government of India meeting their sterling obligations by the purchase of sterling drafts on London, for immediate delivery, by weekly auction on Wednesdays at Calcutta, Bombay, Madras, Rangoon and Karachi Only approved banks and firms could tender at these auctions and allotments were made upto the amount put up to tender. Sterling drafts were also purchased on days other than Wednesdays. Ordinarily most of the amounts offered for sale come from the Exchange Banks.

With the setting up of the Reserve Bank of India, the responsibility for providing funds for the Government of India's expenditure in England has been placed on the bank, and the Government of India do not now purchase sterling in the market, but obtain their requirements from the Bank From April 1935 onwards, the Reserve Bank has been placing itself in funds, to meet this responsibility, by the purchases are made only from the banks named in Schedule II graph as well as at Delhi, on the same lines as before except that the purchases are made only from the banks named in Schedule II to the Reserve Bank of India Act and are subject to a minimum limit of £75,000 in each case.

Import of Sovereigns and of Bullion.

Sovereigns are not at present legal tender in India but are receivable by the Reserve Bank of India at its offices, branches and agencies in India at their bullion value calculated @8 47512 grains troy of fine gold per rupee When the market value of the sovereign is higher, the import of sovereigns, like the import of gold or silver, is more an ordinary commercial, than an exchange, transaction From time immemorial there has been in India a keen demand for the precious metals for domestic purposes, jewellery and the like, and the import of sovereigns and bullion to meet this demand normally operates in exactly the same way as import of other merchandise to reduce a favourable trade balance; only, when the exchange banks are the importers, the proceeds of the sale in the bazar become available to finance exporters' purchases of produce During the war the import of both gold and silver except on Government account was prohibited, so that this method of settling the trade balance ceased to be available, and both gold and silver had to be sold on import to Government at prices notified from time to time These restrictions have since been removed and in normal times the import of sovereigns and of gold bullion takes a prominent place among the methods of settling the trade indebtedness of other countries to India, though, since Britain went off the gold standard in September 1931, the movement of gold has largely been in the opposite direction.

Exporters' bills purchased by the exchange banks instead of being held till maturity are frequently rediscounted on arrival in London, and the banks are thus able to secure a quick turnover of their resources. Indian bills, both import and export, are usually drawn at three months' sight, but bills of four months' usance are not uncommon, and occasionally six months' bills are taken.

The upcountry branches of the exchange banks also engage in the local trade of the places in which they are situate; but their number is not large and for the most part the finance of the internal trade of the country is in the hands of the Imperial Bank of India, of a certain number of joint stock banks, and of the large class of indigenous bankers variously known in different parts of the country as *shroffs*, *mahajans*, *chetties*, etc. An important place in this system is occupied by the Imperial Bank of India, but at the head of the system stands the Reserve Bank of India.

Imperial Bank of India.

The Imperial Bank of India was constituted on the 27th January 1921, by the amalgamation of the three Presidency banks of Bengal, Bombay and Madras under the Imperial Bank of India Act. Up to the end of March 1935, the bank used to carry out the general banking business of the Government of India and hold all the treasury balances of the Government of India at head quarters and at its branches. The total number of branches and agencies of the three Presidency banks prior to the amalgamation was 69. The bank undertook to open 100 new branches within five years of the amalgamation and the total number of branches, pay offices and agencies at present is 164. The bank frequently holds the unemployed cash of the local banks, including the exchange banks; it makes advances to them, when necessary, on Government or other securities and in times of stress it comes to their relief if they are in difficulties

Reserve Bank of India.

The position of the Imperial Bank of India as banker to the Government of India was altered with the setting up of the Reserve Bank of India. The Reserve Bank began to function on the 1st April 1935, under an act of the Indian Legislature and has brought India into line with other important countries where the currency and credit system is controlled by central banks of issue It has replaced the Imperial Bank as banker to the Government of India, and under the terms of its constitution, it also occupies the position of the banker's bank. It has, at present, five offices of its banking department, but has entered into an agreement with the Imperial Bank under which the latter acts as its sole agent at all places in British India where there was a branch of the Imperial Bank on the 6th March 1934 and there is no branch of the banking department of the Reserve Bank. In view of its altered position, some of the restrictions, particularly those relating to exchange business, imposed on the Imperial Bank under its constitution of 1920, have been removed with effect from the 1st April 1935.

The branches of the Imperial Bank of India share with a certain number of old established joint stock banks, such as the Allahabad Bank and the Central Bank of India, in the development of internal trade. But the banking facilities of the country at large are at present so inadequate that there is room for a large growth in the operations of joint stock banks without any undue curtailment of the sphere of the indigenous banker; although in recent years the number of Indian joint stock banks has increased to some extent, it is still the indigenous banker who, with the assistance of the Imperial Bank of India and the more important Indian joint stock banks, is responsible for financing a considerable portion of the internal trade of India.

Hundis.

This trade is financed by the Imperial Bank of India and the other Indian joint stock banks in two ways, either directly by advances against merchandise hypothecated to them, or indirectly through *shroffs* whose *hundis* or internal bills of exchange they purchase. In the latter operation the bank is at the centre of a web at whose extreme circumference may be found the local dealer in grain. Probably the actual shroff from whom a bill is bought will be a man well known to the bank in a presidency town or one of the larger cities; but he will only have to come to the bank for accommodation when he has exhausted his available funds in purchasing or discounting the bills of smaller *shroffs* upcountry, and this process will be repeated possibly more than once, until the village purchaser of grain from a cultivator, the original drawer of the bill, is reached. In the instance taken the bill would be a produce bill, but for approved customers the banks often discount pure finance bills, known as 'hand' bills.

The discount or *hundi* rate generally rises or falls with the bank rate.

Clearing Houses.

The principal clearing houses in India are situated at Calcutta, Bombay, Madras, Rangoon, Karachi, Cawnpore and Lahore. The Reserve Bank of India, the Imperial Bank of India, the exchange banks and most of the English banking agency firms and the better known local joint stock banks at these places constitute the membership of these clearing houses, but no bank as of right is entitled to be a member unless approved by the rest. The Reserve Bank of India is in charge of the clearing house arrangements at Calcutta, Madras, Bombay and Rangoon, and the Imperial Bank of India at Karachi, Cawnpore and Lahore.

The following table shows the total amount of cheques cleared annually at the seven clearing houses. The hectic trade boom of 1920 is strikingly reflected therein.

TABLE No. 26.—*Total amount of cheques cleared annually at clearing houses for 1913, 1914, 1918, 1919, 1920 and from 1925 onwards, in thousands of £* :

Year	Calcutta.	Bombay.	Madras	Karachi.	Rangoon.	Cawnpore. (a)	Lahore. (b)	Total.	Year.
1913	222,013	146,200	15,707	8,327	41,320	..	..	433,567	1913
1914	186,873	115,353	14,240	8,760	33,260	..	..	358,486	1914
1918	496,113	355,747	16,373	16,193	46,180	..	..	930,606	1918
1919	601,660	505,547	20,087	14,793	60,733	.	.	1,202,820	1919
1920	1,022,593	929,293	51,447	21,253	73,473	3,007	..	2,101,066	1920
1925	725,553	343,367	38,653	27,460	83,287	3,867	4,486	1,226,673	1925
1926	632,967	274.387	36,880	20,780	85.426	5,573	5,040	1,061,053	1926
1927	767,940	298,695	42,218	22,928	94,575	5.017	5,625	1,236,998	1927
1928	816.143	402,705	49,635	22,065	90,270	5,775	6,030	1,392,623	1928
1929	748 245	594,630	62,198	20,348	91,628	4,717	6,787	1,528,553	1929
1930	669,855	527.032	39,195	19,058	85,568	4,440	8,025	1,353,173	1930
1931	567,210	479.227	34,215	17.468	61,425	4,065	7,315	1,171,125	1931
1932	566,610	492,435	35,662	19,125	57,750	5,243	6,293	1,183,118	1932
1933	617,768	483,203	38,693	19,147	43,365	5,827	6,847	1,214,850	1933
1934	645,550	512,185	43,209	21,557	43,016	8,127	7,647	1,281,291	1934
1935	699,857	557,909	46,977	22,351	51,382	8,714	7,724	1,394,914	1935

(a) Opened in July 1920.
(b) Opened in April 1921.

PART VII.

IMPORT TRADE.

The outstanding feature of India's foreign trade from the earliest times has been her absorption of the precious metals. The commercial trend has always been towards the West but from the days of the Roman Empire until the enterprise of the East India Company more or less stabilised the sea route round the Cape, exchanges were mainly confined, owing to the difficulties of Land transport, to articles of high value and comparatively small bulk, such as costly muslins, silks, ivory and precious stones With the application of steam to sea traffic and the opening of the Suez Canal the character of the trade was permanetly changed and the greater part of India's international exchanges are now concerned with raw materials of considerable bulk and comparatively low value In the fifty years prior to the outbreak of the great war the excess of exports over imports was persistent During the first four periods, for which figures are given in the table below, the excess was equivalent to 29 per cent and in the twenty years ending 1913-14 to 19 per cent This difference was maintained during the war as well as in 1919-20, for though the high sterling value of the rupee encouraged imports, there were buyers to take exports consisting almost entirely of raw materials regardless of cost Early in 1920-21 the inevitable reaction set in The United Kingdom, the United States of America and Japan, the best customers for India's exports, showed signs of satiety, and owing to the partial failure of the monsoon in 1919 the embargo on the export of food grains could not be wholly withdrawn The total volume of imports exceeded that of exports by £58,932,425 and in the following year by £30,781,115. In 1922-23, import trade, except as regards the precious metals, was stagnant until unsold stocks had been cleared while conditions were favourable for great developments on the export side, had the European markets been able fully to respond The principal reason, however, for the excess of exports over imports, amounting to £6,211,237, was the general fall in prices of imported articles, while the level of export values showed little change In 1923-24 there was an increase of exports (merchandise and treasure) to the extent of £33 3 millions over those of the previous year chiefly due to export of raw cotton at high prices on account of the shortage of the American crop On the other hand the imports of merchandise decreased by £3 3 millions In 1924-25 the exports of merchandise rose to a record figure of £266 6 millions due to increased exportation of jute and food grains and the imports improved by £10·6 millions largely due to increased importations of sugar and cotton piecegoods. There was some falling off in exports in 1925-26 due to reduced shipments of food grains and tea and in 1926-27 due to a heavy fall in the world prices of raw materials particularly of cotton and jute. The favourable balance of trade was maintained and amounted to

Feature of foreign trade.

£107·3 and 52·6 millions in 1925-26 and 1926-27 respectively For the next two years, 1927-28 and 1928-29, there was a steady improvement in the foreign trade of India, both imports and exports recording an increase, with imports showing considerably greater acceleration. The balance of trade in favour of India consequently declined to £37·5 and £39 millions in 1927-28 and 1928-29 respectively. In the latter year an abnormal development in the import trade was an increase in the imports of wheat due to the shortage of the crop in India. The increase in the export of raw and manufactured jute, however, neutralised the effect of the wheat shortage and the favourable balance was maintained at a slightly higher level than that of the preceding year. Up to the year 1928-29, as a result of a series of good monsoons and the establishment of suitable economic conditions, India had enjoyed a fair measure of prosperity. The tide now turned, and the year 1929-30 ushered in an era of trade depression, which was further aggravated by political activity directed against the use of foreign goods, particularly cotton piecegoods The result was clearly reflected in the figures of the foreign trade of India, imports and exports in 1929-30 falling by 5 and 6 per cent and in 1930-31 by 32 and 29 per cent respectively as compared with the preceding year. 1931-32 saw a further decline in foreign trade In 1932-33 there was a slight improvement in imports, but a further decline by 15 per cent under exports In 1933-34 imports instead of maintaining the slight improvement of the previous year declined again by 13 per cent, mainly as a result of the weakening of the demand for foreign textiles Exports during this year improved by 10 per cent due to an increase in the exports of raw cotton and jute The enormous shrinkage in the foreign trade of India during these years was mainly the result of a catastrophic fall in the prices of agricultural produce which reduced both the volume as also the value of the export trade. A very considerable reduction in the purchasing power of the consumers in India followed as a necessary consequence Goods could not, therefore, be imported on anything approaching the scale of the pre-slump years The decline in both imports and exports occurred all along the line but was particularly noticeable on the export side in jute and raw cotton and on the import side in textiles The balance of trade in favour of India fell in 1930-31 to £28·5 millions and in 1931-32 the greater shrinkage in the volume of exports as compared with imports reduced it still further and in 1932-33 would have nearly wiped it out had it not been for the fact that the high price of gold stimulated the exports of hoarded gold from India and helped to bring up the trade balance for merchandise and treasure to £51 millions The exports of gold from India in 1931-32 amounted to £45·7 millions and in 1932-33 to £50 millions The visible balance of trade in merchandise and treasure for the year 1933-34 was in favour of India to the extent of £69 millions, of which exports of gold accounted for £43·5 millions. In 1934-35 the value of imports of merchandise showed a rise of £12·7 millions over the figures for the preceding year. This was largely due to the higher purchasing power of the consumers in India as a result of the general improvement in the world economic conditions The value of exports of merchandise also showed an improvement of £3·4 millions which might be ascribed partly to the effects of the Ottawa Trade Agreement The exports of gold amounted to £40 millions. The year 1935-36 registered a further advance of £1·6 millions in the value of imports of private merchandise, while exports, including re-exports, advanced by £6·8 millions. The visible balance of trade in merchandise and treasure in this year was in favour of India to the extent of £50 millions as compared to £57 millions in 1934-35.

TABLE No. 27 —*Foreign trade of India (quinquennial averages) from 1864-65.*

Year.	Imports. Value in £.	Exports. Value in £.
1864-65 to 1868-69	32,880,000	38,440,000
1869-70 to 1873-74	27,566,666	38,560,000
1874-75 to 1878-79	32,146,666	42,086,666
1879-80 to 1883-84	41,213,338	53,606,666
1884-85 to 1888-89	50,086,666	60,186,666
1889-90 to 1893-94	59,133,333	72,446,666
1894-95 to 1898-99	59,040,000	75,953,333
1899-1900 to 1903-04	73,793,333	91,046,666
1904-05 to 1908-09	104,000,000	116,895,167
1909-10 to 1913-14	132,580,000	155,034,658
1914-15 to 1918-19	132,213,782	155,420,520
1919-20 to 1923-24	212,844,669	213,000,540
1924-25 to 1928-29	213,086,934	249,745,593
1929-30 to 1933-34	130,897,704	180,624,712
1934-35	104,099,341	163,929,862
1935 36	108,200,000	157,700,000

* Including re-exports

History of import trade.

In the first century A D in return for her exports of spices, precious stones and cotton fabrics of the finest texture, India received corals, copper, tin and lead as well as the precious metals and until the seventeenth century these items predominated in the import list The early history of the East India Company is a struggle against bitter opposition, based on the fact that the trade with the East Indies involved the export of bullion from England and did not sufficiently enlarge the market for the latter's woollen manufactures, and to silence this opposition as far as possible the Company had to export woollen goods in excess of the Indian demand and to sell them at a loss Until the spinning jenny was invented, no European looms could compete with those of Dacca and Surat, but the import of cotton goods from India was banned by one Act inimical to the English wool trade and later by another as threatening the infant Manchester weaving industry The Home Government looked to the East India Company to supply saltpetre for its gunpowder and hemp for its shipping, but the Indian silk industry had considerable ups and downs. In the first half of the eighteenth century exports of bullion from England to India agrregated 27 millions, while the value of merchandise exported was only 9 millions A great change was effected by the battle of Plassey when the Company acquired control of the revenues of Bengal Between 1760 and 1809 the total exports of bullion amounted to £14½ millions only, while the value of merchandise shipped to India increased to £48½ millions The first half of the nineteenth century witnessed a remarkable change in the character of the trade between India and England. Henceforward India began to receive those very commodities as imports which had hitherto bulked so largely in her export trade, *viz.*, cotton manufactures and sugar. The Lancashire cotton industry had so developed that by the middle of the century imports of cotton piecegoods represented about half the total imports of foreign merchandise into India. In 1869-70, of a total of £21,946,660 cotton manufactures accounted for £10,846,660, almost all from the United Kingdom The next most important single item was the head which includes wines, beer and spirits which amounted to more than £1,000,000, followed by copper for domestic utensils £906,660, iron and steel £873,330 and salt £500,000. Sugar had then scarcely begun to take its curiously prominent place among the imports into the greatest sugar producing country in the world but in the next half century, the value of arrivals of sugar increased from £476,660 to £5,000,000 and reached a maximum of £12 millions in the year 1928-29. Other classes of imports which have steadily increased in volume and importance are mineral oil (kerosene), which has superseded to a great extent vegetable illuminants even in remote bazaars upcountry, matches and provisions while the arrivals of spices have reached nearly four times the level of India's exports of the same commodities Though progress was suspended temporarily by the war, the most striking feature of the post war period from 1918-29 was the general improvement in imports especially in imports of machinery, railway material and motor vehicles. Since 1930 imports have suffered a set back due to the World economic depression. The policy of discriminating protection to which India is committed and which she has steadily pursued during recent years is further tending to change the character of the import trade.

TABLE No. 28.—*The principal articles of importation into India for 1913-14, 1918-19 and 1932-33 to 1935-36 and their values.*

Name of the article.	1913-14.	1918-19.	1932-33.	1933-34.	1934-35.	1935-36.
	£	£	£	£	£	£
Cotton manufactures—	44,199,510	40,369,871	20,118,462	13,307,565	16,321,329	15,865,101
Grey piecegoods	16,966,515	15,729,434	3,804,961	2,293,343	3,023,721	3,254,701
Coloured piecegoods	11,907,683	7,879,640	6,230,902	3,940,130	5,573,667	4,845,969
White piecegoods	9,523,204	8,753,647	5,419,106	3,549,364	4,099,275	3,734,043
Twist and yarn	2,776,163	5,910,899	2,841,181	1,931,264	2,323,929	2,783,890
Other sorts	3,025,945	2,096,251	1,724,813	1,593,464	1,300,737	1,246,498
Iron and Steel	10,671,928	8,299,919	3,361,399	3,477,019	4,001,019	4,658,082
Sugar	9,971,251	10,409,094	3,171,540	2,032,278	1,581,396	1,430,478
Machinery and Millwork	5,172,206	3,335,597	7,906,805	9,576,965	9,473,997	10,259,174
Mineral oil	2,743,764	2,408,790	5,023,507	4,373,013	4,553,750	4,440,836
Hardware	2,632,089	2,138,897	2,244,117	2,158,754	2,289,728	2,450,682
Woollen manufactures	2,568,168	1,449,492	1,907,630	1,656,288	2,588,395	1,758,268
Silk manufactures	2,067,553	2,472,674	2,370,780	2,151,440	2,097,221	1,649,365
Provisions and Oilmanstores	1,649,087	1,292,074	2,196,553	2,036,693	2,167,925	3,339,025
Copper (excluding ore)	1,373,852	457,538	1,068,520	659,504	1,052,141	876,909
Glass and Glassware	1,296,853	830,711	860,687	916,008	994,233	1,045,494
Instruments and Apparatus	1,214,014	1,445,331	2,885,760	3,015,306	3,544,680	3,882,154
Spices	1,154,875	1,606,131	1,293,737	1,167,512	1,166,187	1,213,294
Apparel	1,140,992	1,223,173	631,586	611,304	618,134	533,127
Haberdashery and Millinery	1,066,551	710,577	508,499	409,268	505,201	442,879
Paper and Paste-board	1,058,454	1,813,779	2,148,344	1,973,923	2,046,110	2,242,608
Motor cars and cycles	1,022,042	259,261	2,425,107	3,060,640	2,880,093	2,808,375
Dyeing and Tanning substances	942,633	1,059,951	1,878,599	1,845,769	2,306,340	2,502,529

Name of the article.	1913-14.	1918-19.	1932-33.	1933-34.	1934-35.	1935-36.
	£	£	£	£	£	£
Spirits	852,670	1,495,902	999,259	1,039,098	1,077,808	1,109,523
Silk (raw)	839,309	693,575	878,201	538,071	430,342	398,919
Drugs and Medicines	780,490	977,962	1,393,736	1,450,662	1,439,253	1,583,740
Fruits and Vegetables	753,583	621,101	874,243	751,026	974,905	1,000,578
Precious stones and Pearls, unset	714,693	252,345	627,281	561,120	375,740	360,474
Coal, Coke and Fuel	710,920	156,933	72,217	101,907	93,740	99,112
Building and Engineering materials	707,139	543,583	580,133	482,624	449,228	545,912
Aniline and Alizarine dyes	699,915	779,566	1,626,560	1,581,080	2,053,963	2,275,296
Chemicals	676,506	1,661,710	2,034,373	2,025,423	2,192,946	2,339,125
Matches	597,651	1,098,353	3,874	5,535	4,658	8,150
Salt	584,432	1,554,018	592,199	373,394	390,576	425,541
Paints and Painter's material	548,869	845,429	691,398	691,439	726,209	765,402
Tobacco	501,923	1,430,736	727,020	541,097	463,683	461,704
Soap	500,400	667,424	619,716	587,802	474,060	257,044
Timber (excluding firewood and wood manufactures).	497,553	431,818	257,688	294,229	252,784	208,089
Stationery (excluding paper, etc.)	466,528	466,447	542,724	496,652	516,035	570,760
Beer, Ale and Porter	439,385	461,137	570,302	515,895	532,441	585,680
Rubber (Raw and manufactures)	352,661	828,174	1,492,912	1,435,142	1,584,632	1,576,679
Tea chests	349,435	606,736	358,311	400,359	390,619	436,281
Belting	281,937	557,548	396,441	345,436	373,695	401,330
Horses	237,934	232,277	96,745	198,897	173,663	136,339
Cutlery	188,882	127,980	182,018	191,261	209,817	215,285
Grain, Pulse, etc.	186,560	749,030	532,346	627,762	1,998,405	1,218,688
Cotton, raw	181,819	802,563	5,442,942	2,667,751	3,962,859	5,056,843
Carriages and Carts	169,169	71,997	43,778	44,374	61,287	70,759

Cotton manufactures.

The traditional customs of the greater portion of the Indian population tend to stereotype the demand for particular classes of cotton manufactures which admit of little variation. The unbleached *dhooties* and *sarees* which are worn by so many millions have been for years the staple articles of import from Manchester. An improvement in later years in the imports of white and coloured goods pointed to a slow but definite change in the public taste, but was probably correctly ascribable to the more effective competition in Bombay mills in the production of grey goods of qualities superior to the T cloths and domestics in which they specialise. The local character of the factors affecting the distribution is emphasised by the fact that Calcutta, the port which serves Bengal, Bihar and the eastern half of the United Provinces and the Central Provinces as well as participating in the rationing of the big up-country entrepots of Delhi and Cawnpore, continues to import a preponderating quantity of unbleached goods In this connection it may be noted that cotton piecegoods which as a whole were imported until 1913-14 almost entirely from the United Kingdom are now imported in large quantities from Japan. The share of this country in the import trade in piece-goods is now well over two-thirds of that of the United Kingdom. Another factor of considerable importance has been the competition from the Indian mills, which have very substantially increased their production as a result of the imposition of the protective duties and the general preference shown for goods made in India The share of the United Kingdom in unbleached goods fell from 98·8 per cent in 1913-14 to 25 6 per cent in 1935-36 as against that of Japan which rose from ·5 per cent. to 74·1 per cent. in the same period. No less than 66 per cent. of the total imports of cotton manufactures into Calcutta in 1913-14 were unbleached goods in a year when her total imports of cotton manufactures represented one half of the imports for all India and in 1935-36 the percentage was 61. The percentage shares of Bombay, Madras and Karachi in the total imports into India of the different classes of cotton piecegoods in the year 1935-36 were as under:—

	Grey.	White	Coloured.
	Per cent.	Per cent.	Per cent.
Bombay	27	17	36
Madras	8	7	5
Karachi	8	52	17

The Rangoon market is *sui generis*. The Burman prefers to wear a lower garment of coloured silk but for work-a-day use he is content with a cotton substitute which, custom demands, should be coloured and the proportion of coloured piecegoods in the total volume of imports of cotton piecegoods was 56 per cent. in 1913-14, of white which is required by the emigrant Indian population, 31 per cent., and of grey 13 per cent. The corresponding percentages for 1935-36 were 64, 29 and 7, respectively.

Sugar.

In 1897-98 the total imports of sugar were 212,000 tons, of which just over half was shewn as beet sugar. The countervailing duties imposed in 1899 and enhanced in 1902, to prevent the ruin of the cane sugar industry by bounty-fed beet sugar, did not diminish the total volume of imports, for as the supply of beet sugar declined, its place was taken by cane. Mauritius, which already supplied more than any other individual country, nearly doubled its shipments by 1903-04, while in the same period Java made a very remarkable advance, increasing its supplies from 7,000 tons to 56,000 tons. Java continued its progress during the next ten years, and in 1913-14 sent 583,000 tons out of total imports of 803,000 tons; Mauritius contributing 138,000 tons only and, although the countervailing duties had meanwhile practically become a dead letter owing to the adherence of most countries to the Brussels Convention, the imports of beet sugar from all sources only amounted to 75,000 tons. Since, as during the war, Java has maintained its position as chief supplier. In 1921-22, 623,300 tons out of 717 600 tons came from this source, the corresponding figures for 1933-34 being 196,827 and 263,712 The demand for imported sugar in the Indian markets has however undergone a remarkable change as a result of the grant of protection to the sugar industry in India. Sheltered behind a protective tariff, the industry has developed its production with considerable success Foreign sugar is being rapidly displaced by indigenous sugar resulting in a considerable shortage of imports. In 1930-31 imports of foreign sugar were over 1 million tons In 1931-32 they amounted to only 556,000 tons, in 1932-33, to 401,000 tons, in 1933-34 to 263,000 tons and in 1935-36 they dropped to 201,000 tons only.

Iron, steel and machinery. Bengal with its jute mills and its collieries and Bombay with its cotton mills divide between them the greater part of the imports of iron and steel and machinery and mill-work which when war broke out had assumed a position only second to that held by cotton manufactures in India's import trade, and since then have continuously maintained that position The protective duties imposed in 1924 have enabled the Indian iron and steel industry to increase its production to a great extent and to displace foreign imports considerably The imports of iron and steel for some years past have thus dropped to nearly one-third as compared with those in the years 1918-19 to 1923-24 There has also been a marked decline in the imports of railway material within the last six years. This was partly due to the acute financial stringency which necessitated partial suspension of railway constructional operations, and partly to the increasing indigenous production. With the development of the protected industries in India the imports of machinery and mill-work have recorded a marked rise within the last ten years particularly in the case of sugar machinery.

Silk and spices. Silk goods are so generally used by the Burmese of both sexes for personal adornment that the imports of that commodity into Burma to some extent reflect the material prosperity of that province. Bombay is, however, by far the biggest market for imported silk manufactures, of which Bengal, Sind and Madras take little. The imports of silk raw and manufactured have been gradually increasing stimulated partly by a considerable fall in their prices. The silk industry in India has recently received tariff protection, but it is yet too early to estimate the extent to which indigenous silk and silk manufactures will displace the foreign products. The chief item which shews Madras in a place much higher than its general position is that of spices, principally betel-nuts.

Regarding private trade as a whole, its division between provinces (including treasure with merchandise) in 1913-14 was as follows:—

Provincial distribution.

Bombay 43 per cent., Bengal 35 per cent., the balance falling in nearly equal shares to the other three maritime provinces. But Bombay figures include practically the whole of the imports of treasure, and if the figures of private merchandise alone are taken, the apportionment should be:—Bengal 39 per cent., Bombay 34 per cent., Madras, Sind and Burma 9 per cent. each. Bengal was the chief importer of salt, and Burma next, the other maritime provinces relying practically entirely on indigenous supplies. The corresponding percentages for 1935-36 are —Bombay 40 per cent, Bengal 29 per cent., Madras 12 per cent., Sind 11 per cent., and Burma 8 per cent. A striking feature of the trade of Burma is the relatively large quantity of provisions and silk manufactures which it imports. The fact that that province took more than half the total Indian imports of milk and butter may be attributable to the national aversion to keeping milch cows, but as an importer of biscuits and canned and bottled provisions as well as of other luxuries, Burma takes a position quite out of proportion to its population, which can only be ascribed to a higher standard of living and to a greater freedom from oriental conservatism.

India's legitimate import requirements were starved while the war lasted, and in many directions return to peace conditions was slow. Comparisons between pre-war and post-war trade are

Features of Post-war Trade.

vitiated to a great extent by the rise in prices which until 1922 continued much above the levels of 1913-14. Since 1922 a gradual decline in the price level has gone on and in many instances prices are now below the pre-war level. A general decline in the volume of imports of cotton piecegoods is noted which may be attributed mainly to the development of the indigenous cotton textile industry In the years 1921-22 and 1922-23 transport difficulties and the increased cost of Indian coal had encouraged abnormal importations of foreign coal Conditions have, however, since changed The reduction in the railway freights, etc, and the fall in prices of Indian coal have contributed to a decline in the imports of foreign coal into India The imports during 1935-36 were 59,437 tons against 531,814 tons in 1913-14 and 881,810 tons in 1922-23 Of 59,437 tons imported in 1935-36 10,291 tons came from the United Kingdom, and 19,203 tons from Natal. In 1918-19 only 400 motor cars were imported The figures for 1933-34, 1934-35 and 1935-36 were 9,759, 14,434 and 13,590 respectively. A considerable advance in imports of chemicals may be explained as due to the development of internal industries which require these articles for their processes The imports of chemicals in 1935-36 were valued at £2,339,125 against £676,506 in the year 1913-14. Matches registered an advance upto the year 1919-20, but the imports have since been declining and are now tending to disappear as a result of the development of the indigenous match industry under the shelter of the protective duties. The imports in 1935-36 were valued at £8,150 against £2,048,823, in the year 1919-20. The imports of tobacco registered an improvement till the year 1920-21 when they were valued at £2,959,123, but they have gradually dropped to £461,704 in 1935-36. This decline can be attributed to the heavy import duties. the change over from cigarettes to *bidis* (country made cigarettes) and increased indigenous production. Imports of mineral oils have been steadily rising in the post-war period due to the development of road transport and increased consumption as illuminants. In 1935-36 their value was £4,440,336 against £2,408,790 in 1918-19 Woollen manufactures have shown a marked increase, the imports in 1934-35 being valued at £2,588,395 against £1,449,492 in 1918-19. In 1935-36, however, the imports dropped abruptly to £1,758,268. Imports of salt rose to £1,554,018 in 1918-19, but they have now declined to £425,541 which is below the pre-war level. The recent decline in the trade is due to the additional import duty imposed on foreign salt in the year 1931. India including Burma has a large surplus of rice and normally imports of that commodity are negligible. For some time past, however, the imports of foreign broken rice into India, especially into the Madras Presidency, have been the cause of some alarm to the Indian rice producer. In the year 1934-35 particularly these imports had reached very considerable proportions, the quantity imported being 282,918 tons. Imported rice, due to its comparatively low price, had come into serious competition with certain of the better grades of rice produced in Madras. In the interests of the Indian rice grower a protective duty has been imposed for a temporary period on the imports of foreign broken rice.

Origin of Imports.

Perhaps the most interesting reflections of the war upon India's import trade is to be found in the redistribution of the business between various countries participating before and since.

TABLE No 29 —*General distribution of import trade showing the percentages borne by the principal countries in the imports of merchandise into India in 1913-14, 1918-19 and from 1932-33 onwards.*

Name of country.	1913-14	1918-19	1932-33.	1933-34.	1934-35	1935-36.
United Kingdom	64·1	45·5	36 8	41·3	40·6	38·8
Germany	6·9	..	7·8	7·7	7·6	9·2
Java	5·8	6·6	2·8	2·1	1·4	1·3
Japan	2·6	19·8	15·4	14·2	15·7	16·3
United States of America	2·6	9·5	8·5	6·2	6·4	6·7
Belgium	2·3	·803	2·6	2·3	1·6	1·8
Austria (*a*)	2·3	.	·5	·4	·4	·3
Straits Settlements	1·9	3·3	2·1	2·3	2·3	2·7
France	1·5	1·1	1·5	1·3	1·2	1·0
Mauritius	1·4	1·5	..	..	..	..
Italy	1·2	·5	3·0	2·5	2·3	1·5
China	·9	1·4	2·2	1·9	1·6	1·4
Netherlands	·8	·1	1·3	1·6	1·0	1·0
Australia	·5	1·3	·8	·9	·7	·9
Hongkong	·5	1·0	·4	·4	·3	·3
Iran	·4	·6	1·5	1·2	1·6	1·7
Ceylon	·4	1·7	1·3	1·1	1·0	1·1
U. S. S. R.	·03	·003	·3	1·4	1·2	1·2

(*a*) Figures for 1913-14 and 1918-19 relate to Austria—Hungary.

The country of import for the purpose of the above table is the country from which the goods have come whether by land and sea or by sea only, without interruption of transit save in the course of transhipment or transfer from one means of conveyance to another.

Even before the war the margin by which the United Kingdom had dominated all other competitors had been subject to gradual reduction. In 1953-54 the United Kingdom sent nearly 76 per cent. of the whole imports, foreign as well as coasting, into Bengal, China coming next with 5 per cent. and 'New Holland' (Australia) with 4 per cent., while France with 3½ per cent. was practically the only European competitor, shipments from Antwerp and Cadiz being very small, from Hamburg even smaller, and from Rotterdam non-existent. Fifty years later, the United Kingdom in 1903-04 supplied 64·9 per cent. of the foreign imports, Belgium coming next with 3·9 per cent., and Germany with 3 4 per cent.; while Russia's percentage was 2·9, that of Austria-Hungary 2·6, of France 1·9, and of the United States and Japan 1·5 each. Ten years later again in 1913-14, as the above table shews, the United Kingdom still retained its position almost unchanged, Belgium's share had fallen to 2·3 per cent and Russia's had become negligible, while Germany's percentage had grown to 6·9 and the United States and Japan had progressed *pari passu* to 2 6 per cent. each. The increase in the trade with Germany was attributed partly to the special technical skill which that country developed in certain lines and partly to the displacement of expensive British goods by cheaper substitutes more readily absorbed in the bazaar. The latter advantage passed after the outbreak of war to Japan and the great benefit, which that country was able to secure from war conditions, is amply illustrated in the percentages for 1918-19 in the above table. As for the United Kingdom the steady decline in its predominance arose directly or indirectly from the same causes, the diminution in the volume of some exports from that country being due to the Home Government's control and of others to the restrictive effect of high prices. Japan and the United States of America owe their advance between 1913 14 and 1918-19 principally to the fact that Indian importers of iron and steel and other hardware were perforce compelled to run to one or other of these countries to replace the supplies which they could no longer obtain from England. After a temporary and partial recovery in the early post-war period, the United Kingdom again experienced a set back and the progressive decrease in its share in the import trade was accentuated in 1926-27 by the prolonged coal strike which seriously affected its industries, its share decreasing to 47·8 per cent. of the total import trade in that year. In the year 1927-28, its position remained very much the same as in the preceding year. The year 1928-29, however, recorded a striking decrease, namely to 44·7 per cent. as compared with the pre-war 64·1 per cent There was a further decline to 42·8 per cent. in 1929-30, 37·2 per cent. in 1930-31, and 35·5 per cent. in 1931-32, the decrease in the last two years being accentuated by the political situation in India. The share of the United Kingdom, has, however, shown an improvement during the last four years due to increased importations of cotton manufactures, iron and steel, motor cars, instruments, mineral oil, sugar, hardware, liquors and paper. Japan and the United States had lost part of the ground captured by them during the War, Japan having received a special set back owing to the commercial crisis of 1920-21. Another cause which had affected the imports from both countries might be traced to the reappearance of old rivals and the restoration of more normal conditions of competition in the Indian markets. The United States of America increased their share from 7·3 per cent. in 1929-30 to 10·2 per cent. in 1931-32 which has again declined to 6·7 per cent. in 1935-36 mainly as a result of a heavy fall in the imports of raw cotton. The share of Japan has again advanced in recent years, the principal articles contributing to this advancement being cotton, silk and artificial silk manufactures, boots and shoes, glass and glassware, and earthenware and porcelain. The depreciation of the Yen was a significant factor in the expansion of Japan's trade during the last few years. Germany has shown a remarkable recovery in recent years. Her percentage share in the Indian import trade was 7·3 per cent. in 1926-27 though it fell slightly, namely, to 6·1 per cent., in 1927-28. It has again gradually advanced to 9·2 per cent. in 1935-36 Belgium and France have practically recovered their old share of the trade but the former has suffered a set-back in the year 1934-35 and 1935-36.

PART VIII.

EXPORT TRADE.

A brief survey of the early history of Indian trade having been made elsewhere, and detailed references to the case of particular exports being subjoined (*vide* p. 141 *et seq.*), it is only necessary to say in general terms that with the growth of mechanical aids to manufacture in Europe, India has since the beginning of the nineteenth century come to be regarded like Argentina chiefly as a producer of primaries. In a year of seasonal prosperity India is able to grow wheat and rice in excess of the needs even of her vast population, and her shipments of food grains with those of raw cotton, raw jute, raw hides and skins and oil seeds constitute one-half of her total exports. The principal exceptions to this classification are jute manufactures, which during the war took an increasingly prominent place in the table, and East India 'kips' (partially tanned hides). During the war circumstances and policy encouraged larger exports of manufactured or partially manufactured goods, and in the post-war boom the percentage of exports of private merchandise, falling under this category, reached its peak. The trend of the trade in later years is marked by variations, and it has now declined below the pre-war level. In the following table the values of the principal articles of Indian merchandise exported from India in recent years are contrasted with the pre-war and post-war figures. Raw cotton is now the most important single item in the list and other articles which have improved their position are tea, metals and ores, oilcakes and timber.

Nature of export trade.

TABLE No. 30.—*Exports of principal articles of Indian merchandise and their values for 1913-14, 1918-19 and from 1932-33 onwards*

Articles.	1913-14.	1918-19.	1932-33.	1933-34.	1934-35.	1935-36.
	£	£	£	£	£	£
Jute—						
Raw jute	20,550,929	8,480,052	7,297,753	8,199,503	8,153,319	10,280,726
Jute manufactures (including twist and yarn).	18,848,759	35,101,466	16,283,826	16,031,199	16,101,238	17,617,088
Cotton—						
Raw cotton	27,361,655	20,655,709	15,279,052	20,645,536	25,873,733	25,327,706
Cotton manufactures (including twist and yarn).	8,079,972	9,360,216	2,468,331	2,044,733	1,986,016	2,195,395
Grain, Pulse and Flour	30,094,279	26,710,384	12,057,665	8,810,890	8,882,990	9,306,531
Rice not in the husk	17,599,582	15,310,023	10,637,838	7,891,052	7,727,130	8,210,550
Wheat and wheat flour	9,589,639	5,045,083	236,396	147,334	195,553	238,120
Barley	1,043,799	1,845,110	97,285	857	69,784	15,947
Pulse	711,009	446,745	778,481	684,831	787,928	691,740
Millets (*Jowar and Bajra*)	576,164	56,182	99,106	36,042	31,020	62,724
Gram	415,104	2,233,414	217,323	193,145	168,973	59,023
Maize	13,969	104,832	382	477	7,960	6,938
Oats	3,391	5,409	379	3,682	2,888	1,292

Seeds—	17,116,959	7,478,903	8,480,113	10,246,147	7,905,740	7,747,862
Linseed	4,457,998	4,391,402	683,307	3,431,335	2,248,181	1,654,663
Groundnut	3,254,246	249,891	5,341,640	4,973,360	4,446,314	4,938,269
Rape	2,851,711	968,811	1,152,983	610,757	317,945	193,408
Sesamum	1,796,841	47,076	146,244	166,456	56,467	20,235
Cotton	1,416,743	11,810	12,528	24,357	2,926	3,391
Castor	1,336,649	1,534,228	930,048	746,470	608,114	623,608
Copra	1,039,826	13,990	1,210	921	1,506	1,324
Mowra	363,634	15	1,618	1	..	11
Poppy	310,589	50,336	11,680	14,248	1,342	980
Mustard	70,724	48,817	45,475	39,738	36,750	30,521
Tea	55,002	14,509	9,572	56	2,366	5,047
Niger	42,926	492	22,432	17,577	10,549	18,203
Coriander	39,099	65,347	11,295	44,572	33,212	46,300
Cummin	30,495	50,499	11,881	44,309	52,684*	54,446
Ajwan	2,983	2,102	488	2,499	736	882
Tea—	9,983,372	11,850,404	12,864,586	14,883,747	15,098,948	14,864,999
Hides and Skins and Leather	10,648,737	12,694,519	5,649,829	6,812,347	6,457,129	7,319,912
Raw	5,530,638	1,742,736	469,528	760,020	821,321	841,260
Tanned	1,058,575	4,744,979	1,215,880	1,806,011	1,482,254	1,717,977
Skins—						
Raw	2,260,244	4,481,107	1,603,388	2,424,264	1,517,972	2,234,348
Tanned	1,758,591	1,701,428	2,281,612	2,428,246	2,433,806	2,189,816
Opium	2,280,031	2,086,049	348,520	846,603	51,101	78
Wool—						
Raw wool	1,669,646	3,594,992	824,471	1,488,616	956,232	1,572,469
Wool manufactures	167,349	117,032	508,537	554,966	688,321	621,729
Metals and ores	1,462,994	2,104,146	3,511,375	4,115,254	4,433,509	5,800,155
Manganese ore	808,763	501,533	361,836	385,042	603,599	993,038
Tungsten ore	..	751,349	(a)	(a)	(a)	(a)
Iron or steel (including iron ore)	300,970	87,766	839,181	970,556	819,533	1,050,155
Lead	59,309	287,122	1,143,709	1,174,167	1,045,882	1,377,107
Zinc all sorts	31,796	..	180,750	253,914	196,933	265,475
Chromite	9,205	82,046	46,002	47,415	56,011	59,722
Lac	1,310,535	1,965,640	931,783	1,848,276	2,474,715	1,187,726
Coffee	1,024,402	795,856	823,606	768,404	445,320	766,468

(a) Not available.

* Other than black.

Articles.	1913-14.	1918-19.	1932-33.	1933-34.	1934-35.	1935-36.
	£	£	£	£	£	£
Oilcakes	920,249	562,941	1,473,801	1,235,409	1,477,420	1,362,742
Wood and Timber	714,092	473,617	421,347	631,811	849,946	1,009,261
Timber	571,636	423,390	333,494	498,486	746,979	892,198
Sandalwood	128,626	10,529	48,054	93,759	60,132	69,400
Dyeing and Tanning substances	693,526	1,366,568	565,761	590,178	537,092	527,653
Myrobalan	379,626	328,936	434,499	444,203	386,322	350,420
Indigo	141,938	832,360	5,386	7,265	8,012	4,910
Turmeric	87,450	111,804	73,562	81,994	74,059	80,095
Cutch and Gambier	62,162	77,189	23,064	28,168	35,749	38,027
Divi-divi (from Madras)	3,288	1,859	(a)	(a)	(a)	(a)
Hemp, raw	682,319	978,641	241,219	270,653	292,710	452,584
Oils—						
Vegetable, non-essential	385,653	1,868,132	287,039	283,635	224,495	268,695
Coconut	155,073	976,987	3,791	3,253	2,998	3,235
Castor	92,504	298,102	130,163	137,743	132,605	161,055
Rape and Mustard	48,624	51,532	33,691	23,150	25,902	25,840
Groundnut	30,013	84,740	107,424	67,651	24,926	29,563
Sesamum	28,699	19,557	10,612	12,494	14,412	18,427
Linseed	17,493	431,018	5,293	8,278	7,805	9,517
Mineral oil	142,732	230,692	73,416	7,406	5,747	4,696
Essential oil	113,992	282,809	109,022	139,501	184,823	203,401
Lemon grass oil	67,955	22,181	31,331	47,244	88,312	94,492
Animal oil	14,708	15,761				563
Fish oil	14,639	6,577	17	246	140	

Manures	629,570	410,216	152,921	190,903	238,221	286,729
Spices—	609,404	728,272	542,466	541,524	580,024	412,387
Pepper	289,943	408,889	170,356	136,793	183,779	57,214
Chillies	134,220	188,170	163,466	165,441	207,143	144,324
Ginger	122,661	65,707	86,313	67,781	62,032	56,605
Cardamom	49,994	51,605	108,805	159,321	114,823	142,008
Betelnut	8,224	8,119	11,004	10,265	10,353	9,554
Cinnamon	1,015	2,329	133	204	150	82
Cloves	231	1,883	40	8	..	23
Coir (excluding cordage and rope)	604,190	237,699	451,793	577,227	598,971	658,539
Rubber, raw	524,486	1,669,527	65,875	233,826	490,700	665,353
Fodder, Bran and Pollards	516,069	63,868	527,146	349,771	579,784	521,312
Coal, Coke and Patent fuel	461,424	104,208	331,442	280,159	221,327	129,939
Paraffin wax	448,736	745,652	1,514,078	1,716,844	1,439,461	1,709,005
Fruits and Vegetables	412,762	398,279	521,426	742,914	808,359	1,234,918
Coconuts	1,517	3,358	579	711	697	306
Provisions and Oilmanstores	362,939	412,026	244,656	210,918	208,978	203,460
Ghi	232,945	235,666	119,275	998,831	109,800	111,905
Butter	38,986	48,584	16,978	13,308	12,898	15,328
Tobacco	319,566	642,206	578,314	703,490	614,277	693,240
Mica	302,564	598,971	236,430	335,529	517,994	626,141
Fish	261,584	293,979	342,795*	386,535*	334,094	341,982
Chemicals and Preparations	219,049	753,915	128,744	133,283	126,637	122,153
Saltpetre	205,598	621,660	91,959	114,474	103,342	98,978
Borax	5,131	10,634	1,142	1,079	590	611
Silk—						
Raw silk	164,943	433,393	8,155	18,575	19,537	33,614
Silk manufactures	37,873	91,239	15,691	6,115	14,954	15,100
Bristles and Fibre	182,045	199,424	282,548	296,214	319,244	335,336
Candles	157,890	203,448	35,560	39,946	37,502	39,779
Drugs and Medicines	138,093	224,778	234,455	178,549	194,655	190,819
Senna	26,425	17,043	80,818	71,870	62,509	75,950
Nux vomica	17,366	57,606	8,787	22,400	29,557	7,063
Cinchona	8,289	706	188	2,219	3,178	473
Sugar	91,649	323,245	15,769	17,821	18,246	17,918

(a) Not available.

(*) Excluding canned fish.

The general distribution of exports, according to the countries participating in it, is illustrated in the table subjoined. In 1913-14, 37 per cent. of the exports went to the United Kingdom and British Possessions and 63 per cent. to foreign countries, the corresponding percentages for 1935-36 being 46.4 and 53.6. In the year 1935-36, about fifty-three per cent. went to Europe and twenty-six per cent. to Asiatic ports while the continents of America, Australia and Africa received fourteen, two, and about five per cent. respectively. Except in the case of Japan, whence the imports amounted to 16.3 per cent. in 1935-36, the import trade is to a much larger extent concerned with Europe, while a feature of the distribution of exports has always been the number of countries participating in it.

The percentage of exports to the United Kingdom rose from the pre-war figure of 23·4 to 29 at the close of the war. It went down to 22 in 1922-23 but has risen to over 31 in 1935-36.

TABLE No. 31.—*General distribution of the export trade showing the shares borne by the principal countries of destination in the exports of merchandise from India in 1913-14, 1918-19 and from 1932-33 to 1935-36.*

Name of countries.	1913-14.	1918-19.	1932-33.	1933-34.	1934-35.	1935-36.
	%	%	%	%	%	%
United Kingdom	23·4	29·2	28·0	32·2	31·6	31·5
Germany	10·6	..	6·5	6·5	4·7	5·8
Japan	9·1	12·1	10·3	8·5	16·0	13·4
United States of America	8·7	13·8	7·4	9·6	8·5	10·1
France	7·1	3·6	6 0	4·9	3·5	4·4
Belgium	4·8	·004	8·3	3·0	2·8	3·4
Austria and Hungary	4·0	·06	..	..	..	..
Ceylon	3·6	4·2	5·0	4·2	4·4	4·5
Italy	3·1	4 0	3 5	3·8	3·8	2·2
Hongkong	3·1	2·0	1·1	·8	·4	·3
Straits Settlements	2·7	2·9	2·7	2·3	2·1	2·3
China	2·3	1·1	2·6	3·0	1·7	1·1
Netherlands	1·7	..	3·0	2·7	2·2	2·3
Australia	1·6	2·6	2·9	2·0	1·8	1·7
U. S. S. R.	·9	..	·3	·1	·1	·2
Java	·8	1·4	·5	·3	·3	·3

The United Kingdom has at no time claimed such a preponderating share of India's export trade as, owing to Lancashire piecegoods and iron and steel, she has done for many years in the import trade. Germany was at the outbreak of war the principal recipient of the raw hides shipped from Calcutta and of rice from Burma, France took the bulk of the South Indian groundnut crop and Japan much of the cotton. While the war lasted enemy countries were of course *hors concours* and the tendency was naturally for the Allies to benefit elsewhere at the expense of neutrals. Increasing quantities of hides went to the United Kingdom and Italy and immense quantities of jute manufactures also to the former destination, and, if Egypt figured largely in the statistics it was only as a most convenient entrepôt, while war lasted, for the Allied forces operating in Italy, Salonika and Palestine. Since the Armistice, trade has with few exceptions returned to the old channels. Germany, considering everything, has shown a remarkable recovery, but trade with France has declined appreciably. The Union of Socialist Soviet Republics in the few years after the war practically ceased to participate in the export trade of India, but is now gradually making a recovery. Japan after a considerable rise, during and after the war, has reverted to the position it held in the pre-war days.

Review of Trade.

It may be of interest here to attempt a summary of the principal features of Indian Trade since the pre-war days.

1913-14.

A severe banking and commercial crisis in northern and western India coupled with an irregular monsoon affected the foreign trade generally. The trade in raw cotton, however, was brisk and there was an unusually large demand from the continent for oilseeds.

1914-15.

A favourable monsoon gave rise to hopes of a general recovery, but, when the war broke out, trade was seriously dislocated. It was not long, however, before the country began to adapt itself to war conditions. With the Allies entering upon an indeterminate period of trench warfare on the Western Front, an enormous demand arose for sand bags. Unlimited quantities of hides were required for the manufacture of boots for the now armies, and, more extensive orders from Japan for raw cotton coincided with an unusually abundant Indian crop.

1915-16.

The monsoon was not altogether favourable, but the export trade, in spite of the restrictions on shipments of food-stuffs, embargo on certain classes of goods, a restricted tonnage and an unprecedented increase in freights and insurance, did extremely well Fresh records were established in the volume of tea, jute bags and cloth and raw wool exported, and large shipments of wheat were made on Government account.

1916-17.

In 1916-17 the value of India's overseas trade showed a noticeable advance, particularly in exports, which increased by 21 per cent., while imports increased by over 13 per cent. The monsoon was particularly good and well-distributed, and crops were, with few exceptions, better than those of the previous year. Improvement was particularly noticed in raw cotton, saltpetre, shellac, indigo and jute manufactures.

1917-18.

The features of 1917-18 were heavier exports of commodities of vital national importance to meet the increasing demands of the Allies. The share of manufactured goods in the export trade, which was less than 24 per cent. in 1913-14 increased to 31 per cent. There was a further fall in the price of raw jute, but the textile industries enjoyed extraordinary prosperity.

The monsoon, which had been unusually favourable in the two preceding years, was a partial failure this year. With the termination of the hostilities in November, a considerable fall in freights followed, but the expectations of increased tonnage were scarcely realised. With so many adverse conditions, the volume of exports was 10 per cent lower than in 1917-18.

1918-19.

With the removal of war prohibitions, and gradual relaxation of restrictions on commercial intercourse with enemy countries, and on the export of such articles as raw jute, oils and oilseeds, and hides and skins, accompanied by an improvement in the freight position, business was brisk in spite of railway and cable congestion, high prices, labour difficulties, unstable exchange and imposition of Governmental control over food stuffs such as wheat and rice. The rainfall was unusually favourable and as compared with 1918-19, exports marked an increase of 80 per cent.

1919-20.

Due to congested stocks and sclackening demands of India's best customers such as United Kingdom, America, Japan, and the impaired credit of Russia and Central Europe, the export trade was badly affected. In March 1920 the value of India's exports had reached the record figure of £21 millions In March 1921, the total was only £12 millions. The year was particularly a disastrous one for the tea trade

1920-21.

Though the monsoon was satisfactory and freights were enormously reduced, 1921-22 was a year of unrelieved depression. In the export trade, the effects of the bad monsoon in 1920 were still noticeable, but the chief factors militating against any trade revival were the economic exhaustion of Europe and the chaotic condition of foreign exchanges. There was. however, a welcome recovery both as regards quantity shipped and prices realised under the head of tea, and the year closed with an improved demand for cotton from Japan and for oilseeds from the continent.

1921-22.

During 1922-23, on the export side, conditions in India favoured a strong revival, to which, however, her overseas customers were only in a position to provide a moderate response. Two years of favourable monsoons rendered a good turnover of exportable surpluses, but, as, before the war more than 50 per cent. of India's exports went to Europe, a return to normal conditions was dependent upon the full recovery of her former markets which were still lacking in purchasing power.

1922-23.

The year 1923-24 marked a slow but distinct advance towards India's commercial recovery. Notwithstanding the unsettled political condition in Europe and the high prices which tended to counteract the even flow of trade, the exports showed an increase of £331 millions over those of the previous year due mainly to the shortage of American cotton crop. Increases were noticed in the exports of raw jute, gunny bags, gunny cloths, food grains and flour, tea, and linseed, while decreases were marked in the exports of oils, metals and ores. indigo, paraffin wax, spices and cotton.

1923-24.

1924-25.

Due to the world-wide tendency towards stabilisation in trade, the year was one of records in the Indian export trade. A good monsoon for the fourth year in succession led to a large increase in the exportable surplus of crops and the total figure of exports of merchandise rose from £2,421 millions to £2,671 millions. The increase was largely in the exports of raw and manufactured jute and food-grains, while decreases consisted mainly in lac, metals and ores and raw cotton.

1925-26.

The total figures of exports of merchandise which reached the record of £2,671 millions in 1924-25 fell to £2,581 millions. Exports of raw cotton, jute manufactures including twist and yarn, registered an increase while there was an apreciable set-back in the export trade of grain, pulse and flour, due chiefly to reduced shipments of wheat and barley, and tea.

1926-27.

This year showed a considerable decrease in the export trade—the reduction being about 20 per cent. over the figures of the preceding year. The most important factor that contributed to this decrease was the heavy fall in the world prices of raw materials, particularly of cotton and jute There was also a noticeable decrease in the value of food-grains exported. Shipments of rice also decreased, while tea showed an improvement in quantity by 23 million lbs and in value by £1·3 millions.

1927-28.

Due largely to a favourable monsoon and a consequential increased output of crops and comparative financial stability, a considerable improvement marked the foreign trade of India this year. Cotton and cotton manufactures proved the depressing feature of the situation, in other sections all round increases though in varied degrees, were noticed

1928-29.

Due to deficiency in monsoon which was particularly unfavourable in the deltaic part of Burma, the exportable surplus of India and Burma together was considerably reduced. Judging by declared values, exports registered on increase of approximately three per cent. over the previous year's figures. Increases were mainly noticeable in the exports of raw and manufactured cotton, oilseeds, hides and skins, lac and raw wool. The export trade in food grains and flour suffered violent reactions, that of rice being adversely affected by an unfavaourable monsoon in Burma and the prohibition of imports into Japan. The adverse statistical position in the world's tea trade was reflected in India, which showed a decrease in value of about £45 thousand though there was a very small decline in quantity

1929-30.

The full advantages of an adequate and generally well distributed monsoon could not be reaped as the economic equilibrium of the country was seriously affected by the disturbed industrial situation due to unsettled labour conditions. The exports registered, on the whole, a decline of 6 per cent. on the previous year's figures. There was a serious depression in the world demand for jute. The total weight of raw and manufactured jute exported fell by 44,000 tons while the total decline under cotton piecegoods amounted to 16 million yards. Improvements were noticed in the exports of rice and linseed. Otherwise there was an all round decline, in some cases, *e.g.*, gunny bags, gunny cloth and tea, the gain in increased shipment was discounted by a fall in prices.

The year under review witnessed one of the worst industrial and trade depressions in history. The depression which started in October 1929 after the Wall Street collapse in America, deepened at an accelerated rate in 1930. Notwithstanding a favourable monsoon, therefore, a decline of 29 per cent. on the values recorded in the previous year, was witnessed in the export trade. Shipments decreased in nearly all the important sections and only slight improvements were noticed in linseed and wheat. The jute trade specially faced a considerable slump while the trade in raw cotton followed the depressed condition of the cotton industry of the world.

1930-31.

The year 1931-32 was even more disastrous than the previous year. The calamitous fall in prices which started in October 1929 continued unabated till September 1931. The consequent disruption of the international trade was partly arrested by the abolition of the gold standard in many countries. In India, the prices of agricultural commodities and raw materials fell comparatively more than those of the manufactured articles, and, as, the former constitutes the bulk of India's exports, the fall in prices of exports was more disastrous than in that of imports. Compared with the figures of the previous year, the value of exports fell by 29 per cent The trade in raw cotton fared worst, but decreases were noticed in all the important branches, *e.g.*, raw and manufactured jute, wheat, tea, oil seeds, hides and skins and lac while slight improvements were found in groundnuts and rape seeds. Export of cotton piecegoods and rice increased in quantity but the gain in increased shipments was counterbalanced by a fall in prices

1931-32.

The depression in the international trade continued in the year under review, and, the slight improvement which followed in the wake of the abandonment of the gold standard by United Kingdom, India and other countries could not be maintained. As in the previous year, the heaviest declines in the commodity prices occurred in respect of raw materials, and, consequently though this year showed an improvement of about 5 per cent in the case of imports, as compared with the previous year's figures, there was a decline of 15 percent. under exports. The downward trend continued in all the important sections particularly raw and manufactured cotton, raw and manufactured jute, food-grains, oil-seeds, hides and skins and lac, while rape-seeds and coffee recorded improvements. Despatches of tea increased in quantity but the value declined owing to lower level of prices.

1932-33.

Signs of progress towards recovery were noticed in the trade conditions but with few exceptions, there was no appreciable improvements in the prices of agricultural commodities. The "export restriction scheme" operated by the Indian Tea Licensing Committee was inaugurated this year, and, resulted in raising the price-level of tea. Despatch of tea contracted, but as the price-level rose, there was a gain in value. Compared with the previous year,

1933-34.

a ten per cent. increase was recorded in the export trade. The improvement was reflected in raw cotton, raw jute, oil-seeds, hides and skins, metals and ores, and lac, while exports of gunny bags and food-grains declined. The trade in soffee increased in quantity but declined in value.

1934-35.

The upward trend of the export trade continued in the year under review. As compared with the preceding year, the exports of raw cotton increased from 2,729 to 3,446 thousand bales. The principal increase was under raw cotton, while the trade in gunny bags, Wolfram ore, raw rubber. oil cakes, fodder, bran, etc., also showed noticeable improvement. On the other hand, seeds, raw skin, tanned or dressed hides, gunny cloth, paraffin wax, coffee, etc., declined.

1935-1936.

A further advance in the export trade as a whole was noticed in the year under review. The principal increase was under jute raw and manufactured, grains, metals, hides and skins, paraffin wax, and lac. The exports of raw cotton and tea, on the other hand, registered a decline.

Principal exports.

Jute and Jute Manufactures.

Jute fibre properly so-called, is obtained from two varieties of *corchorus* (*corchorus capsularis* and *corchorus olitorius*), and India enjoys a practical monopoly as virtually its sole producer. For statistical purposes, however, the fibre obtained from *hibiscus cannabinus*, which is commercially known as Bimlipatam jute from the Madras port from which it is principally shipped, is also included under this head.

Area and production.

Jute growing is confined almost entirely to the Ganges-Brahmaputra delta in the Presidency of Bengal and the province of Assam with the adjoining Indian State of Cooch Bihar though there is some cultivation also of the plant in Bihar and Orissa. River inundation bringing down rich alluvial deposits enables the cultivator to plant this exhausting crop year after year without expenditure on manure. The plants when once established require no attention and grow to the height of 10 to 12 feet The crop is cut before ripening and retted for about three weeks in water before the fibre can be removed by washing and beating. Machine treatment for extraction of the fibre has never got beyond the experimental stage. Jute is generally sown from March to May and harvested from July to September, and though it is customary in the trade to regard the season as ending on June 30th, practically the whole of the season's jute comes into sight commercially by the 31st March when the official year closes. But the special conditions created by the war tended to extend this period. The demand for jute in the world's markets is based upon the fact that no cheaper fibre is procurable for bagging agricultural produce. Some idea of the importance of the trade may be gathered from the fact that in 1913-14, the total value including India's internal consumption of raw jute and jute manufactures. exceeded £40 millions, in 1919-20 over £50 millions, and in 1934-35 over £24 millions.

TABLE No. 32.—*Estimates of the area under and production of jute in 1904, 1914, 1919, 1921 and from 1925 onwards.*

Year.	*Acreage under jute.	*Production in bales (400 lbs.)
1904	2,899,700	7,400,000
1914	3,352,200	10,443,900
1919	2,838,900	8,481,300
1921	1,518,000	3,985,000
1925	3,115,000	8,940,000
1926	3,847,000	12,132,000
1927	3,374,000	10,188,000
1928	3,144,400	9,906,000
1929	3,415,000	10,335,000
1930	3,492,000	11,205,000
1931	1,862,000	5,542,000
1932	2,143,000	7,072,000
1933	2,517,000	7,987,000
1934	2,670,000	8,500,000
1935	1,947,000†	6,372,000†

* Excluding Nepal for which no estimate of area or yield is available. The average annual figure of imports from Nepal is in the neighbourhood of 59,340 bales.

† Figures subject to revision.

The area under jute calculated from the yield of fibre did not exceed 850,000 acres in 1874. The average for the five years ending 1912-13 was estimated at 3,150,400 acres, and in the last pre-war year (1913-14), no less than 3,352,200 acres were appropriated to this crop. The decline which followed, and which was particularly accentuated in 1921 and 1922 is attributable chiefly to economic causes. During the early part of the war, the cultivator saw the prices of jute manufactures soar much higher proportionately than those of the raw material. And the high prices obtainable for rice encouraged larger sowings of this important food-grain at the expense of jute in areas suitable for the cultivation of either. The welcome recovery that followed after the post-war depression received a severe set-back in 1930, and in 1931 the acreage and production receded to the neighbourhood of the minimum figures of 1921. Since then signs of improvement are visible, but, still the pre-crisis level has not been reached. The provincial distribution of the crop and the estimated yield in 1935 are shown in the table below:—

TABLE No. 33.—*Provincial areas under jute and the estimated yield in 1935.*

Provinces and states.	Area (Acres).	Yield (bales of 400 lbs. each).
British Provinces—		
Assam	112,000	257,000
Bengal	1,670,000	5,707,000
Bihar and Orissa	146,000	356,000
Total British Provinces.	1,928,000	6,320,000
Indian States—		
Cooch Behar	18,000	50,000
Tripura	1,000	2,000
	19,000	52,000
GRAND TOTAL	1,947,000	6,372,000

The increasing demand for the fibre may be illustrated by a comparison of the price of raw jute in 1851, when it was the equivalent of Rs. 14½ per bale of 400 lbs, whereas in 1906 the rate was Rs. 57-8. In 1907 there was a drop in value to Rs. 50-12 which was further accentuated in 1908 and 1909, when the price declined to Rs 39 and Rs. 32-8 per bale respectively. In 1912 the average wholesale price was Rs 54-4 and in 1913 Rs. 71 and by April 1914 the rate had gone up to Rs 86-8 or more than three times the price of raw jute in 1880-84 The high prices fetched in 1913 by the cultivators and favourable agricultural conditions led to the production in 1914 of a record crop. Due to the outbreak of war, however, two important consuming countries, Germany and Austria, were closed to India and exports to other destinations were restricted. The market was completely glutted and prices sagged down to Rs. 31 in December 1914. Prices in 1915-16 to 1925-26 ranged between Rs. 35 in August 1917 and Rs 123 in January 1926, then gradually dropped to Rs. 28-4 in January 1931. The record of variations from April 1933 to January 1936, with comparative figures for 1913-14 will be found in the following table:—

Prices.

TABLE No. 34.—*Wholesale price of first grade jute in Calcutta per bale of 400 lbs. for 1913-14 and from 1933-34.*

Article.	Rate	1913-14				1933-34				1934-35.				1935-36.			
		April	July.	October.	January.	April.	July	October.	January	April	July.	October.	January.	April.	July.	October.	January.
Raw Jute First (Calcutta).	400 Lbs	Rs. 59	Rs. 69	Rs 83	Rs 85½	Rs 25½	Rs. 29¾	Rs 25⅛	Rs. 26⅛	Rs. 28¾	Rs 24½	Rs. 24½	Rs 31½	Rs. 31¾	Rs 36	Rs. 31	Rs. 38

The first shipment of raw jute was made apparently in 1795 but the recorded exports in 1828 were 364 cwts. Only in 1832-33, the figure rose to 11,800 cwts. and in 1838 the flax and hemp spinners of Dundee began the manufacture of jute fabrics on power looms. The hand-loom industry in Bengal, however, possessed such vitality that up to 1850 the exports of manufactured jute goods exceeded those of the raw material. The demand for the latter was largely increased by the cutting off at the time of the Crimean war of the United Kingdom from supplies of Russian flax, and the exploitation of jute as a commercial fibre of the first importance dates from that epoch. In 1882-83 the shipments of raw jute amounted to 517,450 tons, and the figures thereafter rose steadily until 1908-09 when they totalled nearly 900,000 tons. The consumption in Dundee had for many years previous to the outbreak of war remained steady in the neighbourhood of 1,200,000 bales say 220,000 tons, annually. In 1913-14 when the exports aggregated 768,000 tons, or about half the total crop, shipments to the continent exceeded those to Dundee, although consignments to the United Kingdom were considerably above the normal.

Exports of raw jute.

TABLE No. 35.—*Distribution and total value of the export trade of raw jute according to countries in 1913-14, 1918-19 and from 1931-32 onwards*

Countries.	1913-14	1918-19.	1931-32.	1932-33.	1933-34.	1934-35.	1935-36.
	(bales).	(bales).	(bales).	(bales).	(bales).	(bales).	(bales).
United Kingdom	1,626,067	1,255,075	864,735	725,323	992,280	923,000	930,000
Germany	886,928	..	732,776	681,576	926,301	761,000	851,000
United States of America	659,366	342,882	275,044	201,314	289,525	289,000	445,000
France	407,165	240,593	290,466	388,918	468,529	465,000	421,000
Italy	211,512	149,144	247,100	209,804	364,425	487,000	275,000
Spain	118,613	73,113	199,477	236,941	199,500	241,000	285,000
Other countries	137,603	168,907	675,462	709,336	949,180	1,048,000	1,112,000
Total { Bales	4,303,326	2,229,714	3,285,060	3,153,152	4,189,740	4,214,000	4,319,000
Total { Tons	768,451	398,146	586,618	563,063	748,168	752,474	771,324
Value £	20,550,929	8,480,052	8,391,022	7,297,763	8,199,503	8,153,319	10,280,726

In 1918-14, Germany, where the fibre is used in the manufacture of blankets, cheap carpets, etc., was next to the United Kingdom, India's best customer for raw jute. In 1914-15 after the outbreak of war, exports to all destinations, except to Italy and Spain shewed a considerable decline. In 1915-16, the volume of exports increased, mainly to the United Kingdom, the United States of America, Italy and Spain. In 1916-17 and 1917-18, due chiefly to the prohibition imposed on the exports of raw jute except under a license granted by the Chief Customs Officer at the port of export, the exports registered a marked decline. The control over exports was partially removed in March 1919 and with effect from the 1st October disappeared altogether. From 1919-20 the volume of exports has been maintained fairly steadily in the neighbourhood of half a million tons annually while prices after two years of marked decline had in 1922-23 nearly recovered to the level of 1919-20. Sterling credits had enabled Germany in 1921-22 and 1922-23 practically to satisfy her pre-war requirements of 800,000 bales annually, while shipments to the United Kingdom were more than 50 per cent. in defect in 1921-22 and 25 per cent. in the following year.

The upward trend which started in 1922-23 continued with small variations, till it reached the record figure of 879,863 tons in 1928-29 after which a decline set in Since 1933-34 however an appreciable increase in exports as compared with the previous years figures has been noticed.

Commercial organisation.

Between the cultivator of jute and the shipper many middlemen intervene. The cultivator disposes of his jute to a *bepari* or petty dealer who has received advances from a *mahajan* or broker (also known as *arathdar*) on the understanding that he gets as much jute as he can for the latter. The intervention of the *bepari* if not that of the *mahajan*, between the cultivator and the wholesale buyer, is unavoidable because the individual holdings are generally very small. The *mahajan* sells to the big buyer who may be the representative of a large exporting firm or of a mill, a baler or another broker, by whom the preliminary sorting, grading and bulking are effected. The most important trade centre upcountry for raw jute is at Narayanganj. Raw jute is transported by river, rail or road to Chittagong and Calcutta. Arrivals of raw jute in Calcutta in the neighbouring mill area in 1934-35 amounted to 9·3 million bales as compared with 10·4 million bales in the preceding year The bulk of the raw jute for Calcutta is despatched in *pucca* bales Jute, unlike cotton, loses only an insignificant percentage of its weight in the process of cleaning and baling.

The raw jute market in Calcutta is operated by brokers who sell either to the mills or to balers who may or may not be exporters also. In 1931, the number of jute presses in India was 110 as compared with 115 in the previous year. All jute is baled for export, the unit of sale as well as of shipment being the bale of 400 lbs though sterling quotations are usually on the basis of a ton, *c.i.f.* Brilliant colour, glossiness and length are the characteristics of good jute Some mills prefer hard and some soft fibre. Though a number of grades are recognised, such as *uttarya*, *deswal*, *dasee* (the standard quality), *deora*, etc., traders' marks play a very important part in the business, while *Narayanganji* and *Serajganji* are fibres named after the localities whence they are obtained. The lowest qualities are sold as *rejections* while *cuttings* represent the hard and woody ends of the plants.

Jute manufactures.

The first power mill in India to spin jute started work at Rishra near Serampur in 1855 and the first weaving mill at Baranagore four years later and the industry progressed steadily until 1875 when there was a temporary set-back owing to a too rapid increase in the number of looms. Since then the record is one of almost uninterrupted progress. Hand weaving has in consequence altogether died out, but the hand spinning of jute twine is still carried on as a cottage industry throughout the jute growing districts. The monthly production of the principal kinds of jute manufactures in Indian mills is shewn in the following table :—

TABLE NO. 36 —*Monthly production of jute manufactures in 1935-36.*

(in millions).

Month.	Hessian.		Sacking.	
	Cloth.	Bags.	Cloth.	Bags.
	Yds.	No.	Yds.	No.
April	94	11	5	46
July	111	8	5	49
October . . .	110	9	4	48
January . . .	113	10	5	46

The consumption of raw jute in Indian mills is more than half of the total production of jute in India, the actual figures for consumption in 1935-36 being about 5,000,000 bales out of an estimated total crop of 6,400,000 bales. The number of jute mills in India has increased since 1870 from 5 to 99, and the number of looms from 1,250 to 59,501. Practically all the mills are in the neighbourhood of Calcutta on the banks of the Hooghly for convenience of cheap water transport, the only mills outside Bengal being three in the Madras Presidency utilising *hibiscus cannabinus* two in Bihar and Orissa and one in the United Provinces. While the chief products of the mills in pre-war times had been gunnies and hessian cloth military demands during the war gave an impetus to the conversion of the latter into sandbags and to a largely increased output of tarpaulins. But perhaps the most interesting development was the manufacture of jute canvas, when the Russian revolution closed the principal European flax market to the allies. Over 5,000,000 yards were made by the Calcutta mills in 1918. The output of jute canvas during 1935-36 was 2·4 million yards.

The record of the jute industry, which is mainly in Bengal, has been, as has been stated, one of almost uninterrupted progress.

Progress of the industry.

In the following table, the quinquennial averages from 1879-80 to 1923-24 for mills, capital, persons employed, looms and spindles are supplemented by actuals for the ten years ending 1933-34, while the figures in brackets represent the variations for each period taking the average for the first quinquennium as 100.

TABLE No. 37.—*Table to illustrate the expansion of the jute industry from 1879-80.*

Year.	No. of mills at work.	Nominal capital (in lakhs of rupees).	Number (in thousands) of		
			Persons employed.	Looms.	Spindles.
1879-80 to 1883 84	21 (100)	270·7 (100)	38·8 (100)	5·5 (100)	88·0 (100)
1884-85 to 1888-89	24 (114)	341·6 (120)	52·7 (136)	7·0 (127)	138·4 (157)
1889-90 to 1893-94	26 (124)	402·6 (149)	64·3 (166)	8·3 (151)	172·6 (196)
1894-95 to 1898-99	31 (148)	522·1 (193)	86·7 (223)	11·7 (213)	244·8 (278)
1899-1900 to 1903-04	36 (171)	680·0 (251)	114·2 (294)	16·2 (295)	334·6 (380)
1904-05 to 1908-09	46 (219)	960·0 (355)	165·0 (425)	24·8 (451)	510·5 (580)
1909-10 to 1913-14	60 (286)	1,200·0 (443)	208·4 (537)	33·5 (609)	691·8 (786)
1914-15 to 1918-19	73 (348)	1,403·6 (519)	259·3 (668)	39·7 (722)	821·2 (933)
1919-20 to 1923-24	82 (410)	2,342·5 (865)	301·8 (777)	44·6 (800)	936·2 (1,062)
1924-25	90 (429)	2,213·3 (818)	341·7 (881)	50·4 (916)	1,067·6 (1,213)
1925-26	90 (429)	2,134·7 (788)	331·3 (854)	50·5 (918)	1,063·7 (1,209)
1926-27	93 (443)	2,119·8 (783)	333·7 (860)	51·0 (927)	1,083·8 (1,232)
1927-28	93 (443)	2,119·8 (783)	335·8 (865)	52·2 (949)	1,105·6 (1,256)
1928-29	95 (452)	2,126·7 (786)	343·9 (885)	52·4 (952)	1,108·1 (1,259)
1929-30	98 (467)	2,186·7 (808)	343·3 (885)	53·9 (980)	1,140·4 (1,296)
1930-31	100 (477)	2,360·7 (872)	307·7 (793)	61·8 (1,123)	1,225·0 (1,392)
1931-32	103 (491)	2,360·7 (872)	276·8 (713)	61·4 (1,116)	1,220·6 (1,386)
1932-33	99 (471)	2,370·7 (878)	* 266 2 (682)	60·5 (1,200)	1,202·2 (1,366)
1933-34	99 (471)	2,370·7 (878)	* 260·0 (667)	59·5 (1,180)	1,194·4 (1,357)

* Figures relate to Calendar years.

During the war, and in its immediate aftermath, the jute industry enjoyed unparalled prosperity. The United Kingdom, Australia, Japan and the United States of America had increasing shares in gunny bags, while the United States of America and the Argentine Republic participated largely in the export trade of gunny cloth.

From 1920-21 to 1928-29 the Indian mills worked short time, and from 1924-25 onwards, they further entered into an agreement not to add to the productive machinery. With the adoption of these remedial measures to stop overproduction the shipments of jute manufactures were generally on the increase. In gunny bags, the United Kingdom and Australia figured as the principal importers, while, the exports to the United States of America, Egypt, China and South Africa generally declined. Shipments to Japan, Cuba and Java fluctuated during the period. In gunny cloth, the principal purchasers were the United States of America and the Argentine Republic, while the United Kingdom and Canada cut down their requirements.

In 1929-30 the mills decided to increase their production, but due to a world wide trade depression, the additional output only accentuated the heavy fall in prices of both raw jute and jute manufactures. The exports of both bags and cloth increased The United Kingdom, Japan and China increased their takings of bags while Australia, Java and Cuba showed reduced shipments. The United States of America, Canada and the United Kingdom took more of cloth while the Argentine Republic and China reduced their demands.

In 1930-31 and 1931-32 the jute industry was faced with an alarmingly increasing world-wide depression in trade and could not find buyers for the comparatively huge turnover of the previous year. The short-time working and voluntary restriction of production of the mills under the inspiration of the Indian Jute Mills Association was only partially successful, until an agreement was entered into with the non-Association mills for regulating the output and eliminating internal competition. Exports of both bags and cloth decreased heavily Australia and the United Kingdom took more bags while shipments to all the other principal destinations were markedly in defect. Consignments of gunny cloth to United Kingdom and Australia showed slight improvements.

The exports of gunny bags increased in 1932-33, while those of gunny cloth decreased. The position was reversed in the following year. In 1932-33 Australia and Japan took more bags while the United States of America and United Kingdom reduced their demands of cloth. In 1933-34 Australia, the United Kingdom, the Union of South Africa cut down the requirements of sacking gunny bags but increased shipments of hessian gunny bags to the United Kingdom and Egypt were noticed. Canada and the United States of America increased their takings of hessian gunny cloth while the Argentine Republic, the United States of America and Egypt enhanced their demands of sacking gunny cloth. The year 1934-35 was one of comparative steadiness for the jute industry. During the year 2½ per cent. of the sealed looms were released. In January 1935 the Indian Jute Mills Association decided to release another 2½ per cent. from the 1st May 1935 and later it was decided to unseal a further 2½ per cent. each from the 5th August and the 11th November 1935 respectively. During the last four months of the year, a definite improvement in the situation was noticed. The total exports of gunny bags increased in number from 402 millions in 1933-34 to 423 millions in 1934-35. The United Kingdom and Australia took more hessian gunny bags but curtailed their requirements of sacking gunny bags. Siam, the Union of South Africa, Cuba, Japan, and the United States of America provided good outlets while exports to Chile, the Philippine Islands, Straits Settlements, Germany and Norway declined. Exports of gunny cloth increased in quantity but declined in value. The United States of America continued to be the largest customer of hessian gunny cloth while the Argentine Republic enhanced her takings. Shipments to the United Kingdom and Canada however declined.

In prewar times the quantity of raw jute exported was nearly equal to the consumption in Indian Mills. As will be seen from the table below the former, after having fallen as low as 1/3rd of the mill consumption in 1917-18, has again revived and reached almost the prewar level.

TABLE No. 38.—*Mill consumption and Export of Raw jute from 1913-14.*

(In 100,000 bales).

Season—July-June.	*Mill consumption.	Exports.
	July-June.	July-June.
1913-14	45	43
1914-15	49	30
1915-16	58	32
1916-17	57	28
1917-18	54	18
1918-19	51	22
1919-20	52	34
1920-21	56	23
1921-22	44	30
1922-23	47	29
1923-24	51	38
1924-25	57	39
1925-26	55	36
1926-27	55	45
1927-28	58	49
1928-29	60	49
1929-30	64	45
1930-31	46	34
1931-32	43	31
1932-33	44	3[illegible]
1933-34	43	43
1934-35	46	44
1935-36	50	41

* Relate to Mills in the membership of the Indian Jute Mills Association.

The diminishing proportion of jute exported from India unmanufactured as compared with manufactured is illustrated by the following table:—

TABLE NO. 39.—*Values, percentages and totals of raw and manufactured jute exported in 1913-14 and 1935-36 contrasted.*

Articles.	1913-14.		1935-36.	
	Value.	Percentage.	Value	Percentage.
	£		£	
Jute—				
Raw . . .	20,551,000	52·7	10,280,726	37
Manufactures . .	18,849,000	47·3	17,617,088	63
Total .	39,400,000	100	27,897,814	100

Details under main heads of jute manufactured exported are given below:—

TABLE NO. 40.—*Details of jute manufactures exported in 1913-14 and in 1935-36.*

Manufactured articles.	1913-14.	1935-36.
No. of bags	368,759,000	458,900,246
Weight . . . . . . tons	*325,700*	*425,726*
Yards of cloth	1,061,152,000	1,218,316,409
Weight . . . . . . tons	*275,200*	*317,971*
Miscellaneous goods—		
Weight . . . . tons	*4,200*	*8,279*
Yards	..	30,883
Total weight .	605,100	751,976
Value of bags . . . . . . £	8,358,000	8,260,975
Value of cloth . . . . . . £	10,396,000	9,177,977
Value of Miscellaneous goods . . . £	100,000	176,401
Total . £	18,849,000	17,615,353

Towards the end of 1916 the Director-General of Commercial Intelligence was appointed Jute Commissioner in Calcutta to effect the purchases of raw jute for the Dundee mills by the various firms among whom the orders were distributed on the basis of their previous Dundee business. The arrangement, which effected considerable economies, was terminated in 1917 when a new scheme was introduced involving purchase in London from selected firms. An officer, designated Jute Controller, was subsequently entrusted with the placing out of contracts in India for the purchase of jute manufactures for army requirements at controlled rates which are calculated to have effected a saving to the Indian and Australian Governments of £1½ millions in 1918 alone. The record of Government orders placed on behalf of the British Indian, Australian and Allied Governments since 1915-16 is shown in the table below Early in 1918 there was also effected a quick shipment of 4 million wheat bags to America on account of the U.S.A. Food Administration In addition one million bags were shipped early in 1919-20 just after control was removed. The appointment of Controller was then abolished

Government buying operations.

Of 221 million bags shipped in 1918-19, 132 million went to the United Kingdom; 74½ million to Egypt 'for orders'; 7½ million to Italy, and 7 million to the Argentine for bagging wheat purchased by the Royal Commission on Wheat supplies. Of the cloth, 118½ million yards went to the United Kingdom, 80½ million yards to the Argentine and 66 million yards to France.

TABLE No 41 —*Shipments on Government account of Jute manufactures from 1915-16 to 1918-19.*

Year.	Bags.	Cloth in yards.
1915-16	297,000,000	35,000,000
1916-17	385,000,000	135,000,000
1917-18	391,000,000	205,000,000
1918-19	221,000,000	269,000,000
Total .	1,294,000,000	644,000,000

The trade names of the principal jute manufactures with their sizes, weight and texture are given below. The terms 'porter' and 'shot' correspond to warp and weft. 'Hessian' is the term applied to the finest quality of jute yarn. The name is said to owe its origin to a fine quality cloth which Dundee used to supply to Hesse. 'Hessians' are made of hessian warp and weft. 'Sacking yarn' is inferior and generally darker in colour and deficient in gloss. 'Fine twill sacking' cloth is often made of hessian warp and sacking weft.

Trade names.

TABLE NO. 42.—*Size, weight and texture of the principal jute manufactures exported.*

Description.	Breadth and length. (in inches)	Weight.	Porter and shot. (in inches.)
A. Twills	44×26½ hd.	15·82	8×9
Twill Bags	51×30 ,,		8×8
A. Twill Bag	26½×18 ,,	16·62	8×9
Australian wool-packs	54×27×27 ,,	23·3	8×9
Australian corn sacks	44×26½ ,,	17·4	8×9
Cape wool packs	54×27×27 ,,	16·5	8×9
Chaff packs	54×27×27 ,,	10·3	5×6
Coal bags	36×28 ,,	..	5×8
Corn sacks (Australian)	44×26½ ,,	17·4	8×9
Cement bags	31½×22 ,,	13	8×8
Cocoa sugar bags	40×29 ,,	14·5	7×9
D. W. Sheets	84×54 selv.	..	7×8
D. W. Packs	72×36×36 hd	..	6×8
Dump packs	33×27×27 ,,	33·5	8×6 to 8
D. W. Bags (flour plain)	56×28 ,,	12·5	8×8
English corn sacks	53×27 ,,	15·82	8×8
Egyptian grain sacks	60×30 ,,	23·4	6×8
Egyptian sugar bags	48×28 ,,	14·5	7×9
Heavy C. Bags (Plain)	40×28 ,,	17·3	8×9
Liverpool Twills	44×26½ ,,	15·82	8×8
Sugar Bags	44×27 ,,	..	8×9
Salt Bags (D. W.)	45×26 ,,	12·4	6×8
Twill bags	27×20 ,,	..	8×9
SACKING CLOTH.			
Cotton Patches	36″×30″	.	2½×2½
Cotton Bagging Cloth	44″	..	1¾×1¼
D. W. Bagging Cloth	29″	..	8×9
Hy. Cee Cloth	29″		8×9
Jute Cotton Bagging Cloth	42″		2×1¼
Jute Cotton Bagging Cloth	44″	..	2·25×2
Plain Twill Sacking Cloth	27″	.	8×9
Twill Cloth	23″	..	10×11
Twill Sacking Cloth	22″	..	8×8
Hessian Cloth	40″	* 8 oz.	9″×10″
Hessian Cloth	40″	* 10½ oz.	11″×12″

Export duty.

With effect from the 1st March 1916 the Government of India decided to levy an export duty on raw jute other than cuttings at a general rate of Rs. 2-4-0 per bale of 400 lbs. equivalent approximately to an *ad valorem* duty of 5 per cent. The duty on cuttings was fixed at 10 annas per bale.

Simultaneously an export duty of Rs. 16 per ton was imposed on hessians and Rs. 10 per ton on sacking, corresponding to the raw jute rate on the material used in the manufacture of each class of goods. With effect from the 1st March 1917 these rates were doubled, and now stand at Rs. 4-8-0 and Re. 1-4-0 for raw jute

* per yard.

and cuttings and Rs. 32 and Rs. 20 for hessians and sacking, respectively. These duties are not applicable to Bimlipatam jute. The amount of export duty realised on Raw jute and jute manufactures in 1935-36 was £2,332,000.

Bimlipatam Jute—(1) Raw.

Though there is no true jute (*corchorus*) grown outside the old Presidency of Bengal and Assam, there is a considerable area in the Bombay and Madras Presidencies, and sporadic cultivation in the Central Provinces of *hibiscus cannabinus* which yields a fibre which is very similar and can be put to practically the same uses. This fibre, which is known as Deccan hemp in Western India, figures more prominently in the export trade under the name of Bimlipatam jute from the port on the Bay of Bengal from which it is chiefly shipped. The area under *hibiscus cannabinus* in the Bombay Presidency was about 125,000 acres in 1914-15 after which separate figures are not available. The area in the Madras Presidency is about 40,500 acres. In Bombay it is chiefly found in the Deccan and Karnatak, although it is a well-known crop in the other districts, and in Madras in the Vizagapatam district. The normal outturn in Madras may be taken at about 700 to 800 lbs. of dry fibre per acre, the percentage of fibre to dry stalks being about 16. The chief ports of export are Bimlipatam and Vizagapatam. The following table shows the figures of exports in recent years as contrasted with the pre-war and post-war exports.

TABLE NO 43—*Exports of Bimlipatam jute (raw) from the Madras Presidency in 1913-14, 1918-19 and from 1931-32 onwards.*

Year.	Quantity.	Value.
	Tons.	£
1913-14	22,003	517,992
1918-19	2,376	60,750
1931-32	1,938	27,095
1932-33	1,454	16,609
1933-34	4,005	47,318
1934-35	899	10,177
1935-36	1,754	25,256

The principal pre-war destinations were the United Kingdom (67 per cent.) and France (8 per cent.) but in 1913-14 Germany took 5,000 tons equivalent to nearly 25 per cent. of the whole. In 1934-35 the chief consumers were the United Kingdom (50 per cent.), Germany (39 per cent.) and the Netherlands (5 per cent.). The shipments of the same fibre from Bombay to foreign ports are negligible and not separately distinguished. The season for shipments in Madras usually runs from January to April and the unit of shipment is the steam pressed bale of about 400 lbs. rope lashed.

(2) Manufactures

There are three jute mills at work in the Madras Presidency, *viz.*, at Chittivlasa near Bimlipatam, Nellimarla near Vizagapatam, and Guntur in the order of their importance having regard to the number of looms and spindles installed in each of them. The exports of jute manufactures are inconsiderable, amounting to £1,689 in 1935-36 but there is a good local demand for gunny bags which compete with products of similar texture from Calcutta mills. There are no mills manufacturing Deccan hemp in Bombay.

Exports of jute and jute manufactures are subject to a cess at the following rates:—

Jute cess.

When exported by sea (whether beyond or within India) from Calcutta or from Chittagong (except raw jute exported to Calcutta):—

Raw jute (including jute cuttings and rejections) . . .	Two annas per bale of 400 lbs
Manufactured jute . . .	Twelve annas per ton of 2.240 lbs.

RAW COTTON.

According to the average for the quinquennium 1929-30 to 1933-34 the exports of raw cotton represent no less than 44·34 per cent of the total value of raw materials exported from India. The extent of the trade depends primarily of course upon the exportable surplus which in turn depends upon the general harvest in India, but the relation of textile activity in Europe and the United States to the supplies available in America and Egypt has such an important bearing upon the prices as to be a factor of scarcely less importance.

Production.

It was felt at one time that the world production of cotton was scarcely keeping pace with the increasing demand for cotton cloth and it would be expedient to explore fresh sources of supply. From this standpoint India undoubtedly offers considerable potentialities for making the additional contribution necessary to restore equilibrium, but the problem is complicated by the doubt as to the extent to which the Indian short staple even with an increased out-turn will really relieve the situation. The Indian cotton committee considered the question in its report of 1919 and the observations are summarised below.

The area under cotton in India covers such a wide climatic range that the season for planting and picking are divergent in different parts of the country, and while in Punjab and Sind, the crop is almost entirely irrigated, elsewhere it depends for the most part upon the sufficiency and the timeliness of the monsoon rainfall. The report of the Indian Central Cotton Committee further dealt with this aspect of the question in 1933-34 and a reference is made to the reservation in the Sukkur Barrage area of nearly 300,000 acres in one block for growing good staple cotton to meet the growing tendency all over the world for mills to take to spinning finer counts.

The Committee has also initiated propaganda for eradication of the spotted boll-worm pest. It has been ascertained that the entire digging up of the roots of plants after the crop is harvested offered immunity to the succeeding crop from the weevil germs.

The area and yield in 1913-14 and 1914-15 were 25,028,000 acres and 5,065,000 bales and 24,595,000 acres and 5,209,000 bales, respectively. The corresponding figures for 1934-35 were 24,023,000 acres and 4,858,000 bales. During the ten years ending 1933-34 the average annual yield per acre in India was 85 lbs. of cotton only, as compared with 169 lbs. in the United States of America and 397 lbs. in Egypt.

In the last pre-war year the value of the Indian cotton crop was estimated at £42½ millions or 15 per cent. of the world's total crop. In 1918-19 with the price of good Broach above 13*d*., the value of the reduced crop gathered was estimated at £76 millions. In 1933-34 with the price of good Broach above 4*d*., the value of the crop is estimated at £36 millions.

TABLE NO. 44.—*Acreage and yield in bales of 400 lbs. each of cotton in each Province from 1930-31 onwards.*

Provinces and States.	1930-31.		1931-32.		1932-33.		1933-34.		1934-35.	
	Area.	Yield.	Area.	Yield.	Area.	Yield.	Area.	Yield.	Area.	Yield.
British Provinces—										
Ajmer-Merwara . .	31,000	11,000	27,000	11,000	33,000	11,000	36,000	13,000	36,000	12,000
Assam . .	41,000	15,000	37,000	15,000	37,000	15,000	37 000	15,000	34,000	14,000
Bengal . .	58,000	17,000	58,000	15,000	59,000	21,000	58,000	21,000	58,000	21,000
Bihar and Orissa (a) .	69.000	14,000	68,000	14,000	65,000	13.000	42,000	8,000	42,000	8,000
Bombay including Sind	3,831,000	712,000	4,321,000	728,000	4,223,000	871,000	4,225,000	824,000	4,200,000	784,000
Burma . . .	373,000	87,000	228,000	34,000	832,000	64,000	445.000	102,000	438,000	92,000
Central Provinces and Berar.	4,750,000	1,136,000	4,620,000	442,000	4,000,000	820,000	4,270,000	758,000	4,240,000	611,000
Delhi . . .	4,000	1,000	4,000	2,000	2,000	1,000	3,000	(c)	4,000	2,000
Madras . . .	2,041,000	378,000	2,204,000	421,000	1,949,000	407,000	2,156,000 (d)	450,000	(d) 2,320,000	477,000
North-West Frontier Province.	13,000	3,000	18,000	4,000	16,000	3,000	21,000	4,000	15,000	3,000
Punjab . . .	2,164,000	667,000	2,160,000	538,000	1,890,000	555,000	2,449,000	927,000	2,347,000	946,000
United Provinces .	822,000	319,000	739,000	205,000	516,000	169,000	805,000	265,000	705,000	192,000
Total British Provinces .	14.197,000	3,360,000	14,484,000	2,429,000	13,122,000	2,950,000	14,547,000	3,387,000	14,439,000	3,162,000

Indian States—										
Baroda . . .	731,000	140,000	693,000	136,000	722,000	144,000	731,000	90,000	800,000	69,000
Bengal States (Tripura)	19,000	2,000	17,000	2,000	17,000	3,000	18,000	3,000	16,000	3,000
Bombay States . .	2,465,000	565 000	2,141.000	573,000	2,507,000	649,000	2,244,000	597,000	2,637,000	606,000
Central India States .	1,284,000	214,000	1,172,000	129,000	1,007,000	133,000	1,152,000	154,000	1,173,000	131,000
Gwalior . . .	619,000	103,000	632,000	76,000	597,000	76,000	614,000	59,000	633,000	58,000
Hyderabad . .	3,527,000	651,000	3,644,000	509,000	3,602,000	534,000	3,696,000	564,000	3,101.000	443,000
Mysore . . .	72,000	10,000	83,000	9,000	88,000	10,000	77,000	8,000	70,000	8,000
Punjab States . .	325,000	100.000	381,000	77,000	371,000	96,000	540,000	178,000	536,000	296,000
Rajputana States .	520,000	73,000	437,000	62,000	419,000	58,000	493,000	65,000	492,000	58,000
United Provinces State (Rampur).	23,000	5,000	14,000	2,000	10,000	1,000	6,000	1,000	10,000	2,000
Madras States (*b*) .	30,000	3,000	24,000	3,000	21,000	3,000	19,000	2,000	(*e*)	(*e*)
Total Indian States .	9,615,000	1,866,000	9,238,000	1,578,000	9,361,000	1,707,000	9,597,000	1,721,000	9,468,000	1,674,000
GRAND TOTAL	23,812,000	5,226,000	23,722,000	4,007,000	22,483,000	4,657,000	24,137,000	5,163,000	23,907,000	4,836,000

(*a*) Excluding certain Orissa States which report an area of 29,000 acres with a yield of 7.000 bales in 1934-35, as against 28,000 acres and 6,000 bales in 1933-34.

(*b*) Includes the State of Banganapalle up to 1925-26 and also Pudukottai from 1926-27

(*c*) Below 500 bales.

(*d*) Includes Madras States for which separate figure is not yet available.

(*e*) Included under Madras.

The average area under cotton in the Bombay Presidency proper, including Indian States, during the five years ending 1934-35 was 6,115,000 acres, of which the share of the British districts was 3,735,000 acres, and that of the Indian States, 2,380,000 acres. In 1934-35, the estimated area in the Presidency proper was 6,267,000, of which 2,610,000 acres are in the Indian States. In Sind, the area sown in 1934-35 is estimated at 705,000 acres, inclusive of 31,000 acres in the Khairpur State. The total area and yield in Bombay (including Sind and Indian States) are estimated at 6,972,000 acres and 1,400,000 bales in 1934-35, as compared with 6,469,000 acres and 1,421,000 bales, the corresponding estimates of the previous year.

Bombay Presidency.

The production of long staple (over 1 inch) cotton in India during the years 1933-34 and 1934-35 was 24,000 and 51,000 bales of 400 lbs. each respectively.

Cotton growing tracts in the Presidency fall into five divisions—

(i) the area comprising the great part of north Gujarat, the adjoining tracts of the Baroda State and the greater portion of Kathiawar where the trade variety *Dholeras* is produced;

(ii) Southern Gujarat, including the Broach and Surat districts in British territory and the Navsari District in Baroda where *Broach* cotton, the barometer of the Indian cotton trade, is grown;

(iii) the Bombay Deccan including the districts of East and West Khandesh, Nasik, Ahmednagar and Sholapur, also the northern part of the Bijapur District of the Hyderabad State where *Khandesh* cotton is cultivated;

(iv) the Karnatak, comprising the districts of Dharwar, Belgaum and the greater part of the Bijapur as well as the Indian States of Kolhapur and Sangli whence *Kumpta-Dharwar* is obtained; and

(v) the territory to the left of the Indus in Sind in the Nawabshah, Thar and Parkar and Hyderabad districts where *Sind* cotton is raised. In parts of the Bijapur district *westerns* are also grown as in the Madras Deccan.

Trade classification.	Staple in inches.	Ginning percentage.	Average area * in acres under cotton.	Average outturn (in bales of 400 lbs. each).
			Acres.	Bales.
Dhollera . . .	5/8" to 7/8" .	33—35	2,351,607	571,696
Broach . . .	5/8" to 1" .	33—36	765,495	165,881
Khandesh . .	4/8" to 6/8" .	33—40	1,136,316	238,120
Barsi and Nagar .	5/8" . .	39—40	211,010	27,817
Westerns . .	5/8" to 6/8" .	25	324,219	38,097
Kumpta and Dharwar	6/8" to 1" .	26—34	1,325,908	187,519
Total .	..	..	6,114,555	1,229,130

* Average of 5 years 1930-31 to 1934-35.

During the five years ending 1933-34, the average area cropped with cotton was 4,544,600 acres, equivalent to about 19 per cent. of the total for India. In 1934-35 the total acreage was 4,201,000.

Central Provinces and Berar.

In the total crop are included some 2,000 bales of Chanda Jari (G.indicum) and about 1,500 bales of *buri* which, if marketed pure, are equal to the 'Middling Americans'. The rest with the exception of about 20,000 bales of the newly introduced medium stapled verum cottons, are all short staple cottons which are commercially classed as *Oomras*. The most important tracts are the four districts of Berar and the adjacent districts of Nimar, Wardha and Nagpur, the main varieties produced being (i) Berar and Central Provinces *jari* in Berar and Central Provinces respectively, (ii) *roseum* in Berar and the adjoining tracts, (iii) *Chanda* jari (G. indicum) as a cold weather crop in the Chanda district and in the Hinganghat Tahsil of the Wardha district and (iv) improved verums which are gradually replacing the *jaris* and *roseum* all over the provinces. The acreage under *buri* is also tending to increase in and around Burhanpur Tahsil. The new improved wilt resistant verums are marketed pure to the extent of about 5,000 bales under Departmental control and obtain an average premium of Rs. 40 (£ 3) over Broach.

Trade classification.	Staple in inches.	Ginning percentage.	Estimated acreage in a normal season	Average outturn (in bales of 400 lbs. each).
"Oomras" Berar and Central Provinces.	5/8" to 6/8" .	35	3,780,000	520,000
Roseum . . .	4/8" . .	38	650,000	170,000
Bani or Chanda jari (G. indicum).	1" to 1-1/8" .	25	10,000	2,000
Improved Verums .	7/8" to 1" .	32	100,000	20,000

K

The following statement shows the average acreage and outturn of cotton in Hyderabad.

Hyderabad.

Trade classifications.	Acreage.	Outturn (in bales of 400 lbs.).
Gaorani	912,639	128,373
Oomras (inclusive of Barsi and Nagar) . .	2,143,866	304,045
Westerns and Northerns	424,457	50,421
Cocanadas	32,939	3,495

Two main varieties of cotton are cultivated, *buri* and *bani*, which both come under the trade description of *Oomras*. *Buri* is said to predominate in the Adilabad, Nizamabad and Karimnagar districts, while *bani*, alternatively known as *Hyderabad gaorani*, is the most important variety in the west, particularly in Parbhani and Nander. In Raichur and South of Gulbarga, the westerns cotton of Madras are found, while south-east of Warangal, *Cocanadas* are grown, and as a mixed crop *Khandesh* also.

Madras.

The estimated average area under cotton in the Madras Presidency for the five years ending 1933-34 was 2,184,000 acres and the estimated average yield 441,500 bales. In 1934-35, the estimated area and yield were 2,320,000 acres and 477,000 bales, respectively. About half of the total crop comes within the Lancashire definition of long staple.

The cotton growing tracts in Madras fall into three well-marked divisions:—

(i) the Deccan tableland including the districts of Bellary, Anantapur, Kurnool and Cuddapah in which *northerns* and *westerns* are grown, the former chiefly in the two first named and the latter chiefly in the two last named districts;

(ii) the Coromandal coast including the uplands of Guntur, Kistna, Nellore and Godavari (of which the first named is much the most important) where *Cocanadas* are grown, and

(iii) the southern districts of Tinnevelly, Ramnad, Madura, Trichinopoly and Coimbatore where (1) *Cambodia* (a variety of American upland, the seed of which was obtained direct from Cambodia about 1905) is grown on red soils, preferably well irrigated, and (2) *Tinnevellies* of which pure *karunganni*, a variety selected by the Agricultural Department, is much the most important, grown on the black soils.

Uppan cotton grown in the Coimbatore district passes under the trade name of *salems*.

Trade Classification.	Staple in inches.	Ginning percentage.	Estimated acreage average of 5 years.	Estimated yield in bales of 400 lbs. lint. (5 years average).	Estimated average of 5 years in bales of 400 lbs.
1. Northerns .	7/8"	26%	928,100	102,000	4,000
2. Westerns .	7/8"	28 to 30%			49,200
3. Cocanadas .	5/8 to 7/8"	24%	182,600	30,300	37,400*
4. Tinnevellies including Karunganni.	7/8"	29 to 31%	539,400	137,000	34,000
5. Cambodia—					
Irrigated .	7/8 to 1"	31 to 34%	167,700	101,600	7,800
Unirrigated .	7/8"	31 to 34%	161,700	33,900	
Salems—					
Uppams .	6/8"	25%	43,000	6,500	12,500
Karunganni .	7/8 to 1"	31%	125,000	28,400	
Nadams . .	5/8 to 6/8"	25%	36,400	1,800	

The Punjab.

For the five years ending 1934-35, the average area under cotton in the Punjab was 2,633,913 acres inclusive of 431,840 acres returned by Indian States. The figures for 1934-35 were 2,883,563 acres (2,347,063 acres in the Punjab and 536,500 acres in Indian States). 92 per cent. of the area under cotton in the British Districts of the Punjab was under irrigation and nearly one-third of it was under medium staple Punjab American cotton chiefly 4F. Long staple 289F was grown on an area of 56,000 acres.

As regards cotton cultivation the British Punjab may be divided into four zones; *viz*:—

I. *The Canal Colonies* which grow both *Desi* and American cottons, comprising the districts of Lyallpur, Montgomery, Jhang, Shahpur, Sheikhupura, Gujrat, Gujranwala, Lahore and Khanewal Tehsil of Multan District,

II. *The Western Punjab* which grows *desi* cotton mainly, comprising the districts of Multan (except Khanewal Tehsil), Mianwali, Dera Ghazi Khan and Muzaffargarh,

III *The Central and North Punjab and Sub-Montane Districts* (which grow *Desi* cotton mainly) comprising the districts of Amritsar, Jullundur, Hoshiarpur, Ludhiana, Sialkot, Jhelum, Rawalpindi, Attock, Gurdaspur and Kangra, and

IV. *The South East Punjab* (which grows *Desi* cotton with the exception of Ferozepore District which grows both Desi and American), comprising the districts of Hissar, Rohtak, Gurgaon, Karnal, Ambala and Ferozepore.

* The excess may be due to the import of other cottons from neighbouring tracts like Hyderabad State, Ganjam and Vizagapatam districts.

The appended table gives particulars of varieties of both Punjab American and Desi cottons as grown in the British Punjab.

Trade classifications.	Staple length.	Ginning percentage.	Area in acres during 1934-35.	Approximate outturn in bales of 400 lbs.
1. *American*—				
(*i*) Punjab 289 F. .	1 1/16″	29	56,000	420,000
(*ii*) Punjab 4 F. and others.	7/8″	32-1/2	784,700	
			840,700	
2. *Bengals*— *Punjab Desi*—				
1. Mollisoni . .	5/8″	36	727,200	580,000
2. Others . .	Below 5/8″	32	779,100	
Total .	..	..	1,506,300	
GRAND TOTAL .	..	..	2,347,000	1,000,000

United Provinces.

For the quinquennium ending 1932-33 the average acreage under cotton was 773,000. In 1932-33 the area was 527,000 acres including Rampur. Practically the whole of the cotton of the province is sold under the commercial name 'Bengals' with a staple of 3/8″ to 4/8″ for ordinary Bengals and 5/8″ to 7/8″ for fine Bengals.

Though grown all over the province the chief areas for cotton lie in the west in the Bulandshahr, Muttra, Aligarh and Agra districts. About half of the total area was irrigated in 1932-33. The chief varieties are:—

1. The U P. Mixed Bengals.
2. The Aligarh white flowered.
3. Cawnpore 520.
4. Cawnpore 402.

Nos. 2 and 3 have been evolved by the Agricultural department.

Trade classification.	Length of staple.	Ginning percentage.	Estimated acreage in a normal season.	Average outturn (in bales of 400 lbs.).
Bengals—				
United Provinces .	4/8″	35	1,000,000	260,000
White flowered Aligarh .	3/8″	39	160,000	32,000
Cawnpore 520 . .	5/8″	38	6,000	1,200
Cawnpore 402 . .	7/8″	37	2,000	270

For the five years ending 1933-34, the area under cotton in the Central India Agency averaged 1,201,000 acres. In addition to this, the average acreage during the quinquennium in Gwalior was 619,000. The estimated area and yield in 1934-35 were 1,178,000 acres and 181,000 bales.

Central India.

The main cotton-growing tract is the southern part of the western of the two detached areas of which the Agency is composed. *Malwa* cotton is grown on the Malwa plateau, and elsewhere the type known as *Central India*, both of which belong to the trade description *Oomras*.

In the Rajputana States, the average area under cotton for the five years ending 1933-34 was 475,000, acres, exclusive of 32,000 acres in Ajmer-Merwara.

Rajputana and Ajmer-Merwara.

No long staple variety of cotton is produced. The cotton tracts of the Agency are in the east adjacent to those of the United Provinces and Central India. The cotton which belongs to the type known as *Rajputana* falls under the trade description of *Bengals*.

The average area under cotton for the five years ending 1933-34 in Mysore was 78,000 acres. Most of the cotton grown satisfies the Lancashire definition of long staple. The chief areas are the Chitaldrug and Shimoga districts, where the types of the adjoining districts of Bombay are produced, *viz.*, *Kumpta* and *Dharwar-American*. The estimated area and yield in 1934-35 were 70,000 acres and 8,000 bales.

Mysore.

During the five years ending 1933-34, the average area in Burma under cotton was 328,000 acres, as compared with about 366,000 acres in the previous quinquennium.

Burma.

The whole crop is of short staple with the possible exception of *wa-gyi* which can be brought under the Bombay description if a regular staple can be evolved. The four chief districts, Sagaing, Lower Chindwin, Meiktila and Myingyan in the dry zone are devoted chiefly to *wa-gale* cotton which forms nearly seven-eighths of the crop.

On the borders of the dry and wet zones in the Thayetmyo and Prome districts *wa-gyi* cotton is cultivated, and in the Shan Hills, the type "Shan Hills". Collectively the three varieties are called *Burmas*.

Trade classification.	Staple in inches.	Ginning Percentage.	Estimated acreage in a normal season.*	Average outturn (in bales of 400 lbs.).*
Burma—				
Wa-gale . . .	4/8" to 6/8"	30 to 32	347 000	70,000
Wa-gyi . . .	6/8"	38 to 40		
Shan Hills . . .	Not known	Not known.		

* Average of 10 years 1924-25 to 1933-34.

Exports of raw cotton from Burma in 1935-36 amounted to 105,684 bales of 400 lbs. each.

Bengal, Bihar and Orissa and Assam.

For the five years ending 1933-34, the average area under cotton in Bengal was 58,000 acres, in Bihar and Orissa 63,000 acres, and in Assam 38,000 acres. In Bengal the chief producing areas are the Chittagong hill tracts, Mymensingh, the districts of Bankura and Midnapore, and in Assam, the Garo and Lushai hills. The product of these areas is known as *Comilla* cotton. The acreage in Orissa is insignificant. In Bihar, the districts of Saran and Ranchi have more than 5,000 acres devoted to the crop.

In 1934-35, the estimated yield of cotton in Bengal was put at 24,000 bales, in Bihar and Orissa at 8,900 bales and in Assam at 13,000 bales, the total estimated area under the crop in the three provinces being 150,000 acres.

Trade classification.	Staple in inches.	Ginning percentage.	Estimated acreage in a normal season.	Average outturn (in bales of 400 lbs each).
Comillas	3/8" to 4"	45	98,000	30,000
Jathia	5/8" to 6/8"	17	Figures not	available.
Bihar and Orissa . .	3 8' to 4/8"	34	74,800	14,300

The exports of raw cotton from Calcutta in a normal year amount to about 45,000 bales.

North-West Frontier Province.

For the five years ending 1933-34, the average acreage under cotton was 17,000 acres. The bulk of the crop is grown under irrigation in the Peshawar and Dera Ismail Khan districts and is known in the trade as *North-West Frontier Province*. Its ginning percentage is 32, and as the length of its staple is only from 5/8" to 6/8", it scarcely satisfies the Bombay standard of long staple.

In 1934-35, the estimated area and yield were 15,000 acres and 4,000 bales.

In the following table the average prices of typical grades of cotton on the Liverpool and Bombay markets are contrasted. In 1913 the figures for Liverpool and Bombay respectively were 7*d.* and 6·3*d.*

TABLE No. 45.—*Average prices of American middling cotton at Liverpool and good Broach cotton at Bombay in 1914, 1918, 1919 and from 1930 onwards, in pence and decimals of a penny per lb.*

Year.	Liverpool	Bombay.
	d.	*d.*
1914	6·50	5·90
1918	23·23	13·30
1919	20·33	13·00
1930	7·10	5·18
1931	5·09	4·32
1932	5·24	4·96
1933	5·43	4·75
1934	6·79	4·60
1935	6·70	5·28

Exports.

The effect of the enormous rise in price during 1918-19 as shown in the preceding table is illustrated by the increased value obtained for reduced exports. Since 1930, the price has fallen below the pre-war level and in the following table, the quantities and values of raw cotton exported in the pre-war, post-war and the recent periods have been contrasted.

TABLE No. 46.—*Quantity and value of raw cotton exported from India in 1913-14, 1918-19 and from 1930-31 onwards.*

Year.	Quantity.	Value.
	Tons.	£
1913-14	531,316	27,361,655
1918-19	183,950	20,655,709
1930-31	701,069	34,746,031
1931-32	423,080	17,585,420
1932-33	364,852	15,279,052
1933 34	503,720	20,645,536
1934-35	615,313	25,873,733
1935-36	606,536	25,327,706

When the trade is classified according to the port from which shipment is effected, the preponderating share of Bombay is clearly emphasised. Exports from Karachi and Rangoon are on the increase while shipments from Calcutta and Madras are marked by variations.

TABLE No. 47.—*Exports of raw cotton from the major ports in 1913-14, 1918-19 and from 1930-31 onwards.*

Year.	Bombay.	Karachi.	Calcutta.	Rangoon.	Madras.
	Tons.	Tons.	Tons.	Tons.	Tons.
1913-14 . . .	380,464	74,686	23,371	8,489	11,791
1918-19 . . .	160,590	7,790	4,647	9,598	168
1930-31 . . .	474,863	180,996	4,588	14,926	14,162
1931-32 . . .	270,980	128,476	4,004	5,197	9,510
1932-33 . . .	206,226	128,666	3,749	13,553	7,278
1933-34 . . .	237,165	200,404	8,548	20,960	8,733
1934-35 . . .	316,539	250,148	6,122	14,387	7,722

The bulk of the shipments of raw cotton has always gone to the Far East and the Continent, but the United Kingdom in recent times is participating in an increasing degree in the trade. Whereas during the war and in its aftermath, the exports to the United Kingdom consisted on an average of 80,000 bales, in 1933-34, no less than 342,000 bales were shipped there Her importation in that year is only next to that of Japan, the biggest consuming country of Indian raw cotton As compared with the figures of 1932-33, China has also increased her takings though she is still far below the average of the previous five years Japan took 37·4 per cent. of the total exports as compared with 52·7 per cent in 1932-33. Great efforts were made in the early part of the last decade to extend the area under cotton in Japan and Korea but the acreage in Japan has been curtailed considerably since 1930-31. Japan's intake of American cotton has fallen slightly. A Convention and Protocol regarding the Commercial Relations between India and Japan was concluded in 1933 and enforced with effect from the 8th January 1934 under which the imports of Japanese cotton piece-goods in India and exports of Indian raw cotton to Japan have been regulated. The main feature of the Protocol is that if in any Calendar year, one million bales of raw cotton are exported from India to Japan, the quantity of cotton piecegoods which may be exported from Japan to India in the corresponding fiscal year shall be a basic allotment of 325 million linear yards. Corresponding adjustments have been provided to cover shipments in excess or defect. Under the Bombay-Lancashire Textile Agreement, 1933, entered into by the British Textile Mission to India and the Millowners' Association, Bombay, further efforts have been made in the United Kingdom to popularise and promote the use of Indian cotton.

India's imports of raw cotton amounted to 42,896 tons in 1933-34 of which more than 56 per cent., mainly Uganda cotton, came from the Kenya Colony.

Nearly 900 tons of foreign raw cotton were exported from India in 1933-34.

Table No. 48.—*Distribution of the exports of raw cotton among principal importing countries.*

Countries.	1913-14.	1918-19.	1932-33.	1933-34	1934-35	1935-36.
	Tons.	Tons.	Tons.	Tons.	Tons.	Tons.
Japan	240,878	139,875	196,686	182,565	359,088	314,187
Germany	84,403	...	27,272	44,087	27,887	47,070
Belgium	56,654	.	22,815	25,826	27,293	40,185
Italy	42,420	22,039	27,373	46,555	49,598	27,539
Austria and Hungary	37,352	.	.	...	11	39
France	26,213	1,822	22,091	29,117	76,391	29,626
United Kingdom	19,246	13,808	29,846	61,037	61,955	81,454
Spain	8,346	123	9,335	10,955	10,774	12,062
Hongkong	5,479	1,050	5	...	12	6
China	4,285	1,652	23,928	60,137	25,269	19,393
Netherlands	1,446	.	6,714	11,649	8,284	7,866
United States of America	1,824	428	2,040	6,178	5,792	10,200
U. S. S. R.	1,316	.				...
Other Countries	1,993	3,158	9,942	22,831	13,514	16,909
Total	531,314	183,950	368,338	489,288	615,313	606,536

With these exports must be contrasted the estimated consumption of indigenous cotton by Indian mills which is arrived at by deducting the quantity of raw cotton imported from the gross figures of mill consumption. No exact estimate of extra-mill or domestic consumption is possible, but 750,000 bales of 400 lbs. each is probably fairly accurate. The quantity of hand-spun cotton is not considerable, as the handloom weavers generally depend for the bulk of their requirements upon yarn from the mills.

Mill Consumption.

Table No. 49.—*Net consumption of indigenous cotton by Indian Mills.*

	(In thousands of bales)					
	1913-14.*	1918-19.*	1932-33	1933-34.	1934-35.	1935-36.
Bombay Island	...	..	571	530	605	666
Ahmedabad	...		336	353	378	305
Bombay Presidency		.	1,105	1,078	1,201	1,177
Madras		..	289	274	296	339
United Provinces	..	.	266	270	289	307
Central Provinces and Berar		.	119	108	121	123
Bengal	.	.	107	103	106	100
Punjab and Delhi			89	72	78	88
Rest of British India			32	33	37	41
Total British India		..	2,007	1,938	2,129	2,176
Total Indian States	.	..	373	352	425	433
Total India	1,800	1,800	2,380	2,290	2,554	2,609

* Detailed figures not available.

A very small percentage of the crop in various parts of the country is delinted by means of hand gins and stone gins. The greater part is machine ginned and chiefly with roller gins. To a small extent the American Saw Gin is used in the Punjab, Sind and Dharwar area. Ginners buy seed cotton and/or gin on commission. The former mode is more prevalent in the Punjab than elsewhere In many of the more important cotton growing centres, big exporters have their own gins.

Ginning.

The ginned cotton is steam pressed in steel hooped bales up-country and railed down to port. The density of the pressing varies from 40 to 55 lbs. per cubic foot. The ginning and pressing of cotton by factories in India (except Burma) is regulated under the provisions of the Cotton Ginning and Pressing Factories Act, 1925.

Baling and Pressing.

Three quarters of the Indian cotton crop is sent to Bombay, where it used to be stored in the open air on the Cotton Green at Colaba exposed not only to the weather but also to serious risk of fire. In March 1923 the new Cotton Depot at Sewri was formally inaugurated. Prior to July 1918, there was no single body controlling dealing in raw cotton and transactions were carried on under the rules of either the Bombay Cotton Trade Association or the Bombay Cotton Exchange, mostly of the former, though adhesion to either set of rules was voluntary In July 1918, all the cotton transactions in Bombay were placed under the control of the Cotton Contracts Board originally appointed under the Defence of India Rules and subsequently constituted under the Cotton Contracts Control (War Provisions) Act (Bombay Act I of 1919) On the repeal of this Act the Bombay Cotton Contracts Act (Bombay Act XIV of 1922) was passed giving the East India Cotton Association, Limited, statutory character to regulate and control transactions in cotton in Bombay and the power to make by-laws having the force of law for regulating and controlling such transactions, not only as regards members of the Association but also as regards every person dealing in cotton in Bombay This regulation and control included regulation and control of transactions, provided such transactions were to be carried out in whole or in part in Bombay By Bombay Act IV of 1932 the East India Cotton Association, Limited, was given further statutory recognition with similar powers, and accordingly now controls and regulates under statutory supervision the immense trade which is done in Bombay in the buying and selling of cotton

Bombay cotton trade control.

Under the Indian Cotton Cess Act (XIV of 1923) and its subsequent amendment, a cess of two annas per standard bale of four hundred pounds avoirdupois or in the case of unbaled cotton of six pies per hundred pounds has been imposed on all cotton produced in India and either exported outside British India or consumed in any mill in British India. The cess was levied at double the above rates for the first three years of the Act The funds derived from the cess are administered by the Indian Central Cotton Committee, the creation of which was recommended by the Indian Cotton Committee of 1917-19. The Committee was constituted originally as an advisory Committee but it was permanently incorporated with the passing of the Indian Cotton Cess Act in 1923 and provided with funds for the purpose of improving and developing the growing, marketing and manufacture of cotton. Its two main functions are (1) to advise the Government of India and Local Governments on matters concerning the growing and marketing of cotton and to bring to their notice matters, which in its opinion, require attention, and (2) to provide funds for research into cotton problems of all-India importance or for large areas where cotton is an important crop, and for the extension and marketing of improved varieties of cotton. In addition to the above, the Committee

Cotton cess.

provides a common meeting ground for all branches of the cotton industry in India.

The Committee also maintains a Technological Laboratory at Bombay, where fundamental research on the physical and chemical properties of the cotton fibre is undertaken and spinning tests conducted on samples of cotton supplied for the purpose by the trade and agricultural departments.

The Committee also undertakes, by means of research scholarships, to train research workers in the several sciences pertaining to cotton.

Unit of sale and shipment. In the Bombay Presidency, the unit of sale is the candy of 784 lbs., and in Karachi, the maund of $82\frac{2}{7}$ lbs.

In the Punjab the maund of $82\frac{2}{7}$ lbs. is the common unit of weight for all cotton transactions and in the United Provinces and the Central Provinces and Berar the maund of $82\frac{2}{7}$ lbs. and the candy of 784 lbs. are the prescribed standards. In the Madras Presidency the standards are the maund of 28 lbs and the candy of 784 lbs.

Shipment is made from Bombay, Karachi, Calcutta and Madras in bales of 400 lbs. usually Cambodia and Tinnevelly cottons are generally shipped in bales of 500 lbs. At Tuticorin shipments are in bales of 392, 500 or 504 lbs

Freight on cotton in fully pressed bales is reckoned on measurement, as a rule one ton being equal to 40 or 50 cubic feet according to the custom of the Port Exceptions to this are shipment to the Far East, where the freight is mostly payable per bale, and some coastal shipments where freight is charged sometimes per Bengal Maund of 82 2/7 lbs. and occasionally per bale. The measurement of bales varies between 25 and 28 tons of 40 cubic feet per 100 bales.

Kapok. Kapok or silk-cotton, which may be conveniently noticed here, is the floss obtained from the seed capsules of the white flowered *eriodendron anfractuosum*,* which grows in the hot moist tracts of western and southern India and of Burma The fibre is too short, light and smooth to be easily spun unless as an admixture with other flosses, and its chief use is in upholstery for filling cushions, etc., where it has the advantage, unlike ordinary cotton, of not readily balling On account of its buoyancy and freedom from water logging, it is also in great demand for life belts The chief sources of supply for the European markets are the Dutch Indies and, to a smaller extent, Ceylon where the tree is widely cultivated for the floss, while in India, no systematic planting has yet been attempted and the export was, until recently, so insignificant that no separate statistical records were kept of it. Even now while the internal trade has developed considerably, the quantity shipped is small and probably the total is swelled by consignment of floss obtained from the *bombax malabaricum*, the red silk cotton tree, which is of much commoner occurrence in India than the white, but is incorrectly called *kapok*. In 1935-36, 39,295 cwts. valued at £51,448 were shipped as compared with 19,032 cwts. valued at £34,890 in the previous year. The bulk of the exports

* Bombax pentandrum, Linn.

goes from Calcutta, with Bombay and Karachi as next in importance. The principal recipients are the United Kingdom, the Netherlands, Italy and China in that order.

Unit of sale and shipment.

The unit of sale in Calcutta is the pound and shipment is made in pressed bales, rope-bound, weighing two maunds nett. In Bombay sales are per candy of 784 lbs. or per maund of 28 lbs. while shipment is effected in pressed bales weighing from 2 to 2½ cwts. Quotations for export to the United Kingdom are per lb. *c.i.f.*

Cotton Manufactures.

Progress of the Industry.

Of the cotton produced in India it may be said in general terms that about one-half is exported raw, while the balance is manufactured into yarn and cloth in Indian mills. The chief centre of the cotton manufacturing industry as of the trade in raw cotton is Bombay. Cotton manufactures now represent about 7 per cent. of the total value of Indian manufactures exported and about 2 per cent. of the total export trade of the country. The first cotton mill in India was started in 1838 at Ghoosery near Calcutta and the first to be opened in Bombay dates from 1853 with 5,000 throstle spindles. At the end of December 1938 the total number of mills in existence was 344, giving employment to 428,658 persons.

Between 1898 and 1918 the number of spindles increased by nearly 50 per cent. and the number of looms by 211 per cent. but the tendency during the last twenty-five years has been more towards enlarging existing mills rather than opening new ones. Indeed India at the outbreak of war ranked as fourth among the countries of the world manufacturing cotton textiles being exceeded by Great Britain, the United States and Germany only. The Indian cotton textile industry has developed considerably since then, and India now ranks third, being exceeded by the United States of America and Japan only. The table below shows the progress made during the last fifty-four years.

TABLE No. 50.—*Progress of the cotton spinning and weaving industry in India since the year 1879-80.*

Year.	Number of mills in existence.	Number of Persons employed.	Number of Looms.	Number of Spindles.
1879-80 . . .	58	39,537	13,307	1,470.830
1888-89 . . .	109	92,126	22,156	2,670.022
1898-99 . . .	174	156,132	37,288	4,463,342
1908-09 . . .	233	236,827	74,592	5,966 530
1909-10 . . .	245	232,381	80,171	6.142.551

Year.	Number of miles in existence.	Number of		
		Persons employed.	Looms.	Spindles.
1913-14 . . .	264	260,847	96,688	6,620,576
1914-15 . . .	255	260,440	103,311	6,598,108
1915-16 . . .	267	275,871	108,417	6,675,688
1916-17 . . .	267	277,370	110,812	6,670,162
1917-18 . . .	269	284,054	114,805	6,614,269
1918-19 . . .	264	290,255	116,094	6,590,918
1919-20 . . .	263	305,511	117,558	6,714,265
1920-21 . . .	255	328,132	117,953	6,652,474
1921-22 . . .	271	341,944	128,314	6,814,273
1922-23 . . .	289	356,758	137,238	7,245,119
1923-24 . . .	310	350,049	147,087	7,903,196
1924-25 . . .	305	376,012	150,680	8,286,206
1925-26 . . .	303	370,617	154,591	8,403,336
1926-27 . . .	306	384,082	158,124	8,412,817
1927-28 . . .	297	388,284	159,289	8,236,280
1928-29 . .	292	380,596	165,384	8,493,310
1929-30 . . .	304	392,532	173,347	9,021,879
1930-31 . . .	310	407,189	171,725	8,802,339
1931-32 . .	317	441,739	173,551	8,908,330
1932-33 . . .	331	(a)453,565	180,704	9,165,848
1933-34 . . .	344	(b)428,658	183,953	9,211,207

Of the total number of mills in India 191 are in the Bombay Presidency; 17 in Bengal, 22 in the United Provinces, 29 in Madras, 11 in the Central Provinces and Berar, 9 in the Punjab, 4 in Delhi, 4 in Ajmer-Merwara, 1 in Burma, 1 in Bihar and Orissa, 3 in French India and the rest in Indian States, chiefly in Central India and Baroda. The mills of the Bombay Presidency (chiefly situated in Bombay city and Ahmedabad) produce 53 per cent. of the yarn spun and 64 per cent. of the cloth woven. The statement below originally compiled by the Industrial Commission and now brought up-to-date indicates that the mill-made and foreign yarn available for handloom weavers averaged in the six years, 1908-09 to 1913-14, over 250 million lbs., and in the last seven years there has been a remarkable increase in this figure as well as in mill consumption.

(a) Relates to the Calendar year 1932.
(b) " " " " 1933.

TABLE No. 51.—*Quantity in thousands of lbs. of mill-made and foreign yarn available for handloom weavers.*

Particulars.	Average of 1896-97-1901-02.	Average of 1908-09-1913-14.	Average of 1917-18-1922-23.	Average of 1929-30-1933-34. •	1934-35.	1935 36.
	lbs.	lbs.	lbs.	lbs.	lbs.	lbs.
1. Yarn imported—						
by sea . .	44,956	41,749	39,388	36,351	34,022	44,570
by land . .	1	80	21	..	..	..
2. Yarn made in Indian mill.	473,000	648,559	661,786	920,939	1,001,420	1,058,297
Total .	517,957	690,388	701,195	957,290	1,035,442	1,102,867
3. *Yarn exported—						
by sea . .	209,398	200,831	94,243	20,994	13,137	9,868
by land . .	7,610	14,632	11,793	10,717	7,400	7,658
Total .	217,008	215,463	106,036	31,711	20,537	17,526
4. Net quantity available in India.	300,949	474,925	595,159	925,579	1,014,905	1,085,341
5. †Cloth made in Indian mills.	98,729	248,918	381,849	633,093	736,649	761,431
6. ‡Equal to yarn .	88,151	222,248	340,937	565,262	657,722	679,849
7. Yarn (mill-made) available for handloom weavers (item 4-6).	212,798	252,677	254,222	360,317	357,183	405,492

Production of Yarn.

The yarn produced in Indian cotton mills in the years 1908-09, 1913-14, 1918-19 and onwards is shown in the next table. The Indian production has enormously increased in the post-war period, the advance being marked in the case of Madras, the United Provinces, the Punjab and the Indian States. Burma commenced production only in 1923 and her annual output of yarn is now approximately 4 million pounds.

* Including re-export.

†All woven goods.

‡Calculated at the rate of 100 lbs. yarn = 112 lbs. cloth.

TABLE No. 52.—*Abstract statement of the quantity (in pounds) of yarn produced in the Cotton Mills in India during the years 1908-09, 1913-14, 1918-19 and onwards.*

Year.	Bombay.	Madras.	Bengal.	United Provinces also Ajmer-Merwara.	Punjab (including Delhi).	Central Provinces and Berar.	Indian States and Foreign territory.	Burma.	Grand Total.
1908-09 .	469,194,256	39,635,423	39,146,723	38,870,997	13,265,405	29,773,277	27,699,078	.	657,585,159
1913-14 .	479,682,975	44,673,626	33,219,947	44,468,505	6,274,754	36,532,870	37,921,174	..	682,776,851
1918-19 .	427,638,345	42,787,344	32,507,148	36,447,155	6,900,776	34,270,946	34,479,750	..	615,040,464
1919-20 .	439,799,625	44,346,268	35,229,179	37,146,135	6,645,641	34,188,442	38,404,983	..	635,760,273
1920-21 .	469,944,960	41,240,677	33,392,116	39,091,048	6,717,075	31,269,565	38,347,156	..	660,002,597
1921-22 .	492,634,404	44,387,583	33,626,236	43,020,649	6,524,002	32,817,846	40,452,279	..	693,462,999
1922-23 .	497,351,824	53,425,405	28,937,591	43,821,522	6,522,193	31,877,488	43,958,000	..	705,894,023
1923-24 .	398,552,000	50,939,000	26,105,000	54,975,000	6,453,000	32,258,000	47,204,000	843,000	618,329,000
1924-25 .	474,292,000	54,221,000	25,672,000	59,584,000	8,210,000	38,116,000	58,228,000	1,067,000	720,390,000
1925-26 .	423,451,000	57,837,000	24,123,000	64,839,000	11,005,000	40,428,000	63,056,000	1,688,000	686,427,000
1926-27 .	512,021,000	64,498,000	31,537,000	73,308,000	13,484,000	38,896,000	72,892,000	480,000	807,116,000
1927-28 .	491,840,000	68,748,000	34,347,000	70,842,000	15,887,000	42,860,000	84,352,000	64,000	808,940,000
1928-29 .	329,856,000	69,036,000	30,022,000	65,320,000	17,336,000	44,057,000	90,621,000	2,048,000	648,296,000
1929-30 .	467,289,000	74,480,000	37,053,000	82,151,000	22,159,000	45,111,000	102,741,000	2,576,000	833,560,000
1930-31 .	475,944,000	76,926,000	37,763,000	91,052,000	23,613,000	45,102,000	133,613,000	3,265,000	867,278,000
1931-32 .	549,039,000	87,729,000	37,620,000	96,693,000	29,643,000	44,143,000	118,247,000	3,259,000	966,373,000
1932-33 .	558,594,709	104,909,653	40,821,488	100,926,527	31,854,058	45,385,349	130,649,685	3,280,395	1,016,421,864
1933-34 .	484,714,674	98,274,069	39,912,399	101,962,564	26,922,993	41,595,480	124,349,193	3,329,251	921,060,623
1934-35 .	523,044,052	103,765,667	41,056,056	108,332,015	28,010,363	45,009,433	148,179,003	4,023,228	1,001,419,817
1935-36 .	548,806,151	113,077,833	40,991,244	118,331,379	31,943,651	46,427,809	155,047,779	3,671,055	1,058,206,901

In the early days of the industry Indian cotton manufactures were concerned chiefly with the production of lower counts of yarn for shipment to China and for use on indigenous handlooms, but the tendency for some years past has been to spin higher counts of yarn, supplementing Indian supplies with imported long staple cotton. The great difference between the Lancashire and Eastern cotton spinning industries may be illustrated by the following. Of the world's spindles 29 per cent. are in the United Kingdom, but they absorb only 10 per cent. of the total world mill consumption of cotton, while India and Japan with one-eighth of the total spindles absorb nearly one-fourth of the world's total mill consumption of cotton.

Imports of Yarn.

It is interesting to compare the imports of coarse, medium and fine yarns with the production of similar descriptions by the Indian mills.

TABLE No. 53.—*Imports and production of cotton yarn in 1913-14 and 1935-36 contrasted.*

Yarn.	1913-14.			1935-36.		
	Quantity in lbs	Percentage of class.	Percentage of total 1	Quantity in lbs.	Percentage of class.	Percentage of total.
Nos. 1 to 25—			85·21	..	..	68·9
Indian	616,688,000	99 65	..	755,658,000	99·92	..
Imported	2,150,000	·35	.	618,000	·08	..
Nos. 26 to 40—	..	..	12·40	.	..	23·7
Indian	62,711,000	69 64	..	238,055,000	91·4	..
Imported	27,344,000	30·36	..	22,307,000	8·6	..
Nos. above 40—	.	..	1·45	..	..	7·4
Indian	2,698,000	25·56	..	58,528,000	72·9	..
Imported	7,859,000	74·44	..	21,653,000	27·1	..
Total	726,269,000*	..	100	1,096,819,000	..	100

In 1912 and 1913 there had been a marked decline in the spinning of counts between 31 and 40 in Indian mills, but while the war lasted Indian mills spun less and less of the lower counts. Of counts 1 to 10 the total was 87 million lbs. in 1918-19, as compared with 130¾ million lbs in 1913-14, and the drop in counts 11 to 20 was about 47 million lbs. There has been in the last ten years a very marked advance in the spinning of counts above 40, the total for 1935-36 being 58.528.000 lbs. as compared with 2,698,000 lbs. in 1913-14, 4,786,000 lbs. in 1918-19 and 2,195,000 lbs. in 1922-23. The production of counts below 40 has also increased to an appreciable extent. It will be noticed that as a result of the development of the indigenous cotton textile industry, the Indian mill production has displaced foreign imports of cotton yarn to a considerable extent.

Production of Woven Goods.

In the next table will be found the estimated production of woven goods in all the power mills in India during the last four years. No exact estimate of the production of the handlooms scattered over the country can be attempted, but it is probably now in the neighbourhood of 464,000,000 lbs.,* as compared with 250,000,000 lbs. which was the figure of production estimated in 1924.

TABLE No. 54.—*Abstract statement of the quantity (in lbs.) of woven goods produced in the cotton mills in India during the last four years.*

Manufactures.	1932-33.	1933-34.	1934-35.	1935-36.
Grey and bleached piecegoods.	531,791,526	495,794,794	570,722,200	587,786,728
Coloured piecegoods .	150,723,944	137,610,496	147,466,140	152,872,906
Grey and coloured goods other than piecegoods.	3,542,296	3,391,982	3,703,737	5,117,609
Hosiery . . .	2,544,339	2,340,336	4,718,435	5,304,435
Miscellaneous .	4,291,948	4,864,133	6,208,320	5,673,448
Cotton goods mixed with silk or wool.	2,007,004	1,859,114	3,830,265	4,676,151
Total .	694,901,057	645,860,855	736,649,097	761,431,277

The corresponding totals in 1915-16 and 1922-23 were 352,000,000 lbs and 405,000,000 lbs respectively The Indian production in respect of almost every description of woven goods has shown a marked increase during the post-war period.

TABLE No. 55 —*Quantity and value of exports of principal cotton manufactures.*

Year.	Yarn.		Piecegoods.	
	Quantity.	Value.	Quantity.	Value.
	(Unit of 1,000 lbs.)	£	(Unit of 1,000 yards).	£
1913-14	197,978	6,554,873	89,233	1,424,583
1918-19	63,798	4,815,549	149,088	4,301,727
1931-32	22,043	958,937	104,636	2,432,514
1932-33	15,108	589,898	66,442	1,564,564
1933-34	16,388	612,870	56,461	1,247,229
1934-35	12,789	470,385	57,693	1,325,237
1935-36	9,668	352,077	71,250	1,522,118

*Calculated according to the formula approved by the Bombay Millowner Association that 100 lbs. of yarn yield 112 lbs. of cloth

Exports of Yarn.

The exports of yarn were, before the war, four or five times as valuable as the exports of piecegoods, but these latter had greatly increased since 1916-17 and in 1922-23 for the first time exceeded the former in value. The exports of yarn have for some years past, shown a steadily declining tendency. The position has consequently reversed, and the exports of piecegoods are now three times as valuable as the exports of yarn. The chief participants in India's export of cotton twist and yarn are Syria, Aden and Iran.

The exports of yarn to foreign destinations in 1935-36 are shown in the statement below according to the port of shipment. Bombay has always enjoyed a preponderating share of the trade.

TABLE NO. 56.—*Quantity of cotton yarn and twist exported in 1935-36 and the share of the principal ports.*

Port.	Quantity.	Percentage.
	lbs.	
Bombay	9,161,123	94·8
Madras	474,891	4·9
Karachi	24,730	·23
Calcutta	7,426	·07
Total	9,668,170	100

Exports of Cotton Manufactures.

The exports of cotton manufactures other than yarn represent nearly 7 per cent. of the total output of the mills. 53 per cent. of the total trade in 1934-35 was from Bombay and 46 per cent. from Madras. The exports of cotton manufactures, classified according to descriptions, have been as follows.

TABLE NO. 57.—*Values of the Exports of cotton manufactures (other than yarn and twist) in 1913-14, 1918-19 and from 1932-33 onwards classified according to descriptions.*

Descriptions of cotton manufactures.	1913-14.	1918-19.	1932-33.	1933-34	1934-35.	1935-36.
	£	£	£	£	£	£
Piecegoods—						
Grey	478,892	1,224,344	95,349	81,335	106,975	135,752
White	11,912	96,080	8,396	6,796	9,560	21,924
Coloured, printed or dyed	938,779	2,980,863	1,460,819	1,159,098	1,208,701	1,364,442
Handkerchiefs and shawls	54,385	50,599	272,961	138,448	94,070	223,129
Sewing thread	11,870	14,027	9,541	7,916	8,780	8,862
Hosiery	9,698	19,994	1,764	2,841	6,325	5,260
Other sorts	24,563	158,759	29,506	35,312	80,861	84,813
Total	1,525,099	4,544,666	1,878,336	1,431,746	1,515,272	1,843,182

The declared valı per yard of grey, white and coloured piece-goods in 1935-36 wa 3 annas 3 pies, 3 annas 6 pies and 4 annas 9 pies, respectively, compared with 2 annas 7 pies, 6 annas and 6 annas in 1913-14, an 5 annas 11 pies, 7 annas 6 pies and 7 annas 6 pies in 1922-23.

Chief Markets.

The chief markets for cotton cloth woven in India are those colonies and countries in which there is considerable Indian immigration. Bombay is the principal port of shipment for *chadars* and *dhooties*, *T. cloths* and *domestics*, drills and jeans and shirtings, the principal destinations being Aden, East Africa, Iran, Zanzibar and the Straits, while coloured *lungis* and *saris* which go chiefly from Madras are shipped mainly to the Straits Settlements, Ceylon and Anglo-Egyptian Sudan.

Madras Handkerchiefs.

As an example of handloom weaving for export, the trade in Madras handkerchiefs may be cited, which are shipped to the United Kingdom, though their ultimate destination is chiefly Africa. These so-called 'handkerchiefs' are made with 40s. to 60s. in pieces 8 yards by 3 feet. The value of these exported in 1935-36 was £222,434.

Cotton Carpets.

Two main varieties of cotton carpets may be distinguished as made in India, one resembling the woollen pile carpet but with warp, weft and pile all of cotton yarn, and the commoner kind without any pile and with the same design on both sides. The latter are produced in three principal forms—*daris* (bed carpets), *shatranjis* (floor carpets) and *jainamaz*† (prayer mats). This distinction of terms is not however strictly observed and all pileless cotton carpets are commonly designated *daris*. In the *dari* proper the pattern generally consists of stripes of various colours, blue and white being the favourite combination, but flowers and geometrical shapes are not infrequently woven into the body of the fabric. The looms on which *daris* are woven are generally horizontal and the dyes formerly in use were indigenous vegetable dyes, principally indigo, but the cheapness of aniline dyes has led to the increasing adoption of the latter. The weavers in most of the provinces are poor Mahomedans or low caste Hindus and the organisation of the trade largely depends on a system of advances by *mahajans* or middlemen who sell the outturn at the big trade centres. *Daris* properly so-called are generally purchased in the piece, while floor carpets are sold by the yard or by weight.

The chief centres of manufacture are Bareilly, Aligarh, Agra, Cawnpore, Farukhabad, Moradabad and Etawah in the United Provinces. The *daris* of Agra are noted for their finish, those of Bareilly for their cheapness and durability and of Aligarh for the closeness of the stitch. The industry has much expanded in Cawnpore where large mills under European and Indian management are manufacturing with machinery larger size suitable for tents and bungalows and turning out considerable quantities for export to England and America. Other provinces where cotton carpets are made are the Punjab, chiefly in the districts of Multan, Amballa and Hoshiarpur, the Delhi Province, the Bahawalpur State, Patna city, and the Champaran

---

* A grey calico, so called from an old trade mark.

† In the Central Provinces, *Ja-namaz*.

and Shahabad districts of Bihar and Ayyampet, Bhavani, Adoni and Kurnool in the Madras Presidency where the local name for these carpets is *jamkulam*. In the Bombay Presidency a not inconsiderable industry is carried on in some of the Deccan districts. It is also a popular jail industry in nearly every province.

No separate statistics are maintained of the exports.

GRAIN, PULSE, AND FLOUR.

Rice.

Although in favourable seasons, barley, millets and pulses are exported in considerable quantities from India, the most valuable exports included under the head "Grain and Pulses" have invariably been rice and wheat, their aggregate values representing more than 91 per cent. of the whole. In 1935-36 rice accounted for 90·9 per cent. of the total quantity of food grains and flour exported as compared with 91·0 per cent. in the preceding year. The world production of cleaned rice has been calculated to be in the neighbourhood of 60,500,000 tons exclusive of an entirely empirical estimate of 30,000,000 tons from China India's share of this grand total of 90,500,000 tons may be taken approximately at over 36 per cent., and, though her average exports are in the neighbourhood of 5 6 per cent. of her total estimated production, she is nevertheless the largest exporter of rice in the world. India's export trade in rice is less susceptible to seasonal influences than is the case of the majority of food grains, because in Burma which contributes the greater part of it, a failure of the rains is unknown. The volume of export to foreign countries is, however, affected by crop shortage in other parts of India.

Production.

The acreage and production of cleaned rice in British India are indicated in the following table.

Acreage.

TABLE No 58.—*Acreage and production of cleaned rice in British India for 1913-14, 1918-19 and from 1930-31 onwards.*

Year.	Area.	Production.	Exports (rice not in the husk).	Percentage of 4 to 3.
1	2	3	4	5
	Acres.	Tons.	Tons.	
1913-14 . . .	76,908,000	30,138,000	2,419,850	8
1918-19 . . .	77,613,000	24,318,000	2,017,900	8
1930-31 . . .	79,467,000	31,277,000	2,253,784	7
1931-32 . . .	80,299,000	31,649,000	2,301,415	7
1932-33 . . .	78,912,000	29,958,000	1,828,196	6
1933-34 . . .	79,224,000	29,745,000	1,732,539	5·8
1934-35 . . .	78,129,000	29,024,000	1,592,537	5·5

In addition, the production in the Indian States has been estimated to be 1,118,000 tons with an acreage of 3,740,000 in 1934-35 as compared with 1,119,000 tons with an acreage of 3,818,000 in 1933-34. The normal yield per acre of cleaned rice in India varies from 648 lbs. to 1,580 lbs. which compares very unfavourably with Japan and Egypt where it is between 2,352 and 2,464 lbs. The area in the principal provinces in 1934-35 and their percentages are shown below. The percentages are, in years of normal rainfall, subject to very little variation

TABLE No. 59.—*Acreage under rice according to provinces in 1934-35.*

Provinces.	Acres.	Percentage.
Assam	(*b*) 4,858,000	6·2
Bengal	20,740,000	26·5
Bihar and Orissa (A)	13,734,000	17·6
Bombay including Sind	2,903,000	3·7
Burma	12,666,000	16·2
Central Provinces and Berar	5,652,000	7·2
Coorg	83,000	0·1
Madras	11,056,000	14·2
United Provinces	6,437,000	8·3
Total British Provinces	78,129,000	100

Terms employed.

Rice in the husk before hulling is known as *paddy*. After hulling it becomes *rough* rice and after pearling it becomes *cleaned* or *white rice*. The broken grains of rice are separated out and sold as *coodie* or *khood*, while the higher grades of rice are subject to a further process of polishing on sheepskins with the object of removing any rice meal which may adhere to the grain. No chemicals whatever are used in this polishing process or in any other process connected with the milling of rice *Cargo rice*, contains 5 to 20 per cent. of unhusked rice, *i e.*, paddy, and, if exported in this form to Europe, is subject to further milling on arrival there. The ratio of paddy to rice by weight depends entirely on the quality of rice produced In the case of *specials* it may be taken as of 8·5, but the ratio for better qualities is lower.

The exports of *boiled* rice to Europe are 65,000 tons on an average, out of which the United Kingdom has a share of 3,500 tons. The total exports of boiled rice were 664,278 tons in 1935-36. The principal demands were from Ceylon, Federated Malay States, Mauritius and Dependencies, and Arabian Native States. There is a considerable demand for the grain in this form in India also. The process may be roughly described as follows. The paddy is soaked in water for forty to eighty hours according to grain and season and boiled for twenty to forty minutes and dried before husking. This business is largely in the hands of small millers in out of the way places where there is plenty of room to spread the rice after steaming

(A) Excluding Feudatory States, estimate for which for 1934-35, is 3,340,000 acres.

(*b*) Including areas under seedlings which were subsequently transplanted.

to dry in the sun, though artificial drying is not unknown. This parboiled rice has a higher nutrient value, owing to its lighter milling and though when husked it has a yellow tinge it becomes white when cooked and keeps better afterwards, which is a great asset when rice is prepared overnight to be eaten the following day. Attempts are being made in Rangoon to evolve a more scientific process for the production of parboiled rice but it cannot be said that any entirely satisfactory plant has yet been devised.

Exports.

For statistical purposes, foreign and coastwise exports of rice are divided up into two heads—rice in the husk (paddy) and rice not in the husk (rice) but the average volume of the former is only 47,000 tons in a year. The demand from Ceylon for paddy is fairly regular, but in 1931-32 and 1932-33, Germany increased her annual takings to 26 and 36 thousand tons respectively. In 1933-34, the demand was considerably reduced; her intake being only 800 tons. The falling off in the European market is partly due to an intensive development of certain tracts in the cultivation of rice. The subsidised exports of Italy and Spain are purchased in quarters which formerly imported Indian rice Rice not in the husk includes boiled rice.

TABLE No. 60.—*Exports of rice (not in the husk) according to provinces in the pre-war and the war periods, in 1919-20 and from 1931-32 onwards in round figures.*

Year.	Provinces.				Total.	
	Burma.	Bengal.	Madras.	Bombay and Sind	Quantity.	Value.
	Tons.	Tons.	Tons.	Tons.	Tons.	£
Pre-war years—						
Annual average for quinquennium-1909-10 to 1913-14.	1,814,000	374,000	121,000	60,000	2,398,000	15,107,000
War years—						
Annual average for quinquennium-1914-15 to 1918-19.	1,271,000	107,000	175,000	131,000	1,684,000	12,588,000
1919-20 . . .	492,000	48,000	2,000	76,000	618,000	6,608,000
1931-32 . .	2,066,000	123,000	61,000	51,000	2,301,000	13,383,000
1932-33 . . .	1,602,000	121,000	65,000	40,000	1,828,000	10,638,000
1933-34 . . .	1,516,000	108,000	78,000	30,000	1,733,000	7,892,000
1934-35 . . .	1,389,000	94,000	73,000	36,000	1,593,000	7,727,[illegible]00
1935-36 . . .	1,205,000	80,000	71,000	37,000	1,394,000	8,211,000

Burma practically has a monopoly of the export trade in rice, and also makes good any shortage in the supply for local consumption in other parts of India because the ratio of acreage under rice to population is so high that her exportable surplus is far larger than that of Bengal, Bihar or Madras who grow more rice but have to meet a much higher internal demand. The Burma trade represents approximately 86 per cent. of the whole. The preponderating share of Burma in the Indian export trade of rice is indicated in the following statement.

TABLE No. 61.—*Total outturn of rice in India and Burma and total exports by sea to foreign countries.*

(In thousand tons.)

Year.	Production.		Exports.			
	Cleaned Rice.		Rice.		Paddy.	
	India Proper.	Burma.	India Proper.	Burma.	India Proper.	Burma.
1913-14 .	24,782	4,037	585	1,835	10	20
1932-33 .	26,201	4,913	226	1,602	4	55
1933-34 .	25,690	5,174	216	1,517	1	10
1934-35 .	25,604	4,533	204	1,389	4	10

The Madras trade is practically confined to Ceylon.

Any failure of the monsoon in India at once creates a remarkable inflation of values in Burma to which the range of prices in foreign markets does not usually respond. Prior to 1910-11 the average export of rice from India did not exceed two million tons; but the trade subsequently expanded and in 1912-13 the total exports amounted to a little less than 2½ millions. The fall from this level between 1919-20 and 1921-22, from which the trade has since recovered, is attributable to the strict control of rice exports enforced by the Government of India.

The principal causes of shrinkage in exports from Burma and Bengal in the first three war years were the loss of enemy markets and shortage of shipping The increasing volume of exports direct to the United Kingdom, which was a feature of the war years, has not been maintained since the armistice

TABLE No 62.—*Direct exports of rice (not in the husk) to the United Kingdom in 1913-14, 1918-19 and from 1931-32 onwards.*

	1913-14.	1918-19.	1931-32.	1932-33.	1933-34.	1934-35.	1935-36.
Tons . . .	161,409	270,143	50,825	75,210	71,415	88,375	50,122

Before the war a good deal of Indian rice was cleaned and polished in Germany and Holland before it reached the United Kingdom. The pre-war freight rate to the United Kingdom from Rangoon for rice was in the neighbourhood of 25 shillings per ton: at the time of the declaration of the armistice the Government rate was 125 shillings and for outside steamers 400 shillings and upwards. The present rate is 26*s* 3*d*.

The principal countries participating in the export trade in rice in the year before the war and in 1935-36 are shown in the subjoined table.

TABLE No. 63.—*Quantities and values of rice exported from India in 1913-14 and 1935-36 classified according to destinations.*

Destinations.	1913-14.			1935-36.		
	Tons.	Per cent.	£	Tons.	Per cent.	£
Ceylon . .	335,059	13·8	3,162,450	423,706	0·4	2,624,333
Straits Settlements (Including Labuan).	284,589	11·8	1,915,029	138,418	9·9	812,850
United Kingdom .	161,409	6·7	1,129,677	50,122	3·6	289,193
Mauritius and Dependencies.	51,344	2·1	503,988	55,091	3·9	358,607
Other British possessions.	198,762	8·2	1,560,638	218,351	15·6	1,397,798
Total British Countries	1,031,163	42·6	8,271,782	885,638	63·4	5,482,771
Netherlands .	333,732	13·8	2,026,221	69,799	5·0	335,490
Germany . .	315,895	13·1	2,096,054	79,209	5·6	412,155
Austria } Hungary } .	211.442	8·7	1,370,032	..	..	..
Japan . . .	160,646	6·6	1,076,886	9,133	0·6	51,637
Asiatic Turkey .	81,057	3·4	665,869	155	..	1,208
Java . . .	39,412	1·6	261,158	4,245	0·3	20,676
France . .	23,679	0·9	152,972	262	..	2,430
Italy . . .	900	0·04	6,110	12,869	0·9	73,320
Other Foreign Countries	221,937	9·26	1,672,498	332,255	24·2	1,830,864
Total Foreign countries.	1,388,700	57·4	9,327,800	507,927	36·6	2,727,780
All Countries .	2,419,863	100	17,599,582	1,393,615	100	8,210,551

Principal recipients.

Of India's total exports about 47 per cent went in pre-war days to Europe, 42 per cent. to other Asiatic countries (Ceylon, the Straits Settlements, Japan, etc.), the remaining 11 per cent. being distributed amongst Africa, the West Indies and South America. In 1935-36 20 per cent. of the exports went to Europe and 60 per cent. to Asia while the remaining 20 per cent. was destined for Africa, the West Indies and South America.*

The exports to Java vary according to the quantities which that country is able to obtain from Indo-China and Siam and the prices ruling in those markets. In 1910-11 and 1911-12 they exceeded a quarter of a million tons and in 1912-13, 160,000 tons. While India exported about 1,400,000 tons to foreign countries in the last pre-war year, Siam and Indo-China, the next most important exporting countries, supplied an almost equivalent quantity to British countries (1,300,000 tons). Ceylon continues to be the best customer for Indian rice, and, in the European market, Germany's takings are the largest, though she has not as yet recovered her pre-war position. The exports to Japan reveal an irregular demand, the fluctuation being

* Shown under foreign countries in 1935-36.

dependent on the intensive cultivation of rice and the presence of large exportable surplus in the adjacent countries. Direct trade with the West Indies developed considerably during the war. The demands of Cuba were previously met by re-exports of Rangoon rice, practically all *Straits quality*, from Liverpool or by German millers with similar or better qualities produced from cargo rice purchased in Burma. In 1934-35 the exports to Cuba and other West Indian Islands exceeded 51,000 tons as against 68,000 tons in the previous year. The condition of the rice trade has been almost consistently becoming worse in the last few years. According to available estimates, the production of rice has increased. This increased supply has not however been met by an adequate demand. Moreover, the substitution of other types of cereals for rice, when there is a decline in the price level of the former, and, restriction on imports, by legislative and other measures, in some foreign countries, have had their adverse effect on the trade.

Export duty.

An export duty of two annas three pies per Indian maund of 82 lbs. avoirdupois weight is levied on all foreign exports of rice, husked or unhusked, including rice flour but excluding rice bran and rice dust (which are exempted from duty), the tax being included in the *f. o. b.* price. The total revenue collected under this head is indicated in the statement below:—

TABLE NO. 64.—*Revenue derived from export duty on rice in 1913-14, 1918-19 and from 1932-33 onwards.*

Year	Revenue.
	£
1913-14	860,000
1918-19	741,000
1932-33	568,000
1933-34	520,000
1934-35	486,000
1935-36	424,000

Rice control.

Early in 1918 the Government of India decided that no exports to Europe of Burma rice should be permitted except for the Royal Commission on Wheat Supplies and a Rice Commissioner for Burma was appointed. In November of the same year, the monsoon rains having been disappointing, a Food Stuffs Commissioner for India was appointed and the Rice Commissioner placed under his orders. The main features of the control scheme were the determination by the Government of India of the quantities to be shipped to any particular destination, and the insistence upon licenses before shipment, which were granted only upon production of satisfactory evidence that the price paid or to be paid was not in excess of the controlled basic price, which was in the first instance fixed at Rs. 335 ex-hopper for the quality known as "big mills specials.". This price had to be raised in May 1919 as the control had threatened to break down owing to the rise in the price of paddy, and again in January 1920, when the control scheme was modified in certain other important particulars.

In 1919-20 the other provinces of India absorbed no less than 80 per cent. of Burma's exportable surplus, the principal foreign destinations being Ceylon, the Straits Settlements, the United Kingdom and Mauritius. Up to the end of 1920 control continued unchanged but the sudden break in the Indian demand led to a reconsideration of the allotment for other countries. In January 1921 all restrictions on the movement of rice coastwise were removed, while shipments to foreign destinations were allowed freely under license. Power was, however, reserved to reimpose control, should prices rise unduly. A notable feature of the year was the reappearance of Germany as a buyer of Burma rice and but for difficulties of finance, despatches would have been even larger than they were. On the other hand, Java and Cuba, which had purchased heavily in the previous year, received very small allotments. There was an unexpected revival in the Indian demand in the early part of 1921. Gambling upon the ultimate removal of control led the latter half of this year to a sensational advance in the price of paddy which the refusal of further licenses for foreign destinations in July failed to arrest. Shipments to Germany again increased while there was a marked fall in the exports to the United Kingdom and Japan. Finally all control over exports of rice from Burma was removed in December 1921, and from India on 1st April 1922. The total net profit accruing from the Rice Control scheme amounted to over 9 crores of rupees (£6 millions) which were placed at the disposal of the Government of Burma for the development of the province

Burma.

Since the British occupation in 1852, rice has been Burma's principal export and Rangoon rice, as it is called, is the standard of the European rice trade About four-fifths of the rice crop comes from Lower Burma where it represents 90 per cent. of the cultivated area From threshing floor to river or railhead the paddy is commonly carted in bulk. It is thence conveyed to the various ports either by rail in bags or more commonly by boat in bulk, measured alongside the mills as discharged, and stored in the mills *godowns*. Paddy prices in Rangoon are quoted with reference to a unit of 100 baskets containing 46 lbs. each, but in the districts the baskets used are not standardised and there is considerable local variance For example, the Akyab paddy basket contains 23 lbs. only

Marketing.

As a rule the paddy is taken over from the cultivator on the threshing floor either by middlemen acting on behalf of the mills, by speculators, or by local traders known as jungle brokers. The beginning of the paddy season corresponds pretty closely to that of the calendar year as harvesting commences generally towards the end of November and the crop comes commercially into sight in January. The crop is all hand-reaped chiefly by coolies from Madras and Bengal, mechanical aids being unknown. The mills which own their own boats advance money to their paddy buyers on the security of the latter's land or other property. In some cases the paddy buyers mortgage their boats against the moneys received. A boat may do three or four trips per month according to the position of the paddy but in bringing paddy from the more distant and outlying districts a full month may be occupied in making one trip. As soon as the buyer obtains a boat he proceeds to the district, buys grain and brings it to the mill for measurement. Measurement is done fairly rapidly and in very few cases occupies more than one day. In fact, generally speaking, the boats which arrive in the morning can return up-country the same day. When a boat of paddy is discharged, a certain number of baskets are weighed and the average weight arrived at therefrom is taken as representing the weight of the whole consignment, credit being given to the seller for any excess over 46 lbs. and deductions being made if the average weight is found to be less than 46 lbs. Storing facilities in the districts, which were formerly limited, are now considerable and at a rough estimate almost half the exportable surplus can be distributed in *godowns* up-country. Paddy deteriorates to some extent as regards colour and grain with lengthy storage, but its merits as a food stuff remain unimpaired. Deterioration in colour is brought about by heating and so far no expedient has been hit upon to overcome this difficulty.

Milling.

In the cargo rice mill, the paddy is put over shakers and sieves in order to remove extraneous matter, such as stones, dirt and straw, and winnowed. It is then hulled, *i.e.*, passed between the grind stones which remove the husk, winnowed again and then becomes what is known as *loonzain*. 'Five parts cargo rice' consists of 80 per cent. *loonzain* and 20 per cent paddy. In white rice mills, the *loonzain* rice is again milled by cones or pearlers, which remove the outer cuticle. The rice then goes through a further process of sieving, the sieves being so arranged and graded that the percentage of broken rice, which it is desired to separate from the whole rice, can be removed and bagged off separately. It is then rewinnowed and bagged. In the higher qualities of rice, usually shipped to Europe, there is a further polishing in cylinders made of wood and wire gauze in which revolve rollers covered with sheep skin. This takes place after the rice has left the cones or pearlers, but before the final sieving process. Formerly the bulk of the rice shipped was cargo rice, but now the proportion of white rice to cargo rice shipped is practically the inverse of what it was quarter of a century ago.

The following are the terms on which rice is sold in Burma:—

Unit of sale and shipment.

When sold locally, at a price per 100 baskets of 75 lbs. each.

When sold to Europe at a price per cwt of 112 lbs nett.

When sold to Java at a price per picul of 136 lbs. nett.

When sold to Manila at a price per picul of 133¼ lbs. nett.

When sold to Straits at a price per coyan of 5,333 ⅓ lbs. nett.

When sold to Japan at a price per picul of 136 lbs. nett. (or per cwt. of 112 lbs nett).

When sold to India at a price per bag (according to weight).

Rice for the United Kingdom is usually on consignment sale through brokers in London. The general level of prices for Burma rice is lower than for any other variety.

The qualities of white rice milled in Burma are known as follows:—

Nos. 1, 2 and 3 Europe rice.
S. Q. (Special Quality) Europe rice.
Small Mills special.
Big Mills special.
Super Rice.
Penang S. Q.

Special grains have their own names, *e g*, *Meedong* rice, *Ngasein* rice, *Yahins* rice, etc.

The following qualities of broken rice or *coodie* are produced from the above:—

From all qualities:—
Nos. 4, 5 and 6 white broken rice.
Cargo broken rice.

From Nos. 1 and 2 Europe rice.—
A 1, A 2 and A 3 white broken rice.

From No. 3 Europe rice and S. Q. Europe rice:—
B 1, B 2 and B 3 white broken rice.

From Small Mills specials and Big Mills specials and Meedong specials:—

C 1, C 2, and C 3 white broken rice.

The barometer of the Rangoon market is the price of big mills special rice which again depends upon and bears a definite relation to the current price of paddy.

The unit of shipment in Rangoon is the bag which varies in weight from 168 to 225 lbs. nett.

The usual busy season for paddy commences about the 15th of January and lasts till somewhere about the 15th of April. By the latter date it is normally reckoned that about half the exportable surplus has been marketed. The remainder of the crop is marketed throughout the year and under normal conditions is delivered at the port of export by the middle of December. There has been a growing tendency, of recent years, which war exigencies have accentuated, to store so as to distribute the business more evenly throughout the year Co-operative Credit Societies have enabled cultivators to hold up part of the harvest instead of rushing it down in the first three months of the season and glutting the market with disastrous results to themselves.

The milling capacity of a typical bigger size Rangoon mill may be put at about 30,000 baskets of 46 lbs. paddy per day of 12 hours.

Mills.

The largest mill at Pazundaung is capable of turning out 700 tons of cargo rice a day. The average milling capacity of the smaller mills in Rangoon may be estimated at about 7,500 to 8,000 baskets of 46 lbs. paddy per day of 12 hours. Mills generally run night and day for about three months in the year and paddy husk is the only fuel used. The quantity of husk produced is always in excess of fuel required and until a year or two ago the surplus husk used to be discharged into the creeks and rivers. Now-a-days, however, when fuel is expensive many other industries are glad to purchase the available surplus.

There are 647 rice mills in Burma employing more than 44,900 persons, and on a conservative estimate the outturn may be put at about 12,000,000 tons of "five parts cargo rice" per annum. In Burma, as in other parts of India, the capacity of mills is considerably in excess of the quantity of grain available for milling.

TABLE No. 65 —*The distribution of the exports of rice from Burma according to countries in 1913-14 and 1935-36 contrasted.*

1913-14.			1935-36.		
Destination.	Tons.	Per cent.	Destination	Tons.	Per cent.
Ceylon . .	44,723	2	Ceylon . .	351,866	29
Straits Settlements .	280,922	15	Straits Settlements	133,369	11
United Kingdom .	139,250	8	United Kingdom	44,893	4
Netherlands . .	325,300	18	Netherlands . .	66,849	6
Germany . .	297,560	16	Germany . .	79,208	7
China and Hong-Kong.	20,429	1	China and Hong-Kong.	76,828	6
Austria-Hungary .	209,417	11	Sumatra . .	74,744	6
Japan . . .	160,643	9	Japan . . .	9,126	
Other countries .	356,701	20	Other countries	368,456	31

The normal distribution of the foreign trade before the war, between the different Burma ports was—Rangoon 68 per cent., Bassein 13 per cent., Moulmein 10 per cent. and Akyab 9 per cent. In 1934-35 the percentages were: Rangoon 85 per cent., Moulmein 7 per cent., Bassein 6 per cent. and Akyab 2 per cent. The total shipment in that year amounted to 1,399,218 tons

Bengal.

Though the average acreage under rice in Bengal and the adjoining province of Bihar and Orissa, which is chiefly served by the port of Calcutta,* amounts to 48 per cent. of the aggregate for British India, the volume of foreign exports has never been comparable with that of Burma, though in a favourable season the Madras figures are generally exceeded. The principal destinations for Bengal rice in pre-war years were Ceylon and Mauritius. Since 1913-14 Natal has taken an increasing share of the trade and a direct trade with Cuba has sprung up. Of the total, 99 per cent. went in pre-war days from Calcutta and the balance from Chittagong. The following table gives the consolidated Bengal figures.

* In 1913-14 and earlier years there were also some shipments from Cuttack.

TABLE No. 66.—*Quantities and values of rice exported from Bengal in 1913-14, 1918-19 and from 1931-32 onwards.*

Year.	Quantity.	Value.
	Tons.	£
1913-14	326,921	3,304,148
1918-19	153,326	1,626,675
1931-32	123,185	1,184,604
1932-33	120,795	983,820
1933-34	107,657	711,623
1934-35	94,151	693,540
1935-36	80,140	657,921

Shipments in 1915-16, 1916-17 and 1917-18 were affected by freight shortage, and in 1918-19, when a better shipping position and a brisk demand for common rice from Ceylon, South Africa, Mauritius and the West Indies encouraged heavier exports, it became necessary to conserve supplies for local consumption in consequence of the partial failure of the monsoon. The Foodstuffs Commissioner, whose appointment became necessary in October 1918, decided that these markets should be rationed as far as possible from Burma.

The chief varieties of Bengal rice on the market are *table* or *white Patna broken table rice* or *Khood*, *Patna* and old hard, while among boiled or brown rices may be mentioned *boiled Patna*, *Kalma*, *ballam*, *raree* and *Kataribhag*, *Kasla*, *ballam* and inferior *Patna* are expo ted to Ceylon and South African Ports, while *Table rice*, *ballam* and *Patna* are shipped mostly to the United Kingdom and the Continent. *Raree* goes chiefly to Mauritius and *boiled Patna* to Persian Gulf.

The unit of sale in Calcutta is the bazaar maund, and shipment is made in bags of 164 or 224 lbs nett, while sterling quotations are based on the cwt. *c.i.f.*

Madras.

Foreign exports from the Madras Presidency are comparatively limited. The following table shows the quantities exported in recent years as contrasted with the pre-war and post-war figures.

TABLE No. 67.—*Quantities and Values of rice exported from Madras in 1913-14, 1918-19 and from 1931-32 onwards.*

Year.	Quantity.	Value.
	Tons.	£
1913-14	155,000	1,570,000
1918-19	97,000	1,126,000
1931-32	61,175	687,293
1932-33	64,894	647,733
1933-34	78,262	601,021
1934-35	72,906	605,335
1935-36	70,664	629,386

Practically the whole of the trade is with Ceylon. The chief ports of export were Dhanushkodi, Adirampatnam, Negapatam, Tirumalaivasal and Cocanada. At Cocanada, the usual grades shipped parboiled, are *mill rice, A. B. and C. grades*, Chabyam or unpolished rice and *bazaar boiled*, which is prepared in local hand mills and is of very inferior quality.

The unit of sale and of shipment is the bag of 164 lbs. nett., generally.

Bombay.

Foreign exports of rice from Bombay are on an even smaller scale than those of Madras. In pre-war days the average shipments did not exceed 26,000 tons a year, the actual figures for 1913-14 being 28,884 tons. The table below shows the quantities and values of rice exported in recent years as compared with the pre-war and post-war figures.

TABLE No. 68.—*Quantities and Values of rice exported from Bombay in 1913-14, 1918-19 and from 1931-32 onwards.*

Year.	Quantity	Value.
	Tons.	£
1913-14	28,884	283,545
1918-19	104,635	1,526,504
1931-32	13,347	191,736
1932-33	11,837	151,432
1933-34	12,680	135,807
1934-35	12,971	142,938
1935-36	13,275	146,292

It will be seen from the above table that the average shipments now amount to 12.000 tons a year, chiefly representing shipments of cleaned rice to the Persian Gulf and African ports. The average unit of sale and shipment of rice is a bag of 165 lbs

Karachi.

The following table shows the quantities and values of rice exported from Karachi to foreign countries in recent years as contrasted with the pre-war and post-war figures.

TABLE No. 69—*Quantities and values of rice exported from Karachi to foreign countries in 1913-14, 1918-19 and from 1931-32 onwards.*

Year.	Quantity.	Value.
	Tons.	£
1913-14	53,739	489,004
1918-19	51,817	729,507
1931-32	37,848	390,603
1932-33	28,339	296,470
1933-34	17,550	158,479
1934-35	23,245	187,792
1935-36	24,197	199,079

There is comparatively little rice grown in the hinterland served by Karachi and the average value of shipments did not exceed £300,000 before 1913-14, when a good harvest in Cutch stimulated foreign exports, the chief customers being Ceylon, Aden, Mauritius.

Red Sea ports, Muscat, and Persia. The embargo imposed in September 1918 on shipments of rice from Burma ports to Calcutta affected despatches in the latter half of 1918-19. The trade in recent years has suffered a decline, but, the new conditions of agriculture in Sind resulting from perennial irrigation under the Lloyd Barrage and Canals systems, and the intensification of agricultural practice in the Barrage areas are expected to stimulate production of rice and lead to expansion of exports.

The unit of sale in the Karachi market is the candy of 656 lbs. and shipment is made in bags of 2 or 2½ maunds nett.

In the official Indian trade returns rice meal or bran is merged in the general heading "Fodder, Bran and Pollards". The total quantity exported under this item in 1935-36 was 250,950 tons. Out of 250,950 tons exported in 1935-36, 248-948 tons were shipped from Burma, and the Burma exports are known to consist entirely of rice meal. Rice bran constitutes more than 95 per cent. of the trade in "Fodder, Bran and Pollards". As in previous years, the United Kingdom continues to be the principal customer for Burma rice meal for use as cattle fodder taking about 180,000 tons each year with the Straits Settlements, Federated Malay States, Germany, Ceylon and Hongkong as next in importance. The average price was Rs. 28 (£2 2*s*.) per ton in 1935-36 as compared with Rs. 8 (10*s* 8*d*.) in 1918-19 and Rs. 69 (£4 12*s*.) in 1921-22. The bulk of the shipments goes from Rangoon.

Rice meal

WHEAT

Though India produces about one-eighth of the world's wheat, this grain is an indispensable article of food to the inhabitants of the Punjab and the United Provinces only. In other provinces extension of cultivation has been dictated more by the prospects of profitable export to Europe than by internal demand. The six principal countries which export wheat are Canada, Australia, Argentine, U. S. S. R., India and the United States of America in that order, while as regards production, India occupies the third place as the table below shows, with about a third of the Russian crop and nearly three times that of Australia

Production.

TABLE No. 70.—**Production and Export of Wheat according to countries in 1935-36.*

Countries.	Estimated Production. †1935. / 1935-36.	Export. 1935-36. / August to July 31.	Percentage of exports to production.
	Tons.	Tons.	
U. S. S. R.	30,314,000	749,000	2·5
United States of Aemerica .	16,683,000	7,000	·04
India	9,435,000	10,000	.1
Argentine Republic . . .	3,736,000	1,754,000	46.9
Canada	7,422,000	6,209,000	83·6
Australia	3,816,000	1,960,000	51·3

* Source.—'Monthly crop report and Agricultural Statistics' of the International Institute of Agriculture, Rome, October 1936.

†Single years refer to N. Hemisphere and double years the S. Hemisphere.

The variety of wheat most commonly cultivated in India is *triticum vulgare*. The larger part of the Punjab crop is under irrigation, particularly in the new canal colonies. Generally the crop is hand-reaped although labour saving machinery has been employed on a few of the big farms. On the land liberally manured and irrigated, yields of from 1,500 to 1,600 lbs. per acre have been obtained but the crop is liable to damage by rust if there is rain or cloudy weather in February. On dry (*i.e.*, un-irrigated) lands 800 lbs. would be a fair average crop.

Harvesting of the crop begins in March and April and winnowing continues until the end of May. In a good year the surplus crop is at once bought up by exporters and no time is lost in putting it on the European market where it bridges the interval between the antipodean harvests of South America and Australia and those of northern latitudes. Good prices are often procurable for early shipments as they arrive at a time when home stocks are practically exhausted. The rush of wheat from the threshing floor to the ports is therefore concentrated in normal years to May, June, July and August and shipments thereafter, except when a good monsoon coincides with a brisk European demand, are comparatively small. The exports have declined considerably during the last four years as will be observed from the subjoined table. This is due to a world-wide progressive over-production of wheat in relation to the demand for it and to the general trade depression. The holding of stocks encouraged by action taken by Government and trade agencies like the Federal Farm Board and the Canadian Wheat Pool has further aggravated the situation The increased rye supplies of Europe and comparatively good crops of rice and other cereals have also affected the position of wheat adversely. Further, the protective measures, such as heavy import duties and the quota system, introduced by many European countries have considerably reduced the consumption of wheat by raising its price within those countries.

TABLE No 71 —*Monthly exports of wheat in 1914, 1919 and during the last three years from Karachi.*

Months.	1914.	1919	1934.	1935.	1936.
	Tons.	Tons.	Tons.	Tons.	Tons.
January . . .	18,670	1,249	83	106	41
February . . .	8,993	543	44	41	36
March . . .	8,479	499	31	33	33
April	7,016	56	20	46	31
May	21,771	597	35	35	396
June	166,997	323	26	27	5,123
July	168,417	455	32	19	4,138
August . . .	41,824	436	5,832	48	8,795
September . .	55,967	601	1,564	2,189	37,385
October . . .	87,742	292	1,247	2,786	53,122
November . . .	54,615	157	323	2,523	(*a*)
December . . .	36,494	595	251	50	(*a*)
Total .	677,016	5,803	9,488	7,903	(*a*)

In the years of plenty the cultivators in the Punjab are generally anxious to realise their money in order that they may pay off

(*a*) Not yet available.

advances, satisfy Government dues and avoid the risk of loss from weevils by storage in the monsoon. In years of famine the local price is generally so high that the parity of prices in Europe is exceeded and the volume of exports falls to a very low figure. In a good season the percentage of exports to outturn may be 10; in a year of scarcity, such as 1908-09, the percentage may fall below 2.

Acreage.

In the five years ending 1912-13, the area under wheat in India averaged 27 million acres with an annual outturn in the neighbourhood of 8 million tons. The corresponding figures for the five years ending 1922-23 were 28 million acres and 9 million tons. The wheat exports of the statistical year are mainly drawn from the crop of the previous year, and in the table which follows this is recognised, as the export figures indicated against each year in the table stand for quantities that actually went forward only in the following year. Though the area under wheat increased by nearly 4½ million acres in 1933-34, the estimated yield, on the other hand, showed a decline of 1 million tons as compared to that for the year 1929-30.

TABLE No 72.—*Area, yield and exports of wheat in India in the last six years.*

Year.	Area. Acres.	Yield. Tons.	Exports. Tons.
1929-30	31,654,000	10,469,000	196,505
1930-31	32,189,000	9,306,000	20,215
1931-32	33,803,000	9,024,000	2,194
1932-33	32,976,000	9,455,000	2,060
1933-34	35,992,000	9,424,000	10,962
1934 35	34,490,000	9,728,000	9,590

Marketing.

India's participation in the world's wheat market dates from 1870, when the opening of the Suez Canal brought the wheat fields of the United Provinces within thirty days of Europe. In the early days of the trade the wheat grown in those Provinces was railed down to Calcutta for shipment until the extension of the railway system enabled Bombay to compete, and then with the expansion of irrigation in the Punjab the trend of exports has gradually drifted north-westward and Karachi where, it is claimed, the cost of handling and storage is lower than at Calcutta or Bombay, has now assumed a commanding position. Wheat is bought at centres up-country, such as Lyallpur, and bagged and railed down to Karachi where it is sold by the candy of 8 mds of 82 2/7 lbs each, manipulated and stored before shipment chiefly to the United Kingdom. Shipment is usually made in bags of 2 cwts. nett In Bombay wheat is sold and shipped in bags varying in weight, from 196 to 210 lbs. nett Quotations to the United Kingdom are generally per quarter of 492 lbs nett Typical descriptions on the Karachi market are—*white*, including 5 per cent. barley, 3 per cent dirt, 30 per cent. red: *red*, including 5 per cent barley and 3 per cent. dirt, and superior grades, *white* and *red* with admixtures in each case of 2 per cent barley and 1½ per cent. dirt only. Though the chief varieties of wheat exported from India fall within the definition of *soft* wheat commercially, there are *hard* wheats (red and yellow) grown in Central India which find a market in Marseilles and Italy, where they are used in the manufacture of macaroni. In the general absence of wheat elevators, Karachi, with a rainfall that seldom exceeds five inches, has great advantages over Bombay, where the monsoon rains are heavy and the general humidity throughout the year much higher. The wheat awaiting shipment in Karachi can be stored at the docks in open sheds with very little risk of damage by rain.

Indian wheat at one time had the reputation of being dirty, but it was established that this was not due so much to careless threshing or handling as to deliberate adulteration to conform to the practice of the English grain trade. Since 1907 there has been a marked improvement in the quality of Indian wheat owing to the new contract of the London Corn Trade Association being on the basis of an admixture not exceeding 2 per cent. of other food grains (in practice chiefly barley) but free from dirt. A specimen of the contract in force in 1934 will be found in Appendix VII.

Exports.

The distribution of the exports of wheat, among the three principal ports interested, is shown in the following table. No less than 81 per cent. of the shipment in 1935-36 went from Karachi, the shares of Bombay and Calcutta in this trade having steadily declined since the war.

TABLE No 73.—*Exports of wheat in 1913-14, 1918-19 and from 1932-33 onwards.*

Principal ports.	1913-14	1918-19.	1932-33.	1933-34.	1934-35.	1935-36.
	Tons.	Tons.	Tons.	Tons.	Tons	Tons.
Karachi . .	893,324	410,127	645	739	9,510	7,833
Bombay . .	235,640	39,613	1,308	1,235	1,280	1,541
Calcutta . .	73,191	25,362	168	74	142	16
Total—						
Quantities .	202,205	476,103	2,194	2,060	10,962	9,590
Values £ . .	8,755,571	4,502,062	28,670	24,522	79,543	71,105

The principal recipient of Indian wheat has always been the United Kingdom In 1935-36, 72 per cent. of the total shipments went to that destination.

Wheat prices are always expressed in India by the number of *seers* (of 2·05 lbs) sold for a rupee and the higher the figures the cheaper the wheat.

Government Control.

There was a general rise of wheat prices all over the world as soon as war was declared and Indian bazaar prices moved up in sympathy. In October 1914 the Government of India by ordinance gave authority to Local Governments to inquire into stocks and take over if necessary any unreasonably withheld. As this did not stay the upwards trend of prices, it was decided to restrict the export of wheat and wheat flour from December 1914 to March 1915 to 100,000 tons. Prices nevertheless continued to soar and in February 1915 were 45 per cent. above the level of the previous July. The promise of an excellent harvest then steadied the market and the measure of increase was reduced to 21 per cent. by the end of March.

In April 1915 the Government decided to prohibit all private exports of wheat so as to remove the link between the Indian and the world market, and created a special appointment of Wheat Commissioner to secure the most advantageous terms for the exportable surplus. While this control was in force the firms which had previously been engaged in the shipment of wheat to Europe were appointed buying agents for the Wheat Commissioner at a fixed commission, the maximum prices to be offered to sellers up-country being fixed by Government from time to time and gradually reduced so as to discourage speculative hoarding. The total quantity purchased on Government account between April 1915 and May 1916, when the arrangements were altered, exceeded 525,000 tons, of which 458,057 tons were shipped from Karachi, 40,870 from Bombay and 29,606 from Calcutta.

With effect from the 1st May 1916 shipment on private account was once more permitted up to the limit of quarterly allotments fixed by the Wheat Commissioner on the basis of pre-war business but this arrangement only continued until the end of October when the Royal Commission on wheat supplies assumed control and made direct purchases until February 1917 and then the Wheat Commissioner was again invested with entire responsibility for buying operations. The wheat harvest of 1917 beat all previous records and in 1917-18 no less than 1,454,400 tons were exported, exclusive of 25,600 tons shipped on military account. The Wheat Commissioner on behalf of the Royal Commission purchased 1,578,346 tons in 1917-18 Though purchases on behalf of the Royal Commission were terminated in October 1918, 384,545 tons were exported on this account in the following year of which 331,464 tons were shipped from Karachi, 229,304 tons were of Punjab wheat and 125,978 tons of wheat from the United Provinces.

The widespread failure of the rains in 1918-19, though it affected the wheat harvest of the Punjab but little, caused a general rise in the price of all food grains in Northern India and to meet the situation the Government of India arranged to take over some of the large stocks of Australian wheat which the Royal Commission had purchased some time ago, but for which no freight could be found During the four months March to June 1919 arrivals of Australian wheat at Indian ports aggregated 168,000 tons. The quantity of wheat exported in 1919-20 was the lowest on record owing to the embargo on exports imposed by the Foodstuffs Commissioner. The harvest of 1919 was also the poorest of recent years, but that of 1920 being above the average the Government of India released 400,000 tons for export between October 1920 and March 1921, but the total actually shipped from Karachi, before the close of the official year was only 229,000 tons. In 1921-22 the failure of the monsoon of 1920 affected the wheat harvest of the following year and exports fell to 80,000 tons while imports of wheat from Australia and the United States of America amounted to 440,000 tons. The Indian wheat crop for 1921-22 was estimated at 9,800,000 tons as compared with 6,700,000 tons in the previous year and in September all restrictions on exports were removed. The total quantity exported by the close of the year was 220,000 tons only as compared with 1,200,000 tons in 1913-14, but it must be remembered that in normal times the heaviest months for shipment are May, June and July when the embargo was still in force.

Wheat Flour.

The exports of wheat flour correspond pretty closely, when uncontrolled, to those of wheat. The products of the mills are known by the vernacular names *maida, atta,* and *sujji* which are statistically shown under the common head of wheat flour. These names represent three grades of flour in order of fineness. *Sujji* is the round, granular meal of inferior quality obtained by grinding wheat which has been moistened overnight and then passing it through a sieve, the bran mixed up with it being later on separated by winnowing. It is used chiefly for making a sort of coarse porridge and as a constituent in certain bazaar sweetmeats. The other two qualities are obtained by regrinding *sujji* and passing it through a second sieve, the finer flour resulting being called *maida*, and the coarser *atta*. While the former is the luxury of the richer classes, the latter baked into coarse cakes called *chappattis* comprises the main food of the poor in many parts of India. The chief destinations for wheat flour before the war were Egypt, Asiatic Turkey, Mauritius, Aden, Ceylon, the Straits Settlements and the United Kingdom, the variety generally shipped being *atta*. Arabia, Straits Settlements, Kenya Colony and Aden are now the principal participants.

TABLE No. 74.—*Exports of wheat flour (Quantities and values) in 1913-14, 1918-19 and 1931-32 onwards.*

Year.	Quantity.	Value.
	Tons.	£
1913-14	79,412	884,068
1918-19	30,942	543,021
1931-32	42,724	434,788
1932-33	20,790	207,726
1933-34	12,536	122,812
1934-35	11,763	110,009
1935-36	18,031	167,015

Unit of Sale and Shipment.

The principal ports concerned in export are Karachi, Bombay and Calcutta in that order. The unit of sale and shipment in Karachi is the bag of 164 or 196 lbs., the latter being the unit commonly accepted in Bombay. In Calcutta sales are made on the basis of the bazaar maund and flour is generally shipped in bags of 196 lbs. nett.

BARLEY.

Area.

Barley (*hordeum vulgare*) is chiefly grown in the United Provinces and Bihar and Orissa with the Punjab and North-West Frontier Province as next in importance. The total area under the crop in British India in 1934-35 was 6·5 million acres in addition to about thirty-seven thousand acres in Indian States—chiefly Hyderabad. Of the four million acres in the United Provinces the greater part is in the

Gorakhpur, Benares, Lucknow and Allahabad divisions. Barley is a *rabi* crop sown in October or November and reaped in March or April. Arrivals in the upcountry markets begin in April and business is brisk till July.

There is such a large internal demand that the volume of exports has never attained any considerable dimensions and Indian barley plays a very humble part in the world market for the grain, though the volume of Indian exports responds at once to any shortage of supplies in the United Kingdom. In 1912-13 as much as 615,177 tons were exported of which 82,872 tons went from Bombay, 154,420 tons from Calcutta, and 377,874 tons from Karachi. The imports of barley in the same year were 720 tons chiefly into Karachi. The negligible exports in the next three years are attributable to control, which was in force from January 1919 until September 1922.

Exports.

As will be seen from the table sub-joined the demand for this article from abroad has fluctuated within very wide limits. In 1931-32, the total exports amounted to 27,000 tons, in 1933-34 only 142 tons were shipped but in 1934-35 a brisk revival was noticed with a shipment of 14,000 tons. In 1935-36 the exports again declined to 3,500 tons.

TABLE No. 75.—*Quantity and value of barley exported in 1913-14, 1918-19, and during the last four years with the share of the different ports.*

Ports.	1913-14.	1918-19.	1932-33.	1933-34.	1934-35.	1935-36.
	Tons.	Tons.	Tons.	Tons.	Tons.	Tons.
Karachi	127,622	215,305	16,578	116	14,076	3,494
Calcutta	54,249	43	11	13	20	18
Bombay	8,519	11,000	9	13	29	4
Rangoon	10	4	..	..	..	..
Total—						
Quantity (Tons)	190,400	226,352	16,598	142	14,125	3,516
Value (£)	1,043,799	1,845,111	79,287	857	69,784	15,947

More than two-thirds of the exports go to the United Kingdom. The bulk of the remainder goes to Arabia.

The unit of sale in Bombay is the bag of 168 to 182 lbs. and in Calcutta the bazaar maund. The wholesale price is generally quoted in Karachi at so much per candy of 8 maunds of 82·2/7 lbs. each. Shipment is made in bags, the weight varying at each port—123 or 186 lbs. in Karachi and Calcutta and 168 or 182 lbs. in Bombay. Quotations for export to the United Kingdom are generally per quarter of 400 lbs gross.

Unit of sale and shipment.

PULSES.

Under the same statistical heading are grouped a great many food grains, the most important being *arhar*, lentils, *dhal*, beans and peas, the three last of which are distinguished by the great number of varieties which are marketed. For gram,* which is also a pulse, separate

Trade Varieties.

*See p. 201 *infra*.

figures are maintained. The lentil or *masur* (*lens esculenta*) is a valuable pulse grown as winter crop all over India, especially in the Central Provinces, Madras and the United Provinces. Flavoured with aromatics and condiments it largely disappears in internal consumption. *Arhar* (*cajanus indicus*) or pigeon pea is generally grown in India as a mixed crop particularly in rotation with cereals. As it enters largely into the vegetarian diet of high caste Hindus, its economic value is great though the volume of exports is negligible. *Dhal* is a common term applied to the split grain of a large variety of pulses, the most common being *pisum sativum* and *phaseolus mungo*. Peas and beans are also of many types, *e.g.*, Rangoon or white beans, French beans, kidney beans, white and green peas.

Rangoon Beans.

The Burma white bean (*phaseolus lunatus*), is locally known as *pebugale*, the trade in which is large and important. The harvesting of white beans begins in February or March, but those grown on the islands, formed when the river falls, are not gathered till April or May and these are of superior quality They are shipped as bought from the cultivator, and were formerly utilized chiefly as feeding stuff for cattle During the war an enhanced demand arose for Burma beans to take the place of the haricot beans so largely grown in the Danubian provinces from which the Allies were temporarily cut off, and large quantities were purchased by the Belgian Relief Commission and shipped to Europe. In 1919-20 the high prices of the previous year encouraged an extension of cultivation and the exports to foreign destinations totalled 109,000 tons chiefly to the United Kingdom, Netherlands and Belgium. Japan and the United Kingdom are now the principal recipients of Rangoon beans, the shares of the other foreign countries being negligible.

Exports.

No separate statistics of acreage or production of any of these pulses are maintained, but the aggregate outturn must be very considerable as every bazaar in India contains one or more varieties. The extent of the export trade in pulses is illustrated in the following table.

All the five principal ports participate. The main recipients are now the United Kingdom, Japan, Ceylon, Straits Settlements and Mauritius though in pre-war days large quantities found their way into Germany, Holland and Belgium. A popular demand for white beans from Burma is evidenced by the fact that Rangoon accounted for 39,000 tons out of the total quantity of pulses (excluding gram) exported from India in 1935-36.

TABLE No. 76.—*Quantity and value of pulses (excluding gram) exported from India in 1913-14, 1918-19 and 1931-32 onwards.*

Year.	Quantity.	Value.
	Tons.	£
1913-14	114,628	711,009
1918-19	159,318	1,970,732
1931-32	76,777	540,035
1932-33	80,723	561,158
1933-34	75,490	491,686
1934-35	87,291	618,955
1935-36	91,822	632,717

The unit of sale and of shipment varies for these pulses in all the ports. In Calcutta sales are made on the bazaar maund, in Karachi per candy of 8 maunds of 82 2/7 lbs. each and in Bombay in bags of 168 to 196 lbs. In Rangoon the unit of sale in the case of red and white beans and Paigyi is a hundred baskets of 69 lbs. each, while in the case of Paihin and other beans, it is a hundred baskets of 72 lbs. each. Quotations for shipments to the United Kingdom are generally based on the quarter of 504 lbs. gross. Shipment is made from Calcutta generally in bags of 205 lbs. nett, Bombay ships in bags of 164 lbs , 206 lbs. and 224 lbs. nett Bombay ships in bags of 168 to 196 lbs nett. In Rangoon shipment to Europe usually takes place in bags of 200 to 224 lbs. nett., and to other places in bags of 180 to 280 lbs. nett each. Butter beans are usually shipped to the United Kingdom in bags of 112 lbs. nett.

Unit of sale and shipment.

Millets.

A number of important food crops grown in India falls within the category of millets, the most important being *jawar (sorghum vulgare)* the great millet yielding an excellent grain which is the staple food of the agricultural population of the Madras and Bombay, Deccan and the adjoining districts of Hyderabad. There are considerable areas under crop in the Central Provinces and Berar, the United Provinces and to comparatively smaller extent in the Punjab and Burma. The total yield of this crop in the whole of India amounted to 6,330,000 tons in 1934-35 as compared with 6,191,000 tons in the previous year. The harvested straw constitutes a popular fodder crop for cattle, but the plants, if grazed, or cut when immature, are sometimes poisonous in their effects. A smaller variety known as *bajra*, the bulrush or spiked millet *(pennisetum typhoideum)* is scarcely less widely cultivated. This crop is quite extensively cultivated in Bombay (including Sind and Indian States), Punjab, Madras, the United Provinces and Hyderabad with the North-West Frontier Province and the Central Provinces and Berar as next in importance. The total yield of the crop in India in 1934-35 amounted to 2,549,000 tons as compared with 2,128,000 tons in the previous year. Neither of these millets is at any time extensively exported. The following table shows the exports of *jawar* and *bajra* in recent years as contrasted with the pre-war and post-war figures.

TABLE No. 77.—*Quantity and value of jawar and bajra exported from India in 1913-14, 1918-19 and from 1931-32 onwards.*

Year.	Quantity.	Value.
	Tons.	£
1913-14	84,294	576,164
1918-19	5,396	56,182
1931-32	58,503	318,664
1932-33	15,530	99,106
1933-34	5,082	36,042
1934-35	4,390	31,020
1935-36	8,543	62,724

The principal ports from which shipments are made are Bombay and Karachi, and, the principal destinations are Aden and Anglo-Egyptian Sudan in the British Empire and Arabia, Netherlands, Germany and Italian East Africa among foreign countries. Restricted shipments to the first named destination owing to the general control of food-stuffs accounts for the drop in the export figures for 1918-19 and subsequent years.

The unit of sale in Karachi is the candy of 8 maunds of 82·2/7 lbs. each, and of shipment the bag of 164 lbs., 206 lbs., and 210 lbs.

Unit of sale and shipment. The unit of sale and shipment varies in Bombay for jawar and bajra, the former being sold and shipped in bags of 168 lbs. and the latter in bags of 168 to 196 lbs. The unit of shipment to Europe is usually the bag of 224 lbs. in Rangoon.

Gram.

Gram (*cicer arietinum*) is probably the most important of the pulses grown in India, being sown over an area of over 17,000,000

Area. acres, of which the Punjab and the United Provinces have the largest shares. The crop is important also in Bihar and Orissa, Central Provinces and Berar, Bombay (including Sind), Hyderabad and Mysore. The total estimated yield in 1934-35 was 3,671,000 tons as compared with 3,779,000 tons in 1933-34. The new crop comes on the market generally in April, and the bulk of the business is put through before the rains. It should be carefully distinguished from the horse-gram (*dolichus biflorus*) grown so largely in Southern India as a substitute for oats.

As in the case of other pulses gram enters so largely into local

Exports. consumption wherever it is grown, that exports, even in years of plenty, are comparatively limited.

TABLE NO. 78.—*Quantity and value of exports of gram in 1913-14, 1918-19 and from 1931-32 onwards.*

Year.	Quantity.	Value.
	Tons.	£
1913-14	69,597	415,104
1918-19	282,193	2,233,414
1931-32	15,890	126,902
1932-33	30,394	217,323
1933-34	28,867	193,145
1934-35	24,743	168,973
1935-36	7,501	59,023

The principal ports participating in the trade are Karachi, Bombay and Rangoon, and the principal destinations are the United Kingdom, Ceylon, the Straits, Mauritius and Aden among British, and France among foreign countries. Before the war, Germany absorbed fairly large quantities, and in 1933-34, after a period of disappearance from the market, she took over 4,700 tons. The phenomenal increase in 1918-19 is to be accounted for by enhanced shipments to Egypt on Government account "for orders" and also to

Italy. Exports were controlled from January 1919 until September 1922, since then the figures show a considerable recovery, though still much below the pre-war level.

Unit of sale and shipment.

The unit of sale in Calcutta is the bazaar maund and in Karachi the candy of 8 maunds of 82·2/7 lbs. each and of shipment the bag of 205 lbs., and 164 lbs., 206 lbs., and 224 lbs., respectively. In Bombay the unit of sale and shipment is the bag of 168 to 196 lbs. In Rangoon gram is shipped in bags of 160 to 224 lbs. and sold per 100 baskets of 65 lbs. each. Quotations to the United Kingdom are generally per quarter of 504 lbs. gross.

Maize.

Area.

Garden plots or patches of maize or Indian corn (*zea mays*) may be found practically all over India, but extensive cultivation is confined to the United Provinces, Bihar and Orissa, the Punjab, the North-West Frontier Province, Bombay (including Sind) and the Central Provinces and Berar in British India and Hyderabad among the Indian States. The total area under the crop in the whole of India, averages about 6,868,000 acres with an estimated annual production of 2,232,000 tons. The new crop begins to appear in upcountry markets towards the end of October and trading is brisk from November to March.

Exports.

The greater part of the crop is locally consumed, and the following table indicates the extent of exports in recent years as compared with the pre-war and post-war figures.

TABLE No. 79.—*Quantity and value of maize exported in 1913-14, 1918-19 and from 1931-32 onwards.*

Year.	Quantity.	Value.
	Tons.	£
1913-14	2,881	13,969
1918-19	13,761	104,832
1931-32	88	829
1932-33	38	382
1933-34	125	477
1934-35	2,592	7,960
1935-36	2,425	6.938

It was only in 1916-17 with the Argentine supplies practically cut off from Europe by difficulties of tonnage and the submarine menace in the South Atlantic, that there was temporarily a great expansion of business. In 1917-18, with these conditions persisting, the total shipments were thirty times the pre-war normal, chiefly to the United Kingdom, Egypt 'for orders' and Greece. In 1918-19 a general shortage of food-stuffs was apprehended in India, owing to the failure of the south-west monsoon, and for the next three years export was controlled

In recent times, the trade in maize had dwindled to insignificant proportions but in the year 1934-35, an enhanced shipment was noticed, though it did not reach the pre-war level. Exports are from Calcutta, Bombay, Karachi and Rangoon.

The unit of sale in Calcutta is the bazaar maund and maize is shipped in bags of 2 maunds nett. In Rangoon the unit of sale is a hundred baskets of 55 lbs. each and that of shipment bags of 200 lbs. In Karachi sales are based on the candy of 8 maunds and shipment is effected in bags weighing 164 lbs., 208 lbs., and 224 lbs. Quotations for export to the United Kingdom are generally based on the quarter of 480 lbs. gross.

Unit of Sale and Shipment.

Oats.

Cultivation.

The cultivation of oats (*avena sativa*) for the grain is confined mainly to the Delhi and Hissar districts of the Punjab and the Meerut districts of the United Provinces where it is grown as a *rabi* crop, but it is raised also to a limited extent in the Poona, Ahmednagar, Satara and Ahmedabad districts of the Bombay Presidency. Elsewhere it is more frequently cut green for cattle fodder. No separate statistics of area or production are maintained and the foreign export trade is normally insignificant in comparison with that of other grains produced in the country, as the following table indicates.

TABLE No. 80.—*Quantity and value of oats exported in 1913-14, 1918-19 and from 1931-32 onwards.*

Year.	Quantity.	Value.
	Tons.	£
1913-14	469	3,391
1918-19	431	5,409
1931-32	176	1,997
1932-33	437	3,792
1933-34	577	3,682
1934-35	491	2,888
1935-36	189	1,292

More than 90 per cent of the exports go from Calcutta and the balance from Bombay. The chief recipients are Ceylon, and Mauritious and Dependencies.

Unit of sale and shipment.

The unit of sale in Calcutta is the bazaar maund and shipment is made in bags of 140 lbs. to 164 lbs. In Bombay, the unit of sale and shipment is the bag of 168 lbs. to 196 lbs.

OILSEEDS.

Exports in General.

The importance and value of the trade of India in oilseeds has now been generally recognised. The annual production of seeds is estimated at over 7,000,000 tons with an aggregate value of over £58,000,000 and 7,000,000 tons with an aggregate value of over £58,000,000 and in the year 1933-34 the exports of oilseeds from India were equivalent to one-fourth of the total world's exports of oilseeds. If the exports of the residual cake and oil are added, the aggregate of India's trade under this head would amount to £18,000,000 in 1913-14, to £19,500,000 in 1922-23, to £11,600,000 in 1933-34, to £9,400,000 in 1934-35 and to £9,200,000 in 1935-36.

The following tabulated statement will give some idea of the actual percentages of the world's demands for seeds that are met from Indian sources.

Seeds.

TABLE No. 81.—*Share of India in the world's trade in oilseeds in 1934-35.*

Seeds.	Total exports from producing countries.	Exports from India.	Percentage.
	Tons.	Tons.	
Linseed	1,770,000	238,000	13
Groundnut	1,760,000	511,000	29
Cotton seed	670,000	636	·1
Rape and Mustard seed	110,000	40,000	36
Castor seed	69,000	69,000	100
Sesame seed	130,000	4,000	3
Nigerseed	1,600	1,600	100

Present Distribution of Trade.

About one-fourth of the total exports is absorbed by the United Kingdom, the principal items being linseed (90,000 tons), cotton seed (50 tons), groundnuts (62,000 tons), and rapeseed (2,000 tons), out of a total of 178,000 tons. Germany, Netherlands, and Italy account for 11 per cent. each, the principal items exported to these countries being groundnuts, linseed and rape-seed. The shares of France, United States of America and Belgium are 23 per cent., 10 per cent., and 3 per cent. respectively. The exports to these countries consist of groundnuts, linseed, rape and mustard seed, sesame and castor seed.

Contracts for the United Kingdom.

The bulk of the oilseeds for the United Kingdom are sold under the terms of the contracts framed by the Incorporated Oil-seeds Association on a pure basis. A specimen of of this Association's linseed contract will be found in Appendix VIII

Oils.

Of very much smaller importance are the exports of oil from India the value of which in 1913-14 was rather less than £400,000 and in 1935-36, £269,000 only. The United Kingdom was the best customer in respect of castor, coconut, cotton seed and groundnut oils. The exports of linseed oil were chiefly to the Straits Settlements, Hongkong, Philippines and Ceylon and of mustard or rape oil to Mauritius and Fiji Islands. Masket territory, Aden, Mauritius and Ceylon were the best customers for sesamum oil.

A great quantity of oil is of course required for internal consumption. Though most of the vegetable oils manufactured are extracted by crude processes in mills worked by bullocks or in hand presses, yet the number of well-equipped modern mills for oil crushing has increased during some years past. There has been a great expansion in recent years of groundnut cultivation, and the development of the crushing industry on up-to-date lines has been taken up.

TABLE NO. 82.—*Exports of oils from India in 1913-14 and 1935-36 contrasted.*

Oils.	1913-14.		1935-36.	
	Quantity. Gallons.	Value. £	Quantity. Gallons.	Value. £
Coconut oil	1,091,477	155,073	32,742	3,234
Castor oil	1,007,001	92,504	1,408,023	161,055
Mustard and Rape oils	407,178	48,624	236,799	25,840
Sesamum oil	208,053	28,699	150,025	18,427
Linseed oil	102,360	17,493	77,866	9,517
Groundnut oil	288,190	30,013	290,803	29,563
Other vegetable oils	137,828	13,247	161,484	21,059

It will be noticed that, except in the case of castor oil and ground nut oil, there has been an appreciable decline in exports.

Oil-Cakes.

The value of India's trade in oil-cakes was at the outbreak of the war in the neighbourhood of £1 million sterling annually, the chief recipients being the United Kingdom, Ceylon and Japan which together accounted for six sevenths of the whole. In 1935-36 the total value of oil-cakes exported from India was nearly £1·4 millions sterling. The value of caster cake and cotton cake shipped amounted to £5,375 and £21,911 respectively, United Kingdom being the chief destination. The exports of coconut cake were valued at £19,075, Belgium being the principal customer. The exports of groundnut cake were valued at £872,274, the principal markets being the United Kingdom, Germany, Belgium, Egypt, Netherlands and Ceylon. The exports of linseed cake, which were valued at £329,537, went chiefly to the United Kingdom and Belgium. Ceylon and Japan were the chief markets for rape and sesamum cake, the exports of which were valued at £108,587.

Linseed.

The feature of the cultivation of *linum usitatissimum* in India is that it is cultivated entirely for its seed and not for its fibre. Practically all the seed and the resultant oil and cake used to be exported but there has been a considerable change in this respect since 1914, and foreign markets are now more of a convenience and less of a necessity than they used to be. The plant is identical with the flax of Europe, but having long been cultivated for its seed only, is sown much more sparsely than on the Continent and has developed a branching habit of growth which would render it useless, or, at any rate, greatly lessen its value as fibre. When sown experimentally for flax in India special seed has always been procured from Europe.

In 1904-05 nearly 560,000 tons of seed were shipped and India practically monopolised the world's production. The increased competition of the Argentine Republic, the United States of America, Canada and Russia have reduced considerably India's share of the trade. The following statement indicates the percentage of India's trade in linseed in certain principal foreign markets.

TABLE No. 83.—*Imports of linseed into the United Kingdom, France and Italy (In thousand quintals).*

	1913.	1914.	1932.	1933.	1934.	1935.
United Kingdom—						
Total . . .	6,550	4,950	3,682	2,526	1,870	2,615
Argentina . .	2,250	2,090	3,495	1,150	447	1,990
India . . .	1,360	2,380	94	1,333	1,418	595
India's percentage .	21%	48%	3%	53%	76%	23%
France—						
Total . . .	2,514	1,337	2,360	2,643	2,366	2,584
Argentina . . .	1,143	546	1,834	2,049	2,055	2,377
India . . .	1,026	617	322	462	216	56
India's percentage .	41%	46%	14%	17%	9%	2%
Italy—						
Total . . .	454	324	686	750	645	Not available.
Argentina . .	133	11	514	537	462	
India (and Ceylon) .	261	282	119	177	132	
India's percentage (including Ceylon).	57%	87%	17%	24%	20%	

The average production of seed in the triennium 1912-1913 and 1914 exceeded half a million tons, of which 75 per cent. was exported, and this proportion may be taken as the normal pre-war percentage. While the war lasted, of course, it was much lower. No linseed is grown in Madras, and the principal producing areas are Bihar and Orissa, the United Provinces, Bengal and the Central Provinces. The area under cultivation in the provinces for which forecasts are available, aggregates ordinarily between 3 and 3½ million acres, inclusive of a mixed crop of about 600,000 acres in the United Provinces, but in years of scarcity, such as 1918-19 the total is much reduced. In a good year the exportable surplus is in the neighbourhood of 400,000 tons.

Production.

The world acreage and production of linseed are approximately 9,000,000 and 1,800 000 tons respectively

TABLE No. 84 —*Acreage under cultivation according to provinces in 1913-14, 1918-19 and from 1931-32 onwards.*

Provinces and States	1913-14.	1918-19.	1931-32.	1932-33.	1933-34.	1934-35.
	Acres.	Acres.	Acres.	Acres.	Acres.	Acres.
Bengal	193,700	144,000	126,000	125,000	124,000	126,000
Bihar and Orissa . .	652,900	595,000	662,000	641,000	631,000	599,000
Bombay (Including Indian States).	178,100	89,000	137,000	125,000	124,000	134,000
			* 10,000	* 6,000	* 6,000	(a) 1,125,000
Central Provinces and Bera	952,100	509,000	937,000	1,008,000	933,000	26,000
Punjab	39,000	27,000	32,000	28,000	32,000	240,000
United Provinces . .	240,600	69,000	321,000	228,000	213,000	622,000
	† 367,000	† 321,000	† 589,000	† 624,000	† 598,000	† 47,000
Bhopal State . .	‡	‡	‡	44,000	37,000	‡
Central Provinces States .	‡	‡	94,000	108,000	128,000	..
Hyderabad State . .	412,600	216,000	306,000	269,000	367,000	399,000
Rajputana (Kotah) .	‡	19,000	95,000	93,000	73,000	92,000
Total — Aecrage . .	3,031,000	1,989,000	3,309,000	3,299,000	3,261,000	3,410,000
Total — Yield (Tons) .	386,200	235,000	416,000	406,000	376,000	420,000

* Figures for Indian States.
† Mixed crop.
‡ Not available.

(a) Including Indian States.

The crop is sown either pure or mixed and the fair average yield may be taken at 435 lbs. to the acre. There are two readily recognised varieties grown, which yield the commercial varieties known as yellow and brown linseed respectively. The bulk of the linseed which is marketed is of the variety known as *brown*, which is graded into *bold*, *medium* and *small*. Bombay exports chiefly *bold* and *small*, and Calcutta, *medium*. The exports from Karachi, which are small, approximate to those from Calcutta in quality. *Yellow* linseed is exported only from Bombay and is generally sold with an admixture of 'bold brown' which may amount to as much as 80 per cent. This *yellow* seed is mostly shipped to Marseilles where it is preferred to the usual Bombay *bold* quality on account of the lighter colour of the resultant oil cake which commands a slight premium in that market.

Trade varieties.

Linseed, as has been noticed, was formerly grown in India largely to meet a foreign demand. The first mention of export from India occurs in 1832 when 3 cwts. were recorded By 1839 the figure had risen to 60,000 tons and in 1880-81 to 300,000 tons. The following table indicates the quantity and value of linseed exported since 1931-32 as compared with the pre-war and post-war figures.

Exports.

Linseed is generally shipped throughout the year but the busy season runs from May to July.

TABLE NO. 85 —*Quantity and value of exports of linseed from India in 1913-14, 1918-19 and from 1931-32 onwards*

Year.	Quantity.	Value.
	Tons.	£
1913-14	413,873	4,457,998
1918-19	292,453	4,391,402
1931-32	120,283	1,148,349
1932-33	72,190	683,307
1933-34	378,868	3,431,335
1934-35	238,365	2,248,181
1935-36	164,743	1,654,663

In 1904-05 there was a record shipment of 559,100 tons valued at £4,219,150.

The fall in 1914-15 was due more to the indifferent harvest of the previous year than to the war. In 1915-16 there was a more substantial contraction with greatly reduced exports to France and Italy and shipments to the United Kingdom at pre-war levels. In 1916-17, however, when an abundant crop coincided with a great shortage of supplies from the Plate, a recovery to 400,000 tons was achieved but in the following year, owing to smaller supplies arriving at the ports from the provinces and partly because of the curtailed demands from the chief importers, the total that left the country was very small. In 1918-19, the increased stimulus imparted to the production of margarine and edible oils to replace butter and to the manufacture of glycerine for explosives, compelled larger exports of linseed from India. The British Ministry of Food made an arrangement by which imports from India were purchased by a Director of Oils and Seeds Supply in London with the Collectors of Customs as agents at the Indian ports concerned to supervise shipments. The total quantity that went to the United Kingdom in 1918-19 was 242,000 tons, or nearly 83 per cent. of the whole. The volume of trade was about the same in the following year but short stocks and high prices in India kept down the volume of exports in 1919-20. Depression in the British oilseed crushing industry and a bumper Argentine crop account for the disappointing figures of 1921-22; but there was a partial, if not complete recovery in 1922-23, with the United Kingdom and France as principal customers, and Italy's takings approximately the same as in 1913-14. In 1923-24, prices were steady, and, there were increased demands from the United Kingdom and the Continent, specially as a large quantity of exportable surplus of Argentine was absorbed by the United States of America, due to the fact that the use of linseed oil in the manufacture of linoleum and oilcloth had rapidly increased. Shipments increased by 34 per cent. in quantity and 31 per cent. in value as compared with the preceding year. In 1924-25, the bumper North American crop led to the curtailment of American demand for Argentine seeds, and, consequently. India's exports to the United Kingdom and France diminished, though she improved her position in the smaller markets of Italy and Australia. A noticeable decrease in the shipments was noticed in the following year owing partly to some continental countries growing more of the seed themselves to meet internal demand. A short Indian crop in 1925-26 accompanied by an abundant crop in Argentine considerably cut down India's exports which decreased by 54 per cent. as compared with the pre-war year. Exports of Indian linseed recovered slightly however in 1927-28 but were still 11 per cent less than the average of the post-war quinquennium. Due to an unfavourable monsoon in 1928-29 the exportable surplus was considerably less than the preceding year's and the European countries, generally, reduced their takings. Though, in the succeeding year, the weather conditions proved unfavourable, exports increased owing to a shortage of supplies in other producing countries. The increased demand continued in the first half of the next year but with the prospect of an abundant new Plate crop in Argentine, the exports dwindled in the latter half. Increased production in Argentine and other countries affected adversely India's exports in 1931-32 and 1932-33. In the latter year a slight improvement was noticed in the exports to the United Kingdom. In January 1933 in pursuance of the Ottawa Trade Agreement a duty of 10 per cent. *ad valorem* was imposed in the United Kingdom on all imports of linseed grown outside the Empire. This preference had a marked effect in the exports of linseed in the following year, in which shipments to the extent of 379,000 tons were registered as compared with only 72,000 tons in 1932-33. The absence of exportable surplus in other countries accentuated the increased demand for Indian linseed. The share of the United Kingdom rose from 20 per cent. in 1932-33 to more than 46 per cent. in 1933-34. Owing, however, to a liberal crop in the Argentine and lesser demand from the United Kingdom, exports from India fell to 238,400 tons during 1934-35. Generally throughout the year 1935-36, Indian prices were above export parity owing to the keen home demand. The total shipment during this year, therefore, amounted to only 164,700 tons. The share of the United Kingdom during the two years 1934-35 and 1935-36 was about 44 per cent. and 55 per cent., respectively.

TABLE No. 86.—*Distribution of the trade in linseed among principal importing countries in 1913-14 and in 1935-36.*

Countries.	1913-14.		1935-36.	
	Quantity.	Percentage.	Quantity.	Percentage.
	Tons.		Tons.	
United Kingdom . .	157,315	38·0	90,144	54·5
Germany . . .	48,326	11·5	8,410	5·1
Netherlands . . .	9,575	2·3	390	0·3
Belgium . . .	38,459	9·3	3,556	2·2
France	115,459	28·0	7,580	4·6
Spain	3,440	0·8	2,586	1·6
Austria and Hungary .	6,500	1·5	..	..
Italy	30,657	7·4	6,696	4·7
Greece	500	0·1	3,479	2·1
Australia . . .	3,360	0·7	9,730	5·9
Other Countries . .	282	0·4	32,172	19·0
Total .	413,873	100	164,743	100

The bulk of the shipment goes from Bombay and Calcutta which share the trade equally between them. In 1933-34, with the commencement of exports from Vizagapatam, Madras figured in the trade for the first time. The shipment from that port however is not yet considerable.

Unit of sale and shipment.

The unit of sale in Calcutta is the bazaar maund and shipment is made in single B twill bags of 164 lbs. or double E bags of 186 lbs. nett. In Bombay, the unit of sale and shipment is the bag of 182 lbs. to 224 lbs. Sterling quotations are for the ton of 2,240 lbs. nett *landed terms* or *c. i. f.*

Linseed oil.

The oil content of linseed varies from 37 to 43 per cent. Of the seed retained in the country for conversion into oil the bulk is dealt with in country mills by primitive methods but while war lasted increasing quantities were consumed in factories working on modern lines under European management. The following table illustrates the course of the export trade.

Table No. 87.—*Quantity and value of exports of linseed oil from India from 1910-11 to 1913-14, 1917-18 to 1922-23 and from 1931-32 onwards.*

Year.	Quantity.	Value.
	Gallons.	£
1910-11	316,111	42,594
1911-12	249,975	49,966
1912-13	106,867	20,823
1913-14	102,360	17,493
1917-18	560,176	127,582
1918-19	1,674,958	431 017
1919-20	438,775	132,773
1920-21	265,848	88,519
1921-22	40,222	11,742
1922-23	30,728	7,203
1931-32	38,009	4,715
1932-33	44,109	5,293
1933-34	67,102	8,278
1934-35	63,682	7,805
1935-36	77,866	9,518

The decline in the volume of exports between 1910-11 and the outbreak of war is due chiefly to the opening of a mill in Melbourne for crushing linseed and the consequent falling off in the Australian demand for oil. At the same time the exports of seed to Australia rose from 700 tons in 1910-11 to 15,850 tons in 1917-18. The recovery in 1917-18 and the phenomenal exports in that year and in 1918-19 are due to a very strong demand, particularly from Australia for oil, in view of the restrictions placed upon shipments of seed. The fall in 1919-20 is attributable partly to a rise of 50 per cent. in the price of the raw material and partly to a reduced demand for Italy, Natal and Australia. Imports of oil crushing and refining machinery into India between 1918-19 and 1920-21 exceeded £150,000 but there was a further fall in the latter year in the exports of linseed oil, and in 1921-22 and 1922-23 new low levels were reached, which is to be regretted, as in the latter year there were increased shipments of linseed to the United Kingdom. In 1923-24, exports increased considerably, after which, the trade gradually declined with an abrupt rise in 1927-28 due to increased demand from the Philippine Islands and the Straits Settlements. In the follownig year, exports decreased by nearly 70 per cent., but in 1929-30 they reached the record figure of 170,000 gallons. An event of some interest in that year was the re-appearance of the United States of America and Siam in the market after a lapse of three years. Since then the trade has fluctuated with alternate rise and fall. In 1922-23, imports of linseed oil from the United Kingdom were 268,000 gallons, but the importation has gradually decreased and in 1935-36 only 136,000 gallons were imported. This is partly due to the growth of the indigenous industries, and partly to the price of the Indian linseed oil being appreciably lower than that of the foreign product. The average quantity imported annually is 165,000 gallons valued at £31,500 approximately.

The unit of sale in Calcutta is the gallon and shipment is made generally in half-cases of 72 lbs. or in drums of 40 gallons, 5 gallons and 4½ gallons. The bulk of the shipments goes from Calcutta, in the neighbourhood of which the principal mills are situated. The distribution of the trade between Calcutta and Bombay is shown below.

Unit of sale and shipment.

TABLE No. 88.—*Share of the principal ports in the export of linseed oil from India in 1935-36.*

Ports.	Quantity.	Percentage.
	Gallons.	
Calcutta	76,496	98·2
Bombay	1,370	1·8

Exports of linseed, rape and sesamum cakes were until the statistical year 1918-19, grouped under one head when the compilation of separate returns for linseed cake was arranged for. The course of the trade is indicated in the following table.

Linseed cake.

TABLE No. 89.—*Quantity and value of linseed cake exported.*

Year.	Quantity.	Value.
	Tons.	£
1918-19	6,142	46,564
1931-32	46,582	281,780
1932-33	81,747	439,925
1933-34	50,844	256,109
1934-35	40,532	210,311
1935-36	71,774	329,537

The distribution of exports was previously confined to two provinces, Bengal and Bombay, but since 1933-34, linseed cakes are exported from Madras also.

TABLE No. 90.—*Provincial distribution of exports of linseed cake in 1935-36.*

Provinces.	Quantity.	Value.
	Tons.	£
Bengal	44,047	198,863
Bombay	16,588	78,451
Madras	11,139	52,222

The main destinations for linseed cake are the United Kingdom, Netherlands and Belgium where they are used for manurial purposes.

The unit of sale for this cake is the bazaar maund and of shipment, the bag of 164 lbs. and 224 lbs. nett. In Bombay, the unit of sale and shipment is the bag of 168 lbs. to 182 lbs.

Groundnut.

The groundnut (*arachis hypogaea*) also known as pea-nut, earth-nut and monkey nut is, though long cultivated in India, probably not indigenous. The appearance of the Indian nut in Europe dates from about 1840, but forty years later the total exports amounted to less than 1,300 tons or little more than 1 per cent. of the aggregate imports into France*. Of 112,000 acres under the crop at this time 70,000 were in Bombay and 34,000 in Madras. In 1895-96 the corresponding figures were, Bombay 164,000 and Madras 248,000 acres. In the last decade of the nineteenth century the trade suffered from a very marked set-back due, it is said, to the marked deterioration of the so-called indigenous varieties of seed which led to a great contraction both in Madras and Bombay in the area cultivated with groundnut, the acreage in the former Presidency declining from nearly 300,000 to less than 100,000 acres. But the successful introduction of disease-resisting seed from Senegal and Mozambique with a much higher oil content is reflected in a remarkable recovery which dates from 1900-01, and under the further stimulus of an increased world demand for seeds yielding edible oils, the trade progressed steadily, particularly in Southern India, until in 1913-14 the total area devoted to the crop was not less than 2,100,000 acres, with an estimated yield of 749,000 tons. The figures for subsequent years are given below.

TABLE No. 91.—*Acreage and yield of groundnut in India for the years 1914-15, 1918-19, and from 1930-31 onwards.*

Year.	Acreage.	Yield.
		Tons.
1914-15	2,413,000	947,000
1918-19	1,407,000	626,000
1930-31	6,579,000	2,766,000
1931-32	5,489,000	2,268,000
1932 33	7,409,000	2,997,000
1933-34	8,226,000	3,330,000
1934-35	5,766,000	1,883,000

*O'Conor's report on the cultivation of groundnut in India. Journ. Agri. Hort. Soc. ed. 1879, Vol. VI, Nos. 97-98.

During the war several causes contributed to fluctuations in the acreage under cultivation. At first there was a marked fall in prices, disorganisation of the labour market at Marseilles and the closing down of several French mills which caused a considerable contraction in area in 1915-16, and after a good recovery in the following year, high freights and the almost complete suspension of sailings to Pondicherry and the smaller Madras ports, which in pre-war times were responsible for so considerable a portion of the exports, led to a further set-back Fortunately, however, the yield when the area was smallest, was so abundant that the estimated outturn of the previous year was actually exceeded and again in 1917-18 the fall in acreage was to a great extent made good by a heavier crop. In 1918-19 there was a marked decline both in acreage and yield, due to failure of rains at sowing time, and the crop afterwards suffered from drought in Madras and Bombay. During recent years there has been a very marked improvement both in the acreage and yield of groundnuts in India, and production is now about three times that of the pre-war period.

The following table gives the exports of groundnuts, oil and cake from India in 1913-14, 1918-19 and during the last four years.

TABLE No. 92.—*Exports of groundnuts, oil and cake from British India in 1913-14, 1918-19, and 1932-33 onwards.*

Articles.	1913-14.	1918-19.	1932-33.	1933-34.	1934-35.	1935-36.
Groundnut (Tons).	278,000	17,000	483,000	547,000	511,000	413,000
Groundnut cake (Tons)	62,000	56,000	159,000	190,000	262,000	194,000
Groundnut oil (Galls.)	288,000	590,000	917,000	716,000	275,000	291,000

On an average 3 cwts. (36 gallons) of oil represent 10 cwts. of nuts crushed.

Exports of Nuts.

The greater portion of the nuts produced in the country is consumed in India, the volume of exports scarcely keeping pace even in normal times with the increased cultivation. Taking the figures for the last pre-war year, *viz.*, 1913-14, it is found that considerably more than half the crop was retained for home consumption, only 278,000 tons out of 749,000, being sent out of the country. Yet in normal times the total exports from India compared very favourably with exports from the other principal producing countries of the world. When the exports from Pondicherry (chiefly grown in British India) are added to those from British Indian ports, India accounted for 458,000 tons out of a grand total of 1,186,000 tons received from all sources in Europe in 1932-33 the principal consuming country being France with a percentage share of 50. The following table shows the percentage borne by exports to outturn in each of the three provinces in which the crop is chiefly grown, calculated on the figures for 1934-35.

TABLE No. 93.—*Relation of provincial outturn to exports on basis of figures for 1934-35.*

Provinces.	Estimated yield of nuts.	Exports of nuts and oil.*	Percentage of exports to yield.
	Tons.	Tons.	
Madras	920,000	437,000	47
Bombay	530,000	78,000	15
Burma	144,000	154	0·1

*Converted at the rate of 36 gallons = 10 cwts. of nuts crushed.

In the table which follows though shipments of Indian groundnuts from Pondicherry and Marmugao are excluded, the predominance of France in the groundnut trade is very marked. In fact Marseilles prices and the Marseilles demand govern the market.

TABLE No. 94.—*Quantity and value of exports from British Indian ports of groundnuts in 1913-14, 1918-19 and 1932-33 onwards, and the principal destinations.*

Destinations.		1913-14.	1918-19.	1932-33.	1933-34.	1934-35.	1935-36.
		Tons.	Tons.	Tons.	Tons.	Tons.	Tons.
France		222,380	2,553	219,447	188,080	99,262	140,697
Belgium		16,608	...	8,627	13,491	13,951	9,196
Netherlands		...	...	87,474	100,855	114,813	95,161
United Kingdom		480	402	31,643	52,821	134,196	62,399
Germany		9,436	..	48,129	97,249	65,116	71,268
Italy		1,225	2,030	28,214	72,413	54,870	17,765
Other countries		27,778	12,214	9,478	21,637	29,486	16,081
Total	Quantity	277,907	17,199	433,012	546,546	5,511,194	412,567
	Value £	3,254,246	1,249,891	5,341,640	4,973,360	4,446,314	4,988,269

Shipping.

The decorticated kernels are generally shipped from Madras in bags weighing 80 kilogrammes, equal to 176 English lbs. nett, and are sold in Marseilles in francs per unit of 100 kilos. The groundnuts both in shell, and decorticated, are usually sold in the more southerly producing districts of the Madras Presidency at so much per French candy of 529 109 English lbs., but in the northern area the unit is the English candy of 500 lbs. Sterling quotations are generally per ton of 2,240 lbs. nett, *c. i. f.* Until some years ago the universal method of decorticating was to damp the groundnuts and beat them with sticks to separate the brittle shells from the kernels, a method which involves considerable damage to the latter. Further, once the kernels have been wetted they are liable to discolouration and fermentation, when the oil produced from them is rancid. The use of machinery for decorticating has grown in popularity, as by this method the seed is decorticated in the dry state and the kernels are uninjured, and consequently command a much better price in foreign markets than hand decorticated kernels. There are several satisfactory types of decorticators, and the percentage of seed for export now decorticated by machine instead of by hand has increased.

The best grades of oil in Europe are obtained from nuts shipped in the shell, but this method is not general from India owing to the heavy sea freights. The nuts when shipped in the shell occupy nearly double the space on the steamer than they take when shipped as kernels, and in this respect India is handicapped in comparison with the west coast of Africa where, the freight consideration being negligible, the bulk of the crop has always been shipped undecorticated. The want of adequate facilities for shipping at the minor ports in the Madras Presidency is a drawback to the South Indian trade, steamers having to lie at considerable distance from the shore owing to the shallow and surf-beaten nature of the coast and the cargo has to be carried from the shore in lighters and small boats which facilitate speculation. In 1935-36 the exports were nearly one and a half times those of the last pre-war year, over half of them going to France and the Netherlands.

Groundnut Oil.

Before 1916, when the Burma figures swelled the total for the first time, practically the only shipments of groundnut oil from India were from Madras and for the use of Indian *coolies* working in Mauritius and Ceylon. The bulk of the oil crushed is still consumed internally for domestic purposes. The substantial increase in the foreign exports of oil from India, while the war lasted, could not be maintained for some years after the war, but during recent years, the exports of oil showed considerable expansion and in 1932-33 reached the peak figure of 917,000 gallons. In the following year a slight decline was noticed and in the year 1934-35 exports of oil dropped to a very low level as a result of the market for the oil in Europe showing signs of contraction. If the gallonage is converted into the weight of seeds assumed necessary to produce it, according to the formula already given, it will be seen that the oil exported represents an almost negligible percentage of the total tonnage. The oil content of the shelled nut is about 40 per cent.

TABLE No. 95.—*The percentage share of the exports of groundnuts and oil to the total yield in India in 1913-14 and 1934-35.*

Year.	Yield.	Exports.			
		Nuts.		Oil.	
	Tons.	Tons.	Percentage to yield.	Gallons *converted into tons.	Percentage to yield.
1913-14 . . .	749,000	278,000	37·1	4,003	·53
1934-35 . . .	1,883,000	511,900	27·1	3,819	·2

*Converted at the rate of 36 gallons = 10 cwts. of nuts crushed.

Ground nut Cake.

The question of further expansion of seed crushing in India on up-to-date lines appears to be limited by the difficulty of finding more remunerative markets for the cake. Machine pressed cake is regarded with more favour by agriculturists in India as a cattle feed than the produce of country mills, because it is less adulterated, but four-fifths of the cake retained in India is used for manurial purposes and only one-fifth as fodder. The bulk of the groundnut cake exported is taken by the United Kingdom, the other principal markets being Germany, Netherlands, Belgium and Ceylon. Burma's principal customer is the United Kingdom while Ceylon, where the cake is admirably suited for tea plantations, relies for her supplies on Madras and Bombay. In the home market, the cake from the East Indies is known by the name of *Coromandel* to distinguish it from Rufisque derived from the African nut.

Madras.

Taking the provinces, where groundnut is cultivated, in order of their importance, we find that in Madras the annual acreage is about 3,500,000, yielding on an average about half a ton of unshelled nuts per acre, or between 1,000,000 and 1,125,000 tons of kernels. The general trade name for the nuts exported from Southern India is *Pondicherry* which are classed as *small*, while a *bold* grade of the *Bombay* nut (*i.e.*, shipped from that port) is also recognised. The crop is sown between July and September and comes into sight commercially between January and March. The exports from Pondicherry in 1934-35 amounted to 57,417,000 Kilogs. or 56,513 tons, valued at £430,626.

TABLE No. 96.—*Exports of groundnuts, foreign and coastwise in 1933-34 from Pondicherry and principal Madras ports.*

Ports.	Quantity.	Value.
	Tons.	£
Pondicherry	40,220	303,445
Madras Ports—		
Madras	154,190	1,345,500
Cuddalore	71,515	615,150
Porto Novo	3,373	32,550
Negapatam	34,335	327,300
Vizagapatam	13,742	110,550
Calicut	41,515	369,075
Cocanada	48,116	469,200
Bimlipatam	19,916	166,200
Other ports	72,542	684,600
Total (Madras Ports)	459,244	4,120,125

Since 1919-20 there has been a gradual revival of trade in groundnuts as a result of removal of all restrictions on the export after the war, the abundance of available tonnage, and the gradual decline in freight rates. Consequently the exports from Madras ports in 1921-22 and 1922-23 were considerably above the pre-war normal. Since then the exports have been steadily rising as a result of increased consumption in Europe.

Foreign exports of groundnut oil from Madras ports amounted in 1913-14 to 280,000 gallons, valued at £29,000, of which 48 per cent. went to Ceylon and 50 per cent. to Mauritius. In 1917-18 the total was 626,242 gallons, but with France eliminated and the United Kingdom, a smaller buyer, the total for 1918-19 shrank to the pre-war level. In 1935-36 the exports amounted to 18,000 gallons, valued at £1,231. Machine-pressed oil does not fetch such good prices as that pressed in *Chekkus* (country mills) which is cold drawn. Groundnut oil is generally sold per candy of 500 lbs. and shipped in cases of 80 lbs. at Negapatam and in tins of 40 lbs. at Dhanushkodi. Cochin casks holding 700 to 750 lbs. have gone out of favour and are now rarely used on account of their greater liability to leakage. In the case of coastwise exports, the unit of shipment is the drum of 400, 500, 550 or 560 lbs.

There is a large coastwise export of groundnut oil from Madras the exports in 1935-36 amounting to 1,063,000 gallons. Groundnut oil is largely used to adulterate *ghi* and other vegetable oils, and for Indian confectionery.

The foreign exports of cake in 1913-14 amounted to 23,600 tons, valued at £106,000. The corresponding figures for 1935-36 were 38,745 tons, valued, at £182,090. The cake is sold either per ton or per candy of 500 lbs. and shipped generally in bags containing 1½ cwts. nett.

Burma.

During the last twenty-five years Burma has evinced a growing interest in the cultivation and crushing of groundnut. The centre of the trade is at Myingyan in the dry zone. The estimated yield in Burma in 1913-14 and the following year was in the neighbourhood of 90,000 tons from an acreage of 256,000. In 1915-16 the yield soared to nearly 120,000 tons and the estimate for 1916-17 was only slightly less. The figures for the four years 1931-32, 1932-33, 1933-34 and 1934-35 have been 117,000 tons, 151,000 tons, 144,000 tons, and 144,000 tons respectively. Exports from Burma for the corresponding periods were respectively (1913-14) 26,912 tons, (1915-16) *nil*, (1916-17) 2,158 tons, (1931-32) 27 tons, (1932-33) 7 tons, (1933-34) 40 tons and (1934-35) 62 tons. It will be observed that in recent years foreign trade has dwindled to insignificance

In 1935-36 the exports of cake from Rangoon amounted to 54,561 tons, out of which 53,182 tons went to the United Kingdom. The foreign exports of Burma oil which is regarded as superior in quality to Madras oil amounted in 1915-16 to 77,000 gallons and the following year to 495,000. In 1917-18 the total was 297,000 gallons, of which 211,336 gallons went to the United Kingdom. In 1918-19, with shipments to the United Kingdom practically suspended, the aggregate was 76,836 gallons, and in 1922-23, 92 gallons only. In 1935-36, the exports of groundnut oil from Rangoon amounted to 240 gallons, the chief destinations being the Straits Settlements and the Federated Malay States

Units of Sale and Shipment.

The unit of sale in Burma for groundnuts is a hundred baskets of 25 lbs. each and of groundnut oil and cake, a hundred viss of 360 lbs. Groundnut kernel is very seldom exported from Burma. It is generally imported from India into Burma in 146 to 150 lbs. bags. Groundnut oil is shipped from Rangoon in tins of 4 gallons and also in casks of 40 to 80 gallons. Groundnut cake is shipped in bags of 200 to 224 lbs. nett.

Bombay Presidency.

The groundnut trade in Bombay has not made anything like the headway it has in Madras since the beginning of the present century. In 1895-96 three-quarters of the groundnuts exported were shipped from Bombay; in 1917-18 they represented less than 38 per cent. of the whole and in 1934-35 about 15 per cent. only.

The area under groundnut cultivation in the Bombay presidency in 1934-35 was 1,516,000 acres (inclusive of 654,000 acres in Indian States) equivalent to about 26 per cent. of the total area under the crop in India. The average yield on the basis of figures for the five years ending 1934-35 is 707,000 tons. The crop in Bombay is sown about six weeks earlier than in Madras and is harvested about November. Two grades of nuts are recognised—*bold* and *small*, which are sold either shelled or unshelled. The following table illustrates the volume of the trade in groundnuts, oil and cake from the Presidency for 1913-14, 1914-15, 1918-19 and from 1932-33 onwards.

TABLE No. 97.—*Exports of groundnuts, oil and cake from the Bombay Presidency for 1913-14, 1914-15, 1918-19 and 1932-33 onwards.*

Articles.	1913-14.	1914-15	1918-19	1932-33.	1933-34.	1934-35.	1935-36.
Groundnuts Tons	53,670	21,178	6,042	82,994	91,073	74,677	80,240
Groundnut oil Galls.	166	8,421	132,384	907,685	649,043	241,663	263,100
Groundnut cake Tons.	8,031	5,112	4,263	93,975	114,298	149,563	96,706

In the last pre-war year, more than 50 per cent. of the nuts went to France, the balance being divided mainly between Belgium and Germany, the share of the United Kingdom being only 40 tons. In 1916-17, however, the United Kingdom percentage of the trade rose to 20, the major quantity still finding its way to France, *viz.*, 59,000 tons. Bombay suffered less than Madras ports and Rangoon from the shortage of freight in this year, and her total shipments of groundnut were considerably higher than in the year preceding the war. In 1934-35, Italy and France took 25 per cent. each of the total exports of groundnuts from the Bombay Presidency. The percentage shares of the United Kingdom, Germany and Netherlands were 20, 13 and 9, respectively, while Belgium and Egypt accounted for 2 per cent. each. The trade in oil, which rose to 132,000 gallons in 1918-19, fell again five years later to inconsiderable dimensions (6,000 gallons), the chief customers being Mauritius and Mesopotamia. In the years which followed, the exports of groundnut oil rose very considerably and reached a figure of 907,685 gallons in 1932-33, after which there was again a rapid decline, the quantity exported in 1935-36 being 263,100 gallons. The United Kingdom and Mauritius are the principal customers which take about 70 per cent. of the total exports. Egypt, Italy and Aden share between themselves 20 per cent. of the trade. The export trade in groundnut cake has also developed to a marked extent during the past ten years. In 1935-36, 96,706 tons were exported as compared to 8,031 tons in the pre-war year. The United Kingdom and Germany were the only two customers for the cake in 1913-14, the greater part going to the former. The United Kingdom now takes 50 per cent. of the exports. The other chief customers are Germany and Belgium, their percentage shares in the trade being 17 and 14, respectively.

Unit of sale and shipment.

The unit of sale in Bombay for groundnuts is the bag of 168 to 196 lbs. for oil, the maund of 28 lbs., or the cwt., and for cake, the cwt. Shipment for the decorticated nuts is made in bags of 168 to 196 lbs., and the undecorticated nuts in bags weighing 85 lbs. or less, while the oil is packed for export in tins of 84 lbs. or drums of 6 or 8 gallons. Cakes are shipped in hydraulic pressed bags of 180 lbs. or in native pressed bags of 161 or 168 lbs. Sterling quotations for the nuts are generally based on the ton of 2,240 lbs. nett, *c. i. f.*

RAPE AND MUSTARD SEED.

The term rapeseed is commercially often indifferently used to denote, at least two sub-species of *brassica campestris, viz.*, Indian cozla or *sarson* and Indian rape or *toria*, while mustard seed is derived from a closely allied species, *brassica juncea*. The chief qualities of rapeseed recognised by the exporters are *toria*, brown bluish in colour, chiefly exported from Karachi, Ferozepore brown, brown Cawnpore, chiefly shipped from Bombay and Calcutta, *brown Delhi*, mainly exported from Bombay and Karachi, *yellow bold*, from Bombay and *yellow small* from Bombay and Calcutta.

Trade varieties.

Separate figures are not available in respect of the acreage of Rape and Mustard, but the subjoined table shows the area and yield of the combined crops, Rape and Mustard, in the British Provinces, and the Indian States. Rape and Mustard are *rabi* (spring) oilseeds, being sown from August to October and harvested from January to April. The crops are grown either pure or mixed almost entirely on unirrigated land. The normal yield per acre varies in different provinces as is indicated in the table below. When rape is cultivated by itself as a pure crop, the yield is probably appreciably higher. In parts of the country the crop is cut green in January for cattle fodder. In up-country markets the bulk of the crop is disposed of between March and July and the principal trade centres are Cawnpore in the United Provinces and Ferozepore in the Punjab where supplies are collected for export *via* Bombay and Karachi.

Area and production.

TABLE NO 98.—*Area and yield of Rape and Mustard from 1930-31.*

Provinces and States.	Normal yield per acre.	1930-31.		1931-32.		1932-33.		1933-34.		1934-35.	
		Area.	Yield.	Area.	Yield.	Area.	Yield.	Area.	Yield.	Area.	Yield.
	lbs	Acres.	Tons.	Acres.	Tons.	Acres	Tons.	Acres.	Tons.	Acres.	Tons.
British Provinces.											
Assam	459	363,000	64,000	302,000	46,000	271,000	43,000	330,000	57,000	345,000	54,000
Bengal	624	769,000	139,000	770,000	139,000	716,000	154,000	693,000	164,000	724,000	180,000
Bihar and Orissa (a)	492	657,000	147,000	645,000	136,000	627,000	140,000	598,000	135,000	600,000	137,000
Bombay including Sind	625 { *376 (g) *362 (h)	191,000	23,000	142,000	14,000	190,000	23,000	187,000	19,000	127,000	10,000
Central Provinces and Berar	..	64,000	(d)	70,000	16,000	71,000	15,000	74,000	16,000	71,000	17,000
Delhi	325	8,000	(e)	8,000	500	8,000	(e)	4,000	(e)	5,000	1,000
North-West Frontier Province	320	83,000	9,000	107,000	10,000	126,000	7,000	112,000	9,000	67,000	6,000
Punjab	428	889,000	141,000	1,150,000	184,000	1,158,000	151,000	1,099,000	131,000	673,000	101,000
United Provinces	600	240,000	32,000	273,000	48,000	327,000	58,000	219,000	31,000	206,000	30,000
	..	3,230,000@	423,000@	2,659,000@	419,000@	2,484,000@	438,000@	2,594,000@	372,000@	2,444,000@	357,000@
Total—British Provinces	...	3,264,000	555,000	3,467,000	593,000	3,494,000	591,000	3,313,000	562,000	2,818,000	536,000
	...	3,230,000@	423,000@	2,659,000@	419,000@	2,484,000@	438,000@	2,594,000@	372,000@	2,444,000@	357,000@
Indian States											
Baroda	..	20,000	2,000	21,000	2,000	20,000	2,000	40,000	3,000	15,000	1,000
Bombay States	...	17,000	3,000	23,000	4,000	46,000	6,000	37,000	5,000	23,000	4,000
Hyderabad	.	11,000	(e)	10,000	(e)	10,000	(e)	12,000	(e)	12,000	(f)
Rajputana (Alwar)	.	90,000	5,000	40,000	7,000	40,000	5,000	38,000	1,000	20,000	2,000
Total—Indian States	..	138,000	10,000	94,000	13,000	116,000	13,000	127,000	9,000	70,000	7,000
GRAND TOTAL	...	6,632,000	988,000	6,220,000	1,025,000	6,094,000	1,042,000	6,034,000	943,000	5,332,000	900,000

(a) Excluding Feudatory States, estimates for which for 1934-35 are 76,000 acres and 5,000 tons, as against 82,000 acres and 6,000 tons in 1933-34.

(@) The figures represent "mixed crop".
(d) Not available.
(e) Below 500 tons.
(f) 500 tons.
(*) Refers to Sind.
(g) Irrigated.
(h) Unirrigated.

The average world production of Rape seed is 180,000 tons with an acreage of 500,000. Japan, Rummania, and Poland are the principal countries concerned in cultivation of this crop with France and Hungary as next in importance.

Export of rapeseed.

India has always been the principal source of rape-seed imported into Europe in supplement to the supplies of Poland (chiefly ravison) Roumania (chiefly colza) France and Hungary. The most important country in addition to the above contributing to the world's exportable surplus is Japan and to a smaller extent, Germany and Netherlands. The statement below shows the percentage of India in the import trade of rapeseed in the United Kingdom, Belgium, Italy, and France.

TABLE No. 99.—*Percentage of India in the import trade of rapeseed in 1913, 1914 and 1932 onwards in foreign countries.*

(In thousand quintals.)

—	1913.	1914.	1932.	1933.	1934.	1935.
United Kingdom—						
Total	530	620	248	208	208	309
India	190	210	179	150	180	..
India's percentage	36%	34%	72%	72%	87%	..
Belgium—						
Total	94	..	42	55	42	54
Roumania	14	..	13	11	..	1
Argentine	3	..	..	1	2	19
India	67	..	17	32	24	4
India's percentage	72%	..	40%	58%	57%	7%
Italy—						
Total	102	220	752	114	71	(a)
India (including Ceylon)	95	183	735	110	52	
India's percentage	93%	83%	98%	96%	73%	
France—						
Total	538	404	103	158	139	103
India	482	303	67	103	87	44
India's percentage	90%	75%	65%	65%	63%	43%

Most of the seed grown in Bengal and Bihar would appear to be retained for local consumption. The principal exporting centres are Karachi and Bombay. Only a small percentage of the total production is exported, as the following statement would indicate.

(a) Figures not available.

TABLE No. 100.—*Percentage of export of rape and mustard to total production.*

Article.	Pre-war average.	War average.	Post-war average.	1933-34.	1934-35.
Rape and Mustard .	23	8	19	8	4

The figures of export for all ports are combined in the table below, which shows the principal destination for the seed.

TABLE No. 101.—*Exports and destinations of rapeseed from India for 1913-14, 1918-19 and from 1932-33 onwards.*

Countries.	1913-14.	1918-19.	1932-33.	1933-34.	1934-35.	1935-36.
	Tons.	Tons.	Tons.	Tons.	Tons	Ton
United Kingdom .	14,099	54,488	10,680	19,710	12,171	2,046
Germany	58,199	..	9,058	9,779	4,194	4,700
Belgium	98,869	..	2,775	4,348	2,604	950
France	53,943	10,729	8,305	11,073	5,193	3,274
Italy	13,726	4,068	70,497	9,672	3,433	156
Japan	1	9,906	100	..	..	..
Netherlands . .	..	..	11,300	14,531	6,945	2,459
Other countries . .	10,168	471	1,831	4,350	2,394	5,436

Though Belgium was, before the war, nominally the principal market, there is little doubt that a great deal of her imports *via* Antwerp found their way eventually to Holland and Germany. The effect of the war on the trade was very perceptible. In 1914-15, only 97,000 tons were exported as against 249,000 tons in the previous year, a partial revival being experienced only in 1916-17 when 122,000 tons were sent out of the country. Of this the greater portion was taken by the United Kingdom and France, both of which countries formerly relied for their supplies on Russia to a great extent. There was a great set-back again in 1917-18 owing to lack of tonnage. With the United Kingdom trade reduced by two-thirds and with France's requirements much curtailed, it was easy to satisfy a fleeting interest on the part of Japan in the crushing of rapeseed for oil. An interesting feature of the post-war trade was the increasing participation of Germany, Netherlands and the United Kingdom with a considerable decline in the share of Belgium. In 1923-24, a record shipment of 336,920 tons was registered with Germany, Italy and the United Kingdom as the principal recipients. There was a considerable falling off in the overseas demands immediately afterwards and since 1925-26, the trade suffered a decline, till 1932-33, when, due to an abrupt demand from Italy, exports improved by more than 50 per cent. as compared with the preceding year. Since then the trade has suffered another set-back.

Unit of sale and shipment.

In Karachi, the unit of sale is the candy of 8 maunds and of shipment the bag of 164 lbs., 206 lbs. and 186 lbs. In Bombay, the unit of sale and shipment is the bag of 182 lbs. to 196 lbs. In Calcutta, shipment is generally made in bags of 160 lbs. Sterling quotations are generally on the basis of the ton of 2,240 lbs. nett, *c.i.f.*

The average quantity of mustard seed exported does not usually exceed 5,000 tons a year and even that is believed to contain a very large admixture of rapeseed. In the last pre-war year it was 5,104 tons and in 1916-17, 6,174 tons. The bulk of the exports goes from Bombay packed in bags of 182 lbs. to 196 lbs. and France is the chief customer, more than 50 per cent. being appropriated by her every year. Occasional shipments were made to Germany in pre-war days. From South India there is a small trade with Ceylon and to a limited extent with France, the ports of export being Madras, Cocanada, and Tuticorin. The unit of sale in Bombay is the bag of 182 lbs. to 196 lbs.

Exports of mustard seed.

Large quantities of rape and mustard seed are annually crushed in India for local consumption in the form of oil which is commonly used, particularly in Bengal for cooking purposes and generally by Hindus to anoint the body. Indian seed is assumed to yield from 42 to 45 per cent. of oil. Mustard oil is not uncommonly adulterated in the bazaars, if not for the export market, with gingelly, mowra and *pakra* which is obtained from the seeds of *schleichera trijuga* (*kusumb*). The refining of rapeseed oil, as colza is refined in Central Europe, for the manufacture of margarine, has not yet been taken up in India. Pre-war exports from India averaged about 400,000 gallons (including mustard oil) of which practically the whole went to British Possessions and nearly three quarters to Mauritius and Natal alone for the Indian *coolie* population in those colonies. In 1915-16, 352,969 gallons, out of a total of 465,735 gallons, went to these two destinations. Large quantities are also sent out for the same reason to Fiji and British Guiana. In 1916-17 the total quantity of oil exported exceeded 574,000 gallons and in 1917-18, 488,000 gallons. In 1922-23 despatches amounted to 426,700 gallons. In 1924-25, shipments reached the record figure of 512,604 gallons but since 1926-27, the trade has considerably receded and during recent years the average quantity exported has declined to only 235,000 gallons in a year.

Rape and mustard oil.

TABLE NO. 102.—*Quantities and values of rapeseed and mustard seed and rape and mustard oil exported in 1913-14, 1918-19 and from 1932-33 onwards.*

Article.	1913-14.	1918-19.	1932-33.	1933-34.	1934-35.	1935-36.
Rape Seed—						
Quantity (Tons)	249,005	79,662	114,546	73,463	36,934	19,021
Value (£) . .	2,851,711	968,811	1,159,983	610,757	317,946	193,408
Mustard Seed—						
Quantity (Tons)	5,104	1,888	3,655	3,389	2,773	2,117
Value (£) . .	70,724	48,821	45,457	39,738	36,750	30,521
Rape and Mustard Oil—						
Quantity (Galls.)	407,178	265,672	226,187	262,933	295,095	236,799
Value (£) . .	48,624	56,532	26,192	23,148	25,901	25,840

Karachi, Bombay, and Calcutta, are the principal ports concerned. The unit of sale is the Indian maund at the former port and the bazaar maund at the latter, while shipment is made from Calcutta in half-cases of 78 lbs. and from Karachi in tins of 17½ seers to 18 seers.

Rapeseed cake.

Rapeseed cake, though accepted on the Continent as cattle fodder, is chiefly used in the United Kingdom for manurial purposes. Japan has always been a good market for Indian rapeseed cake, with Ceylon as next in importance. The quantity of rapeseed cake (together with sesamum cake) exported in 1935-36, was 20,638 tons, valued at £108,587 the principal recipients being Japan and Ceylon. The bulk of the shipments goes from Bengal and Madras.

Sesamum.

Area and production.

The seed of *sesamum indicum*, an annual plant thriving in the tropical and sub-tropical parts of the world and variously known to the trade as *til*, *teel*, *gingelly* or *sesame*, yields a valuable oil. The seed is generally grown in India, except in the United Provinces, as a pure crop. The normal yield per acre varies in different provinces, as is indicated in the statement below.

TABLE No. 103.—*The Normal yield per acre of sesamum in different provinces.*

Ajmer-Merwara.	Bengal.	Bihar and Orissa.	Bombay.	Burma.	C. P. and Berar.	Madras.	United Provinces.
lbs.	lbs.	lbs.	lbs.	lbs.	lbs.	lbs.	lbs.
72	610	350	400 *{ 284 (*g*) 320 (*h*)	160	210	301	280

* Refers to Sind.

(*g*) Irrigated.

(*h*) Un-irrigated.

Cultivation extends to almost all the provinces of India but the crop is raised most extensively in Bombay, Burma, Madras and in the Central Provinces. The all-India total in a good average year may be placed at 6,000,000 acres, and the output at 525,000 tons. The following table illustrates the distribution of the crop and the annual yield in 1913-14, 1918-19 and from 1931-32 onwards.

TABLE No. 104.—*Acreage and yield of sesamum in 1913-14, 1918-19 and from 1931-32 onwards.*

Provinces and States.	1913-14.	1918-19.	1931-32.	1932-33.	1933-34.	1934-35.
Ajmer-Merwara	(a)	(a)	20,000	21,000	24,000	21,000
Bengal . .	241,000	218,000	161,000	161,000	158,000	158,000
Bihar and Orissa (b) . .	219,700	194,000	200,000	200,000	205,000	202,000
Bombay (including Sind) .	851,200*	217,000*	234,000	256,000	229,000	186,000
Burma . .	(a)	(a)	1,308,000	1,600,000	1,609,000	1,439,000
Central Provinces and Berar . .	865,700	497,000	505,000	604,000	570,000	338,000
Madras . .	809,300	681,000	747,000	836,000	836,000	653,000
Punjab . .	144,000	51,000	162,000	137,000	93,000	108,000
United Provinces .	378,400 850,000†	207,000 925,000†	330,000 882,000†	388,000 839,000†	438,000 902,000†	257,000 1,057,000†
Baroda State .	(c)	26,000	81,000	71,000	75,000	69,000
Bhopal State .	..	..	..	131,000	85,000	9,000
Bombay States .	(c)	(c)	457,000	372,000	462,000	431,000
Hyderabad .	612,000	512,000	508,000	601,000	581,000	509,000
Rajputana (Kotah) .	(a)	42,000	44,000	39,000	40,000	38,000
Other Provinces	104,600	15,000	..	..	..	..
Total Acreage	5,076,000	3,585,000	5,639,000	6,256,000	6,307,000	5,218,000
Total Yield (Tons)	403,500	278,000	476,000	551,000	541,000	405,000

(a) Not available.
* Including Bombay States.
† Mixed crop.
(b) Excluding Orissa States estimates for which for 1934-35 are 209,000 acres and 13,000 tons as against 233,000 acres and 16,000 tons in 1933-34.
(c) Included under Bombay.

The new crop comes on to the up-country markets towards the end of November and sales are heavy till March. Five qualities are known to the trade, *white*, *black*, *mixed*, *yellow* and *red*, of which the first named is regarded as having the highest oil content. The chief port of export for this variety is Bombay.

In the last pre-war year the exports of sesamum seed from India amounted to 112,200 tons, only exceeded by China with 121,000 tons. Between 1870 and 1890 France was the principal customer for Indian sesamum and took nearly 75 to 85 per cent of the exports, but this proportion has declined since groundnuts displaced sesamum in the Marseilles market and the trade of the quinquennium, 1910-11 to 1914-15, indicated an average import of only 33,000 tons, out of India's total of 100,000 tons. In 1912-13 the position of the trade was as follows. The total exports amounted to 78,000 tons, of which 21,700 tons went to France, and 19,000 to Austria-Hungary and about 18,000 to Belgium, other importers being Italy and Germany with very much smaller quantities. The trade has gradually declined as a large proportion of the seed is retained for local consumption. The following statement indicates the percentage of exports to production.

Exports.

TABLE No. 105.—*Percentage of exports to production.*

Article.	Pre-war average.	War average.	Post-war average.	1933-34.	1934-35.
Sesamum . .	25	8	6	3	1

The increasing competition which Indian sesamum has to face in the world market from Chinese sesamum, West African palm kernels and the tendency of soap makers to utilize groundnut in preference has also accentuated the fall in exports. The following table shows the percentage of exports from India and China in the import trade of the two principal importing countries.

TABLE No. 106.—*Imports of sesamum seed into France and Italy (in thousand quintals).*

Countries.	1913.	1914.	1932.	1933.	1934.	1935.
France—						
Total imports . .	278	261	12	5	8	22
India . . .	228	251	1	..	..	..
India's percentage .	82%	96%	8%	..	..	..
China . . .	10	2	..	..	..	..
China's percentage .	4%	7%	..	..	..	..
Italy—						
Total imports . .	*	*	141	135	218	*
India (including Ceylon) . .	*	*	75	78	113	*
India's (including Ceylon) percentage	*	*	53%	58%	52%	*
China . . .	*	*	3	24	55	*
China's percentage .	*	*	2%	18%	25%	*

* Not available.

The distribution of the trade in the last four years as compared with the pre-war and post-war figures is indicated in the following table. There have never been exports of any magnitude to any other part of the British Empire except Ceylon.

TABLE No. 107.—*Share of the principal importing countries of sesamum in 1913-14, 1918-19 and from 1932-33 onwards.*

Countries.	1913-14.	1918-19.	1932-33.	1933-34.	1934-35.	1935-36.
	Tons.	Tons.	Tons.	Tons.	Tons.	Tons.
Belgium	33,800	..	..	..	3	1
France	22,200	150	183	167	62	..
Austria-Hungary .	19,000	..	..	..	..	..
Germany. . . .	16,000	..	200	385	110	..
Italy	14,000	..	4,596	8,454	783	5
Ceylon	1,517	613	416	802	680	198
Egypt	1,242	67	2,763	3,273	568	380
Aden	879	246	38	243	491	46
Other Countries .	3,563	1,308	2,126	1,937	1,551	670
Total Quantity (Tons) .	112,201	2,384	10,322	15,261	4,245	1,300
Total Value (£) .	1,796,841	46,076	146,243	166,456	56,467	20,235

The total exports of the world in 1934 amounted to 1,360,000 quintals of which India's contribution was 82,798 quintals only. The bulk of the shipment goes from Bombay through Sind. Madras and Burma have a small share.

Unit of sale and shipment.

In the Madras Presidency the unit of sale as well as of shipment is generally the single gunny bag of 164 lbs. nett. while in Bombay the weight varies from 168 lbs. to 182 lbs. The unit of sale in Karachi is the candy of 8 maunds and of shipment the bag of 164 lbs. and 168 lbs. Quotations for export are per ton of 2,240 lbs. nett. *c.i.f.*

Sesamum oil.

The percentage of oil in *til* seed is assumed to be in the neighbourhood of 40. Though the oil is generally extracted in crude mills, worked by bullocks, the better qualities are clear and nearly colourless. Most of it is retained in India for cooking purposes and as an illuminant or for anointing the body. The average annual export of oil from India was in the neighbourhood of 200,000 gallons before the war, but since then the trade has suffered a considerable decline and the average annual export now amounts to 100,000 gallons only. The distribution of the trade among the principal provinces in the last pre-war year and in 1935-36 is contrasted in the table below.

TABLE No. 108.—*Distribution of the exports of sesamum oil according to provinces in 1913-14 and in 1935-36.*

Provinces.	1913-14.		1935-36.	
	Quantity.	Value.	Quantity.	Value.
	Galls.	£	Galls.	£
Bombay	153,680*	20,991*	118,325	13,951
Sind	..	..	27,153	3,797
Madras	53,102	7,520	4,423	658
Bengal. . . .	911	128	88	13
Burma. . . .	360	60	37	7
Total .	208,053	28,699	150,025	18,426

* Including Sind.

The Bombay trade, which is the most important, is mainly with Maskat territory and Mauritius and the war has not created any alteration in the direction of exports. Pre-war shipments from Karachi averaged only 3,000 gallons but the average had increased to 26,000 in the quinquennium 1929-30 to 1933-34. The destinations are mainly Aden and Maskat.

In Madras the principal ports of shipment are Tuticorin for the Ceylon market and Madras, Cuddalore and Negapatam for the Straits, and the demand is chiefly on behalf of the Indian *coolie* population in these colonies but the market is a small one. The following table shows exports from India in 1913-14, 1918-19 and from 1932-33 onwards, classified according to destinations.

TABLE No. 109.—*Share of the principal importing country of sesamum oil in 1913-14, 1918-19 and from 1932-33 onwards.*

Countries.	1913-14. Galls.	1918-19. Galls.	1932-33. Galls.	1933-34. Galls.	1934-35. Galls.	1935-36. Galls.
Maskat Territory and Trucial Oman	63,570	27,304	33,973	44,716	29,906	35,474
Aden and Dependencies	35,657	2,561	9,358	22,851	45,656	41,230
Ceylon	31,609	4,894	3,080	10,005	5,227	4,449
German East Africa	10,443	3,531	..	..	..	..
Straits Settlements	15,367	693	933	913	..	..
Mauritius and Dependencies	6,986	16,327	5,002	12,828	17,311	17,064
Natal	5,662	2,070	..	..	.	..
United Kingdom	4,196	79	18	9	8,580	71
Other Countries	34,633	55,041	22,691	12,779	19,640	51,737
Total Quantity (Galls.)	208,113	112,500	75,055	104,101	126,320	150,025
Total Value (£)	28,699	19,557	10,613	12,494	14,412	18,427

Unit of sale and shipment.

The unit of sale of the oil in Bombay is the maund of 28 lbs. and of shipment, the barrel of 400 lbs. Shipment is made in Karachi in tins of 17½ seers to 18 seers. In Tuticorin the oil is shipped in cases of 8 gallons and in Dhanuskodi in tins of 4 gallons.

Sesamum cake.

The export trade in sesamum cake is practically confined to Japan and Ceylon and to a small extent to the United Kingdom, where it is used for manurial purposes. The bulk of the shipment goes from Bengal and Madras. In India it is more commonly used as cattle fodder either alone or in conjunction with *poonac* (coconut cake). The combined total volume of exports of sesamum and rape cake in 1935-36, was 20,638 tons, valued at £108,587.

Cotton Seed.

Production.

In the matter of production of cotton seed, India occupies a position next only to that of the United States of America, contributing annually about 2,000,000 tons of the world's total of 11,000,000, but scientific utilization of the greater part of her supplies has scarcely yet been attempted.

Export.

Exports of cotton seed from India vary from year to year according to the season, for when there is any scarcity it is hoarded as winter feed for cattle, but even in a year of plenty they probably do not exceed 15 per cent. of the seed available. About 200,000 tons are required annually for sowing; and the normal consumption in the Punjab, as food for milch-cows, has been estimated at about the same figure. Considerable quantities are also crushed for oil and cake. The balance, available for export, which is estimated at 150,000 tons per annum, far exceeds the average annual exports for the last four years. The trade in cotton seed may be described as of modern growth, originating in inquiries from the United Kingdom for Indian seed, about the year 1900, in consequence of German competition in the Egyptian cotton seed market at a time when a scarcity of olive oil and sesamum in the market and the necessity of finding substitutes for the preparation of lard and margarine coincided with the discovery of a new process of hulling the seed cheaply. From 1901-02 onwards the value of exports progressed steadily until 1913-14. In 1900-01 the total was 11,250 tons only, but it rose in the following year to 101,800 tons and in 1910-11 to nearly 300,000 tons. A considerable proportion of the requirements of the United Kingdom—which has been the chief market for Indian cotton seed—are now met from Egypt at comparatively low prices. Indian exports of cotton seed have therefore precipitately declined during recent years, the quantity exported in 1934-35 being 636 tons only. The figures of total quantity and value and the percentage of shipment to the United Kingdom in 1913-14, 1918-19, 1919-20 and during the last five years are given below:—

TABLE No. 110.—*Quantity and value of exports of cotton seed and percentage of shipments to the United Kingdom for 1913-14, 1918-19, 1919-20 and from 1931-32 onwards.*

Year.	Quantity. Tons.	Value. £	Percentage to the United Kingdom.
1913-14	284,327	1,416,743	98
1918-19	1,454	11,810	*Nil*
1919-20	248,749	2,437,085	98
1931-32	11,655	44,636	92
1932-33	2,389	12,527	63
1933-34	5,575	24,356	60
1934-35	636	2,926	*Nil*
1935-36	730	3,391	7

The United Kingdom percentage in 1900-01 was 62 which rose to 98 in 1913-14, and the following two years. While the war lasted there was a progressive decline in the total exports of cotton seed, due partly to freight difficulties and partly to a fall in prices, but 1919-20 marked a recovery almost to the pre-war levels, which however, was not sustained in 1920-21 and the subsequent years. About 95 per cent. of the cotton seed exported in a normal year goes from Bombay, 3½ per cent. from Karachi and 1 per cent. from Madras ports Shipments of the seed are usually effected between January and July.

Trade Varieties.

The usual qualities of seed obtained in the market are (1) *Bombay*, (2) *Delhi-Cawnpore*, (3) *American* (from seed originally imported from America), all shipped from Bombay and known as *Bombay* in the United Kingdom market, (4) *Comilla* (Eastern Bengal) chiefly shipped from Calcutta and (5) *Rangoon*, exported from Burma. Of these (2), (4) and (5) are generally regarded as inferior as they contain a larger percentage of damaged and worm-eaten seeds. The *American* quality commands normally a small premium over *Bombay*, though it is the latter that is most extensively exported. Shipments from Karachi are mostly of varieties (2) and (3). Indian cotton seed generally belongs to the class known as 'white' or 'fuzzy', as in addition to the outer layer of true cotton fibre, it has on it an underlayer of fluff or lint which is not removed before shipment. It is valued in Europe on the basis of 18 per cent. oil, but the average yield of oil in India is considerably lower. In Burma the oil content is normally assumed to be 10 per cent. only.

Unit of Sale and Shipment.

The unit of sale in the Bombay market is the bag of 112 to 140 lbs., while contracts with the United Kingdom are per ton of 2,240 lbs. *c.i.f.* In Karachi sales are based on the standard maund of 82 2/7 lbs. Shipment is made from Bombay in bags of 112 to 140 lbs., from Karachi in bags of 110 to 165 lbs., from Tuticorin in bags of 210 lbs., from Cocanada in bags of 150 lbs. and from Dhanuskodi in bags of 121 or 123 lbs.

Cottonseed Oil.

In comparison with other vegetable oils, the production of cotton seed oil in India is very limited. The seed is not decorticated before crushing. In 1913-14 only 2,507 gallons were shipped, the entire quantity being from the Bombay Presidency, but while the war lasted there was an appreciable development of the trade in Burma where a good quality of oil was produced, the residue known as *foots* being sold in Rangoon for the manufacture of cheap soap. The oil was packed in Rangoon in 40 lb. tins at the factory and shipped mostly to the United Kingdom, but a considerable quantity also found its way to Australia. The following table illustrates the vicissitudes of the trade which had steadily reached a figure of 132,000 gallons in 1919-20 Due to the elimination of the United Kingdom market, the trade since suffered a marked decline, but in 1933-34 the United Kingdom suddenly reappeared with a big demand amounting to 354,000 gallons which was met by exports from Burma alone.

TABLE No. 111.—*Quantity and value of cotton seed oil exported in 1913-14, 1918-19, 1919-20 and from 1931-32 onwards.*

Year.	Quantity.	Value.
	Galls.	£
1913-14	2,507	347
1918-19	9,356	1,183
1919-20	132,486	25,762
1931-32	24,877	2,099
1932-33	172	27
1933-34	368,777	28,009
1934-35	122,932	9,591
1935-36	86,650	9,232

In Bombay cotton seed oil is sold in tins of 42 lbs. each. Sales are made in Rangoon per 100 viss of 360 lbs. and shipment in drums of 400 lbs. nett.

There is no considerable market in India for cottonseed cake as cattle fodder, as it is usual to give milch-cows the uncrushed seed, and there should be considerable quantities available for export, if fresh markets for the oil could be found. 10,000 tons valued at £50,000 were exported in 1913-14 to which Burma contributed half, though in point of production of seed her share was only 1 per cent., 90 per cent. of this went to the United Kingdom. In 1914-15 the effects of the war began to be felt and the value of the cake exported was only £31,000 and in the following year it dropped still lower to £23,000. The totals for 1916-17 and 1917-18 were £15,500 and £800, with a partial recovery in 1918-19 to £7,000. In 1920-21, 8,720 tons were exported, valued at £62,354, chiefly to the United Kingdom and Japan, and the corresponding figures for 1935-36 were 6,213 tons and £21,911, the principal destination being the United Kingdom. Outside Burma, the trade in cotton seed cake is confined almost entirely to Bombay, whence shipment is made in bags of 168 to 182 lbs. gross. The unit of sale in Burma is a 100 viss of 360 lbs. and shipment is effected in bags, weighing 200 to 224 lbs. nett.

Cottonseed Cake.

CASTOR SEED.

The castor oil plant (*ricinus communis*) has long been cultivated in India, but until the beginning of the nineteenth century there were considerable imports, doubtless for medicinal purposes, of the oil and no recorded exports either of oil or seed. Foreign trade in the Indian seed is indeed of comparatively recent growth. The plant is widely grown over India but the cultivation is most extensive in Southern India, *viz.*, Madras, Hyderabad and Bombay. The following table shows the acreage and yield of the crop in each province for the quinquennium 1930-31 to 1934-35.

Production.

TABLE No. 112.—*Area and yield of Castor Seed from 1930-31 onwards.*

Provinces and States.	1930-31.		1931-32.		1932-33.		1933-34.		1934-35.	
	Area.	Yield.	Area.	Yield.	Area.	Yield.	Area.	Yield.	Area.	Yield.
	Acres.	Tons.	Acres.	Tons.	Acres.	Tons.	Acres.	Tons.	Acres.	Tons.
British Provinces.										
Bihar and Orissa	55,000	8,000	54,000	8,000	52,000	8,000	56,000	9,000	55,000	8,000
Bombay including Sind	60,000	9,000	77,000	12,000	81,000	12,000	65,000	8,000	44,000	4,000
Central Provinces and Berar	46,000	9,000	38,000	8,000	39,000	7,000	37,000	7,000	32,000	6,000
Madras	283,000	28,000	330,000	33,000	355,000	38,000	305,000	31,000	278,000	23,000
United Provinces *	7,000	2,000	10,000	3,000	15,000	3,000	8,000	2,000	7,000	2,000
Total—British Provinces	451,000	56,000	509,000	64,000	542,000	68,000	471,000	57,000	416,000	43,000
Indian States.										
Baroda	60,000	6,000	66,000	6,000	78,000	7,000	81,000	5,000	76,000	2,000
Bombay States	43,000	6,000	46,000	7,000	48,000	9,000	51,000	8,000	76,000	8,000
Hyderabad	792,000	45,000	856,000	63,000	838,000	61,000	825,000	67,000	786,000	47,000
Mysore	111,000	7,000	106,000	6,000	111,000	6,000	106,000	6,000	94,000	5,000
Total—Indian States	1,006,000	64,000	1,074,000	82,000	1,075,000	83,000	1,063,000	86,000	1,032,000	62,000
GRAND TOTAL	1,457,000	120,000	1,583,000	146,000	1,617,000	151,000	1,534,000	143,000	1,448,000	105,000

* Excludes estimates for the mixed crop for which no reliable data are available.

The normal yield per acre which varies in different provinces, is indicated in the statement below:—

TABLE No. 113.—*Normal yield per acre in different provinces.*

Bihar and Orissa.	Sind.	Central Provinces and Berar.	Madras.
lbs.	lbs.	lbs.	lbs.
350	225	400	231

The average annual outturn may be put at 135,000 tons. The crop is sown from May to July and harvested in January and February; a late variety is also grown which is generally sown in September and harvested in March and April. Two principal varieties of the plant are cultivated. The oil, which, before the invasion of kerosene and electric light, was in scarcely less demand than coconut oil as an illuminant for the houses of Europeans and Indians alike, is deprived chiefly from the large-seeded variety: the wellknown medicinal oil from the small-seeded. The seeds after picking are sun-dried and husked and are then ready for the market. Four chief qualities are recognised by the trade, namely, *Bombay small seed (Deccan)*, *Madras small seed (Deccan)*, *Cawnpore and Calcutta*, The two-first-named are very similar and only differ in the port of shipment. The characteristics of Calcutta quality is a *bold* seed, and this is even more marked in the case of Cawnpore. Neither quality gives such a high yield of oil as the smaller seed. The crop comes on to the markets up-country in March and April but the bulk of the sales are completed by the end of May.

Though Java, Indo-China and Manchuria grow castor on a commercial scale, India yet commands a preponderating share of the world's export trade in the seed. The first recorded export was some 225 tons in 1877-78, but in the next year 11,880 tons were shipped and in 1913-14 134,888 tons. War conditions then emphasized the disadvantages of shipping raw material instead of the less bulky and more valuable manufactured product and while the exports of oil temporarily shewed satisfactory expansion, those of seed fell away. In pre-war times the United Kingdom took nearly half the exports About 80 per cent of the arrivals in the United Kingdom went to Hull to be crushed and the balance was re-exported to Russia and the United States. The United States trade, direct and through United Kingdom ports, has always been very steady The volume of exports to Germany in 1913-14 was, it should be remarked, nearly 100 per cent. above the average for the previous five years. A feature in recent years has been the improved demand from the United States of America and Spain; but the United Kingdom, France, Belgium and Germany have considerably cut down their requirements, as compared with the pre-war figures. The table below indicates the distribution of the trade in recent years as contrasted with pre-war and post-war exports.

Exports.

TABLE No. 114.—*Exports of Castor Seed from India according to destinations in 1913-14, 1918-19 and from 1932-33 onwards.*

Destinations.	1913-14.	1918-19.	1932-33.	1933-34.	1934-35.	1935-36.
	Tons.	Tons.	Tons.	Tons.	Tons.	Tons.
United Kingdom .	55,675	62,838	22,732	27,092	26,380	22,409
France . . .	20,989	16,735	16,788	13,025	9,180	14,578
United States of America . .	20,279	..	28,434	23,451	13,883	4,003
Belgium . .	14,822	..	4,010	300	..	733
Italy . . .	11,788	1,127	6,176	7,890	5,058	6,693
Germany . .	9,671	..	1,562	4,472	3,273	522
Spain . . .	975	..	2,803	2,325	2,826	2,820
Australia . .	589	1,278	963	869	1,850	1,969
Other countries .	1	11	2,422	2,135	6,299	6,241
Total { Quantity (Tons) .	134,789	81,989	85,890	81,559	68,749	59,968
Total { Value (£) .	1,336,649	1,534,228	930,048	746,470	608,114	6,23,608

The bulk of the seed is exported from Madras. The trade is centred at Cocanada The small seeded varieties, locally known as *coasts* and *verangals*, go from the former port, and, *salems*, which are large seeded from the latter. The export trade from Bombay comes next in importance, and, comprises the production of Berar and Hyderabad, in addition to that of the Presidency. The exports from Calcutta are usually from Bihar and the United Provinces.

In 1918-19 to satisfy the increasing demands of the Air Ministry, the Director of Oils and Seeds Supply in London made arrangements for the purchase of Indian castor seed on lines similar to those for linseed. Under this scheme, over 40,000 tons of castor seed were shipped from Bombay, 11,000 tons from Madras and 3,200 from Calcutta.

The distribution of the trade among the principal maritime provinces in the last pre-war year is contrasted below with that for 1935-36. It will be noted that the share of Madras has increased remarkably at the expense of that of Bombay.

TABLE No. 115—*Share of the principal provinces in the export of Castor Seed from India in 1913-14 and 1935-36.*

Provinces.	1913-14.		1935-36.	
	Quantity.	Percentage.	Quantity.	Percentage.
	Tons.		Tons.	
Bengal.	9,989	7	10,066	17
Bombay	115,389	85	31,197	52
Sind	..	..	320	·5
Madras	9,428	7	18,385	30
Burma.	..	..	..	..

The unit of sale as well as of shipment in Bombay is the bag of 168 to 196 lbs. In Calcutta the unit of sale is the bazaar maund while shipment is effected in bags of 180 lbs. In Madras the unit of shipment is the bag of 165 lbs. Quotations for export are per ton of 2,240 lbs. nett, *c.i.f.*

Unit of sale and shipment.

Castor oil figured in India's export trade much earlier than castor seed, 20,207 lbs. being sold at the East India sales in 1804 at a price which works out at 22*s*. 6*d*. a gallon. In 1889-90, 2,664,990 gallons of oil were exported, but the primitive methods of extraction and inferior quality of the oil (due in part to deliberate adulteration) turned the scale thereafter in favour of the export of seed and the pendulum did not swing back again until after the outbreak of war. In 1912-13 the total had fallen below a million gallons, of which nearly the whole went to the United Kingdom and British Possessions, particularly to Australia and New Zealand. The following table shows the figures of export for the last four years as contrasted with the pre-war and post-war shipments. The oil content of castor seed is about 40 per cent.

Castor Oil.

TABLE No. 116 —*Quantity and value of castor oil exported in 1913-14, 1918-19 and from 1932-33 onwards.*

—	1913-14.	1918-19.	1932-33.	1933-34.	1934-35.	1935-36.
Quantity (Galls.).	1,007,001	1,658,539	1,124,608	1,334,773	1,213,039	1,408,023
Values (£)	92,504	298,102	130,163	136,736	132,605	161,055

A good deal of the country-pressed oil is retained for home consumption, chiefly as a lubricant and an illuminant. Large quantities are also utilized for dressing leather and in the manufacture of Turkey red oil. A considerable quantity of Madras-grown castor seed is railed to Calcutta for crushing. There are a great number of small oil mills in the neighbourhood of Calcutta working with castor, in addition to a few European-managed concerns.

Even with the improvement in the volume of export between 1915 and 1918, the figures of 1889-90 were not attained, and, after the armistice, there was again a marked set-back, though the great enhancement in price, which meanwhile took place, raised the total values above the pre-war level. The trade had been subject to fluctuations but in recent years, there has been a steady improvement in the overseas demands, and the shipments have exceeded the pre-war level, though they are still below the post-war figures. The distribution of the trade is illustrated in the following table.

TABLE NO. 117.—*Exports of Castor Oil from India in 1913-14, 1918-19 and from 1932-33 onwards according to countries.*

Countries.	1913-14.	1918-19.	1932-33.	1933-34.	1934-35.	1935-36.
	Galls.	Galls.	Galls.	Galls.	Galls.	Galls.
Australia . . .	360,252	14,977	8,244	10,845	13,985	6,611
New Zealand . .	146,659	58,997	34,555	30,000	30,848	19,550
Straits Settlements .	141,414	3,073	8,067	9,654	9,178	8,351
Mauritius . . .	92,050	17,069	13,865	27,339	22,131	18,135
United Kingdom . .	87,256	893,776	766,976	752,876	612,381	957,656
Ceylon . . .	73,730	11,930	23,416	27,222	18,223	17,524
Union of South Africa .	59,659	26,530	26,625	43,265	36,577	63,585
Siam	16,273	336	..	..	120	..
Portuguese East Africa	8,365	..	2,618	1,871	169	..
Italy	..	627,173	..	19,920	27,312	..
Denmark . . .	..	..	21,856	16,691	21,876	19,103
Belgium . . .	..	..	15,539	22,572	38,148	25,080
Germany . . .	..	..	158,520	240,452	260,864	152,985
Netherlands . .	..	..	6,000	52,849	51,040	27,054
Sweden . . .	..	..	2,496	12,420	27,304	25,779
United States of America	..	..	6,733	3,600	..	3,000
Canada . . .	..	..	24,656	53,444	20,353	6,240
Other Countries . .	21,043	4,678	4,442	9,753	22,530	57,370

The total imports of castor oil into the United Kingdom in 1914 and 1915 were only 196,000 and 177,000 gallons, respectively, but with the increasing demand for herself and her Allies of this oil for the lubrication of areoplane engines the total for 1916 was over 1,300,000 gallons, of which India supplied 1,220,000 gallons The figures for 1917-18 and 1918-19 were 1,086,000 and 893,800 gallons, respectively. The feature of the returns in recent years is the preponderating share once more taken by the United Kingdom.

Unit of sale and shipment.

In 1933-34, 70 per cent. of the oil was shipped from Bombay. 19 per cent. from Madras and 11 per cent from Calcutta. The Unit of sale in Bombay is the tin of 7 lbs. and 40 lbs and that of shipment the barrel of 400 lbs. In Cocanada shipment is made in drums of 400 lbs. and in Dhanushkodi in tins of 4 gallons. In Calcutta the unit of sale is the bazaar maund and shipment is made in cases containing 17 gallons or half-cases of 8½ gallons or in 5-gallon drums.

Castor Cake.

The actual production of castor cake is difficult to estimate, but the internal consumption for manurial purposes is considerable, particularly for tea and sugarcane. The presence of a poisonous substance, called ricin, remaining in the cake after the oil has been extracted, renders it unsuitable for cattle fodder In pre-war years the average quantity exported was in the neighbourhood of 6,000 tons. This fell to less than a thousand tons in 1932-33 but during the years 1933-34 and 1934-35 there was a marked improvement as is illustrated in the following table.

TABLE No. 118.—*Exports of Castor Cake in 1913-14, 1918-19 and from 1931-32 onwards.*

Year.	Quantity.	Value.
	Tons.	£
1913-14	4,902	19,385
1918-19	4,284	23,297
1931-32	1,813	6,841
1932-33	835	3,693
1933-34	2,434	8,564
1934-35	3,043	9,449
1935-36	1,704	5,375

Shipments are made from Bengal, Bombay and Madras and more than 90 per cent. of the total exports goes to Ceylon for manurial purposes in the tea estates. In Cocanada shipment is made in bags of 164 lbs. and in Dhanushkodi in bags of 168 lbs

Copra.

Coconuts, Area and Production.

It is estimated that the value of the products of the coconut in the world's markets in the year before the outbreak of war exceeded £70 million or nearly double the value of the world's output of rubber. The coconut palm (*cocos nucifera*) makes four principal contributions to commerce, *viz.*, (*a*) *copra*, the dried kernel of the nut, (*b*) *coconut oil*, the oil extracted from (*a*), (*c*) *poonac*, the residual cake, and (*d*) *coir*, the fibre derived from the husk surrounding the nut. A well distributed rainfall, a sandy soil containing plenty of decayed vegetable matter and not liable to become water logged and protection from strong winds are essential to the growth of the coconut The mean temperature should be from 75°F. to 85°F., and the mean annual rainfall should not be less than 50 inches. Coconuts grow particularly well close to the sea, but there is no reason why a plantation should not be successful up to an altitude of 2,000 feet provided that other requirements are fulfilled In India the tracts where the coconut flourishes best are the Kathiawar, Kanara and Ratnagiri districts of Bombay, and Malabar and South Kanara districts and the Godavari delta in Madras, the Indian States of Travancore and Cochin, the lower basins of the Ganges and the Brahmaputra in Northern India and the Irrawaddy delta in Burma. The total area under coconut cultivation in India has been estimated at 1,388,000 acres.

Whereas in exceptionally well-situated areas the yield of a single mature tree may run up to 200 nuts, the average may be placed at 50 to 75 nuts a tree and the outturn per acre may range from 4,000 to 5,000 nuts equivalent to one ton of copra. The acreage under coconut cultivation in the Madras Presidency has been estimated at 539,000 (of which more than half is assigned to Malabar alone) with a total annual yield of approximately two milliards of nuts. There are no large plantations under one management, and the industry has hitherto been almost entirely in the hands of small Indian cultivators. The produce of the Coromandel coast, as of Bombay and Bengal, largely disappears in local consumption. The total internal consumption of coconuts in India has been roughly estimated at 400 million nuts a year, but is probably much higher.

The most important coconut product, copra, which is the trade name for the dried kernel of the nut, had nearly doubled in price during the five years preceding the war. Malabar copra* is sun-dried in the sand by the sea-shore or in cemented yards (known as *barbecues*) under nets, the process taking from 5 to 10 days and at seasons when non-liability to damage from rain is practically assured.

The exports of copra from India never at any time represented more than a seventh of the world's trade in this article and have always been considerably smaller than those of Ceylon, whose exports in 1935 exceeded 48,000 tons.

Exports of Copra.

The value of the exports from the Malabar Coast ports trebled between the years 1908-09 and 1913-14, but since then has been steadily declining and during recent years exports have entirely disappeared.

It would seem that shippers have been experiencing great difficulty in securing supplies at prices acceptable to purchasers in the United Kingdom and on the Continent in competition with the Ceylon and Manilla product. Although coconut cultivation on the West Coast is extending and increasing the potential supplies of copra in the market, the exportable surplus has dwindled into insignificance. So far as this elimination of the export trade represents a larger internal demand for crushing purposes, it is to India's benefit, but it is not reflected in any larger shipments of coconut oil.

TABLE No. 119.—*Exports of Copra and Coconut Oil in 1913-14, 1918-19 and from 1931-32 onwards.*

Year.	Copra.	Coconut Oil.
	Tons.	Galls.
1913-14	38,191	1,091,477
1918-19	451	7,198,407
1931-32	27	36,174
1932-33	35	29.278
1933-34	33	31,611
1934-35	59	39,127
1935-36	48	32,742

In the five years preceding the war Germany took nearly 73 per cent of the exports of copra and only 33 per cent. of the exports of Coconut Oil. The copra was crushed at Hamburg, and in 1913-14 alone 30,236 metric tons of oil were shipped thence to the United Kingdom for conversion into margarine. The copra trade was therefore hard hit by the elimination of Germany as a customer, but the shipping season of 1914-15 was over before the war was declared. France developed a limited demand, but the United Kingdom took little until 1919-20. In the following table are shown the quantities exported in 1913-14, 1918-19 and during the last four years with the share of the principal ports.

*i e o'. the copra of the west coast from Mangalore to Cape Comorin.

Table No. 119-A.—*Exports of copra in 1913-14, 1918-19 and from 1932-33 onwards showing the share of the principal ports.*

Ports.	1913-14.	1918-19.	1932-33.	1933-34.	1934-35.	1935-36.
	Tons.	Tons.	Tons.	Tons.	Tons.	Tons.
Madras Ports . .	38,086	1	..	..	..	..
Bombay Ports . .	85	322	35	32	56	46
Total Madras and Bombay . .	38,171	323	35	32	59	46
Total All India .	38,191	451	35	33	59	48

Exports of copra experienced a serious set-back in 1918-19, owing to the difficulty of securing freight for such a bulky and unpopular cargo, and the only foreign shipment in the year from Madras ports was a paltry 13 cwts. to the Bahrein Islands, while the total for all India was only 451 tons. In 1920-21 and the following year the falling off is attributed to the high prices prevailing locally for copra but in 1922-23 Germany was an active buyer as well as the United Kingdom and a considerable, if temporary, recovery was recorded. Thereafter the exports have been declining and are now of scarcely any importance, the exports in 1935-36 being 48 tons only, the principal destination being Iraq.

Unit of sale and shipment.

The unit of export is uniformly the bag of 126 lbs., the copra being sliced into small pieces and so packed, but as it loses some weight in transit (about 2 to 3 per cent.) between India and Europe, payments are usually made on the basis of delivered weights. The unit of sale in Cochin is the candy of 600 lbs., and in Madras the Dutch candy of 672 lbs. Copra is practically all sold forward on *c.i.f.* contracts either to the United Kingdom or to Continental ports, but the majority of these contracts are put through in the commercial sale rooms in Mincing Lane, as the business is financed from London and worked almost entirely through London brokers. The season for shipment lasts from October to May in Cochin and from December to May in other ports, inconsiderable shipments being also made from Madras and Cocanda.

Malabar copra has for years commanded a higher price than any other in the world's markets, because it is wholly sun-dried, which is said to secure a higher oil content as well as a better colour, whereas elsewhere, as in Ceylon, owing to the uncertainty of the weather, much of the copra is dried artificially under cover over grills or in kilns or hot-air rotary machines.

Coconut Oil.

Copra has a very high oil content (from 60 to 70 per cent.) and the resultant product is not only in great demand for the manufacture of edible oils and fats but also in connection with soap making. The best Malabar copra yields a higher percentage of oil than that of Ceylon, West Africa or the Philippines. Before kerosene came into general use coconut oil was India's principal illuminant. It is still widely employed for toilet purposes. The export trade before the war was practically confined to the Malabar littoral, where the oil, though extracted for the most part in *chekkus* or primitive country mills of the pestle and mortar type, was of excellent quality and under the trade name of *Cochin Oil* commanded a premium of 15 to 20 per cent. in the world's markets as against *Ceylon oil*. There are now a number of power-driven concerns, known as 'chuck'* mills in Cochin, Calicut and Alleppey working on practically the same principle, except that the mortar and not pestle revolves, driven by small oil engines. While the yield of hot pressed oil is higher, cold pressed oil is of a better colour. The best Cochin oil, which is filtered before shipment, is so clear as to be scarcely distinguishable from water. The obstacle to shipment by tank steamer is the fact that coconut oil solidifies at about 70°F. The oil from Cochin and Calicut is shipped in puncheons of 8 or 10 cwts., in Hogsheads of 5 cwts, in cases of 74 or 78 lbs. or in cylinders of 5 or 10 cwts. The unit of sale in Cochin is the candy of 600 lbs. but the price usually quoted for export is so much per ton *f.o.b.* Cochin, the ton being according to the Cochin tonnage scale of 14 cwts. The unit of shipment in Calcutta is the 5 gallon drum, or cases and half cases containing 17 and 8½ gallons of the oil respectively. In the following table the exports and the principal destinations in the last pre-war year are contrasted with those for 1935-36.

TABLE No 120.—*Exports of coconut oil (Quantity and value) and the principal destinations in 1913-14 and 1935-36.*

Destinations.	1913-14.		1935-36.	
	Quantity.	Value.	Quantity.	Value.
	Galls.	£	Galls.	£
United Kingdom	223,756	31,759	14,167	1,335
United States of America	447,664	63,070	..	..
British Possessions	30,132	4,687	315	36
Germany	163,632	22,857	..	..
Netherlands	29,283	4,116	7,260	635
Belgium	43,571	6,212	..	..
Sweden	119,541	16,996	..	..
France	8,492	1,214	..	..
Italy	5,566	795	..	..
Other countries	19,840	3,367	11,000	1,228
Total	1,091,447	155,073	32,742	3,234

The United Kingdom, Netherlands and the United States of America are now the principal markets for Indian Coconut Oil. Coco-butter of good quality is being manufactured on a commercial scale at Pondicherry and at Ernakulam, and there is an increasing demand for the oil in connection with the numerous small factories making soap by the cold process, which have sprung up all over India

Ports of Shipment.

The trade has always centred in Cochin. Out of 1,091,477 gallons exported from India in 1913-14, the share of this port was 1,056,532 gallons. In 1934-35, 27,403 gallons were shipped from Cochin out of the total exports from India of 39,127 gallons. (The exports from Ceylon in 1913 exceeded 6½ million

* A corruption of the Malayalam word 'chekku' meaning 'a small mill' mentioned above.

gallons and in 1934-35, 15½ million gallons). A feature of the last two years of the war was a marked increase in the exports from Calcutta, where the mills to a great extent depended upon Ceylon for their supplies of Copra, whereas in 1915-16 and 1916-17 the exports of oil from Calcutta were in the neighbourhood of 23,000 gallons only, in 1917-18 the total rose to nearly 471,000 gallons and in 1918-19 to 2,500,000 out of an all India total of 7,200,000 gallons In recent years the share of Calcutta has shown a steep decline, the exports therefrom in 1935-36 being 93 gallons only out of the total exports from India of 32,742 gallons. Madras accounts for 75 per cent. of the exports, the balance of the trade being distributed equally between Bombay and Karachi.

Exports from Madras Presidency.

The exports of coconut oil from all Madras ports to foreign destinations declined in the quinquennium before the war whereas nearly 2,000,000 gallons went out in 1910-11, the total for 1913-14 was only 1,060,000 gallons. The same conditions however, which operated generally in respect of oilseeds, led to increasing quantities going forward during the war, and also to a larger proportion of the shipments of Cochin oil being made from other than Madras ports. Exports to foreign countries have shown a heavy decline in the post-war period owing particularly to smaller shipments to Europe consequent upon cheaper supplies being available from other sources. The exports in 1935-36 were 24,000 gallons only as compared to 1,060,000 gallons in 1913-14 and 3,885,000 gallons in 1918-19. Increased local consumption is also partly responsible for the decline in foreign exports. The coastwise trade has also declined to an appreciable extent during recent years, the exports in 1935-36 being 2,257,000 gallons against 6,970.000 gallons in 1918-19. The following table gives a conspectus of the trade of the Madras Presidency in the oil during 1913-14, 1918-19 and from 1932-33 onwards. For conversion purposes 240 gallons may be taken as the equivalent of one ton.

TABLE No. 121.—*Foreign and coastwise exports (quantities and values) of coconut oil from the Madras Presidency.*

Year.	Foreign.		Coastwise		Total.	
	Quantity (in thousands of gallons).	Value.	Quantity (in thousands of gallons).	Value	Quantity (in thousands of gallons).	Value
		£		£		£
1913-14 .	1,060	149,800	3,386	474,900	4,446	624,800
1918-19 .	3,885	464,640	3,085	392,800	7,970	857,500
1932-33 .	20	2,213	1,514	176,965	1,534	179,178
1933-34 .	23	2,219	2,587	208,872	2,610	211,091
1934-35 .	29	1,896	2,793	206,644	2,822	208,540
1935-36 .	24	2,267	2,257	199,013	2,281	201,280

The residue of the chuck mills mixed with a little gum arabic is *poonac* or coconut cake, valuable both as a food stuff for cattle and as a manure. Most of the cake remains in the country, but before the war there were inconsiderable exports to Germany. At that time the value of *poonac* as a cattle food was scarcely known in England, but since the war what little has been exported from India has found its way into the United Kingdom, Germany, Belgium and France

Poonac.

TABLE No 122.—*Exports of coconut cake in 1913-14, 1918-19, and 1931-32 onwards*

Year.	Quantity.	Value.
	Tons	£
1913-14	4,208	26,965
1918-19	1,100	5,428
1931-32	2,989	14,481
1932-33	2,795	13,314
1933-34	2,965	14,320
1934-35	3,457	16,549
1935-36	3,825	19,075

It will be noticed that the exports have again risen during recent years, the total quantity exported in 1935-36 being 3,825 tons against 1,100 tons in 1918-19.

The chief ports of export are Cochin, Calicut, Cocanada, Masulipatam and Vizagapatam. The unit of sale on the West Coast is the candy of 560 or 600 lbs. Shipment is made in bundles, each containing 168 lbs. to 170 lbs. nett or in bags of 1 to 1¼ cwts nett.

The following table shows the exports of coconut palm products from India in 1913-14 and 1935-36, respectively There are in addition considerable exports from the Travancore port of Alleppey, which during the war, largely diverted to Tuticorin and Cochin.

Exports of Coconut Products.

The trade in desicated coconut which has attained to such considerable dimensions in Ceylon has never yet been successfully exploited in India.

TABLE No. 123—*Quantity and value of coconut products exported from British India in 1913-14 and 1935-36.*

Products.		1913-14.		1935-36.	
		Quantity.	Value.	Quantity.	Value.
			£		£
Coconuts	No.	344,111	1,517	68,635	306
Coir fibre	Cwts	14,812	11,449	3,620	2,348
Coir Manufactures	,,	772,262	592,741	684,467	656,191
Cordage and rope	,,	60,420	70,189	48,163	51,393
Copra	Tons	38,191	1,039,826	48	1,324
Coconut cake (poonac)	Cwts.	84,166	26,965	76,500	19,075
Coconut oil	*Tons	4,548	155,073	136	3,234
Total value		..	1,897,760	..	733,871

* For purposes of conversion 240 gallons have been taken as the equivalent of one ton.

Mowra Seed.

Mowra, mowhra mowa or mahua seed is obtained from three species of *bassia*, *viz.*, *latifolia*, a deciduous tree, widely distributed in the Central Provinces, Chota Nagpur and Western India, the bulk of the seeds, exported from Bombay and from Calcutta belonging to this variety, *longifolia* in Hyderabad and Madras, and *butyracea*, grown in the sub-Himalayan tracts. Two grades of seed are recognised, known as *first* and *second* quality respectively, the former consisting of brown, yellowish seeds with a small percentage of damaged seeds, while the seeds in the latter are dark brown with anything up to 20 per cent. damaged and slightly damaged grains. The crop usually comes into sight in the month of June and the market is brisk until September.

Between 1907-08 and 1912-13 the exports of mowra seed from India averaged about 27,000 tons but the trade was marked by great variations. In 1913-14, 33,000 tons were shipped, of which Germany took 85 per cent. for soap and candle manufacture and Belgium accounted for most of the balance. In 1914-15 the crop is said to have been indifferent, and with Germany out of the market, only 7,500 tons were exported, of which over 5,000 tons went to the United Kingdom, which had not hitherto taken any interest in these seeds. Shipments in 1915-16 and 1916-17 averaged 4,200 tons only and practically nothing was shipped in 1917-18 or 1918-19, 5 000 tons were exported in 1920-21, but only 1,000 in the following year.

Exports.

Almost 60 per cent. of the shipments in 1922-23 went to Germany and Belgium and France shared the balance. Since then, the trade suffered a gradual decline, till 1926-27, when, due to an abrupt demand from Netherlands for nearly 9,000 tons, a considerable improvement was noticed. The recovery was, however, of a transient nature, and in 1929-30 the exports diminished to less than a thousand tons. In the next year, there was a slight increase, after which the trade practically dwindled into insignificance, registering no shipment in the last three years.

A country spirit is distilled from the flowers of the mowra, which are also a favourite article of food, particularly in the Central Provinces.

The seeds contain a large quantity of edible oil, which from the ease with which it solidifies is often called 'mahua butter'. It is largely used all over India as a *ghi* substitute or adulterant.

Poppy Seed.

While it is doubtful if the poppy plant would be cultivated in India were it not for the opium derivable from it, poppy seed at the same time forms an important secondary crop. The decline in the area under poppy will be discussed in detail in the article on opium.* The only areas in British India where the cultivation of

*See page 280 infra.

the poppy is permitted, under license, are the United Provinces and the Punjab Hills. Ninety-nine per cent. of the whole acreage is in the United Provinces. The average produce (at 70 per cent.) per acre is 20 lbs.—The table below shows the acreage and production of poppy in recent years. Three qualities of seed are recognised, *white*, *blue* and *red*, but the two latter are very difficult to obtain The seeds come on to the market generally in April and most of the business for the year is concluded by July. A great deal of poppy seed is consumed as food and the oil is widely used for culinary purposes, while poppy cake is realised by the poorer classes and by cattle alike.

Area and Production.

TABLE No. 124.—*Acreage and production of poppy from 1932 onwards.*

—	1932.		1933		1934		1935.	
	Acreage.	Produce at 70°.	Acreage.	Produce at 70°	Acreage.	Produce at 70°.	Acreage.	Produce at 70°.
		lbs.		lbs.		lbs.		lbs.
British India	37,012	856,608	27,227	656,045	15,611	267,316	8,268	135,591
Punjab Hills	831	3,170	1,235	2,314	1,821	2,973	1,463	1,874

Export figures not unnaturally have been on the decline since 1911-12 when 34,900 tons were exported, equivalent to about 16 per cent. of the estimated then available crop France, where the oil is extracted by the cold process for table purposes and as an ingredient in paints, has always taken the bulk of the crop, Belgium, Netherlands and Germany being the only other countries at any time interested in the trade. As in the case of other seeds dependent upon a Continental demand there was a very marked decline in the volume of exports while the war lasted. In recent years, there has been a precipitate decline in the volume of exports of poppy seed, due mainly to the deliberate policy of reducing the acreage under poppy cultivation in the country. The percentage of oil content by weight is 30. Seeds, the capsules of which have not been scarified for opium, give a higher yield than those which have. No figures are available regarding the exports of poppy oil from India which is generally extracted by the cold process, or of the residual cake.

Exports.

The bulk of the shipments goes from Bombay and the balance from Calcutta. In Bombay, the unit of sale and shipment is the bag of 168 lbs. to 196 lbs. The unit of sale in Calcutta is the bazaar maund, and of shipment, single heavy C bags of 155 lbs. nett. Quotations for export are generally per ton of 2,240 lbs. nett *c.i.f.*

Niger Seed.

Niger seed is obtained from *guizota abyssinica*, a native of tropical Africa which, since its acclimatisation in India, has become the chief source of European supplies. It has not and is never likely to be an article of first rate importance, as sesamum, which is grown in the same localities, gives a better return per acre. It is a spring crop, largely

Area and production.

sown mixed, the chief producing areas being Chota Nagpur, the Central Provinces, the Deccan and north-eastern Madras. From its resemblance to sesamum it is sometimes called *kala-til* (or black sesamum). The normal yield per acre may be taken at 300 lbs. and the percentage of oil to seed by weight as 35. No separate statistics of production or cultivation are available. Most of the seed is locally crushed and used for cooking, anointing the body and mixing with sesamum and other more valuable oils. The relative cheapness of the oil encourages its use as an adulterant.

Exports.

The history of the export trade in recent years is marked by variations. Shipments fell from 10,000 tons in 1911-12 to 5,000 in the following year. In 1913-14 there was again a slight shrinkage and in 1915-16 the total was no more than 589 tons. At one time half of the exports used to go to the United Kingdom but in the years immediately preceding the war an increasing share of the trade was taken by Germany and Austria-Hungary. The trade suffered a set-back in the post-war period but in recent years a gradual expansion in the volume is noticeable, though it is still far below the pre-war level. The following table shows the exports of niger seed according to destinations in 1913-14, 1918-19 and from 1933-34 onwards.

TABLE No. 125.—*Distribution of the trade in niger seed among principal importing countries in 1913-14, 1918-19 and from 1933-34 onwards.*

Destinations.	1913-14.	1918-19.	1933-34.	1934-35.	1935-36.
	Tons.	Tons.	Tons.	Tons	Tons.
Germany	2,029	..	1,265	830	836
France	1,047	.	15	20	95
Hungary	566	..	..	..	..
United Kingdom	367	10	331	244	334
Italy	50	..	.	1	..
Other Countries	48	14	636	494	734
Total Quantity (Tons)	4,107	24	2,247	1,589	1,999
Total Value (£)	42,926	492	17,577	10,540	18,203

The bulk of the shipments goes from Madras and the balance from Bombay.

Unit of sale and shipment.

The seed is chiefly shipped from Bimlipatam and Vizagapatam in bags of 168 lbs. The usual grade of quality is fair average of season, Europe cleaned. The unit of sale and shipment in Bombay is the bag of 168 lbs. to 182 lbs. The London quotations are generally per quarter of 376 lbs. in Madras, but in Bombay, it is the ton of 2,240 lbs. nett. *c.i.f.*

Coriander.

Coriander (*coriandrum sativum*) is cultivated all over India on account of its fruit and leaves. It is sown at different seasons in different provinces, frequently as a mixed crop, and perhaps on that account no estimate of the area under the plant or the annual outturn seems to have been attempted. The fruits commonly but erroneously called seeds yield a spice and a volatile oil, while the leaves are eaten as a vegetable and form a common ingredient in curries. The volume of the trade, though it has attained no great dimensions, was in the neighbourhood of 5,000 tons on an average in a year, till 1928-29. The trade shrank to less than 2,000 tons from 1929-30 to 1931-32, after which an improvement is noticed. The following table indicates the course of the trade in recent years, as compared with the pre-war and post-war figures The season generally runs from January to July.

TABLE No. 126.—*Quantity and value of coriander exported from India in 1913-14, 1918-19 and from 1931-32 onwards.*

Year.	Quantity.	Value.
	Tons.	£
1913-14	4,777	39,099
1918-19	4,839	65,347
1931-32	1,750	31,725
1932-33	2,571	33,793
1933-34	3,667	44,572
1934-35	3,273	33,212
1935-36	4,092	46,300

Foreign markets for Indian seeds were restricted, at any rate before the war, because their oil content is much lower than that of the coriander grown in Eastern Europe. The bulk of the traffic is from Bengal and Bombay with Madras and Burma, in that order, as next in importance The principal recipients are Ceylon and Straits Settlements.

Unit of sale and shipment.

In Cocanada the unit of shipment is the bag of 100 lbs., while in Bombay the unit of sale and shipment is the bag of 112 lbs. The unit of sale in Calcutta is the bazaar maund and the seed is shipped in bags weighing 164 lbs.

Cummin Seed.

Trade varieties.

Commercially there are two varieties of cummin seed distinguished in India *viz.*, the true cummin (*cumminum cyminum*) and black cummin (*nigella sativa*), to which perhaps may be added another variety which, on account of its appearance and its vernacular name (*shiyah zirah*), is very often confounded with black cummin There is good reason to believe that none of these varieties are indigenous, the original home of the plant being Egypt and the Mediterranean littoral and islands. True cummin is grown chiefly in the United Provinces and the Punjab but it is found in almost every province, the chief trade centres being Jubbulpore, Gujarat and Rutlam. Black cummin is not so widely distributed

No statistics of acreage or production are available in respect of either variety, but the internal consumption of both as a spice in confectionery and curries is considerable, and over 20,000 cwts. of true cummin and 15,000 cwts. of the black variety are exported annually, chiefly to Ceylon and the Straits Settlements. Practically nothing goes to the United Kingdom or to the Continent because of the extensive cultivation in Europe of caraway (*carum carui*). The exports of cummin (other than black) during the last six years are shewn in the following table. The chief ports of export are Bombay and Calcutta.

Exports.

TABLE No. 127.—*Quantity and value of cummin seed (other than black) exported from India from 1930-31 onwards.*

Year.	Quantity.	Value.
	Tons.	£
1930-31	836	51,844
1931-32	661	36,653
1932-33	258	10,791
1933-34	1,084	43,076
1934-35	1,211	52,684
1935-36	1,265	54,446

Shiyah zirah (*carum indicum*) grows throughout north-western India from Kashmir to the United Provinces and large quantities of the seeds are collected by hill tribes and brought to the towns for sale to *mahajans* It is considered superior in taste and fragrance to ordinary cummin seed and so much disappears in internal consumption that all attempts to export the seed on a considerable scale have hitherto proved abortive

Shiyah zirah.

Ajwan Seed.

Ajwan seed, the source of the valuable antiseptic *thymol*, is obtained from *carum copticum*, a herbaceous plant cultivated all over India as a *rabi* crop, belonging to the same genus as caraway. Two qualities of seed are generally recognised on the market, known respectively to the trade as *Indore* and *Kurnool*, of which the latter is regarded as superior. No statistics of acreage or production are available but the internal consumption is fairly large as the aromatic fruits are much in request for admixture in curries, etc., and in *pan supari*. A liquid obtained by distillation from the seeds known as *omam water* is commonly retailed in every considerable town up-country as well as an essential oil.

The export trade in this seed is marked by great variations. In the pre-war period, no more than 10,000 cwts. were shipped, during the war, the exports increased to more than 13,000 cwts., but in the immediate aftermath of the war, the trade dwindled to less than 2,000 cwts. Since the beginning of the last decade, however, the trade gradually expanded till 1925-26, when, it reached the record figure of 40,000 cwts. The volume then suffered an abrupt shrinkage to less than 500 cwts. and in recent years the average annual exports amount to only 1,000 cwts.

Exports.

Bombay and Calcutta are the principal ports concerned in the trade. The principal recipients in pre-war times were Germany, whose distilleries absorbed 80 per cent. of the shipments from India, the United States of America and, to a limited extent, Ceylon and the Straits. Little was directed to the United Kingdom, except during the war. Germany and the United States of America considerably increased their takings during the boom period of the trade.

In Bombay the unit of sale and shipment is the bag of 140 lbs. and in Calcutta shipment is effected in Single B. Twill bags of 140 lbs. nett. Quotations are generally based on the ton of 2,240 lbs. nett. *c.i.f.*

Thymol.

Ajwan oil is specific in cholera and colic. In the process of distillation a crystalline substance separates itself and settles on the surface which is known commercially as *thymol*, which is a valuable antiseptic. It is prepared on a fairly extensive scale in Central India and sold locally as *ajwan-ka-phul* or *flowers of ajwan*. The percentage of oil in the seed is low and usually does not exceed 3 to 4. The amount of *thymol* extracted from a given quantity of seed varies from 20 to 30 per cent of the yield of oil. High grade thymol crystals comparable with those manufactured in pre-war years in Germany were during the war successfully manufactured by two firms in India. Statistics of export previous to June 1917 are not available, but the quantity exported from Calcutta between June 1917 and June 1919 aggregated 10,500 lbs valued at £16,000. The principal destinations were the United States of America and the United Kingdom. The trade in *thymol* has diminished in recent years.

Bye products.

One of the bye-products obtained from the distillation of *ajwan* is the *thymene* which is a cheap scent utilised in the manufacture of soap. The demand in India for this oil is very limited, but in pre-war years German distillers made a profit out of the sale of *thymene* and the spent seed which enabled them to sell *thymol* itself at a price which barely covered the cost of the seed and the expense of distillation.

The spent seed makes an excellent cattle food, but so far it has not found much favour among Indian agriculturists, as the seed is not crushed or distilled to any appreciable extent. The whole seed is however used as a medicine for cattle.

Kardi (Safflower) Seed.

The seeds of the safflower plant (*carthamus tinctorius*), the flowers of which are utilised for the extraction of safflower dye, yield, when crushed, the *kusum* or *carthamus* oil of trade. In some localities, *e.g*, the Deccan, distinction is made between two species, one sown essentially for oil and the other for dye The former is extensively produced in Bombay: indeed, at the beginning of the century it was regarded as perhaps the most important oilseed grown in that Presidency, the chief centres of cultivation being the alluvial loams of Ahmednagar, Poona, Satara and Bijapur. It is also widely distributed in the Central Provinces and the Madras-

Presidency. The areas cultivated with the dye-yielding variety have shrunk in recent years, owing to the competition of chemical substitutes. Safflower being chiefly grown as subsidiary to some other crop, no statistics of area or production of seed are available. The export trade in this seed is not considerable. In recent years no shipment is reported from Madras while about 1,500 to 2,000 tons valued at £11,250 were exported in each year from 1931 to 1933 and about 600 tons valued at £8,148 during the year 1934 from Bombay.

In Bombay, the unit of sale and shipment is the bag of 168 lbs. to 180 lbs. and quotations are generally made on the basis of the ton of 2,240 lbs. nett *c.i.f.*

Carthamus oil.

The oil is extracted in two ways (1) by cold-dry pressure either before or after the seeds have been husked, and (2) by crude distillation in two earthen pots, one above the other, the percentage of oil in the seed being about 25. The cold drawn oil is of a clear straw colour and it is largely used for culinary purposes as an adulterant of *ghi* or tilseed oil and as an illuminant, while the hot drawn oil is converted into *roghan*, chiefly employed as dubbin for greasing well-ropes, leather etc. The seeds are excellent for fattening poultry, but the cake is more highly valued as manure than as a cattle feed.

TEA.

The trade in tea (the leaf of a species of *camellia*) represents a considerable proportion of the export trade of British India: and in 1935-36 amounted to 313 million lbs. equivalent to 12·3 per cent. of the total exports, an individual total only exceeded by cotton and jute.

The world demand for tea has been estimated as in the neighbourhood of 880 million lbs. annually and approximately 40 per cent. of the total is supplied by India.

Though the China crop is difficult to estimate with any approach to accuracy, as there are no annual statistics of production, India is now probably the largest tea producer in the world. The following table indicates the shares of the principal tea-producing countries in the world trade in recent years as contrasted with the pre-war and post-war figures.

TABLE No 128.—*Quantity of tea, exported to foreign countries in 1913-14, 1918-19 and from 1930-31 onwards, from India, Ceylon, China and Java.*

Year.	India.	Ceylon.*	China.†		Java.†
			Black and green.	Brick tablet and dust.	
	lbs.	lbs.	lbs.	lbs.	lbs.
1913-14 .	291,715,041	197,419,430	109,259,733	82,274,400	64,938,907
1918-19 .	326,645,780	180,817,744	43,422,933	10,445,866	61,853,000
1930-31 .	362,094,438	243,107,474	61,981,067	30,558,667	135,367,509
1931-32 .	348,316,264	243,969,970	65,154,000	30,556,800	145,292,100
1932-33 .	385,394,897	252,823,755	56,236,533	30,904,267	141,470,350
1933-34 .	329,151,630	216,060,773	60,095,366	32,379,625	130,910,988
1934-35 .	343,767,641	218,694,956	66,454,788	37,241,649	113,184,216

* Figures from 1918-19 onwards relate to the calendar year.

† For calendar year.

In the latter half of the eighteenth century, the most profitable trade of the East India Company with the United Kingdom was in tea from China, of which it had the monopoly, though the exorbitant import duty encouraged a great deal of smuggling. In 1787 over 20,000,000 lbs. were shipped and in the following year the suggestion emanated from Kew that experimental cultivation should be made in India, so that in the event of trouble with the Chinese authorities an alternative source of supply might be available. Little however was done until 1834 when Lord William Bentinck, the then Governor General, unaware, that the tea-plant was indigenous in Assam, warmly took up the matter, and appointed officers to proceed to China and collect tea seed and expert Chinese labour. Three missions in all were sent to China and much money unprofitably spent on exploiting imported in preference to indigenous seed. The first samples of teas grown on the Government plantations in Assam were sent to England in 1838 and the first Calcutta sale held three years later. It was not until 1852 that it was established that Indian tea was in a position to compete on the London market with China tea, but thereafter progress was so rapid that the Government's direct connection ceased in 1865. In 1868, the exports totalled 8,000,000 lbs. The first private company to be formed was the Assam Company in 1839 with a capital of £500,000, which purchased the Government plantations at Sibsagar in the following year. Tea was experimentally started in the Darjeeling district in 1840 and in the same year introduced into the Chittagong district The first garden in Cachar was opened in 1855. The industry in the Terai started in the year 1862 and in the Western Duars, where the climate and soil have proved extremely suitable for tea cultivation, twelve years later. The early years of tea planting were marked by many failures, and when in 1853 the tide turned there was such reckless extension of tea cultivation and speculation in gardens. that another severe crisis occurred in 1866. The chief elements of weakness were then eliminated and subsequently the history of the tea industry in Assam and Bengal has been one of almost uninterrupted prosperity. In Northern India tea is cultivated only on a small scale, in the United Provinces in the Districts of Dehra Dun, Almora and Kumaon Garhwal, in Nepal and in the Chota Nagpur district of Bihar and Orissa. In the Punjab it is to be found in the Kangra valley, the States of Mandi and Sirmur and to a very small extent in the Simla Hills.

History of cultivation.

Tea has also been profitably cultivated in Southern India since 1853, chiefly in the Wynaad, the Nilgiris, and latterly in the Anamalais and the high range of Travancore, and depreciation in coffee values in the early part of the present century has led to the conversion of considerable areas, formerly under that plant, into tea gardens.

The production of tea in Burma is insignificant, and returns from that area have since 1920, when the acreage was less than 2,000, been discontinued. The tea grown in the Shan States is chiefly used for making *letpet* or pickled tea, which is eaten as a condiment and not drunk as a decoction.

Most of the more important gardens in north-east India are managed and financed by Calcutta agency firms, and the same tendency is extending in Southern India where the majority of estates used to be privately owned. Every garden of any importance has its own factory where tea is prepared for the market, as it is essential that the various processes should be carried through immediately after the leaf has been plucked. The better organised factories are elaborately equipped with highly specialised plant and are under the supervision of expert tea makers.

Method of cultivation.

The object of tea cultivation being to secure the maximum quantity of leaf of the best liquoring quality, the bushes are periodically pruned to ensure constant and plentiful 'flushes,' which is the term applied to the young tender shoots, which are hand plucked, chiefly by women and children

Acreage and production.

The total area under tea in 1934 was 820,700 acres, as compared with 818,100 acres in the preceding year. The area abandoned in the year was 11,800 acres, while the new extensions including replantations in previously abandoned areas, amounted to 14,400 acres, showing a net increase of 2,600 acres. Seventy-six per cent. of the total area lies in the Brahmaputra and Surma valleys of Assam and in the two contiguous districts of Darjeeling and Jalpaiguri in Northern Bengal. The elevated region over the Malabar coast in Southern India (including the States of Travancore and Cochin and the districts of Malabar, Nilgiris and Coimbatore in British India) contains nineteen per cent of the total.

The following table shows the acreage and production of tea in the quinquennium 1930—34. Black tea accounted for 395,576,000 lbs. in 1934.

TABLE No. 129.—*Area and production of tea according to provinces and States from 1930.*

Provinces and States.	1930.		1931.		1932.		1933.		1934.	
	Area.	Yield.	Area.	Yield.	Area.	Yield.	Area.	Yield.	Area.	Yield.
	Acres.	lbs.	Acres.	lbs.	Acres.	lbs.	Acres.	lbs.	Acres.	lbs.
British Provinces.										
Assam . . .	432,900	233,416,100	431,000	243,229,300	428,400	257,057,900	430,400	219,341,100	431,800	232,835,400
Bengal. . . .	199,100	96,991,100	198,400	88,482,100	199,000	108,876,300	199,800	96,658,500	199,900	98,402,000
Bihar and Orissa . .	3,700	809,200	3,700	886,500	3,400	672,000	3,900	1,094,100	3,900	1,032,800
Coorg	400	167,500	400	174,300	400	219,800	400	209,400	400	198,700
Madras . . .	69,900	26,439,500	72,400	27,508,500	74,000	29,660,800	75,800	29,295,300	75,500	29,342,000
Punjab . . .	9,700	1,896,300	9,700	1,902,200	9,700	1,368,600	9,600	2,111,100	9,600	2,339,700
United Provinces . .	6,300	1,822,700	6,300	1,366,600	6,300	1,299,800	6,200	1,732,900	6,300	1,786,000
Total—British Provinces . .	722,000	361,542,400	721,900	363,549,500	721,200	399,155,200	726,100	350,442,400	727,400	365,936,600
Indian States.										
Cochin . . .	500	61,700	500	59,200	500	88,800	1,600	515,400	1,600	553,200
Mysore . . .	4,000	199,000	4,000	187,500	4,200	153,800	4,000	198,400	4,400	192,600
Travancore . . .	68,600	28,028,300	71,000	28,673,100	74,700	32,641,000	76,300	30,735,000	77,300	31,112,700
Tripura (Bengal) . .	8,400	1,249,400	8,500	1,614,200	8,900	1,630,500	9,900	1,783,200	9,900	2,300,500
Total—Indian States .	81,500	29,538,400	84,900	30,534,000	88,300	34,514,100	91,800	33,232,000	93,200	34,159,000
GRAND TOTAL .	803,500	391,080,800	806,800	394,083,500	809,500	433,669,300	817,900	383,674,400	820,600	400,095,600

The total quantity of green tea produced in 1934 was 4,519,500 lbs. as compared with 4,923,900 lbs. in the preceding year. The quantity manufactured in each tract in 1933 and 1934 is shewn in the statement appended below.

TABLE No. 130.—*Quantity of green tea manufactured in each tract in 1933 and 1934.*

Countries.	Production.	
	1933 (1,000 lbs.).	1934 (1,000 lbs.).
Northern India	3,357	3,358
Surma and Brahmaputra Valley	885	519
Bengal and Bihar and Orissa	682	643
	4,924	4,520

Of the total area of 820,700 acres in 1934, 765,300 acres were reported to have been plucked, as against 755,300 acres in the preceding year.

The total number of plantations were 5,132 in 1934 as against 4,974 in the previous year. The sizes of the plantations vary in different provinces. The acreage under the plantations in 1934 in different provinces is indicated in the following statement.

TABLE No. 131.—*Number and area of tea plantations in 1934 in India.*

Provinces. 1	No. of plantations. 2	Total * area (acres). 3	Average * area per plantation (acres). 4
British India—			
Assam	1,046	430,417	412
Bengal	385	199,796	519
Bihar and Orissa	26	3,884	149
United Provinces	42	6,226	148
Punjab	2,564	9,628	4
Madras	798	75,753	95
Coorg	1	415	415
Total—British India	4,862	726,119	..
Indian States—			
Tripura (Bengal)	49	9,953	203
Travancore	200	76,296	381
Mysore	14	4,070	291
Cochin	7	1,627	232
Total—Indian States	270	91,946	..
GRAND TOTAL	5,132	818,065	..

* The figures in columns 3 and 4 of the statement relate only to tea-bearing areas and do not include the area in the occupation of planters but not utilised in the cultivation of tea.

Evidence of the prosperity enjoyed by the tea industry during the war is furnished by the extension of gardens in the chief tea-producing districts. In Assam, the area under tea has increased since 1914 by 63,000 acres, in Bengal by 43,700 acres, in Madras by 48,700 acres and in Travancore by 38,900 acres.

Tea cultivation postulates a warm, sub-tropical humid climate, and a well-distributed rainfall of not less than 60 inches annually. In India the tea plant is raised not from cuttings or layers but from seed, and the bushes, which are allowed to grow more than three feet high and trained to give a good spread of plucking surface, are in full bearing by the sixth or eighth year. The average yield from Indian tea gardens per acre plucked has increased in the last forty-six years from 334 to 523 lbs. The highest production in 1934 was in Lakhimpur (Assam), namely, 684 lbs. per acre, and the lowest in Hazaribagh, namely, 21 lbs.

Out of 5,132 tea-plantations, returns of area and production were furnished in 1934 by 5,035 planters.

Manufacture
(1) Black Tea.

Black tea is prepared from young shoots (composed of one, two or three leaves and the bud), of the tea plant *Thea Sinensis*, which after plucking from the bush are withered by spreading on wire netting or on hessian cloth frames in a withering house The shoot is thereby reduced to a flaccid condition for rolling, and its moisture content is reduced under normal conditions from about 75 per cent. to 60-65 per cent. in about 18 hours. The leaf is then rolled and fermented. Rolling bruises the tissues and exposes the leaf juices to atmospheric oxidation whereby the characteristic red brown colour of tea liquor is produced. Rolling occupies usually between 1 and 1½ hours and is followed by 1 to 3 hours fermentation on any clean surface in a cool place usually on a cement or tiled floor. The leaf is then dried in a machine, by a draught of air heated usually to between 180°F. and 200°F. It is then cut and sorted into grades. These are normally Broken Orange Pekoe, Orange Pekoe, Orange Fannings (fine tippy grades), Broken Pekoe. Pekoe, Broken Pekoe Souchong, Pekoe Fannings and Dust (coarser grades). Other grades not made in general, are Flowery Orange and Broken Orange Pekoes, Pekoe Souchong and Broken Tea.

The grades are packed in paper and metal—lined chests of 3-ply wood.

(2) Green tea.

During 1934 only 4·52 million lbs. of green tea were manufactured in British India, as compared with 4·92 million lbs. in the preceding year It is not necessary to comment at length on the stages of manufacture beyond stating that the object is to prevent the possibility of fermentation, and that instead of being withered the pluckings are steamed. Seventy-four per cent. of the green tea produced in India in 1934 came from Northern India, nearly half the quantity being from the Kangra valley (Punjab), and the remaining quantity from the Dehra Dun (United Provinces), Ranchi (Bihar and Orissa), Nowgong and Sylhet (Assam) and Jalpaiguri (Bengal), in that order.

The principal leaf grades are Young Hyson, corresponding to Orange Pekoe, Hyson No. 1 to Pekoe, Hyson No. 2 to Pekoe Souchong, Gun-powder, Twankay, Fannings and Dust.

The trade in green tea has never been considerable, on an average 600,000 lbs. were shipped annually, the principal recipients being the United Kingdom, Canada and the United States of America. In the last few years, the trade has dwindled into insignificance.

Brick tea.

No separate statistics are maintained in respect of the acreage, production and exports of brick tea Small quantities of brick tea are made in the Darjeeling and Kumaon divisions for the Tibetan and Bhutan markets, but practically the trade has no commercial value. There was however a considerable trade in 'dust' tea to the Chinese ports of Hankow and Shanghai, where it was manufactured into brick tea for the Russian market. The pre-war average was about 8,000,000 lbs annually, and the war average over 6,000,000 lbs. During the last four years only two shipments of 78 and 221 lbs. respectively are recorded.

Labour.

As regards the labour force employed on the tea gardens, the most recent report on the production of tea in India gives the total as 905,555, of which 847,858 were permanently employed and 57,697 temporarily employed, equivalent roughly to one cooly per acre of area under cultivation. Compared with the figures of the preceding year, there was an increase of 39,995 in permanent employees, and of 1,057 in temporary hands. The distribution of the labour in different provinces is indicated in the statement below.

TABLE No 132—*Distribution of labour in different provinces.*

Provinces.	Persons employed (daily average).		
	Garden labour (permanent).	Outside labour (permanent).	Outside labour (temporary).
Assam	479,210	28,023	33,180
Bengal	182,968	5,181	6,608
Bihar and Orissa	1,405	714	602
United Provinces	1,912	600	1,234
Punjab	1,128	2,806	6,794
Madras	60,340	3,389	5,950
Coorg	370	..	..
Tripura (Bengal)	5,353	1,156	1,608
Travancore	66,572	1,151	1,247
Mysore	1,550	2,400	400
Cochin	1,630	.	74
Total	802,438	45,420	57,697

The question of labour is one of much difficulty. Speaking generally, all the important districts have to obtain their labour from considerable distances, and this involves a heavy outlay and an elaborate machinery to control recruitment. Assam has always had to contend with special difficulties in view of its remoteness from the recruiting districts in the United Provinces, the Central Provinces. Bihar and Orissa and the East Coast.

Following the recommendations of the Royal Commission on Labour in India, the Tea Districts Emigrant Labour Act. 1932 (XXII of 1932) was introduced. Act VI of 1901 being repealed. Important changes have been made in the recruitment of labour for Assam. There are now no restrictions on the *personnel* to be employed in recruiting but certain regulations have been imposed governing the forwarding of emigrants to Assam. 'Assisted emigrants' *i.e.*, persons who are going up to tea estates for the first time or after more than two years absence from Assam have been given the right of being repatriated with their families to their homes at their employers' expense after working for 3 years on a tea garden. The Assam Labour Board has been abolished and the new office of Controller of Emigrant labour has been instituted to supervise the working of the Act.

The average monthly wages of labourers employed in the tea gardens in Assam in 1934-35 are stated below.

	Settled labourers		Faltu or Basti labourers.	
	s.	*d*	*s.*	*d.*
Men	10	1·2	6	7·4
Women	7	3·5	6	5·3
Children	4	8·3	4	0·2

The earnings are supplemented by private cultivation and gratuitous supply of certain necessaries, such as fuel and grazing.

Transport and Shipping.

In Northern India tea is now transported by means of railway and river. Assam is served by the River Steam boat services on the Brahmaputra river; and the North Lakhimpur district, which possesses no railway, by a subsidiary service on the Subunsiri river, a tributary of the Brahmaputra. On the south bank of the river the Assam Bengal Railway and its branches and the Dibru Sadiya Railway run through the tea districts, and on the north bank the newly opened branch of the Eastern Bengal Railway has greatly facilitated transport in the Darrang district. Generally speaking tea for the Calcutta market is borne by steamer and the tea for direct shipment to London goes *via* Chittagong by the railway. The same applies to the Cachar and Sylhet districts which lie south of the Assam hills.

Teas from Darjeeling and Dooars are almost entirely transported by rail, and reach Calcutta, whether for sale or direct shipment, by the Eastern Bengal Railway, which has for its feeders the Darjeeling Himalayan Railway and the Bengal Dooars Railway in addition to its own branches.

On arrival at Calcutta rail-borne teas go to the Hyde Road Warehouse and river-borne teas to the Sale Tea Warehouse of the Tea Transit Sheds, Kidderpore Docks, where if for auction they are stored and lotted, and whence after sale they are eventually shipped.

Tea seed.

India has been an exporter of tea seed for some considerable number of years past and had been the means of supplying other producing countries with a superior type of plant. Figures are available from 1895-96 but the trade shows marked fluctuations. In that year exports aggregated 3,238 cwts. and in 1897-98, 5,371 cwts. but only 601 cwts. were shipped in 1902-03. The table below shows that the trade, which had recovered by 1913-14, showed a steep decline in 1932-33, since when exports have been almost eliminated as a result of the prohibition on export imposed with effect from the 26th May 1933. Shipments to Java in the two years prior to the outbreak of the war were peculiarly heavy, and in the following decade, very considerable extensions were made of the area under tea in the Dutch East Indies, to a large extent with British capital.

TABLE No. 133.—*Exports of tea seed from India in 1913-14, 1918-19 and from 1931-32 onwards.*

Year.	Quantity.	Destinations.
	Cwts.	
1913-14 . . .	7,847	Chiefly to Java, Ceylon and Sumatra.
1918-19 . . .	1,268	Ditto.
1931-32 . . .	12,620	Chiefly to U. S. S. R. and Egypt.
1932-33 . . .	1,300	Chiefly to Java.
1933-34 . . .	..	....
1934-35 . . .	120	To Kenya Colony.
1935-36 . . .	240	To Kenya Colony and Tanganyika Territory.

Month of shipment.

In a normal trade year the principal months for tea shipments are from July to December inclusive; but appreciable quantities also go forward in June, January and February. The curtailment of shipping facilities owing to tonnage scarcity altered all this even after the export trade in tea was controlled, and though the total volume of shipments during the war approximated to pre-war levels, the seasonal distribution of exports ceased to be so clearly defined.

Tea control.

Early in 1917 it became necessary, owing to the reservation of freight for articles of the first importance, to restrict the export of tea from India to the United Kingdom As a considerable balance of the 1916-17 crop was still unshipped, prospects were gloomy, but in November 1917 the Food Controller formulated a scheme for the purchase and shipment of 40 per cent. of the Indian tea crop between November 1, 1917, and May 31, 1918, which was operated through a Tea Commissioner in Calcutta. So successful was this scheme that the Food Controller raised his requirements by another 25 million lbs. and ultimately took all the tea that offered to fill the available tonnage. The feature of the trade in 1917-18 was the increase in direct shipments to the United States of America, where considerable quantities of Java tea had been dumped in the previous year. The embargo, placed by the Commonwealth Government on the import into Australia of China and Java teas, encouraged larger purchases from India as well as Ceylon. Persian buyers were also strongly in evidence. In the following year the Tea Commissioner took 66 per cent. of the 1918 crop including purchases on War Office account and the balance shippers were left to dispose of themselves.

All restrictions upon the export of tea to the United Kingdom were removed in March 1919, and in the year of record shipments, which followed, despatches to that destination exceeded by 54,000,000 lbs. the total of the previous twelve months. In no year have the exports of tea from British India been so great as in 1919-20, when 382 million lbs. were sent away by sea and across the land frontier. About 15,000,000 lbs. were sent direct to Canada and the United States of America in addition to nearly three quarters of a million *via* the United Kingdom ports. A reduction in army requirements accounted for smaller despatches to Mesopotamia. In 1920-21, the tea industry suffered a severe set back. The United Kingdom market was glutted with stocks, and the high percentage of coarse pluckings, which the pooling of all grades had encouraged when shipments were under control, led to such a slump that the price of common Pekoe Souchong fell from 1*s*. 3*d*. in March 1920 to 4*d*. in September. The complete elimination of Russia and the difficulties of finance on a rapidly falling exchange were other disturbing factors. Good prices, however, continued to be offered for the finer qualities of tea, and strenuous efforts were made to reduce the quantity and improve the quality of pluckings during the following season. The total shipments for the year fell to 286 million lbs. The tide began to turn again in 1921-22. As a result chiefly of deliberate policy, pluckings were materially reduced and the general range of qualities was unusually high, and practically the whole of a short crop had been sold by the end of February 1922 at prices sufficient to enable most gardens, inspite of the higher cost of production, to show a profit on the year's working. This favourable position was further consolidated in the following year, the most satisfactory feature of which was the steady advance in the price of common teas. Other contributory causes were careful plucking, the absence of any great variation in the rate of exchange and a reduction in freights. The prosperity of the tea industry reached its zenith in 1924-25. The world-wide reactions which attacked commerce after the immediate prosperous post war year began to make themselves felt in the tea producing countries in 1927 and during the next five years matters went from bad to worse as a result of overproduction by tea growers in their efforts to lower the costs of production to meet existing market prices, which reached their lowest point in 1932. At this stage tea was sold in the world markets at below costs and stocks had accumulated to such an extent on the London market that it was estimated that at the commencement of the next season, *i.e.*, 1933, when exports of new season tea would begin to arrive, there was over 7 months' supply of previous season's tea unabsorbed by distributors.

Later history.

The disastrous results of this overproduction by India were brought into sharp relief by an examination of the average prices obtained for teas in the Calcutta Auctions during season 1932-33 and the preceding four seasons:—

	Per lb. *s.* *d.*
1928-29	1 0·75
1929-30	0 11·34
1930-31	0 10·69
1931-32	0 7·41
1932-33	0 5·81

The prices obtained on the London market reflected a similar position in respect to teas imported from India, Ceylon and the Netherlands East Indies—the chief tea producers of the world.

Owing to this state of affairs a large number of estates in the three countries were on the verge of closing down with consequent repercussion on the economic system of their respective countries in the shape of unemployment, and the grave financial considerations involved in the prospect of the loss of so much capital.

International Tea Committee.

At this stage representatives of the tea industry in India, Ceylon and Java formulated a scheme whereby the exports of tea and tea seed from their respective countries and extensions of tea areas should be regulated for a period of five years commencing from 1st April 1933 in order to restore equilibrium between supply and demand, and which was to be enforced by legislation in each country before becoming effective. An agreement was reached by the three countries.

This was not the first time during these years of depression that the three countries had collaborated to improve the situation, as in 1930 an agreement was arrived at and put into execution for the voluntary restriction of crop. This however was not continued as it was impossible to enforce the terms of the agreement.

International Tea Agreement.

The International Tea Agreement embraced the following articles *viz.*:—

1. That the exports of tea from the producing countries be regulated in order to restore equilibrium between supply and demand.
2. That the Government of the respective countries will undertake to prohibit exports in excess of the quotas agreed upon.
3. That the standard upon which regulation is based shall be fixed on the maximum exports from each country reached in any of the three years 1929, 1930, or 1931.
4. That the commencing degree of regulation for the first year shall be 85 per cent. of the standard export, and that a Committee shall be set up representing all the Associations interested, which taking into due consideration stocks and the price of tea, shall fix—prior to the expiry of each year—the figure of regulation for the following year.
5. That the agreement shall be for a period of five years.
6. That it will be part of the agreement that the existing tea areas must not be extended during the said period of five years except in special cases where the existence of an estate would otherwise be imperilled, and that no further areas must be sold or leased out for tea cultivation and that no planting of tea must take place on land now carrying other products. Under no circumstances should such extensions and new planting exceed one-half of one per cent. of the present total planted tea area of each territory, and the respective Governments should be asked to make a binding regulation to the above effect.

7 That the conclusion and continuation of the agreement should be made dependent on the enforcement of the regulation by the Governments of all the territories concerned.

Standard Year Basis for Export Quota.

In accordance with Article 3 of the International Tea Agreement India selected 1929 as her standard year when she exported by sea and land 382,594,779 lbs. of tea and by Article 4, her total export quota for the first year of regulation was 325,205,562 lbs. of tea.

Legislation. Indian Tea Control Act.

In accordance with one of the provisions of the 1932 agreement each of the Governments of the contracting parties duly legislated to implement the terms of the agreement. In the case of India, due to pressure of business in the Legislature it was not found possible immediately to enact a statute and in consequence the Government of India enforced the required control over exports overseas by means of notifications under the Sea Customs Act. During the latter part of the year the necessary legislation was enacted which superseded the Customs Notifications. The Indian Tea Control Act (XXIV of 1933) came into force on the 15th November 1933. Prominent features of the control legislation are (a) that a tea estate is the unit of the scheme, (b) that an application for an export quota is to be made each year—the year being from the 1st April to 31st March, (c) that the right of the owner of a tea estate, to which an export quota is granted, to obtain export licenses is transferable subject to necessary proof of the transfer in accordance with the procedure laid down by the Licensing Committee being provided by the contracting parties, and (d) that teas covered by an export license but not placed on board ship on or before the 31st March in any year can be exported after this date by means of special export licenses valid up to the 30th June next.

Indian Tea Licensing Committee.

The administration of the Indian Tea Control Act was placed in the hands of a Committee representative of the various Tea Associations in India called the Indian Tea Licensing Committee, who appointed two executive officers to carry out their duties under the Act at their offices established at Calcutta in North India and Coonoor in South India.

Control of exports overseas.

India's position as an exporter differs in one respect from that of the other signatories to the International Tea Agreement. She is part of a continent and has, in addition to a vast sea-board, land frontiers in the North, North-East and North-West over which tea is exported in not inconsiderable quantities. In acceding to India's tea growers' request for legislation, the Government of India made it clear that they considered that the frontier trade was of a domestic nature, and that any tea exported was for the consumption of the inhabitants of the adjacent countries and did not affect the world markets, and such being the case they were not prepared to legislate to restrict land exports. They however indicated that should tea exports across the frontiers increase materially beyond the figures of previous years and in such a way as to show that the frontiers were being used to evade the sea export restriction and so affect world markets, they would be prepared to reconsider the question afresh in the light of such circumstances as were brought to their notice.

Accordingly India's standard year of exports taken to be 1929-30 was apportioned as between Sea and Land as follows:—

	lbs.
Overseas	**377,141,885**
Overland	**5,452,894**

and the first year of regulation of exports saw India entitled to export the following quantities of tea:—

	lbs.
Overseas	**320,570,560**
Overland	**4,635,003**

Allotment of Export Quota.

In order to apportion India's overseas export quota equitably amongst tea producing estates it was enacted that each estate's yearly quota should be based on the accepted maximum production of that estate in any one of the four years 1929, 1930, 1931 and 1932, allowances being made for young tea. This maximum was called the estate's crop basis. The yearly quota would then bear the same ratio to the crop basis of the estate as the total India overseas export quota bears to the total of India's crop basis. Along these lines Tea Estates were allotted an export quota for the first year, *i.e*, 1st April 1933 to 31st March 1934, of 64 per cent. of their accepted crop basis.

Issue of Export Licenses.

The procedure adopted by the Licensing Committee to facilitate the export of tea is designed to provide for the needs of both producers and distributors in India In the case of producers exporting direct from the garden overseas, a Direct Shipment Export License is issued on application to the Joint Controllers' offices covering a stated quantity of tea, which is set against the quota allotted to the garden for export. The export license is then delivered to the Customs Authority at the port of shipment by the shipper and thereafter the tea is placed on board ship. These licenses are issued throughout the season provided the unexhausted balance of quota is sufficient to meet the application. The needs of distributors are provided for by the method of crediting to deposit accounts opened by them with the Licensing Committee, the weight of teas purchased for export from producers and charging a similar weight to the export quota accounts of the producers concerned Export Licenses are then issued on application to the Joint Controllers' offices to export a stated quantity of tea, as required, provided a sufficient balance is available in the account to cover the weight so stated The above described system appears to have worked effectively as it is of a nature which enabled the Licensing Committee to meet such representations as the tea trade made from time to time in respect to difficulties which arose in the course of their business.

Considerable areas under tea are situated outside British India and are located in several of the large Independent States, chiefly in Southern India. As the control legislation is only applicable to British India, a means had to be found to lift the hardship which would have ensued had they been unable to export their teas. Accordingly each of these independent States enacted legislation along the lines of the British India Act and so enabled the Indian Tea Licensing Committee to allot export quota to their tea estates and exercise control over extensions of tea cultivation.

Control in Independent Indian States.

The Indian Tea Control Act regulates the internal movement of teas from British India to the Foreign Settlements within India. The Licensing Committee are empowered to issue a "no objection" permit for export of teas to these settlements. The permit takes the form of a guarantee against re-export and may be refused if it is thought that the quantities are excessive or that there is a danger that re-export may take place.

Control of exports in relation to Foreign Settlements and Independent Indian Maritime States in India.

Similar provisions are extended to the Maritime Indian Independent States whose ports do not come within the control of the Customs Authorities in British India or with whose Government there exists no agreement with British India to control the movements of tea through their ports.

As already stated elsewhere exports of tea across India's land frontiers were not controlled at the time the International agreement came into operation. As the overland exports were showing a tendency towards abnormal expansion, restrictions have now been placed on the export of tea, including green tea, from British India across the land frontiers to Iran. The trade with Afghanistan, Nepal, Bhutan and Sikkim is still considered to be of a domestic nature and unlikely to affect world markets. Generally speaking, the restriction scheme has yielded good results as will be seen from the following statement relating to the average prices of Indian tea sold at the Calcutta Auction Sales.

TABLE No. 134 —*Average prices of Indian Tea at Auction Sales in Calcutta, and average declared values of exports in 1913-14, 1918-19, 1924-25 and from 1932-33 onwards.*

—	1913-14.	1918-19.	1924-25.	1932-33.	1933-34.	1934-35.
	d.	*d.*	*d.*	*d.*	*d.*	*d.*
Average price of Indian Tea-price per lb. .	7·75	8	15·91	5·81	10·8*	9·9*
Average declared value of exports by sea—						
Value per lb. .	8·25	8·75	15·75	8·15	11·25	11·16

* With export rights.

TABLE No. 135.—*Exports of tea by sea from India in 1900-01 and every fifth year thereafter upto 1910-11 and 1913-14, 1918-19 and from 1931-32 onwards.*

Year.	Grand total of exports.		Exports to the United Kingdom.	
	Quantity.	Value.	Quantity.	Value.
	lbs.	£	lbs.	£
1900-01 . .	190,305,490	6,367,286	166,171,556	1,768,524
1905-06 . .	214,223,788	5,898,402	166,591,433	4,593,454
1910-11 . .	254,301,089	8,276,912	182,935,424	5,982,589
1913-14 . .	289,473,591	9,983,372	209,050,771	7,232,049
1918-19 . .	323,659,710	11,850,404	282,205,196	9,859,050
1931-32 . .	342,385,304	14,596,292	292,004,265	12,711,717
1932-33 . .	379,827,446	12,917,828	331,531,870	11,136,739
1933-34 . .	318,291,068	14,904,128	276,679,265	13,190,932
1934-35 . .	325,069,940	15,109,305	286,966,102	13,619,535

NOTE.—All the figures include shipments from the State of Travancore.

Supplementary details showing the distribution of re-exports from the United Kingdom to other countries are subjoined.

TABLE No. 136.—*Quantity of Indian tea re-exported from the United Kingdom to principal foreign countries in 1913, 1919 and from 1932 to 1934.*

Countries.	1913.	1919.	1932.	1933.	1934.
	lbs.	lbs.	lbs	lbs.	lbs.
Re-exported to—					
Irish Free State . .	...		15,140,863	15,407,702	13,700,680
U. S. S. R. . . .	6,979,883	1,057,057	5,471,580	3,167,713	880,271
Denmark . . .	269,872	955,988	429,868	3,94,881	377,185
Germany . . .	764,954	159,712	2,778,591	2,572,642	1,748,520
Netherlands . . .	2,026,331	6,390,984	1,633,621	1,239,304	1,269,428
Belgium . . .	115,575	357,081	141,477	141,064	125,066
France	124,649	191,835	107,597	121,855	68,907
Austria and Hungary .	259,119	74,506	88,294	54,870	42,900
Turkey (European)	81,954	328,886	187,356	185,993	93,425
Turkey (Asiatic) . .	170,992	51,593			
Portuguese East Africa .	184,743	2,105	...	...	...
United States of America	2,175,972	157,562	6,773,701	5,693,147	4,661,185
Canada	2,262,313	519,718	4,048,043	4,144,544	2,969,750
Chile	1,393,651	74,220	191,084	52,418	290,219
Argentine . . .	955,949	113,999	343,305	373,749	380,104
Channel Islands . .	792,082	382,582	1,713,779	1,695,715	1,122,485
Union of South Africa .	1,593,440	82,824	2,311	144,395	1,824
Newfoundland . .	71,330	9,227	39,853	22,697	21,818
Other Countries . .	1,607,665	1,860,615	2,463,788	2,815,208	2,284,819
Total—Re-exported .	21,829,974	12,769,989	41,555,111	38,226,347	30,038,081

The enhanced demands from the Irish Free State, Channel Islands, Germany and the United States of America account partly for the difference in the pre-war, post-war and the recent figures.

There are shipments of tea from all principal ports but 85 per cent of the trade goes from Calcutta and Chittagong while the

South Indian ports, including the ports of Travancore, account for the bulk of the remainder. No tea is grown in the Bombay Presidency, but some tea is railed from Calcutta to Bombay for shipment.

TABLE No. 137.—*Quantity of Indian tea shipped from the different ports in India in the years 1932-33 to 1934-35 with the pre-war and the war average.*

Ports.	Average pre-war quinquennium.	Average war quinquennium.	1932-33.	1933-34.	1934-35.
	lbs.	lbs.	lbs.	lbs.	lbs.
Calcutta	190,543,887	236,215,439	234,043,202	197,046,493	199,522,135
Chittagong . . .	55,205,248	52,454,854	89,781,504	73,775,533	76,939,842
South Indian ports including Travancore . .	19,009,766	24,961,267	55,827,614	47,273,487	48,375,435
Bombay and Karachi .	1,789,609	9,070,021	166,986	187,250	217,119
Burma ports . . .	173	9,612	8,140	8,305	24,409

The distribution of the export trade between Calcutta and Chittagong is not without interest. In the pre-war quinquennium, the ratio was about four to one, during the war the ratio increased to nearly five to one, but since then the share of Chittagong has increased, and the recent shipments indicate a ratio between three and two to one.

Trans-frontier trade. The following table shews the exports of tea across the land frontiers of India.

TABLE No. 138.—*Exports of tea across the land frontiers of India in 1914-15, 1919-20 and from 1931-32 onwards.*

Year.	* Exports.
	lbs.
1914-15	2,431,296
1919-20	3,238,256
1931-32	5,931,000
1932-33	5,567,000
1933-34	10,361,000
1934-35	18,698,000

Unit of sale and shipment. The unit of sale is uniformly the lb. *c.i f.* for London and *f.o b* for America. The unit of shipment is the full chest or half chest which varies in weight according to the fineness or coarseness of the quality packed. In Calcutta, coarse tea is usually packed in chests of 80 lbs. Finer teas, fannings, and dust are generally shipped in half chests weighing 60 lbs. Chests of 120 lbs. are also sometimes used In Madras, shipment is effected in full chests of 115 to 120 lbs., half chests of 80 to 85 lbs. and cases of 90 lbs.

* Some amount of green tea was exported by land across the frontier of India in 1933-34, but no accurate statistics are available.

The statement below shows the course of freight charged on tea from Calcutta to London during the quinquennium 1930-34. The rates are the minimum ones (per ton of 50 cubic ft.) obtaining in August of each year—the month in which the largest quantity of tea is ordinarily shipped.

TABLE No. 139.—*Rates of freight charged on tea from Calcutta to London from 1929.*

Year.	Rate. £	s.	d.
1930	2	5	0 (*a*)
1931	2	0	0 (*a*)
1932	2	0	0 (*a*)
1933	2	0	0 (*a*)
1934	2	5	0 (*a*)

(*a*) Subject of a rebate of 10 per cent. not exceeding 5*s*. per ton.

Tea auctions.

Shipments of tea from India fall into two classes: (*a*) consignments direct from the garden to London where they are sold by auction in Mincing Lane: (*b*) consignments sold at auction in Calcutta and shipped thence chiefly to what are known as 'outside' destinations. *i.e.*, countries other than the United Kingdom. The Calcutta tea auctions commence in May and continue weekly until January or February in the following year. The following tables show the details according to districts of sales at Calcutta in the recent years as contrasted with pre-war and post-war figures. In 1933-34, Darjeeling teas with export rights averaged 14·25*d*. per lb and at the other end of the scale Tipperah teas 9·46*d*. per lb.

TABLE No. 140.—*Quantity of tea (in package) sold at the auction sales in Calcutta in 1913-14, 1918-19 and from 1930-31 onwards.*

Principal districts.	Number of packages sold in 1913-14	1918-19	1930-31	1931-32.	1932-33	1933-34	1934-35.
Assam	209,686	267,816	256,117	251,855	250,797	185,551 (*a*) 118,309 (*b*)	191,534 (*a*) 102,883 (*b*)
Cachar . .	133,540	66,334	59,104	79,352	70,233	48,629 (*a*) 16,262 (*b*)	42,645 (*a*) 19,941 (*b*)
Sylhet .	116,197	73,941	85,701	116,482	100.915	60,804 (*a*) 37,008 (*b*)	58,901 (*a*) 37,792 (*b*)
Duars . .	240,169	127,848	240,579	206,378	243,175	203,206 (*a*) 67,688 (*b*)	199,410 (*a*) 74 758 (*b*)
Darjeeling . .	85,877	34,605	38,306	28,866	27,659	20,257 (*a*) 6,505 (*b*)	17,872 (*a*) 20,575 (*b*)
Chittagong .	9,647	3,924	7.453	6,472	9.558	5,015 (*a*) 2,466 (*b*)	4,787 (*a*) 3,514 (*b*)
Terai . . .	36,709	16,775	50,525	48,976	56.213	44,036 (*a*) 10,844 (*b*)	39,682 (*a*) 13,592 (*b*)
Chota Nagpur . .	1,387	13	2,917	2,927	2,686	3,418 (*b*)	62 (*a*) 2,189 (*b*)
Kumaon and Kangra .	2,089	158					
Dehra Dun . .	9,217	1,831	750	12	. .	614 (*a*)	1,141 (*a*)
Madras . . .	518	142				72 (*a*)	
Nepal . .	1,069	4[illegible]4	1,074		. .	308 (*a*) 105 (*b*)	445 (*a*) 4 (*b*)
Tipperah (Bengal) .	.	. .	11,836	11,841	11,607	7,217 (*a*) 5,030 (*b*)	10,855 (*a*) 7,743 (*b*)
Other Places . .	974	765	338	206	.	.	
Total .	847,079	594,586	754,700	746,367	772,848	575,709 (*a*) 267,635 (*b*)	566,834 (*a*) 282,991 (*b*)
Average price per lb. (in pence) . . .	7·75	8	10·5	7·2	5·8	10·8 (*a*) 5·4 (*b*)	9·8 (*a*) 5·8 (*b*)

(*a*) With export rights.
(*b*) For internal consumption.

These figures may be compared with those obtained in Mincing Lane in 1913-14 and from 1930-31 onwards.

TABLE No. 140-A.—*Quantity (in packages) and average price per lb. of Indian Tea sold in London in 1913-14 and from 1930-31 onwards.*

Year.	Number of packages sold.	Average price per lb.
		(*d*.).
1913-14	1,791,451	9·25
1930-31	1,992,693	12·84
1931-32	1,960,948	11·05
1932-33	2,204,911	9 78
1933-34	1,790,223	14·26
1934-35	1,848,836	11·99

Tea Cess.

Exports of tea were subject to a cess of ¼ pie (1/48*d*.) per lb. imposed by the Indian Tea Cess Act (Act IX of 1903), which was introduced at the request of the Indian Tea Association to furnish funds to advertise and stimulate the tea drinking habit, and by the appointment of agents in India and abroad to push the sales of Indian grown tea From 8th April, 1921, the rate was fixed at four annas per hundred pounds, and from the 21st April 1923, to 6 annas per 100 lbs (¾ pie or 1/16 *d*. per lb.) From 16th September 1933, the rate was increased to eight annas per 100 lbs. (1 pie or 1/11 *d*. per lb), and from 13th April 1935, it was further raised to 12 annas per 100 lbs (1½ pies or 3/22 *d* per lb) Under the provisions of the Indian Tea Cess (Amendment) Act, 1936, the cess is leviable at a rate not exceeding one rupee and eight annas per hundred pounds. Government acts in the matter purely as a revenue collecting agency, and the whole of the amount collected is made over to a fund known as the Tea Cess Fund, which is placed at the disposal of the Indian Tea Market Expansion Board. The total amount collected in 1934-35, was £120,750 as against £91,425 in 1933-34 and £105,975 in 1932-33.

The cess collections are utilised for propaganda work in India and abroad In 1934-35, the allotments were £48,750 for India, £50,000 for America, and £10,000 with an additional £1,000 for the United Kingdom.

Export duty.

In addition to the cess, an export duty of Rs. 1/8 per 100 lbs. (equivalent to about a farthing a lb) was levied with effect from the 1st March 1916. The duty was abolished on the 1st March 1927. The industry was made liable to income tax so far as the whole of the non-agricultural portion of its income was concerned, the presumption that only 25 per cent. of the income is derived from business was negatived. The rule has been subsequently modified and at present, income derived from the sale of tea grown and manufactured by the seller in British India is computed, as if, it is an income derived from business and forty per cent. of such income is deemed to be income, profits and gains liable to tax, due allowance being made in respect of replacement of bushes.

A considerable amount of black tea is consumed in India itself. The following statement shows the percentage of exports to production, and, ordinarily, the remaining quantity *plus* the imports and stocks from previous years and minus the stock left at the end of the year represents the volume of internal consumption.

Consumption of tea in India.

TABLE No. 141.—*Percentage of exports to production.*

Article.	Pre-war average.	War average.	Post-war average.	1933-34.	1934-35.
Tea	96	89	95	83	87

Burma in addition to leaf tea, consumes a considerable quantity of pickled tea (*letpet*) mostly imported from the Northern Shan States. The total imports of *letpet* into Burma in 1924-25, the latest year for which statistics are available, amounted to 21 million lbs.

At the instance of the Indian Tea Market Expansion Board the Government of Bengal have prescribed a standard for tea An attempt has been made in the subjoined table to estimate the amount of tea available for internal consumption in India

TABLE No. 142.—*Quantity of tea, green and black, available for consumption in India in 1913-14, 1918-19 and from 1930-31 onwards (in millions of lbs.).*

Year.	Quantity available for consumption
1913-14	22
1918-19	51
1930-31	49
1931-32	63
1932-33	63
1933-34	66
1934-35	70

There has been a marked increase in tea shops not only in Calcutta, Madras and other big cities but also in the smaller towns, and inspite of higher prices, there is reason to believe that the tea drinking habit is gradually extending among all classes of Indians.

Imports of tea.

The imports of tea, black and green, into India by sea amounted to 5,126,447 lbs. in 1935-36 as compared with 3,074,987 lbs in 1934-35 and 4,716,054 lbs. in 1933-34, valued at £187,298. £128,447 and £188,486 respectively. The importations are mainly from Ceylon in respect of black tea, while China (including Hongkong) supplies the bulk of green tea. The following table shows the re-exports by sea of foreign tea in recent years as compared with the averages of pre-war and war periods.

TABLE NO. 143.—*Quantity of foreign tea re-exported from India by sea in 1932-33 to 1935-36 with pre-war and war averages.*

Destinations.	Pre-war average.	War average.	1932-33.	1933-34.	1934-35.	1935-36.
	lbs.	lbs.	lbs.	lbs.	lbs.	lbs.
Re-exported to—						
Iran . . .	97,407	452,072	5,831	8,967	5,000	1,983
Maskat . .	64,178	128,550	1,559	14,424	4,818	} 4,158 (Maskat, Turkey-Asiatic, Iraq, Other Countries)
Turkey-Asiatic .	} 182,017 (Turkey-Asiatic and Iraq)	} 205,293	..	..	..	
Iraq . . .			515	..	20*	
Other Countries .	180,493	97,803	1,649	4,925	1,609	
Total .	524,095	883,718	9,554	28,316	11,447	6,141

* Black Tea.

In the result, the figure of net imports by sea was 5,120,306 lbs. in 1935-36, as compared with 3,063,540 lbs. in 1934-35 and 4,687,738 lbs. in 1933-34.

Finance.

The capital of joint stock companies invested in tea in India in 1934-35 was approximately £39 millions, chiefly in sterling companies. The following table indicates the number of companies incorporated in India and the United Kingdom and elsewhere and the aggregate paid-up capital in recent years.

TABLE NO. 144.—*Number of companies engaged in the tea industry in India from 1931-32 onwards.*

Year.	Companies incorporated in India.		Companies incorporated in the United Kingdom and elsewhere		Total.		
						Paid-up capital.	
	Number	Paid-up capital (Rs 1,000)	Number.	Paid-up capital (£1,000)	Number	Columns 3 and 5 (Rs 1,000).	Equivalent of column 7 in sterling (£1,000)
1	2	3	4	5	6	7	8
1931-32 .	486	13,16,90	187	28,739	673	51,48,77	38,616
1932-33 . .	471	13,36,35	186	28,531	657	51,40,48	38,554
1933-34 . .	458	12,92,14	185	27,457	643	49,53,07	37,148
†1934 35 . .	443	12,74,78	182	27,335	625	49,19,45	36,896

† Provisional

All teas bought at the Calcutta Auctions have to be paid for on or before the Prompt day, which is ten days after the sale. Firms which purchase teas for export draw through their Banks to the value of the teas against shipping documents.

Tea waste.

Tea waste or refuse is the chief source commercially of caffeine. Before 1931-32, the principal demands were from the United States of America and the United Kingdom, but in recent years, considerable quantities are shipped to Germany and Belgium, while the share of the United Kingdom has dwindled. The bulk of the shipments goes from Bengal and the balance from Madras.

TABLE No. 145.—*Exports of tea waste from India in 1913-14, 1918-19 and from 1931-32 onwards.*

Year.	Quantity.	Value.
	lbs.	£
1913-14	3,084,288	17,907
1918-19	1,641,320	26,368
1931-32	2,698,752	13,779
1932-33	2,870,423	10,748
1933-34	5,782,678	22,055
1934-35	3,210,650	10,579
1935 36	3,909,414	13,419

Tea chests.

A number of Himalayan woods have at different times been used for making tea chests, particularly *toon* (*cedrela toona*) and *simal* (*bombax malabaricum*), but certain varieties have the reputation of tainting the teas, and others require prolonged seasoning before they can be considered suitable. Formerly Burma teak shooks were largely employed for this purpose, but by 1908-09 this trade had died out, and the tendency since has been to rely more and more upon patent tea chests from Europe. Steel chests have proved too expensive for general adoption.

The import trade in wooden tea chests was valued at £298,000 in 1911-12, of which 95 per cent came from the United Kingdom, though made largely of Russian birch and alder. During the war, until communications by the Trans-Siberian Railway, were cut off. large shipments of shooks were made *via* Vladivostok, instead, of, as previously, *via* the United Kingdom. The value has fluctuated from year to year but with an upward tendency and, at the outbreak of war, had stood at £347,000: in 1915-16, at £554,000 and in 1916-17, as a result of great appreciation in prices, at £579,000. The figures for 1917-18 and 1918-19 were £628,000, and £606,500, respectively. In the last six years the values of the imports were:

	£
1930-31	455,600
1931-32	356,078
1932-33	355,671
1933-34	392,369
1934-36	379,318
1935-36	398,589

The value of the metal chests imported in the last pre-war year was only £2,137, in 1918-19, £173, but in 1931-32, £21,288, in 1932-33, £2,640, in 1933-34, £7,991 in 1934-35, £11,300 and in 1935-36, £37,691. The importations are mainly from the United Kingdom with Esthonia, Finland and Germany, as next in importance. The bulk of the tea chests is imported in Bengal and the balance in Madras. Tea chests, to save space and freight, are shipped in the form of shooks, cut to size, with clamps, etc., which are made up locally and lined with thin sheet lead. After filling they are carefully soldered and made air-tight so that the tea will not absorb moisture and become mouldy.

HIDES AND SKINS.

The term *hides* in general parlance denotes the raw, dressed or tanned skins of bullocks, cows, buffaloes, horses, camels, etc. while the term *skins* is restricted to those of calves, sheep, goats deer and other wild animals. Statistically and commercially, however, calf skins are treated as hides. It has been calculated that in India there are about 200 million head of cattle and 93 million sheep and goats. The internal trade in hides is greatly affected by the seasons and, when there is any shortage of fodder or general scarcity the market is unusually brisk. The exports of raw hides and skins largely exceeded the tanned before the war, and they are even now about double the latter as the following figures for 1935-36 indicate.

TABLE No. 146.—*Quantity and value of hides and skins exported in 1935-36.*

Descriptions.	Hides.		Skins.	
	Quantity.	Value.	Quantity.	Value.
	Tons.	£	Tons.	£
Raw	22,677	841,260	21,195	2,234,345
Tanned . . .	14,029	1,717,977	6,275	2,183,315

It has been estimated that the internal absorption of tanned hides and skins in local manufactures is equal to the entire volume exported, making the total turn-over in hides and skins about £10 millions in 1934-35 as compared to £13 millions in the pre-war year. In round figures out of every 100 tons of hides and skins exported, only 32 tons are exported tanned.

Raw Hides.

In the two years preceding the outbreak of war, there was a marked advance in the prices of dry and salted hides due to a world shortage and an increased demand. This advance was particularly marked in the case of buffalo hides, which appreciated by 50 per cent. between 1912 and 1913. There is evidence in fact of considerable overtrading (doubtless deliberate) on the part of Germany and Austria with a consequent accumulation of stocks in Europe, while the United States market was almost bare. In 1913-14 the distribution of the exports of raw hides was as indicated in the table below.

TABLE No. 147.—*Distribution of exports of raw hides in 1913-14.*

Destinations.	Quantity.	Percentage.	Value.
	Cwts.		£
Germany	388,000	35	2,044,000
Austria-Hungary	238,000	21	1,229,000
United States of America . .	155,000	14	698,000
Italy	107,000	10	563,000
Spain	49,000	5	296,000
United Kingdom	42,000	3	166,000
Holland	41,000	3·5	197,000

The declaration of hostilities caused in the first instance an accumulation of stocks in Calcutta, Agra, Cawnpore and other hide-collecting centres in Northern India, enabling Madras tanners to buy at reasonable prices the finer qualities of raw hides previously shipped to the German and Austrian markets, and send large consignments of tanned 'kips' to the United Kingdom where unfortunately the market again became congested as there were not enough curriers available to work them up into commercial leather. Gradually, however, the capacity of the English tanneries was extended to deal with the increased supplies of raw hides from India, and when the Indian Munitions Board took over the control of export in June 1917, fresh openings were found in Italy and the United States of America, in spite of the difficulties of freight and finance, for considerable quantities of raw hides which formerly used to go to the Central Powers. The table below indicates the percentage share of the various importing countries of raw hides in 1918-19 and from 1932-33 onwards.

TABLE No. 148.—*Percentage share of the various importing countries of raw hides in 1918-19 and from 1932-33.*

Destinations.	1918-19.		1932-33		1933-34		1934-35		1935-36	
	Quantity.	Percentage.	Quantity	Percentage	Quantity.	Percentage.	Quantity.	Percentage	Quantity.	Percentage.
	Tons.		Tons.		Tons.		Tons		Tons	
United Kingdom.	10,888	57	1,361	10	3,051	15	3,236	13	4,743	21·0
Germany	..	.	3,671	28	5,606	28	5,257	23	6,531	29·0
Netherlands	..	...	739	6	1,152	6	1,783	8	755	3·3
Spain	178	1	852	6	718	3	579	2	817	3·6
Italy	5,039	26	2,876	21	3,939	20	4,968	22	2,431	11·0
Greece	403	2	1,168	9	1,644	8	1,419	6	1,026	4·5
United States of America.	2,073	11	..	...	349	2	337	·6	328	1 5
Other Countries	516	3	2,681	20	3,816	18	5,666	25·4	6,046	26·1
Total	19,097	100	13,348	100	20,275	100	22,589	100	22,677	100

It will be noticed that Germany has practically recovered the premier position which she occupied in 1913-14. Italy and Netherlands have increased their share in the post-war period. On the other hand the trade with the United Kingdom has considerably declined since 1918-19 while exports to the United States of America have dwindled into insignificance.

The following table indicates the total volume of the export trade in 1913-14, 1918-19, 1919-20 and from 1931-32 onwards with the distribution under different heads.

Exports.

TABLE No. 149.—*Total volume of the exports of raw hides in 1913-14, 1918-19, 1919-20, and from 1931-32 onwards, classified according to descriptions.*

Year.	Cow hides.	Buffalo hides.	Calf skins.	Total quantity.	Total value.
	Tons.	Tons.	Tons.	Tons.	£
1913-14	37,152	17,293	1,306	55,787	5,530,638
1918-19	14,200	3,949	948	19,097	1,742,736
1919-20	39,427	11,655	3,640	54,738	5,501,599
1931-32	13,570	2,702	347	16,628	686,251
1932-33	11,439	1,563	343	13,348	469,528
1933-34	16,866	2,974	451	20,275	760,019
1934-35	19,271	2,838	480	22,589	821,321
1935-36	19,462	2,693	522	22,677	841,260

The totals under the head cow hides are inflated somewhat by the shipment of large calf-skins under that head, because they obtain better prices under the former designation.

The remarkable figures for 1919-20 were due partly to the removal of the embargo which had been enforced with increasing strictness during the war upon raw hides and partly to a considerable rise in prices. The total shipments (54,000 tons) of raw hides had only been exceeded in 1912-13 and 1913-14. In the following year there was a lamentable reaction to which the heavy stocks accumulated during the boom, particularly in the United Kingdom, declining prices, adverse exchange conditions and the dullness of the Continental market were the chief contributory causes. In Calcutta, which is accustomed to work on stocks of 300,000 to 400,000 pieces of cow hides, unsold stocks accumulated to twice the higher of these figures, and the trade was in such a perilous condition that the question of removing the export duty was urged and seriously considered.

The slight improvement recorded in 1921-22 was only achieved at the expense of a further fall in prices, while in 1922-23 the record was one of rather better rates, but smaller shipments particularly to Germany, the United Kingdom and Spain. The exports had since been rising gradually from the low level of 1920-21 and in 1927-28 reached a figure of 40,664 tons. There was again a steady decline in the five years which followed, the exports in 1932-33 coming down to 13,348 tons only. In the past three years there has been a welcome change from diminishing demand and falling prices that had characterised the hides trade in India in the preceding year. This improvement was due to the interplay of numerous economic forces, the most important of which was the reaction set up by the depreciation of the American dollar. There was thus a larger demand for supplies from India which was reflected in the total exports of 22,589 tons in 1934-35. The distribution of the trade according to ports of shipment in 1913-14 is contrasted below with that of 1918-19 and 1935-36.

TABLE No. 150.—*Quantity and percentage share of the various ports in the export of raw hides in 1913-14, 1918-19 and 1935-36.*

Ports.	1913-14.		1918-19.		1935-36.	
	Quantity.	Percentage	Quantity.	Percentage.	Quantity.	Percentage.
	Tons.		Tons.		Tons.	
Calcutta .	43,617	78·1	9,750	51·0	14,351	63·3
Rangoon	7,158	12·8	3,824	19·8	5,223	23·0
Karachi .	3,983	7·2	4,881	25·6	2,496	11·0
Bombay .	837	1·5	630	3·3	580	2·5
Madras .	192	·3	12	·2	27	·1

During the war Karachi captured a portion of the Calcutta pre-war trade, notably in the case of *daisic* and *dakhin* classes from the United Provinces. Calcutta has recovered her share to a great extent in the post-war period while there has been a corresponding decline in the case of Karachi.

Trade Organisation.

Indian hides vary a good deal in size according to the breed of cattle and province of origin. Large numbers are depreciated in value owing to the owners of the animals, from which they have been taken, having wantonly branded them. The pelts of those used for draught purposes or allowed to die of old age or starvation are also deteriorated. Indeed it may be said that improvements in the general quality of the hides marketed have scarcely kept pace with developments in the organisation of agencies for collecting them.

Hides are collected up-country from slaughter-houses or cultivators by *beparis* who consign them to *arathdars* in the big markets, such as Cawnpore, Lahore and Calcutta. These *arathdars* are the large dealers in the bazaar, who finance the up-country *beparis* and eventually sell the hides to the large European and Indian exporting houses and to the tanneries. Endeavours have been made by Government to teach the up-country collectors of hides better flaying and cleaner curing, for the primitive methods generally employed were a great handicap to the trade, but they have not yet achieved much success The share of Madras in the export of raw hides has always been negligible

Descriptions.

Three principal descriptions of hides are recognised, cow hides, buffalo hides, and calf-skins Hides after being flayed, are cured either for transport by rail or for shipment to other countries by three methods·

(i) wet salting;

(ii) dry salting;

(iii) air-drying and arsenication.

Hides are scarcely ever shipped wet-salted but are preserved in this way for local transport by rail to tanneries.

Dry salted hides receive a number of applications of a solution of salt and water which is eventually left to dry on the hides, the salt used being generally *khari* (*i.e.*, sodium sulphate). This method of cure has encouraged adulteration in certain markets, extraneous matter in the form of mud, lime, etc., being plastered on the hides to give them additional weight; but the Calcutta Hides and Skins Shippers' Association has been giving a great deal of attention to this matter without so far any lasting effect.

Hides are air-dried in the drier parts of India, the finest qualities being stretched on frames and known in the trade as 'framed' hides. Before exporting, air-dried hides are always arsenicated, i e., treated with a solution of arsenic and water at the port of shipment. In the rainy season when sun-drying is impossible, a salt lotion is applied in lieu. The chief varieties of dry salted hides known to the trade are *Daccas*, *Meherpurs*, *Dinajpurs*, *Rangpurs* and *Daisie*, and of arsenicated, *Agras*, *North-Westerns*, *Darbhangas*, *Purneas*, *Ranchis*, *Patnas*, *Sambalpurs*, etc , the first two grades being frame-stretched hides superior in quality. *Patnas* are divided into *crumpled* and *uncrumpled*, the former being low grade hides, the appearance of which has been spoilt by careless drying after flaying. For export hides are again classified as *slaughtereds*, *deads*, *rejections* and *double rejections* The hides of animals which are slaughtered, fetch better prices than those which die natural death and they are distinguished commercially by the terms 'kills' and 'commons' All hides, classified as 'slaughtered' and 'kills.' are not necessarily, however, from slaughtered animals but may be dead hides sufficiently fine in quality and condition to warrant the description. It should be noted that only a very small percentage of Indian raw hides are from animals actually killed and slaughtered, these being principally from the Municipal slaughter-houses in the large cities and the army slaughter-houses at the big military centres and also from Saugor, Agra and other towns in the United Provinces and Bihar where dry and barren cows are killed for the 'jerked' meat trade with Burma

The very finest types of slaughtered hides are known as 'Commissariats', a designation due to the fact that for many years the Indian Government purchased large quantities of cattle to supply the British troops with beef, the hides of which were branded with the letter 'C' The Indian Government no longer buys cattle but the term still stands for the best quality of slaughtered hides.

Unit of sale and shipment.

In Calcutta raw hides are usually sold in the bazaar at prices per unit of 20 lbs though some buyers prefer to purchase per *corga* of twenty pieces. The export houses always quote per lb. *c.i f.* or *c f.* The unit of shipment for cow hides is the bale containing 100 to 200 pieces*, for buffalo hides 40 to 50 pieces, and for calf-skins 500 pieces In Bombay the unit of sale is the lb. but in Karachi as in the Punjab and the United Provinces the maund of 28 lbs , shipments being made from both the ports in bales containing 1,000 to 1,200 lbs nett. In Rangoon local transactions are generally done on the basis of 100 viss of 360 lbs and sometimes also per 100 pieces; while the unit of sale to foreign port is the lb Shipment of dry hides is effected in bales of 600 to 700 lbs. and of wet hides in bags of 200 to 300 lbs.

* In case of hides weighing less than 4 lbs. a piece, 300.

Half tanned or 'crust' tanned hides, known in the trade as East India 'kips', the product for the most part of Indian hand-tanneries in Madras and Bombay were in pre-war days exported in considerable quantities to the United Kingdom where they were curried and turned into finished leather. The tannage used was chiefly the bark of *cassia auriculata* (known as *avaram* in the Madras Presidency and *tarward* in Bombay), of which there are abundant supplies only in the two presidencies named and in the adjoining Indian States of Hyderabad and Mysore.

Tanned Hides.

As soon as the value of these hides as upper leather for army boots was realised, every effort was made to stimulate the export, and in August 1916 the Government of India assumed control of the trade and purchased the whole supply for shipment direct to the War Office. The scale of prices was revised from time to time, but so pitched as to encourage the production of army selection leather as much as possible Steps were also taken to prevent adulteration and improper weighting The average outturn before the war was only 1,500,000 'kips' annually equivalent to 27,000,000 feet of upper leather The output at one time during the war was in the neighbourhood of three million 'kips' and at least three-fifths of the upper leather, used for the boots, of the Allies was made from Indian hides.

Government Control.

The statement below gives a very good idea of the expansion of business while the war and the trade boom, which followed it, lasted, though the figures are weighted with a small proportion of tanned buffalo hides and calf-skins which formed part of the Government purchase scheme In 1922-23, after two disastrous years, there was a satisfactory recovery to pre-war levels in volume, with prices, if much lower than in 1919-20, at any rate appreciably higher than in 1913-14. This recovery has been maintained all through. Although during recent years the trade has shown some weakness due to the general depression, it is still above the pre-war level.

Exports.

TABLE No 151.—*Exports of tanned hides contrasted in pre-war year, war period, post-war years and from 1931-32 onwards.*

Year.	Quantity shipped.	Value.
	Tons.	£
1913-14	8,701	1,058,575
1914-15	10,851	1,606,649
1915-16	13,600	2,041,582
1916-17	16,183	2,995,561
1917-18	18,257	3,269,595
1918-19	25,455	4,744,979
1919-20	24,022	5,252,798
1920-21	4,074	765,549
1921-22	6,314	972,124
1922-23	9,952	1,543,178
1931-32	10,300	1,594,914
1932-33	9,036	1,315,879
1933-34	13,156	1,806,010
1934-35	11,370	1,482,254
1935-36	14,029	1,717,977

If the 1913-14 figures are represented by the index number 100, the 1918-19 figures indicate an increase of 193 per cent. in quantity and 348 per cent. in value. The greater part of the output was from Madras tanneries and shipped from that port. Instead of eight or nine separate tannages formerly recognised, such as *Bangalores*, *Cocanadas*, etc.. Madras tannages for War Office shipments were classified into four main grades, *primes*, *best*, *good*, and *ordinary*, each of the first three being again sub-divided into two classes, according to growth and spread. In 1916-17, 99 per cent. of the exports of tanned hides went to the United Kingdom and in 1919-20, 93 per cent. In 1922-23 the United Kingdom's takings of tanned hides increased to 9,100 tons from 5,200 tons, being 91 per cent. of the trade. In 1935-36, 13,592 tons of tanned hides were exported to the United Kingdom whose share represented 97 per cent. of the total exports.

Unit of sale and shipment.

The unit of sale alike in Madras and in Bombay is the lb. and shipment is made in bales of 500 lbs. nett from Bombay and in pressed, gunnied, roped bales, each containing generally 600 lbs., from Madras. Quotations for export are based on the lb. *c.i.f.*

India occupies a much stronger position in the skin than she does in the hide market.

Raw Skins.

India's exports of raw sheep and goat skins have greatly expanded during the last thirty years owing to the introduction of chrome leather tanning in the United States and the increased demand in Europe for glacé kid Being largely obtained from animals slaughtered for food, Indian skins, and goat skins in particular, compare more favourably than Indian hides with similar classes of pelt from other parts of the world. The condition of the trade in 1913-14, 1918-19 and from 1931-32 onwards is illustrated by the following table

TABLE No 152 —*Exports of raw skins from India in 1913-14, 1918-19, and from 1931-32 onwards*

Year.	Quantity in tons.			Total.		Average value per ton.
	Goat skins.	Sheep skins.	Others.	Quantity in tons.	Value.	
					£	£
1913-14	22,668	1,653	7	24,328	2,260,244	92·9
1918-19	21,345	3,622	15	24,982	4,481,107	179 4
1931-32	15,613	520	331	16,464	2,053,536	124·7
1932-33	12,152	636	528	13,316	1,602,388	120 3
1933-34	18,183	1,244	482	19,909	2,424,263	121 8
1934-35	13,874	1,176	110	15,160	1,517,971	100 1
1935-36	20,108	933	154	21,195	2,234,345	105·4

The export of goat skins, raw and tanned from India represents about one-third of the world's supply. The United States of America has always been India's best customer for raw skins, her share of the trade often exceeding 75 per cent. of the total exports. Next comes the United Kingdom, while Continental countries like France, Netherlands, Germany and Belgium, which differentiate against tanned skins by their tariffs, absorb considerable quantities. The fall in the quantity exported in the first two years of the war was of no great moment, and in 1916-17 there was a marked increase in the volume and an even more marked increase in the value of the skins which left India, although by a notification of the 12th August 1916 the only destinations to which shipments were permitted were the United Kingdom, the United States, France and Italy. When an apprehended shortage of tanning materials in India seemed likely to prejudice the output of East India 'kips' for the War Office, the tanning of sheep and goat skins in the Madras and Bombay Presidencies was prohibited with effect from the 28th April 1917 and this was followed up by an embargo upon the export of tanned skins to all destinations with effect from the 15th May, but the exports of raw skins were below the level of the previous year, chiefly owing to the scarcity of freight and prohibitions subsisting in the principal markets against such imports. As in the case of hides, a boom in 1919-20 was followed by a severe set-back in 1920-21 and shipments of goat skins alone are responsible for the improved figures for 1921-22 and 1922-23, with a lower range of prices in the latter year. This improvement was generally maintained till 1928-29 when exports amounted to 22,891 tons Since then exports have declined due, as in the case of hides, to the general economic depression About half of the total exports of raw skins from India are shipped from Calcutta alone, while the percentage shares of Karachi and Bombay are 26 and 20 respectively Madras accounts for only 8 per cent of the total export trade and shipments from Rangoon are negligible. The pre-war distribution is contrasted in the following table with that for 1935-36.

TABLE No 153.—*Quantity and percentage share of the various ports in the exports of raw skins from India in 1913-14 and 1935-36 contrasted.*

Ports.	1913-14		1935-36	
	Quantity.	Percentage	Quantity.	Percentage.
	Tons.		Tons	
Bombay	6,878	28 3	4,212	20·0
Karachi	5,681	23·6	5,604	26·4
Calcutta	10,347	42·7	9,732	46·0
Madras . .	1,390	5·0	1,643	7·6
Rangoon . .	25	·4	4	..

Goat and sheep skins are either dry-salted with Glauber's salt (*khari*), wet-salted with common salt, or, if purchased air-dried, arsenicated by dipping in a solution of arsenic and water. Indian goat skins are generally larger, heavier and of better texture than sheep skins. The best qualities of dry-salted goat skins sold in the Calcutta market are *Daccas, Kushtias, Dinajpurs and Muzaffarpurs* all of which are very suitable for the production of glacé kid. Other classes are *Darbhangas*, *Patnas*, *daisies* and *Chourichauras*, the last of which are indifferent and command poor prices. *North-Westerns*, the principal centres for which are Cawnpore and Delhi, are generally wet salted and run to a very much larger size than skins from Bengal and Bihar. The hair is coarser and the pelt thinner. *Amritsars*, which are also dry-salted, usually have a good spread. From Hyderabad and the Deccan strong medium size skins are obtainable which are mostly sent to the tanneries in Southern India where they are cured for export, but are also shipped untanned from Bombay. The export of goat skins is much larger than that of sheep skins which come mainly from the Darbhanga District of Bihar and Orissa and from Rajputana In Madras the skins are mostly dry-salted with the hair on, but are sometimes flint-dried and very occasionally are wet-salted in the hair or unhaired and then pickled in a solution of alum and salt These are then sorted according to substance of skin and condition into *firsts* and *seconds*, the consignments usually consisting of definite proportions of each The trade names of the best Madras skins are *Cocanadas*, *Bangalores*, *Mysores*, *Trichinopolys* and *Coimbatores*

Unit of sale and shipment.

The unit of sale in Madras is a hundred skins and the unit of shipment is the pressed bale packed in mats and gunnies, generally containing 750 lbs nett or, in the case of salted and pickled skins, the cask. The lb is a recognised unit of sale in Bombay and Karachi, but in the latter market sales are also conducted on the basis of a score of 22 numbers In Calcutta, on the other hand, skins are sold at the rate of 100 pieces and shipped in bales of 500 pieces or casks containing 125 to 150, quotations for export being made per piece, *c i f* or *c f* High freights have discouraged shipment in casks and wet-salted skins are frequently washed on arrival at the Calcutta depots, treated with a fresh solution of salt, sun-dried and baled Wet-salted skins are known in the American market as *soft stock* and dry-salted as *hard stock*. In Bombay the unit of shipment varies according to quality, dry skins being shipped in bales of 1,000 to 1,200 lbs nett, sun-dried and salted skins in bales of 600 to 700 lbs and wet-salted in casks of 560 lbs In Karachi all raw skins are shipped in bales of 950 to 1,400 lbs Each skin should be at least 21 inches wide if two sets of upper sides are to be obtained from it when it has been converted into glacé kid.*

Tanned Skins.

Tanned skins, commercially speaking, mean sheep and goat skins only, though there some inconsiderable shipments of other pelts from Indian ports As in the case of tanned hides, the existence of the bark of *cassia auriculata* in the Madras and Bombay Presidencies created a large industry in lightly tanned skins, which flourished for the first two-and-a-half years of the war with very high prices in England, the United States of America and Japan. In 1917-18 the embargo upon the export of tanned skins, already referred to reduced the volume of these exports from 166,000 to 34,000 cwts and was lifted only in September 1918, too late to effect more than a partial recovery in the figures for 1918-19. In the early part of 1922-23 Indian tanned skins were in good demand but the year closed with

*Report of the Indian Industrial Commission, Appendix D.

large stocks in hand both in London and New York. The export trade in tanned skins has gradually expanded in recent years as will be apparent from the following table.

TABLE No. 154.—*Exports of tanned skins in 1918-19 and from 1931-32 onwards with value and index numbers.*

Year.	Quantity. exported.	Index No.	Value.	Index
			£	
1918-19	Tons.	100	1,701,428	100
1931-32	2,984	184	2,352,675	138
1932-33	5,494	184	2,281,612	134
1933-34 . . .	5,485	220	2,428,246	143
1934-35	6,516	219	2,433,806	143
1935-36 .	6,275	210	2,183,315	128

It will be noticed that the exports in 1935-36 were more than double those of 1918-19 The prices have also risen to an appreciable extent.

The export of tanned goat skins usually exceeds the export of tanned sheep skins, but not to the same extent as in the case of raw skins The finest qualities of tanned sheep and goat skins come from the Trichinopoly and Coimbatore districts and the Dindigul sub-division of the Madura District of the Madras Presidency, where the tanners are very expert and produce skins, unexcelled as regards texture, colour and pliability. The finest qualities of Madras tanned skins are specially suitable for the production of light weight leathers finished in light colours In other parts of the Madras Presidency and in Hyderabad there is a large outturn of tanned skins but they are much commoner in type India's chief market for tanned skins is the United Kingdom which took 95 per cent. and 83 per cent. of the total exports of goat and sheep skins, respectively, in 1935-36. The Japanese market for tanned sheep-skins is a post-war development The distribution of trade according to countries from 1932-33 onwards is shewn in the following table, goat and sheep skins being separately distinguished.

TABLE No 155.—*Percentage distribution of the trade in tanned goat and sheep skins among importing countries*

Countries	Goat skins.				Sheep skins.			
	1932-33.	1933-34.	1934-35.	1935-36	1932-33	1933-34	1934-35	1935 36.
United Kingdom .	99 0	96·0	97 0	94 6	76·0	78·0	74·0	82·7
Japan	.	·5		·5	19·0	18·0	21·0	15·3
France	·3	1·1	.	1·7	..	.	..	·2
United States of America	·2	2·4	1·6	2 0	..	1	..	..

As in the case of tanned hides, the greater portion of the exports goes from Madras, the percentages from Madras and Bombay in 1913-14 being 82 and 18, and in 1935-36 94 and 5 respectively.

Unit of sale and shipment. Tanned skins are usually sold in Bombay market per lb.

and shipment is made in bales of 500 to 550 lbs. nett. The unit of sale in Madras is the lb. and that of shipment the pressed bale wrapped in gunnies and roped, weighing 500 lbs in the case of both sheep and goat skins. Quotations for export are per lb. *c.i.f.* or *c.f.*

With effect from the 11th September 1919 an export duty of 15 per cent. *ad valorem* was imposed on all shipments of raw hides and skins from British India based on tariff valuations.

Export Duty.

A rebate to the extent of two-thirds of the duty, however, was allowed in the case of exports to the United Kingdom and British Possessions including mandatory territories upon production of evidence that the hides or skins had been tanned within them. From the 1st March, 1923 the duty was fixed at an all-round rate of 5 per cent as a revenue measure This duty, which was originally intended to assist the tanning of Indian hides and skins within the Empire, did not succeed in that object On the other hand, it proved a serious handicap to the export trade in raw hides and skins. The trade in hides was more seriously affected and it was found possible to abolish the export duty on hides in the budget of 1934-35. The export duty on skins was removed in March 1935

OPIUM.

The opium yielding poppy (*papaver somniferum*) is an annual which grows to a height of from two to four feet The capsules or seed pods from which the drug is obtained, are, while still green, carefully scarified with a four-bladed instrument, which causes them to exude a gummy sap and this operation is repeated three or four times at intervals of two or three days until the discharge is exhausted. The juice is scraped off and when coagulated forms crude opium, for which the flower petals, carefully collected and steamed, are used as packing

The trade formerly recognised two descriptions of opium, based on the area of cultivation of the poppy · *Bengal* opium, obtained from certain districts of the United Provinces and Bihar (which once formed part of the old Bengal Presidency) and *Malwa* opium the product of certain Indian States in Central India, particularly Indore, Gwalior, Bhopal, Jaora, Dhar, Rutlam, Mewar and Kotah.

In Central India the opium collected is sold by the cultivator to middlemen, from whom the large dealers again obtain their supplies For export purposes the drug, which was of 90° to 95° consistency, was made up into balls of twelve ounces each and packed in half chests for despatch about the end of September. No statistics of the area under poppy were maintained, and no control was exercised by the British Government over either cultivation or manufacture; but as the States in which this opium is produced have no access to the sea, except through British territory, the regulation of exports to China, the chief market for Malwa opium, used to be effected by making the issue of passes for transport to Bombay depend upon prior payment of duty by the successful bidders at auctions, held monthly at the latter port A few chests were also shipped annually

Malwa Opium.

to Zanzibar. The duty was at the rate of £40 per chest until 1912, when it was raised to £80. The last auction was held in January 1913 and the last shipment made in December of that year

Bengal opium.

In British India cultivation is permitted only under license granted to cultivators who obtain advances from Government free of interest to meet the cost of production, on the understanding that the whole of their outturn is sold to the Government Factory at Ghazipur (United Provinces) at a rate fixed by Government which was in 1935-36 Rs. 9 (13s 6d.) per seer for opium of 70° consistency. The opium trade was created a Government monopoly in 1773 and in 1817 the cultivation of the poppy except on account of the East India Company was forbidden All opium was auctioned with the stipulation that it should be exported.

In British India, as in Indian States, the area under opium has since 1907 been much curtailed owing to the agreement come to with the Chinese Government for the suppression of opium traffic with that country, and the opium factory at Patna closed. In 1908 an arrangement was made with China by which the total exports of opium from India were to be reduced annually by 5,100 chests from an assumed standard of 67,000 chests and by a further agreement in 1911, the reduction was accelerated by further limitations, and exports to China have been discontinued altogether since 1913 In British India the cultivation of the poppy is now restricted to the United Provinces and the product is known as Benares opium While 488,548 acres were under the crop, yielding 71,340 maunds of opium in 1907-08, in 1911-12 the area was reduced to 200,672 acres, producing 31,473 maunds and in 1913-14 to 145,000 acres The following table shows the cultivation and produce during the seven years 1928-29 to 1934-35

TABLE No 156.—*Cultivation and produce during the five years 1928-29 to 1934-35.*

Year.	Area of cultivation (excluding failures).	Damdeta produce at 70°.
	Acres	lbs.
1928-29	42,186	589,051
1929-30	36,613	585,102
1930-31	36,537	629,945
1931-32	37,012	850,953
1932 33	27,227	650,680
1933-34	13,792	261,915
1934-35	6,805	135,936

The area sown in British India in 1934-35 is 4·7 per cent. of that in 1913.

Small quantities of opium are also grown in the Punjab Hills where the area under poppy cultivation measured 1,285 acres, and the opium produced amounted to 2 314 lbs in 1933

As a result of Shan States (Burma) Opium Order of 1923, satisfactory progress has been made in the restriction of opium cultivation. The total production in the Shan States amounted to 49,046 lbs. in 1933.

The seed is broadcast in October and November and the capsules harvested in March and April.

In July 1914, when the cost of manufacture was about Rs. 500 per chest the price realised was about Rs. 1,578, but upon the outbreak of war the market became much disturbed. At the August auction the average price realised was only Rs. 1,212 a chest. The decision was then taken to fix an upset price of Rs. 1,600, and though this arrested any further decline, 1,352 chests were left unsold at the close of the year Between 1916 and 1920 there was a marked advance in price and the figures for the past three years, if not so high as in the boom year, are yet thrice as high as the average for 1913-14.

Prices.

At the Calcutta sales the number of chests sold in the year 1922-23 totalled 2,890, a remarkable improvement on the 935 sold in 1921-22 and 1,550 in 1920-21, but considerably less than the 3,600 sold in 1919-20 The highest and lowest prices obtained during the year for *Benares* opium were Rs. 4,910 and Rs. 4,500, respectively In 1924, the average auction price per chest was Rs. 4,666, and in 1925 Rs 4,617. Since April 1926, the auction sales of opium have ceased

The following table shows the declared values of opium for exports in the last six years:—

TABLE No 157.—*Declared value per hundredweight of opium exported.*

Year.	Values.					
	Rs.	A	P.	£	s	d.
Pre-war average	1,945	11	0	129	14	3
1929-30	3,200	1	0	240	1	0
1930-31	3,196	7	0	239	14	8
1931-32	3,201	14	0	240	2	10
1932-33	3,205	11	0	240	8	6
1933-34	3,200	0	0	240	0	0
1934-35	3,213	14	8	241	0	0

6 pies and more have been taken as 1 anna.

At the Ghazipur factory, three classes of opium are manufactured: (*a*) *Provision* opium which is intended for export, (*b*) *excise* opium for home consumption, the duty on which varies in different provinces, and (*c*) *medical* opium for export to London and for supply to the Medical Department in India for medical purposes. *Provision* opium is made up in balls or cakes weighing 3½ lbs. each. 40 cakes going to the chest It is generally of 71° consistency. *Excise* opium which is of 90° consistency is made up in cubic packets of one seer each, 60 packets to the chest. Medical opium is made up in cakes, each weighing 2 lbs. at 87·50° consistency.

In the year ending the 30th September 1933, in the Ghazipur factory, the total quantity of opium at 70° dealt with was 650,680 lbs. Benares, 626,249 lbs. Malwa, and 110,504 lbs. Hard Mewar. During this year 75,604 *provision* opium cakes, equivalent to 1,890 chests, were manufactured as against 48,040 cakes in the preceding year. This increase in manufacture was due to the decision of the Government of French Indo-China to take half of their 1933 quota of 660 chests in 1934 in addition to the quota of 1934. And since the full quota was ready of the *provision* opium cakes required up to the end of 1935, when their sales finally ceased, the manufacture practically ceased.

The unit of sale as well as of shipment of provision opium is the chest of 140 lbs. The exports of opium on private account (quantities and values) in 1913-14, 1918-19 and from 1931-32 onwards are shown in the table below:—

Exports.

TABLE No. 158.—*Exports of opium on private account in 1913-14, 1918-19, and from 1931-32 onwards.*

Year.	Quantity.	Value.
	Cwts.	£
1913-14	16,858	2,280,031
1918-19	15,345	2,086,049
1931-32	2,715	651,985
1932-33	351	84,390
1933-34	2,270	544,803
1934-35	212	51,101
1935-36	..	73

The principal event in the history of the opium trade in 1922-23 was the issue of a Notification by the Government of India in pursuance of the resolution adopted by the Assembly of the League of Nations, that every application for the export of opium from India should, from the 1st January 1923, be accompanied by a certificate from the Government of the importing country that the consignment is approved by that Government and is required for legitimate purposes The only transactions with countries that have not adopted the certificate system were the exports of small quantities of certain medicinal preparations to certain places on the Persian Gulf.

Under the Rules framed by the Government under section 7 (2) of the Dangerous Drugs Act, 1930, exports of opium by air are prohibited. Exports by sea are permissible only on an authorisation certificate, on behalf of the Governor-General in Council.

At the request of the Government concerned the Government of India are under agreement to supply Ceylon, Hongkong, Singapore, British Borneo, Siam, and the Dutch East Indies with a regular stipulated supply of opium at a fixed price.

The quantities and values of opium shipped on Government account are, as the table below shows, declining.

TABLE NO 159 —*Quantities and values of exports of opium on Government account in 1918-19 and from 1931-32 onwards.*

Year.	Quantity.	Value.
	Cwts.	£
1918-19	9,609	715,015
1931-32	1,758	422,829
1932-33	1,100	264,130
1933-34	1,252	301,800
1934-35	613	147,982
1935-36	321	76,875

The revenue derived by the Government of India from opium since 1913-14 is shown in the following table.

TABLE NO 160 —*Revenue derived from opium by the Government of India since 1913-14.*

Year.	Amount.
	£
1913-14	1,624,878
1914-15	1,572,218
1915-16	1,913,514
1916-17	3,160,005
1917-18	3,078,903
1918-19	3,289,111
1919-20	3,037,481
1920-21	2,356,082
1921-22	2,048,320
1922-23	2,526,138
1923-24	2,832,110
1924-25	2,531,745
1925-26	2,766,639
1926-27	2,887,583
1927-28	2,958,919
1928-29	2,449,457
1929-30	2,280,734
1930-31	1,937,060
1931-32	1,555,615
1932-33	673,961
1933-34	1,192,258
1934-35	539,565
1935-36	458,277

RAW WOOL.

Trade Centres.

Indian wool falls for the most part in the lowest of the three classes into which the article is classified for trade purposes (*viz*., merino, crossbreds and carpet wool) and the exports from India are generally destined for the manufacture of blankets, rugs, carpets and felt only, though some of the better quality Bikaner wool is good enough to be utilised for clothing As compared with cotton, the internal consumption of wool in India is comparatively small, as it is unsuitable as a clothing material in the climatic conditions prevailing over the greater part of the country. Further and perhaps for the same reason, the wool of the Indian sheep is short stapled and in every respect inferior to that of Europe and Australia. The estimated production of wool in India has been placed in the neighbourhood 87 million lbs. per annum on the basis of 2 lbs. per sheep, as compared with 7½ lbs. the average weight of an Australian fleece. The chief centres of the trade in raw wool in India are the Punjab, particularly the Hissar district; the United Provinces, particularly Garhwal, Almora and Naini Tal; Sind, Baluchistan and the Bikaner State The largest marts for indigenous wool are at Fazilka and Beawar, at the former of which it is subjected to a certain amount of cleaning and, if intended for shipment, pressed and baled also In the Bombay Presidency, the black Deccan and Khandesh wools and the white wools of Sind, Gujarat and Kathiawar have a recognised commercial value and in Southern India wool-bearing species of sheep are found in the Mysore State and the Bellary Kurnool and Coimbatore districts of the Madras Presidency. In other parts of the country the sheep yield hair without any felting qualities. A good deal of the wool which comes into the Indian market is dead wool. *i.e.*, wool that has been removed from the carcases of slaughtered sheep and not shorn.

Imports.

As regards imports, a great deal of wool enters India from Afghanistan of fairly good quality, but the indiscriminate intermixing of black and white wool of different staples tends to lower the export value of what is shipped at Karachi From Tibet, in addition to large quantities of ordinary wool, there is a considerable trade in shawl wool or pashm, the silky under-fleece of a particular species of goat which is superior in quality to any Indian wool Quetta, Shikarpur, Amritsar and Multan are the chief collecting centres for wool received by land from Afghanistan and Central Asia, while the principal purchasing centres for Tibetan wool are Kalimpong on the Teesta Valley branch of the Darjeeling-Himalayan Railway and Tanakpore on the Oudh and Rohilkhand Railway The mills in India also import considerable quantities of wool chiefly from Australia, the United Kingdom and Persia, for the manufacture of woollen goods for which the indigenous material is not suitable. A good deal of the raw wool grown in, or brought across the frontier into India goes into internal consumption but the export trade though considerably less in value than that in raw cotton, is nevertheless of considerable interest and importance It is estimated that the total supplies of wool in India, indigenous and imported, are about 950,000 cwts. of which 594,000 cwts are exported and the balance goes into mill and domestic consumption

War Restrictions.

The first recorded export of raw wool from India was in 1834 and the total quantity was rather less than 70,000 lbs. Two years later the figure was 1,200,000 lbs. and in 1872, 24 million lbs., and the advance since had been steadily progressive Very soon after the outbreak of war restrictions were placed on the exports of raw wool, chiefly in the interests of manufactures in India executing Army clothing contracts, and in respect of all varieties of Tibet wool and the black and grey varieties of Madras wool, the prohibition on export was made absolute with effect from the 15th January, 1915, shipment of other descriptions being allowed under license, subject to limit of quantity. The embargo as regards Tibetan wool was in abeyance between September 1915 and January 1916 and so great was the general demand for wool created by the war, particularly as clothing for troops, that the total volume of exports of wool from India (including re-exports), in spite of restrictions, rose from 54½ million lbs. in 1914-15 to nearly 82 million lbs. in the following year, practically all for the United Kingdom. Of the re-exports in this year no less than 15 million lbs. were shipped from Karachi. Early in April 1916 the export of wool was prohibited except to the United Kingdom and the sudden closure of the United States and other markets caused an immediate slump in prices But the decline in exports both of Indian and transfrontier wool during the next twelve months was due rather to difficulties of freight and finance than to any embargo 1920-21 was a dull year as it was in most lines of trade In the year that followed, the trade was marked by great fluctuations. It reached a record figure in 1928-29 when total shipments amounted to more than 68 million lbs. The trade suffered a decline in the next two years, after which a slight improvement was noticed. In 1933-34 shipments exceeded the pre-war levels, the total quantity exported being 66½ million lbs. The export trade in Indian raw wool in the year 1934-35 was divided between Karachi and Bombay in the proportion of something like 67 and 28. Of the re-exports Karachi had 33 per cent. and Calcutta 66 per cent , the share of Bombay being negligible.

The exports and re-exports of wool in 1913-14, 1918-19, 1919-20, 1920-21, and from 1931-32 onwards are indicated in the following table —

TABLE No. 161.—*Quantity and value of Indian and foreign wool exported from India in 1913-14, 1918-19, 1919-20, 1920-21 and from 1931-32 onwards.*

Year.	Exports.	Re-exports.	Total.	
	Quantity.	Quantity.	Quantity.	Value.
	Lbs.	Lbs.	Lbs.	£
1913-14 . . .	48,922,061	10,245,538	59,167,599	2,000,156
1918-19 . . .	47,376,163	15,662,076	63,038,239	4,590,128
1919-20 . . .	36,319,126	15,984,490	52,303,616	3,698,923
1920-21 . . .	23,042,603	8,934,049	31,976,652	2,016,126
1931-32 . . .	41,265,157	9,066,516	50,331,673	2,354,878
1932-33 . . .	32,248,819	3,863,002	36,111,821	921,799
1933-34 . . .	55,888,567	10,616,581	66,505,148	1,722,551
1934-35 . . .	34,075,204	6,313,202	40,388,406	1,074,472
1935-36 . . .	49,352,285	11,346,951	60,699,236	1,782,519

The chief customer for Indian wool in pre-war days was the United Kingdom, though there were some exports *via* Calcutta of Tibetan wool to the United States of America, and to a limited extent Germany and France were also recipients. 75 per cent. of the shipments of Indian wool in 1934-35 were to the United Kingdom and 16 per cent. to the United States of America. About 80 per cent. of the exports of foreign wool from India went to the United States of America and 14 per cent. to the United Kingdom.

Trade Organization.

In India the rearing of sheep and the production of wool are entirely in the hands of village shepherds who depend upon middlemen to purchase the clip from them. These middlemen, as is usual in other Indian trades, make monetary advances to the shepherds, about six months or even earlier before the actual clipping season, up to as much as 50 per cent. of the total price to be paid. The middlemen, after delivery of the wool, consign it to one of the principal Indian markets for sale outright there, though some of the bigger merchants arrange to forward the wool to Liverpool for sale on a consignment basis, through exporting agencies at Karachi and Bombay, each individual parcel being auctioned on its merits. The exporting firms who undertake this business, arrange the freight and insurance and generally pay, through a guarantee broker on the basis of a sterling bill at 3 months' sight, a percentage advance in rupees on the estimated price of the wool, which therefore virtually remains the property of the merchant till it has been warehoused, valued and sold No sale by private treaty is permitted unless the wool fails to find a buyer at auction, and when a final settlement of accounts is made the shipper claims a net commission of 2 per cent. in Bombay and 3 per cent in Karachi, of which 1 per cent in each case is paid to the broker. The rates of commission are. however, subject to variation with different circumstances These auction sales were suspended during the war, though the arrangements, other than as regards freight and insurance between the consignor and the exporting firms, were not disturbed

The principal varieties of East Indian wool as shown in the Liverpool price market returns are *Bikaner*, *Joria Kandahar*, *Marwar* white and yellow, *native* black and grey, *Rajputana* white and yellow, *Peshawar* white and yellow, *Bibruk* and *Harnai* white, and *Beawar* and *Jaisalmere*. As the consignments represent assorted and clean wool, the designations under which they are marketed should be regarded as trade names rather than indicating the district of origin.

Unit of sale and shipment.

Raw wool is generally picked and cleaned up-country, but exporting houses make advances against pressed bales as soon as they come into their possession The unit of sale in the Karachi Market is the maund of 84 lbs and in Bombay the candy of 21 Bombay maunds Shipment is made from both ports in bales of 3 cwts gross In Madras sales are made per lb and wool is shipped in bales of 300 to 350 pounds. In Bombay, while a good deal is pressed up-country, some of the wool intended for export reaches the port in *borahs*, and is sorted. pressed and graded there. It is usually made up in small lots, a consignment of more than hundred bales being exceptional.

WOOLLEN MANUFACTURES.

At the end of 1934, there were 13 woollen mills working in India employing 75,085 spindles and 1,595 looms. Some of these mills manufacture all classes of woollen and worsted goods while others manufacture blankets only. The market for their manufactures is almost entirely in India itself. During the war all the woollen mills in India were employed to their fullest capacity in meeting Government's war requirements, and in particular in supplying greatcoat cloth, serges and putties, flannels, blankets and hosiery. There are also in India considerable quantities of hand manufactures of felts and blankets as well as of *Puttoo* and *Pashmina* in Kashmir, North-West Frontier Province, the Punjab, the United Provinces and a few parts of the Mysore State. In the past handloom weaving was generally done with hand spun yarn, but for many years now, except in Kashmir, the use of handspun yarn for the finer fabrics has become less and less, and the substitution of fine mill-spun cross bred and merino yarns has enabled the weavers to produce a cheaper article of very similar appearance and quality With the exception of carpets, the exports by sea of woollen manufactures from India have never been of importance Apart from a special export of woollen piece-goods to the United States of America in 1932-33 (90,000 yards) the average annual exports have never exceeded 10,000 yards. Exports of woollen manufactures other than piece-goods, which include blankets, namdahs and hosiery, amount to an average of 288,000 lbs. The export trade in shawls, at one time considerable, is now insignificant, the number exported being 80,450 in 1908-09 and 4,860 only in 1933-34 The exports of woollen goods of all kinds by land during the three years ending 31st March 1935 averaged 245,300 lbs per annum.

Woollen Mills.

One of the results of the great exhibition of 1851 in London was to stimulate an interest in Indian pile carpets These carpets which are for the most part handknotted in the Punjab and the United Provinces are generally composed of a woollen pile on a cotton warp, though woollen warps with a silk pile are occasionally made to special order The chief centre of the industry is Amritsar. The wool used, which comes chiefly from Bikaner or from Kerman in Iran *via* Nushki, is locally spun and dyed with vegetable colours Other centres outside the Kashmir State are Multan in the Punjab, Jaipur and Bikaner in Rajputana, Agra and Mirzapur in the United Provinces, and Ellore in the Madras Presidency Carpet manufacture is also a feature of a number of jails, as for example Lahore, Agra, Yeroada (near Poona) and Vellore In Northern India the weavers are for the most part Kashmiri Mahomedans. Rugs and carpets from beyond the frontier have for many years found their way into Northern India and the two most important trade centres for these imports, which come chiefly from Iran, Russia and Turkestan, are Peshawar, the capital of the North-West Frontier Province, and Quetta. In 1886-87 the exports of carpets did not exceed £20,000 in value At the beginning of the century there was an American boom and in 1903-04 the total exceeded £173,000, but this level was not touched again until 1910-11. The returns for 1913-14, 1918-19 and from 1930-31

Carpets.

onwards are given in the table below. The exports have risen to a considerable extent during recent years. The phenomenal rise since the year 1933-34 reflects the benefit to the Indian carpet industry of the preference given by the Ottawa Trade Agreement:—

TABLE No. 162.—*Exports of carpets and rugs from British India in 1913-14, 1918-19 and from 1930-31 onwards.*

Year.	Quantity.	Value.
	Lbs.	£
1913-14	1,640,770	153,446
1918-19	944,132	98,466
1930-31	4,231,526	502,822
1931-32	4,766,797	425,438
1932-33	5,963,304	476,277
1933-34	8,452,443	545,006
1934-35	10,093,364	673,602
1935-36	9,347,108	604,848

The chief recipients have always been the United Kingdom and the United States of America and it is probable that many carpets consigned in the first instance to the former country were subsequently re-shipped to New York The Amritsar Carpet Manufacturers in particular specialise for the American market Beautiful re-productions are made there and at Agra of famous old carpets in the Vienna, South Kensington and other museums

METALS AND ORES.

Manganese.

Occurrence.

The exploitation of the manganese deposits in India dates from 1892. These deposits may be classified geologically as follows —

(*a*) deposits associated with rocks of the kodurite series, worked for export in the Vizagapatam district of the Madras Presidency;

(*b*) deposits associated with rocks of Dharwar age, chiefly the gondite series, found in (1) the Balaghat, Bhandara, Chindwara and Nagpur districts of the Central Provinces, (2) the Panch Mahals district in the Bombay Presidency, (3) the Gangpur State in Bihar and Orissa and (4) Jhabua in Central India; and

(*c*) lateritoid ores found in (1) the Singhbhum district in Bihar and Orissa, (2) the Jubbulpore district in the Central Provinces, (3) the Bellary district and the Sandur State in the Madras Presidency, (4) the Chitaldrug, Kadur, Shimoga and Tumkur districts of the Mysore State, and (5) Goa (also in true laterite).

Manganese quarrying began in Vizagapatam in 1892 and in the following year over 3,000 tons were exported. In 1900-01, 90,000 tons were shipped, but since then water troubles as the workings grew deeper and lower prices have made further exploitation of the ores, which are not first grade, less profitable. The Central Provinces are normally the largest producers of manganese although in the years 1932 and 1933 the largest quantity was obtained from the Madras Presidency.

Before the year 1926, the record production of manganese-ore in India took place in 1907, when 902,291 tons were raised. In 1926 the output rose to 1,014,928 tons, valued at £2,463,491 *f. o. b.* Indian ports; the rise in output was however, accompanied by a decrease in value In 1927 the production rose to the highest figure yet recorded, 1,129,353 tons, accompanied by a rise in value to the peak figure of £2,703,068 During the year 1928, the upward tendency was not maintained, the output falling to 978,449 tons valued at £2 198,895. In 1929, the output improved to 994,279 tons, but the value deteriorated to £1,571,030. In 1930 the output declined to 829,946 tons with a heavy fall in value to £1,200,236, and this tendency was aggravated in 1931 when the output was reduced to 537,844 tons with a value of £726,954 This was followed by a disastrous fall in 1932 to 212,604 tons with a value of £140,022. In 1933 the output rose slightly to 218,307 tons but the value fell to £123,171 These are the smallest quantities and values reported since 1901 when the output was 120,891 tons valued at £122,831 The full magnitude of this catastrophe to the Indian manganese industry is perhaps best realised from the fact that whilst the quantity of the production in 1933 was a little over one-fifth of that of the peak year of 1927, the value was less than one twenty-second part of the value of 1927 production. This continued fall in the price of manganese-ore is to be correlated with the fact that from 1924 to 1927 the rate of increase of the world's production of manganese-ore was much greater than the rate of increase in the world's production of pig-iron and steel And although there was a fall in the world's output of manganese-ore in 1928, there was a very large increase in 1929, greater than was justified by the increased production of iron and steel in that year, and it is evident that the world's available supplies of manganese-ore are now much in excess of requirements. There is a steady consumption of manganese-ore at the works of the three principal Indian iron and steel companies, not only for use in the steel furnaces of the Tata Iron and Steel Company, and for the manufacture of ferro-manganese, but also for addition to the blast furnace charge in the manufacture of pig-iron. The consumption of manganese-ore by the Indian iron and steel Industry in the year 1935 amounted to 67,442 tons The following table shows the quantity and value of manganese-ore produced in India in 1935:—

TABLE No. 163 —*Quantity and value of manganese-ore produced in India in 1935.*

Province.	Quantity.	Value f o.b. at Indian ports.	Value per ton.
	Tons.	£	£
Central Provinces . . .	385,179	657 304	1·7
Bombay Presidency . . .	4,866	7,927	1·6
Bihar and Orissa . . .	74,996	91,315	1·2
Mysore	871	957	1·2
Madras Presidency . . .	175,571	193,127	1·1
Total .	641,483	950,630	1·5

The number of workers employed in the manganese quarries reached the high figure of nearly 32,000 in 1929, but, as a result of the increasing depression in the industry during the succeeding years, it fell to about 4,500 in 1933 The year 1934 shows an appreciable improvement, the corresponding figure being 8,549. The workings in British India are subject to a royalty of 2½ per cent. on the sale value at the pit's mouth. As a result of fluctuations in the market price of manganese-ore the royalty actually levied in the Central Provinces, varied between 1·8 and 6·0 *annas per ton during the five years 1929 to 1933 The royalties in Indian States are generally considerably higher, varying from 4 to 10 annas per ton.

In Mysore, labour is easily obtainable, but in the Central Provinces, Central India and Sandur it has frequently to be imported. Work is generally done through contractors who are paid at a fixed rate per 1,000 cubic feet of stacked and cleaned ore and for dead work at a given rate per 1,000 cubic feet of cavity made in the quarry or of waste measured, according as the 'deads' are hard or soft.

Exports. The following were the exports of manganese-ore in 1913-14, 1918-19, 1920-21 and from 1930 onwards, according to ports:—

TABLE No. 164.—*Share of the ports in the exports of manganese-ore in 1913-14, 1918-19, 1920-21 and from 1930 onwards.*

Year.	Vizagapatam	Bombay.	Calcutta.	Mormugao.
	Tons	Tons.	Tons.	Tons.
1913-14	36,750	606,724	74,575	86,747
1918-19	..	180,376	204,935	(a)
1920-21	12,410	391,650	375,582	25,745
1930	4,500	297,738	300,211	170,577
1931	4,331	88,681	153,535	171,410
1932	3,200	58,145	131,399	108,508
1933	61,940	51,747	146,121	116,546
1934	149,380	57,089	183,827	115,582
1935	412,683	64,100	225,504	162,411

India has all along been a big exporter of manganese ore, the highest exports during the post-war years being 964,489 tons (inclusive of exports from Mormugao) in 1929 Since then there has been a very sharp decline in exports, which receded to 301,252 tons in 1932, due mainly to the world's available supplies of manganese ore being much in excess of requirements, increased competition from Russia at comparatively low prices and to the disastrous decline in the activities of the Iron and Steel Industry of the world. There has been a marked improvement during the last few years. The exports from British Indian ports alone amounted to 455,000 tons in 1934-35, the relative shares of principal consuming countries being the United Kingdom, 155,000 tons, France, 113,000 tons, Japan, 99,000 tons and Belgium 37,000 tons, the balance being absorbed by other countries.

The unit of sale is the percentage of Mn. (manganese) contained in each ton of ore and shipment is made by the ton. Ore containing

Unit of sale and shipment. 48 per cent and upwards of Mn. is considered first grade, 45 to 48 per cent. second grade and below 45 per cent. third grade. The price per

(a) Figures not available.
* An anna is the equivalent of 9/8 *d.* at the current rate of exchange.

unit in July 1914 for ore of these three grades, delivered at a port in the United Kingdom was respectively 9¼ to 9⅜*d.*, 9 to 9½*d.* and 8¾ to 9*d.* In September, 1935, the market prices ruling at Bombay were as follows:—

1st Grade Gujarat	6¼ to 6⅜*d.* F. A. S.
2nd Grade Gujarat	6 to 6 1/8*d.* F. A. S.
3rd Grade Gujarat	5 to 5⅜*d.* F. A. S.

Iron and Steel.

Iron and Steel Manufacture.

Deposits of iron ore of good quality have been proved to exist in different parts of India and for some years ending 1929, the production thereof had been steadily increasing India is now, in fact, only next in importance to the United Kingdom in the British Empire In 1930, the prevailing world depression was reflected in a decrease in the Indian output of 23·8 per cent over the previous year amounting to 678,930 tons followed by a further fall of 224,742 tons (12·1 per cent) in 1931. In 1932, a slight rise in output was noticed. Though there was a slight set back in 1933, the production advanced to an appreciable extent in the years 1934 and 1935. The following table shows the quantity and value of iron ore produced in India in recent years:—

TABLE No. 165.—*Quantity and value of iron ore produced in India from 1932 onwards.*

Province.	Producers.	1932.		1933.		1934.		1935.	
		Quantity.	Value.	Quantity.	Value.	Quantity.	Value.	Quantity.	Value.
		Tons.	£	Tons.	£	Tons.	£	Tons.	£
Bihar and Orissa—									
Keonjhar State	United Steel Corporation of Asia Ltd.	186,173	13,998	195,944	14,733	397,461	29,884	283,489	21,315
Mayurbhanj State	Tata Iron & Steel Company Ltd.	891,193	160,448	341,502	47,529	645,108	75,076	876,939	96,672
Puri	....	..	..	..	..	..	..	..	..
Sambalpur	Tata Iron & Steel Company Ltd.	7	4	4	2	..	..	..	..
Singhbhum	Indian Iron & Steel Company Ltd.	666,874	116,633	616,946	104,043	810,547	100,179	1,155,965	136,046
	*Bengal Iron Company	..	..	..	..	..	..	..	..
Burma—									
Northern Shan States	†Burma Corporation Ltd.	6,560	(a) 1,973	36,293	(a) 10,915	23,930	(a) 7,197	23,085	(a) 6,943
Central Provinces	....	803	181	777	175	898	203	800	180
Madras—									
East Godavari	....	4,496	335	2,118	97	..	..	..	..
Mysore State	....	4,395	1,148	35,041	10,319	38,974	10,904	24,019	5,786
		1,760,501	294,720	1,228,625	187,813	1,916,918	223,443	2,364,297	266,942

(*a*) Estimated.
* Bengal Iron Company suspended production since November 1931 but resumed manufacture of Pig Iron from March 1935.
† The output is used as a flux in lead smelting.

Iron smelting by primitive methods was at one time a widespread industry all over the sub-continent, and pig iron has been turned out at Kulti since 1875, but it was not until 1914 that the manufacture of steel in India by modern processes was successfully demonstrated. The imports of iron and steel (including galvanised iron, tin plates, railway plant, etc.) in 1913-14 amounted to over 1,250,000 tons valued at £17 millions. In addition the value of machinery imported exceeded £5,000,000 including prime movers £558,000, electrical machines £845,000 and textile machinery £2,186,000 After the grant of protection in 1924, the Indian Iron and Steel industry was able to increase its production and to displace foreign imports to a considerable extent. The total production of iron and manufactures in India amounted to 550,696 tons in 1933-34, 627,358 tons in 1934-35 and 676,691 tons in 1935-36 There are four concerns which are equipped for the manufacture of pig iron in India, *viz.*, The Tata Iron and Steel Company, the Indian Iron and Steel Company, the Bengal Iron Company and the Mysore Iron and Steel Works Of these, the Bengal Iron Company suspended production in November, 1931 but resumed manufacture of pig iron from March 1935. The Bengal Iron and Steel Company's works were opened in 1875, but were not a paying concern in the earlier years. With four blast furnaces they have a potential output of 320 tons of pig iron a day, equivalent to a normal production of nearly 10,000 tons a month. In 1930 the output rose to 103,929 tons. 28,211 tons of sleepers and chairs and 32,760 tons of pipes and other castings were manufactured from their pig iron in 1931 as against 3,153 tons and 34,833 tons respectively, in 1930 In 1933, their output of products from pig iron amounted to 12,511 tons of sleepers and chairs and 23,263 tons of pipes and other castings against 3,371 tons and 17,266 tons, respectively in 1932 The Tata Iron and Steel Company, which was floated in 1907, owns valuable iron ore concessions in the Mayurbhanj State in Orissa and the Raipur district of the Central Provinces, manganese ore deposits in the Balaghat district of the Central Provinces, magnesite and chromite in Mysore, and coal in the Jharia field The works were completed in 1911, in September 1912 a second blast furnace was blown in, and in August, 1919, a third (the Batelle furnace), but the full effect of these additions was not felt until 1921 Before the works were started the Government of India placed a standing order with the works for 20,000 tons of steel rails annually for ten years for State Railways, but the demands of the Munitions Board during the war largely exceeded this figure In 1918 the works produced 198,061 tons of pig iron and 71,069 tons of rails In 1933 the company produced 793,953 tons of pig iron as compared with 699,931 tons in 1932 with increases in the production of steels (including steel rails) from 430,333 tons in 1932 to 505,429 tons in 1933 and of ferro-manganese from 366 tons in 1932 to 7,725 tons in 1933 The Indian Iron and Steel Company, with an authorised share capital of £1 million manufactures pig iron, steel, ferro-manganese, etc, at Burnpore, near Asansol, 130 miles from Calcutta near an important railway junction and close to the Raniganj, Jharia and Barakar coal-fields. The initial plant includes two blast furnaces capable of producing 300 tons of pig iron or 200 tons of ferro-manganese daily and by-product recovery coke ovens. The Company commenced turning out pig iron, railway sleepers and railway "chairs" in November 1922, and increased their production of pig iron from 198,700 tons in 1932 to 249,079 tons in 1933. The output of pig iron by the

Mysore Iron and Steel Works rose slightly from 14,683 tons in 1932 to 14,805 tons in 1933. The total production of pig iron in India rose from 918,314 tons in 1932 to 1,057,887 tons in 1933.

A new company known as the National Iron and Steel Co., Ltd., was registered in October 1934, and has started a factory at Belur near Calcutta for the manufacture of mild steel rounds, bolts, nuts, etc. It also proposes to manufacture structural materials and other steel products such as steel bars, high class alloy steel and steel castings in the near future.

Exports.

The exports of pig iron, ferro-manganese and iron and steel manufactures in 1913-14, 1918-19 and from 1931-32 are shown in the table below

TABLE No. 166.—*Quantities and values of exports of pig iron, ferro-manganese, and of iron and steel manufactures in 1913-14, 1918-19 and from 1931-32, onwards.*

Year.	Pig Iron.		Ferro-manganese.*		Iron and Steel manufactures	
	Quantity.	Value	Quantity	Value	Quantity.	Value.
	Tons	£	Tons	£	Tons.	£
1913-14	82,592	282,418		..	828	12,725
1918-19	9,596	70,497	10,878	272,045	813	17,268
1931-32	350,858	920,241	.		194,329	199,238
1932-33	218,384	557,383		.	118,682	1,031,267
1933-34	377,514	637,689		.	138,806	332,457
1934-35	417,059	695,066	.		58,940	122,995
1935-36	538,153	932,874	.	...	58,902	116,207

The bulk of the shipments goes from Calcutta Madras and Burma in that order, have considerable shares in the export trade of re-manufactured iron or steel. In recent years, no export is recorded of ferro-manganese, the last shipment of 3,200 tons being in 1929-30, wholly from Madras to Belgium and France The chief markets for pig-iron are Japan, United Kingdom, United States of America and China, while iron and steel manufactures go mainly to the United Kingdom and Japan

Gold.

Chief Producing Areas.

India contributes only about 2 per cent of the world's production of gold and occupies the seventh position among the gold producing countries of the world Over 99 per cent of the Indian output is obtained from the Kolar field in eastern Mysore, about forty miles from Bangalore where there is a single gold-bearing reef of quartz some four miles long The prosperity of the Kolar gold field dates from 1885 and the high water mark of output was reached twenty years later, when 631,116 ozs valued at £2,373,457 were recovered and £1,066,615 was paid out in dividends by the five companies working the reef Since then there has been on the whole a decline in the output, though with intermittent recoveries, and the price of gold being considerably higher than it was before the war values are still in the neighbourhood of £2,000,000 annually.

Electrical power provided from the falls of the Cauvery River at Sivasamudram, 92 miles distant, was brought to the field in 1902

* Not recorded separately before 1916-17.

and has since been considerably increased. In addition the Kolar mines power station, originally started to supplement the hydro-electric supply with electricity generated by steam power, is a valuable stand-by in the event of any interruption to the main transmission line.

The mines are thoroughly well equipped and efficiently managed. The cyaniding process is employed to deal with the tailings. The Champion Reef and the Ooregum mines, the two deepest on the field reached vertical depths of 7,811 feet and 7,661 feet respectively, below field datum on the 31st December 1934.

The royalty paid to the Mysore Government has, in recent years, risen to over £100,000 annually and, following the introduction of a higher scale of royalties in 1934, a further increase may be expected The number of persons employed in 1935 was 22,271. The whole of the output of gold was until 1914-15 exported from Bombay in the form of ingots for refining, but during the war a considerable portion of it was taken over by the Bombay mint for coinage purpose This latter practice was, however, discontinued a few years after the war and since then the output of gold has been exported

In 1918, 2,109,660 gold mohurs, equivalent in weight and fineness to the sovereign, were coined at the Bombay mint, and thereafter upto April, 1919, when minting was suspended, 1,295,644 sovereigns were coined Between the years 1914-15 and 1918-19 over 2½ million ounces of mint standard gold were received by the Bombay mint from the South Indian mines

In 1931 over 1¾ million ounces of mint standard gold were purchased from the public under section 4 of the Currency Act, 1927.

The following table shows the value of gold produced in India during 1917, 1918 and from 1932 onwards classified according to provinces —

TABLE No 167 —*Value of gold produced in India during 1917, 1918 and from 1932 onwards.*

Provinces.	1917.	1918	1932.	1933	1934.	1935.
	£	£	£	£	£	£
Mysore	2,067,541	1,936,785	1,905,522	2,076,352	2,195,419	2,676,862
Hyderabad	52,013	44,936		...	..	...
Madras	87,066	67,219	..	..	..	..
Burma	4,248	739	271	272	4,756	8,689
Punjab	857	541	36	62	6	66
United Provinces	31	27	20	31	29	13
Bihar and Orissa	10,133	9,905	274	1,484	626	218
Total	2,221,889	2,060,152	1,906,123	2,078,201	2,200,836	2,285,848

Silver.

Silver has only since 1909 been added to the list of metals won within the confines of the Indian Empire Nearly the whole output comes from the Bawdwin mine in the Northern Shan States in Upper Burma but is quite insignificant in comparison with the country's requirements, India being by far the largest consumer of silver in the world

Production.

TABLE No. 168 —*Production and value of silver in India in 1918 and from 1932 onwards.*

Province.	1918.		1932.		1933.		1934.		1935.	
	Quantity.	Value.	Quantity.	Value.	Quantity.	Value.	Quantity.	Value.	Quantity.	Value.
	Oz.	£	Oz.	£	Oz.	£	Oz.	£	Oz.	£
Burma—										
Bawdwin	1,970,614	295,592	5,998,956	468,640	6,054,047	494,338	5,792,019	559,736	5,825,913	766,524
Madras Presidency—										
Anantapur	1,169	104	..	..	..	..	..	..	..	..
Mysore										
Kolar	..	..	27,781	2,917	26,172	2,873	25,491	3,120	24,477	2,928
Bihar and Orissa—										
Manbhum	..	..	..	..	22	2	14	1	16	2
Total	1,971,783	295,696	6,026,737	471,557	6,080,241	497,213	5,817,524	562,857	5,850,406	769,454

The output of silver at Bawdwin has as the above table shews. increased considerably as compared to that in 1918. Silver has only recently appeared among the returns from Kolar. There has been no production of silver from Anantapur field since 1928. Manbhum in Bihar and Orissa has just entered the field with an insignificant production of 22 ozs. in 1933, 14 ozs. in 1934 and 16 ozs. in 1935.

Most of the silver from Burma is purchased by the Government of India for minting purposes.

Tungsten.

Tungsten is necessary for the manufacture of high speed steel, and in the form of wire for the filaments of incandescent lamps, while tungstates are employed in dyeing and fire proofing and other industrial processes. Until about two decades ago the chief source of supply of the metal was the United States of America but to the estimated total world's production of 10,000 tons of tungsten concentrates, carrying 60 to 70 per cent of tungstic trioxide (W. O_3) in 1917, Burma contributed about a third.

Production.

The exploitation of the Tavoy and Mergui districts for this metal which occurs in the form of wolframite, to the existence of which attention had been drawn by the Geological Survey, only began in 1909. The output for the statistical year ending on the 31st March 1910 was 100 tons and though 262 tons were obtained during the remaining months of 1910, progress was for a time hampered not only by lack of communication and difficulties of transport but also by short-sighted and wasteful methods of extraction, the labour employed being chiefly Chinese and Telegu The production figures for 1914, 1919 and from 1930 onwards for the Tavoy district are given in the following table

TABLE No 169.—*Output of wolfram concentrates from Tavoy in 1914, 1919, and from 1930 onwards*

Year.	Quantity. Tons.
1914	1,977
1919	2,731
1930	1,433
1931	870
1932	751
1933	762
1934	1,202
1935	2,089

Until the outbreak of the war practically the whole of the wolfram won was shipped to Germany for metallurgical treatment. During the war the wolfram deposits of Burma were of supreme importance to the Home Government, and between 1914 and the armistice no less than 17,642 tons of a total value of £2,323,000 were exported. Of this quantity, over 14,000 tons came from the Tavoy field. For some years after the war the industry suffered from great discouragement and falling prices and in 1921 and 1922 India produced only 898 tons and 943 tons, respectively (including an output of 12 tons in 1921 and 5 tons in 1922 in Mergui and Southern Shan States). Although the output from Tavoy field has declined during recent years, the total Indian production during the last four years was above the pre-war level consequent on a substantial increase in the output from Mawchi in the Southern Shan States. The total Indian output in 1935 was 3,837 tons which included 1,288 tons from Mawchi, calculated to be the proportion of wolfram in concentrates (assumed to contain 43 per cent. of wolfram and 57 per cent. of cassiterite) derived from the mixed wolfram-scheelite-cassiterite-ore.

The Tavoy deposits are worked by many different methods, from the cobbing hammer, pan and sluice box on the one hand to machine drills, modern concentrating mills and hydraulic plant on the other.

The wolfram bearing veins of Thaton are in two well-marked series—one in granite, and the other in the sand-stones of the long mountain ridge which runs parallel to the coast through this district. They differ markedly from those of Tavoy, in that they carry tourmaline Four parallel veins, only a few inches thick, have been traced for the unusual distance of 2½ miles The well-known Mawchi mine is situated in the Southern portion of the Bawlake state of Karenni. It possesses at least ten important veins varying from 2½ to 5 feet in thickness, which are all in granite Outside Burma, there are wolfram occurrences in the Singbhum district of Bihar, at Agargaon in the Central Provinces, and at Degana in the Marwar district of Rajputana, but these deposits are insignificant, compared with those in Burma.

TABLE No 170.—*Quantity and value of Tungsten ore produced in India in 1935.*

Province	Quantity.	Value.
Burma—	Tons	£
Mergui	223·1	11,725
Thaton, Yamethin and Karenni States	1,524·9	120,023
Tavoy	2,089 1	164,945
Total	3,837·1	296,693

The total mine production from 1930 was 1930, 2,451 5 tons, 1931, 2,247·7 tons, 1932, 2,022·9 tons; 1933, 2,147·1 tons, 1934, 3,328·5 tons, and 1935, 3,837·1 tons. The figures of export which are compiled for the statistical year (April to March) amounted to 3,811 tons in 1930-31, 4,384 tons in 1931-32, 3,366 tons in 1932-33, 4,242 tons in 1933-34, 5,644 tons in 1934-35 and 7,825 tons in 1935-36 About 90 per cent. of the concentrates go to the United Kingdom, the balance being shared by Germany, Belgium, Sweden and France.

Exports.

The unit of sale is the percentage of WO_3 in the concentrate. Each shipment is assayed and this percentage determined and the price per ton arrived at The price before the war was about 35 shillings per unit and during the war it was fixed by Government at 55 shillings and subsequently at 60 shillings equivalent, with an assay of 60 per cent. WO_3, to £180 a ton. In August 1935, the price of wolfram in

Unit of sale and shipment.

London was reported to be 30 *sh.* to 31 *sh.* per unit. The Unit of shipment of the concentrate is the bag, varying in weights from 56 to 112 lbs.

Tin.

Tin mining is an established industry in Burma. Following a series of years of practically continuous increase, a slight decrease in the production of tin ore in Burma was reported in 1931 The output in that year amounted to 4,255·2 tons valued at £259,806. In the succeeding two years, production increased to 4,525 tons valued at £339,097 and 4,960·4 tons valued at £533,082 respectively. This is the highest quantity and total value yet recorded in any one year. The considerable increase in the total value is mainly due to the rise in the price of the metal resulting from the restriction scheme in operation in the five leading tin-producing countries, namely, Malaya, Netherlands East Indies, Bolivia, Nigeria and Siam. India is not a participant in the scheme. Milling operations were suspended at Mawchi in the Southern Shan States in August 1927 pending the installation of additional plant and further development. Milling was resumed in February 1930 The total figure for 1933 includes 1,738; 5 tons from Mawchi, calculated to be the proportion of tin-ore in 3,050 tons of concentrates derived from mixed wolfram-scheelite-ceessiterite-ore There was no reported output of block tin.

Production.

The following table shows the quantities and values of tin-ore produced in India in recent years.—

TABLE No. 171 —*Quantities and values of tin-ore produced in India from 1932 onwards.*

Producing areas.	1932		1933		1934.		1935.	
	Quantity.	Value	Quantity.	Value	Quantity.	Value	Quantity	Value.
	Tons.	£	Tons	£	Tons	£	Tons	£
Burma—								
Amherst	19 2	1,708	23 0	2,549	32 6	3,807	39·7	4,468
Mergui	598	40,927	978 7	95,579	1,357 3	172,188	1,755·9	228,272
Karenni State	(a) 1,557 3	116,701	1,282 0	137,743	1,894·0	(a) 249,666	1,456·9	(a) 189,726
Tavoy	2,349 6	179,687	2,215 8	247,668	2,512 0	388,351	2.601·7	344,988
Thaton	·9	75	4 4	495	5·3	676	5·5	627
Total	4,525·0	339,097	4,503 9	484,084	5,801 2	764,688	5,859·7	763,081

All the exports of tin-ore to foreign destinations from India are from Burma, where cassiterite is obtained by washing alluvial gravels, chiefly in the Tavoy and Mergui districts Some of the tin won in the Mergui District is smelted locally by Chinamen in small native furnaces and the block tin obtained goes into local consumption in India and Burma, but practically the whole of the ore from other localities is exported in the form of high grade concentrates. In the case of mixed tin and wolfram concentrates chiefly from Tavoy the ore used formerly to be shipped in the first instance to the Straits Settlements for separation.

(*a*) **Estimated.**

TABLE No. 172.—*Exports of tin unwrought and tin ore from Burma in 1913-14, 1918-19 and from 1929-30 onwards.*

Year.	Foreign.		Coastwise.	
	Quantity.	Value.	Quantity.	Value.
	Cwts.	£	Cwts.	£
1913-14	4,212	24,482	1,466	13,729
1918-19	7,423	62,268	1,880	25,165
1929-30	66,623	482,902	6,116	55,863
1930-31	50,480	253,222	6,699	37,644
1931-32 . . .	47,240	182,443	8,259	45,736
1932-33 . . .	50,560	214,320	(a)10,699	(a)73,535
1933-34 . . .	64,410	437,421	(a)11,491	(a)122,936
1934-35 . . .	71 780	530,969	(a)11,492	(a)136,034
1935-36	83,720	609,995	10,821	(a)128,960

Lead.

Occurrence.

The exports of lead from India are entirely confined to Burma and are the produce of a single mine, that of Bawdwin in the Northern Shan States, the control of which passed into the hands of the present lessees, the Burma Corporation Limited, in 1914 The corporation was registered on December 1919 with an authorised capital of £13 1/3 millions The ore reserves in the Bawdwin mine, as calculated on the 1st July 1935, totalled 3,965,199 tons, against 4,062,511 tons at the end of June 1934, with an average composition of 24·2 per cent of lead, 15·1 per cent of zinc, 0·87 per cent. of copper and 18·7 ozs. of silver per ton of lead Included in this reserve, there are approximately 250,000 tons of copper-ore The existence of this mine had long been vaguely known and it had been worked by Yunnanese for its silver until about 60 years ago When the concession over this area was first taken up in 1902 enormous heaps of lead slag were found which had been abandoned by the Chinese after extracting some of the lead and nearly all the silver.

Until the end of 1908 practically no smelting was carried on, but in 1909 a light railway from the mine to Nam Yao on the Shan States branch of the Burma Railway, close to Lashio, was completed, and nearly 12,000 tons of lead slag and 485 tons of ore, obtained from open-cut working, were transported to Mandalay, and 5,030 tons of lead and 27,000 ozs of silver obtained from them.

At the end of 1911 the smelting plant was transferred from Mandalay to Namtu, which is about 15 miles from Bawdwin and 36 miles from Namo Yao, and a refining plant also set up Hydro-electric power is derived from the Mansam falls over a transmission line about 20 miles long. The ores, which are very rich, consist of argentiferous galena and zinc-sulphide and a small quantity of copper pyrites, with traces of antimony and nickel

A large staff of about 3,000 persons daily is employed at the Smelta Plant and crushing and concentrating Plant at Namtu, while the coolies are for the most part Shans or Yunnanese

(a) Includes wrought tin also.

The downward trend in the output since 1930 was checked in 1933 when the production increased from 372,586 tons in 1932 to 454,791 tons in 1933, and the total amount of metal extracted from 71,202 tons of lead (including 642 tons of antimonial lead) valued at £826,736 in 1932 to 72,045 tons (including 1,485 tons of antimonial lead) valued at £869,317 in 1933 The quantity of silver extracted from the Bawdwin ores rose slightly from 5,998,956 ozs., valued at £468,640 in 1932 to 6,057,047 ozs., valued at £494,338 in 1953 The value of the lead per ton rose from £11·6 to £12·07 while the value of the silver per ounce rose from 18 75*d* to 19·6*d*. in 1933.

The production of lead ore in 1934 and 1935 amounted to 443,489 tons and 460,886 tons, respectively. 72,060 tons of metal valued at £1,037,479 was extracted in 1935 against 71,815 tons valued at £803,476 in the previous year. 5,825,913 ozs of silver valued at £766,524 was extracted from the Bawdwin ores in 1935 against 5,792,019 ozs valued at £559,736 in the year 1934. The value of lead per ton rose from £11·19 in 1934 to £14·39 in 1935 whilst that of silver per ounce rose from 23 19*d* in 1934 to 31·6*d*. in the following year.

Imports.

Between 1908-09 and 1913-14 the average value of lead imported into India was £140,000, chiefly in the form of sheet lead for tea chests but also lead for pipes, sheets, and tubes and pig lead In 1934-35 the imports excluding ore increased in quantity from 28,313 cwts in 1933-34 to 28,414 cwts but decreased in value from £40 817 to £35,422 The imports of ore decreased both in quantity and value from 362 tons at £8,222 in 1933-34 to 256 tons at £5,135 in the following year

Exports.

The following table shows the quantity and value of lead in 1913-14, 1918-19 and from 1931-32 onwards exported from India to foreign destinations Germany came into the market, for the first time since the war, in 1921-22 but the chief recipients are Japan, the United Kingdom, China and Ceylon

TABLE No 173 —*Quantity and value of foreign exports of lead in 1913-14, 1918-19 and from 1931-32 onwards*

Year	Quantity.	Value.
	Cwts.	£
1913-14	69,862	59,309
1918-19	185,951	287,121
1931-32	1,321,350	1,344,956
1932-33	1,249,986	1,143,709
1933-34	1,343,592	1,174,168
1934-35	1,255,989	1,045,883
1935-36	1,361,876	1,377.107

Zinc.

Occurrence.

The principal occurrence of zinc in India is in association with the silver-lead ores of Bawdwin in the Northern Shan States The zinc won from this mine was until the outbreak of war chiefly exported to Antwerp and Hamburg in the form of ore for conversion into spelter, and when these outlets were closed there was temporarily a large accumulation of stocks at Rangoon. A great deal of zinc was formerly lost in the lead smelting works partly by volatilisation and partly in the residual slag. Zinc ore has a particular value for India apart from its metallic content as a potential source of sulphur. In 1917-18 experimental work, in connection with zinc concentrates began at Namtu and a year later the Government of India was interested in a proposal to erect zinc smelting works at Jamshedpur, where the zinc concentrates from Bawdwin would be dealt with, and the spelter and sulphuric acid yielded, made available to the Tata Iron and Steel Company for their own purposes and for subsidiary companies but unfortunately the scheme fell through. The production of zinc concentrates by the Burma Corporation Limited rose in 1935 to 78,590 tons valued at £285,666. The quantity is the greatest hitherto recorded, but the value is much below those of the years 1926 to 1929 (£559,412 in 1928). The following table shows the exports of zinc in recent years as compared with the pre-war and post-war figures.

TABLE No 174.—*Quantity and value of zinc exported from India in 1913-14, 1919-20, and from 1931-32 onwards.*

Year.	Quantity.	Value.
	Cwts.	£
1913-14	153,204	31,796
1919-20	1,005	159
1931-32	1,126,350	211,219
1932-33	964,000	180,750
1933-34	1,406,194	253,914
1934-35	1,505,236	196,933
1935-36	1,703,230	265,475

In recent years almost entire shipment went from Burma, the principal recipients being Belgium, the United Kingdom, Germany and Japan

Copper.

Production.

Copper was formerly smelted in considerable quantities in Southern India, in Rajputana and at various places along the outer Himalayas in which a persistent belt of killas-like rock is known to be copper bearing in numerous places, as in Kulu, Kangra, Nepal, Sikkim and Bhutan Though the internal consumption of copper is estimated at about £1 million, attempts to work commercially the indigenous deposits of the mineral have met with limited success. Copper is found at Bawdwin in the Northern Shan States of Burma. The reserves of copper-ore therein were reported in 1928 to amount to 350,000 tons averaging about 13 per cent. of lead, 8 per cent of zinc, 7 per cent of copper and 18 ounces of silver to the ton The Namtu Smelting Works of the Burma Corporation produce regularly a considerable quantity of copper matte. In 1933 the production increased from 9,729 tons valued at £148,985 in 1932 to 12,550 tons valued at £225,863. The existence of considerable quantities of copper in Sikkim has been established, but one of the chief obstacles to a successful exploitation of the ores, is the inaccessibility of the areas and the lack of adequate communication. In the Singhbhum district of Bihar and Orissa, a copper-bearing belt persists for a distance of some 80 miles. These copper ores have been the subject of exploitation on European lines by various companies during more than fifty years past. The Cape Copper Company actively developed the Rakha Hill Mines and during the five years from 1919-1923, when the mining operation ceased, the total production of copper ore and metal from the Rakha mines amounted to 130,797 and 354,976 tons respectively. Two other companies commenced operations in the Mosabani and Sideshur-Kendadih areas in Singhbhum between 1920 and 1922, but in 1924, the companies were amalgamated as the Indian Copper Corporation Limited with a capital of £225,000. The average number of persons employed daily by the Corporation is over 800. Operations continued successfully on the Mosabani mine and on the Corporation's milling and smelting plant at Maubhander Ghatsila. During 1933 there was an initial production of ore from Dhobani where a lode parallel to that at Mosabani was opened up. In that year the total output of copper was 201,722 long tons valued at £166,388, as compared with 175,010 long tons valued at £188,652 in 1932 The total ore reserves at the close of the year 1933 amounted to 686,402 short tons with an average assay value of 3·06 per cent of copper In 1932, 365 tons of copper ore valued at £519 were produced in the Nellore district, Madras There was no recorded production in 1933.

TABLE No 175.—*Output of copper ore in 1914, 1919, and from 1929 onwards.*

Year.	Quantity.	Value.
	Tons.	£
1914	4,400	6,600
1919	32,756	34,940
1929	76,831	108,862
1930	123,749	180,413
1931	153,636	168,292
1932	175,010	188,652
1933	201,722	66,388
1934	328,676	257,133
1935	350,801	262,316

In 1935, 334,589 short tons of ore were treated in the mill, and the production of refined copper amounted to 6,900 long tons as compared with 6,300 long tons in 1934 and 4,800 long tons in 1933.

Chromite.

Occurrence.

Chromite is mined in Baluchistan, in the Mysore, Shimoga and Hassan districts of Mysore, and the Singhbhum district of Chota Nagpur in the province of Bihar and Orissa There are also occurrences in the Andaman Islands and in the Salem district, Madras Presidency. The ore is used in the manufacture of ferro-chrome and chrome steel, while chromium salts are in large demand in connection with tanning and dyeing. Chromite is also used in the manufacture of chromite bricks. The quantity and value of chromite produced in 1933, 1934 and 1935 are shown in the following table:—

TABLE No. 176.—*Quantity and value of chromite produced in India during 1933, 1934 and 1935.*

Provinces.	1933.		1934.		1935.	
	Quantity.	Value.	Quantity.	Value.	Quantity.	Value.
	Tons.	£	Tons.	£	Tons.	£
Baluchistan . .	2,702	3,047	2,346	2,646	7,642	8,335
Bihar and Orissa .	7,068	7,662	7,010	6,935	11,397	9,512
Mysore . . .	5,756	6,076	12,220	13,732	20,088	18,240
Total .	15,526	16,785	21,576	23,313	39,127	36,087

Exports.

The pre-war average did not exceed 6,000 tons annually which went to Hamburg, whence it probably found its way to Essen. At the outbreak of war a German firm in Calcutta had a large quantity collected and ready for shipment. In 1916-17 six thousand tons were shipped, and in 1917-18 nearly fifteen thousand and more would have probably gone forward, if freight had been available, the deposits at Hindubagh being by then linked up *via* Khenai with the Bostan-Bolan section of the North Western Railway. 82 per cent. of the whole went to the United Kingdom and the balance to Italy and Japan. In 1918-19, the total shipments from India aggregated 39,381 tons, of which 12,740 tons of Mysore ore valued at £28,000 were shipped from Madras (in the absence of freight from Mormugao) chiefly to the United Kingdom for munition purposes. The exports reached a record figure of 52,471 tons in 1922-23 after which there has been a decline. In 1935-36 the exports amounted to 26,091 tons as compared with 24,273 tons in 1934-35 and 20,395 tons in 1933-34. Sweden and Norway were the two principal purchasers, taking 5,100 tons and 4,353 tons, respectively. France took 1,213 tons, Germany 3,445 tons and the United States of America 4,800 tons. Of the total quantity exported 15,933 tons were shipped from Karachi while Madras and Calcutta accounted for 6,109 tons and 4,049 tons, respectively.

Unit of sale and shipment.

The price is governed in the United Kingdom by the percentage of sesquioxide of chromium contained in the ore, payment being generally made on a 50 per cent. basis after analysis. A return of 2 shillings to 2*s*. 6*d*. per unit above or below 50 per cent. is usually made to the seller or buyer, as the case may be, after the percentage has been ascertained. The demand in the United Kingdom is for ore with 48 to 52 per cent. chrome content, and India's chief competitors in the London market are New Caledonia and Rhodesia.

Corundum.

Production.

The occurrences of corundum in India (chiefly in the form of crystals) are widely distributed, but little organised mining has yet been attempted and the returns of production are manifestly incomplete. Corundum was formerly found in considerable quantities in Mysore and the other chief areas of occurrence were the Khasi and Jaintia hills in Assam, the Coimbatore, Anantapur, South Canara, and Salem districts of the Madras Presidency, and Pipra in the Rewah State in Central India. The Pipra mines, from which a peak production of 1,860 cwts. was obtained in 1913, have not been worked since 1920. Small quantities of corundum were produced in the Bhandara district of the Central Provinces in 1925, 1926 and 1927. Of the production of corundum recorded from the Madras Presidency, 211 cwts. from Coimbatore and 478 cwts. from Trichinopoly made up the supply for 1914, but throughout the remainder of the period (1915—18) the whole of the output, averaging 31½ cwts. annually, came from South Kanara. During the quinquennium 1919—23 there was no output from Madras. In 1926 to 1930 small outputs were reported from the Salem district, but there has been no output since then. The average annual production from the Mysore State during the quinquennium 1914—18 was 523 cwts. valued at £104, but there has been no recorded output for the past 16 years. The reported output of corundum from the Khasi hills was 12,660 cwts in 1919, 3,320 cwts. in 1920 and 1,277 cwts. in 1921, but no production is reported for the last 13 years. The production of 'corundum with sapphire patches' in Kashmir State amounted to 1·6 cwts. in 1926, 11 cwt. in 1927 and 1 cwt. in 1928. Small production was also reported from Mahbubnagar, Gulbarga and Nalgonda in Hyderabad.

The total production of corundum in India amounted to 30 tons valued at £162 in 1930, the whole of which came from the Salem district in the Madras Presidency, but since then there has been no production until 1935, when 28 tons valued at £465 were produced.

Corundum, on account of its use as an abrasive, used to be a regular item of trade in most Indian cities, where the lapidary flourished and it used to be collected in a casual way by agriculturists and cowherds who disposed of it through the village *banias* to the larger dealers of the great *cities. Owing to the competition of carborundum manufactures in the United States and the commercial extraction of corundum from felspar in Canada, the Indian export trade has never attained any considerable dimensions. No separate statistics of exports have been maintained.

Monazite.

Occurrence.

The monazite sands of Travancore owe their economic importance to the fact that they contain a percentage of thoria, from which thorium nitrate, used in the manufacture of incandescent gas mantles, is derived, ceria and other rare earths. The percentage of thoria in monazite varies between 1 and 12 but mineral containing less than 3½ per cent. can not be profitably used in the manufacture of thorium nitrate. In 1911 the occurrence of these sands near Cape Comorin was exploited by a concern which eventually came under German control, and the concentrates to the extent of 3,200 tons, extracted during 1911 and 1913 were said to have been shipped to Hamburg, the manufacture of thorium nitrate in India having never yet been attempted. Previous to the discovery of monazite in Travancore,

* Pascoe's Mineral Production of India, 1924—28, p. 382.

Brazil enjoyed a monopoly. The Brazilian industry suffered a set-back during the war and in the post-war years. In 1919—22 the average production was only 437 metric tons. The production of monazite in India increased to 2,117 tons in 1918, after which there has been a gradual decline till 1925 when the output amounted to only 1 cwt. There has been an appreciable revival since 1925, due to the increasing demands for ilmenite, a mineral associated with monazite and obtained as a kind of by-product of the latter. Monazite also occurs in the sands to the east of Cape Comorin in the Tinnevelly district of the Madras Presidency and again near Waltair in Vizagapatam. A crystalline variety containing only 2¼ per cent. of thorium has been found in pegmatites of the Bangalore district in the Mysore State. Deposits have also been found to exist in the Gaya district of Bihar and Orissa and Tavoy and Mergui in Burma.

The following table indicates the production of monazite from 1914 onwards:—

TABLE No. 177.—*Quantity and value of monazite produced in India from 1914 onwards.*

Year.	Quantity.	Value.
	Tons.	£
1914	1,186	41,411
1915	1,108	33,238
1916	1,292	37,714
1917	1,940	56,489
1918	2,117	58,819
1919	2,024	40,475
1920	1,641	32,821
1921	1,260	30,959
1922	125	1,871
1923	246	3,697
1924	622	9,301
1925	(a)	..
1926	64·2	947
1927	280	3,810
1928	103	1,242
1929	180	1,800
1930	14	140
1931	90	890
1932	654	6,147
1933	139	1,592
1934	1,009	3,769
1935	3,819	12,453

Exports.

Exports from Travancore in the period between 1911 and 1918, foreign and coastwise, amounted to 7,706 tons of an approximate value of £220,000. German interests have, of course, long since been eliminated. The exports, amounting to 604 tons, valued at £27,999, and 882 tons valued at £40,000 in 1917-18 and 1918-19, from Tuticorin, were probably for the most part of Travancore monazite. The principal recipient was the United States of America and next to her came the United Kingdom. Small quantities were also taken by Japan. In recent years, the export trade in monazite has practically ceased, the last shipment of 212 tons valued at £1,909 from Madras being

(a) The production amounted to 1 cwt. only.

recorded in 1929-30. In association with monazite are found ilmenite and zircon. Ilmenite was formerly considered as a bye-product of the monazite industry, but since 1922, except in 1933, the production of this mineral has expanded almost continuously so that in both quantity and value it is more important than monazite and zircon. This steady increase in the output is due to the demand for its contents of titanium dioxide in the manufacture of titanium paints. In 1933 the output decreased from 50,053 tons valued at £58,134 in 1932 to 43,384 tons valued at £43,384. The output of zircon in that year amounted to 603 tons valued at £3,018 as compared with 491 tons valued at £3,805 in 1932.

Magnesite.

Occurrence.

The principal occurrence in India of magnesite, which is of value as a source of carbon dioxide and as a refractory material, is over an area of about 4½ square miles in the Chalk Hills near Salem, in the Madras Presidency. Magnesite is also known to occur at several other places in Southern India, always as veins traversing periodities, for example, at Seringala in Coorg, on the Cauvery above Fraserpet, in other parts of the Salem district, in the Trichinopoly district, and in the Hassan and Mysore districts of the Mysore State. Analysis of Salem magnesite shows an average content of magnesium carbonate of between 96 and 97 per cent. and in picked samples 99 per cent. The mineral is won by open quarrying operations and is calcined on the spot to produce (a) lightly calcined or caustic magnesia obtained at a temperature of about 800° C, and (b) dead-burnt, sintered or shrunk magnesia, obtained by calcination of about 1,700° C Roughly speaking two tons of the crude ore produce a little less than one ton of caustic magnesia, while about two and a half tons are requisite for the manufacture of one ton of dead-burnt magnesia. The latter kind contains less than ½ per cent. carbon dioxide and averages at least 87 or 88 per cent. of magnesium oxide. The Indian form is considerably higher in grade and is comparatively free from the impurity of the lime content Its main use is as a refractory lining for steel furnaces. The greater proportion of magnesite produced is utilised in a dead-burnt form.

Other uses for magnesite are the preparation of medicinal compounds, and the manufacture of certain varieties of vitreous porcelain, of fire-resisting paints, of non-conducting materials for steam pipe and boiler laggings and of sulphite paper pulp.

While 3,450 tons of crude magnesite were mined in 1902, the figure for the following year was 825 tons only and in 1909, 737 tons. In 1910, 5,182 tons and in 1911, 3,490 tons were recovered. There was thereafter a marked development in 1912 and 1913 (the output being 15,379 tons and 16,198 tons, respectively), and again in 1916 and 1917. In 1918 there was again a marked set-back with a partial revival in the two following years. The average annual production during 1919-23 amounted to 18,039 tons valued at £14,388, during 1924-28 it rose to 25,717 tons valued at £19,358 with a record production in 1926 of 30,461 tons valued at £26,444.

The following table shows the quantity and value of magnesite produced in India in recent years, as compared with the pre-war and post-war figures.

TABLE No. 178.—*Quantity and value of magnesite produced in India in 1914, 1919 and from 1930 onwards.*

Year.	Quantity.	Value.
	Tons.	£
1914	1,680	557
1919	17,126	13,152
1930	16,523	6,277
1931	5,333	2,026
1932	13,864	5,470
1933	15,206	7,344
1934	14,975	7,385
1935	16,984	7,918

Exports.

In 1913-14, 3,824 tons of calcined magnesite valued at £8,922 were exported as compared with 1,147 tons valued at £5,822 in 1918-19. Figures of export of calcined magnesite in recent years are not available In 1934-35, 3,466 tons of magnesite valued at £25,976 were shipped as against 3,668 tons valued at £31,484, in the previous year. During 1934-35, 84 per cent. of the total export went to the United Kingdom and 9 per cent. to the United States of America. In 1935-36 the exports of magnesite amounted to 3,940 tons valued at £31,473 of which 77 per cent. went to the United Kingdom.

In Madras shipment is made in bags of 185 or 190 lbs. or in drums of 224 lbs.

LAC.

Cultivation.

Lac is the resinous exudation of certain scale insects of the genus *tachardia*, frequenting particular trees, the nature of the host being an important factor in the resultant crop. The name is derived from the Sanskrit word *laksha* (lakh) meaning a hundred thousand, referring to the vast numbers of minute insects at the time of swarming. The best lac is obtained from the *schleichera trijuga* (*kusumb*) but very large quantities are derived from other species such as the *butea frondosa* (*palas*), *acacia arabica* (*babul*) *zizyphus jujuba* (*beer*) and *zizyphus xylopyrus* (*ghont*) while the *albizzia lebbex* (*siris*), *shorea robusta* (sal), *ficus religiosa* (*pipul*) *acacia catechu flemingia congesta* and *cajanus indicus* (*arhar*) are also suitable hosts for the insect. The cultivation of lac is probably one of the oldest minor industries in India, and if the dye was originally valued more than the resin it yielded, the latter is referred to as a wood varnish as far back as the beginning of the 16th century in the *Ami-i-Akbari*.

Area and Occurrence.

Lac is obtained in India from four main areas, (1) the Central India area including Chota Nagpur and the adjoining districts of Orissa, Bengal and the United Provinces, the north eastern forests of the Hyderabad State and the Central Provinces generally, and the Chattisgarh and Nagpur divisions in particular (*palas* and *kusumb*), (2) Sind (*babul*) (3) Central Assam (*pipul* and *arhar*) and (4) Upper Burma and the Shan States (*pipul* and *palas*). There is sporadic cultivation elsewhere, for example, in the Punjab (*beer*) and Mysore, and the principal factories are situated in the United Provinces (Mirzapur) and Bihar (Balarampur and Imamganj). There are also two factories in Calcutta where shellac is manufactured by special processes on a considerable scale. In certain grades the best machine-made lac cannot compete with hand-made.

Production.

Until recent years no actual estimate of production was possible owing to the difficulty of obtaining reliable statistics of stick-lac crop, and this uncertainty made lac a highly speculative trade and led to frequent fluctuation in the market values. According to the information collected by the Indian Lac Cess Committee, the total Indian production in the year 1934 amounted to 1,027,500 maunds (752,300 cwts.) of stick-lac.

The following table gives the prices of T. N. Shellac in Calcutta in 1914, 1918, 1920 and from 1931 onwards.

TABLE No 179.—*Prices of T. N. shellac in Calcutta per bazaar maund in 1914, 1918, 1920 and from 1931 onwards.*

Year.	Highest		Lowest.	
	Month.	Price.	Month.	Price.
		Rs.		Rs.
1914	January	43¼	October	23
1918	December	100	May	83
1920	January	255	April	155
1931	April	31	July	28
1932	January	27½	July	17½
1933	July	25	April	18
1934	July	50	April	34¼
1935	January	41	April	24

There are four distinct crops of shellac in India known as *bysaki*, *kushmi*, *katki* and *jethwa* respectively, in order of commercial importance, though the katki crop is generally larger than the *kushmi*. *Kushmi* and *jethwa* apply to the produce of *schleichera trijuga* only, and the others to lac from *butea frondosa* and other hosts. Lac collected before the insects swarm is known as *ari* after they have swarmed as *phunki*. The normal annual production of stick-lac in India, as estimated by the Indian Lac Cess Committee, is in the neighbourhood of 1½ million maunds (1 million cwts). The only other lac producing countries are Siam and Indo-China. A maund (forty seers) of stick-lac yields on an average about eighteen seers of shellac.

Trade Descriptions.

Stick-lac is the incrustation on the twigs of the tree which contains three main constituents, lac resin, the outermost portion of the incrustation, lac wax, secreted from specially localised regions, and lac dye contained in the body of the insects itself. Stick-lac, when ground and sifted and washed free of so much of the dye as is soluble, becomes *seed-lac* or *grainlac* which is converted into *shellac* by fusing it over a slow fire. A small quantity of orpiment is frequently added to produce the light yellow colour required in the finer grades, and an admixture of rosin (colophony) is also occasionally made to lower the melting point. The mixture is then fused by twisting it in long narrow bags before an open fire and the molten liquid is squeezed through the bags and spread out uniformly on porcelain cylinders. When cold these sheets are assorted according to colour, the thick pieces and impurities being punched out and cast into the bags for remelting. To produce button-lac, the molten lac is dropped on to a smooth surface instead of being stretched. The only other commercial forms of lac which need be noticed are *garnet-lac*, which is a dark red lac made from Assam or Burma stick-lac by the spirit or wet process, usually with about 10 per cent. rosin, but without orpiment, *tongue lac*, and *kiri*, the residue remaining in the bags after melting. Button and tongue lac are usually made from medium to good quality stick-lac, while shellac is made in all grades.

In India there is a considerable demand for *kiri* in connection with the manufacture of bangles, bracelets, toys and articles of domestic utility, the ornamentation of ivory and metalware, or as a cement.

Exports.

Repeated attempts to cultivate lac in Japan, Formosa and German East Africa having proved fruitless and the produce of Siam and Indo-China together representing only a small percentage of that of India, the latter enjoys a practical monopoly of the trade. The following tables show the quantity and value of the exports of manufactured and unmanufactured lac, respectively, in 1913-14, 1918-19 and from 1931-32 onwards:—

TABLE No. 180.—*Exports of manufactured lac by sea from British India to foreign countries in 1913-14, 1918-19 and from 1931-32 onwards.*

Year	Shellac.		Button-lac		Other kinds (except lac-dye).		Total.		Average value per cwt.
	Cwts	£	Cwts	£	Cwts	£	Cwts	£	£
1913-14	275,357	1,131,876	21,865	87,130	23,646	29,095	320,868	1,248,110	3·9
1918-19	222,889	1,866,268	3,520	37,538	6,575	12,530	232,984	1,916,326	8·2
1931-32	297,012	973,844	18,164	71,107	31,050	30,650	346,226	1,075,601	3 1
1932-33	261,733	625,386	17,432	51,330	14,109	9,991	293,274	686,707	2 3
1933-34	529,075	1,456,870	19,100	51,799	23,727	15,695	571,902	1,524,364	2·7
1934-35	431,937	2,002,048	15,722	80,827	44,627	30,257	492,286	2,113,132	4 3
1935-36	284,582	766,833	29,373	86,056	40,564	23,967	354,469	876,356	2·5

TABLE No 181.—*Exports of unmanufactured lac by sea from British India to foreign countries in 1913-14, 1918-19 and from 1931-32 onwards.*

Year	Stick-lac.		Seed-lac		Total.		Average value per cwt.
	Cwts	£	Cwts	£	Cwts	£	£
1913-14	1,196	3,449	17,097	58,975	18,293	62,424	3·4
1918-19 . . .	4	27	6,111	49,287	6,115	49,314	8·1
1931-32 . .	12,841	22,738	104,657	281,222	117,498	303,960	2·6
1932-33 . . .	4,204	6,108	120,822	238,966	125,026	245,074	2·0
1933-34	6,872	11,558	152,214	312,353	159,086	323,911	2 0
1934-35	5,081	12,733	88,635	348,850	93,716	361,583	3·9
1935-36	7,270	14,014	125,842	287,356	133,112	301 370	2·3

Government control.

When the war had been some time in progress it became necessary in order to secure sufficient supplies for the Ministry of Munitions (whose annual requirements for the United Kingdom and the Allies were estimated at 50,000 cwts.), to come to an agreement in January 1917 with the shellac shippers in Calcutta, whereby the shipment of lac was prohibited to all destinations, but licenses were freely given on condition that against every export on private account a consignment of shellac, corresponding to 20 per cent. of the quantity exported and of a certain specified quality, was guaranteed to Government at a fixed *f.o.b.* price of Rs. 42 per maund. Owing to the difficulty of obtaining sufficient quantities of the Government quality, the Ministry of Munitions eventually agreed to take a certain portion of their requirements in commercial T. N. London standard. In the matter of export of other qualities of lac, the Government percentage was calculated on the assumed percentage of shellac in each variety, *viz.*, 90 per cent. in the case of seed-lac, 70 per cent. in that of stick-lac and 40 per cent. of refuse lac, giving 18 per cent. 14 per cent. and 8 per cent. as the proportion due to Government in respect of each. Through the co-operation of the shellac shippers this scheme worked very successfully and resulted in the supplying of 80,000 cwts. to the Ministry of Munitions. Though prices remained fairly constant in Calcutta during the period of control, the London quotation rose from 144*s*. in January 1917 to 450*s*. in April 1918, and stood at the Armistice at about 320*s*. Shortly after the suspension of hostilities control was discontinued, and the restrictions on export were also removed, but nevertheless shipments from India in 1918-19 were not particularly heavy owing to railway congestion between the manufacturing districts and Calcutta, and to a markedly small bysaki crop in 1918. The London price, which had fallen to 205*s*. in April 1919, began to soar again and in January 1920 touched 880*s*. before the inevitable reaction set in. In the year 1934, the highest and the lowest prices were 120*s*. and 81*s*. respectively.

The distribution of the exports in the last pre-war year and in 1935-36 is shown in the following table:—

TABLE No. 182.—*Distribution of exports of lac in the years 1913-14 and 1935-36.*

Country.	1913-14.			1935-36.		
	Manufactured.	Unmanufactured.	Total.	Manufactured.	Unmanufactured.	Total.
	Cwts.	Cwts.	Cwts.	Cwts.	Cwts.	Cwts.
United States of America . . .	142,663	10,766	153,429	92,222	80,223	172,445
United Kingdom .	91,160	6,404	97,564	63,746	16,169	79,915
Germany . . .	52,298	466	52,764	45,042	9,557	54,599
France . . .	12,202	81	12,283	10,925	1,624	12,549
Japan . . .	4,246	37	4,283	54,101	..	54,101
Other countries . .	18,299	539	18,838	88,433	25,539	113,972

United States of America is the best customer for Indian lac. It will be noticed that the demand for lac has, as compared to the pre-war period, increased considerably especially from the United States of America and Japan, where extensive use is made of it in the manufacture of gramophone goods, varnishes, lithographic ink and for insulating purposes in the electrical industry. But the outstanding feature of the export trade in lac has been the uncertainty regarding the demand for shellac. In the case of this commodity the demand is so variable and so precariously elastic, that any uncontrolled orgy of inflation can but lead to one result—the increased concentration on the development and use of synthetic substitutes. Taking a long view of the past, shellac which was intensively sought after as a raw material in the manufacture of paints and varnishes is now being displaced from its position of pre-eminence through the rise of cellulose finishes. Even in the electric and plastics industries where newer uses were found for the natural product, a large part of the field is being increasingly appropriated by thermosetting plastics and similar synthetic resins. With the intensive research in new synthetic compositions it is doubtful if the consuming interests will tolerate for long a position in which they are at the mercy of an uncertain supply.

Lac Dye.

Exports of lac dye have for several years practically ceased though crude cake dye continues to be sold in the bazaars. Against 18,000 cwts. recorded in 1868-69 only 18 cwts. were exported in 1910-11 the last recorded Lac dye (crimson *lake*) gives a fast bright red tint to silk and wool, and if supplies were available in a reasonably pure state should command a considerable market.

Lac Wax.

Lac wax is in demand in connection with boot polish but is not usually separated from the resin in the treatment of stick-lac, as it is believed to affect prejudicially the quality of the resultant shellac. No separate statistics are maintained of the exports of lac wax.

Imports.

Imports of lac into India are on a comparatively small scale and are practically limited to stick-lac from Siam and Indo-China *via* the Straits Settlements, for conversion into shellac averaging about 48,500 cwts. per annum during the last six years.

Marks and Standards.

The major portion of the lac that leaves India is in the form of a dark orange shellac known as T. N. (probably from the mark of a firm called Tularam Nataram). T. N. is made from all kinds of stick-lac including Burma and Siam. In London a sample, representing the average quality of the lots of common shellac, arriving from India, is standardised and quotations are made on the T. N. basis. The London standard for T. N. generally remains unaltered except in very exceptional circumstances

T. N. on the London market is sold with the addition of 3 per cent Rosin and upto 3 per cent. inpurities or insoluble matter is not penalised; allowances are, however, payable if either or both these quantities are exceeded In New York T. N. is sold in 3 grades, Heart, USSA TN and TN Pure. The first and last grades are sold free of Rosin and if the insoluble matter exceeds 3 per cent. penalties are enforced. USSA TN is sold with the addition of 3 per cent Rosin and impurities should not exceed 3 per cent. If the quantity of Rosin exceeds 1 per cent. in the former two grades or 4 per cent. in the latter, the buyer has the option of rejection. In the case of Heart grade, the buyer can reject if the impurities exceed

4 per cent., while in the case of the other two grades impurities are limited to 5 per cent. Seed-lac is now largely taking the place of TN Pure in the New York market and this is sold on a basis of 5 per cent. impurities free and with a rejection limit of 8 per cent.

Organization of the Trade.

The lac trade like so many others in India is encumbered by the large number of middlemen who intervene between the actual collector and the manufacturer or shipper. By a system of advances, the collector of stick-lac and the small manufacturer are bound to *banias* or middlemen to whom alone they can sell, and brokers again intervene at the port of shipment. Shellac is sold on drafts of 3 months' sight for shipment to Europe and 4 months' sight for the United States of America against letters of credit in London. Contracts are on a *c.i.f.* basis to Europe but in the case of America only *c.f.* as insurance is usually arranged by the importers themselves. Occasional shipments are also made on consignment sale.

Shellac is packed for export in two maund cases (one maund =82 2/15 lbs) which weigh approximately 1½ cwts., or in double gunnies. The local unit of sale is the bazaar maund, but for export the cwt in the case of shipments to the United Kingdom, and the lb. for the American market.

Calcutta has always enjoyed a preponderating share in the export trade in lac as is illustrated by the following table.

TABLE No. 183.—*Exports of lac from British India (principal ports and percentage) in 1913-14, 1919-20 and 1935-36.*

—	1913-14.		1919-20.		1935-36.	
	Quantity.	Percentage.	Quantity.	Percentage.	Quantity.	Percentage.
	Cwts.		Cwts.		Cwts.	
Calcutta . . .	328,892	96·9	373,476	99·4	486,481	99·8
Rangoon . . .	4,068	1·3	1,307	·3	1,060	·2
Karachi . . .	3,664	1·0	870	·2	21	} ..
Bombay . . .	1,296	·4	41	} ·1	30	}
Madras . . .	1,240	·4	12	}	...	..

Burma.

Before the war there were occasional shipments chiefly of seed lac to the United States of America, which purchased in this market when the margin between the prices in India and Burma lac made it profitable to do so Over 7,500 cwts. went to the United States of America in 1912-13. The overland imports in 1913-14, 1918-19 and from 1931-32 onwards into Burma, which constitute the bulk of what is known commercially as Burma lac, are shewn in the table below:—

TABLE No. 184—*Overland imports of lac into Burma in 1913-14, 1918 19 and from 1931-32, onwards.*

Year.	Imports. Cwts.
1913-14	11,364
1918-19	15,793
1931-32	31,553
1932-33	16,480
1933-34	54,356
1934-35	37,482
1935-36	31,764

There is only one company in Burma engaged in shellac manufacture and the quantity of stick-lac, exported coastwise to Calcutta for conversion into shellac, amounted in 1931-32 to 30,778 cwts. in 1932-33 to 14,310 cwts in 1933-34 to 63,101 cwts. in 1934-35 to 46,799 cwts. and in 1935-36 to 32,085 cwts. A royalty is levied at the Customs Houses in Burma on all exports by sea of stick-lac and manufactured lac from Burma at the rate of one anna in the rupee, based on the average market price in Calcutta of standard T. N. Shellac, and credited to Forest revenues.

Lac Cess.

With effect from the 1st January 1922, a cess of four annas per maund on shellac and two annas per maund on refuse lac was imposed From the 23rd August 1936, the rates of cess were increased to 7 as. per maund in the case of shellac and 5 as per md in the case of refuse lac. Until the year 1931, the net proceeds of the cess were handed over to the Indian Lac Association for expenditure on research. The Association, which was chiefly composed of manufacturers and shippers in Calcutta and on which the interests of the cultivators were not represented, did not consider itself in the best position to control effectually the future conduct of in the lac industry, and the Royal Commission on Agriculture also emphasised in their Report the importance of bringing together the various interests, especially those of cultivators, in that industry A statutory committee called the Indian Lac Cess Committee was accordingly constituted under the provisions of section 4 of the Indian Lac Cess Act, 1930, which came into force on the 1st August 1931, to which all monies and properties vested in the Indian Lac Association were transferred, the latter body having been dissolved The total collections on account of lac cess adjusted during 1934-35 totalled Rs 2,13,579 (£16,018).

COFFEE.

Coffee is derived from a rubiaceous plant belonging to the same family as cinchona and *madder* The bulk of the coffee grown in India is *Coffea Arabica* but there has been an increased interest of recent years in *Coffea Robusta* on account of its vigour and high yield and the existence of some demand in India for the produce despite its lower quality It is used mainly to replace unthrifty *Coffea Arabica* and the present average, apart from small patches, probably does not exceed 2,000 acres. There appears to be some room for extension at the lower elevations. Hybrids between *Coffea Arabica* and *Coffea Liberica* are grown on a very small area, having mainly been used as "supplies" in poor Arabica areas.

According to tradition Baba Budan, returning from a pilgrimage to Mecca in the 16th century, brought seven seeds and planted them on the hills, now called after him in the Kadur district of Mysore, but the systematic cultivation of coffee in India dates only from 1830 when Mr. Cannon opened a plantation near Chickmugalur and during the next 30 years a large area was put under coffee not only in Mysore but also in Coorg, the Nilgiris and Shevaroy Hills, the Wynaad and Travancore. In 1862 the coffee industry in Southern India had reached its zenith, but three years later the borer beetle made its appearance in the Wynaad and Coorg, and the leaf blight (*hemileia vastatrix*), which ruined the Ceylon coffee estates, followed. Between 1877 and 1887 no less than 263 plantations in the Wynaad were abandoned and those in South Travancore practically wiped out by the industry elsewhere if it has made no headway in the last thirty years, has at least lost little ground, despite the competition of Brazil, Guatemala and Costa Rica, chiefly because East India coffee is generally of superior quality. Indeed the coffee from certain Mysore estates commands higher prices than even so-called Mocha, much of which, if the truth were known, is Native cherry exported by dhow from Mangalore and Tellicherry to Red Sea ports. When railway communication between the coffee growing area and the coast is established, the heavy cost of transport by cart with the attendant risk of theft will be greatly reduced. The Nilgiri Railway is utilised by the neighbouring plantations in transporting Coffee to the Coast, but it is not yet of much use to any estates in the district which is off the line. The following table shows the acreage under coffee cultivation in recent years :—

History of Coffee Growing in India.

TABLE No 185.—*Area under coffee in India for the years (ending 30th June) 1931 to 1935.*

Provinces and States.	Area (in acres).				
	1930-31.	1931-32.	1932-33.	1933-34.	1934-35.
British Provinces—					
Coorg . .	37,500	38,400	38,600	39,400	38,600
Madras . .	37,800	41,300	39,900	40,900	42,400
Total British Provinces.	75,300	79,700	78,500	80,300	81,000
Indian States—					
Cochin . .	1,800	1,900	1,900	2,100	2,000
Mysore . .	82,400	89,800	93,300	100,700	101,500
Travancore .	800	800	800	900	1,000
Total Indian States .	85,000	92,500	98,000	103,700	104,500
GRAND TOTAL .	160,300	172,200	176,500	184,000	185,500

NOTE.—From 1931-32, statistics of plantations having an area between five and ten acres have been included.

The area under coffee under the stimulus of better prices, has increased by nearly fifteen per cent. since 1930-31, the Mysore acreage having risen from 82,400 to 101,500, the Madras from 37,800 to 42,400 and the Coorg from 37,500 to 38,600. In 1934-35, 4,170 acres of new land were put under coffee, while the area of old cultivation abandoned was 2,668 acres. Of the total area under coffee during 1934-35, Mysore accounted for 55 per cent., Madras 23 per cent., Coorg 21 per cent. and Cochin and Travancore together 1 per cent.

The yield of coffee varies considerably according to the season and the estate. On the best plantation in a good season as much as 12 cwts. to the acre has been recorded, but 400 lbs. of clean coffee per acre may be taken as a fair average yield. The total reported production of cured coffee in 1934-35 was 32,856,861 lbs , as compared with 34,586,658 lbs. reported in 1933-34 and 32,490,790 lbs. in 1932-33. Of the total production in 1934-35, 2,298,115 lbs. were reported for smaller plantations having an area between five and ten acres. The yield per acre of plucked area is 120 lbs. (270 lbs.) in Cochin, 204 lbs. (266 lbs) in Madras, 241 lbs. (235 lbs) in Coorg, 167 lbs. (213 lbs) in Travancore and 187 lbs. (198 lbs) in Mysore The figures for 1933-34 have been shown in bracket. The bulk of the coffee produced in India is exported, the most important markets being France, the United Kingdom, Germany, Norway and Belgium in that order. The number of plantations on the 30th January 1935 was 6,781, of which 2,180 were in British India and the remaining 4,601 in the Indian States. The following statement shows the number and area of plantations and the number of persons employed in each district in India in 1934-35.—

TABLE No 186—*Statement showing the number and area of plantation and the number of persons employed in each district in India during the year ending 30th June 1935.*

District.	Number of plantations.	Total area of plantations.	Persons employed (daily average).		
			Garden labour (permanent).	Outside labour (permanent).	Outside labour (temporary).
Madras—	No.	Acres.	No.	No.	No.
Vizagapatam	6	622	27	..	6
Madura	468	12,009	2,238	2,130	2,478
Tinnevelly	8	12,672	218	1	40
Coimbatore	12	12,281	1,638	215	245
Nilgiris	331	38,345	5,534	1,262	1,830
Salem	79	14,784	3,381	910	697
South Kanara	1	12	10	..	..
Malabar	82	24,837	1,693	674	500
Total Madras	987	115,562	14,739	5,192	5,796
Coorg	1,193	64,492	9,451	3,835	7,541
Total British India	2,180	180,054	24,190	9,027	13,337
Mysore—					
Mysore	3	534	228	..	..
Hassan	1,567	43,669	5,237	3,742	8,132
Kadur	3,001	95,477	13,762	6,989	14,346
Total Mysore	4,571	139,680	19,227	10,731	22,478
Travancore	13	2,520	471	11	38
Cochin	17	5,848	1,344	91	59
Total Indian States	4,601	148,048	21,042	10,833	22,575
GRAND TOTAL	6,781	328,102	45,232	19,860	35,912

Coffee is sown and transplanted in the rainy season. The crop begins to ripen in October and hand-picking continues until January. The berries which have fallen on the ground and are collected at the end of the season are known as jackal coffee. The ripe coffee bean or *cherry* consists usually of two seeds or berries, but in a certain percentage is found only one, which on account of its shape is distinguished by the name of *peaberry*, After plucking, the fruit is either dried and pounded or immersed in water and pulped by the wet method before it is bagged and sent down to the coast. The outer covering is known as the pulp and the inner adhesive layer as parchment, while the seed coat within the *parchment* is the ***silver skin.***

Some coffee is sent in parchment direct to Europe, but the bulk of the coffee grown in Mysore, Coorg and the Wynaad, the Nilgiris, Palni and Shevaroy Hills is prepared for export at Mangalore, Tellicherry, Calicut and Coimbatore. Altogether there are eighteen large curing works employing about two hundred men and women apiece. The parchment coffee which is brought down to the coast in carts is spread out on barbecues which consist of asphalt platforms in open yards slightly sloped from the centre and divided by low barriers. After being well sundried the coffee is pulped or peeled by machinery and then winnowed by either machinery or hand labour, and sized. It is next 'garbled' by women who eliminate all the broken and imperfect beans. When the garbling is over the coffee is weighed and bagged in double sacks or put into casks. Commercially two kinds of coffee are recognised, (1) *cherry* usually from Indian-owned estates, where the whole fruit is dried and not put through pulpers, and (2) *plantation* coffee, cured at the coast ports according to the process already described. Most of the cherry goes to France and of the plantation coffee to the United Kingdom The three recognised sizes are known as A, B, and C, exclusive of peaberry, while the broken and imperfect beans are classified as *triage*. Typical pre-war prices were Rs. 50—60 for *plantation* and Rs. 40—50 for *native cherry f.o.b.*, West Coast ports; or 80 and 70 shillings respectively *c.i.f.*, London. When bagged, coffee is put up in gunnies containing 170 to 182 lbs. at the West Coast ports (Cochin, Calicut and Mangalore) in the Madras Presidency In Bombay the unit of sale and shipment is the bag of 168 to 182 lbs. The following table shows the quantity and value of coffee exported in recent years as contrasted with the pre-war and post-war figures.

Coffee curing.

TABLE No. 187.—*Quantities and values of coffee exported from India in 1913-14, 1918-19 and from 1931-32 onwards.*

Year.	Quantity.	Value.	Average value per cwt.
	Cwts.	£	£
1913-14	259,900	1,024,402	3·9
1918-19	218,504	795,058	3·6
1931-32	155,600	708,758	4·5
1932-33	173,177	823,606	4·8
1933-34	185,995	768,404	4·1
1934-35	140,963	545,302	3·8
1935-36	215,951	766,466	3·5

In the next table the quantities of coffee shipped from each province and the proportionate share of each in the last pre-war year and in 1935-36 are contrasted. It will be seen that the bulk of the shipment goes from Madras.

TABLE No. 188.—*Share of each province in the export trade of coffee in 1913-14, and 1935-36 contrasted.*

Province.	1913-14.		1935-36.	
	Quantity.	Percentage.	Quantity.	Percentage.
	Cwts.		Cwts.	
Madras	257,375	98·7	213,654	98·9
Bombay	2,439	·9	2,168	1·05
Burma	22	·1	129	·05
Bengal	64	·3	..	..
Total	259,900	100	215,951	100

In 1917 it was found necessary to restrict the exports of coffee, and the suggestion of large purchases by the military authorities for the troops in the eastern theatre of war, as an alternative to tea, provoked so much opposition that it was not persevered in. An unusual feature of the 1918 shipping season was the purchase of 2,000 tons by the Greek Government, for which freight was found in a Greek vessel, and this contract was followed in 1919 by a second for 3,500 tons. The importation of coffee plants, coffee seeds and coffee beans into British India is prohibited, except for experimental planting purposes. The restriction does not apply to roasted and ground coffee.

Coffee Cess.

By the Indian Coffee Cess Act, 1935, provision has been made for the levy of a customs duty at the rate not exceeding Re. 1 per cwt on all coffee produced in India and taken by sea or by land to any place beyond the limits of British India or to Burma. A Statutory Committee called the Indian Coffee Cess Committee has been constituted under the provisions of the above Act to which the net proceeds of the Coffee Cess are handed over for meeting the expenses of the Committee and the cost of such measures as it may consider advisable to undertake for promoting the sale and increasing the consumption in India and elsewhere of coffee produced in India and also for promoting agricultural and technological research in the interest of the coffee industry in India.

TIMBER.

The Indian forests are a source of considerable profit to the State, yielding a net revenue in 1931-32 of £2,998,797 as compared with £3,550,080 in 1930-31 and £4,593,852 in 1929-30. The corresponding charges were £1,733,492, £2,549,491 and £2,606,464. The area covered by reserves under the control of the Forest Department in India was about 106,000 square miles in 1931-32.

The outturn of timber and fuel in 1931-32 was about 306 millions cubic feet, of which Burma accounted for more than 83 millions. Other important timbers extracted include deodar (*cedrus deodara*), Sal (*shorea robusta*), shisham (*dalbergia sissoo*), rosewood (*dalbergia latifolia*), eng (*dipterocarpus tuberculatus*), *matti* (*terminalia tomentosa*), padauk (*petrocarpus macrocarpus*), *pyinkado* (*xylia dolabriformis*), and Indian mahogany (*cedrela toona*). The total area regenerated amounted to more than 200,000 acres. The most important, apart from rubber, of artificial plantations is, perhaps, the teak plantation at Nilambur in the Malabar district of the Madras Presidency (started in 1842) and the numerous copues for fuel purposes of casuarina, eucalyptus and deodar. The following table shows the area of forest lands and outturn of forest produce in the years 1930-31 and 1931-32.

TABLE No. 189.—*Area of forest lands and outturn of forest produce in 1930-31 and 1931-32.*

Year.	Total area of provinces †	Forest Area				Proportion of forests to total area.	Outturn of produce	
		Reserved.	Protected.	*Unclassed State.	Total.		Timber and fuel.	Minor produce.
	Sq. miles.	Sq. miles.	Sq. miles.	Sq. miles.	Sq. miles.	per cent.	C.ft.	C.ft.
1930-31 .	1,102,602	107,753	6,263	135,694	249,710	22·6	322,852,820	12,586,854
1931-32 .	1,101,902	105,960	6,682	133,189	245,831	22 3	305,911,538	11,327,397

The foreign exports of timber are almost entirely of teak from Burma but in 1923 there was a marked improvement in the demand for other varieties in the London market, particularly for *pyinkado* from Burma, rosewood from Madras, *padauk* from the Andamans. In 1913-14 the exports from Rangoon amounted to 42,406 cubic tons valued at £426,200 and from Moulmein 6,122 cubic tons valued at £65,300. The United Kingdom took 27,416, and Germany 6,282 tons Owing to the increasing scarcity of supplies, prices had been rising for several years past and stocks growing depleted The coastwise exports were from Rangoon 78,763 cubic tons, valued at £493,400, and from Moulmein 34,328 tons, valued at £251,400.

Exports.

The foreign trade was dislocated by the war, and in 1916-17 exports from Burma had declined to 23,944 cubic tons, valued at £304,300 from Rangoon and 74 cubic tons, valued at £733 from Moulmein, but owing to increased demands for military and building purposes from India proper, the coastwise exports totalled 145,518 cubic tons, valued at £1,109,600. A certain amount of teak from Siam forests close to the Burma frontier is floated down the Salween River to the timber yards at Moulmein and is re-exported from there. The total quantity so brought down rose from 7,153 cubic tons in 1917-18 to 17,549 tons in 1918-19. The foreign exports of timber other than teak from Burma have hitherto been comparatively small but considerable quantities of *eng* and *pyinkado* are shipped in normal times to Bombay and Calcutta.

* Unclassed state forests include in many provinces all unoccupied waste. The figures do not therefore necessarily represent the wooded area.

† Excludes Delhi Province and the British Pargana of Manpur (Central India).

The exports from Burma on Government account during the last two years of the war amounted to nearly 150,000 tons. A good deal of the teak went to Mesopotamia, and other theatres of war supplied with scantlings, etc., were Salonica and East Africa.

The quantity and value of timber exported in the last few years is contrasted below with the pre-war and post-war figures.

TABLE No. 190.—*Quantity and value of exports of timber in 1913-14 1918-19, and from 1931-32 onwards.*

Year.	Quantity.	Value.
	Cubic tons.	£
1913-14	58,672	571,636
1918-19	33,313	423,390
1931-32	22,113	424,602
1932-33	17,348	301,357
1933-34	26,738	459,800
1934-35	44,736	700,993
1935-36	59,306	846,475

The bulk of the shipments goes from Burma, the principal recipient being the United Kingdom.

Imports.

Apart from Siam teak imported in considerable quantities into Bombay, there have always been large quantities of comparatively cheap foreign timber coming into India for various purposes, such as furniture making, packing cases, etc. Wooden railway sleepers imported on Government and private account which are registered under a separate statistical head, have been included in the next table for the sake of completeness Of the cheaper timbers the principal are Oregon pine imported from America and Deal and firewood from Jugo-slavia. The following table shows the imports of the principal kinds of timber in recent years as contrasted with those of the pre-war and post-war.

TABLE No 191.—*Imports of timber including railway sleepers into India in 1913-14, 1919-20 and from 1931-32 onwards.*

Year.	Quantity.		Total Value.
	Timber. Deal and Pinewood Jarrah and Teak.	Railway sleepers.	
	Cubic tons.	Cwts.	£
1913-14	62,581	1,090,063	632,377
1919-20	45,430	15,420	629,360
1931-32	17,096	..	143,192
1932-33	12,601	..	85,373
1933-34	19,851	120	122,764
1934-35	19,673	..	113,509
1935-36	13,797		64,656

Unit of sale.

In Burma the unit of sale in the case of round log as well as of converted timber is the ton of 50 cubic feet.

SANDALWOOD.

East Indian sandalwood is the heartwood of *santalum album*, an evergreen tree whose occurrence is practically limited to a restricted area in Southern India, chiefly in Mysore and Coorg and the Coimbatore and Salem districts in the Madras Presidency, and to a more limited extent in Travancore and Sandur States.

Occurrence.

Sandalwood is mentioned in ancient Sanskrit literature and, long before the exploitation of the East by European traders, was a principal article of commerce. The heartwood (equivalent to about one-third of the felled tree by weight) is employed in the manufacture of small caskets and picture frames and for carved work in general. Considerable quantities are also utilized for religious rites and ceremonies. Hindus all over India smear sandal paste on their foreheads and upper parts of the body and the wealthier burn billets of it when cremating their dead. The wood is also used in the fire temples of the Parsees. The oil content of the heartwood varies from 5 to 7 per cent. This essential oil has valuable medicinal properties and considerable use in also made of it in perfumery and in the manufacture of superior toilet soaps. The local demand of sandalwood for these various purposes has been estimated at between 500 and 600 tons annually out of a total of 2,750 tons coming commercially into sight in pre-war times During the war this total fell to about 2,050 tons. In recent years the exports averaged less than 1,000 tons.

In Mysore and in Coorg all the trees are State property, and in Madras, though private ownership is recognised, production is almost a monopoly of the Government Forest reserves. All wood collected during the year in the three provinces was formerly sold by public auction, the average quantity thus disposed of ranging between 2,500 and 3,000 tons annually. At the sales held at the end of 1912 (for statistical purposes 1912-13), indication of a powerful competitor having entered the market was revealed by the disposal of 2,418 tons for £151,200 and these greatly enhanced values were more than maintained in the following year It is now known that the enhancement in the rates offered for sandalwood in 1912 was entirely due to competition on behalf of German buyers, who were either desirous of accumulating stocks against the day believed to be not far distant when the market would be closed to them by war, or had set themselves out to obtain a virtual monopoly of the supply of East Indian sandalwood for distillation purposes. With this competition eliminated, the auctions at the end of 1914 proved a complete fiasco, though some small sales were effected early in 1915 at prices almost up to pre-war levels and at the next auction 2,000 tons were disposed of for £113,300 owing to American purchases, partly it is believed, on German account. Before the auction took place in the following year, the Bangalore factory had opened and the Mysore Government materially enhanced the upset price. Though only 1,347 tons were sold, no less than £158,300 were realized. Since then Mysore auctions have been suspended. The quantity sold in Madras is not separately recorded. In Coorg 380 tons were disposed of in 1915-16 for £23,330, and in 1917-18, when

Production and Sales.

Mysore competition was for the first time eliminated, 800 tons realized rather more than £35,000. The average price per ton realized at auction nowhere much exceeded £38 before 1912, when buyers acting on behalf of Messrs. Schimmel raised it to over £60. In 1913-14 the average was £70 in Mysore and £66 in Coorg, and 1916-17 £114 and £105. In 1932-33, six hundred and forty-eight tons of sandalwood were sold for £44,599 in the Madras Presidency as against six hundred and seventy tons for £45,960 in the preceding year. The average price realised was £69 per ton as against £68 per ton in the previous year. The market for this article of luxury is rather uncertain, as it is considerably affected by overseas demand and the competition of sandalwood substitutes at home and abroad. Attempts made by the Forest Department to establish direct contact with European consumers have so far not materialized appreciably. The retail sales of sandalwood in the Madras Presidency have not yielded satisfactory results.

In pre-war days the Government of Mysore sold their Sandalwood by auction at different Koties maintained by the Forest Department of the Mysore State Mysore happens to have virtually the monopoly of the finest species of East Indian Sandalwood *viz.*, *Santalum Album*, seven-tenth of the world's demand being met by it, the supply being almost inexhaustible Sandalwood is a monopoly of the Government of Mysore.

Sandalwood Oil.

On account of the disturbed conditions in Europe during the Great War, the demand for Sandalwood slackened and the Government of Mysore decided to start their own factories. A small factory was first started in Bangalore and later on due to increased demand for the oil, it was found necessary to have a larger and a more up-to-date factory in the City of Mysore. The second factory was planned with a view to concentrate the work in one single factory. The Bangalore Factory was closed in January 1931, and all the distillation work is being conducted at the Mysore Factory since then.

The values of the exports of sandalwood and sandalwood oil in recent years are contrasted in the next table with pre-war and post-war figures. The shipments are made from Bombay and Madras.

TABLE No. 192.—*Values of sandalwood and sandalwood oil exported in 1913-14, 1918-19 and from 1931-32 onwards.*

Year.	Values.	
	Sandalwood.	Sandalwood oil.
	£	£
1913-14	128,626	..
1918-19	10,529	274,845
1931-32	96,597	136,114
1932-33	48,054	56,054
1933-34	93,759	69,336
1934-35	60,130	73,348
1935-36	69,400	83,241

The average quantity of sandalwood exported annually in recent years amounts to over 700 tons, and that of sandalwood oil, to about 10,000 gallons.

The principal destinations for the wood in pre-war days and in 1934-35 are contrasted in the table below. During the war the United Kingdom and the United States of America appropriated between themselves more than 75 per cent. of the quantities shipped, and Japan also increased her demands.

TABLE No. 193.—*Distribution of the trade in sandalwood among importing countries in 1913-14 and 1935-36.*

Destination.	Percentage.	
	1913-14.	1935-36.
Germany	43·4	..
United Kingdom	21·7	4·3
United States of America	15·5	66·0
France	7·7	·7
Netherlands	3·1	..
Ceylon	·4	..
Egypt	3·8	·6
Japan	·3	13·0

As regards sandalwood oil, the earliest Mysore shipments went almost exclusively to the United Kingdom with Japan which received 4,231 gallons in 1918-19 as the chief competitor. The distribution of the trade in oil in 1935-36 is shown in the next table.

TABLE No 194.—*Exports of sandalwood oil in 1935-36 showing the share of the principal recipients*

Destinations	Quantity.	Value.
	lbs.	£
United Kingdom	59,708	53,508
Japan	32,888	23,039
Other countries	9,475	6,694
Total	102,071	83,241

Imports.

The average annual imports of sandalwood amount to 350 tons approximately The importations are mainly from Australia, with Kenya and Straits Settlements as next in importance. More than 80 per cent goes to Bombay and the bulk of the balance to Burma. The shares of the other provinces are negligible The sandalwood is mainly used for religious and ceremonial purposes.

Unit of sale and shipment.

The unit of sale varies at the different West Coast ports. In Calicut and Tellicherry sales are made per cwt. and shipment takes place in bundles of 1½ to 1¾ cwts., while in Madras shipment is effected in bags of one cwt. In Madras and Calcutta the unit of sale of the oil is the lb. and of shipment cases of 60 to 75 lbs. at the former port and in tins packed in cases varying in weight from 48 to 60 lbs. at the latter.

DYEING AND TANNING SUBSTANCES.

Myrobalans.

Trade Descriptions.

Myrobalans, the commercial name indiscriminately applied to the fruit of *terminalia chebula*, *terminalia belerica* and *phyllanthus emblica*, which are widely distributed over India, are a valuable tanning agent. Considerable difference exists in the percentage of tannin contained in the dried fruit. The best qualities are oval and pointed and solid in structure while the less valuable are round and spongy. On the English market there are five chief kinds recognised, called after the localities where they are marketed: *Bimlies* shipped from Bimlipatam in Madras, *Rajapores* and *Vengurlas* from Bombay, *Jubbulpores* from the Central Provinces, and *Madras* On the London market *Madras No. 1 whole nuts* used to command the highest price, while tanners held different opinions as to the relative value of *Bimlies* and *Jubbulpores* which are abbreviated and referred to as B1 or J2, the figure representing the quality.

Unit of sale and shipment.

The fruits are generally picked over for shipment and contracts made on the basis of fair average of season, the unit of sale in Madras being the candy of 500 lbs. and of packing the bag of 160 to 168 lbs. In Calcutta the nuts are shipped in ½ cwt packets and sales are made per bazaar maund, while in Bombay the unit of sale and shipment is the bag of 1½ cwts.

Myrobalan Extract.

High freights first encouraged shipments of crushed myrobalans, *i.e*, with the kernels removed, and myrobalans extract The concentrated extract containing 50 to 60 per cent. tan is usually shipped in solid blocks. In 1934-35, 36,499 cwts. valued at £27,303 were shipped, as compared with 32,946 cwts valued at £24,716 in 1933-34, and 20,517 cwts valued at £16,544 in 1932-33. In 1935-36, 42,265 cwts valued at £31,555 were exported. The bulk of the exports usually goes to the United Kingdom. The extract is packed for shipment in bags or cases weighing about one cwt each.

Exports.

The following table shows the quantity and value of myrobalans exported in recent years as constrasted with the pre-war and post-war figures

TABLE No. 195 —*Quantity and value of myrobalans exported in 1913-14, 1918-19 and from 1931-32 onwards.*

Year.	Quantity.	Value.
	Tons	£
1913-14	61,819	379,626
1918-19	41,195	328,936
1931-32	63,542	496,380
1932-33	53,102	417,955
1933-34	61,835	419,489
1934-35	67,777	359,018
1935-36	74,117	350,429

In Calcutta the season for shipment runs from December to June. The chief markets before the war were the United Kingdom, Germany, the United States of America, Belgium, France and Austria-Hungary, though the exports to the United Kingdom were diminishing and those to the Central Powers and Belgium increasing. In 1935-36 the principal recipients were the United Kingdom, the United States of America and Germany in that order. Of the total exported in 1913-14, 32,652 tons went from Bombay, 28,500 from Bengal and 5,667 tons from Madras, while of that in 1935-36, 36,282 tons were shipped from Bombay, 35,205 tons from Bengal and 2,630 tons from Madras.

There is a large coastwise trade in Western India, chiefly from the smaller ports such as Bankot, Jaigad, Viziadurg and Vengurla in the Ratnagiri District and Tadri and Honawar in the Kanara District into the main port of Bombay.

The figures of exports from these districts during the three years ending 1934-35 will be seen below:—

	Ratnagiri District.		Kanara District.	
	Quantity.	Value.	Quantity.	Value.
	Cwts.	£	Cwts.	£
1932-33	218,176	36,954	3,239	749
1933-34	180,781	23,250	3,432	318
1934-35	209,883	22,662	1,870	436

INDIGO.

History of Cultivation.

Indigo is the produce of several species of plants belonging to the genus *indigofera*, especially *indigofera arrecta, tinctoria* and *sumatrana*, which yield the well known dark blue dye of commerce. Until 1907-08 indigo represented more than half the total value of dyeing and tanning materials exported, but no more than one-fifth in 1913-14. The historical record of indigo goes back almost to the beginning of the Christian era and the process of manufacture is described by many early travellers to India. Originally the industry in Western India was in Portuguese hands, but about 1778 the East India Company revived it in Bengal and gave it direct encouragement for the next twenty years, and when about 1837 the industry migrated to Tirhoot and the United Provinces, India recovered the foremost place among indigo producing countries of the world from which she had been temporarily ousted by the West Indies India's position remained unassailed though there was cultivation also on a considerable scale in Java, until German laboratories, thanks to an accident, found themselves in 1897 at last in a position to produce indigo (which had actually been synthesized nearly thirty years earlier) on a commercial scale. The fate which had already overtaken the *madder* and lac dye industries thereupon threatened the factories of Bihar. A decline in the exports of natural indigo from India (and also in Java) began almost immediately, and though at one time it was hoped that the introduction of the Natal-Java plant (*indigofera arrecta*) giving a higher yield of indigotin with improved methods of cultivation and extraction might stem the tide, this retrogression proceeded steadily until the declaration of hostilities in 1914. By 1910 the Java industry was dead, and in 1913-14 the area under cultivation in India was scarcely more than a tenth of that in 1895-96.

Prices.

Soon after the outbreak of war the shortage of dye stuffs among the Allies (except perhaps in Japan) became acute, and in India when the Calcutta indigo sales were resumed in December 1914 the prices realised were nearly four times as great as those of previous March. In January 1915 the quotation was £70-10s. and the rate continued in the neighbourhood of £61 until March 1917. Since then the prices have undergone great fluctuations The trend of prices in recent years is indicated in the subjoined table.

TABLE No. 196.—*Wholesale prices of *Indigo in Calcutta from 1933-34 onwards*

Month.	Prices per cwt.					
	1933-34.		1934-35.		1935-36.	
	£	s.	£	s.	£	s.
April	18	11	14	16	14	16
July	14	16	14	16	14	16
October	14	16	14	16	14	16
January	14	16	14	16	14	16

Area and Production.

With this encouragement to exporters and with the Indian dyers finding supplies of aniline increasingly difficult to obtain and then only at extravagant rates, the area under cultivation increased by over 100 per cent. in 1915-16 and again by another 100 per cent. in the following year. But even then the total was less than half the high water mark reached twenty years before and the output was scarcely proportionately raised as the increase in cultivation was chiefly in Madras and the United Provinces where, owing to the dye being manufactured in more primitive fashion, the outturn is generally lower than in Bihar. A reaction had set in even before the armistice. The dye shortage in the United Kingdom led to the reopening of the Badische branch works at Ellesmere Port for the manufacture of aniline and alizarine dyes, as soon as the secrets of manufacture had been re-discovered by English chemists, and now Germany is once more in a position to export her dye stuffs freely. In 1917-18 there was a fall in the acreage under the plant, and a marked fall in prices, and in 1918-19 these elements of weakness became even more accentuated. The following table shows the total area under indigo, the estimated production and the exports in

*Refers to "Bengal and Tirhoot Middling to good 60 to 66 per cent".

1896-97 and in recent years as constrasted with the pre-war and post-war figures:—

TABLE No. 197.—*Area, yield and exports of indigo in 1896-97, 1913-14, 1918-19 and from 1929-30 onwards.*

Year.	Area.	Yield.	Exports.
	Acres.	Cwts.	Cwts.
1896-97	1,688,901	168,673	169,523
1913-14	172,600	26,800	10,939
1918-19	292,000	48,600	32,707
1929-30	75,700	14,400	867
1930-31	69,800	13,000	934
1931-32	53,500	9,900	799
1932-33	60,800	11,100	342
1933-34	43,900	7,500	502
1934-35	59,600	10,200	544

The following statement illustrates the percentage of exports to total production:—

TABLE No. 198.—*Percentage of exports of Indigo to total production.*

Article.	Pre-war Average.	War. Average.	Post-war Average.	1932-33.	1933-34.	1934-35.
Indigo	40	44	27	5	7	5

The area and production in the various provinces at the outbreak of war, as compared with those in 1934-35, are given in the next table.—

TABLE No. 199.—*Area and yield of indigo in each province in 1914-15 and 1934-35.*

Province.	1914-15.		1934-35.	
	Area	Production.	Area.	Production.
	Acres.	Cwts.	Acres.	Cwts.
Madras	71,700	13,600	54,000	9,300
Bihar and Orissa	38,500	5,500	1,000	200
Punjab	20,400	3,400	3,000	500
United Provinces	12,300	1,500	1,300	200
Bombay and Sind (including Indian States).	4,200	1,000	300	(a)
Bengal	1,300	200	.	..
Total	148,400	25,200	59,600	10,200

NOTE.—In estimating the yield of indigo, an allowance of 10 per cent. of the area is made for seed in the United Provinces and Bombay. In the Punjab, the rate varies widely from district to district.

It will be seen that by far the largest area under the crop is in Madras where (as in the Punjab and the United Provinces) it is for

(a) Less than 50 cwts.

the most part cultivated in small holdings and the inferior dye produced largely disappears in local consumption, though there has always been a definite market for the better grades, particularly in the Levant There is also an appreciable but not definitely ascertainable area under indigo in Travancore.

The Bihar crop usually comes on the market in December and the export season is completed before the end of the statistical year, while the Madras season for the best grades runs from July to February. The trade names for the two principal varieties of indigo sold on the Calcutta market are *Bihar cake* (also known as *Bengal and Tirhoot*) and *Oudh and Benares*, while the Madras indigo for which occasional quotations are made is known as *kurpah*.

Exports.

The province which contributed chiefly to the foreign export trade before the war was Bihar where the dye is more systematically extracted and marketed under European supervision. The bulk of the indigo produced in the factories of Bihar is in normal years exported and the Calcutta trade returns are a very fair gauge of the total production of that province When in 1894-95, 237,449 cwts. were produced from 1,688,042 acres, 106,830 cwts. were exported from Calcutta and in the last pre-war year the all-India exports amounted to 10,939 cwts. when 8,752 cwts came from the factories of Bihar

The following table shows the distribution of the export trade among the principal ports concerned.

TABLE No. 200.—*Share of the principal ports in the exports of indigo in 1915-16, 1919-20, and from 1931-32 onwards*

Ports	1915-16	1919-20.	1931-32.	1932-33	1933-34*	1934-35*.	1935-36.*
	Cwts.	Cwts.	Cwts.	Cwts.	Cwts.	Cwts.	Cwts.
Calcutta	13,137	15,739	554	154	351	278	104
Madras . .	26,171	12,132	208	160	151	266	241
Bombay .	2,565	4,179	.	..	..	..	5
Total (including other ports).	41,932	32,687	799	342	502	544	350

The feature of the export trade in 1915-16 was the heavy shipments from Madras, greatly in excess of those from Bihar, which went chiefly to the United Kingdom but also to Egypt, Iran and the United States of America. In recent years an increasing participation by Greece is noticeable with the United Kingodm as next in importance.

Indigo Cess.

In 1918 by an Act of the Imperial Legislature, an indigo cess was imposed at the rate of one rupee per bazaar maund (of 82 2/15 lbs. avoirdupois) on all Indian indigo exported the proceeds of the duty to be expended by the Government of India for scientific research work in connection with the cultivation and manufacture of indigo, a corresponding cess being imposed on all exports from Travancore to ports outside British India or to Aden. The rate of cess was changed to Re 1-8-0 per cwt. of 112 lbs. avoirdupois with effect from April

*Shares of respective provinces have been shown.

1st, 1921. Investigations were conducted at the Pusa Research Institute by the Indigo Research Chemist to the Government of India but these were terminated and the cess abolished with effect from the 1st August, 1923. In 1922-23 the cess yielded £533 and in the four months from April to July 1923, £212 only.

Unit of sale and shipment.

Prices are quoted in Calcutta at so many rupees *f.o.b.* or pounds *c.i.f.* sterling per lb. for London, the unit in the local bazaar being the factory maund of 74⅔ lbs. The paste is shipped in cases containing 4 or 4½ maunds each. The unit of sale in Madras is the maund of 25 lbs. but the unit of shipment varies according to destination. Egypt requires cases weighing from 80 to 120 lbs. while European countries require chests weighing 76½ to 246 lbs.

Turmeric.

Production.

Turmeric is derived from *curcuma longa* which is extensively cultivated in India for the sake of its rhizomes, which are edible, and also yield a valuable dye. The total area under the crop was estimated some years ago to be at least 100,000 acres*, but this is probably very much under the mark. In 1902-03 the exports from India amounted to 126,000 cwts. valued at £66,666. Next to Formosan turmeric, the Indian product commands the best prices. In pre-war days quotations on the European market fluctuated between 12 shillings and 26 shillings per cwt. The turmeric known in the European trade as Cochin is grown at or near Alwaye in the Travancore State. Other varieties with special quotations are known as *daisee*, *Masulipatam*, *Madras* and *Gopalpur*, while on the Calcutta market there are two descriptions, *Pabna* and *country*, of which the former commands better prices. The root is marketed as *fingers* or *bulbs*, the former being superior in quality to the latter Five per cent. bulbs may be included in a shipment of fingers. The normal outturn per acre varies from two to four thousand lbs of dried and cured rhizomes, and the Madras Presidency alone is estimated to produce a hundred thousand tons.

Exports.

The bulk of the exports go to Ceylon, Straits Settlements, Iran, France, the United Kingdom and the United States of America, the ports participating in the foreign traffic being Bombay, Madras, Tuticorin, Cochin, Rangoon and Calcutta. In the following table are shown the quantities exported in 1935-36 and the ports from which they were shipped.

TABLE No. 201.—*Exports of turmeric in 1935-36 with the share of the ports of shipment.*

Ports.	Quantity.	Value.
	Cwts.	£
Bombay	48,202	53,960
Madras ports (including Tuticorin and Cochin)	36,121	24,708
Rangoon	1,057	467
Calcutta	1,124	897
Karachi	90	62
Total	86,594	80,094

*Imperial Gazetteer. Indian Empire, Vol. III, P. 183.

In 1913-14, 115,027 cwts. valued at £87,450 were exported. There was a decline in exports in subsequent years, only 64,000 and 67,000 cwts. being shipped in 1914-15 and 1915-16. A revival was experienced in 1916-17 when over 103,000 cwts. valued at £105,000, left the country. In 1917-18 and 1918-19 the quantities exported were 77,000 and 79,500 cwts. respectively, after which the trade gradually declined and the average exports in the six years ending 1924-25 amounted to less than 560,00 cwts. There was again a revival in 1925-26 when 108,672 cwts. were shipped. Since then the trade has steadily declined. The average annual exports during the four years ending 1934-35 were 74,000 cwts.

Shipment is made in bags containing 3 cwts. nett from Madras, 1½ cwts. from Cochin, 2 cwts. from Negapatam, 1⅓ cwts. from Dhanushkodi, 1 5/8 cwts. from Tuticorin, ½ cwt. from Calcutta and 1⅓ or 1⅔ cwts. from Bombay. The unit of sale in Madras is the candy of 500 lbs and on the West Coast the candy of 600 lbs. In Bombay it is the candy of 21 Bombay maunds and in Calcutta the bazaar maund.

Unit of sale and shipment.

Cutch.

Cutch or *khari* is derived from *acacia catechu* which is found in the Western Himalayas and in Burma. The tree is felled and the heart wood cut into little chips and boiled in a cauldron until the fluid attains the consistency of syrup when it is taken off and cooled. A ton of wood is said to yield 250 to 300 lbs. of cutch. As the trade is largely in the hands of small manufacturers and dealers no trustworthy returns are available regarding the output. In 1895-96 the total exports to foreign countries were 183,729 cwts. valued at £246,407, but since then the traffic has considerably declined. In a normal year Burma contributes a preponderating share of the whole, in which province a royalty is levied on exports at the rate of Rs. 4 per 100 viss of 360 lbs. The bulk of the consignments are usually made to the United Kingdom, other customers being France, Germany and Holland. The exports in 1913-14, 1918-19 and from 1931-32 onwards are shown in the table below.

TABLES No. 202.—*Quantities and values of exports of *cutch in 1913-14, 1918-19 and from 1931-32 onwards.*

Year.	Quantity.	Value.
	Cwts.	£
1913-14	58,859	62,162
1918-19	58,125	77,189
1931-32	35,292	31,393
1932-33	29,066	23,063
1933-34	31,237	28,167
1934-35	34,707	35,749
1935-36	37,651	38 027

*Inclusive of small quantities of gambier for which no separate statistics are available.

The chief ports of export are Rangoon and Calcutta. In Calcutta prices are quoted per bazaar maund and shipment is made in cases of one cwt. gross or 74 lbs. nett. In Rangoon the unit of sale is the cwt. and shipment takes place in cases weighing 56 to 112 lbs. nett.

Unit of sale and shipment.

RAW HEMP.

The term hemp is used to denote the fibre of at least three important varieties of plants, namely, *cannabis sativa*, *agave sisalana* and *crotalaria juncea* which occur in India, but so far as her export trade is concerned it is the last named known generally as *sann* hemp which ranks first in importance, while the *agave sisalana*, commercially known as *sisal* comes next The fibre of *hibiscus cannabinus*, or *Deccan* hemp is better known perhaps as *Bimlipatam jute* from the port from which it is principally exported, and as it actually competes in certain classes of manufactures, *e g* , heavy C's.* with the products of Bengal mills, it is classified statistically with *corchorus* and has been dealt with already. No official forecasts of the hemp crops are published but in 1917 the Director of Statistics instituted a special inquiry to ascertain the area and estimated production in 1916-17, the results of which are tabulated below

Trade varieties.

TABLE No 203 —*Area and estimated yield of hemp in 1916-17.*

Provinces.	Area.	Yield.
	Acres.	Cwts.
Madras	197,900	1,230,680
Bombay and Sind	150,900	997,097
Central Provinces and Berar†	161,100	1,064,648
United Provinces	176,900	947,745
Bengal	32,300	189,372
Punjab	49,200	181,078
Bihar and Orissa	15,200	63,960
Burma	600	1,467
North-West Frontier Province	700	1,316
Delhi	500	1,586
Total	785,300	4,678,679

From the 'Season and Crop Reports" of the different provinces. it has been estimated that the total area under hemp in 1933-34 was 595,054 acres.

The true hemp *cannabis sativa*, commonly spoken of as *Indian hemp*, is both indigenous and cultivated The preparation known as *bhang* and *ganja*, are made from the native products, whereas the preparation known as *charas* is imported overland from Central Asia (Yarkand). *Ganja* is produced in the provinces of Madras, Bengal, Bihar and Orissa, Central Provinces and Bombay

Area and production.

*A hemmed bag 40" long by 20" broad, 2¼ lbs. in weight, 8 porter, 9 shot usually containing a coloured stripe.

†No estimate of average yield being available, the outturn has been calculated at the rate for Bombay.

Presidency proper. The total area in 1938 was 919 acres. No reliable figures are available as to the area of cultivation of the plant from which *bhang* is prepared. There is no Government factory for the production of *ganja* and *bhang*, but the cultivation of the plant and the collection of the wild product are governed by the issue of licenses. The drugs are stored after collection in Government depots and issued to licensed vendors under conditions similar to those applying to the vend of opium. The import of Indian hemp and *bhang* and of galencial preparations of Indian hemp is subject to restrictions, and their export is allowed only on the production of an import certificate from the importing country stating that the consignment is required for legitimate purposes and that the resin or its preparations will not be re-exported.

Botanical and historical evidence points to *crotalaria juncea* being indigenous to India and at a time when the value of jute as a fibre had not been commercially recognised, it received the early attention of the East India Company who procured their supplies from Salsettee near Bombay and made attempts to introduce it into England as a substitute for Russian hemp. It is now widely grown in Bombay, the Central Provinces and the United Provinces. Of the 200,000 acres devoted annually to the crop in Southern India, the chief districts producing the fibre are the Godavari, Kistna and Tinnevelly districts of the Madras Presidency, and Hyderabad State, but it is grown for cattle fodder as well as for fibre Throughout India it is grown as a *kharif* crop, *i e* , sown about the commencement of the rains and cut at the end of September or beginning of October. The fibre is obtained by retting the stems in water bruising with stones, and re-soaking until the fibre strips off easily. The average yield of fibre ranges from 500 to 800 lbs. per acre and it has been calculated that the percentage of fibre to dry stem is about 8. The *sann* hemp exported from Calcutta is classified for trade purposes as (1) *Benares*, (2) *Green* or *Raigarh*, and (3) *Bengal*, the bulk of the shipments being made between October and May The pre-war shipments of Benares *sann* hemp averaged about 85,000 bales of 350 lbs each. The Bombay trade amounted in normal times to about 80,000 pressed bales of 3½ cwts. each, the principal trade descriptions being *Pilibhit* (*United Provinces*), *Central Provinces* [including *Itarsi* (*Seoni*) and *Jubbulpore*], *Devgad* and *Gulbarga* All descriptions are hackled or combed in Bombay and shipped under private marks as *combed* or *tow*, the latter term being applied to the short ends of the hemp which are put to special uses in certain trades such as shipbuilding. The chief grades shipped from Madras ports arranged in order of relative importance are—(1) *Cocanada*, (2) *Gopalpur*, (3) *Warangal*, and (4) *Upper Godavari*. Except in the case of Gopalpur the colour is generally uniform, but shorts and tow are graded separately.

Sann hemp is essentially a cordage fibre and much superior in durability to jute. It is put to a variety of uses in India, being converted into floor mats in the United Provinces and cordage in most districts of India for local consumption. In the Central Provinces and Madras Presidency, it is made into canvas and bags by cottagers. If flax spinning machinery were introduced, there is reason to hope that the production in India of all the coarser materials such as hose-pipes, belting and canvas for which the country has hitherto depended on imported flax manufactures might be commercially successful. Hitherto all the exports of *sann* hemp have been in the form of raw fibre. Experiments in the improvement of *sann* hemp retting and handling are in progress in several provinces and the recent trade reports show that there has been a definite improvement in the quality of the Indian hemp now shipped to London.

Sisal hemp is obtained from the spiny leaves of *agâve sisalana*, which is commonly grown as a hedge in many parts of India, particularly on railway lines. The exploitation of the plant on a commercial scale has been attempted in Sylhet, Tirhoot, Bombay, and Southern India, but probably because the right species was not cultivated, these efforts have generally proved unsuccessful. In the Mysore State, *henequen* hemp of Yucatan (agave rigda *Var* Sisalava) is grown with success on waste lands. The fibre is extracted by hand and is used locally in making ropes required by the agriculturists.

Exports.

The bulk of the shipments of raw hemp of which statistics are given below has hitherto consisted of *sann* hemp.

TABLE No. 204.—*Quantities and values of hemp exported in 1913-14, 1918-19 and from 1931-32 onwards.*

Year.	Quantity.	Value.
	Cwts.	£
1913-14	711,548	682,319
1918-19	489,420	978,641
1931-32	223,994	201,718
1932-33	280,879	241,219
1933-34	387,923	270,653
1934-35	437,041	292,710
1935-36	642,932	452,584

In 1913-14, the distribution among the provinces was as follows: Bengal 429,469 cwts., Bombay 224,790 cwts. and Madras 57,289 cwts. The United Kingdom before and during the war was the principal individual customer for *sann* hemp, but considerable quantities always went to the Continent. In recent years the principal recipients are Belgium and the United Kingdom with Germany, Italy, and Greece as next in importance. In 1935-36, 488,283 cwts. were shipped from Bengal, 129,893 cwts. from Bombay and 24,756 cwts. from Madras.

TABLE No. 205.—*Distribution of the trade in hemp among principal importing countries in 1913-14 and 1935-36.*

Countries.	1913-14.		1935-36.	
	Quantity.	Value.	Quantity.	Value.
	Cwts.	£	Cwts.	£
United Kingdom . .	297,444	294,694	167,901	128,837
Belgium . . .	140,221	129,090	200,181	133,196
Italy	103,333	97,789	11,231	7,078
France . .	69,242	61,006	67,332	44,941
Germany . . .	68,341	69,408	68,141	46,908
Greece . . .	7,887	6,870	44,384	26,033
Denmark . . .	7,639	6,806	16,381	12,051
Other Countries . .	17,441	16,656	67,381	53,540
Total .	711,548	682,319	642,932	452,584

Hackling and combing.

The question of adulteration was taken up by the London Hemp Association in 1913 with the Government of India, who pointed out in their reply that buyers should insist upon getting the clean article and be prepared to pay higher prices for it. In 1916 the question was raised again by the Board of Trade who suggested to the India Office that grading might be controlled by legislation. This the Government of India pointed out would be a matter of considerable difficulty as so many different gradings are recognised in the Indian trade. The private marks of the bigger shippers carry with them a sufficient guarantee of consistent grading to satisfy most buyers. Hackling or combing as practised particularly at Bombay get rid of the dust and dirt due to retting in dirty water.

Unit of sale and shipment.

The bulk of the South Indian exports goes from Cocanada and Tuticorin. From the former port, shipment is usually made in bales of 400 lbs. while bundles of 1½ cwts. are used in the latter. In Bombay, it is sold per candy of 25 Bombay maunds and shipped in bales weighing from 336 to 392 lbs. The unit of sale as well as of shipment is generally the bale of 400 lbs. Quotations for export are generally per ton *c. i. f.*

Imports.

There have always been considerable imports of raw hemp into India, chiefly of Manilla hemp from the Philippines. There are three mills in Calcutta and one in Bombay which utilise imported fibre. Between 1913-14 and 1917-18 the value of these imports averaged about £69,000 but in 1918-19 it rose to nearly £171,000. The total for 1934-35 was £16,821. In addition, the average annual imports of hemp manufactures amount to £3,500.

MINERAL OILS.

Production. The production of petroleum in India increased from 118½ million gallons in 1904 to 277½ million gallons in 1913, 305½ million gallons in 1921 and 311 million gallons in 1930, due chiefly to the greater productivity of the Yenangyaung, Yenangyat, Singu and Minbu fields in Burma, Digboi field in Assam and at Attock in the Punjab. The production in 1930 was the highest ever recorded. There was a slight decline in the following years, the total production in 1933 being 306 million gallons. With an enormous Indian market adjacent, in which the use of kerosene for domestic consumption in supersession of vegetable oil illuminants has been assiduously exploited by competing interests, the export trade has always been comparatively small; and practically confined to benzine or petrol in bulk, fuel oil and lubricating oil. The Indian demand for kerosene now exceeds even the greatly increased indigenous production, and imports into India from foreign countries averaged 79½ million gallons per annum during the six years ending 1934-35.

Exports. In 1910-11 the exports scarcely exceeded 2½ million gallons, but they rose in the following year to nearly 15 and aggregated in 1913-14 22 million gallons, valued at £142,000, as compared with the coasting trade of 119 million gallons, valued at £2,840,000 The foreign trade in fact consisted largely of benzine, though oil fuel for the Navy and lubricating oil which, prior to 1st April 1914, were also included in the same statistical head, helped to swell the total. In 1914-15 over 20 million gallons of benzine, benzol, petrol and other motor spirit were exported to the United Kingdom and the shipments in the following year (all to the United Kingdom) exceeded £150,000, in value. The exports, foreign and coastwise, other than from Burma, are negligible Military requirements, chiefly of petrol, in Mesopotamia were largely met by re-export from Bombay to Persian Gulf ports and therefore do not figure in the statistics of foreign exports from Burma, though from 1917 until the end of the war there were considerable direct shipments to Egypt from Rangoon. In 1918-19, 24,845,000 gallons were exported, and in 1919-20, 37,854,000 gallons, France and Italy being large recipients, and more than twelve million gallons going to Egypt 'for orders'. The average annual exports during the five years ending 1924-25 amounted to 20,273,000 gallons. In the following quinquennium the average annual exports declined to 2,201,000 gallons. There has been a further decline in exports in recent years, and the average annual shipments during four years ending 1933-34 did not exceed 84,000 gallons. This precipitate fall in the exports of mineral oils is attributable to the greatly increased demand in India due to the development of road transport and increased consumption as illuminants in place of vegetable oils. In the following table the distribution of the trade in 1913-14 and 1935-36 is contrasted.

TABLE No. 206.—*Distribution of the trade in mineral oils in 1913-14 and 1935-36 contrasted.*

Countries.	1913-14.		1935-36.	
	Quantity.	Value.	Quantity.	Value.
	Gallons.	£	Gallons.	£
United Kingdom	15,268,640	93,014	1,984	87
Holland	3,066,663	19,167	..	..
United States of America	2,920,459	18,254	..	..
Germany	922,586	5,772	..	..
Australia	40,084	2,567	..	..
Ceylon	39,644	1,600	770	169
Straits Settlements	32,406	1,143	51,487	4,337
Total (including other countries)	22,308,700	142,732	55,705	4,696

The arrangements under which foreign consignments of benzine are marketed make it impossible to say, until some months after shipment, what price has actually been realised. In 1913-14 values were calculated at the conventional rate of 1½ annas (1½*d.*) per gallon, the declared value at the time of export, but from 1919-20 onwards the price adopted has been that current for wholesale shipments from India less excise duty.

The unit of sale in Burma of fuel oil is the ton of 2,240 lbs. and of other oils the gallon Shipment of fuel oil from Burma takes place usually in drums of 42 gallons.

An excise duty of 10 annas (11¼*d*) per gallon is at present levied on all motor spirit produced in India and Burma, and a corresponding duty of the same amount on foreign imports. An excise duty of 2 annas 9¾ pies (3 16d) per gallon is levied on kerosene The import duty on kerosene is at present 3 annas 9 pies (4 22*d*) per gallon.

FISH OIL.

On the West coast of the Madras Presidency the *clupea longiceps*, (sardines), appears in numerous and sometimes very large shoals between August and June. The small fish is also known as "oil-sardine". The adult fish, which is generally fat, yields from 10 to 15 per cent of oil when boiled and pressed in mere manual presses. The oil sardines are also found to some extent about the same season of the year on the East coast north of Cocanada Formerly large quantities of oil sardines used to be converted into manure by the wasteful and offensive method of sun-drying on the open beach as the excessive oil content rendered the fish unsuitable for edible purposes. In 1907-08 the Madras Department of Fisheries interested itself in the subject and based experiments and suggestions on early American practice, *viz.*, that of boiling the fish in large pans, pressing the mass for the oil in manual presses and drying the press cakes as fertiliser. Nine smaller but similar works sprang up in the same year, and, in 1920 the number exceeded six hundred, while the output of dry fertiliser was approximately 20,000 tons and that of oil 5,000 tons. In 1933-34 one hundred and sixty nine private oil

Production.

and guano factories worked in the South Kanara district against twenty-five in 1932-33. The number of factories in Malabar that worked during 1933-34 was one hundred and thirty-two. During 1932-33 no factory worked in Malabar.

The oil from sardines, like that from Japanese "iwashi" menhaden, pilchard, and herring, is made from the body of the fish and is technically known as body oil or "fish oil". Fish oil from its cheapness is often used as a cheap illuminant either directly or indirectly when converted into gas. The commoner sorts, usually brown or almost black, are largely used as baths in tempering steel, and in batching jute, while the better sorts, brown to yellow, are extensively used in leather dressing, in the manufacture of saddle and harness soap, for lubrication and paints The name "guano" has been generally employed to distinguish the residue (scrap) obtained by drying the tissue and osseous material which is left after boiling and pressing the fish, for oil, from the "fish manure" obtained by simply drying the whole fish on the beach The "guano" when commercially dry, contains about 20 per cent of nitrogen and 9 per cent. of phosphoric acid The presence of nitrogen and phosphoric acid renders it a valuable fertiliser. Every ten tons of sardines treated should yield 1½ tons of fish oil and 1½ tons of dry fish guano In the better equipped factories steam heating is employed and a clear yellow oil with a high stearine content is obtained. Over open fires the oil yielded is very dark in colour. Oil sardines after a continuous absence for a number of years, appeared in abundance in the Madras Presidency in 1933-34 The following statement shows the quantity of fish oil and guano produced in Malabar and South Kanara in that year.

TABLE No 207.—*Quantity of fish oil and guano produced in Madras Presidency from 1930-31 onwards.*

	Oil.	Guano
	Tons.	Tons.
Malabar	1,500	5,000
South Kanara	820	5,000

The price for fish oil ranged between £3 and £9 per ton and that for guano between £1. 10s. and £2. 5s. per ton

TABLE No. 208 —*Exports of fish guano from the West Coast of the Madras Presidency from 1930-31 onwards.*

Year.	Quantity.	Value.
	Tons.	£
1930-31	275	3,333
1931-32	22	198
1932-33	6	45
1933-34	2,346	11,288
1934-35	1,219	7,332
1935-36	139	616

Negapatam and Calicut are the chief ports of export of fish guano.

The unit of sale of the oil on the West Coast is the ton or the maund of 28 lbs., shipment being made in tins of 28 to 36 lbs.

LEMON GRASS OIL.

Occurrence.

The extraction of the essential oil contained in lemon grass (*cymbopogon flexuosus*) is an industry of considerable promise in Southern India as the oil which contains a large percentage of *citral* is utilized largely in the manufacture of soaps and artificial scents. Cultivation may be described as a monopoly of the West Coast of the Madras Presidency, the main producing areas being the Indian States of Travancore and Cochin and the southern part of the Malabar district. Lemon grass is both wild and cultivated. The hill sides on which it flourishes are fired in January. The first crop is ready to be harvested in July and the season for distillation extends to October, furnaces and stills being set up in the neighbourhood of the plantations. The method of distillation is generally crude, and the resultant oil highly coloured and so adulterated that the citral content seldom exceeds 50 per cent as compared with 83 per cent in the pure article. The trade which was inconsiderable until the beginning of the present century received a great impetus about 1903-04, but the temptation of high prices encouraged crude methods of distillation and subsequent adulteration and when the demand in Europe was discovered to be unequal to the absorption of the quantity which Travancore and Malabar were prepared to export, a fall in prices which followed made distillation scarcely profitable There was some revival again before the war both in prices and in the volume of the trade, and private efforts, supplemented by those of the Travancore Darbar to obtain a better quality of oil have proved that there is a steady and increasing demand in Europe and America for the purer product which is yielded by redistillation. Travancore oil used in pre-war times to be shipped either from Alleppey or Cochin, but no export statistics are available for the former port The quantities that went forward from ports in British India, mainly Cochin, in the pre-war year, 1918-19 and in the last five years are shewn in the following table.

TABLE No 209.—*Quantity and value of lemon grass oil exported in 1913-14, 1918-19 and from 1931-32 onwards.*

Year.	Quantity.	Value.
	Gallons.	£
1913-14	47,522	67,955
1918-19	17,049	22,181
1931-32	50,670	36,043
1932-33	43,098	31,331
1933-34	45,416	47,244
1934-35	77,790	88,311
1935-36	98,877	94,492

The principal pre-war destinations were France, which accounted for more than 50 per cent of the total, Germany, the United Kingdom and the United States, and the war did not cause any material alteration in the distribution of the trade except that Germany was eliminated and a new market apparently found in Switzerland. During the post-war period France, the United States, and the United Kingdom have maintained their position as the principal recipients, and Germany has made her re-appearance. In 1933-34 the United States of America took 48 per cent of the total exports, the United Kingdom 31, France 12, and Germany 7.

Unit of sale and shipment. The unit of sale on the West Coast is a dozen bottles of 22 oz. each, the unit in Madras being the lb. Shipment from Cochin is made in drums containing 67½ dozen bottles In Bombay lemon grass oil is sold in tins of 28 lbs and bottles of 1 lb. each, while shipment takes place in copper pots of 125 to 250 lbs.

MANURES.

The Indian cultivator is generally too poor and his holding too small to make intensive manuring profitable. Green manuring is common and the benefits to the soil from the cultivation of nitrogenous plants is not unrecognised, but dried cow dung which is the commonest manure available is too commonly preferred as fuel for domestic purposes. The chief internal demand for manures is therefore from the tea and coffee planting industries for whom, in addition to the supplies available in the country, over 66 thousand tons of artificial and other kinds of manures valued at £502,913 were imported in 1934-35, as against 50 thousand tons valued at £393,148 in 1933-34.

Fish manures. Of the animal manures produced in India, the principal are derived from fish and bones The fish manure industry on the Malabar Coast has already been separately noticed*. The total exports from India of fish manure (including an inconsiderable quantity of guano derived from the excrement of birds and bats) are shown in the table below. Prices, it will be noticed, are much higher than those obtaining in the post-war period, though there has been a marked diminution in quantity.

TABLE No. 210.—*Quantity and value of fish manure and guano exported in 1913-14, 1918-19 and from 1931-32 onwards.*

Year	Quantity.	Value.
	Tons.	£
1913-14	16,284	64,044
1918-19	18.185	143,415
1931-32	5,646	41,205
1932-33	3,194	18,561
1933-34	7.227	35,733
1934-35	6.383	35,838
1935-36	6,304	33,249

* *Vide* page 237.

The trade is distributed between Madras, Burma and Sind, the shares of Bombay and Bengal being negligible. Shipments are mainly directed to Ceylon and the Straits Settlements.

In 1933-34, 9,600 tons of fish manure were produced in South Kanara and 4,000 tons in Malabar in the Madras Presidency. The prices of fish manure in that year ranged between 10s. and £3 per ton.

The unit of sale in Madras is the cwt., the ton or the candy of 600 lbs and shipment, chiefly from Mangalore is made in bags of 2½ qrs. and rarely, of one cwt.

Bone manure.

There was a considerable demand before the war for crushed bones in France and Belgium for the manufacture of bone-black, buttons, etc. Bone meal was also exported in pre-war days to Hamburg, while a coarser quality went to Liverpool and Hull for the manufacture of superphosphates. The war which cut off India from external supplies encouraged the internal demand. In 1931, 21 mills for bone crushing and manure were in existence in India, of which 6 (553) were in Madras, 5 (1,009) in Bombay, 8 (1,386) in Bengal, 1 (210) in the United Provinces and 1 (56) in Hyderabad. The figures in brackets indicate the number of persons employed.

The following table shows the distribution of the trade in recent years as compared with the pre-war and post-war figures. It will be seen that shipments since 1931-32 have been fairly steady.

TABLE No. 211.—*Quantity and value of exports of bones and bone-meal from India in 1913-14. 1918-19 and from 1931-32 onwards.*

Year.	Quantity.	Value.
	Tons.	£
1913-14	105,413	522,223
1918-19	16,734	84,409
1931-32	37,778	174,062
1932-33	21,563	101,194
1933-34	24,819	108,614
1934-35	36,474	151,771
1935-36	42,894	179,958

Figures prior to 1931-32 include crushed bones.

The provincial distribution of the trade in the last pre-war year was as follows · Bengal 43,337 tons, Sind 25,506 tons, Bombay 25,364 tons, Madras 9,425 tons and Burma 1,681 tons, the chief destinations being Belgium, France, the United Kingdom, Japan and Germany. In 1933-34 the provincial distribution was: Bengal 12,959 tons, Bombay 1.514 tons, Sind 4,267 tons, Madras 4,919 tons and Burma 1,160 tons, the chief destinations being the United Kingdom, Ceylon and Belgium.

The unit of sale in Calcutta and Madras is the ton of 2,240 lbs. though Karachi sells on the standard maund. The unit of sale as well as of shipment in Bombay is the bag of 168 lbs. In Calcutta bone-meal, steamed and unsteamed, and crushed bones are exported in bags of 224 lbs. nett From Madras ports as well as from Karachi shipment is made in bags of 2 cwts.

Unit of Sale and shipment.

Exports of dried blood or "blood-meal" according to trade classification are not separately recorded, but, appreciable quantities obtained from the slaughter houses in big cities such as Calcutta, Madras and Bombay are shipped It has been estimated that 150 tons valued at £750 are exported from Bombay in each year Dried blood is sold in bag of 140 to 168 lbs in Bombay. Animal meal is sold per unit of 8 to 10 per cent. nitrogen and horn meal 12 to 13 per cent nitrogen The average annual exports of horn meal amount to approximately 2,000 tons valued at £11,845. The bulk of the shipments goes from Bengal with Sind and Bombay as next in importance, the recipients being Japan and the United Kigdom

Blood-meal.

Crude saltpetre is extracted from the earths containing usually not more than five per cent of nitrate. This crude saltpetre, which may contain from 30 to 50 per cent of foreign matter is used as a fertiliser. In 1924, the latest year for which figures of production are available, 8,542 tons were manufactured. Excepting a few hundred tons required for internal consumption as fertiliser, most of the output is exported to foreign countries The quantity exported in 1933 amounted to 189,567 cwts valued at £117,136 as compared with 165,782 cwts valued at £92,272 in the preceding year The principal recipients were the United Kingdom, Ceylon, and Mauritius. The only other mineral manures exportd in any quantity are sulphate of ammonia, sulphate of potash and kainite.

Mineral manures.

The following statement shows the figures of production of ammonium sulphate in recent years

TABLE No. 212.—*Production of sulphate of ammonia from 1932 onwards.*

Article.	1932	1933.	1934.	1935.
	Tons.	Tons.	Tons.	Tons.
Sulphate of Ammonia . .	9,474	9,885	11,775	15,398

In 1934-35, 3,053 tons valued at £19,851 were exported as compared with 2,121 tons valued at £13,366 in 1933-34 and 303 tons valued at £2,625 in 1932-33 Practically the whole quantity goes to Ceylon from Bengal. The unit of sale is generally the ton and shipment is made in bags of 2 cwts. nett

Of the other manures exported from India, the principal are oilcakes, the chief items being linseed, castor, groundnut, sesamum and rape cakes. These have already been dealt with in the respective articles on seeds.

Other manures.

SPICES.

Pepper.

The trade in pepper is perhaps the oldest, and during the Middle Ages was one of the most important branches of commerce between Europe and the East. Then and even earlier the West Coast of India enjoyed a practical monopoly, there being evidence that it was flourishing as early as the fifth century A.D., but by the beginning of the nineteenth century the competition of the Malay Archipelago had proved too strong and it had lapsed into comparative insignificance. Yet even now the average value of the exports from the British Indian ports approximates to £326,000 a year.

Pepper is the berry of a vine-like climbing plant (*piper nigrum*) which grows wild in the forests of Malabar and Travancore and is extensively cultivated by Europeans and Indians in and below the Western Ghats from Karwar to Cape Comorin. It thrives in a hot, moist climate with an abundant rainfall. In Bengal, pepper is grown to a very limited extent only in the northern parts of Jessore, while in Assam, except in Sylhet and the southern slopes of the Khasia Hills, very little is produced. In Bombay the area under the crop in 1904-05 amounted to 6,736 acres and in 1905-06 to 7,483, practically the whole of which was in Kanara. In Madras, the principal producing areas are Malabar, Cochin and Travancore, and, to a small extent, Coorg and South Kanara. The vines are usually propagated from cuttings and the first crop is obtained in the third year, the berries ripening in March. A vine in full bearing in a good year will carry about 1,000 clusters of fruit yielding 4 lbs. of dried pepper* The yield from some of the Kanara gardens in the Bombay Presidency is probably rather higher. The life of vine is about seven years. To obtain *white* pepper the berries after being plucked are soaked in water for seven or eight days until the pulp ferments. The mass is then trampled under by *coolies* to remove the pulp from the stone, and sun-dried. Little or no *white* pepper is produced in India. *Black* pepper is derived from the unripe berry picked green, heaped and dried when the skin and pulp adheres as a wrinkled covering to the stone. Two grades of quality are known on the West Coast, *viz.*, *Alleppey* and *Tellicherry*, of which the latter in normal times commands a slight premium over the former, as the pepper is bolder and heavier.

Area and Production.

The total exports of Indian pepper during the period 1900-1907 averaged 12,000,000 lbs. valued at about £275,000. In 1913-14,

---

*Imperial Gazetteer. The Indian Empire, Vol. III, page 54.

13,880,000 lbs. valued at £290,000 (average value 5d. per lb). were exported. During five years ending 1922-23, the average annual exports amounted to 11,298,000 lbs. valued at £284,000. In the following quinquennium 13,587,000 lbs. of pepper valued at £553,000 were shipped at an average per year. During the seven years ending 1934-35, the average annual exports amounted to 9,626,000 lbs. valued at £370,000. The export trade in 1913-14, 1918-19 and in the last five years is illustrated by the following table.

Exports.

TABLE No. 213.—*Quantity and value of pepper exported from India in 1913-14, 1918-19 and from 1931-32 onwards.*

Year.	Quantity.	Value.	Average value per lb.
	lbs.	£	d.
1913-14	13,879,964	289,943	5·0
1918-19	12,846,748	408,889	9·0
1931-32	10,538,864	280,414	6·4
1932-33	6,689,200	170,355	6·1
1933-34	6,597,808	136,793	5·0
1934-35	8,295,840	183,779	5·3
1935-36	2,958,480	57,214	4·6

The average value, which had declined during some years after the armistice, has again reached the pre-war level in recent years.

The chief importing countries in the last pre-war year and in 1935-36 are shewn in the following table

TABLE No 214 —*Distribution of the trade in pepper among principal importing countries in 1913-14, and 1935-36 contrasted*

Countries	1913-14.		1935-36.	
	Quantity	Value.	Quantity.	Value.
	lbs.	£	lbs.	£
United Kingdom	1,579,274	32,399	116,144	2,451
Germany	3,110,541	64,571	18,480	495
Italy	2,896,660	60,730	2,241,568	41,225
Iraq	*650,956	*16,172	14,224	195
Egypt	192,280	4,296	336	10
United States of America	2,352,228	45,973	179,200	4,150
Other countries	3,098,025	65,802	388,528	8,688
Total	13,879,964	289,943	2,958,480	57,214

The principal shipments to Germany in 1913-14 were unusually heavy. Pepper, we have since learnt, is an ingredient in the manufacture of tear shells. In 1935-36, Italy and the United States of America took 76 and 6 per cent., respectively of the total exports, while the United Kingdom and Germany accounted for 4 and ·6 per

*Figures for Persian Gulf area of Asiatic Turkey.

cent, respectively. Tellicherry pepper which is derived from two varieties of vine known in the vernacular *Kalluvalli* and *Balankotta* is not only shipped from Tellicherry, but also from the neighbouring ports of Calicut, Cannanor and Badagara, while Cochin, Alleppy and Tuticorin are the outlets for the pepper grown in the Cochin and Travancore States. The distribution of the trade in 1913-14 and 1935-36 among the provinces is given in the table subjoined. Madras has always taken a preponderating share of the trade.

TABLE No. 214-A.—*Distribution of the trade in pepper among the various provinces in India in 1913-14, and 1935-36 contrasted.*

Provinces.	1913-14.		1935-36.	
	Quantity.	Value.	Quantity.	Value.
	lbs.	£.	lbs.	£.
Madras	12,065,786	246,177	2,793,168	52,993
Bombay	1,683,024	40,636	101,920	2,354
Sind	6,748	144	5,040	83
Bengal	123,734	2,959	57,456	1,736
Burma	672	27	896	48
Total	13,879,964	289,943	2,958,480	57,214

Unit of sale and shipment.

Pepper is packed for export from Madras ports in bags of 1¼ cwts. nett, from Bombay in bags of 140 to 168 lbs. nett and from Calcutta in bundles of 224 lbs. nett. The unit of sale in Tellicherry is the cwt. and in Cochin the 600-lb. candy. Bombay sells in bags of 140 to 168 lbs and Calcutta on the bazaar maund.

Imports.

In addition to the foreign trade, movements by rail and river and coastwise by sea between the provinces for internal consumption have always been considerable. During the three years ending 1934-35 the coastwise imports by sea averaged about 19 million lbs., of which Calcutta and Bombay took 8 million lbs. each, and Sind 2 million lbs. Imports from foreign countries were mainly from the Straits Settlements, the total quantity in 1932-33 being 1,427,000 lbs., in 1933-34, 1,290,000 lbs. and in 1934-35, 711,000 lbs.

Chillies.

Cultivation.

Originating in tropical America and introduced into India somehere about the middle of the seventeenth century by the Portuguese, there are at present many varieties of *capsicum* disseminated over large tracts in India, both as garden and field crops. No separate statistics of production or of acreage are available but in Madras, the province with by far the largest production, the area has been estimated at not less than 300,000 acres annually; and while the distribution is pretty general, cultivation is particularly large in the Guntur district and the uplands of Godavari and Kistna Outside Madras the chief producing areas are in Eastern and Northern

Bengal, in the Kayaukse, Sagaing and Myingyan districts of Burma and in Bombay where there is extensive garden cultivation particularly in the Dharwar, Belgaum, Khandesh, Satara, Poona and Sholapur districts. To a limited extent the crop is raised in the Punjab, where when grown at an elevation, the chillies are said to acquire a greater pungency to which perhaps is due the popularity of the so-called 'Nepal' cayenne. The yield is subject to great variations in different localities.

Unit of Sale and Shipment.

The pods are sun-dried and packed for the market in Southern India in gunnies each containing 70 to 75 lbs. or in bags weighing 168 lbs gross, and shipment takes place in bags of 54 lbs or in bundles of 1½ cwts each. In Bombay the unit of sale and shipment is the bundle of 168 to 196 lbs each while in Calcutta it is the bundle of 1 maund gross The unit of sale in Rangoon is a hundred viss of 360 lbs. and chillies are packed for export in bags weighing from 100 to 170 lbs. nett

Exports.

Of course the bulk of the chillies grown disappears in local consumption as an ingredient in curries, chutneys and other food preparations The dried fruit reduced to powder is the red pepper or cayenne of commerce The export trade does not greatly interest any large firms and the business is chiefly in the hands of Indians with branches or correspondents in Ceylon and the Far East The distribution and volume of the trade varies little from year to year The average shipments have for a long time been in the neighbourhood of 15 million lbs a year but in 1918-19 the total was only 9,217,000 lbs due to failure of this crop in the Guntur District of the Madras Presidency and the consequent restrictions placed upon export to prevent depletion of stocks for local consumption In 1933-34 and 1934-35 the exports were 16,564,000 lbs and 17,746,000 lbs, respectively In the following table the quantities and values of chillies exported in 1913-14 with the shares of the principal recipients, are contrasted with those in 1935-36. Values, which had appreciated by over 100 per cent in the first decade after the out-break of the war, have in recent years come down to the pre-war level.

TABLE No 215 —*Share of the principal importing countries of chillies in 1913-14, and 1935-36 contrasted.*

Principal countries.	1913-14.		1935-36.	
	Quantity.	Value.	Quantity.	Value.
	lbs.	£	lbs.	£
Ceylon	10,674,719	90,813	19,486,096	134,643
Straits Settlements	3,552,346	28,474	321,216	2,455
United States of America	690,284	5,218	..	..
Italian East Africa	380,988	3,181	72,016	771
Mauritius and dependencies	280,483	2,048	94,752	586
Aden and dependencies	204,036	1,671	176,176	2,109
United Kingdom	9,789	93	12,096	99
Other countries	310,440	2,722	379,568	3,661
Total	16,103,08	134,220	20,541,920	144,324

The only noticeable alteration in the course of the trade during the war was the transitory interest taken by the United Kingdom which took 10,000 lbs. only in 1913-14, while her total for 1916-17 was 1,108,000 lbs. This rise was not maintained in the post-war period and exports to the United Kingdom have now declined to the pre-war level In 1935-36, 70 per cent of the exports went from Bengal, 24 per cent. from the Madras Presidency and 3 per cent. from Burma, the principal ports concerned being Calcutta, Tuticorin, Negapatam, Madras and Rangoon. Ceylon and the Straits Settlements continue to be the chief recipients.

Ginger.

Ginger (*zinziber officinale*) has been cultivated in India for centuries, but no statistics as to area of cultivation or outturn are available. On the Malabar Coast which has long been famous for its ginger, cuttings are planted in May and the rhizomes dug up in the following November Other parts of India where there are considerable quantities grown are the Surat and Thana districts of the Bombay Presidency, the Rangpur district in Bengal and the Kumaon district of the United Provinces. In a good year 2,000 lbs. of dry ginger to the acre is a fair average yield. The rhizomes are purchased from the cultivator by dealers who either sell them again as *green* or *dried* ginger. Dried ginger again is either bleached or unbleached according as it is parboiled or scraped before being exposed to the sun. Uncoated (*i e*, scraped) Cochin ginger is reputed the best marketed in India.

Cultivation.

The export trade does not attain to any great dimensions, but ginger is to be found in almost every bazaar and the internal consumption for curries and medicinal purposes must be very great The chief external markets for Indian ginger are Aden, Arabia, the United Kingdom, Germany, Anglo-Egyptian Sudan, Ceylon, Italian East Africa and the United States of America Ginger is usually packed for export from Cochin and Tuticorin in bags containing 112 lbs each, and from Calicut in bags of 140 lbs each, the unit of sale at the former two ports being the candy of 600 lbs and at the latter the cwt. From Calcutta it is shipped in bags of 2 maunds and from Bombay in bags of 112 to 140 lbs

Exports.

In the following table are shown the quantity and value of ginger exported in 1913-14, 1918-19 and from 1931-32 onwards

TABLE No 216.—*Quantity and value of exports of ginger in 1913-14, 1918-19 and from 1931-32 onwards.*

Year	Quantity.	Value.
	lbs.	£
1913-14	9,214,471	122,661
1918-19	3,842,677	65,707
1931-32	6,108,592	96,352
1932-33	6,339,312	86,312
1933-34	5,244,288	67,780
1934-35	4,400,256	62,032
1935-36	2,818,816	56,605

Of the quantity exported in 1913-14, 4,220,551 lbs. went from Bombay, 3,158,653 lbs. from Calicut, 1,275,421 lbs. from Cochin and 314,356 lbs. from Calcutta. The substantial decline in the volume of shipments in 1918-19 was attributed chiefly to the greatly reduced tonnage available at West Coast ports in that year. The total shipments for the Madras Presidency in 1918-19 aggregated less than 300,000 lbs. During the three years 1931-32 to 1933-34 the volume of exports averaged 5,897,000 lbs. to which Bombay contributed 71 per cent. and Madras Presidency 28 per cent.

Imports.

While India exports on an average about 6,000,000 lbs. of ginger every year, her imports averaged 207,000 lbs. per annum during 5 years ending 1933-34, chiefly from Japan into Bombay and Calcutta. A marked improvement in the imports was noticed in 1934-35 when 1,449,504 lbs. were imported against 142,352 lbs. in the previous year.

Cardamoms.

Cultivation.

The cardamoms which enter in the export trade of India are obtained from the capsules of perennial herb (*elettaria cardamomum*) indigenous to the humid forests of Western and Southern India where it is extensively cultivated at elevations from 500 to 5,000 feet. Two varieties of cardamoms are recognised, Mysore, round, smooth-skinned capsules and Malabar, long, rough-grained capsules, known as *shorts* and *short longs*. The former are preferred and command a higher price.

Uses.

Cardamoms are chiefly used for medicinal purposes, for flavouring cakes and liquors and as an ingredient in German sausages. The essential oil used medicinally as a carminative and in connection with perfumery in France and the United States of America is derived not from the Malabar nor Mysore cardamom, but from the so-called 'greater cardamom' of Nepal (*amomum subulatum*).

Method of Marketing.

The capsules which ripen in September and October are hand-gathered and sent down to the ports, and while some are dried and bleached in the sun before export, better qualities are generally cured more elaborately After being sulphur-bleached the stalk end of each pod is carefully clipped and the capsules are then graded. Such cardamoms usually fetch in London about double the price per lb. of the less carefully prepared pods In some quarters there has been an increased demand lately for dried green cardamoms which are supposed to be more highly flavoured than the bleached cardamoms.

Cardamoms are packed for export from Madras ports in cases of 56 lbs. to 1 cwt each in the case of shipment to London, Australia etc., and in bundles of 120 to 300 lbs. in the case of shipment to the Straits Settlements The unit of sale in Bombay is the Surti maund of 39·2 lbs. and shipment is made in bags containing 140 lbs. nett.

The following table shows the chief ports of export and the proportionate share of the trade enjoyed by each in the year preceding the outbreak of war and in 1935-36.

TABLE No. 217.—*Share of the ports in exports of cardamoms in 1913-14 and 1935-36 contrasted.*

Ports.	1913-14.		1935-36.	
	Quantity.	Percentage.	Quantity.	Percentage.
	lbs.		lbs.	
Bombay . . .	191,769	51·0	404,208	30·0
Calcutta . . .	63,905	17·0	6,160	·5
Madras Ports . .	105,648	27·0	929,488	69·0

Exports from Calcutta were in 1913-14 considerably above the average, owing to greater facilities for shipment, large quantities being railed up from the West Coast for despatch from this Port.

The next table shows the foreign trade, quantity and value, in 1913-14, 1918-19, 1919-20 and from 1931-32 onwards.

TABLE No. 218.—*Quantity and value of cardamoms exported from India in 1913-14, 1918-19, 1919-20 and from 1931-32 onwards.*

Year.	Quantity.	Value.
	lbs.	£
1913-14	373,401	49,994
1918-19	641,650	51,605
1919-20	1,854,048	176,388
1931-32	723,856	92,785
1932-33	935,872	108,804
1933-34	1,341,760	159,320
1934-35	1,039,024	114,825
1935-36	1,340,304	142,008

Though the volume of exports from Madras ports declined from over 100,000 lbs in 1913-14 to 21,000 lbs. in 1917-18, very large shipments from Calcutta and Bombay, chiefly to the United Kingdom, raised the all-India total (893,186 lbs.) in the latter year to nearly three times that for 1916-17 (311,790 lbs.) and shipments in 1919-20 were phenomenal, though values were below pre-war rates. In the triennium 1931-32 to 1933-34 exports of cardamom averaged 1,000,496 lbs of which Sweden took 26 per cent. and the United Kingdom 12 per cent. The other principal direct customers for Indian cardamoms are Germany, the United States of America and Arabia.

Betelnuts.

The betelnut, which is the fruit of the arecapalm (*areca catechu*), forms in conjunction with the leaf of the betel vine (*piper betle*) and a little lime and clove or nutmeg, the common masticatory of the East, known all over India as *pan supari*. Statistically both the betelnut and the betel leaf are regarded as spices and the internal demand for the former is so great that the import trade is of much greater moment than the export, though there is some traffic outwards with colonies where Indian emigrants abound. Though supplies of betel leaf, which are derived from a climbing plant belonging to the same family as pepper; are drawn from considerable distances by rail and river, the fact that they have to be chewed green, limits foreign exports, which are negligible, to the island of Ceylon. The areca palm is confined almost entirely to the moist tropical tracts that fringe the coastline and it is seldom found more than 200 miles from the sea. No statistics of area or production are available, but the number of trees must be very large as the demand is practically universal. In Southern India a full-grown tree is calculated to yield 250 to 300 nuts annually, but elsewhere, as for example in Burma, the average output is very much lower. The nut is prepared in a great variety of ways for sale, being sometimes marketed sun-dried only, and sometimes plucked unripe and boiled and sliced The Indian tariff recognises eight different classes with different valuations for purposes of import duty.

Exports.

The following table illustrates the insignificant extent of the export trade as compared with the import trade

TABLE No. 219 —*Exports and imports of betelnuts in 1913-14. 1918-19. and from 1931-32 onwards.*

Year	Exports.		Imports	
	Quantity.	Value.	Quantity.	Value
	lbs.	£	lbs.	£
1913-14	439,886	8,224	127,464,241	819,068
1918-19	362,419	8,119	142,527,683	1,141,269
1931-32 .	295,120	7,717	123,314,240	1,085,628
1932-33 . .	367,248	11,003	125,143,088	891,983
1933-34	382,144	10,264	133,773,696	784,408
1934-35	394,128	10,352	137,480,560	767,201
1935-36	426,160	9,354	147,777,504	729,014

The principal recipients of Indian betelnuts are the Union of South Africa, Kenya Colony, Aden and Fiji Islands, and the chief ports of export Bombay and Madras. The bulk of the imports come from the Straits Settlements, Ceylon, Java and Hongkong

Unit of Sale and Shipment.

The unit of sale in Calcutta is the bazaar maund and the nuts are shipped in bags weighing 2 maunds. In Bombay the unit of sale is the candy of 21 Bombay maunds or the maund of 28 lbs, shipment being made in bags of 168 to 182 lbs.

Cinnamon.

Marketing.

The true cinnamon of commerce is the dried bark of *cinnamomum zeylanicum*, a native of Ceylon but found also on the Western Ghats in Southern India at altitudes up to 6,000 feet. The plant exists under cultivation as a coppiced bush. The bark after removal is pressed in bundles until slight fermentation sets in, which allows of the scraping of the outer covering and the pulp underneath. These strips are then cut into lengths of about twelve inches and dried, when they contract into the

shape of *quills* under which name they are sold. Thicker pieces of bark from the larger shoots are sold as chips which command lower prices as the flavour is inferior. Three valuable essential oils are also obtained from the tree, one from the bark, one from the leaves, known as *clove oil*, and one from the root, all with medicinal properties. No statistics of area or production of cinnamon are maintained but the yield per acre is said to be 150 lbs.

The provinces contributing to the insignificant export trade are Madras and Bengal the chief port in the former presidency being Tellichery on the West Coast. The true cinnamon is very commonly adulterated, specially in powder form, with *cassia lignea* the bark of *cassia cinnamomum* common in East Bengal, the Khasia Hills and Burma, and the exports from Bengal would most probably seem to be of this origin It will be noticed from the following table that there has been a marked decline in the volume of exports during recent years. The principal destination of the exports is the United Kingdom.

Exports.

TABLE No. 220.—*Quantity and value of exports of cinnamon from India in 1913-14, 1918-19 and from 1931-32 onwards*

Year.	Quantity.	Value.
	lbs.	£
1913-14	33,170	1,015
1918-19	71,579	2,329
1931-32	10,528	424
1932-33	4,480	132
1933-34	6,496	204
1934-35	8,960	150
1935-36	5,376	82

The unit of sale in Calcutta is the bazaar maund and shipment is made in bags of 2 maunds. On the West Coast sales are on the basis of the candy of 600 lbs or the maund weighing 28 lbs, while exports are made in bags of 100 or 168 lbs.

Unit of Sale and Shipment.

Cloves.

Cloves are the dried, unexpanded flower buds of *eugenia caryophyllata* plucked when they assume a bright pink or scarlet colour and generally dried in the sun with or without scalding, the yield from each tree being about 6 or 7 lbs of dry cloves. There is no systematic cultivation in India and no statistics of acreage or yield are separately recorded. Cloves are chiefly grown in the foothills of the Western Ghats in the Madras Presidency A valuable essential oil is obtained from the dry buds which is largely employed in perfumery.

Zanzibar and Pemba contribute four-fifths of the world's supply of cloves and India on an average imports over 7 million lbs. valued at about £267,000 from these two countries Exports from India on the other hand are small and in value seldom exceed £600. In 1913-14 the total quantity shipped reached barely 10,000 lbs. The total rose to 21,000 lbs. in 1915-16 while in 1917-18 and the following year 19,000 lbs. went out from Calcutta probably on account of freight being more readily obtainable there than in Madras which used to enjoy a monopoly of this trade. In recent years the exports have declined steeply.

Exports.

The average annual exports during five years ending 1931-32 amounted to 5,000 lbs. In 1932-33, 784 lbs. were exported and in 1933-34, 112 lbs. only. In 1934-35, there were no exports while 784 lbs. were shipped in 1935-36. Bengal now enjoys a monopoly of the export trade. The chief post-war destinations are the Straits Settlements, Mauritius, and Fiji.

Unit of Sale and Shipment. The unit of sale in Calcutta is the seer and shipment is made in bundles weighing 2 bazaar maunds.

Coir.

Of the products derivable from the coconut, the exports from India of coir fibre and manufactures thereof were at the outbreak of war, second in importance to those of copra, and of considerably greater value than the shipment of coconut oil The coir industry then underwent severe eclipse, but the premier position temporarily usurped, while war lasted, by coconut oil is now claimed by coir manufactures

Coir fibre. In recent times, the coir industry is most developed in Travancore and least developed in South Kanara On the West coast, Mysore, Orissa and in parts of Bombay coir is manufactured to a smaller extent. The total number of persons employed in the coir industry was in 1931, 224,788, of which 154,312 were women. For the manufacture of coir, mainly the green husk is used. but an inferior grade of coir is also made from the dry husk and the green husk which is beaten and converted into yarn without retting. The inferior qualities are not however commercially important. Husk of a particular stage of maturity is required for the manufacture of the best grades of coir. The husks should be buried for at least eight months in pits on the foreshore of rivers or backwaters, where there is a good scour and then removed and beaten on stones till the pith and all extraneous particles are removed The better qualities of fibre are obtained by this method. The varieties of coir known in the trade as *unsoaked*, which are generally inferior, are obtained by treating the husks immediately after the nuts have been extracted or alternatively, storing the whole nuts in a dry place for six or seven months and after the kernels have been extracted, immersing the husks in water for twelve hours or so before beating The cost of retting three to four thousand husks ranges from 4 sh to 10 sh To obtain a candy of six cwts. of yarn three to four thousand green husks are required The fibre is separated from the pith by beating the husks on a block of wood with a small stick The fibre is then dried and again lightly beaten. Properly retted fibre does not usually lose its colour on exposure. Five or six nuts should yield one lb. of dried clean fibre.

Exports. Shipments of coir fibre are inconsiderable but such as there are, go forward usually in hydraulic pressed bales of 200 to 224 lbs. In recent years the shipments have declined considerably as compared with the pre-war despatches. In 1934-35 only 54 tons valued at £730 were exported as against 746 tons valued at £11,450 in 1913-14 and 300 tons valued at £4,353 in 1918-19. Cochin has practically a monopoly of the comparatively small exports of this fibre from India in the raw state having a share of 49 tons out of the total quantity of 54 tons exported in 1934-35.

It is more usual to export the fibre in the form of yarn rope. In the former case it is spun to the required length either by hand as is the case in Malabar, or on the spinning wheel as in Travancore. The husks of nuts about ten months old yield better material than older or immature nuts. And tidal backwaters furnish the best soaking pits. The best yarns *Anjengo* (superior or ordinary), *Alapat*, *Vycome*, *Astatamudy*, originally named after the localities where they were produced or collected but now obtainable from other places as well, are easily distinguishable by their colour and twist.

Coir yarns.

Between the spinner and the shipper the yarn passes through many hands. The first middleman may be a petty shopkeeper who has accepted yarn in payment for rice or salt, or the owner of a shed in which half a dozen or more piece-workers wash and spin the fibre from his coir pits. Eventually the yarn, which is all in short hanks, reaches dealers who sort it roughly according to colour and thickness and put it up in bundles weighing a standard maund or multiples thereof, before disposing of it to the big dealers at the coast ports from whom the shippers get their supplies, or to the manufacturers. The shipper is obliged, when the yarn has been examined and graded by women according to size and colour, to get it rewinded into long hanks of 450 yards weighing 2½ lbs each at a cost of about Rs. 10 per ton because the village workers cannot be persuaded to do so. These hanks are then tied across and made into bundles each weighing one cwt., which again are baled and hydraulically pressed before shipment. Inferior yarns are done up in bundles known as dholls of 5 or 7 lbs. for acceptance as broken stowage. The middlemen arrange for sales through brokers on payment of commission which varies from 1 sh. 6d to 3 sh per six hundredweights. The yarn is sold at Alleppy on spot cash basis or stock system. The yarn intended for overseas exports is supplied by the contractor on the "baled weight" basis. These bales are made according to the firm's grades. The principal ports of shipment are Alleppy, Cochin and Calicut.

Trade organisation.

The exports of manufactured coir exclude rope (which is separately classified in the trade returns) and consist chiefly of yarn. The following table shows the quantity and value exported in recent years as contrasted with the pre-war and post-war figures.

Export of manufactured coir.

TABLE No. 221.—*Quantity and value of manufactured coir, excluding rope in 1913-14, 1918-19 and from 1931-32 onwards.*

Year.	Quantity.	Value.
	Tons.	£
1913-14	38,610	59[illegible],610
1918-19	13,16[illegible]	233,346
1931-32	26,390	565,036
1932-33	26,904	45[illegible],284
1933-34	31,102	577,104
1934-35	31,3[illegible]9	598,241
1935-36	34,223	656,192

The following statement shows the exports of coir goods from the Travancore State, by all routes.

TABLE No. 222.—*Export of coir goods from Travancore State by all routes.*

Year.	(Year ending middle of August)						Number of husks required.
	Coir fibre.	Coir ropes.	Coir yarn.	Coir mats.	Coir matting, rugs and druggets.	Grand total.	
	Cwts.	Cwts.	Cwts	Cwts	Cwts	Cwts	Thousands.
1930-31 . .	1,608	280	583,723	173,390	130,890	895,801	447,900
1931-32 . .	2,846	11,227	569,287	175,650	164,,000	913,010	456,505
1932-33 . .	4,967	306	549,019	296,017	209,709	1,060,018	630,009

NOTE.—(1) Mattings, rugs and druggets have been converted from yards into cwt. at the rate of 33·3 yards per cwt.

(2) 3,000 husks have been taken to yield a candy of coir 6 cwts.

Before the outbreak of war Germany took rather more and the United Kingdom rather less than 30 per cent. of the whole, the balance going in about equal shares to Holland, Belgium and France. In 1918-19 tonnage was scarce and the exports were restricted chiefly to matting. In recent years, the principal recipients are the United Kingdom, Germany, Netherlands, Belgium, France and Italy.

The West Coast ports are practically closed to traffic during the south-west monsoon, and the season for shipment therefore runs from September to May. The yarn is shipped from Cochin in coils of 1 cwt. and bales of 3 cwt., from Cocanada in bales of 280 and 288 lbs. and from Calicut in bales of 3 cwts. The unit of sale in Cochin is the candy of 600 lbs., in Calicut the cwt., and in Cocanada the candy of 500 lbs.

Of the ports participating in the trade, Cochin, it will be seen, continues to enjoy a preponderating share. The pre-war percentage of Cochin was 76 and of Calicut 21.

TABLE No. 223.—*Quantity and percentage share of the principal ports in the exports of manufactured coir in 1934-35.*

Ports.	Exports.				Percentage.
	Coir yarn.	Coir mats and mattings.	Coir manufactured other sorts.	Total.	
	Cwts.	Cwts.	Cwts.	Cwts.	
Madras Presidency—					
Cocanada . .	6,336		..	6,336	1
Cochin . . .	376,286	62 898	9,580	448,764	71
Calicut . . .	164,940	5	554	165,499	26
Mangalore . .	1,810	..	..	1,810	·3

The signs of quality are colour, which should be golden, strength, length and lightness. On the Malabar Coast about a dozen different grades are recognised, which may be placed roughly as follows in order of merit

Grades of yarn.

Alapat	Fine hand-twisted.
Anjengo Aratory Ashtamudy Kuruva or Curwa	All wheel-twisted.
Vycome Beach Calicut (fine unsoaked) Beypore Quilandi Kadalundi Poonani Chowghat Ariyalur Kallai Parapanangadi	Weaving yarns, hand-twisted.
Cochin	Roping yarn.

All the above yarns are two-ply and so is the loosely twisted yarn of inferior quality shipped from Cocanada to the extent of about 400 tons annually. *Alapat* coir is probably the finest in the world and has always commanded a higher price than any other variety on the European market. There is also *Divi* coir which is brought over to the mainland to the extent of four to five thousand cwts. annually by the Laccadive and Amindivi islanders and taken over by Government at privileged rates in lieu of tribute. This coir is thereafter sold by auction at Mangalore, and though it varies very much in quality the best is only inferior to Alapat and Anjengo. The importance of the industry on the Malabar littoral is illustrated by the table subjoined which gives details of the foreign exports.

TABLE No. 224 —*Quantity and value of manufactured coir (excluding rope) exported in 1913-14, 1918-19 and from 1931-32 onwards.*

Year.	Quantity.	Value.
	Tons.	£
1913-14	38,300	587,000
1918-19	13,090	232,000
1931-32	26,251	560,740
1932-33	26,683	448,374
1933-34	30,981	574,111
1934-35	31,149	594,032
1935-36	34,064	652,594

Mats and matting of every description are woven from coir yarn on handlooms at Alleppey and Cochin for which there is normally a good demand from all parts of India. The export trade expanded very considerably during the war with increased shipments from Cochin. In 1934-35, 63,222 cwts. valued at £142,224 were shipped, as compared with 48,289 cwts. valued at £100,438 in the previous year. The bulk of the shipments goes to the United Kingdom.

Coir matting.

Quantities of coir rope and cordage (all hand-made) are also produced, but apart from coast-wise traffic chiefly to Bombay whose trade amounted in 1917-18 to £36,000 in value, the trade is insignificant since coir rope cannot compete with Manilla in most foreign markets.

Coir rope and cordage.

TABLE No. 225.—*Exports of coir rope and *cordage in 1913-14, 1918-1919 and from 1931-32 onwards (quantities and values).*

Year.	Quantity.	Value.
	Tons.	£
1913-14	3,021	70,189
1918-19	2,717	78,448
1931-32	2,228	64,014
1932-33	2,295	57,949
1933-34	2,115	49,149
1934-35	2,649	55,200
1935-36	2,408	51,393

Coir rope is made up into lengths of 60 or 120 fathoms and sized by circumference. The unit of sale in Calicut is the cwt. and in Cochin the candy of 600 lbs., while shipment is made from the former port in coils of 1 to 2 cwts. and from the latter in coils of ½ cwt.

In the last two years of the war about 150,000 sq. yards of coir screening (similar to Kentish hop screening) were supplied monthly to the military authorities in France for *camouflage* purposes. Other manufactures of coir include mesh bags which are very useful for the carriage of tanning bark and other produce from one part of India to another

Rubber.

Though a number of rubber yielding trees are indigenous to Indian forests they are not sufficiently abundant to justify exploitation, and, apart from two plantations in Assam under *ficus elastica*, the spasmodic efforts made to grow rubber on a commercial scale never got beyond the experimental stage before 1900. There are two tracts enjoying very similar climate and rainfall scarcely less favourable than Malaya which pre-eminently offer potentialities for rubber growing in India, *viz* , the Tenasserim coast in Burma and the Malabar coast below the Western Ghats from Mangalore to Cape Comorin. The more southerly districts have a more evenly distributed rainfall, closely approximating to that of Ceylon. In cultivation and transport facilities Southern India enjoys considerable advantages over Burma where communications are very backward and labour, other than imported, not easy to obtain. In Travancore the Shencottah and Mundakayam districts and the Rani valley are the chief centres of the industry, the pioneer estate at Thattakad on the Periyar River being opened up in 1902 with *Para* rubber (***hevea brasiliensis***) which has generally proved by far the most suitable variety for cultivation in

History of cultivation.

*Including rope and cordage manufactured from other vegetable fibre.

Southern India. In the last seventeen years there has been a great deal of exploitation, particularly in Travancore, but also to some extent in Cochin, Malabar, Coorg and the slopes of the Shevaroy Hills in the Salem district, while the Burma Government plantation at Mergui, having demonstrated that *Para* rubber could be successfully grown in Burma, was about 1910 sold to a limited company, and other areas have since opened up there and in the neighbourhood of Rangoon.

Acreage and producton. The following table shows the acreage and production of rubber in recent years.

TABLE NO. 226.—*Area and yield of *rubber from 1930 onwards.*

Provinces.	Quantities.	1930.		1931.		1932.		1933.		1934.	
		Area.	Yield.	Area.	Yield.	Area.	Yield.	Area	Yield.	Area.	Yields.
		Acres	lbs	Acres.	lbs.	Acres	lbs.	Acres.	lbs.	Acres.	lbs.
Burma	Hevea	112,489	9,958,542	109,490	8,446,354	109,056	4,578,461	105,056	7,867,113	106,187	10,274,981
	Ceara	...		...		...	...	24	...	24	1,215
	Ficus elastica	3	700	8	(a)	8	(a)	8	(a)	7	(a)
Madras	Hevea	15,650	1,991,512	12,415	606,296	11,261	31,500	11,374	397,131	11,785	1,128,653
	Ceara	...	...		...	...	...	...	...	...	...
	Ficus elastica	230	(a)	230	(a)	230	(a)	230	(a)	230	(a)
Coorg	Hevea	2,986	404,216	2,986	147,031	2,786	(a)	1,538	(a)	1,738	108,846
	Ceara	...	...	...	...	...	...	...	...	...	...
	Ficus elastica	...	...	...	...	...	...	...	...	...	...
Mysore	Hevea	607	18,200	607	2,300	586	(a)	586	(a)	586	(a)
	Ceara	10	(a)	10	(a)	...	...	...	...	...	...
	Ficus elastica	...	...	...	...	...	...	...	...	...	...
†Travancore	Hevea	48,287	8,825,446	47,275	9,382,632	42,996	1,248,983	95,832	3,717,930	95,832	23,390,080
	Ceara	2,436	593,415	1,565	39,650	1,523	175,626	...	...	...	...
	Ficus elastica	96	6,090	10	(a)	2,032	(a)		...	...	...
Cochin	Hevea	9,571	2,553,422	9,571	1,482,806	9,571	346,786	9,530	932,988	9,530	1,825,747
	Ceara	...	...	...	...	...	...	...	...	...	...
	Ficus elastica			...	...	...	...	...	...	...	...
Total, India	Hevea	189,590	23,751,338	182,344	20,077,419	176,256	6,205,730	223,916	12,915,162	225,658	36,718,807
	Ceara	2,446	593,415	1,575	39,650	1,523	175,626	24	(a)	24	1,215
	Ficus elastica	329	6,790	24	(a)	2,270	(a)	238	(a)	237	(a)

* Production figures relate to dry rubber.

† There is some uncertainty about the proportion of the area under hevea and ceara rubber in the State.

(a) No area was tapped during the year—hence there was no production.

NOTE.—The above statistics are based on data furnished by rubber planters. Owing to the existence of a large number of small holdings devoted to rubber cultivation and the voluntary nature of the returns on which the statistics are based, it cannot at present be stated to what extent the information given is complete.

The total area under rubber in 1934 was 225,919 acres, which is about 1 per cent. above the area of the previous year and of this area only 175,419 acres were tapped. Of the total area under cultivation 47 per cent. was in Burma, 43 per cent. in Travancore, 5 per cent. in Madras, 4 per cent. in Cochin and 1 per cent. in Coorg and Mysore. The total production of raw rubber in 1934 was 36,719,522 lbs., as compared with 12,915,162 lbs. in the preceding year. The yield per acre of tapped area was 297 lbs. in Coorg, 252 lbs. in Travancore, 224 lbs. in Cochin, 181 lbs. in Madras and 151 lbs. in Burma.

The number of plantations in 1934 was 15,650, of which 4,261 were in British India, as against 4,637 in the preceding year. The daily average number of persons employed in the plantations during 1934 was returned at 30,274 of which 23,562 were employed permanently and the remaining 6,712 temporarily. New lands planted with rubber amounted to 611 acres in 1934.

Exports.

The export trade in raw rubber is marked by great variations. In 1913-14, the aggregate exports amounted to 2,605,000 lbs., in 1918-19 these increased to 13,907,000 lbs. and from 1919-20 to 1922 23 owing to the slump in prices, the exports averaged 12,500,000 lbs. in a year. In the following quinquennium an improvement was noticed, the average annual exports amounting to 14,000,000 lbs. Since then the exports gradually increased up to 1930-31. The trend of the trade in recent years is indicated in the following table.

TABLE No. 227.—*Quantity and value of raw rubber exported from British India from 1931-32 onwards.*

Year.	Quantity.	Value.
	lbs.	£
1931-32	15,104,991	334,329
1932-33	6,903,923	65,875
1933-34	16,205,857	233,826
1934-35	23,756,734	494,180
1935-36	30,647,783	665,353

Since 1934, India has become a party to the International Agreement for the restriction of exports, stocks and production of rubber, and under the provisions of the Indian Rubber Control Act, 1934, exports of rubber are restricted, with effect from the 1st June 1934, to consignments covered by certificates of origin and export licenses issued by the Indian Rubber Licensing Committee (for the whole of India excluding Burma) and the Burma Rubber Licensing Committee (for Burma). The permissible exportable amount for any year is the quantity of rubber equivalent to the percentage fixed for that period by the International Rubber Regulation Committee as the percentage of the basic quota which may be exported during that period. If the net exports are in excess or deficit, adjustments are made from the permissible amounts of the next year. The basic quotas allotted to India (excluding Burma) and Burma are shewn in the following statement.

TABLE No. 228.—***Basic quotas allotted to India and Burma from 1934 onwards.***

	1934.	1935.	1936.	1937.	1938.
	Tons.	Tons.	Tons.	Tons.	Tons.
India (excluding Burma) .	$\frac{7}{12}\times 6{,}850$	12,500	12,500	12,500	13,000
Burma	$\frac{7}{12}\times 5{,}150$	8,000	8,500	9,000	9,250

The share of the principal ports in the export trade of raw rubber is indicated in the following table.

TABLE No. 229.—*Share of the principal ports in 1933 and 1934.*

Ports.	1933.	1934.
	lbs.	lbs.
Madras—		
Cochin	2,323,853	9,959,013
Calicut	291,984	828,277
Dhanuskodi	..	28,427
Other ports	3,920	9,350
Burma—		
Rangoon	1,756,093	3,723,210
Mergui	2,544,477	3,849,600
Moulmein	2,820,055	4,246,746
Tavoy	369,600	747,099
Victoria Point	33,600	242,726
Travancore—		
Alleppey	603,596	2,022,079
Total .	10,747,178	25,656,527

Nearly two-thirds of the total shipments goes from Burma and the balance from Madras. Shipments of rubber are either in the form of crepe or sheetings. The share of the principal recipients in 1913-14 and 1934-35 are contrasted below. A striking commentary on the fall in rubber prices during the two decades is afforded by the fact that though the volume of exports has increased enormously, the total value has declined.

TABLE No. 230.—*Share of the principal recipients of rubber raw exported from India in 1913-14 and 1935-36.*

Destinations.	1913-14.		1935-36.	
	Quantity.	Value.	Quantity.	Value.
	lbs.	£	lbs.	£
United Kingdom	1,718,752	336,113	10,892,489	240,870
Ceylon	784,112	171,664	5,428,570	131,732
Straits Settlements	75,264	11,891	7,716,851	147,394
Holland	22,400	4,169	..	..
United States of America	3,696	519	212,230	4,587
Germany	1,232	120	1,937,986	38,432
Total (including other countries).	2,605,568	524,468	30,647,783	665,353

In 1935-36, the United Kingdom took 35 per cent. of the total, Ceylon 18 per cent., the Straits Settlements 25 per cent., Germany 6 per cent. and the United States of America 1 per cent. The average declared value was 4 annas 8 pies (5*d*.) per lb. in 1935-36 as compared with 4 annas 5 pies (5*d*.) in 1934-35.

Unit of Sale and shipment.

The unit of sale is the lb. From Burma shipment is made in chests, varying from 200 to 224 lbs. nett and also in gunnies of varying weights The unit of shipment in Cochin and Calicut is a bundle, a case or a chest varying in weight from 150 lbs. to 240 lbs. Quotations for export are generally based on the lb. *c.i.f.*

Coal.

Occurrence.

The Indian coalfields are classified according to the two geological divisions, namely, the Gondwana system of strata, chiefly composed of sandstones and shales deposited in fresh water and by rivers, and the Tertiary (or cretaceous) beds. The bulk of the coalfields belong to the former system, as is indicated in the following statement

TABLE No. 231 —*Origin of Indian coal raised in 1934 and 1935.*

	Average of five years ending 1933.	1934.	1935.
	Tons.	Tons.	Tons.
Gondwana coalfields	21,389,321	21,691,404	22,607,552
Tertiary Coalfields	386,832	366,043	409,143
Total	21,776,153	22,057,447	23,016,695

The Jharia and the Raniganj are the two principal coal-fields and from them were derived in 1935 over 72 per cent. of the total output. The latter lies chiefly in the Burdwan district of Bengal and the first working dates from 1820, while mining on the Jharia field, which is in the adjoining province of Bihar, began in 1893. Next to them are the Bokaro and Giridih coalfields in Bihar and Orissa, Pench Valley coalfields in the Central Provinces and Singareni coalfields in the Hyderabad State. Of the tertiary deposits those at Makum in Assam and in the Mianwali district of the Punjab are the most considerable.

Value of coal.

The value of the coal produced in India is reported annually by mine-owners and represents the actual or estimated wholesale price of coal at the pit's mouth. The qualities of coal commonly sold on the Calcutta market are *Desherghur* (from the seam of that name which runs through the Raniganj field) and *selected Jharia*. In the following table the average value of all the coal produced is contrasted with that of the declared export value at the ports of shipment:

TABLE No. 232.—*Average value of coal at the pit's mouth contrasted with that declared at the time of export.*

Year.	Value at the pit's mouth per ton.		Declared value per ton.	
	s.	*d.*	*s.*	.
1913	4	8	13	1
1919	6	0	15	10
1930	5	10	16	11
1931	5	9	16	9
1932	5	1	14	11
1933	4	8	14	5
1934	4	4	14	9
1935	4	3	12	10

The average value at pit's mouth for the quinquennium ending 1935 was 4*s.* 9*d*. In the following statement this is contrasted with the average value of coal at pit's mouth in some foreign countries.

TABLE No. 233.—*Average value of coal in India as contrasted with that in some foreign countries.*

Countries.	Value.	
	Rs.	As.
India	4	9 (*a*)
United Kingdom	13	2 (*a*)
Australia	13	11 (*b*)
Japan	7	11 (*a*)
United States of America	9	1 (*b*)
Union of South Africa	5	6 (*a*)

(*a*) Average of five years ending 1935.
(*b*) Average of five years ending 1934.

Due mainly to the accessibility and the cheapness of labour, Indian coal has a lower value.

The average prices of Indian, Welsh and Natal coal at the chief ports are contrasted in the following table.

TABLE No. 234.—*Average price per ton of Indian, Welsh and Natal coal at chief ports.*

Year.	Calcutta.		Bombay.						Karachi.					
	Desherghur. (Delivered into Wagons)		Desherghur.		Cardiff.		Natal		Indian (Trimmed into Bunkers		South Welsh (Trimmed into Bunkers)		Natal (Trimmed into Bunkers)	
	s.	*d.*	*s.*	*d.*	*s.*	*d.*	*s.*	*d.*	*s.*	*d.*	*s.*	*d.*	*s.*	*d.*
1932 . .	7	0	(*a*)23	0	No quotation.		No quotation.		25	5	35	11	26	4
1933 . .	5	8	(*b*)18	2	Do.		Do		22	0	34	6	23	9
1934 . .	5	8	(*c*)17	6	(*d*)29	6	Do.		20	4	34	6	21	0
1935 . .	4	11	(*c*)17	9	(*d*)29	10	(*e*)21	10	21	2	34	6	22	2
1936 (Six months)	4	8	(*c*)17	5	(*d*)30	10	(*e*)23	8	21	8	No quotation.		22	3

(*a*) Ex-scales, average for three months.
(*b*) *C.i.f.*, average for nine months
(*c*) Selected grade Jheria, net *c. i. f.*, Bombay.
(*d*) Average declared value of coal imported into Bombay Presidency (excluding Sind) from the United Kingdom
(*e*) Average declared value of coal imported into Bombay Presidency (excluding Sind) from the Union of South Africa.

Production.

The total production in 1935 amounted to 23,016,695 tons, exclusive of the more or less empirical estimate of 575,000 tons taken by the miners for their own use. In 1935-36, the total monthly raisings amounted to 20,873,000 tons.

The output of coal in each of the principal coal bearing provinces and Indian States is shewn in the table below.

TABLE No. 235.—*Production of coal in each province and Indian State (in tons).*

Year.	British Provinces.						
	Assam Tons.	Bihar and Orissa. Tons.	Bengal. Tons.	Punjab. Tons.	Baluchistan. Tons.	Central Provinces. Tons.	Total. Tons.
1926	300,506	13,942,404	5,187,688	68,048	9,131	635,252	20,093,024
1927	322,517	14,494,550	5,554,990	62,704	8,945	666,758	21,110,464
1928	297,501	14,789,216	5,639,993	46,152	11,217	732,353	21,516,432
1929	321,545	15,085,689	5,965,104	43,136	10,984	882,331	22,308,739
1930	358,035	14,995,452	6,316,528	50,619	11,301	952,371	22,684,306
1926-30 (Average)	*320,000*	*14,661,000*	*5,723,000*	*54,000*	*10,000*	*774,000*	*21,542,000*
1931	274,278	13,390,482	5,810,184	54,840	13,472	973,040	20,516,296
1932	208,802	11,593,680	5,782,603	72,857	13,957	1,049,238	18,721,087
1933	192,036	10,941,445	5,691,189	94,099	9,141	1,234,523	18,162,433
1934	186,313	12,323,760	6,159,486	125,266	10,519	1,438,980	20,244,324
1935	(a)218,830	12,438,058	6,682,752	144,423	4,946	1,526,690	21,015,699

(a) Includes figures for Act-mines in the Khasi and Jaintia Hills which are situated within the British territory.

Year	Indian States.								
	Assam (Khasi and Jaintia Hills). Tons	Bihar and Orissa (Talcher State). Tons.	Central Provinces (Korea State and Raigarh State). Tons.	Baluchistan (Kalat State) Tons.	Hyderabad Tons.	Rajputana (Bikaner). Tons.	Central India (Rewah) Tons.	Total. Tons.	Grand total. Tons.
1926	555	13,371	..	6,455	637,779	31,275	216,708	906,148	20,999,167
1927	825	23,316	...	5,499	707,213	17,358	217,661	971,872	22,082,336
1928	588	38,237	...	6,714	734,765	27,386	218,750	1,026,440	22,542,872
1929	970	47,505	...	5,238	815,875	35,275	205,132	1,109,995	23,418,734
1930	1 005	68,973	(a) 3,517	4,593	812,298	35,123	193,233	1,118,742	23,803,048
1926-30 (Average)	*1,000*	*38,000*	...	*6,000*	*742,000*	*29,000*	*210,000*	*1,027,000*	*22,569,000*
1931	743	142,312	(a)31,351	3,082	757,575	38,148	226,928	1,200,139	21,716,435
1932	1,233	253,586	113,858	4,971	781,121	37,043	240,488	1,432,300	20,153,387
1933	2,118	316,539	266,388	2,321	753,402	33,194	252,768	1,626,780	19,789,163
1934	3,214	306,649	403,512	4,221	769,636	36,510	289,381	1,813,123	22,057,447
1935	(b)1,907	309,282	591,987	4,612	729,414	34,425	329,369	2,000,996	23,016,695

(a) Korea State only.
(b) Excludes figures for Act-mines in the Khasi and Jaintia Hills which are situated within the British territory.

Labour.

The following table shows the total average number of men, women and children employed daily in the coal mines in India in recent years.

TABLE No. 236.—*Average number of persons employed daily in the coal mining industry in India from 1930 onwards.*

Year.	British Provinces.				Indian States.	Grand Total.
	Men.	Women	Children.	Total.		
1930 Below Ground .	92,847	23,917	1	116,765	9,654	
1930 Above Ground .	39,308	12,962	..	52,270	5,651	
				169,035	15,335	184,370
1931 Below Ground .	91,035	21,099	..	112,134	10,316	
1931 Above Ground .	34,770	11,363	..	46,133	4,592	
				158,267	14,908	173,175
1932 Below Ground .	89,456	16,901	..	106,357	12,279	
1932 Above Ground .	32,245	9,951	2	42,198	4,733	
				148,555	17,012	165,567
1933 Below Ground .	89,595	14,487	..	104,082	12,844	
1933 Above Ground .	31,328	9,354	..	40,682	5,565	
				144,764	18,409	163,173
1934 Below Ground .	95,903	12,559	1	108,463	13,364	
1934 Above Ground .	33,061	9,949	10	43,020	4,507	
				151,483	17,871	169,354
1935 Below Ground .	102,313	11,092	2	113,407	14,634	
1935 Above Ground .	34,355	11,473	12	45,840	5,271	
				159,247	19,905	179,152

The classes from which colliery labour is recruited being largely agricultural, supply is adversely affected by a favourable monsoon as the cultivator only turns to mining when his crop has failed and his savings are exhausted In 1935, the average daily labour employed showed a general increase There was an increase of 1,710 persons in the coalfields of Bihar and Orissa, 5,294 in Bengal, 1,261 in the Central Provinces, 1,155 in Hyderabad, 133 in Assam and 162 in Central India The average annual output per head of labour was in 1935, 128 tons (above and below ground) and 180 tons (below ground only) as compared with 289 tons and 370 tons in the United Kingdom, 203 tons and 298 tons in France, and 217 tons and 314 tons in Belgium, respectively. In 1934 the figure in the United States of America was 657 tons and in Japan 212 tons and 290 tons. The *per capita* output of Indian labour has decreased considerably in recent years, as compared with the figures in 1929 when the outturn was 130·4 tons and 187·8 tons, respectively. In 1935 the number of coal cutting machines, operated by electricity was 95, as compared with 106 in the previous year. The machines were utilised by 36 mines and the total area undercut was 6,634,100 sq. ft. The number of collieries using electric energy was 120. The aggregate horse power employed increased by 5·9 per cent. over that of the preceding year from 77,491 to 82,038.

Exports.

Almost all the coal shipped as private merchandise from India goes from Calcutta. Ceylon and the Straits Settlements used to be the principal markets but in recent years, the exports to the latter country have declined considerably, as a result of Japanese competition. In January 1921, shipments to Singapore, Penang, Sabang, Aden, and Perim were totally stopped and Colombo was given reduced allotments which terminated in the month of March and strictly rationed thereafter. As a result of these restrictions more coal was made available for Indian industries which in spite of unprecedented arrivals of Welsh coal were at one period threatened with complete stoppage. The embargo was removed with effect from the 1st January 1923. The total quantities exported in recent years are shewn in the table below with the shares of the principal recipients.

TABLE No. 237.—*Exports of coal on private account according to destinations, in 1913-14, 1918-19 and from 1931-32 onwards.*

Year.	Ceylon.	Straits Settlements (including Labuan).	Hong-Kong.	United Kingdom.	Other Countries.	Total.
	Tons.	Tons.	Tons.	Tons	Tons.	Tons.
1913-14 .	393,889	183,501		107	144,259	721,756
1918-19 .	81,310	45,763	7,098	..	9,456	143,627
1931-32 .	272,680	23,431	162,265	11,955	44,786	515,117
1932-33	169,081	20,550	188,571	31,529	42,342	452,073
1933-34	222,996	5,391	99,286	15,329	..	372,894
1934-35 .	215,605	29,719	55,384	18	7,963	308.689
1935-36 .	132,618	16,589	41,270	..	7,548	198,025

The figures of bunker coal and coal on Admiralty and Royal Indian Marine shipping account are not included in the statistics of foreign exports. The following statement shows the exports of bunker coal.

Bunker coal.

TABLE No. 238.—*Exports of bunker *coal.*

Year.	Quantity.
	Tons.
1931-32	592,746
1932-33	558,623
1933-34	495,592
1934-35	502,012
1935-36	547,426

* Coal shipped for the use of steamers engaged in the foreign trade.

The bulk of these shipments goes from Calcutta with Bombay as next in importance.

The consumption of coal on Admiralty and Royal Indian Navy accounts was 29,000 tons in 1935.

Coke and patent fuel.

Coke is produced mainly in the area covered by the Bihar and Orissa coalfields from low-grade coal, but only small quantities are exported. In 1935, the quantity of soft coke despatched from the Bengal, Bihar and Orissa coalfields amounted to 888,493 tons as compared with 860,478 tons during 1934. The exports during 1934-35 and 1935-36 were 2,034 tons and 1,799 tons, respectively, the chief recipients being the Straits Settlements, Ceylon and Hongkong The Indian Soft Coke Cess Committee are carrying on intensive propaganda in the country for the popularisation of soft coke as a domestic fuel. There have been no recorded exports of patent fuel

Soft coke cess.

A cess at the rate of 2 annas per maund is levied on all soft coke despatched by rail from collieries in the provinces of Bengal, Bihar and Orissa. the cess is collected by the railway administrations concerned by means of a surcharge on freight, and is paid to the Soft Coke Cess Committee.

Imports.

The imports of foreign coal into India amounted in 1913-14 to 531,814 tons, of which 155,390 tons were from the United Kingdom and the balance chiefly from Natal, Portuguese East Africa, Japan, Holland and Australia. During the war these imports declined from 379,000 tons in 1914-15, to 115,000 tons in 1915-16 and 48,000 tons in 1916-17. In 1917-18, there was a further drop to 23,600 tons. but there was a revival in the following year to 67,600 tons In 1919-20 the imports again fell to 38,000 tons, but rose in the three succeeding years to 86,000 tons in 1920-21, 1,489,000 tons in 1921-22, and 882,000 tons in 1922-23. In the quenquennium ending 1929-30, the imports suffered a decline, the average quantity imported amounting to 2,25,000 tons in a year. The downward trend continued in the succeeding years but in 1933-34 there was a slight improvement, imports registering 56,351 tons as compared with 34,800 tons in the previous year. In 1934-35, this improvement was maintained, the total quantity imported amounting to 56,754 tons In 1935-36, 59,437 tons were imported.

Coal consumption.

The total available supply of coal (Indian and foreign) arrived at by adding imports (minus re-exports) to the total production and deducting exports therefrom amounted in 1935 to 22,876,000 tons as compared with 19,428,000 tons in 1933 and 21,799,000 tons in 1934 The statement below gives the Director General of Commercial Intelligence's estimate of the distribution of this supply among railways and industrial concerns and the percentage under each head to the whole Of the 7 million tons consumed by Indian railways, with the exception of 1,500 tons all were Indian coal.

TABLE No. 239.—*Estimated consumption of coal in 1935.*

Consumers.	Quantity.	Percentage.
	(000 Tons.)	
Railways	(a)7,293	31·9
Admiralty and Royal Indian Navy Shipping Accounts	29	0·1
Bunker Coal	1,020	4·5
Cotton Mills	1,531	6·7
Jute Mills	653	2·9
Iron Steel and brass foundaries (including engineering workshops)	5,583	24·4
Port Trusts	135	0·6
Inland Steamers	551	2·4
Brick and tile factories (including potteries and cement works)	792	3·5
Tea Gardens	186	0·8
Paper Mills	171	0·7
Consumption at Collieries and wastage	1,220	5·3
Other forms of industrial and domestic consumption	3,712	16·2
Total	22,876	100

(a) For official year 1935-36.

It has been estimated that the consumption of coal per head of population was ·06 ton in 1935 as against ·05 ton in 1933 and ·06 ton in 1934.

Government control of coal.

The distribution of coal throughout India became a matter of acute difficulty in 1917 on account of the special conditions set up by the war. Before the war the bulk of the coal consumed on the western side of India was carried by sea from Calcutta and the railways serving the coalfields of Bengal and Bihar and Orissa were laid out and equipped for transporting some 3 million tons of coal per year to the Calcutta docks for shipment. When shipping failed, all this coal, with the exception of a very small percentage sent by sea on Admiralty account, had to be transported by rail across India

In the first instance a Coal Committee was appointed to deal with the situation which introduced a system of distribution by priority, but as the work in connection with the distribution of coal to industrial concerns in India, in addition to meeting demands on Admiralty and military account, became heavier and more complicated, the Government of India decided in November 1917 to vest all powers in a single officer designated Coal Controller.

The main difficulty with which the Coal Controller was faced at the outset was a shortage of labour in the coalfields. He therefore imposed restrictions on the output of a large number of collieries producing the inferior classes of coal in order to prevent labour being diverted from collieries producing better class of coal. Some collieries were restricted as to the monthly tonnage which they might raise and despatch while others were only allowed to manufacture soft coke for domestic purposes.

To save railway wagons for the movement of grain and fodder about India, the Coal Controller also prohibited the transport of brick-burning coal and dust except for purposes of very special importance, and throughout the year 1918 public lighting in the streets of Calcutta and Bombay was reduced to a minimum.

The supply of wagons for the transport of coal is now controlled by the Coal Wagon Supply Committee. The Committee have fixed the bases of collieries for the purpose of allotment of wagons on representation from railways and collieries. Priority in wagon supply is granted according to the merits of each case.

The Indian Coal Grading Board is responsible for maintaining the standard of coal. In 1935-36, the Board granted shipment certificates for 1,782,015 tons (including coal for Railways).

Requisitioned coal.

A certain quantity of coal was originally requisitioned on Government account at the end of 1916, but the whole output of all collieries working first class coal was requisitioned in June 1917 and, owing to a shortage, the output of a certain number of collieries working second class coal was temporarily placed under requisition early in 1918.

During 1918 the bunkering of steamers in Bombay, Karachi and Calcutta was also controlled by Government.

Relaxation of control.

Control began to be relaxed early in 1919, and in April of that year was abolished, when the onerous responsibilities of the Coal Controller in connection with the transportation of coal by rail were transferred to the Chief Mining Engineer, Railway Board

PARAFFIN WAX.

The trade in paraffin wax, which is one of the most valuable of the refinery products of petroleum, has developed to a marked extent during the last two decades with the expansion of the Burma oil industry, and the foreign demand has always absorbed a great deal of the outturn. In 1912-13 the volume of exports exceeded 260,000 cwts valued at £400,000 and ten years later the corresponding totals were 547,000 cwts valued at £822,000 In recent years, there has been a further improvement in the export trade, the shipments in 1935-36 amounting to 1,080,120 cwts. valued at £1,709,005.

TABLE No. 240.—*Exports of paraffin wax (quantities and values) to all destinations in 1913-14, 1918-19 and from 1931-32 onwards*

Year.	Quantity.	Value.
	Cwts.	£
1913-14	303,153	448,736
1918-19	486,476	745,652
1931-32	1,034,540	1,738,066
1932-33	904,660	1,514,078
1933-34	1,083,660	1,716,843
1934-35	929,060	1,439,461
1935-36	1,080,120	1,709,005

In 1914-15 Japan was the next best customer after the United Kingdom, while the United States and China each doubled the total of the previous year. In 1915-16 owing to the demand for paraffin wax for munition purposes, the volume of exports from Burma, in spite of restrictions and freight shortage, was about the same. The United Kingdom took 124,000 and Japan 63,000 cwts., as compared with the absorption in the coastwise trade of 13,000 cwts. only. In 1916-17 there was some relaxation of the embargo and a very largely increased demand for the wax, especially from Japan, to which country over 100,000 cwts. were shipped, and with these factors persisting, there was a slight appreciation in the aggregate and in the volume of exports to Japan in 1917-18. In 1918-19, on the other hand, scarcity of tonnage to Japan reduced exports to that country to 39,000 cwts., but there were increased exports to the United Kingdom, South Africa and Portuguese East Africa. In the quinquennium 1919-20 to 1923-24, Japan had replaced the United Kingdom as principal customer. Since 1924-25, the latter has again regained her position, while there has been a precipitate fall in the volume of exports to Japan during recent years. In 1933-34 there were no exports to Japan and in 1934-35 a trivial quantity of 600 cwts. was exported to that country. The consumption of paraffin wax in India continues comparatively insignificant.

TABLE No. 241.—*Distribution of the trade in paraffin wax among principal recipients in 1935-36.*

Countries.	Quantity.	Value.
	Cwts.	£
United Kingdom	386,320	615,732
Netherlands	111,680	179,889
Belgium	64,640	102,535
Italy	31,180	46,533
China	39,000	61,425
Union of South Africa	53,440	83,100
Portuguese East Africa	90,600	142,040
Canada	32,500	51,187
United States of America	23,000	36,201
Mexico	71,000	112,612
Other Countries	176,760	277,751
Total	1,080,120	1,709,005

About 90 per cent. of the exports go from Rangoon and the balance from Calcutta.

Unit of sale and shipment. The unit of sale in Calcutta is the bazaar maund and shipment is made in packages of 168 lbs. Sales are made in Rangoon on the basis of the lb. and the wax is shipped in bags weighing 140 lbs. nett. Quotations for export are generally made per cwt. *c.i.f*

PROVISIONS AND OILMANSTORES.

Butter. Of the articles exported from India which fall under this heading the only items of importance are butter and *ghi*, the value of which ordinarily makes up five-eighths of the total. Indian butter is generally made either from curdled boiled milk (*dahi*) or from milk that has been only scalded. Climatic considerations practically prevent preparation from the cream of fresh milk as in Europe but, with the development of dairy farming in Western India, cream separators have been introduced in many large towns, and the resultant butter is tinned for internal distribution as well as for the export trade The centres of this industry are Bombay and Aligarh. Thirty years ago over a quarter of a million lbs of butter were imported annually. The figures for the last pre-war year were 374,000 lbs., valued at £28,500 and for 1934-35, 701,680 lbs., valued at £46,774. Large quantities of butter obtained from *dahi* are however exported. Buffalo milk is richer in butter than that from the Indian cow. Butter is used by all classes and castes, and the bulk of the supply is home made. No estimate is possible of the proportion of such butter to the total exports.

Exports. The export traffic, which was very brisk in 1916-17 and the following year, has since declined and is now considerably below pre-war levels.

TABLE No. 242.—*Quantity and value of exports of butter from India in 1913-14, 1916-17, 1917-18, 1918-19 and from 1931-32 onwards.*

Year.	Quantity.	Value.
	lbs.	£
1913-14	702,318	38,986
1916-17	1,472,471	82,025
1917-18	1,522,880	95,624
1918-19	690,142	48,584
1931-32	322,448	22,710
1932-33	250,992	16,978
1933-34	214,032	13,307
1934-35	212,576	12,897
1935-36	256,368	15,328

Practically the whole quantity is shipped from Bombay. The principal destinations are Ceylon, Tanganyika Territory and Iran.

Dairy butter is usually put up in tins of from one to five lbs and sold by the lb. Country butter is shipped in wooden cases containing two new tins with a capacity of 18 lbs. each, and sold by the cwt.

Ghi. The internal consumption of *ghi* in India greatly exceeds that of butter *Ghi*, which is known as *neyi* in Southern India, is clarified butter prepared by practically every house hold by heating butter over a slow fire until an oil is formed that rises to the surface while the refuse (mostly casein) settles down as sediment. This oil is then decanted and has the great advantage over butter that it will keep almost indefinitely. Butter loses about 25 per cent. in the process of clarification. The chief producing areas are the United Provinces, Bengal, Rajputana, Central India and the Punjab. *Ghi* is used for all purposes to which butter is put in Europe and is also extensively employed in the preparation of bazaar sweetmeats. Adulteration is largely practised with the aid of vegetable oils like that of coconut, groundnut, nigerseed, poppy and sesame and also with animal fats and starch. Vegetable *ghi* is also being used as an adulterant of *ghi* and as a *ghi* substitute. The bulk of the quantity of *ghi* produced is locally consumed and supplies are reinforced by a considerable transfrontier trade, as well as by imports by sea from Iran and the Persian Gulf.

Exports.

Though the exports have declined during recent years, the export trade is nevertheless of considerable importance as the following table indicates, though the figures include 'imitation *ghi*' which contains a certain percentage of pure *ghi* and costs about half the unadulterated article.

TABLE No. 243.—*Quantity and value of exports of ghi from India.*

Year.	Quantity.	Value.
	lbs.	£
1913-14	5,568,809	232,945
1918-19	4,389,352	235,666
1931-32	3,056,928	167,003
1932-33	2,445,744	119,274
1933-34	2,734,816	99,831
1934-35	2,858,912	109,800
1935-36	2,691,360	111,906

The trade is not centred in any particular port, though Calcutta accounts for about 64 per cent. of the traffic, followed by Bombay, Negapatam, Dhanushkodi, Cocanada, and Madras in that order. About nine-tenths of the exports go to British Possessions, particularly to those colonies with a large Indian immigrant population, such as the Straits Settlements, Federated Malay States, Ceylon, Hongkong, Union of South Africa, Mauritius and British West India Islands

Unit of sale and shipment.

The local unit of sale is the bazaar maund, quotations for export being generally made per case containing two new tins weighing 40 to 50 seers either *c.i.f.* or *f.o.b.* This case of two tins is also the common unit of shipment.

TOBACCO.

Cultivation.

The Portuguese are credited with having conveyed the tobacco plant and the knowledge of its properties to India about the year 1508. The only two species cultivated in India are *nicotiana tabacum* and *nicotiana rustica.* The former is the more common and is grown all over the country. The plant is pink-flowered with large sessile leaves and forms the most important source of tobacco of commerce. The latter is widely cultivated in Eastern Bengal, Assam, the United Provinces, the Punjab and Kashmir. This species differs from the other by being a smaller and hardier plant with yellowish flowers and stalked smaller leaves. It gives a higher yield of leaf and matures earlier than the other. The important tobacco tracts are few in number and are situated in the provinces of Bengal, Madras, Bihar and Orissa, Burma and Bombay. In Bengal, the main tobacco-growing areas are in the districts of Jalpaiguri and Rangpur and in the State of Cooch Bihar. Nearly three-fourths of the area is under *nicotiana tabacum*, the rest being under *nicotiana rustica*. About 500 acres are used in the cultivation of Sumatra wrapper and the Burmese Havana Manilla and Pensylvania filler tobaccos. In Madras, the most important tobacco-growing centre is the Guntur district where about 100,000 acres are annually under this crop, Vizagapatam, Coimbatore, East Godavari, and Madura are next in importance. Adcok and white Burley varieties of virginian tobacco are also grown in the Guntur district. As in Bengal *Nicotiana tabacum* is the chief variety cultivated in Madras. In Bihar and Orissa, the most important districts are the Mazaffarpur and Darbhanga, where the crop covers a compact block of about 70,000 acres The district of Purnea comes next in importance with an acreage of 46,000 acres. In Burma, two varieties of tobacco namely Burmese tobacco and Havana tobacco are cultivated. There is no inland cultivation in Burma, but the tobacco-growing tract is along the big rivers on land fertilised by flood water during rains. In Bombay the tobacco-growing regions are the Kaira, Belgaum and Satara districts and the Baroda and other Indian States.

The crop is suited only to small holdings as it requires considerable attention and liberal manuring The following table shows the area and yield of tobacco in India in recent years.

TABLE NO. 244.—*Area and yield of tobacco in India from 1930-31.*

	1930-31		1931-32.		1932-33		1933-34		1934-35.	
	Area.	Yield	Area.	Yield	Area	Yield.	Area	Yield.	Area	Yield.
British Provinces—	Acres	Tons	Acres	Tons	Acres	tons	Acres	Tons	Acres	tons.
Assam	14,000	6,000	14,000	5,000	13,000	5,000	14,000	5,000	13,000	5,000
Bengal	284,000	120,000	293,000	122,000	281,000	139,000	286,000	123,000	308,000	144,000
Bombay (including Sind)	146,000	107,000	158,000	144,000	137,000	118,000	144,000	107,000	184,000	146,000
Bihar and Orissa	136,000	65,000	141,000	63,000	161,000	58,000	140,000	53,000	133,000	50,000
Burma	111,000	49,000	87,000	39,000	88,000	39,000	103,000	45,000	102,000	45,000
Central Provinces and Berar	16,000	4,000	16,000	4,000	17,000	4,000	13,000	4,000	15,000	4,000
Delhi	1,000	300	1,000	1,000	1,000	1,000	1,000	1,000	1,000	1,000
Madras	243,000	122,000	269,000	142,000	256,000	138,000	248,000	129,000	292,000	153,000
North-West Frontier Province	11,000	(a)	13,000	(a)	8,000	(a)	6,000	(a)	14,000	(a)
Punjab	71,000	27,000	85,000	30,000	66,000	30,000	49,000	20,000	88,000	38,000
United Provinces	73,000	44,000	67,000	47,000	83,000	55,000	81,000	50,000	100,000	65,000
Total British Provinces	1,106,000	544,300	1,144,000	597,000	1,111,000	587,000	1,085,000	537,000	1,250,000	651,000
Indian States— Baroda	41,000	8,000	32,000	7,000	39,000	8,000	44,000	5,000	(a)	(a)
Hyderabad	87,000	17,000	78,000	16,000	76,000	18,000	73,000	15,000	75,000	16,000
Khairpur (Sind)	.	..		..	...	..	..	..	2,000	1,000
Mysore	23,000	4,000	25,000	3,000	25,000	3,000	25,000	4,000	23,000	3,000
Total Indian States	151,000	29,000	135,000	26,000	140,000	29,000	142,000	24,000	100,000	20,000
Grand Total	1,257,000	573,300	1,279,000	623,000	1,251,000	616,000	1,227,000	561,000	1,350,000	671,000

(a) Not available.

The following statement shows the outturn per acre of cured leaves. The average yield per acre is roughly 1,000 lbs. of dry leaf.

TABLE No. 245.—*Outturn per acre of cured leaves in different provinces.*

Bengal.	Madras.	Bihar and Orissa.	Burma.	Bombay.
Lbs.	lbs.	lbs.	lbs.	lbs.
700 to 1,000	800 to 1,000(*a*) up to 1,500 (*b*)	up to 1,200	400 to 1,000	400 to 750

(*a*) Unirrigated. (*b*) Irrigated.

Though harvesting goes on in some localities as late as June, the bulk of the crop is gathered between February and April. The leaves are dried, sorted and then stacked and allowed to ferment, different qualities of tobacco being produced by varying the degree of fermentation allowed.

Trade Varieties.

The best quality of Indian tobacco on the Calcutta market is known as *Rangpur* after the district of that name in which it is chiefly grown. *Poolah* and *bispath* are varieties of Rangpur tobacco, the latter being of inferior quality. Other trade varieties known to exporters are *golden leaf* from Guntur for cigarette making and *thindoor* and *sindine* from Burma for cheroot wrappers and fillers.

Exports.

(1) Unmanufactured Tobacco.

The bulk of the tobacco grown in India disappears in local consumption, but the export trade chiefly from Madras and Rangoon is of considerable value. The total value of the exports of tobacco, manufactured and unmanufactured, in 1913-14, exceeded £319,000, of which roughly two-thirds was unmanufactured, the corresponding figures for 1934-35 being £614,277, of which nine-tenths was unmanufactured. The following table shows the value of India's export trade in unmanufactured tobacco, which for the most part consists of crudely cured leaf, from 1931-32 onwards as compared with the pre-war and post-war figures.

TABLE No. 246.—*Quantity and value of unmanufactured tobacco exported in 1913-14, 1918-19 and from 1931-32 onwards*

Year.	Quantity.	Value.
	lbs.	£
1913-14	27,817,000	211,800
1918-19	31,506,000	549,600
1931-32	25,426,632	604,630
1932-33	20,892,804	550,562
1933-34	29,206,470	675,975
1934-35	26,349,287	581,644
1935-36	28,742,628	659,676

The principal destinations in 1913-14 were Aden and its dependencies, Hongkong, France, the Straits Settlements (including Labuan), the Federated Malay States, Holland and Germany. Burma tobacco was at one time used in the manufacture by the French Government of the *caporal* cigarette, the supplier being on the outbreak of war a German American. Exports to France from Rangoon amounted to over 3 million lbs. in 1913-14. In 1918-19 France was by far the largest customer for Indian tobacco with over 13 million lbs., followed by Aden with 6,400,000 lbs. and the Straits Settlements with just over and the United Kingdom a little less than three million lbs. In recent years, France has practically disappeared from the market while Japan and Hongkong have increased their takings considerably. The share of the United Kingdom is now the largest with Aden and Japan as next in importance. In 1934-35 the United Kingdom took more than 9 million lbs. as compared with 13 million lbs in the preceding year Japan increased her takings from over 3 million lbs. in 1933-34 to 5·9 million lbs. in 1934-35, Aden and its dependencies from 5·4 million lbs. to over 6 million lbs. The share of the various provinces is shown in the following table.

TABLE No 247.—*Provincial share of exports of unmanufactured tobacco in 1913-14 and 1935-36 contrasted.*

Province.	1913-14.		1935-36.	
	Quantity.	Percent.	Quantity.	Percent.
	lbs.		lbs	
Burma	11,655,612	42	993,004	3·5
Bombay and Sind .	9,913,490	35·5	*9,912 7,385,252	*·04 25·7
Bengal	4,013,705	14·0	327,769	1·16
Madras	2,234,511	8·5	20,026,691	69·6

Unit of sale and shipment. The unit of sale in Calcutta is the maund of 82 2/15 lbs. and of shipment the bale of 400 lbs. nett. In Bombay sales are effected in cases of 40, 60 and 100 lbs. the unit of sale being the maund of 82 2/7 lbs. The unit of shipment is the package of 50 lbs. or more. In Rangoon tobacco is shipped to Europe in bales of 200 to 250 lbs. Rolled tobacco is also shipped in cases containing 175 to 400 lbs. In Madras, shipment is made in casks of 880 lbs., in Negapatam in bundles of 224 lbs and in Cocanada in bales of 250 to 270 lbs.

(2) Manufactured Tobacco. As regards manufactured tobacco, the value of imports has always exceeded that of the exports. Among the manufactured products, the most important item is cigarettes and the United Kingdom is the principal supplier of imported cigarettes. The imports of these amounted to over 4 million lbs. in 1919-20 but gradually fell to 2¾ million lbs. in 1924-25 due partly to the increasing development of the cigarette manufacturing industry in India. In the following

*Refers to Sind.

quinquennium, the volume increased to 5¼ million lbs. in 1929-30. The abrupt shrinkage in 1930-31 to 3 million lbs. was due partly to trade depression and partly to the boycott of foreign goods. Since then the consumption of indigenous cigarettes has increased with a corresponding diminution in the volume of imports. In 1931 there were 22 tobacco factories in India employing nearly 8,000 persons. There are also considerable imports into Bombay and Calcutta of cigars from the Philippines and Netherlands. There was formerly a good market for 'Burma' and 'Trichy' cheroots in the Far East but in recent years the demand from the United Kingdom is by far the largest. When the import duty on foreign leaf was enhanced the principal factory producing "Trichy" cigars for export was temporarily transferred to Pondicherry and later, these were manufactured at Dindigul in bond under customs supervision. They are now manufactured in the factory at Dindigul out of country tobacco, but duty-paid tobacco leaf cleared from the warehouse is used as covering for cigars. In 1907, the Bengal Agricultural Department opened a farm in the Rangpur tobacco tract for purposes of improvement of leaf tobacco by the method of selection and investigation into the possibilities of introducing suitable varieties of exotic cigar tobacco, Virginia tobacco and Turkish tobacco. The coastwise exports of Indian unmanufactured tobacco to Burma amounted to 11,465,854 lbs. in 1934-35 as compared with 11,114,795 lbs. in the previous year The share of Bengal in that year amounted to 4,262,825 lbs. and that of Madras 2,171,199 lbs The lowest qualities of Indian tobacco are shipped to Europe for tanning purposes The chief customers for Indian cigars in pre-war times and in 1935-36 are contrasted below·—

TABLE No. 248 —*Principal countries importing Indian cigars in 1913-14 and 1935-36*

Countries.	1913-14. Quantity.	1935-36. Quantity.
	lbs.	lbs
Straits Settlements and Federated Malay States	1,602,041	8,854
United Kingdom	86,033	42,700
European Turkey	30,663	..
Siam	14,584	
Gibralter	13,950	..
Germany	9,506	.
Aden	7,830	5,252
Ceylon	5,990	10,070
Iraq	..	2,192
Total (including other countries)	1,825,635	73,356

The largest demand used to be from the Straits Settlements but the trade has gradually suffered a decline and in 1935-36 the total quantity of exports to that country fell from 27,810 lbs. in the year 1932-33 to 8,854 lbs. The quantity and value of manufactured tobacco (which includes cigarettes and 'other sorts' as well as cigars) exported in recent years are contrasted below with the pre-war and post-war figures.

TABLE No. 249.—*Quantity and value of manufactured tobacco exported in 1913-14, 1918-19 and from 1931-32 onwards.*

Year.	Quantity.	Value.
	lbs.	£
1913-14	2,206,000	107,800
1918-19	1,477,000	93,206
1931-32	834,617	36,056
1932-33	729,846	27,753
1933-34	753,430	27,515
1934-35	1,027,797	32,633
1935-36	855,472	33,564

The distribution of the export trade in manufactured tobacco among the various provinces is shown in the table below.

TABLE No. 250.—*Provincial share of exports of manufactured tobacco in 1913-14 and 1935-36 contrasted.*

Countries.	1913-14.	1935-36.
	Per cent.	Per cent.
Burma	38	6
Bengal	15	52
Madras	45	40
Bombay and Sind	2	2
	100	100

The bulk of the shipments goes from Calcutta and Madras.

In pre-war times the principal customers of Indian-made cigarettes were Zanzibar and East Africa, but in recent years the trade is almost wholly confined to the British Empire—Ceylon, Federated Malay States and Straits Settlements being the chief markets.

MICA.

Area and production.

Twenty-two years ago, three-fifths of the world's production of mica was derived from India, the bulk of the balance being contributed by the United States of America and Canada though German East Africa was making considerable headway A feature of the war was the considerable development of mica mining in Brazil. Practically all the mica mined in India is muscovite, though small quantities of phlogopite are won in Travancore

Muscovite mica is obtained from two principal areas: (1) the Bihar mica belt, a strip of country about 12 miles broad and 60 to 70 miles long, running obliquely across the districts of Hazaribagh, Monghyr and Gaya in the provinces of Bihar and Orissa, and (2) the Nellore district of the Madras Presidency. The mica mines in Nellore are situated on the eastern half of the Madras coastal plain over a tract of country about 60 miles long and 8 to 10 miles broad. The garnets of both Nellore and Hazaribagh are of the same variety although they have different crystal shapes. Mica is also obtained from workings in the Eranial Taluk of Travancore, the Hassan district of Mysore and Ajmer in Rajputana. It is impossible to give accurate figures of production from these different fields, which differ considerably not only in the quantity but also in the quality of their output. The following table shows however the declared production of mica in recent years:—

TABLE No. 251.—*Quantity and value of mica produced in India from 1932 onwards.*

Place of origin.	1932.		1933.		1934.		1935.	
	Quantity	Value.	Quantity	Value.	Quantity	Value	Quantity	Value.
	Cwts.	£	Cwts.	£	Cwts.	£	Cwts.	£
Bihar and Orissa—								
Gaya .	8,597	29,595	8,402	17,286	12,679	21,729	10,524	34,263
Hazaribagh	15,500	48,259	24,266	77,376	33,300	105,058	37,679	125,603
Manbhum . .	...	..		...	...	...	29	66
Monghyr			6	13		..	442	876
Madras—								
Nellore . .	8,318	28,726	7,932	29,884	9,114	27,643	9,452	29,126
Nilgiris . .	51	592	73	923	75	634	43	536
Travancore State	..	...	.	...	.		41	263
Rajputana—								
Ajmer-Merwara	177	490	326	762	387	386	384	466
Jaipur State .	70	263	70	226	151	685	160	727
Shahpur State				.	..			...
Total .	32,713	107,925	41,075	126,470	55,706	156,135	58,754	191,926

Bihar mica exported from Calcutta is principally of the *ruby* variety, the higher qualities of which known as *clear* and *slightly stained* are regarded as the finest micas in the world and are of great importance in certain electrical industries for their high dielectric co-efficient. Nellore mica is principally *green* mica and is shipped from Madras. The following statement gives the quantities and average values per cwt of mica shipped from each area in the years 1913-14 and 1935-36.

TABLE No. 252.—*Quantities and average values per cwt. of mica shipped from the principal ports in 1913-14 and 1935-36.*

Ports.	1913-14.		1935-36.	
	Quantity.	Average value per cwt.	Quantity.	Average value per cwt.
	Cwts.	£ s. d.	Cwts.	£ s. d.
Calcutta . . .	41,313	5 14 7	151,217	3 12 0
Madras .	10,871	5 3 9	15,096	5 4 0
Bombay . . .	1,707	5 10 1	336	18 6 0
Total (including other ports).	53,891	5 12 3	166,649	3 15 0

The following statement compares the quantities and average values per cwt. of Indian mica imported into the United Kingdom with the quantities and average values of mica from the United States of America, Canada and Brazil.

TABLE No. 253.—*Quantities and values of imports into the United Kingdom of Indian mica contrasted with those from the United States of America, Canada and Brazil.*

Country of Origin.	1913.		1919.		1932.		1933.		1934.	
	Quantity.	Average value per cwt	Quantity.	Average value per cwt.	Quantity.	Average value per cwt	Quantity.	Average value per cwt.	Quantity.	Average value per cwt.
	Cwts.	£ s d.	Cwts.	£ s. d.	Cwts.	£ s. d.	Cwts.	£ s. d.	Cwt.	£ s. d.
British India .	40,178	3-11-7	59,013	9-1-5	22,240	6-6-8	20,460	8-4-8	28,360	8-1-9
Canada . .	1,383	6-9-6	780	15-9-0	*		*	..	*	...
United States of America	889	1-3-0	2,755	2-9-5	240	9-4-8	10,240	1-1-2	7,140	1-5-4
Brazil . .		..	217	21-18-10	60	14-7-4	*	...	*	...

Mining.

The methods of mining in Bihar and Nellore are not identical. In the latter field, owing to the flat nature of the ground, will be found large open quarries, while in Bihar, where the surface is irregular, veins are followed up by winzes, shafts, stops and drives Exploitation has often been haphazard and uneconomical, but some of the wealthier firms engaged in the industry have during recent years introduced more scientific methods, and labour-saving machinery has been successfully introduced to assist the inadequate supply of local labour for the removal of water and debris Altogether mica mining in India gives employment to about 12,000 persons.

Preparation for market.

After being raised to the surface, mica has to be prepared for the market Madras mica is *shear-trimmed* into rectangular plates, while Bihar mica is *sickle dressed, i.e.* trimmed by means of the country sickle. This method produces irregular shapes as all cracks and flaws are cut out, but is also less wasteful, for it leaves no square corners to fray out, the blocks are more easily split and it has this additional advantage that sickle-dressed mica is not considered as 'manufactured mica' for tariff purposes on import into the United States of America. After trimming with the sickle, Bihar mica is sized, a process which is based on the greatest number of square inches which can be measured as a rectangular figure, the irregularities due to cutting being left out of account. The largest size is known in trade as 'extra special' (over 48 sq. inches), while blocks containing from 36 to 48 sq. inches are classed as 'special' and below that there are eight grades, the lowest (No. 7) being less than 1 sq. inch. Each size is then graded according to quality—*clear, slightly stained, fair stained, heavily stained, black spotted, etc.*

* Information not available.

Originally all the smaller sizes of mica, *i.e.*, under one square inch, had little or no commercial value. These, with the trimmings and other waste, were dumped close to the mine or factory. It is now unusual to discard clear or slightly stained mica of above one square inch and this is recovered even from mica dumps. The installation of grinding plants to convert these trimmings into boiler and pipe lagging, etc., has scarcely been attempted in India in the absence of an assured market for their consumption though, it is stated, they form part of the equipment of almost every mine of any size in America.

Scrap mica.

For the manufacture of micanite, mica splittings (generally No 6 and No. 7 size) are stuck overlapping each other with shellac dissolved in spirit. They are thus cemented together either alone, or on cloth or paper backing and built up under pressure into sheets of any required size and thickness These varieties are most commonly known as micanite 'board', 'cloth' and 'paper' respectively. The micanite is normally steamed, rolled and trimmed and finally shaped. Women and children are extensively employed in the mica fields for the preparation of splittings from mica block. Micanite was made at Kodarma but has been discontinued for many years as it has been found more convenient to make it in England where the market can be more quickly supplied with sheet or pressed ware The same reasons apply to condenser plates, funnels and other mica manufactures which would otherwise be undertaken in India.

Micanite.

At present exports are chiefly in the form of block mica and splittings which are packed in boxes lined with paper and calculated to weigh about 1 cwt nett each, the unit of sale being the bazaar maund in Calcutta. From Madras shipments are made in cases of 90 to 170 lbs., from Tuticorin in cases of 100 lbs. and from Calicut in cases of 83 lbs. Quotations for export are generally based on the lb. *f.o.b.* The following are the statistics of export of mica from India in recent years as compared with the pre-war and post-war figures. There are, it will be noticed, considerable variations in the average value from year to year partly attributable to the proportion of block mica to splittings in the shipments.

Exports.

TABLE No. 254—*Exports of mica from India in 1913-14, 1918-19 and from 1931-32 onwards.*

Year.	Quantity.	Value.
	Cwts.	£
1913-14	53,891	302,564
1918-19	55,992	598,971
1931-32	53,368	295,187
1932-33	40,466	236,430
1933-34	65,718	335,529
1934-35	104,502	517,994
1935-36	166,649	626,141

The internal consumption of mica in India is very small and probably does not exceed two or three hundred tons per annum. Of the principal ports participating in the export trade, the percentage shipped from Calcutta in 1933-34 was 84·8 and that from Madras 15. In 1914 Germany held a predominant position in the electrical industry and the world's mica market was about to be transferred from London to Hamburg. The distribution of the trade according to the Custom House statistics would suggest that nearly 60 per cent. of the whole went to the United Kingdom, 19 per cent. to the United States and rather less than 16 per cent to Germany, but not less than half of the shipments to the United Kingdom were re-exported to Germany whose consumption of Indian mica in the calendar year 1913 was 47,000 cwts. in addition to about 10,000 cwts. obtained from her colonies. The outbreak of hostilities suspended the activities of a German merchant who had begun to build up a big business in the mining and shipping of mica from the Nellore field. The mica sent direct to the United States was of higher average value than to other destinations, as only the superior grades can stand the heavy import duty.

Distribution of the trade.

The first effect of the war was to discourage the output and diminish the volume of the exports of mica, but a considerable demand soon grew up for Indian mica for munition purposes To secure adequate supplies for the British Government, exports to destinations other than the United Kingdom were prohibited in September 1915, and in June 1916 a scheme to purchase on Government account was brought into force. The Government of India also took great interest in exploiting mica-producing areas hitherto untouched or incompletely developed

Control.

All restrictions on the export of mica were removed in October 1919. In the following year 86 per cent. of the exports went to the United Kingdom and 12 per cent to the United States of America, while the average value per cwt declined owing to heavy consignments of splittings In 1934-35, the chief recipients were the United States of America (44 7 per cent) the United Kingdom (30 5 per cent.) and Germany (9·5 per cent.)

CHEMICALS AND PREPARATIONS.

Saltpetre.

Saltpetre (potassium nitrate) is in considerable demand for industrial purposes, *e g.*, in connection with the manufacture of glass, for food preservation and for manurial proposes in addition to its importance as a constituent of gunpowder. The production of saltpetre in India is practically confined to the areas covered by the three provinces of Bihar, the United Provinces and the Punjab in all of which places the manufacture is controlled under a system of licenses by the Northern India Salt Revenue Department. Farrukhabad in the United Provinces may be cited as the main centre of manufacture, though the refined saltpetre produced in the Punjab excels that of

Area and production.

any other province. Small quantities sufficient only for local consumption are obtained in Madras as well as in a few Indian States in the north. With the outbreak of the war the Indian output was stimulated by a reduction of license fees for crude manufacture and the opening of fresh areas for the production, and other concessions to encourage manufacture. Later on the export of saltpetre exceeding 10 per cent. refraction (impurity) was prohibited and the export of saltpetre of lower 'refraction' restricted to the United Kingdom, at prices subject to fixed maxima, until the 4th January 1919, when all restrictions were removed. The number of refineries decreased from 327 in 1913-14 to 193 in 1934-35, of which 105 are in Bihar, 56 in the United Provinces and 32 in the Punjab. The production of refined saltpetre in factory maunds (of 74·67 lbs. each) may be indicated by the following statement. Production in Bihar and the United Provinces has declined, while there has been a considerable increase in the Punjab.

TABLE NO. 255.—*Production of refined saltpetre in factory maunds of 74·67 lbs. in 1913-14, 1918-19 and from 1931-32 onwards.*

Year.	Bihar.	United Provinces.	Punjab.
	Factory maunds.	Factory maunds.	Factory maunds.
1913-14	185,373	169,756	87,010
1918-19	204,681	289,485	206,882
1931-32	29,670	58,060	120,393
1932-33	40,164	49,935	145,134
1933-34	62,871	59,999	183,494
1934-35	63,312	66,523	163,993
1935-36	88,500	58,300	231,800

The total realisation on account of license fees for refinement of saltpetre amounted to £488 in 1934-35 as compared with £478 in the preceding year The issue of licenses for the manufacture of crude saltpetre has been abolished since October 1931

Manufacture.

Crude saltpetre is extracted from nitrous earths scraped during the dry season from the roads, walls, etc , in and around villages where a large quantity of nitrogen is derived from the excreta of men and animals and decayed vegetable matter. This earth is laid in shallow filter beds of clay and water poured over it and the resulting liquor after settling is concentrated in large open pans over a slow fire (as in the United Provinces and Bihar) or evaporated by solar heat (as in the Punjab), crystallizing out in the form of crude saltpetre which contains a considerable admixture of common salt. The terms of the license issued to the *nooniah* (crude saltpetre licensee) do not allow him to carry the process any further. Refining is carried out in licensed premises either by continuing the process applicable to the manufacture of crude saltpetre till the eduction of the salt mixed up with it, or by heating to boiling point a solution of crude saltpetre, when the potassium nitrate dissolves and the common salt contained in it crystallizes out. By evaporating the remaining solution, fairly pure saltpetre may be obtained. The process chiefly in vogue in the Bihar refineries is the former, and the product so obtained is known as *kuthia*. It has a refraction of from 20 to 40 per cent. and a good demand for it exists for manurial purposes and for the manufacture of fertilizers. A much more highly refined article is produced in the Punjab with a refraction in the neighbourhood of 4 per cent., while in Bihar anything better than 8 per cent. is seldom achieved The crude product of the United Provinces and Bihar yields as a rule from 40 to 50 per cent. refined saltpetre, but the percentage in the Punjab is no more than 30.

Exports.

Up to the year 1860, India enjoyed a monopoly in the saltpetre trade when artificial manufacture from the nitrate deposits of South America and German potash knocked the bottom out of the export trade which fell from 35,000 tons in 1859 to 13,400 tons in the last pre-war year. India's chief customers used to be China, the United Kingdom, Mauritius and dependencies and Ceylon but China has since dropped out of the market while the Straits Settlements has increased her takings in recent years.

The following table shows the exports and countries of destination in recent years as contrasted with pre-war and post-war figures.

TABLE No. 256.—*Destinations and quantities of saltpetre exported in 1919-20 and from 1932-33 onwards*

Countries.	1913-14	1919-20.	1932-33	1933-34	1934-35	1935-36.
	Cwts.	Cwts.	Cwts	Cwts.	Cwts.	Cwts.
United States of America.	27,800	33,580	1,220		.	
China . . .	80,680	44,620			.	
United Kingdom .	49,280	110,640	64,372	57,094	37,544	47,941
Mauritius and Dependencies	28,740	46,020	48,167	88,054	70,257	71,931
Ceylon .	44,480	99,200	23,582	21,108	40,409	19,704
Straits Settlements .	.		3,087	4,296	4,577	4,927
All other Countries . .	37,080	36,920	18,632	17,560	19,856	21,281
Total .	268,260	370,980	159,060	188,112	172,643	173,784

With the outbreak of the war, the trade was mainly diverted to the United Kingdom, whose chief sources of supply, Germany and Belgium, had been cut off and the Ministry of Munitions looked to India to meet its constantly increasing demands. Whereas the share of the United Kingdom was 55 per cent. in 1914-15, it was 80 per cent. in 1915-16, and in 1916-17, when the new restrictions on export became effective, 87 per cent. Small quantities were permitted to go to Australia and New Zealand for meat preservation and to Mauritius and Ceylon for manurial purposes, but with this exception India's whole output of saltpetre was earmarked for the use of British or Allied manufacturers of munitions.

The following table shows the value of saltpetre exported in recent years as compared with the pre-war average.

Prices.

TABLE No. 257—*Value of saltpetre exported in recent years per hundredweight from 1930-31 onwards.*

Year.	Rs. A. P.	£ s. d.
Pre-war average	11 7 6	0 16 3
1930-31	9 0 5	0 13 6
1931-32	7 14 5	0 11 10
1932-33	7 11 4	0 10 11
1933-34	8 1 10	0 12 2
1934-35	8 1 2	0 12 1
1935-36	7 9 6	0 11 5

Early in 1916 owing to a marked rise in prices as a result of market manipulation for the benefit of the middlemen rather than of the manufacturer, the Government of India intervened and fixed maximum rates for exports, *viz.*, Rs. 13-12-0 (18*s*. 4*d*.) for a factory maund of 5 per cent. (or less) refraction and Rs. 12-14-0 (17*s* 2*d*) for 10 per cent refraction *f.o b.*, the refraction values being determined by the Chemical Examiner, Calcutta Custom House, upon samples drawn from the consignments which were under Customs control; but there is reason to believe that there was a good deal of evasion practised in order to defeat these restrictions

The revision of these rates was under consideration when the armistice was declared and with it the United Kingdom's demand for munition purposes ceased and shortly afterwards all restrictions on the export of saltpetre of all grades were removed

TABLE No 258—*Exports of saltpetre (quantities and values) to all destinations in 1913-14, 1918-19 and from 1931-32 onwards*

Year.	Quantity.	Value.
	Cwts.	£
1913-14	268,060	205,600
1918-19	478,000	621,660
1931-32	133,938	79,344
1932-33	159,060	91,959
1933-34	188,112	114,474
1934-35	172,643	103,342
1935-36	173,784	98,978

The bulk of the shipments goes from Bengal with Sind and Bombay, as next in importance in that order. The unit of sale in Calcutta is the factory maund but sterling quotations to the United Kingdom are per ton *c.i.f.* The unit of shipment in Calcutta is the bag of 224 lbs nett, while the unit of sale as well as of shipment in Bombay is the bag of 2 cwts. nett.

BORAX.

Borax (sodium bi-borate) is not found in British India but is obtained in conjunction with salt on the banks of certain lakes in Tibet or as a deposit in conjunction with sulphur of certain hot springs in Ladakh, Kashmir. The latter supplies enter India generally *via* Kulu and are refined at Sultanpur, or alternatively through Chamba to Kashmir and Lahore while *tincal*, the Tibetan product which constitutes nine-tenths of the trade, is brought into the United Provinces by Bhutia traders and is refined at Ramnagar. The trans-frontier imports of borax (through the United Provinces, Bihar and Orissa, Bengal and Assam with Tibet, Nepal, Sikkim, and Bhutan) have been in the neighbourhood of 6,000 cwts a year. The figures for 1933-34 and 1934-35 being 6,328 cwts. and 6,775 cwts. respectively. The annual imports of refined borax by sea, chiefly from the United Kingdom, average about 23,000 cwts.

Imports.

The export (strictly re-export) trade has been steadily declining in recent years owing to the discovery of inexhaustible supplies of calcium borate in Nevada and California, but the internal consumption for medicinal purposes and as a mordant in dyeing and calico printing and other industrial purposes has somewhat increased, the balance struck by deducting shipments from the sum of the trans-frontier and sea-borne imports giving a total of about 28,000 cwts. per annum.

Exports.

The quantity and value of borax exported in recent years are contrasted below with the pre-war and post-war figures.

TABLE No 259 —*Quantity and value of exports of borax from India in 1913-14, 1918-19 and from 1931-32 onwards.*

Year.	Quantity.	Value.
	Cwts.	£
1913-14	4,270	5,131
1918-19	4,939	10,634
1931-32	1,230	1,683
19 2-33	749	1,142
1933-34	915	1,079
1934-35	602	590
1935-36	644	611

Formerly the principal destinations were the Straits Settlements and Hongkong and the war has not materially affected the distribution of the trade. Over 90 per cent. of the exports have always gone from Calcutta. The unit of sale in Calcutta is the bazaar maund and shipment is made in cases weighing 1 cwt. each. Quotations for export are per maund *f.o.b.*

RAW SILK.

The rearing of mulberry feeding silk worm (*bombyx mori*) is now mainly confined to the Bangalore, Mysore, Tumkur and Kolar districts of the Mysore State, the Kollegal taluk of the Coimbatore district of the Madras Presidency, the Kashmir and Jammu State and the Malda, Murshidabad, Rajshahi and Birbhum districts of Bengal and a few scattered

Producing Areas.

areas in Assam, Burma and submontane Punjab.* Besides the *tasar* silkworm is reared in the forest areas of Bihar and Orissa, the Central Provinces and the Mirzapur district in the United Provinces, the *muga* worm in Assam and the *eri* silkworm in Bengal and Assam and a few places in Bihar and Orissa and Madras. All these are purely indigenous. The *tasar* is a wild silk worm never successfully domesticated; the *muga* is semi-domesticated silk worm feeding in the open, chiefly on two particular species of laurel; while the *eri* is a domesticated silk worm feeding on castor, the silk from which cannot be reeled but has to be carded and spun. Both in Bengal and Southern India the silk is the produce of a multivoltine worm fed on the leaves of the shrub mulberry. The Mysore industry, supposed to have been started by Tippu Sultan with seed received from China, with that in the adjoining district of Coimbatore, is now responsible for over two-fifths of the total output of silk in India. A good deal of experimental work has been done in Bengal and Mysore in recent years under the direction of French and Japanese experts, and the area of land under mulberry cultivation in Bengal has been found to have increased by about 33 per cent. since 1913. In Kashmir, where mulberry trees are abundant and the historical records of the industry go back to the sixteenth century, only uni-voltine worms chiefly from seed imported every year from France and Italy are now grown. The industry is a State monopoly, and the only limit to its expansion is the amount of food available for the worms. The output of silk in Kashmir in the year 1931-32, as estimated by the Indian Tariff Board, was 200,000 lbs. of reeled silk. The following table shows the acreage under mulberry, number of persons depending on silk worm rearing, number of country reeling machines, power driven filatures and filature basins, and the number of persons engaged in reeling and connected branches in the various provinces in India in the year 1931-32.

TABLE No. 260.—*Production Statistics 1931-32 in Round Figures.*

Name of area.	Acreage exclusively under Mulberry	Number of persons depending on silk worm rearing (mostly part time)	Number of country reeling machines of one basin each	Number of power driven filatures	Number of power driven filature basins.	Total number of basins.	Number of persons engaged in reeling and connected branches.
Mulberry silk—							
1. Bengal	25,000	160,000	5,000	..	..	5,000	15,000
2. Mysore	37,000	240,000	4,000	2	58	4,058	12,152
3 Kashmir	..	124,000	...	4	992	992	2,250
4 Jammu	.	33,000	79	1	15	94	350
5 Madras	6,105	120,000	500	1	40	540	2,000
6. Assam		12,000	50	..	.	.	200
7. Punjab	.	1,900	6	...	..	6	25
Total for Mulberry silk	68,105	690,900	9,635	8	1,105	10,690	31,977
Tasar silk—							
Bihar and Orissa	...	160,000	...	...	No information. Mostly primitive hand appliances.		
Central Provinces	...	30,000	...	...			
United Provinces	...	1,200	...	...			
Total for *tasar silk*	...	191,200	...	...			
Other silk—							
Assam *Muga* } Assam *Eri* }	...	150,000	...	...			
GRAND TOTAL		1,032,100					

The Indian Tariff Board's estimate of the production of silk in India in 1931-32 is given in the table below.

Production.

TABLE No. 261.—*Estimated production of silk in India in 1931-32.*

Name of Area.	Production of cocoons.	Silk reeled.	Silk waste.
	lbs.	lbs.	lbs.
Mulberry silk			
1. Bengal	14,500,000	1,000,000	500,000
2. Mysore	9,620,000	740,000	376,000
3. Kashmir	2,016,000	200,000	98,000
4. Jammu	640,000	32,000	15,000
5. Madras . . .	1,260,000	90,000	45,000
6. Assam . .	102,400	6,400	..
7. Punjab	16,000	1,000	750
Total Mulberry silk production .	28,154,400	2,069,400	1,034,750
Tasar silk.			
1. Bihar and Orissa . .	..	240,000	No information.
2. Central Provinces . .	250,000	160,000	160,000
3. United Provinces . .	1,000	1,000	No information.
Total known *tasar* silk production	..	401,000	..
Other silk.			
1. Assam *Muga*	..	100,000	No information.
2. Assam *Eri*.	..	50,000	"
Total wild silk production . .	..	551,000	..
GRAND TOTAL .	..	2,620,400	..

14 pounds of mulberry silk cocoons would appear to yield one pound of reeled silk.

Exports.

In the early days of the East India Company silk was an important article of the export trade from Bengal and in the time of Warren Hastings the exports averaged over 500,000 lbs., it is believed, of reeled silk alone; but the trade was subject to great fluctuation. Between 1866 and 1874 the average annual exports amounted to over two million lbs. including not only reeled silk but also *chasam* (silk waste) and cocoons.

The average exports for decennial periods, from the statistical year 1864-65 onwards, are shewn in the following table.

TABLE No. 262.—*Exports of raw silk during decennial periods from 1864-65 onwards.*

Average for ten years.	Exports of raw silk.
	lbs.
1864-65 to 1873-74	2,065,272
1874-75 to 1883-84	1,401,025
1884-85 to 1893-94	1,744,109
1894-95 to 1903-04	1,717,601
1904-05 to 1913-14	1,740,023
1914-15 to 1923-24	1,171,074
1924-25 to 1933-34	1,006,366

The above figures would suggest that since 1884 the trade had, until the war broke out, remained very steady, but unfortunately the proportion of reeled silk in the total (except for a temporary recovery in 1906-07 and the following year) had greatly declined and with it the average value of the whole. There was a remarkable fall in 1913-14 to 160,222 lbs., as compared with 382,081 lbs. in 1912-13, but this was largely ascribable to the Srinagar fire in July 1913 in consequence of which the exports from Kashmir in the following year were chiefly in the form of cocoons In 1914-15 the effect of the war was greatly felt, as so much of the trade is in normal times with Southern France The exports of raw silk *chasam* and cocoons from India in 1913-14, 1918-19 and from 1932-33 onwards are shown in the following table With higher prices and a larger demand from France in 1918-19 there was something of a recovery in the shipments of reeled silk and a corresponding fall in the volume of cocoons exported In recent years there has been a very sharp decline in the exports of raw silk from India This is due mainly to a catastrophic fall in the world demand for silk, to increased Indian consumption and to the severe competition from China and Japan in the world market The increased use of artificial silk is another factor which has affected Indian exports of silk adversely. The exports of *chasam* and cocoons have also declined to nearly half the pre-war level.

TABLE No. 263.—*Quantity of exports of raw silk,* chasam *and cocoons from India in 1913-14, 1918-19 and from 1932-33 onwards*

Articles.	1913-14.	1918-19.	1932-33.	1933-34	1934-35.	1935-36.
	lbs.	lbs.	lbs.	lbs.	lbs.	lbs.
Raw silk .	160,222	290,089	5,432	11,642	22,954	37,382
Chasam .	909,077	551,299	73,796	429,090	664,292	531,976
Cocoons .	133,789	112,680	39,755	7,806	56	5,000

The principal destinations are the United Kingdom, France and Italy. The chief ports participating in the trade are Karachi, which has superseded Bombay as the principal entrepôt for the Kashmir trade (though there are still considerable exports from Bombay), Calcutta for Bengal and Assam silk, and Madras for *chasam* and cocoons from Mysore, shipments of raw silk from the last named port having practically ceased since 1906-07.

Unit of Sale and Shipment.

In Karachi the unit of sale is the lb. and of shipment the bale of 165 lbs. (two standard maunds nett) while in Calcutta raw silk is sold by the factory seer and shipped in bales of 150 lbs. each. *Chasam* is shipped in 300 lb. bales Shipment is made from Madras in bales of 212 lbs. each to the United Kingdom, 300 lbs. each to France and 336 lbs. each to Italy.

SILK MANUFACTURES.

Industrial Centres.

The decrease in the exports of silk manufactures from India has been even more noticeable in recent years than that of raw silk. Complete statistics regarding the total number of persons at present employed in the silk spinning and weaving industry are not available. The annual value of production of silk goods in India (excluding Burma) has been estimated by the Tariff Board at £5,390,629 There are at present three small mills in India—one in Calcutta, one in Bombay and one in Mysore—in which silk fabrics are manufactured on power driven looms, but the quantity of raw silk consumed in these mills constitutes an insignificant proportion of the Indian production Under existing conditions it would (for all practical purposes) be correct to regard the hand loom weaver in India as the consumer of the bulk of the raw silk produced in the country. The chief silk weaving centres are Amritsar, Jullundhar, Multan in the Punjab, Benares and Shahjehanpur in the United Provinces, Murshidabad, Malda, Bankura, Vishnupur in Bengal, Nagpur in the Central Provinces, Bhagalpur in Bihar and Orissa, Mandalay in Burma, Surat, Ahmedabad, Poona, Yeola, Belgaum, Dharwar, Hubli, Sholapur, Bagalkote in Bombay, Bangalore and Mysore in Mysore State, Dharmavaram, Berhampur, Kumbakonam, Conjeevaram, Trichinopoly, Salem and Tanjore in Madras and Srinagar in Kashmir. While the quantity of raw silk annually imported chiefly from China and Hongkong is about the same as it was sixty years ago, the bulk of the imports consists now-a-days of fine weaving qualities, whereas it was formerly coarse and suitable only for embroidery Most elaborate patterns are worked out with the aid of dobbies and jacquard harness, and the beautiful silk brocades (known as *kincobs*) liberally interspersed with metallic threads for which Benares and Madura are famous, command appreciation even in the West. In Burma, where the material is worn by all but the poorest of both sexes, the absorption of silk piece-goods is remarkable. In recent years the silk weaving and spinning industry in India has experienced severe competition from Japanese and Chinese silk and artificial silk manufactures. The industry has been the subject of an exhaustive enquiry by the Indian Tariff Board in 1933, and in pursuance of their recommendations, protective duties have been imposed from May 1934 on imported silk and silk manufactures.

The consumption in India of foreign reeled silk is estimated at 1,923,000 lbs. and of Indian raw silk at 2,065,000 lbs. With this silk which is worth about £1,550,000, piecegoods worth nearly £6,000,000 are produced. The exports of manufactures, which on an average were valued at £11,000 per annum during six years ending 1934-35, represent an insignificant proportion of the total production in India, the bulk of the output of the Indian silk weaving industry is absorbed in the country itself.

Raw Silk Consumption.

There has as remarked above been a general decline in the exports of silk manufactures in recent years. In 1893-94 the total exports from British India were valued at £162,000 and in 1903-04 at £55,000. The exports in 1913-14, 1918-19 and from 1931-32 onwards are shewn in the following table. About 49 per cent. of the shipments in 1933-34 were from Madras, 48 per cent. from Bengal and 3 per cent. from Bombay.

Exports.

TABLE No. 264.—*Quantity and value of silk manufactures exported in 1913-14, 1918-19 and from 1931-32 onwards.*

Year.	Quantity.	Value.
	yds.	£
1913-14	566,367	37,740
1918-19	823,282	82,364
1931-32	18,124	2,331
1932-33	273,155	11,900
1933-34	60,912	5,282
1934-35	201,471	14,254
1935-36	393,885	14,172

The above table includes goods made of silk mixed with other materials but is exclusive of small quantities of sewing thread and "other sorts" of silk manufactures, averaging in the four years ending 1934-35 about 2,895 lbs. in weight valued at £1,470 per year. The principal recipients are Ceylon, the United Kingdom, Aden, Tunis, and the United States of America.

In the transfrontier trade there are not inconsiderable exports of raw silk and silk piecegoods across the borders of Burma to the Southern Shan States, against which may be set similar imports from Siam and Western China.

BRISTLES AND FIBRE.

Among the other raw materials exported are bristles and fibre for brushes and brooms.

The bristles are chiefly pigs' bristles which are collected in the United Provinces, graded, and either absorbed by the local trade or shipped from Calcutta and Bombay for the foreign market which takes certain qualities for which there is no demand in India. In 1931, there were two factories at Cawnpore in the United Provinces with an average

Bristles.

daily employment of 478 persons which manufacture household and toilet brushes with these bristles. Bristles plucked as in the United Provinces from the living animals are rated superior to those obtained from carcases. The quantities and values of exports in recent years are shown in the subjoined table.

TABLE No. 265.—*Exports of bristles (quantities and values) in 1913-14, 1918-19 and from 1931-32 onwards.*

Year.	Quantity.	Value.
	Cwts.	£
1913-14	4,093	92,948
1918-19	2,746	117,897
1931-32	2,900	87,484
1932-33	2,944	102,403
1933-34	4,009	131,035
1934-35	4,406	175,608
1935-36	4,542	170,859

The bulk of the shipments goes from Bombay and the rest from Bengal and Sind in that order. More than ninety per cent. of the exports are absorbed by the United Kingdom, while Germany receives the bulk of the balance. In Calcutta the unit of sale is the bazaar maund, but shipment is usually made in cases weighing one cwt. nett In Bombay, sales are made by the lb. and bristles are shipped in cases weighing 50 lbs nett Sterling quotations are generally per lb *c i.f*

Palm fibre.

Palm fibre is derived chiefly from the palmyra (*borassus flabelliformis*), the bulk of it being exported from Tuticorin and Cocanada to the United Kingdom, to be made up into brooms It is obtained from the leaf stalks of seedling palmyras which are widely distributed over Southern India, but the only tracts in which the industry is important are the uplands of Kistna and Godavari, Tinnevelly, the Palghat sub-division of Malabar, and south Travancore The fibre is chiefly exported from Cocanada in bales of 1 cwt , from Calicut in bales of 3 cwts and from Tuticorin in ballots of 1 cwt and bales of 3 cwts The exports of fibres for brushes and brooms in recent years are contrasted below with the pre-war and post-war figures

TABLE No 266 —*Quantities and values of fibre exported in 1913-14, 1918-19 and from 1931-32 onwards.*

Year.	Quantity.	Value.
	Tons.	£
1913-14	4,022	89,097
1918-19	2,919	81,527
1931-32	5,728	152,259
1932-33	7,141	180,144
1933-34	7,291	165,179
1934-35	7,025	143,637
1935-36	8,142	164,476

Before the war Germany took 37 per cent., Belgium 30 per cent., the United Kingdom 18 per cent. and Holland 7 per cent. of the exports of this fibre. In 1934-35, the percentages of the principal countries participating were: Japan 25·5 per cent., Belgium 15·8 per cent., United Kingdom 15 per cent., Germany 14·2 per cent., and United States of America 8·1 per cent.

The bulk of the shipments goes from Madras.

CANDLES.

Candles are manufactured either of stearine, or of paraffin wax with an admixture of stearine as at Syriam near Rangoon. In the latter case the purified wax is melted and run direct to the mixing tubs where a percentage of stearine, which is generally small, though in some makes as much as 50 per cent. by volume, is added to increase the rigidity of the candle and to impart a skin which it would not otherwise possess on leaving the moulds. The wax is then poured into rows of block tin moulds and supplied with wicks, an average machine being capable of turning out 360 candles every fifteen minutes Stearine candles are manufactured in Calcutta, Madras, Mysore, Bilimora (Baroda State), etc The following table shows the quantity and value of candles of all kinds exported from India in recent years as compared with the pre-war and post-war figures.

Production.

TABLE No. 267 —*Quantity and value of exports of candles from India in 1913-14, 1918-19 and from 1931-32 onwards*

Year	Quantity.	Value.
	lbs	£
1913-14	8,395,078	157,890
1918-19	9,787,492	203,618
1931-32	1,435,482	30,399
1932-33	1,682,142	35,560
1933-34	1,885,052	39,946
1934 35	1,766,570	37,502
1935 36	1,879,369	39,779

More than 95 per cent. of the exports go from Burma with Bombay and Bengal as next in importance The principal destinations are Ceylon, the Straits Settlements, Federated Malay States and Mauritius and dependencies in the British Empire and Iraq, Siam, and Iran among foreign countries Sales of paraffin wax candles are usually made per case of 25 packets for the Calcutta market and of 30 packets for the Madras, Bombay and Karachi markets, the weight of a packet varying with the weight of the single candle For foreign markets packings are scarcely standardised yet.

DRUGS AND MEDICINES.

Senna.

The senna of the British Pharmacopœia is derived from the leaves of *cassia angustifolia* and the chief source of supply outside the Sudan is the Tinnevelly district of the Madras Presidency.

The plant is cultivated on special plots of land. No estimate of the area under cultivation, however, can be made but it has been stated that on dry land 700 lbs. of leaves per acre and on garden lands under wells as much as 1,400 lbs. may be obtained. Plucking commences generally 60 days after sowing, the leaves being stripped from the stalks, and if the flower buds are nipped off a heavier flush of leaves follows. After picking, the leaves are dried in the shade for a week or ten days and the senna is then ready for sale. Between the cultivator and the shipper is the inevitable middleman who mixes the leaves and bags them before selling to the exporter who has therefore to re-sort according to size and quality before baling. The usual season for collection runs from June to December.

The volume and value of the exports of senna in 1913-14, 1918-19 and from 1931-32 onwards are shewn in the table below. It will be noticed that there has been an appreciable rise in exports during recent years.

TABLE No 268.—*Quantities and values of exports of senna in 1913-14, 1918-19, and from 1931-32 onwards.*

Year.	Quantity.	Value.
	Cwts.	£
1913-14	26,450	26,425
1918-19	11,990	17,043
1931-32	40,788	54,303
1932-33	60,539	80,818
1933-34	59,179	71,869
1934-35	51,141	62,508
1935-36	67,118	75,950

Indian senna has a good reputation for quality and price In pre-war times the principal customers for senna were the United Kingdom, the United States of America, Germany and France. In 1933-34 the chief recipients were Germany taking 32 per cent of the total exports, United States of America taking 24 per cent., the United Kingdom 14 per cent, France 11 per cent., Belgium 5 per cent, and Italy 3 per cent. 98 per cent of the exports of senna go from Tuticorin, the unit of sale at the port being the candy of 500 lbs. and that of shipment, bales of 300 to 400 lbs. each.

Unit of sale and shipment.

Nux Vomica.

Nux vomica, which is commercially important as the source of the alkaloids strychnine and brucine, is the name given to the seeds of a deciduous tree widely distributed over India known as *strychnos nux vomica*. The fruits are collected between November and January and the seeds taken out and dried in the sun, the busy season for export on the West Coast running from February to the middle of May. Shipments are chiefly from Cochin, Madras, Cocanada,

Bombay and Calcutta. Figures for the foreign trade in 1913-14, 1918-19 and from 1931-32 onwards are given in the following table.

TABLE No. 269.—*Exports of nux vomica from India in 1913-14, 1918-19 and from 1931-32 onwards.*

Year.	Quantity.	Value.	Average value per cwt.
	Cwts.	£	£ s.
1913-14	46,149	17,366	0 8
1918-19	62,158	57,606	0 18
1931-32	20,789	8,502	0 8
1932-33	19,978	8,787	0 9
1933-34	59,058	22,400	0 8
1934-35	65,041	27,058	0 8
1935-36	17,093	7,063	0 8

The prices, which rose to an appreciable extent during the war period and some years after it (the average value per cwt. in 1921-22 being £1 17*s.*) have again declined to the pre-war levels. The chief countries participating in the trade in pre-war times were the United Kingdom, Belgium, Germany, Holland and France, and in 1933-34 the United States of America, (52 per cent), the United Kingdom (24 per cent) and Netherlands (18 per cent.). 'Fair general average of season, Europe cleaning' is usual quality exported.

Unit of sale and shipment.

In Madras and Cocanada nux vomica is exported in bags containing 168 lbs. and 182 lbs. each while on the Malabar Coast, the unit is the packets of 28 lbs or 56 lbs. It is exported from Bombay in bags of 140 to 168 lbs. The unit of sale in Calcutta is the bazaar maund and in the South the candy of 500 lbs. or 600 lbs , generally, garbled or ungarbled.

Cinchona.

Area and production.

All the varieties of cinchona from which the commercial barks of to-day are obtained are represented in India, namely, *cinchona ledgeriana* (yellow bark), *cinchona succirubra* (red bark) and *cinchona officinalis* (pale bark) and hybrids therefrom The plantations were first started in 1862 at the initiative of the Government from seed introduced from South America, but since then private efforts on the part of tea and coffee planters have been responsible for some part of the increased production and consequent fall in price The price of quinine which was Rs. 20 (£1-6-8) an ounce in 1878 had fallen to Rs. 12 (16 shillings) per lb. in 1890, and practically similar conditions prevailing in Java have kept the price at that level or lower ever since. The main areas in British India to which cultivation is now confined are the Nilgiri Hills, Coimbatore and Tinnevelly in the Madras Presidency, the Darjeeling District of Bengal and the Mergui district in Burma. The acreage in the Madras and Bengal Presidencies in 1913-14 was 2,452 and 2,200, respectively. *Cinchona ledgeriana* is the species mainly cultivated in Bengal, while *officinalis* is more frequently grown in Southern India. The whole of the cinchona plantations in Burma and Bengal belong to Government, while in Southern India, 1,786 acres are in Government ownership. The area under cinchona in Bengal is 2,686 acres.

Method of marketing.

The plant is generally raised from seeds and infrequently from cuttings or layering. The first crop is usually obtained between the third and fifth year after planting by thinning out the plantation, when about 25 per cent. of the trees are uprooted and barked. Proper bark harvesting however does not begin until at least ten years after planting.

Harvesting is conducted in one of two ways, either by (1) lopping off branches or uprooting trees, and removing the bark from root-stem and branches, or by (2) coppicing.

The bark collected in whatever form is either exported or bought by Government. The chief products of the two Government factories at Neduvattam near Ootacamund in the Nilgiris, and at Mungpoo in the Darjeeling district are sulphate of quinine, and cinchona febrifuge. These factories meet to some extent the large internal demand for quinine from malarial stricken areas in India. Sulphate of quinine manufactured in India is now on sale at Post Offices all over the country. It is sold either in the form of powder in packets or in tablet form put up in small glass phials.

Extension of the area under cinchona is necessary in order to make the British Empire independent of Java and other foreign sources of supply. An officer was placed on special duty some years back to suggest suitable localities for new plantations As a result of his enquiry, Government have opened certain plantations in Mergui district in Burma.

Exports.

Exports of the bark which are practically confined to the United Kingdom averaged about 600,000 lbs. annually valued at £10,000 before the war. Bengal has no exportable surplus and all the shipments are from the Madras Presidency. Exports, chiefly in the form of bark, are sold at a price calculated on the percentage of quinine sulphate contained in each lb , the unit being 1 per cent. Shipment is usually made in bales of 225 to 325 lbs. each.

TABLE No 270—*Exports of Cinchona bark from British India in 1913-14, 1918-19 and from 1931-32 onwards.*

Year.	Quantity.	Value.
	lbs.	£
1913-14	605,102	8,289
1918-19	27,468	706
1931-32	89,038	2,528
1932-33	9,029	188
1933-34	94,841	2,219
1934-35	141,798	3,178
1935-36	24,118	473

Imports into India are chiefly in the form of quinine and its salts. The total quantity in 1935-36 amounted to 103,610 lbs. valued at £196,338. The imports were chiefly from the United Kingdom, Germany, Netherlands, Switzerland and Java.

Imports.

SUGAR.

Production.

India was probably the original home of sugarcane The area under sugarcane is larger than in any country in the world. The average yield per acre has been so low and the demand from a population that is largely vegetarian so great that the country had to depend to an increasing extent on the imports of foreign sugar and until recently India's apathy in fact had proved Java's opportunity. Due to the increasing adoption of improved varieties of sugarcane the average yield per acre has steadily advanced in recent years. The adverse condition of the sugar industry in other important producing countries would have caused serious dislocation in the Indian market but for the reason that this market has, for some time past, been less responsive to influences abroad. The demand for imported sugar in Indian markets has undergone a remarkable change since the grant of protection to the sugar industry in India in 1932 as a result of which the Indian industry has developed its production steadily The total imports of sugar into India in 1934-35 amounted to 222,932 tons against 939,600 tons in 1929-30 and 803,000 tons in 1913-14 Prior to 1932-33 there were only 31 cane factories in operation but 27 and 65 new factories were added during 1932-33 and 1933-34, respectively and another 19 new factories were built for working in 1934-35, making a total of 142 factories in India, an increase of over 350 per cent. in three years Until 1906-07 the majority of imports into India were of German and Austrian beet sugar; but though the world prices for sugar continued to be regulated until the outbreak of war by the price of 88 per cent. Hamburg, cane gradually secured the bulk of the Indian trade and imports of sugar into India in 1913-14 were almost entirely from Java and Mauritius, the figures being 670,330 tons from Java and 142,395 tons from Mauritius out of a total of 896,869 tons. The area under sugarcane in India in that year was only 2,536,900 acres representing a decline of 8 per cent on the totals for 1890-91, but the large purchases by the United Kingdom of Mauritius and Java sugar and the apprehended shortage of supplies and rise in values while war lasted made cultivation more remunerative and in 1918-19 a recovery was made to the acreage of thirty years ago and the area under sugarcane was 2,901,000 acres. The acreage has risen appreciably during recent years. The area under sugarcane in India in 1934-35 was 3,596,000 acres. The severe earthquake which occurred on the 15th January 1934, caused very extensive damage to the sugar industry in Bihar, but it is again showing signs of vigorous growth

Consumption.

India's net production of gur (unrefined sugar) for direct consumption has been calculated at 3,692,000 tons in the season 1934-35 which became available for consumption in 1935-36. In addition to this, some 130 modern sugar factories produced 578,115 tons of sugar direct from cane. Sugar manufactured by refineries and indigenous process is estimated at 40,000 tons and 150,000 tons, respectively during the season 1934-35. The total production of sugar may thus be put at 768,115 tons. To supplement this supply 222,000 tons of sugar were imported, chiefly from Java, the total arrivals of beet sugar amounting to no more than 26,811 tons.

Re-export of foreign refined sugar by sea amounted to 2,604 tons. There were also 363 tons of refined Indian sugar exported by sea and 34,034 tons exported by land. The exports by sea of molasses (including cane and palmyra Jaggery) amounted to 1.153 tons and exports by land to 4,176 tons. The position as regards refined sugar is summarised in the following table*.

TABLE No. 271 —*Estimated consumption of refined sugar in India in 1934-35.*

Total Gross Supply.	Tons.
Initial stocks on 1st April 1934	25,350
India's Production of Sugar of the previous year (1933-34) for consumption during 1934-35—	
(a) Direct from cane	453,965
(b) Refined from *Gur*	61,094
(c) Made by indigenous process	200,000
Imports of sugar by Sea	222,900
Imports of Sugar by sea into Kathiawar ports	110,963
Total Supply	1,074,272
Quantity to be deducted.	
Re-exports of sugar by sea	2 604
Exports of sugar by sea	363
Exports of sugar by land	34,034
Closing stocks on 31st March 1935	22.373
Total to be deducted	59,374
Net quantity available for consumption in 1934-35	1,014,898

Exports.

The exports of Indian sugar are chiefly in the form of crude molasses or *gur* for which there was formerly a considerable demand from Ceylon, and the Straits Settlements and Fiji for the Indian population there who prefer this adulterated product to commercial sugar. The trade is in the hands of Indian merchants and the principal ports of export are Madras, Dhanushkodi, Vizagapatam, Tuticorin and Bombay. Sugar is shipped from Bombay in bags containing 168 to 224 lbs. each, and from Madras ports in bundles of 168 lbs. each.

Of the greatly reduced shipments in 1934-35, 1,436 tons were from Madras ports, chiefly to Ceylon.

**Vide* Review of the Sugar Industry in India in 1934-35 by R. C. Srivastava, Sugar Technologist, Imperial Council of Agricultural Research, India.

TABLE No. 272.—*Exports of sugar, quantity and value in 1913-14, 1918-19, and from 1931-32 onwards.*

Year.	Quantity.	Value.
	Tons.	£
1913-14	9,597	91,649
1918-19	12,052	323,245
1931-32	966	14,388
1932-33	1,256	15,768
1933-34	1,626	17,821
1934-35	1,516	18,246
1935-36	1,415	17,918

With effect from 1st April 1934 an excise duty has been levied at the rate of 10 annas per cwt. on *khandsari* sugar and Rs. 1/5 per cwt. on all other sugar except Palmyra sugar produced in factories in British India. Imported sugar is at present subject to a protective duty of Rs. 9/1 per cwt. The import duty on molasses is 31¼ per cent. *ad valorem.*

GUTS AND CASINGS.

Though it has to contend with many difficulties the Indian export trade in guts and casings is of some importance. The term *casings* is, generally speaking confined to the viscera of cattle, while the viscera of sheep and goats are called *guts*, though the guts of certain sheep are sold salted as casings, as for example, those of the fat tailed Delhi rams This distinction, however, is not strictly observed in practice and the two terms have become more or less interchangeable.

Production.

There is little or no internal demand for casings, but it has been calculated that the average exports do not represent more than the viscera of one and a half million animals; while from 4 to 5 million cattle hides, raw or partially tanned, are annually exported. The chief reason for this difference is the difficulty of working up in the tropics a market for viscera except in cities of considerable size where the meat trade is centred in slaughter houses. *Beparis* may profitably collect the hides of single animals from village butchers or even the hides of cattle which have died a natural death, but deterioration sets in very quickly if casings are not treated immediately after the animal is disembowelled. Climatic conditions for a great part of the year also affect casings more prejudicially than hides In view of all these considerations it is doubtful whether the volume of trade is capable of much expansion though considerable improvements might be effected in the methods of marketing. Casings are exported either dried or wet salted, but on account of the higher freight charged the bulk of the shipments are dried.

Preparation for market.

Casings are usually purchased direct from the slaughter houses and treated without delay on adjacent premises. After the fat has been carefully cut off they are turned inside out, scraped clean with a wooden scraper and well washed. One of the open ends is then tied and each gut is blown, and when the other end has been tied is sun-dried. When dry they are deflated, bound up in bundles of 100 *klafters** or 200 yards, packed in cases and pressed. A half

* One *klafter* = 1·80 metres or roughly 2 yards.

case usually contains about 20,000 yards and a full case about 40,000 yards. The process is the same in the case of salted casings up to the point of inflation; in lieu of inflation the casings are sorted and packed in casks known as *tierces* in brine. The casks generally used in India are about 40 gallons in capacity and 2½ to 3 tierces go to the ton. Before packing, dry casings are sorted according to the measurement in millimetres of half the circumference, while in the case of salted casings the diameter is measured.

Trade Varieties. Five different varieties of casings are recognised, namely—

(1) *Runners*, the main gut 20 or 30 yards long in whorls open at both ends;

(2) *Middles*, a straight gut with a maximum length of about 4 yards open at both ends;

(3) *Bungs*, a curved gut with a maximum length of about one yard with a bulbous closed end. The bung skin from which gold beaters' skin is obtained is a tissue which is removable from either side of this bulbous end;

(4) *Bladders* used chiefly to cover cheese; and

(5) *Throats* (known in England as *weasands*) about one to three feet in length

The preparation of bladders is impossible during the rains and they are at other times particularly subject to damage from insects.

Guts. Indian sheep and goat guts are generally of inferior quality. They are usualy dried, packed in bundles of one or two lbs each and shipped in cases containing from 150 to 200 lbs. No standard size is recognised · they are sorted according to colour and are shipped both split and unsplit.

In the following table are shewn the exports of guts and casing from Calcutta to each foreign country in recent years as compared with the post-war year. Indian casings have a fair reputation in the world's market but were not considered in pre-war days so good as those from Southern Russia The principal centres in the export trade are Calcutta, Bombay and Madras.

TABLE NO. 273—*Quantity and value of guts and casings exported from Calcutta in 1919-20, and from 1931-32 onwards.*

Countries.	1919-20		1931-32		1932-33		1933-34		1934-35	
	Quantity	Value	Quantity	Value	Quantity	Value	Quantity	Value	Quantity.	Value.
	Cwts	£	Cwts	£	Cwts	£	Cwts	£	Cwts.	£
Germany	...		2,060	8,385	1,843	8,390	2,242	10,797	2,737	13,317
United Kingdom	22	178		...	...	...		...	11	66
France	1,023	3,637	...	...	...	...	20	38	28	60
Spain	393	5,567	23	350	35	680	125	2,026	47	1,344
Switzerland	14	74	...	...	...	...	...	...	...	...
United States of America.	9	100	...	...	...	...	...	...	4	388
Italy			...	...	...	...	3	15	...	...
Japan	1,180	473	...	...	...	...	...	...		...
Czecho-Slovakia	...	...	...	...	...	...	...	...	109	410
Portugal	...	...	...	...	...	...	...	...	21	470
Netherlands	...	...	...	...	...	...	...	...	100	130
Total	2,041	10,029	2,083	8,735	1,878	0,070	2,390	12,876	3,057	16,135

TURPENTINE.

The turpentine industry in India had only just passed the experimental stage when war broke out and the reduction of imports of American turpentine direct and *via* the United Kingdom greatly encouraged the production of Indian turpentine.

Centres of industry.

At present the distillation of crude resin derived from *pinus longifolia*, which abounds in Himalayas, is mainly confined to two factories in which the Government have part interests, one at Jallo in the Punjab, and the other at Bareilly in the United Provinces. The Jallo factory employs on the average 90 persons daily as compared with 95 at Bareilly. There are two other factories at Jammu in Kashmir which also manufacture rosin. That there is an enormous scope for the development of the industry is evidenced by the estimated area under *pinus longifolia* under Government-owned forests which is put at about 400,000 acres, while the acreage under Indian States can be scarcely less. Other species of the resin-yielding pines are also available in the Himalayas, in the Assam Hills and in Burma, and there is no reason why the ultimate annual production of Indian turpentine should not exceed 1½ million gallons and of rosin (colophony) 400,000 cwts. Owing to the low prices obtaining recently the production was greatly reduced The tapping season for the pines extends from March to November, the yield being about a cwt of crude resin per acre which yields at Jallo 70 per cent by weight of rosin and 3 gallons of turpentine oil. The chief constituents of resin are rosin and turpentine oil, which must be separated from each other by steam distillation Turpentine is sold in three qualities through agents at Calcutta, Bombay and Karachi working on a commission basis. There is a large demand for turpentine in the patent varnish trades and also in medicine, while rosin is used for shellac adulteration, in paper mills, soap factories and in the production of cheap varnishes.

The following table shows the exports in recent years

Exports.

TABLE No 274.—*Quantity and value of rosin exported from India from 1929-30 onwards.*

Year.	Quantity.	Value.
	Cwts.	£
1929-30	46,075	43,728
1930-31	13,151	12,456
1931-32	14,428	14,226
1932-33	22,060	20,199
1933-34	10,352	8,419
1934-35	12,812	9,723
1935-36	9,411	5,867

The bulk of the shipments goes from Bengal and the balance mainly from Sind. The principal recipients are the United Kingdom and Australia. Shipments of Turpentine are separately recorded from April 1934 and in 1934-35, 18,102 cwts. were exported. In that year, 166,646 gallons of Turpentine and 54,236 cwts. of Rosin were produced in the United Provinces, as against 189,822 gallons and 46,708 cwts. in 1933-34, 151,294 gallons and 48,645 cwts. in 1932-33 and 145,203 gallons and 44,268 cwts. in 1931-32, respectively. In the Kashmir State, the average annual production of rosin amounts to nearly 20,000 cwts. In 1934-35, 174,826 gallons of Turpentine and 71,503 cwts. of Rosin were produced in the Punjab, as against 214,236 gallons and 88,016 cwts. in 1933-34, 136,474 gallons and 56,765 cwts. in 1932-33 and 132,570 gallons and 55,187 cwts. in 1931-32 respectively.

Imports of Rosin and Turpentine.

In 1907-08, 76,525 cwts. of rosin were imported; and in 1917-18, 31,496 cwts. equivalent to about two-thirds of the Indian output in those 12 months. The imports amounted to 33,805 cwts in 1934-35, as compared with 34,538 cwts. in 1933-34 and 15,653 cwts. in 1932-33. In 1907-08, 333,500 gallons of turpentine were imported and in 1913-14, 193,937 In 1915-16, and 1916-17, the figures were: 86,700 and 80,000 respectively which is considerably less than the Indian output, and in 1917-18, under 50,000. The figure for 1918-19 was 65,000 gallons. In 1934-35, 3,973 cwts. of genuine turpentine were imported as against 2,766 cwts. and 2,174 cwts respectively in the preceding years.

PEARLS.

The only pearl and chank fisheries of any importance in India are in the extreme South and in the Mergui archipelago. The nineteen banks in Palk Bay comprising the third or northern division of the Madras Pearl Bank were inspected in 1933-34 and found to be bare of oysters A cursory inspection was also made of the Tuticorin banks and a few oysters were found The Ceylon Fisheries Department also conducted the inspection of the Ceylon banks on the other side of the Gulf of Manaar entirely by dredging The survey revealed a promising sign of repopulation of the bank. The small branches of oysters, though not of any fishable value by themselves, are important in that they may conduce to the repopulation of the bank. In the Tinnevelly chank fishery, 441,520 shells (fullsized) were fished in 1933-34 as against 309,226 shells in the previous season. The conch or chank shells (*turbinella pirum*) which are obtainable in the Ramnad and Tinnevelly districts of the Madras Presidency go chiefly to Bengal to be made into bracelets, armlets and charms, the headquarters of the industry being Dacca The import of pearls, chiefly from the Bahrein Islands and Maskat, into Bombay exceed £100,000 annually They escaped separate registration until 1922-23 as they are usually despatched by insured letter mail. The aggregate value of pearls unset imported in that year amounted to £640,000. In 1934-35, the value was £82,401 as against £103,447 in 1933-34 and £78,708 in 1932-33. Exports of pearls were absolutely prohibited for financial reasons in 1918; but this embargo was lifted within a few months of the armistice. The exports of precious stones and pearls unset declined considerably in the years 1931-32 to 1934-35, but in 1935-36 they suddenly rose to £5,008 as is indicated in the following statement.

Table No. 275.—*Value of precious stones and pearls unset from 1929-30 onwards.*

Year.	Value.
	£
1929-30	4,395
1930-31	1,395
1931-32	406
1932-33	295
1933-34	71
1934-35	173
1935-36	5,003

PRECIOUS STONES.

India was known to the Romans for its beryls, and in later times the diamond mines of Golconda (Hyderabad) are believed to have produced the Koh-i-noor, but latterly the only precious stones mined in any quantity have been rubies, sapphires and spinels at Mogok in Upper Burma. The Burma Ruby Mines Limited went into liquidation and finally ceased operations in 1931 and since then, reliable statistics of production of gem stones in the Mogok Stone Tract are not available. The work is still continued by local miners; in addition a certain amount of work is being done under extra-ordinary licences. The figures of production of ruby and sapphire are shewn in the following table.

Table No. 276.—*Quantity and value of ruby and sapphire produced in India from 1932 onwards.*

Place of Origin.	1932		1933		1934		1935	
	Quantity.	Value	Quantity.	Value	Quantity	Value	Quantity	Value.
	Carats.	£	Carats	£	Carats.	£	Carats	£
Burma	..	..	1,103 (Rubies)	44	21,622 (Rubies)	2,708	98,753 (Rubies)	8,287
	...	..	...	.	153 (Sapphires)	25	202 (Sapphires)	25
	...	...	...		...	...	6,687 (Spinels)	289
Kashmir State	..	.	1,494,285 (Sapphire with corundum)	6,917	1,071,869 (Sapphires)	10,448	798,929 (Sapphires)	(a)
Total	.	..	1,435,388	6,961	1,093,644	13,181	904,571	8,601

(a) Value not yet determined

In 1932 no returns are available except that a fine ruby of 17 carats was found at Chaunggyi near Mogok and a fine sapphire of about 90 carats and a good star sapphire of 453 carats were mined at Katha. For 1933 the only return was of 1,103 carats of rubies from Katha. For 1934, however, there is a reported production of 21,622 carats of rubies and 153 carats of sapphire, and for 1935, 98,753 carats of rubies, 202 carats of sapphires and 6,687 carats of spinels. The smaller and inferior stones are generally sold locally while the larger and better are despatched to London. The pigeon blood ruby of Mogok is considered superior to any other in the world. There are some aquamarines found in Sind and the Punjab, sapphires in Kashmir, and jadeite (for which there was formerly a good market in China) in Burma.

PART IX.

MISCELLANEOUS.

Coinage.

The units of Indian coinage are the pie, the pice (three pies), the anna of four pice and the rupee of sixteen annas. When the exchange value of the rupee is one shilling and four pence, the anna corresponds exactly to the English penny. The weight and fineness of silver coins and the weight of the cupro-nickel and bronze coins minted are shewn in the table below.

TABLE No 277.—*The weight and fineness of silver, curpro-nickel and bronze coins minted in India.*

Denomination.	Silver Coins.		Cupro-nickel Coins			Bronze Coins.	
	Fine silver Grains	Alloy Grains	Standard weight Grains.	Denomination	Standard weight Grains	Denomination	Standard weight Grains.
Rupee	165	15	180	8 anna coin	120	Pice.	75
Half-rupee	82½	7½	90	4 anna coin	105	Half-pice	37½
Quarter-rupee or four anna piece	41¼	3¾	45	2 anna coin	90	Pie	25
Eighth of a rupee or two-anna piece.	20⅝	1⅞	22½	1 anna coin.	60		

The four-anna and one-anna nickel coins have scollopped edges with 8 and 12 scollops, respectively. The two-anna nickel is a square coin with rounded corners The silver ⅛ rupee and the 8-anna nickel coin are being gradually withdrawn from circulation and no more of these coins are minted.

The 4-anna nickel coins will also not be minted in future, but they are not withdrawn from circulation. One hundred thousand rupees are known as a *lakh* of rupees and a hundred lakhs as a *crore*.

By Act XXII of 1899 gold coins, sovereigns and half sovereigns were legal tender on payment of account at Rs. 15 for each sovereign, but as a result of the recommendations of the Babington Smith Committee this ratio was in 1920 reduced to Rs. 10. The legal tender quality of these coins has been removed by the Currency Act IV of 1927. They are received however at any Government currency office and at any Government Treasury and paid for at the bullion value at the rate of 8·47512 grains troy of fine gold per rupee. Since 1893, the Indian mints have been closed to unrestricted coinage for the public. The branch of the Royal Mint established at Bombay in 1918 for the coinage of sovereigns was closed down in April 1919. Prior to the opening of this branch of the Royal Mint, a number of 15 rupee gold *mohurs* were minted at Bombay, the weight and fineness of these being the same as of sovereigns.

The denominations of currency notes in circulation are Rs. 5, 10, 50, 100, 500, 1,000 and 10,000.

Weights and Measures.

Weights and measures in India vary not only from district to district but also for different commodities within the same district, and though the railways have given a lead to the adoption of a uniform system, the country is so vast that the differences are likely to persist for many years to come. The principal units in all the scales of weights are the maund, seer and the tola, and the standard weights for each of these are 82·28 lbs., 2·057 lbs. and 180 grains troy. The tola is the same weight as the rupee. In addition to these weights, there is the viss of 3·60 lbs or 140 tolas and the candy of 500 to 840 lbs. It is not necessary for the purposes of this volume to detail any variations of the weight of the maund, except those which enter into the export trade. It will be sufficient to say that in any particular city there are probably as many different maunds as there are articles to weigh The only varieties which need be considered in connection with the foreign trade are the Bengal or railway maund already specified, the factory maund of 74 lbs 10 ozs. 11 drs., the Bombay maund of 82 lbs 2 ozs 2 drs., and the Madras maund of 25 lbs. In October 1913 the Government of India appointed a Committee to inquire into the whole question, and their majority report, which was presented in the following year, recommended the extension of the railway system based on the 180 grains tola, while the minority report advocated the adoption of the metric system. The views of the Provincial Governments on these reports were obtained and the Government of India in their Resolution dated the 3rd January 1922, declared themselves in favour of the ultimate adoption in India, excluding Burma, of a uniform system of weights based on the scale now in use on the Railways It has been decided that no new measures prescribing all-India measures of weight or capacity should be introduced at present but that the local Governments should take such executive action as they can to educate public opinion in favour of the standard maund and seer. The Bombay Government have already taken necessary steps towards this end by a notification issued under the provisions of Section 2 (2) of Part I of the Bombay Weights and Measures Act, 1932 bringing into force with effect from the 1st August 1935, the standard weights and measures on the basis of the scale now in use on the railways in India.

In the table below an attempt has been made to present within a small compass the principal weights and measures employed in the Indian export trade.

Table No. 278.—*Principal weights and measures in use in the export trade.*

Name of unit.	British Imperial Value.	Commodities.
General.		
Tola	180 grains troy.	
Seer (Standard or Railway or Indian).	2·057 lbs.	
Seer (Factory)	1 lb. 13·5 oz.	
Viss	3·60 lbs.	
Maund (Standard or 40 seers Railway or Indian)	82 lbs. 4 oz. 9 dr.	
Maund (Factory)	74 lbs. 10 oz. 11 dr.	
Local Variations.		
Calcutta.		
Seer—80 tolas	2·053 lbs.	
Bazaar Maund	82 lbs. 2 oz. 2 dr.	
Bombay.		
Seer—80 tolas	2·053 lbs.	
Maund—40 seers	82 lbs. 2 oz. 2 dr.	
Maund (Surti)	39·2 lbs.	Cardamoms.
Maund	82 2/7 lbs.	Tobacco unmanufactured.
Bag	112 lbs.	Coriander.
	168 to 182 lbs.	Sesame. Barley.
	182 to 196 lbs.	Rape and Mustard seed.
	168 lbs.	Myrobalans, Jowar.
	168 to 196 lbs.	Groundnut, chillies, pulse, castor seed, bajra, gram.
	1½ or 1¾ cwts.	Turmeric.
	140 to 168 lbs.	Pepper, Nux Vomica.
	196 to 210 lbs.	Wheat.
	112 to 140 lbs.	Cotton seed.
Candy	588 lbs.	Raw Wool.
Karachi.		
Bag	224 lbs.	Bone manures.
Maund	28 lbs.	Hides raw.
	84 lbs.	Wool.
Candy	8 maunds of 82 2/7 lbs. each.	Oilseeds, wheat, barley, sesame.
Madras.		
Candy (Dutch)	672 lbs.	Copra.
Maund	25 lbs.	Indigo.
Tuticorin.		
Tulam	14 lbs.	Groundnut cake.
	15 lbs.	Chillies.
	20½ lbs.	Sugar.
Negapatam.		
Seer—24 tolas or 8 palams	9 3/5 oz.	Chillies, ginger, etc.
Cocanada.		
Maund	25 lbs.	Turmeric.
Cuddalore.		
Candy (French)	530 lbs.	Groundnut.
Cochin.		
Candy	600 lbs.	Copra, etc.
Mangalore.		
Maund	28 lbs.	Coconut oil.
	32 lbs.	Copra.

Freights.

The following statement shews the rate per ton for London, current at the several ports named, during that month of the year in which shipments of the stated article of produce are usually the heaviest.

TABLE NO. 279.—*Rates of freight per ton for certain articles from India to the United Kingdom in 1914, 1918 and from 1933 onwards.*

Ports, articles and destinations.	1914	1918.	1933.	1934.	1935.	1936.
	£ s. d.	£ s. d.	£ s. d.	£ s. d.	£ s. d.	£ s. d.
Calcutta.						
Linseed to London (June).	0-17-0	(*f*) 8 15 0	(*a*) 1 7 6	(*a*) 1 10 0	(*k*) 1 8 9	(*l*) 1 8 9
Jute to London (August).	(*g*) 2 3 9	20 0 0	(*a*) 1 17 6 (per ton of 50 c ft)	(*a*) 1 17 6 (per ton of 50 c. ft)	(*m*) 1 17 6 (per ton of 50 c. ft.)	(*n*) 1 17 6 (per ton of 50 c. ft.)
Bombay.						
Cotton to Liverpool (January).	0 15 6	15 5 0	1 1 0 (40 c. ft.)	(*b*) 1 1 0 (40 c ft.)	1 1 0 (40 c. ft.)	1 10 0 (40 c ft)
Seed to London (December)	0 17 6	No quotation	(*b*) 1 1 0 (16 cwt and over.)	1 2 0 (16 cwt. and over).	(*o*) 1 2 0 (16 cwt. and over).	No quotation (16 cwt. and over).
Karachi						
Wheat to Liverpool (May)	0 12 6	12 10 0	1 3 0 (18 cwt)	1 1 0 (18 cwt.)	No quotation	No quotation
Madras.						
Groundnuts to Marseilles (January)	1 7 6	No shipment	(*c*) 1 5 0	1 5 0 to 1 6 8	1 6 8	1 5 0 to 1 7 6
Hides and skins to London (October)	2 8 0	(*i*) 6 5 0	(*j*) 3 7 6 (50 c. ft.)	(*j*) 3 7 6 (50 c ft)	No quotation	No quotation
Rangoon						
Rice to London (February).	1 1 0	(*h*) 6 5 0	(*d*) 1 7 6	(*e*) 1 6 3	(*p*) 1 5 0	(*q*) 1 7 6

(*a*) Less 10 per cent. rebate not exceeding 5*s*. per ton.
(*b*) For February 1934.
(*c*) For February 1933.
(*d*) For March 1933.
(*e*) For March 1934.
(*f*) Rate fixed by Ministry of Shipping as only Government shipments allowed.
(*g*) Inclusive of 25 per cent. surtax.
(*h*) Controlled rate for Government purchases only
(*i*) Tanned hides per ton of 40 c. ft. shipped on behalf of War Office.
(*j*) Less 10 per cent.
(*k*) July 1935.
(*l*) January 1936.
(*m*) July 1935.
(*n*) January 1936.
(*o*) April 1935.
(*p*) January 1935.
(*q*) January 1936.

APPENDICES

I. Tonnage Schedules.
II. Merchandise Marks Law.
III. Principal Railways in India.
IV. Concessions to Commercial Travellers.
V. Crop Forecasts
VI. Glossary of Indian terms.
VII. East Indian Wheat Contract.
VIII. East Indian Linseed Contract.
IX. List of Publications consulted.

APPENDIX I.

TONNAGE SCHEDULES FOR STEAMERS.

For the ports of Calcutta, Bombay, Madras and Karachi.

Name of the article.	Calcutta.	Bombay.	Madras.	Karachi.
	Per ton nett.	Per ton.	Per ton nett.	Per ton.
Aloes	...	In kegs, 40 c. ft.	In bags, 20 cwt. In cases, 50 c. ft.	In kegs, 40 c. ft.
Alum	...	In bags, 16 cwt.	20 cwt.	In bags, 16 cwt.
Aniseed	In bags, 8 cwt.	.	...	...
Annato	...	In c/s, 40 c. ft.	...	In cases, 50 c. ft.
Apparel	...	...	50 c. ft.	Do.
Arrowroot	. .	In cases, 40 c. ft.	In c/s, 50 c. ft.	Do.
Assafœtida	...	In cases, 40 c. ft.	In bags, 20 cwt In cases, 50 c. ft.	In cases, 40 c. ft.
Bajree	...	In bags, 18 cwt.	...	In bags, 18 cwt.
Barilla	...	...	...	16 cwt.
Bark	...	. .	In bags, and bundles, 8 cwt.	. .
Barley	20 cwt.	In bags, 16 cwt.	..	In bags, 16 cwt.
Beans	...	17 cwt	..	
Beeswax	20 cwt.	In cases, 40 c ft.	20 cwt.	In bags, 40 c ft.
Betelnuts	20 cwt.	In bags, 13 cwt	18 cwt.	In bags, 18 cwt.
Blackwood	...	In straight square logs, 40 c ft Otherwise 16 cwt.	... ...	In straight square logs 40 c ft. Otherwise, 16 cwt.
Bonemeal, etc.	20 cwt.	Meal and dust, 20 cwt	20 cwt.	Meal and dust 20 cwt.
Bonemeal II	...	...	...	In bags or wheat sacks as per standard preserved in the Chamber, 17 cwt.
Bones	...	Meal in bags (in accordance with the average quality of which a standard is preserved by the Chamber), 20 cwt.	...	Crushed in bags as per standards preserved in the Chamber, (Note 4 on p 416), 15 cwt, 17 cwt and 18 cwt.
Bones	Crushed 20 cwt or 50 c ft (at steamer's option)	Crushed in bags as per the Chamber standard. A 11 cwt. B 14 cwt C 17 cwt. (See note 2 on p. 416)	Bone Sinews, in bales, 50 c. ft.	Loose 8 cwt. (See note 4 on p. 416). ... ...
Books	...		50 c ft	40 c ft.
Borax (or Tincal)	20 cwt	In cases 40 c ft In bags, 16 cwt	In bags 20 cwt. In c/s, 40 c ft	In c/s, 40 c ft. In bags, 16 cwt.
Bran	14 cwt.	In bags, pressed 10 cwt (See note 2 on p 416) In bags, unpressed, 9 cwt	... ...	In bags pressed. (See note 4 on p. 416), 10 cwt. Unpressed in bags 9 cwt.
Brimstone	...		20 cwt	. .
Bristles	50 c. ft.	. .	...	..
Buffalo horns (See horns).	...	..	..	In bundles, 6 cwt.
Bullion	*Ad valorem*	*Ad valorem*	*Ad valorem*	At per cent.
Camphor	In c/s, 50 c. ft.	In cases 40 c ft	In c/s, 50 c. ft.	In c/s, 40 c. ft.
Canes or rattans (See also Rattans).	Rattans for dunnage, 20 cwt or 50 c. ft. (at steamer's option).	In bundles, 13 cwt	...	In bundles, 13 cwt.
Carbonate of Potash.	50 c. ft.	...	...	...
Cardamoms	In robbins, 8 cwt. In boxes, 50 c. ft.	In bundles 40 c ft. . .	... In cases, 50 c ft. In bags, 10 cwt.	In bundles, 40 c.ft. . .
Carpets	50 c ft.	.	50 c. ft.	...
Cassia	In boxes, 12 cwt.	Cassia, lignea, fistula and buds, 40 c ft.	In cases, 50 c. ft. In bags, 12 cwt.	Cassia, Lignea, Fistula and buds, 40 c. ft.

Name of the article.	Calcutta.	Bombay.	Madras.	Karachi.
	Per ton nett.	Per ton.	Per ton nett.	Per ton.
Castor seed	15 cwt.	*Bold Cawnpore* description and mixture containing more than 2 per cent. of such, 10 cwt Othersorts not containing more than 2 per cent. of *bold Cawnpore* description 13 cwt. (12 cwts. with effect from 1st October 1924)	20 cwt.	14 cwt.
Chasam	50 c. ft.	8 cwt.	...	8 cwt.
Chillies	(Dry) in bags, or bundles, 8 cwt.	In bags 4 cwt In borras 40 c ft	In bags, 12 cwt In robbins, 14 cwt	...
Chinaroot	...	In cases, 40 c ft.	In bags, 11 cwt In cases, 50 c ft	In c/s, 40 c ft. ...
Chiretta	In bundles, 50 c ft.		In bales, 50 c. ft.	. .
Chrome ore	20 cwt	...	. .	...
Cigars	..	40 c ft	50 c ft.	40 c ft.
Cinnamon	.	In bales or cases, 40 c ft	...	In c/s, 40 c. ft.
Cloves	In bags, 8 cwt. In cases, 50 c ft	In cases, 40 c ft In bags or frazils, 8 cwt.	In bags, 8 cwt. In cases, 50 c. ft.	In c/s, 40 c. ft. In bags or frazils, 8 cwt
Coal	20 cwt.		20 cwt.	20 cwt
Cochineal	50 c ft		50 c. ft.	
Cocoa	. .	In bags, 16 cwt.	...	In bags, 10 cwt.
Coconut Oil (See oil)	...		...	11 cwt.
Coculus Indicus	..	In bags, 13 cwt.	...	In bags, 13 cwt.
Coffee	In bags, 18 cwt	In c/s, 40 c ft In bags or frazils, 14 cwt	In bags, 18 cwt. In c/s, 17 cwt.	In c/s, 40 c ft. In bags or frazils, 12 cwt
Coir	In dholls, 10 cwt	In bales, 40 c ft. In bundles or loose, 5 cwt	Yarn and fibre, in bales, 50 c. ft. In bundles and dholls, 10 cwt.	In bales, 40 c ft. In bundles or loose, 5 cwt.
Coir rope	..	In coils, 40 c. ft		In coils, 40 c ft.
Coke	20 cwt		..	
Colocynth	...	In cases, 40 c ft.	...	In c/s, 40 c. ft.
Colombo root	.	In bags, 8 cwt	...	In bags, 8 cwt.
Copper ore	20 cwt.		...	...
Copra or coconut kernel	12 cwt.	In robbins, or bags 8 cwt Cut copra in bags, 10 cwt	In bags, 12 cwt. ...	In robbins, 8 cwt. Cut, in bags 11 cwt
Copra cake or Coconut cake.	20 cwt.	...	...	In bags, 15 cwt.
Coral	.	Rough (not specimen) in bags 16 cwt	...	Rough (not specimen) in bags, 16 cwt.
Coriander seed	12 cwt.	10 cwt	20 cwt.	...
Corundum ore	20 cwt.	..	20 cwt.	..
Cotton	50 c. ft.	In bales, 40 c ft.	In bales, 50 c ft.	In bales, 40 c. ft. Dessi & Punjab American.
Cottonseed	14 cwt.	13 cwt. (See note 2 on p. 416).	20 cwt.	13 cwt Sind American 11 cwt.
Cotton in yarn	. .	...	50 c ft.	. .
Cotton piece-goods	...	...	50 c. ft.	...
Cow and Goat Hair	...	...	In bales, 50 c ft.	.
Cowries	20 cwt.	In cases, 40 c. ft. In bags, 16 cwt.	20 cwt.	In c/s, 40 c ft. In bags, 16 cwt.
Cubebs	...	10 cwt.	...	10 cwt.
Cumminseed	8 cwt.	In c/s, 40 c. ft. (In bags, 11 cwts. with effect from 1st October 1924)	...	In c/s, 40 c. ft.
Cutch	In bags, 18 cwt. In c/s 50 c. ft., not exceeding 20 cwt. gross.	And gambier (terra japonica) in bags or baskets, unscrewed 13 cwt.	In bags, 17 cwt.	And gambier (terra japonica) in bags or baskets unscrewed 13 cwt.
Cylindrical packages, rolls, etc.	...	40 c. ft. (See note 2 on p. 416).	...	40 c. ft. (see note 4 on p. 416).
Dates	Wet 20 cwt. Dry, 16 cwt.	Wet, 16 cwt. Dry, 13 cwt.	... ...	Wet, 16 cwt. Dry, 13 cwt.

Name of the article.	Calcutta.	Bombay.	Madras.	Karachi.
	Per ton nett.	Per ton.	Per ton nett.	Per ton.
Dhall	20 cwt.	Crushed in bags, 17 cwt.	20 cwt.	Crushed or split in bags, 17 cwt.
Dragon's blood	...	In cases, 40 c. ft.	...	In c/s, 40 c. ft.
Ebony	...	Square and straight 40 c. ft. Otherwise 16 cwt.	.. ...	Square and straight 40 c. ft. Otherwise, 16 cwt.
Elephants' teeth	...	In cases, 40 c. ft. In bundles, 14 cwt Loose, 16 cwt.	. In c/s, 50 c ft. ..	In c/s, 40 c ft. In bundles, 14 cwt. Loose, 16 cwt.
Fennel seed	...	10 cwt.	...	10 cwt.
Fenugreek (Methie Seed)	...	17 cwt.	20 cwt	17 cwt.
Fibres, all sorts	50 c. ft.	...	Palmyra fibre in bales 50 c. ft. In ballots or bundles, 10 cwt.	...
Fish Manure	...	...	...	As per sample lodged with the Chamber, 9 cwt.
Fishmaws or Isinglass.	...	...	...	In c/s, 40 c. ft.
Flour	...	In bags, 18 cwt Middlings or sharps in bags, 12 cwt.	... .	18 cwt. Middlings or sharps in bags 14 cwt
Furniture	...	.	...	40 c. ft.
Galingals.	...	10 cwt	...	10 cwt.
Galls	...	In bags, 13 cwt. In cases, 40 c ft.	.. ...	In Bags, 13 cwt. In c/s, 40 c ft.
Ganja	50 c ft.	5 cwt	50 c ft.	...
Garlic or onions	12 cwt.	..	..	...
Ghee (Ghi)	...	.	...	In dubbas or casks, 40 c ft
Ginger	16 cwt.	Dry in cases 40 c ft Dry in bags, 10 cwt.	In bags 12 cwt. In c/s, 50 c. ft.	Dry in c/s, 40 c. ft. Dry in bags, 10 cwt.
Gram	20 cwt	In bags, 18 cwt.	20 cwt	18 cwt. Crushed 16 cwt.
Groundnuts	...	Shelled, 13 cwt. (14 cwt with effect from 1st October 1924) Unshelled, 6 cwt.	... Kernels & unshelled, 20 cwt.	Shelled, 13 cwt. Unshelled 6 cwt.
Gums	In c/s, 50 c ft.	Of all kinds in cases, 40 c. ft. Gum olibanum in bags, 13 cwt. (Gum Persian) in double bags and Gum (Arabic) in double bags, 17 cwt	In c/s, 50 c ft In bags, 20 cwt.	Of all kinds in c/s, 40 c. ft. Olibanum in bags, 13 cwt.
Gunny bags and gunny cloth.	Gunnies. 50 c. ft or 20 cwt. gross (at steamer's option)	..	In bales, 50 c. ft..	...
Hemp	In bales, 50 c. ft.	In screwed bales, 40 c ft Loose or in bundles, 5 cwt.	In bales, 50 c. ft. ...	In screwed bales 40 c ft. Loose or in bundles, 5 cwt.
Hides and Skins (See also Skins)	In bales, 50 c. ft.	In bales, bundles or casks, 40 c. ft. Hides and skins loose and in small bundles, 40 c. ft.	Hides, 50 c. ft. tanned and dry. ...	In screwed bales hides and skins, 40 c. ft. Hides and skins loose and in small bundles, 40 c. ft.
Hide cuttings	In bales, 50 c ft.		50 c. ft.	..
Hoofs, horns, etc.	Hoofs, cow and buffalo, Horns and Horn tips, loose, 20 cwt. Ditto in bags or bundles 50 c ft. Horns, deer, in bags, or bundles, 50 c ft.	Horns, buffalo and cow, loose, 13 cwt Ditto in bundles or bags, 6 cwt. Horns, deer, loose, 6 cwt. Horn tips, of any kind, 13 cwt.	Hoofs, horns shavings and tips, 20 cwt. Horns, cow, buffalo and deer, 20 cwt.	Hoofs crushed in bags, 13 cwt. Horns in bags 8 cwt. Horns buffalo and cow loose 13 cwt. Horns, deer loose, 6 cwt. Horn tips of any kind and hoofs, 13 cwt.

Name of the article.	Calcutta.	Bombay.	Madras.	Karachi.
	Per ton nett.	Per ton.	Per ton nett.	Per ton.
Hurtall (Orpiment).	..	...	...	In c/s, 40 c. ft.
India Rubber	Rubber, in c/s, 50 c. ft.	..	In c/s 50 c. ft. Scrap in bags, 20 cwt	...
Indigo	50 c ft.	In cases 40 c ft	50 c ft.	In c/s, 40 c ft.
Iron (See Metals)	...	20 cwt.	...	Old or scrap 20 cwt. Or steel rails, 20 cwt.
Jackwood (See Timber).	...	40 c. ft.	...	40 c. ft.
Jaggery	..	18 cwt.	...	18 cwt
Jowaree	..	In bags, 17 cwt.	...	In bags, 18 cwt.
Jute	50 c ft.	.	50 c. ft.	...
Kapok	50 c. ft.	..	...	...
Kapok seed	14 cwt.	.	...	...
Khorassan	...		...	16 cwt
Lac	Button, seed, stick and shellac, in bags, 16 cwt	Lac dye in shells or cases, 40 c ft.	Cake lac in bags, 16 cwt.	Lac dye in shell or c/s, 40 c ft.
		Lac Seed 10 cwt		
	Button, seed, stick and shellac, in cases, 50 c ft.	...	Lac dye, 50 c. ft.	Lac (seed) in bags, 13 cwt.
	Kiri lac or lac refuse, in bags, 20 cwt	...	Seed lac in c/s, 50 c ft	...
	Lac dye, in cases, 50 c ft.	...	Seed lac in bags, 16 cwt	...
			Shellac in c/s, 50 c ft	...
			Shellac in bags, 16 cwt	...
			Stick lac in c/s, 50 c ft	...
			Stick lac in bags, 16 cwt.	...
Lang (Vetch)	...	In bags, 18 cwt Crushed in bags, 17 cwt	... ...	In bags, 18 cwt. Crushed in bags, 17 cwt
Lard	20 cwt	.	50 c ft	...
Leather	In cases or bales, 50 c ft	...	In bales, 50 c. ft	...
Lentils	20 cwt.		...	20 cwt.
Linseed	20 cwt.	In bags, 16 cwt	20 cwt	In bags, 16 cwt.
Mace	...	In cases, 40 c ft	In c/s, 50 c. ft.	In c/s, 40 c ft.
Machinery	...	...	20 cwt or 50 c ft (at Steamer's option)	...
Magnesite	...	...	In bulk or bags, 20 cwt.	...
Maize	20 cwt.	In bags, 15 cwt	.	In bags, 17 cwt.
Manganese	20 cwt.	.	...	...
Metals (see Iron separate).	...	.	20 cwt	...
Methie seed (*vide* Fenugreek).	...	...	...	...
Mica (See Talc)	...	..	...	...
Molasses	20 cwt gross	.	20 cwt.	...
Mother of pearl	In bags or cases, 20 cwt. gross	In tins or cases, 40 c ft	In bags, 20 cwt.	In c/s 40 c ft.
Motor car	..	In bags, 16 cwt.	In chests, 20 cwt. 50 c ft.	In bags, 16 cwt.
Mowra	Seed, 20 cwt.	Flowers, 18 cwt. Seed in bags, 13 cwt.	20 cwt. ...	Flowers, 18 cwt. Seed in bags, 13 cwt
Mutter (*Dhal*)	...		...	18 cwt.
Munjeet (Dye)	Dye, in cases, 50 c. ft.	Or Madder root in cases or bales, 40 c. ft	50 c. ft.	Or Madder root in c/s or bales, 40 c ft.
		Or Madder root in bundles or bags, 8 cwt.	...	Or Madder root in bundles or bags, 8 cwt.
Musk	.	In cases, 40 c. ft	...	In c/s, 40 c. ft.
Masur (*Dhal*)	...	In bags, 20 cwt (19 cwt. with effect from 1st October 1924).	...	In bags, 20 cwt.
Mustard seed	20 cwt.	15 cwt.	20 cwt.	16 cwt.

Name of the article.	Calcutta. Per ton nett.	Bombay. Per ton.	Madras. Per ton nett.	Karachi. Per ton.
Myrobalans	Whole or crushed, 20 cwt.	In bags, 13 cwt. (14 cwt with effect from 1st October 1924) Crushed in bags, 11 cwt. (See note 2 on p. 416). Powder, 15 cwt.	20 cwt.	In bags, 13 cwt.
Nigerseed	20 cwt.	14 cwt	20 cwt	14 cwt
Nutmegs	In c/s. 50 c. ft.	In cases, 40 c. ft.	In cases, 50 c ft	In c/s, 40 c. ft
Nux Vomica	Seed, 16 cwt.	In cases, 40 c ft. In bags, 13 cwt.	20 cwt. ...	In cases, 40 c. ft. In bags, 13 cwt.
Oats	16 cwt.	12 cwt.	20 cwt.	
Oil (See Coconut oil and cotton-seed oil separate).	In c/s, 50 c. ft. In casks or drums, 50 c. ft. Essential *ad valorem*.	Of any kind in casks, 40 c. ft. ...	In c/s, 20 cwt. or 50 c ft. (at steamer's option). In casks, 20 cwt. Essential, *Ad valorem*	Of any kind in cases, 40 c. ft. ...
Oilseed cake (See cotton-seed cake separate)	20 cwt.	Oil cake powder, 16 cwt. Oilcake, expeller 16 cwt. Oilcake, rotary or ghanny 15 cwt. Oilcake hydraulic pressed 16 cwt	Poonac, 20 cwt.	Oilcake in cakes or lumps (in bags), 16 cwt.
Olibanum (See Gum).				
Onions (See Garlic).				
Opium	Per chest	Per chest	...	Per chest
Ore of all descriptions.			20 cwt.	Loose or in bags, 20 cwt.
Paddy	16 cwt.	In bags, 13 cwt.	In bags, 20 cwt.	In bags, 13 cwt.
Palmyra fibre (See Coir and fibres of all sorts).				
Peas	20 cwt.	17 cwts with effect from 1st October 1924	20 cwt.	White, 18 cwt.
Pepper	Long, 12 cwt Black, 14 cwt.	In bags, 13 cwt.	In bags, 16 cwt.	In bags, 13 cwt.
Pig Iron and Pig Lead.	20 cwt.		...	...
Pimento	...	12 cwt	...	12 cwt.
Planks and deals	...	...	50 c ft.	...
Plumbago	...	In bags 16 cwt.	...	In bags, 16 cwt.
Pollards	...	In bags, 10 cwt	20 cwt.	...
Poonac (See oil seed cakes also).	...	...		...
Poppyseed	20 cwt.	In bags, 13 cwt	20 cwt.	In double bags (1½ cwt), 13 cwt In single bags (1½ cwt), 14 cwt In double bags (1½ cwt), 14 cwt In bags, (1½ cwt), 14 cwt.
Rails, Iron or steel (See Iron)				
Rapeseed	20 cwt.	15 cwt	20 cwt.	Rapeseed, Sita-, Jamba and other kinds, 16 cwt.
Rattans (See Canes also).	For dunnage, 20 cwt. or 50 cwt. or 50 c ft (at steamer's option).	In bundles, 13 cwt.	20 cwt.	In bundles, 13 cwt.
Redwood (Dye)	For dunnage, 20 cwt or 50 c. ft. (at steamer's option).	Ground, 13 cwt. 13 cwt.	... For dunnage, 20 cwt.	Ground, 13 cwt. 13 cwt.
Rhea	...	...	In bales, 50 c. ft.	...

Name of the article.	Calcutta.	Bombay.	Madras.	Karachi.
	Per ton nett.	Per ton.	Per ton nett.	Per ton.
Rhubarb	...	In c/s, 40 c ft.	...	In cases, 40 c. ft.
Rice	20 cwt.	In bags, 18 cwt	In bags, 20 cwt.	In bags, 18 cwt.
Roping (See Coir, etc.).	Rope in coils, or bundles, 50 c. ft.	...	In coils, 50 c. ft.	...
Rubber (See Indian Rubber).				
Rum	...	...	In casks, 20 cwt.	...
Safflower	50 c ft.	In c/s, 40 c ft In screwed bales 40 c.ft In bags, 8 cwt.	20 cwt.	In c/s, 40 c. ft. In screwed bales 40 c. ft. In bags, 8 cwt.
Safflower seed (Kardi).	...	Seed in bags, 13 cwt.	..	13 cwt.
Sago	...	In cases, 40 c. ft.	In c/s, 50 c. ft. In bags, 20 cwt.	In c/s, 40 c. ft.
Salammoniac	In bags or boxes, 20 cwt. gross.	In cases, 40 c. ft.	...	In c/s, 40 c. ft.
Salt	20 cwt.	In bags, 15 cwt. 28 Indian mds. of 82 2/7 lbs.	... 20 cwt.	In bags, 15 cwt. 28 Indian mds. of 82 2/7 lbs.
Saltfish	...	...	...	14 cwt.
Saltpetre	20 cwt.	20 cwt.	20 cwt.	20 cwt.
Sandalwood	...	9 cwt. Roots and chips, 7 cwt.	... ...	11 cwt. ...
Sapanwood (Dye).	For dunnage, 20 cwt. or 50 c. ft. (at steamer's option).	9 cwt.	...	11 cwt.
Sealingwax	...	In cases, 40 c ft.	...	In c/s, 40 c. ft.
Senna	In bales, 50 c ft.	In bags, 5 cwt In bales, 40 c. ft.	In bales, 50 c. ft. ...	In bags, 5 cwt. In bales, 40 c. ft.
Sharks and Fins	..		16 cwt.	...
Shells	.	Rough in bags, 16 cwt.	In bags, 20 cwt.	Rough in bags, 16 cwt.
Silk	Raw in bales, 10 cwt. In cases or bales, 50 c. ft. Waste, 50 c. ft. Chasam 50 c. ft Piecegoods, *Ad valorem* or 50 c ft. (at steamer's option).	In bales, 8 cwt. In cases, 40 c. ft.	Raw in bales, 50 c. ft Piecegoods and waste 50 c. ft	In bales, 8 cwt. In c/s, 40 c. ft.
Silver, specie and/or valuable cargo	*Ad valorem*	...	*Ad valorem*	...
Sita oil seed (See Rapeseed).				
Skins (See Hides)	In casks, 20 cwt. gross. In bales, 50 c. ft.	... ...	Tanned and dry 50 c. ft. Wet salted and pickled in casks, 50 c. ft.	Tanned skins in pressed bales, 40 c ft. ...
Soap	In bags, 15 cwt. In cases, 50 c ft.	In cases, 40 c. ft	Country, in c/s, 50 c. ft.	In c/s, 40 c ft.
Sugar (See Jaggery).	20 cwt.	In double bags, 19 cwt.	Including Jaggery, in bags, 20 cwt	In bags, 19 cwt.
Talc.	In cases, 20 cwt gross.	16 cwt.	Mica Talc and splittings, in cases 50 c ft Mica waste, in bags, 20 cwt.	16 cwt.
Tallow	In c/s or casks, 20 cwt. gross.	40 c ft.	...	40 c. ft.
Tamarind	In cases or casks, 20 cwt. gross.	15 cwt.	In cases and casks, or bundles 20 cwt	15 cwt.
Tamarind skins	...	...	..	In bundles 8 cwt. In pressed bales 40 c. ft
Tapioca	...	...	50 c. ft.	..
Tea	50 c. ft. Waste, as broken stowage, 16 cwt.	In chests, 40 c. ft.	50 c ft.	In chests, 40 c. ft.
Tilseed or Gingelly.	20 cwt.	15 cwt. (14 cwt. with effect from 1st October 1924).	20 cwt.	15 cwt.
Teak (See Timber).	...	...	...	Teak square planks and poon, 40 c. ft.

TONNAGE SCHEDULES FOR STEAMERS—*concld.*

Name of the article.	Calcutta.	Bombay.	Madras.	Karachi.
	Per ton nett.	Per ton.	Per ton nett.	Per ton.
Timber (See also Teak and Jack wood separate)	50 c. ft. . .	...	20 cwt or 50 c. ft. (at steamer's option)	...
Tobacco . .	In bales, or cases, 50 c. ft.	In bales, 40 c. ft.	In bales, 50 c. ft. .	In bales, 40 c. ft.
Tortoise shells (See shells).	..	In chests, 40 c. ft.	In cases, 50 c. ft. .	In chests, 40 c. ft.
Turmeric. .	16 cwt. . .	In bags, 11 cwt. .	In bags, 16 cwt. .	In bags, 11 cwt,
Tutenague .	. .	16 cwt. . .	..	16 cwt.
Twine . .	In cases, 50 c. ft.	...	..	...
Unrated wood .	...	11 cwt. . .	..	11 cwt
Wax . .	20 cwt. . .	.	...	...
Weed seed .	...	In bags, 10 cwt. (11 cwts. with effect from 1st October 1924).	...	...
Whanghees (*vide* canes).	...	13 cwt . .	...	13 cwt.
Wheat . .	20 cwt. . .	18 cwt . .	...	18 cwt
Wine and spirits	.	In casks and cases, 40 c ft.	.	In casks and cases 40 c ft.
Wolfram .	20 cwt. . .	.	.	. .
Wool . .	50 c. ft. . .	In bales, 40 c. ft.	In bales, 50 c ft. .	In screwed bales 40 c ft.
Woollen cuttings	.	. .	50 c ft . .	. .
Zedoary . .		16 cwt. . .	.	16 cwt.
All other articles not enumerated.	50 c ft. or 20 cwt gross, at steamer's option.	...	20 cwt , or 50 c ft at steamer's option	...

NOTE 1. **Calcutta** —(*a*) Measurement, and when necessary, weighment shall be made by the Bengal Chamber of Commerce, Licensed Measurer's Department in accordance with their rules, and their certificate shall be final, and freight shall be payable in accordance therewith

(*b*) Goods in casks or cases to be calculated at gross weight when paying freight by weight

(*c*) The term ' dead weight ' shall be understood to mean the following articles only : Sugar, Saltpetre, rice, wheat, gram, dhall, and peas.

NOTE 2. **Bombay** —*Tonnage scale.*—At a general meeting of the Bombay Chamber of Commerce held on 20th July 1883, the following Resolution was passed .—' That the Tonnage Scale for steamers shall be on the basis of 40 cubic feet to the ton, but in no case to exceed 20 cwt. dead-weight '

Bones, etc —These standards are for guidance only In case of disagreement either shipper or steamer may claim survey by the Chamber which may fix any scale as per standards intermediate or otherwise and that this alteration be given effect to in the supplements now being printed for publication with the report for the past year. A survey fee of Rs 30 shall be paid on a submission of the case.

Pressed bran —Pressed bran to be understood as not less than 5 maunds (of 28 lbs) in a bag of 45½ × 25 inches

Cottonseed —The following Resolution was adopted at the annual general meeting on 6th March 1901 . That cottonseed cleaned, be for the present omitted from the Chambers' tonnage scale, and that this alteration be given effect to in the supplement now being printed for publication with the report for the past year

Cylindrical packings.—On and after 1st April 1902 the following formula shall be recognized for the calculation of the cubical contents of cylindrical packings, *viz* , the square of the diameter be multiplied into the length and one-fifth deducted from the product (Resolution, dated 12th March 1902)

Crushed myrobalans —At the annual general meeting held on 4th March 1909 it was resolved that the footnote to the item crushed myrobalans in the Chambers' tonnage scale be amended to read as follows :—(as in footnote to Bones).

NOTE 3. **Madras**' —When cargo is measured prior to shipment, callipers should be used for measuring, and the rope or Iron hoop on the one side of the package should be taken in, and left out on the other side. Half inches should be given and taken alternatively. The Callipers should be laid on the package to be measured and the sliding arm pressed lightly, *i.e.*, without using force, against the side of the package.

NOTE 4 **Karachi** —*Tonnage Scale.*—The Karachi tonnage scale for steamers shall be on the basis of 40 cubic feet to the ton, but in no case to exceed 20 cwts dead-weight, except in the case of salt.

2 The dead-weight ton of 2, 240 lbs. shall be considered as the equivalent of 1016 Kilos.

3. The freight on oil to be paid on the full-gauge of the cask ascertained at the port of discharge.

4. When freight is payable on weight, the same is to be on the net weight delivered.

5. When cotton is shipped at a rate per bale, in the absence of special agreement, if the average measurement exceeds 13 feet per bale, the ship shall be entitled to proportionate extra freight, but in no case shall be compelled to take bales larger than 14 feet.

Bones, etc.—The scale for grades differing from the standards to be settled by private arrangement between shippers and steamer agents. Any disputes between them to be referred to and decided by the Committee of the Chamber.

Pressed bran.—Pressed bran to be understood as not less than 5 mds. (of 28 lbs.) in a bag of 45½ × 25 inches.

Cylindrical packages.—On and after 1st March 1903, the following formula shall be recognised for the calculation of the cubical contents of cylindrical packages, etc., *viz* , that the square of the diameter be multiplied by the length and one fifth be deducted from the product

Landing charges in the case of imported goods and shipping charges in the case of exported goods are now payable to the Port Commissioners on a general basis at over-head rates instead of as formerly at varying rates according to the class of goods.

With but few exceptions, such charges are now payable by weight (20 cwts. per ton) or measurement (50 c. ft. per ton) according to the basis on which freight has been paid or is payable.

Charges payable are clearly set out in the Port Commissioners' tariff from which the following is extracted :—

Port of Rangoon—Landing Charges for Imported Goods.

Description of goods.	Landing Charge Weight or Measurement. Per ton. Rs.	A.	P.	cwt. Per c. ft. Rs.	A.	P.
All goods shewn in Commissioner's standard list as chargeable by weight or on which vessels' freight was charged by weight up to a maximum of 1 ton for a single package	2	3	0	0	1	9
Over 1 ton up to 2 tons	2	8	0	0	2	0
Over 2 tons up to 3 tons	2	13	0	0	2	3
Over 3 tons up to 4 tons	3	2	0	0	2	6
Over 4 tons up to 5 tons	3	7	0	0	2	9
Over 5 tons up to 10 tons	3	12	0	0	3	0
Over 10 tons up to 15 tons	4	2	8	0	3	4
Over 15 tons up to 20 tons	4	9	4	0	3	8
All goods shewn in Commissioner's Standard list as chargeable by measurement or on which vessel's freight was charged by measurement up to a maximum of 50 c. ft. for single package	2	1	4	0	0	8
Over 50 c. ft. up to 100 c. ft.	2	9	8	0	0	10
Over 100 c. ft. up to 150 c. ft.	3	2	0	0	1	0
Over 150 c. ft. up to 200 c. ft.	3	10	4	0	1	2
Over 200 c. ft. up to 250 c. ft.	4	2	8	0	1	4
Over 250 c. ft.	4	11	0	0	1	6
Exceptions to general charges above.						
Pyrites and ores in bulk (chargeable by weight)	2	6	0	0	1	10
*Coal and Coke in bulk (chargeable by weight)	0	5	0	0	0	3
*Salt in bulk (chargeable by weight)	0	5	0	0	0	3
Loose, if packed charged by weight or measurement:						
Bicycles, per 5	2	3	0	..		
Bricks, fire per 500 } Bricks, salt glazed, per 500	2	3	0	..		
Carriages, each	3	0	0	..		
Casks and barrels, empty per 12 } Drums, empty, up to 12 ins. dia. per 100 } Drums, empty over 12 ins. and upto 24 ins. dia. per 50. } Drums, empty, over 24 ins. in dia. per 10 } Earthenware pots and chatties per 1,500	2	3	0	..		
Motor cycles, unpacked each	1	0	0	..		
Motor cycles with side car unpacked each	2	0	0	..		
Motor cars and tractors unpacked on own wheels, each	5	0	0	..		
Motor lorries and buses unpacked on own wheels, each	10	0	0	..		
Rickshaws, per 2 } Sampans, each.	2	3	0	..		
Shingles per 2,500	2	1	4	..		

Description of goods.	Landing Charge. Weight or Measurement. Per ton.			cwt. Per c. ft.		
	Rs.	A.	P.	Rs.	A.	P.
Loose, if packed charged by weight or measurement. Tiles, Marseilles, flooring and country roofing per 1,000; Tiles, Mangalore and Marseilles, roofing per 750; Tins, kerosene and petrol, empty, per 250	2	3	0	..		
*Cocoanuts, per 500	0	5	0	..		
Buffaloes, each	5	0	0	..		
Baby elephants under 5 ft. high each	10	0	0	..		
Elephants, each	20	0	0	..		
Horses, mules, cows and other cattle, each	4	0	0	..		
†Ponies, donkeys and calves, each	2	0	0	..		
Sheep, goats, dogs and other small animals, each	0	6	0	..		
Canaries and other small birds, each	0	2	0	..		
Turkeys and geese, loose per dozen	0	4	9	*		
Fowls and ducks, loose per dozen	0	2	0	*		
Aeroplanes and hydroplanes	Charged on one-half measurement as above.					
Bidee leaves; Betel leaves; Chillies; Cotton seeds	Charged on twice weight as above.					
Excepted articles	1/8 per cent. *ad valorem* per package subject to a minimum charge of Rs. 1-8-0 per package.					

*Minimum charge Anna 1.
† Does not include handling.

Port of Rangoon—Shipping Charges for Exported Goods.

Description of goods.	Shipped from the wharves by Commissioners' labour. Weight or measurement. Per ton.			cwt. Per c. ft.		
	Rs.	A.	P.	Rs.	A.	P.
All goods shewn in Commissioners' standard list as chargeable by weight or on which vessel's freight was charged by weight up to a maximum of 1 ton for a single package	2	3	0	0	1	9
Over 1 ton up to 2 tons	2	8	0	0	2	0
Over 2 tons up to 3 tons	2	13	0	0	2	3
Over 3 tons up to 4 tons	3	2	0	0	2	6
Over 4 tons up to 5 tons	3	7	0	0	2	9
Over 5 tons up to 10 tons	3	12	0	0	3	0
Over 10 tons up to 15 tons	4	2	8	0	3	4
Over 15 tons up to 20 tons	4	9	4	0	3	8
All goods shewn in Commissioners' Standard list as chargeable by measurement or on which vessel's freight was charged by measurement up to a maximum of 50 c. ft. for a single package	2	1	4	0	0	8

Description of goods.	Shipped from the wharves by Commissioners' labour. Weight or measurement. Per ton.	cwt. Per c.ft.
	Rs. A. P.	Rs. A. P.
Over 50 c. ft. up to 100 c. ft.	2 9 8	0 0 10
Over 100 c. ft. up to 150 c. ft.	3 2 0	0 1 0
Over 150 c. ft. up to 200 c. ft.	3 10 4	0 1 2
Over 200 c. ft. up to 250 c. ft.	4 2 0	0 1 4
Over 250 c. ft.	4 11 0	0 1 6
Exceptions to general charges above		
Lead	2 11 0	0 2 1·4/5
Ores in bulk or bagged (including zinc concentrates copper matte, speiss, lead slag, lead concentrates and wolfram)	2 7 0	0 1 11·2/5
Exceptions to general charges above		
Loose, if packed charged by weight or measurement.		
Bicycles, per 5 }		
Bricks, fire, per 500 }	2 3 0	..
Bricks, salt glazed, per 500 }		
Carriages, each	3 0 0	..
Casks and barrels, empty, per 12 }		
Drums, empty, up to 12 ins. dia., per 100 }		
Drums, empty, over 12 ins. and up to 24 ins. dia., per 50. }	2 3 0	..
Drums, empty, over 24 ins. dia., per 10 }		
Earthernware pots and chatties, per 1,500 }		
Motor cars and tractors, unpacked, on own wheels, each	5 0 0	..
Motor cycles, unpacked, each	1 0 0	..
Motor cycles with side car, unpacked each	2 0 0	..
Motor lorries and buses, unpacked, on own wheels, each	10 0 0	..
Rickshaws, per 2 }	2 3 0	
Sampans, each }		..
Shingles, per 2,500	2 1 4	..
Tiles, Marseilles flooring and country roofing, per 1,000. }		
Tiles, Mangalore and Marseilles roofing, per 750 }	2 3 0	..
Tins, kerosene and petrol empty, per 250 }		
* Buffaloes . . . each	5 0 0	..
* Baby elephant under 5 feet high ,,	10 0 0	..
* Elephants ,,	20 0 0	..
* Horses, mules, cows and other cattle ,,	4 0 0	..
* Ponies, donkeys and calves ,,	2 0 0	..
* Sheep, goats, dogs and other small animals ,,	0 6 0	..
* Canaries and other small birds ,,	0 2 0	..
Aeroplanes and hydroplanes	Charged on one-half measurement as above.	
Bidee leaves }		
Betel leaves }	Charged on twice weights as above.	
Chillies }		
Cotton seeds }		
Excepted articles	1/8 per cent. *ad valorem* per package subject to a minimum charge of Rs. 1-8-0 per package.	

*Not handled by Commissioners' labour.

The landing and shipping charges are subject to a rebate of 10 per cent.

Port of Rangoon.

Charges on goods landed from or shipped into inland vessels over the Commissioners' premises.

(Lighters, cargo-boats or other vessels used for the purpose of landing or shipping goods at the Commissioners' premises from or into sea-going vessels are not inland vessels for the purposes of this schedule). .

Description of goods.	Quantity to a ton.	Charge per ton.
		Rs. A. P.
All descriptions of goods except those named below.	Weight or measurement according to Commissioners' Standard List.	}
Bamboos up to 1 inch diameter	500	}
Bamboos over 1 inch. diameter	250	}
Bicycles, loose	5	}
Bricks, loose	500	}
Carriages	1	}
Carts, hand or bullock	2	}
Casks and barrels, empty	12	}
Cocoanuts	500	}
Drums, empty, up to12 inches diameter .	100	}
Drums, empty over 12 inches and up to 24 inches diameter.	50	} 0 5 0
Drums, empty over 24 inches diameter . .	10	}
Earthernware pots and chatties . . .	500	}
Grass, fresh	40 bundles	}
Matches in cases	6 cases.	}
Matches in tins	72 tins.	}
Motor cars and tractors, unpacked, on own wheels.	one-half.	}
Motor lorries and buses, unpacked, on own wheels.	one-fifth.	}
Motor cycles	2	}
Motor cycles, with side car, unpacked . .	1	}
Rickshaws, loose	2	}
Sampans	1	}
Shingles	2,500	
Tiles, Marseilles flooring and country roofing .	1,000	
Tiles, Mangalore and Marseilles roofing . .	750	
Tins, kerosene and petrol, empty . . .	250	

Live stock.	Number.	Rs. A. P.
Buffaloes	Each.	0 5 0
Cows, bullocks, horses, ponies, mules and donkeys . .	„	0 3 0
Calves	„	0 2 0
Elephant	„	3 0 0
Baby elephants under 5 feet high	„	1 8 0
Sheep, dogs, goats and other small animals . . .	„	0 1 0
Canaries and other small birds	„	0 0 6
Turkeys and geese	One dozen	0 1 0
Fowls and ducks	„ „	0 0 6

APPENDIX II.

Merchandise Marks Law.

Part I.—Principal provisions of the Indian Merchandise Marks Act, 1889 and connected Acts relating to merchandise marks.

Prohibitions on Importation.

Sea Customs Act, 1878, section 18.—No goods specified in the following clauses shall be brought, whether by land or sea, into British India :— **Indian Merchandise Marks Act, 1889, Section 10.**

* * * * * *

(*d*) Goods having applied thereto a counterfeit trade mark within the meaning of the Indian Penal Code, or a false trade description within the meaning of the Indian Merchandise Marks Act, 1889.

(*e*) Goods made or produced beyond the limits of the United Kingdom and British India, and having applied thereto any name or trade mark being, or purporting to be, the name or trade mark of any person who is a manufacturer, dealer or trader in the United Kingdom or in British India, unless—

(*i*) the name or trade mark is, as to every application thereof, accompanied by a definite indication of the goods having been made or produced in a place beyond the limits of the United Kingdom and British India, and

(*ii*) the country in which that place is situated is in that indication indicated in letters as large and conspicuous as any letter in the name or trade mark, and in the same language and character as the name or trade mark.

(*f*) Piecegoods, such as are ordinarily sold by length or by the piece, which—

(*i*) have not conspicuously stamped in English numerals on each piece the length thereof in standard yards, or in standard yards and a fraction of such yard, according to the real length of the piece, and

(*ii*) have been manufactured beyond the limits of India, or

(*iii*) having been manufactured within those limits, have been manufactured beyond the limits of British India in premises which, if they were in British India, would be a factory as defined in the Indian Factories Act, 1881.

Note.—For definition of piecegoods, see Part II.

Definitions.

Indian Merchandise Marks Act, 1889, Section 2 (1).—Trade Mark has the meaning assigned to that expression in Section 478 of the Indian Penal Code as amended by this Act.

Trade mark.

Indian Penal Code, Section 478.—A mark used for denoting that goods are the manufacture or merchandise of a particular person is called a trade mark, and for the purpose of this Code the expression 'trade mark' includes any trade mark which is registered in the register of trade marks kept under the Patents, Designs and Trade Marks Act, 1883, and any trade mark which, either with or without registration, is protected by law in any British Possession or foreign State to which the provisions of the one hundred and third section of the Patents, Designs, and Trade Marks Act, 1883, are, under Order in Council, for the time being applicable. **Section 3 of the Indian Merchandise Marks Act, 1889.** **46 & 47 Vict. C., 57.**

Counterfeit.

Indian Penal Code, Section 28.—A person is said to 'counterfeit' who causes one thing to resemble another thing intending by means of that resemblance to practice deception, or knowing it to be likely that deception will thereby be practised.

Explanation 1.—It is not essential to counterfeiting that the imitation should be exact.

Explanation 2.—When a person causes one thing to resemble another, and the resemblance is such that a person might be deceived thereby, it shall be presumed until the contrary is proved, that the person so causing the one thing to resemble the other thing intended by means of that resemblance to practice deception or knew it to be likely that deception would thereby be practised.

Indian Merchandise Marks Act, 1889, section 2 (2).—'Trade description' means any description, statement or other indication, direct or indirect,—

Trade description.

(*a*) as to the number, quantity, measure, gauge or weight of any goods, or

(*b*) as to the place or country in which, or the time at which, any goods were made or produced, or

(*c*) as to the mode of manufacturing or producing any goods, or

(*d*) as to the material of which any goods are composed, or

(*e*) as to any goods being the subject of any existing patent, privilege, or copy right;

and the use of any numeral, word or mark which according to the custom of the trade is commonly taken to be an indication of any of the above matters shall be deemed to be a trade description within the meaning of this Act.

(3) 'False trade description' means a trade description which is untrue in a material respect as regards the goods to which it is applied, and includes every alteration of a trade description, whether by way of addition, effacement or otherwise, where that alteration makes the description untrue in a material respect, and the fact that a trade description is a trade mark or part of a trade mark shall not prevent such trade description being a false trade description within the meaning of this Act.

False Trade description

Indian Merchandise Marks Act, 1889, section 4 (1)—The provisions of this Act respecting the application of a false trade description to goods or respecting goods to which a false trade description is applied, shall extend to the application to goods of any such numerals, words or marks, or arrangement or combination thereof, whether including a trade mark or not, as are or is reasonably calculated to lead persons to believe that the goods are the manufacture or merchandise of some person other than they really are and to goods having such numerals, words or marks, or arrangement or combination, applied thereto

Provisions supplemental to the definition of false trade description.

(2) The provisions of this Act respecting the application of a false trade description to goods, or respecting goods to which a false trade description is applied, shall extend to the application to goods of any false name or initials of a person and to goods with the false name or initials of a person applied in like manner as if such name or initials were a trade description, and for the purpose of this enactment the expression false name or initials means, as applied to any goods, and name or initials—

(*a*) not being a trade mark, or part of a trade mark, and

(*b*) being identical with, or a colourable imitation of, the name or initials of a person carrying on business in connection with goods of the same description and not having authorised the use of such name or initials.

(3) A trade description which denotes or implies that there are contained in any goods to which it is applied more yards, feet or inches than there are contained therein standard yards, standard feet or standard inches is a false trade description.

Section 11 of the Indian Merchandise Marks Act, 1889.

Sea Customs Act, 1878, section 19A (3).—Where there is on any goods a name which is identical with, or a colourable imitation of, the name of a place in the United Kingdom or British India, that name, unless accompanied in equally large and conspicuous letters and in the same language and character, by the name of the country in which such place is situate, shall be treated for the purposes of section 18 .... as if it were the name of a place in the United Kingdom or British India.

Identical names of places.

Indian Merchandise Marks Act, 1889, Section 5 (2).—A trade description shall be deemed to be applied whether it is woven, impressed or otherwise worked into or annexed or affixed to the goods or any covering label, reel or other thing.

Application of trade description.

(3) The expression 'covering' includes any stopper, cask, bottle, vessel, box, cover, capsule, case, frame or wrapper, and the expression 'label' includes any band or ticket.

Covering.

Indian Merchandise Marks Act, 1889, section 2 (4).—'Goods' means anything which is the subject of trade or manufacture.

Goods.

(5) 'Name' includes any abbreviation of a name.

Name.

General Clauses Act, 1897, section 3 (39).—'Person' shall include any company or association or body of individuals, whether incorporated or not.

Person.

Indian Merchandise Marks Act, 1889, section 21.—In the case of goods brought into British India by sea, evidence of the port of shipment shall, in a prosecution for an offence against this Act or section 18 of the Sea Customs Act, 1878, as amended by this Act, be *prima facie* evidence of the place or country in which the goods were made or produced.

Evidence of origin.

Indian Merchandise Marks Act, 1889, section 21—An officer of the Government whose duty it is to take part in the enforcement of this Act shall not be compelled in any Court to say whence he got any information as to the commission of any offence against this Act.

Information as to commission of offenses.

Sea Customs Act, 1878, Section 19-A.—Clauses (2), (4), (5), (6) enable the Governor General in Council to make regulations respecting the conditions, if any, to be fulfilled before such detention and confiscation, to determine the information, notices and security to be given, the evidence requisite for any of the purpose of the section and the mode of verification of such evidence, as well as the reimbursement of public officers and the State by an information for expenses and damages incurred in respect of any detention made on his information, and of any proceedings resulting therefrom. Section 19A (1) authorises the Customs authorities to require regulations so issued to be complied with before taking proceedings.

Rules and Regulations

Indian Merchandise Marks Act, 1889, section 16 (1)—The Governor General in Council may, by notification in the *Gazette of India* and in local official Gazettes, issue instruction for observance by Criminal Courts in giving effect to any of the provisions of this Act.

(2) Instructions under sub-section (1) may provide, among other matters, for the limits of variation, as regards number, quantity, measure, gauge or weight, which are to be recognised by Criminal Courts as permissible in the case of any goods.

NOTE—Such instructions are also a guide to Customs Officers.

Indian Merchandise Marks Act, 1889, Section 19.—For the purposes of section 12 of this Act and clause (*f*) of section 18 of the Sea Customs Act, 1878, as amended by this Act, the Governor General in Council may, by notification in the *Gazette of India*, declare what classes of goods are included in the expression 'piece goods' such as are ordinarily sold by length or by the piece.

Indian Merchandise Marks Act, 1889, section 20.—This section enables the Governor-General in Council to make rules regulating with respect to any goods the first selection and testing of samples, the value of the evidence so obtained, the conditions under which a further selection and testing may be made, and the value of the further evidence so obtained.

For goods not covered by such rules the section enables Customs officers to issue orders having a similar effect, namely :—

(2) The . officer of Customs having occasion to ascertain the number, quantity, measure, gauge or weight of the goods, shall, by order in writing, determine the number of samples to be selected and tested and the manner in which the samples are to be selected.

(3) The average of the results of the testing in pursuance of ... . an order under sub-section (2) shall be *prima facie* evidence of the number, quantity, measure, gauge or weight, as the case may be, of the goods.

(4) If a person having any claim to, or in relation to, any goods of which samples have been selected and tested in pursuance of . .. .an order under sub-section (2) desires that any further samples of the goods be selected and tested, they shall, on his written application and on the payment in advance by him to the .... officer of Customs.. ....of such

sums for defraying the cost of the further selection and testing as the............... officer may from time to time require, be selected and tested to such an extent as................... ..... the officer of Customs may determine in the circumstances to be reasonable, the samples being selected in manner prescribed under........... sub-section (2).................

(5) The average of the results of the testing referred to in sub-section (3) and of the further testing under sub-section (4) shall be conclusive proof of the number, quantity, gauge or weight, as the case may be, of the goods.

Part II.—Notifications under the Indian Merchandise Marks Act, 1889, and Connected Acts.

No. 1430, dated the 6th April, 1891, as subsequently amended.—In exercise of the powers conferred by section 19-A, sub-section (2), of the Sea Customs Act, 1878 (as amended by section II of the Indian Merchandise Marks Act, 1889), and sections 19 and 20 of the Indian Merchandise Marks Act, 1889 (as amended by Act IX of 1891), the Governor-General in Council is pleased to make the subjoined rules and orders :—

Stamping of piece-goods

1. Piece-goods, such as are ordinarily sold by length or by the piece, shall be deemed to include cotton piece-goods and woollen piece-goods of all kinds, except the descriptions noted below :—

Alhambras.
Blankets
Blind cloth.
Bookbinding cloth in cut pieces.
Buckrams.
Carpets (in rolls).
Counterpanes
Dusters in woven pieces.
Embroidered Flounces
Embroidered Voile Sarries
Filter Cloth
Glass Cloths in woven pieces
Handkerchiefs in woven pieces
Lace Curtain Cloth
Madras Muslin Cloth
Penelope Canvas
Pillow Calico (Tubular)
Prayer Mats.
Press Cloth.
Quilts
Rugs
Sarongs up to 2½ yards in length.
Shawls (finished), with ends hemmed or fringed, imported singly or in pieces containing two or more shawls.
Sponge Cloth (for swabs).
Tapestry Cloth.
Teddy Bear or imitation Seal Skin Cloth
Towels in woven pieces.
Undershirt Cloth.
Woollen Clearer Cloth
Woollen Knitted Cloth.
Woollen Roller Cloth.
Woollen Sizing Flannel.

Provided that the Collector of Customs shall not detain any unstamped piece-goods if he is satisfied that, although they are not named in the preceding list, they are of such a nature that they would be liable to serious depreciation in value, if stamped

NOTE 1.—Whenever a Collector exercises his discretion under this proviso, he should forthwith report the case, sending a sample of the goods, to the Government of India, through the Central Board of Revenue, so that the question of issuing general orders in favour of such goods may be considered

NOTE 2.—The mention of any item in the list of exemptions has no bearing upon the question whether that item, if consisting of cotton, is assessable under the Tariff head "Cotton piece-goods".

2. Unstamped cotton and woollen piece-goods imported for the personal use of individuals or private associations of individuals and not for trade purposes shall not be detained.

3. Examinations of packages to ascertain whether the goods mentioned in Rule 1 are stamped shall be made at frequent intervals at the discretion of the Customs Collector and either under his personal instructions or under general orders and instructions given by him to an Assistant Collector.

4. The piece-goods contained in the packages so examined need not be examined, when found to be stamped, to test the accuracy of the stamping, except on information received, or when the Customs Collector has reason to suspect that the stamping is false.

5. All measurements of piece-goods shall be made on the table.

6. Yarns need not be examined or measured, except on information received, or when the Collector has reason to suspect that the trade description is false.

Testing of yarns.

7. An examination of yarns to test the accuracy of the description of count or length shall be made, in the first instance, up to the limit of one bundle in every one hundred bales or fraction of one hundred bales in the consignment.

8. If, on such examination, the difference between the average count or length and the described count or length is in excess of the variations permitted in paragraphs III and IV of the Notification of the Government of India in the Home Department, No. 1474 (Judicial), dated the 13th November 1891, the importer may require a further examination to be made up to the limit and on the condition stated in Rule 9.

9. The test to determine length of yarns shall be applied as follows :—

From every one hundred bales, or fraction of 100 bales, in a consignment one bundle should be selected at random The hanks in this bundle should then be measured on the wrap-reel, one after the other, in the presence of a representative of the importer, and the lengths noted, the process being continued (within the limits of the bundle) until either the importer is satisfied that the yarn is short, or the average of the lengths noted shows that it is of full length.

When the importer is dissatisfied with this test he may, on payment of the cost, require the Customs Collector to measure more hanks up to 1 per cent. of the total number of hanks in the consignment, such hank being taken at random by an officer of Customs out of any bundles in the consignment.

10. The Customs Collector may require from any informant a security not exceeding five hundred rupees. If the Collector should be satisfied that the information given is wilfully false, the security shall be forefeited.

No. 1474, dated the 13th November 1891, as subsequently amended.—In exercise of the powers conferred by section 16 of the Indian Merchandise Marks Act, *IV of* 1889 and in expression of all existing orders on the subject, the Governor-General in Council directs that Criminal Courts, in giving effect to the provisions of the Act in respect of trade descriptions of quantity, measure, or weight of the goods specified hereunder, shall observe the following instructions :—

Trade description of length and width.

I.—A trade description of length stamped on *grey, white or coloured cotton piece-goods* shall not be deemed to be false in a material respect, unless—

(*a*) where a single length is stamped, the description exceeds the actual length by more than—

4 inches in pieces stamped as 10 yards long and under;

5 inches in pieces stamped as above 10 yards and up to 23 yards long;

7 inches in pieces stamped as above 23 yards and up to 36 yards long;

9 inches in pieces stamped as above 36 yards and up to 47 yards long;

18 inches in pieces stamped as above 47 yards long;

Provided that the average length of the goods in question shall not be less than the stamped length;

(*b*) where a maximum and a minimum length are stamped, the described maximum length is greater than the actual length by more than—

9 inches in piece-goods under 35 yards long;

18 inches in piece-goods 35 yards and up to 47 yards long;

36 inches in piece-goods above 47 yards long;

Provided that no such piece shall measure less than the minimum stamped length.

II.—A trade description of width stamped on *grey, white or coloured cotton piece-goods* shall not be deemed to be false in a material respect, unless the description exceeds the actual width by—

half an inch in pieces stamped as 40 inches or less in width;

three-quarters of an inch in pieces stamped as over 40 inches or under 59 inches in width;

one inch in pieces stamped as 59 inches or more in width;

Provided that the average width of the goods in question shall not be less than the stamped width.

Trade descriptions of count

III.—A trade description of count or number, length or weight, aplied to *grey* or *bleached cotton yarn*, shall not be deemed to be false in a material respect, unless—

(*a*) the described count or number is greater or less than the actual count or number by more than 5 per cent., provided that the average count of the whole of the yarn in question is not greater or less than the described count; or

(*b*) (*i*) in a bundle of *grey* yarn, the average length of the whole number of single hank is less than 840 yards and of double hanks is less than 1,680 yards; or

(*ii*) in a bundle of *bleached yarn* the average length of single hank is less than 819 yards and of double hanks is less than 1,638 yards; or

(*c*) (*i*) in a bundle of yarn of any count under 50, described as being 10 lbs in weight, the number of knots of 20 hanks each is not half of, or the number of knots of 10 hanks each is not the same as, or the number of knots of 5 hanks each is not double, the described count or number of the yarn; or

(*ii*) in a bundle of yarn of any count under 50, described as being 5 lbs in weight, the number of knots of 20 hanks each is not a quarter of, or the number of knots of 10 hanks each is not half of, or the number of knots of 5 hanks each is not the same as, the described count or number of the yarn; or

(*iii*) in a bundle of yarn of any count from 50 upwards, the number of knots of 20 hanks each is not half, or the number of knots of 40 hanks each is not a quarter, when the described weight is 10 lbs., or is not a quarter or an eighth, when the described weight is 5 lbs., of the count or number of the yarn, or

(*d*) in the case of bleached yarn, the described weight exceeds the actual weight by more than—

10 per cent in counts up to 24;

8½ per cent. in counts from 25 to 40,

7½ per cent in counts of 41 and upwards;

the allowance being 1 per cent. less than that specified in each of the above cases if the bleached yarn in the bundle is two fold :

Provided that for the purposes of applying any of the sub-clauses of clause (*c*) to importations of single yarn in double hanks and of two-fold yarn in single and double hanks, one single hank of two-fold yarn, one double hank of single yarn, and one double hank of two-fold yarn shall be taken respectively as two, two and four hanks of single yarn, but the described count or number shall contain a definite indication that the yarn in the bundle is two-fold or in double hanks or both, as the case may be.

IV. A trade description of count or number applied to a bundle of *dyed cotton yarn* shall be accepted as indicating length only, the hank being taken to measure 840 yards, and it shall be deemed to be false in a material respect if the average length of the hanks in a bundle is less than 819 yards.

V. A trade description of length applied to *thread of any kind* (of cotton, wool, flax, or silk) shall not be deemed to be false in a material respect, unless it exceeds the actual length by more than 1 per cent.

VI. The dimensions of goods on which their length or width is stamped shall be determined by measurement in imperial yards of thirty-six inches.

REWARDS.

The grant of rewards is controlled by rules issued with Resolution, No. 342-D., dated the 6th December 1918, as amended by Resolution No. 4514, dated the 11th July 1921, which are applicable generally to all cases under the Sea Customs and Indian Merchandise Marks Acts. The Resolution states that it is undesirable in practice to grant rewards to gazetted officers, but it was held in letter No. 4080-S R., dated the 3rd August, 1901, to the Government of Madras that the prohibition does not apply to gazetted officers below the rank of Assistant Collector.

APPENDIX III.

THE PRINCIPAL RAILWAYS IN INDIA AND THE AREA AND TRADE CENTRES SERVED BY THEM.

Railways and Headquarters.	Mileage open or in the course of construction on 31st March 1934.	Gauge. @	Area served with principal internal trade centres.
*Bengal Nagpur Railway. (Calcutta).	3,412	A (2,467 miles) C (926 miles). D (19 miles).	Eastern half of the Central Provinces, Bihar and Orissa and down to Vizagapatam in Madras Presidency. Raipur, Nagpur, Jubbulpore, Amraoti.
*Bombay, Baroda and Central India Railway. (Bombay).	3,692	A (1,260 miles). B (2,208 miles). C (224 miles).	Northern half of the Bombay Presidency, Central India and Southern Rajputana, Surat, Broach, Ahmedabad, Muttra, Delhi.
*Eastern Bengal Railway. (Calcutta).	1,998	A (893 miles). B (1,068 miles). C (37 miles).	Eastern Bengal, the north-western portion of Assam and the northern Gangetic plain in Bengal to the foot of the Himalayas. Naihati, Murshidabad, Patna, Goalundo, Narainganj, etc.
*East Indian †Railway. (Calcutta).	4,395	A (4,329 miles). B (66 miles).	Southern end of the Punjab, United Provinces, Bihar and Western Bengal. Asansol, Dhanbad, Gaya, Patna, Mirzapur, Benares, Allahabad, Cawnpore, Agra, Fyzabad, Lucknow, Saharanpur, Aligarh, Delhi, etc.
*Great Indian Peninsula Railway. (Bombay).	3,727	A (3,483 miles) C (244 miles).	Central portion of Bombay Presidency, Hyderabad, western half of Central Provinces, Central India, lower part of the United Provinces and some part of Rajputana. Poona, Raichur, Ahmednagar, Nasik, Sholapur, Akola, Amraoti, Nagpur, Jubbulpore, Katni, Gwalior, Agra, etc.

*Indicate State Railways.

† Also contains the line formerly known as the Oudh and Rohilkhand Railway the two lines being amalgamated on 1st July 1925.

@A Standard gauge 5′ 6″. B Metre gauge 3′ 3 3/8″. C Narrow gauge 2′ 6″. D Narrow gauge 2′ 0″.

Railways and Headquarters.	Mileage open or in the course of construction on 31st March 1934.	Gauge. @	Area served with principal internal trade centres.
Madras and Southern Mahratta Railway. (Madras).	3,230	A (1,150 miles). B (2,080 miles).	North-eastern and central parts of the Madras Presidency, a small part of Hyderabad, and the southern part of Bombay Presidency and Mysore. Bangalore, Guntakal, Poona, Guntur, Bezwada, Ellore, Cocanada.
Nizam's Guaranteed State Railway. (Secunderabad).	1,348	A (688 miles) . B (660 miles).	Hyderabad State. Bezwada, Singareni, Hyderabad.
*North Western Railway. (Lahore).	6,949	A (6,263 miles) C (686 miles).	Sind, the Punjab, North-West Frontier Province, Baluchistan. Hyderabad (Sind), Larkana, Shikarpur, Jacobabad, Quetta, Rawalpindi, Lahore, Amritsar, Lyallpur, etc.
South Indian Railway. (Trichinopoly).	2,526	A (599 miles) . B (1,828 miles). C (99 miles).	Whole of Southern India, south and west of the Jolarpet Section of the Madras and Southern Maharatta Railway connecting *via* Dhanuskodi with Ceylon. Trichinopoly, Madura, Salem, Coimbatore, Calicut and Tuticorin.
Assam-Bengal Railway. (Chittagong).	1,306	B	The Province of Assam. Naraingunj, Sylhet, Silchar, Gauhati, etc.
Bengal and North-Western Railway. (Gorakhpur, U. P.)	2,113	B	Northern portions of the United Provinces and of Bihar. Monghyr, Gorakhpur, Allahabad, etc.
*Burma Railways. (Rangoon.)	2,056	B	Upper and Lower Burma. Prome, Pegu, Myingyan, Mandalay, Bassein, Martaban (for Moulmein), etc.

* Indicate State Railways.

@ A standard gauge 5′ 6″. B Metre gauge 3′ 3/8″. C Narrow gauge 2′ 6″. D Narrow gauge 2′ 0″.

APPENDIX IV.

COMMERCIAL TRAVELLERS' SAMPLES—CUSTOMS FACILITIES.

I. *Regulations governing the admission into and re-exportation from British India of Commercial Travellers' Samples and Specimens.*

A.—IMPORTATION.

(i) *Dutiable articles.*

1. Articles liable to customs duty imported from any of the undermentioned countries as Commercial Travellers' Samples or Specimens (whether or not accompanied by the Commercial Traveller) are temporarily admitted without payment of the duty to which the goods are liable, subject to the amount thereof being deposited in cash or secured by bond before their delivery out of official charge.

The privileged countries are :—

All parts of the British Empire.
Austria.
Belgium.
Brazil, United States of.
Bulgaria.
China.
Czechoslovakia.
Denmark.
Estonian Republic.
Egypt.
Finland.
France.
Germany.
Greece.
Holland.
Hungary.
Iran.
Iraq.
Italy.
Latvia.
Labuan.
Luxemburg.
Morocco (French Protectorate)
Norway.
Poland
Roumania.
Serbs, Croats and Slovenes, Kingdom of.
Siam.
Sweden.
Switzerland.
Syria.
Tunis (French Regency).

2. (*a*) The Commercial Traveller or his agent is required to produce a list containing a description, sufficiently full for identification purposes, of the samples or specimens imported and, in the case of goods liable to duty on an *ad valorem* basis a statement of their value. The list (and statement where necessary) should be officially attested by the proper authority in the country of exportation.

(*b*) If the Commercial Traveller is unprovided with the list referred to in sub-paragraph (*a*), he may be required to produce before the Customs Collector a certificate or letter of identity from his principals, or otherwise satisfy the Collector of his eligibility for the concession If the Collector is so satisfied, a list may be compiled at the port of importation, in which case documentary evidence of value must be produced for any of the samples or specimens which are liable to duty on an *ad valorem* basis

3. Examination of the samples and specimens will be limited to ascertaining that they are fully described on the list and, in the case of goods chargeable on an *ad valorem* basis, that their value is correctly stated.

4. If the samples and specimens bear the marks, stamps or seals of the country of exportation, no additional marks or seals for purposes of identification will as a rule, be affixed by the Customs Collector. If the samples or specimens bear no marks, stamps or seals, they may be marked or sealed for future identification.

5. The list of samples or specimens will be signed and dated by the Customs Collector, who will affix a statement bearing an official seal or stamp and showing—

(*a*) the port of importation and the amount of duty chargeable; also whether duty was deposited in money or bond given;

(b) the marks, if any, applied by him to the samples or specimens;

(c) the date on which the duty deposited will be carried to the public account, or recovered under the security given, unless it is proved that the samples or specimens have been previously exported or placed in bond. This date will be not later than twelve months from that upon which the samples or specimens were imported.

No charge is made for the document issued or certified by the Customs Collector or for marking for identification.

(ii) *Non-dutiable articles.*

6. The list referred to in paragraph 2 need not be produced for samples or specimens of goods not liable to customs duty, and the examination of such samples or specimens will be restricted to verifying that they are not dutiable.

B.—EXPORTATION OF IMPORTED SAMPLES.

7. Samples and specimens of dutiable articles imported under the above regulations may be produced to the Customs Collector at any of the under-mentioned ports for examination prior to exportation therefrom, and to obtain refund of the deposit or release from the bond given on importation, subject to deduction in respect of any samples or specimens not produced for re-exportation. The list and statement referred to in paragraph 5 must be produced with the goods.

(Non-dutiable samples or specimens are not required to be produced on shipment.)

The ports are :—

Karachi.	Madras.
Bombay.	Calcutta.
Tuticorin.	Chittagong.
Dhanushkodi.	Rangoon.
Negapatam.	Moulmein.

8 Prior to the re-exportation of goods chargeable to duty on an *ad valorem* basis a declaration signed in the presence of a Customs Officer must be produced with the goods stating that they have not been used in British India for any purpose other than as Commercial Travellers' samples or specimens, and that they are in all respects identical with the goods imported.

C.—SAMPLES RETAINED IN INDIA.

9. If the samples or specimens of dutiable goods are not re-exported or placed in bond within the prescribed time [*see* paragraph 5 (c)], the duty deposited will be brought to account, or the bond put into force.

NOTE —The above regulations apply with equal force to samples re-imported by a Commercial Traveller on a second visit to British India The re-importation of samples in such circumstances by commercial travellers who have not been eligible for the privileges of these regulations, or who have not taken advantage on them, is governed by the regulations published with the Finance Department (Central Revenues) Resolution, No 33, dated the 11th June 1927.

II.—Regulations governing the exportation from British India and subsequent re-entry of Commercial Travellers' Samples and Specimens

Commercial Travellers proceeding out of British India to any of the countries mentioned in Part I, rule 1, may have their samples and specimens sealed and the list thereof certified by the officers of the Customs Department under the following regulations :—

(1) On prior application by the firm concerned, the samples, accompanied by a list in duplicate containing a full description thereof, including quantity and value, may be produced at the Customs House at

any of the ports mentioned in Part I, rule 7, for examination. A declaration as to the accuracy of the values stated on the lists must be made by the Commercial Traveller or a member of the firm concerned.

(2) The list, after verification by a comparison with the samples, will be signed and officially stamped, and the samples sealed or marked.

(3) The samples may be re-imported at any of the ports mentioned in Part I, rule 7. The list referred to in paragraph 1 must be produced; and if the samples are found to correspond therewith, they will be delivered forthwith after removal of the official seals.

(4) The examination and sealing of samples and specimens will be allowed at private premises before exportation, and re-examination and removal of seals after re-importation on prior application being made. The expenses of the Customs Officer's attendance in such cases must be borne by the applicants.

(5) The above regulations will only apply to samples and specimens on which no drawback, rebate or remission of customs or excise duty has been claimed at the time of exportation.

2. The following regulations governing the exemption from payment of customs duty of re-imported commercial travellers' samples on which duty has already been paid on previous importation into British India were communicated by the Government of India to Local Governments with Commerce and Industry Department letter No. 8595-82, dated the 9th October 1907, and are republished for general information They now apply to samples brought by a commercial traveller from any foreign country that is not one of the privileged countries referred to in the regulations published with Finance Department (Central Revenues) Resolution No. 32 of 11th June 1927 or by a commercial traveller from any of those privileged countries, who has not taken advantage of the privileges conferred by those regulations at the time of the previous importation of the samples.

Regulations.

1. Samples of goods, not intended for sale, re-imported by commercial travellers into British India shall be passed free of duty, provided that the Collector of Customs at the port of re-importation is satisfied :—

(1) that duty was paid on first import;

(2) of the identity of the articles;

(3) that no drawback was paid on export;

(4) that the ownership in the articles has not changed since its first import; and

(5) that no more than six months have passed since the articles were exported.

2. In order to be able to claim the benefit of this concession, commercial travellers must observe the following procedure :—

(1) When the samples are first imported into British India, commercial travellers will be required to produce to the Collector of Customs a certificate or letter of identity from their principals or otherwise satisfy the Collector of their eligibility for the concession. An invoice in duplicate, showing each article in detail, should be filed at the Customs House. The original will be retained by the Customs authorities. Each page of the duplicate will be stamped with the Custom House seal, and will be endorsed, over the signature of a Customs Officer, with a reference to the Bill of Entry on which the samples were assessed to duty. It will be returned together with a certified copy of the Bill of Entry to the travellers.

(2) The certified copy of the Bill of Entry must, on each occasion on which the samples are exported from a port in British India, to a foreign port, be produced to the Customs Collector of the port of export, who will endorse, after such examination of the samples, as he may think necessary, the copy of the Bill of Entry with a certificate that no drawback had been paid, together with the date of exportation. On re-importation from a foreign port the Bill of Entry must similarly be produced to the Collector of Customs, who will endorse, after such examination of the samples, as he may think necessary, the date of re-importation on the Bill of Entry.

3. When the samples are finally exported under claim of draw-back, a certificate of examination shall be recorded on the certified copy of the Bill of Entry by a Custom Officer after verification of the necessary particulars in regard to the identification of the articles and payment of duty. The certified copy of the Bill of Entry and the duplicate copy of the invoice shall be forwarded to the port of first importation.

APPENDIX V.

GOVERNMENT CROP FORECASTS.

The following statement shews the dates on which provincial forecasts of crops are transmitted by Local Governments and the dates on or about which general memoranda are issued by the Commercial Intelligence Department :—

Provinces and crops concerned.	Issue by Local Government.		Issue of consolidated forecast by Director-General of Commercial Intelligence.
Rice.			
1st report.			
Bengal, Bihar and Orissa and Assam. Summer*	April	.	October 20 (1st memorandum).
Bengal, Bihar and Orissa and Assam. Autumn† , Winter	September	30	
Bombay	October	1	
Central Provinces and Berar	,,	3	
Burma, Madras and United Provinces	,,	15	
Hyderabad	,,	15	
Baroda	,,	15	
Bhopal (Central India)	,,	15	
2nd report.			
Burma (2nd report)‡	November	15	December 20 (2nd memorandum).
Bombay	December	1	
Bengal, Bihar and Orissa and Assam [Autumn† (Final) and Winter]	,,	15	
Burma (3rd report)	,,	15	
Madras and United Provinces	,,	15	
Central Provinces and Berar (Final)	,,	15	
Hyderabad	,,	15	
Baroda	,,	15	
Bhopal (Central India)	,,	15	
3rd report.			
Burma (4th report)‡	January	15	February 20 (Final memorandum).
Bengal, Bihar and Orissa and Assam (Winter)	February	15	
Bombay (Spring)	,,	15	
Burma (Final)	,,	15	
Madras, United Provinces and Coorg	,,	15	
Mysore (Preliminary)	,,	15	
Hyderabad	,,	15	
Baroda	,,	15	
Bhopal (Central India)	,,	15	
4th report.			
Mysore (Final)	April	.	Not issued.
Hyderabad	May	.	
Wheat			
1st report.			
Punjab, United Provinces, Central Provinces and Berar, Bombay, North-West Frontier Province, Bengal, Bihar and Orissa, Ajmer-Merwara, Delhi, Mysore, Hyderabad, Central India, Rajputana, Baroda, Gwalior	January	20	January 31 (1st memorandum).
2nd report.			
All provinces mentioned above	March	1	March 15 (2nd memorandum).

* With other rabi crops in the case of Bengal and Bihar and Orissa.

† With other autumn or bhadoi crops in the case of Bengal and Bihar and Orissa.

‡ Not utilised in All-India General Memorandum.

Provinces and crops concerned.	Issue by Local Government.		Issue of consolidated forecast by Director General of Commercial Intelligence.
Wheat—*contd.*			
3rd report			
All provinces mentioned above . . .	April	10	April 20 (3rd memorandum).
4th report.			
All other provinces mentioned above . .	May	15	May 30 (4th memorandum).
North-West Frontier Province . . .	,,	22	May 30 (4th memorandum).
5th report.			
All provinces mentioned above . . .	August	1	August 10 (Final memorandum).
Cotton.			
1st report.			
Punjab, United Provinces, Central Provinces and Berar, Madras, Burma, North-West Frontier Province, Assam, Bengal, Bihar and Orissa, Ajmer-Merwara, Hyderabad, Rajputana, Central India, Mysore, Delhi, Baroda, Gwalior and Bombay (early) .	August	10	August 15 (1st memorandum).
2nd report.			
All provinces mentioned above . . .	October	10	October 15 (2nd memorandum).
3rd report.			
All provinces mentioned above . . .	December	10	December 15 (3rd memorandum).
Madras (Condition report only)* . .	January .		
4th report.			
All provinces mentioned above . . .	February	10	February 1st (Final memorandum).
5th report.†			
Madras	April	15	April 15 (Supplementary memorandum).
Bombay	,,	15	April 15 (Supplementary memorandum).
Hyderabad	,,	15	April 15 (Supplementary memorandum).
Linseed Rape and Mustard (Winter Oil Seeds).			
1st report.			
Hyderabad	December	20	January 1 (1st memorandum).
Punjab, Bengal, Bihar and Orissa . .	,,	20	January 1 (1st memorandum).
United Provinces and Bombay (rape and linseed)	,,	20	January 1 (1st memorandum).
Central Provinces and Berar (linseed) .	,,	20	January 1 (1st memorandum).
Assam (rape and mustard)	,,	20	January 1 (1st memorandum).
North-West Frontier Province and Alwar (rape seed)	,,	20	January 1 (1st memorandum).
Delhi and Baroda (rape and Mustard) .	,,	20	January 1 (1st memorandum).
Kotah and Bhopal (linseed) . . .	,,	20	January 1 (1st memorandum).

* Not utilised in the All-India General Memorandum.

† Provinces and States other than those mentioned are required to send in returns only when there is a material change in the condition of the crop since the February forecast.

Provinces and crops concerned.	Issue by Local Government.	Issue of consolidated forecast by Director General of Commercial Intelligence.
Linseed, Rape and Mustard (Winter Oil Seeds)—*contd.*		
2nd report.		
Hyderabad	March 1	March 15 (2nd memorandum).
Punjab, Bengal, Bihar and Orissa	,, 1	
United Provinces and Bombay (rape and linseed)	,, 1	
Central Provinces and Berar (linseed)	,, 1	
Assam (rape and mustard—) (Final)	,, 1	
North-West Frontier Province (rape seed)	,, 1	
Delhi, Baroda (rape and mustard)	,, 1	
Kotah and Bhopal (linseed)	,, 1	
Alwar (rape seed)	,, 1	
3rd report.		
Punjab, Bengal, Bihar and Orissa	May 15	June 1 (Final memorandum).
United Provinces and Bombay (rape and linseed)	,, 15	
Central Provinces and Berar	,, 15	
Kotah and Bhopal (linseed)	,, 15	
Delhi and Baroda (rape and mustard)	,, 15	
North-West Frontier Province (rapeseed)	,, 22	
Alwar (rape seed)	,, 15	
Sesame (Til or Gingelly).		
1st report.		
Bengal (early crop)	July 31	September 1 (1st memorandum).
Burma (early crop)	August 10	
Bombay, Madras, Central Provinces and Berar, United Provinces, Ajmer-Merwara, Punjab, Bihar and Orissa, Baroda, Kotah, Bhopal and Hyderabad	,, 15	
2nd report.		
Burma (early and Late)	October 10	October 20 (2nd memorandum).
All other provinces mentioned above except Bengal	,, 15	
3rd report.		
Burma (late crop)*	December 10	January 15 (Final memorandum).
Bengal (late crop)	,, 31	
All other provinces mentioned above	January 1	
Hyderabad	,, 5	
Madras	,, 12	
Burma (early and late—4th Report)	,, 10	
4th report		
Burma (early and late—Final)	February 10	April 20 (Supplementary memorandum).
Madras	April 15	
Groundnut.		
1st report.		
Madras*	April 13	August 20.
Madras* (Summer and early—Condition Report)	July 13	
Burma	August 10	
Bombay	,, 15	
Madras (2nd report)	,, 13	
Hyderabad and Mysore	,, 10	

* Not utilised in the All-India General Memorandum.

Provinces and crops concerned.	Issue by Local Government.		Issue of consolidated forecast by Director General of Commercial Intelligence.
Groundnut—*contd.*			
2nd report.			
Burma	October	10	October 20 (1st memorandum).
Bombay	"	15	
Madras (3rd report)	"	13	
Hyderabad and Mysore	"	10	
3rd report.			
Burma*	December	10	February 15 (Final memorandum).
Bombay	January	15	
Madras (Final)	February	13	
Burma (Final)	"	10	
Central Provinces and Berar	"	10	
Hyderabad and Mysore	"	5	
4th report.			
Hyderabad*	April	5	
Sugarcane.			
1st report.			
Bengal, Bihar and Orissa, Assam, Madras, United Provinces, Punjab, North-West Frontier Province, Bombay, Central Provinces and Berar, Delhi, Baroda and Bhopal	August	15	August 20 (1st memorandum).
Hyderabad	August	.	
2nd report.			
All provinces mentioned above	October	15	October 20 (2nd memorandum).
Hyderabad	October	.	
3rd report.			
All the provinces mentioned above	January	31	February 5 (Final memorandum).
Mysore (preliminary)			
Hyderabad	January	.	
Mysore* (Final)	April	.	
Jute.			
1st report.			
Bengal, Assam, Bihar and Orissa	..		July 15.†
2nd report.			
Bengal, Assam, Bihar and Orissa	..		September 21.†
Castor Seed.			
Final report.			
Hyderabad* (1st report)	October	10	
Madras	January	.	
Bombay, Bihar and Orissa, Central Provinces and Berar, United Provinces, Mysore, and Baroda	February	15	February 20.
Hyderabad (2nd Report)	February	10	

* Not utilised in the All-India General Memorandum.

† Issued by the Director of Agriculture, Bengal.

APPENDIX VI.

Glossary of Indian Terms used in this Book.

A

Abkari	Excise of liquors and drugs.
Ajwan	An essential oilseed obtained from *carum copticum.*
Ajwan-ka-phul	Thymol (*lit.* flowers of ajwan).
Arathdar	From *arath* a warehouse—a middleman.
Arhar	The pigeon pea (*cajanus indicus*).
Ari	Lac collected before the insects swarm.
Atta	Coarse wheat flour used by the poorer classes, intermediate in quality between *maida* and *sujji* (q. v.).
Attar	The fragrant essential oil of roses, jasmine and other flowers.
Avaram	The Tamil name for the bark of *cassia auriculata* extensively used in Southern and Western India for tanning hides and skins. Called *tarwad* or *tarwar* in the Bombay Presidency.

B

Babul	A thorny tree (*Acacia arabica*) which in Sind is a common host of the lac insect. The bark is used for tanning.
Bajra	The bulrush millet (*pennisetum typhoideum*), known as *cumbu* in South India.
Ballam	A particular quality of boiled rice, long-grained.
Bania	A petty shop-keeper or money-lender.
Bhang	The dried leaves and flowering shoots of *cannabis sativa* which ground to a paste and taken as an emulsion are a powerful narcotic.
Beer (ber)	A thorny shrub (*zizyphus jujuba*), which in the Punjab is a common host of the lac insect.
Bepari	A small trader, who acts as a middleman in the marketing of grain, hides, etc.
Biri (bidi)	Country made cigarette.
Bispath	An inferior quality of tobacco obtained in Bengal
Borah	A bamboo basket in which wool is transported.
Bysaki	One of the four lac crops called after the Bengali month 'Bysak' corresponding to April—May, when it comes commercially into sight.

C

Catamaran	A floating raft made of logs tied together.
Chabyam	A quality of unpolished rice obtainable in Southern India.
Chadar	A shawl, of cotton, wool or silk.
Chapati (Chaupatti)	An unleavened cake made generally of atta or coarse wheat flour.
Charas	The narcotic resin of *cannabis sativa* used for smoking.
Chasam	Silk waste.
Chauki	An outpost for the collection of revenue.
Chekku	A Malayalam word, meaning 'a small mill' corrupted into chuck-mill.
Chetty	A caste in South India, money-lenders or merchants by profession.
Cooly	An Indian labourer.
Cholam	The Tamil name for the large millet (sorghum vulgare) known as *jowar* in Northern India.
Copra	The dried meat of the coconut.
Corge	A score.
Crore	Ten million, generally applied to the currency. A crore of rupees =£750,000.

D

Dahi (Dayi)	Curdled boiled milk.
Dari	A pileless cotton carpet.
Deodar	The Himalayan cedar (*cedrus libaniv.* deodara.)
Deshi (daisee)	An Urdu word meaning 'indigenous' applied as a trade name to varieties of jute and other produce.

Dhall . .	A generic term applied to various pulses.
Dhak . . .	Butea frondosa, a common host of the lac insect, known as *palas*.
Dholl . . .	A bundle or package.
Dhooti . . .	Piece of cloth in varying lengths with coloured border worn by men.
Dhow . . .	A small country boat.
Dowd Khani .	A variety of boiled brown Bengal rice.

E

Eng (Ing) . . .	A deciduous forest tree (*iplerocarpus tuberculatus*) yielding valuable timber, grown chiefly in Burma,
Eri	A variety of silk-worm (Assam).

G

Ganja . .	A narcotic derived from the unfertilised flowers of the female plants of *cannabis sativa.*
Ghi (ghee) . .	Clarified butter.
Godown . . .	A warehouse.
Gur	Crude molasses.

H

Hundi (hoondee) .	An Indian bill of exchange.

J

Jainama (ja-namaz)	A pileless cotton prayer mat
Jamkalam .	A pileless cotton carpet made in Southern India.
Jaridar . .	Embroidered.
Jethwa . .	The lac crop which comes on the market in June-July, called after the corresponding Bengali month ' Jaistha '.
Jowar . .	See *cholam*

K

Kainit . . .	A mineral manure
Kala-til . . .	Niger seed, lit. ' black til ' from its resemblance to sesame or til
Kapok . . .	The floss of the white silk cotton tree (*eriodendron anfractuosum*). A Malay word.
Katki . . .	A lac crop that comes commercially into sight in November, called after the corresponding Bengali month ' Kartik '.
Kazla (kajla) . .	The commonest variety of boiled rice obtainable in Bengal
Khadder . . .	Cloth made from hand-spun yarn.
Khair . .	Cutch, obtained from the heart-wood of *acacia catechu.*
Khari . . .	Glauber's salt or sodium sulphate.
Kharif . .	The crop sown just before or during the South-West monsoon.
Khood (coodie) . .	Broken rice.
Kiri . . .	Residue left over in the manufacture of shellac, containing about 50 per cent of lac.
Kurpa (Cuddapah) .	A quality of Madras indigo sold in Calcutta
Kushmi . . .	One of the four lac crops marketed in November-December.
Kusum (oil) . .	Carthamus oil, obtained from *carthamus tinctoria*.
Kusumb . . .	A forest tree (*schleichera trijuga*) the host of the lac insect from which the best lac is derived.
Kutcha (kaccha) .	An Urdu word meaning inferior or bad.
Kuthia . . .	Inferior quality of saltpetre of from 20 to 40 per cent. refraction.

L

Lakh . . .	One hundred thousand.
Lanka . . .	A variety of tobacco grown in South India.
Let-pet . . .	Pickled tea, eaten as a condiment in Burma and the Shan States.
Lungi (Loongi) . .	A tubular piece of cloth of silk or cotton worn as a waist cloth.

M

Masula . . .	A small boat (South India).
Maddar . . .	Applied to two different varieties of plants whose roots yield a red dye.
Mahajan . . .	A money-lender or big merchant who advances money to the cultivator against his crops.
Mahua (mowra) . .	A forest tree (*bassia latifolia*) whose dried flowers are eaten as food or distilled into liquor.
Maida . . .	Wheat flour superior to atta obtained by regrinding sujji or coarse flour and passing it through fine sieves.
Masur . . .	The lentil (*lens esculenta*).
Maund (man) . .	A weight varying in different localities (see under weights and measures, p. 405.)
Mohur . . .	A gold coin (see coinage, p. 404).
Monsoon . . .	Periodical rain-bearing winds. Applied to the two rainy seasons in India: the South-West monsoon from June to September and the North East from October to December.
Muga . . .	A variety of silk-worm (Assam).
Mung . . .	A common variety of pulse (*phaseolus* radiatus).

N

Neyi . . .	The South-Indian term for *ghi*.
Numya (Noonia) .	The producer of crude, unrefined saltpetre.

O

Omam (water) . .	Liquor obtained by distillation from *carum copticum*.

P

Padauk . . .	A valuable timber tree (*pterocarpus macrocarpus*) grown in Burma.
Paka (oil) . . .	Oil obtained from the seeds of *schleichera trijuga*.
Palas . . .	See *dhak*.
Pan supari . .	The universal masticatory composed of *pan* (leaf of betel vine), and *supari* (fruit of betel palm), with an admixture of lime, cloves, etc.
Pashm . . .	The fine underwool of a species of Tibetan goat.
Pashmina . . .	Woollen cloth obtained from *pashm* wool (see above).
Pebugale . . .	The Rangoon white bean (*phaseolus lunatus*).
Phunki . . .	Lac collected after the insects have swarmed.
Pipul . . .	A sacred tree (*ficus religiosa*) an occasional host of the lac insect.
Poolah . . .	A variety of tobacco grown in Bengal.
Poonac . . .	Strictly speaking the residual cake left in the *chekkus* or mills after extracting coconut oil from copra, but also applied to linseed, gingelly and other oil cakes.
Pothi . . .	A variety of tobacco grown in South India.
Pucca . . .	An Urdu word meaning good, correct, substantial, of standard quality or measurement, as contrasted with *Kutcha*.
Putto . . .	Thick woollen cloth made from the coarser wool of the sheep.

R

Rabi . . . The spring crop sown during or after the North-East monsoon and harvested in March or April.

Raree . . . A quality of boiled brown rice, obtainable in Bengal.

S

Sal . . . . A fine timber-yielding tree (*shorea* robusta) which is also a common host of the lac insect.

Sangtara . . . A variety of loose-skinned oranges.

Sann (hemp) . . Fibre obtained from *crotalaria juncea*.

Sari . . . . A piece of cloth of varying lengths with broad coloured borders worn by Indian women.

Sarson . . . Indian colza, a subspecies of *brassica* campestris, commercially called rape.

Seer . . . . A weight or measure varying in size in diffrent parts of the country (see under weights and measures, page 405).

Shatranji . . . A pileless cotton floor mat.

Shisham . . . A timber tree (*dalbergia sissoo*).

Shiyah-zirah . . The seeds of carum indicum, the Indian caraway.

Shroff . . . A banker or money-changer.

Simal . . . The red silk cotton tree (*bombax malabaricum*).

Sindine . . . A variety of tobacco obtainable in Burma.

Sirdar . . . A headman or overseer.

Siris . . . . A forest tree (*albizzia lebbek*), a host of the lac insect.

Sujji . . . A quality of wheat flour.

T

Taluk . . A revenue sub-division of a district (Bombay, Madras and Mysore).

Tasar . . . Wild silk worms, *antheroea paphia*, also applied to the cloth made from their silk.

Tarward (tarwar) . See *avaram*.

Thindoor . . . A variety of tobacco obtainable in Burma.

Til (teel) . . . Gingelly or *sesamum indicum*, the sesame of commerce.

Tincal . . . Crude borax.

Tola . . . . The weight of a rupee equivalent to 180 grs. troy.

Toon . . . A valuable timber tree also known as the Indian mahogany (*cedrela toona*).

Toria (Tori) . . Rape (*brassica campestris*).

Z

Zamindar . . . A landholder under the Permanent Settlement.

Missing

Page

APPENDICES VIII - 443-446

APPENDIX VIII.

THE INCORPORATED OILSEED ASSOCIATION.

EXCHANGE CHAMBERS, ST. MARY AXE, LONDON, E. C. 3.

CONTRACT FOR EAST INDIAN LINSEED.

To U. K. PORTS

1933,

Pure basis—Sound Delivered. ... 3A.

London 19 .

1. this day the following Linseed, viz.—About tons say tons (of 2,240 lbs. each) shipment from during by steamer or steamers direct or indirect with or without transhipment *Via* Suez Canal.

At per ton of 2,240 lbs. net, delivered sound, *ex-ship* in including the usual 2¼ lbs B. twill bags, and/or 2¼ lbs. heavy C bags at sellers' option at an allowance to the Buyers of one-half-penny per bag

If bold Calcutta seed be appropriated, the Incorporated Oilseed Association shall decide whether the seed comes under the denomination of bold or not. The basis shall be 145 grains to the gramme, and any excess shall be allowed for at the rate of 0·15 per cent. off the Contract Price for Bold Seed for every grain over 145 up to 160 Over 160 to be considered as Ordinary Seed and to carry an allowance of 2½ per cent off the contract price for Bold Seed.

If Bombay Linseed be appropriated the seed shall be warranted to contain not more than 25 per cent of small grains, any larger proportion to be allowed for at the rate of 05 per cent for every 1 per cent. of such excess; the percentage of small grains to be ascertained by the Incorporated Oilseed Association

For the purposes of this contract the words steamer or steamers are intended to include any full powered primarily engine driven vessel.

Each shipment to be regarded as a separate contract

Should any of the within mentioned quantity form part of a larger quantity of the same bulk or mark shipped on board the vessel by the same shipper in the same or a different period of shipment no separation or distinction shall be necessary.

Bill of Lading to be proof of date of shipment in the absence of evidence to the contrary

Declaration of shipment.

2. Appropriation giving Steamer's name, date of Bill or Bills of Lading, and approximate weight shall be made by sellers in Europe (or their Agents) not later than 14 days from the date of the Bill of Lading. Any error proved to be due to a *bona fide* error in cable transmission may be rectified after receipt of documents. Appropriations from intermediate Sellers shall be accepted by Buyers although received by them after 14 days from date of Bill of Lading if from the 14th day such appropriations have been passed on without delay, and by wire if Buyers and Sellers do not reside in the same town Further particulars with marks and number of bags shall be given within seven days of arrival of the documents in Europe. Should steamer report before appropriation and extra expenses be incurred, such expenses to be paid by the sellers Buyers shall not object to slight deviations in marks so long as the seed can be identified on arrival as the *bona fide* parcel intended to be delivered on the declaration Any expenses incurred in consequence of such marks not being in accordance with the declaration shall be paid by the sellers When an appropriation is made of less quantity than 600 bags, an allowance of one shilling and six pence per ton to be made to the Buyers on such appropriation, but if the net weight delivered exceed 45 tons no allowance to be given. Provisional Invoice to be computed upon net shipping weights For the purposes of this Clause the official closing hours of business shall be 5 P.M. on week days and 12 NOON on Saturdays.

3. Payment to be made in London, on vessel's reporting in by net cash, in exchange for shipping documents and/or delivery order (the latter to be countersigned by Banker, Shipbroker, Captain or Mate if so required) and policy or policies of insurance effected with approved underwriters and/or approved letter of insurance, interest at 5 per cent., or at Bank of England rate if over 5 per cent., at 10 A.M. on day of payment, to be allowed for unexpired portion of prompt of 21 days from vessel's reporting. The original Marine Insurance shall extend to goods in lighter during the ordinary course of transit from ocean steamer to destination within the precincts of the port for a period not exceeding 15 days. After the goods have passed into possession of the buyers the Insurance documents shall be returned to the Sellers if and when required. Buyers to have the power of retaining a margin of 4 per cent. accounting for same on final settlement. Should documents be retired before vessel's reporting at port of discharge, interest to be allowed up to date of reporting at Bank of England rate on day of arrival. Interest at 5 per cent. or at average Bank of England rate if over 5 per cent. to be paid on any balance due on final invoice from date of prompt up to date of settlement. Notice to retire documents shall be given by Buyers before 11-30 A.M. on day of payment, except on Saturdays when the time shall be 10-30 A.M.

Payment.

4. Should the sellers be prevented from delivering the seed sold, or the Buyers from taking delivery, by reason of Riots, or Strikes, or Lock-outs at the place named for delivery, the time for delivery and payment shall be extended until the operation of the causes preventing delivery has ceased. Buyers to pay interest at half Bank of England rate for said extension. A strike of the receiver's men only shall not exonerate him from any demurrage for which he may be liable if by the use of reasonable diligence he could have obtained other suitable labour, and in case of any delay by reason of the before-mentioned causes, no claim for damages for such delay shall be made by the receiver of the seed.

Strikes &c.

Should the shipment of the seed sold under this contract be prevented by reason of strikes, riots, or lock-outs at spot of shipment, or on any railways feeding such port, shippers shall be entitled at the termination of such riot, strike, or lock-out, to an extension of time for shipment of as much time as was left for shipment prior to the outbreak of such riot, strike or lock-out.

In case of non-fulfilment under above conditions, the date of default shall be similarly dealt with.

Shippers shall give notice by cable within two days after the last day for shipment if he claims an extension of time of shipment.

5. Buyers to be allowed 24 hours from vessel's reporting to lodge documents and apply for delivery and the Company in whose dock the ship discharges shall be ordered by sellers to weigh 5 sound and undamaged bags in every 100 as they rise from the ship and 2 in every 100 shall be emptied to ascertain the tare (said bags being weighed together) Buyers to give the sorting orders and failing then so doing the seed to be invoiced as sound, and sweepings to be for Buyers' account. Should the seed be sorted the damaged shall be taken by Buyers with the following allowances, *viz.*—1st class damaged at 4 per cent., 2nd class at 8 per cent., 3rd class at 12 per cent., and lower class damages at a valuation, or by arbitration. Slack bags to be weighed separately. Buyers to have the option of weighing the whole of the bags and the sweepings at their own expense. If in Hull, the Corporation Sworn Meters and Weighers to be employed, or the Dock Company, at Sellers' option, and the certificate of those employed shall settle the weight to be invoiced. Buyers to have the option, to be declared previous to ship's reporting, of taking the Linseed all weighed, *ex*-quay or warehouse at Sellers' option, at landing weights, paying all current charges; prompt to be 7 days from seller's notice of being ready for delivery. The Dock Company—or if in Hull, the Corporation Sworn Meters and Weighers, or the Dock Company, at Sellers' option—shall be instructed to take a fair average sample of the bulk out of the bags emptied for taring, and to seal and forward it to the Incorporated Oil Seed Association, who upon such sample shall determine, by analysis, the quantity and description of the substance other than Linseed contained therein.

Discharge, Sampling and Analysis

Should there be no dock Company or Sworn Meters at port of discharge, samples (or sample) shall be taken and sealed jointly by Buyers' and Sellers' Agents, and shall remain under their mutual control and be deposited daily with the local Exchange Committee or similar Corporation, Harbour Master, or other independent party agreed upon (any charges incurred to be equally divided between buyers and sellers), and immediately after final discharge the whole set of samples shall be forwarded to the Incorporated Oil Seed Association. In the case of seed damaged by water samples of wet seed shall be drawn in sealed bags in the usual way for arbitration and if required by either party, duplicate samples of such wet seed shall be drawn in sealed bottles to be tested by the Incorporated Oil Seed Association for moisture content solely for the information of the arbitrators. The samples (or sample) when delivered to the Incorporated Oil Seed Association to become and be their absolute property; the charges for sampling, average weighing, taring, sorting and analysing to be divided between Buyers and Sellers Port Dues, if any, to be for Buyers' account.

Basis of Admixture.

6 The percentage of admixture having been ascertained, non-oleaginous substances shall be considered valueless, and oleaginous as worth half the Contract price of the Linseed The basis shall be pure Linseed and the Buyer shall receive an allowance equal to the percentage of admixture so ascertained. If the percentage of pure Linseed is less than 92, there shall be an additional allowance to the Buyer equal to the excess of the calculated allowance over 4 per cent

Notice of Arbitration

7. Notice of Arbitration with particulars of claim and name of Arbitrator, to be given by party claiming arbitration within 21 days from date of ship's reporting the other party to name and instruct his Arbitrator within 7 days from receipt of such notice. Intermediate Buyers and Sellers to pass on all communications within 24 hours of receipt. Such arbitration to be held within 28 days from date of certificate of analysis, unless Buyers' and Sellers' Arbitrators, or Umpire, agree to extend the time

Cancellation.

8. This contract is to be void as regards any portion shipped that may not arrive by the ship or ships declared against this Contract and also if shipment or delivery be prevented by embargo, hostilities, prohibition of export or blockage; except that if owing to any cause beyond the control of the sellers the voyage be terminated at some port other than the original destination, the parcel must be transhipped promptly at the Sellers' expense and accepted by Buyers on the original tender.

Default.

9. In default of fulfilment of contract by either party the other party at his discretion shall after giving notice in writing have the right to sell or purchase as the case may be against the defaulter who shall make good the loss if any on such sale or purchase on demand. If the party liable to pay shall be dissatisfied with the price of such sale or purchase or if the above right is not exercised the damages if any payable by the party in default shall be settled by arbitration and such damages shall be limited to the difference between contract price and market price unless the default consists of a failure by a seller to tender documents after an appropriation has been made in which case in assessing damages Arbitrators may in their absolute discretion have regard to any loss of profit or any liability incurred by Buyer under any sub contract he may be entered into. If either party shall suspend payment of his debts or commis any act of bankruptcy or being a Company shall have a Receiver appointed or go into liquidation voluntarily or otherwise (except a voluntary winding up of a solvent Company for the purpose of reconstruction) he shall be deemed to be in default and the other party shall after giving notice in writing as aforesaid and notwithstanding notice of any act of bankruptcy be entitled immediately to sell or purchase as the case may be against the party deemed to be in default and to recover against him or prove against his estate, whether wound up in bankruptcy or otherwise, any loss or shall account for any profit occasioned by or resulting from such sale or purchase.

Circle.

10 Where a seller re-purchases from his buyer or from any subsequent buyer the same goods or part thereof, a circle shall be established as regards the particular goods so re-purchased, and the provisions of the Default Clause shall not apply.

Subject to the terms of the Cancellation Clause in the Contract if the goods are not declared, or having been declared documents are not delivered, the invoices based on 96 per cent. of the Contract quantity shall be settled between each buyer and each seller in the circle by a payment by each buyer to his seller of the excess of the seller's invoice amount over the lowest invoice amount in the circle. Such settlement to be made on the last day for tendering 21 days' interest at 5 per cent per annum. Should any party in the circle suspend payment or become bankrupt, or make a composition with creditors, or being a company shall have a Reciever appointed or go into liquidation voluntarily or otherwise (except a voluntary winding up of a solvent Company for the purpose of reconstruction), the invoice amount for the goods, calculated at the market price on the last day for tendering, shall be taken as the basis of settlement instead of the lowest invoice amount in the circle, such market price to be fixed if necessary by an arbitrator or arbitrators appointed by the Executive Committee of the Incorporated Oil Seed Association. As between the buyers and sellers in the circle the non-delivery of documents by each seller to his buyer shall not be considered a breach of Contract.

Domicile &c

11. Buyers and sellers agree that, for the purpose of proceedings, either legal or by arbitration, this contract shall be deemed to have been made in England and to be performed there, any correspondence in reference to the offer, the acceptance, the place of payment or otherwise notwithstanding, and the Courts of England or Arbitrators appointed in England, as the case may be, shall, except for the purpose of enforcing any Award made in pursuance of the Arbitration Clause thereof, have exclusive jurisdiction over all disputes which may arise under this contract Such disputes shall be settled according to the law of England, whatever the domicile, residence, or place of business of the parties to this contract may be or become Any party to this contract residing or carrying on business in a foreign country shall, for the purpose of proceedings, be considered as ordinarily resident or carrying on business at the Consulate in London of the country of his residence or place of business Any party to this contract residing or carrying on business either in Scotland or Ireland or any Colony or Dependency of the United Kingdom, shall, for the purpose of such proceedings, be considered as ordinarily resident or carrying on business at the Office of the Incorporated Oil Seed Association and being a party residing or carrying on business in Scotland shall be held to have prorogated jurisdiction, as against himself, to the English Courts, and being a party residing or carrying on business in Ireland, shall be held to have submitted to the jurisdiction, and to be bound by the decision of the English Courts The service of proceedings upon a party residing or carrying on business in a foreign country, by leaving the same at such Consulate, and upon a party residing or carrying on business either in Scotland or Ireland, or in any Colony or Dependency of the United Kingdom, by leaving the same at the Offices of the Incorporated Oil Seed Association, together with the posting, in a registered cover, of a copy of such proceedings to the address abroad or in Scotland or Ireland or in any Colony or Dependency of the United Kingdom, of such party, shall be deemed good service, any rule of law or equity to the contrary notwithstanding

Arbitration

12 All disputes from time to time arising out of this Contract, including any question of Law appearing in the proceedings, whether arising between the parties hereto, or between one of the parties hereto, and the Trustee in Bankruptcy of the other party, shall be referred to arbitration according to the Rules appended to this Contract, and this stipulation may be made a Rule of any of the divisions of His Majesty's High Court of Justice in Ireland on the application of either contracting party, for the purpose of enforcing an Award against a party residing or carrying on business in Ireland Neither Buyers, Sellers, Trustee in Bankruptcy nor any other person claiming under either of them shall bring any action against the other of them in respect of any dispute until such dispute has been settled by Arbitrators, Umpire, or Committee or Board of Appeal, as the case may be, and it is expressly agreed that the obtaining an Award from either tribunal, as the case may be, shall be a condition precedent to the right of either contracting party to take any legal proceedings against the other in respect of any claim arising out of this contract All costs of or connected with the stating and argument of any Special Case for the opinion of the Court on any question of law arising in the course of the reference shall be borne and paid by the party requiring the same to be stated unless or except so far as otherwise determined by the Award to be made in the reference.

13 Should the time limited for doing any act or giving any notice expire on a **Non-Business Days** Sunday, Public Holiday, or the Saturday before any Public Holiday which shall fall on a Monday, or on any day which the Incorporated Oil Seed Association shall declare to be a non-business day, the time so limited shall be extended until the first business day thereafter

Signature

RULES

Arbitration

I. Any dispute arising out of a contract embodying these rules shall be referred to arbitration in London, each party appointing one arbitrator, who shall be a member of the Association or a partner in a member's firm, or a director of a company represented by a member, and such arbitrators shall have the power to appoint an umpire, who shall be a member of the Association, or, a partner in a member's firm, or a director of a company represented by a member, whose decision in case of disagreement is to be final.

II. The arbitration fees to be paid by the party against whom the decision is given, except when allowances are fixed by arbitration on country damaged or on seed damaged during the voyage in such cases the fees to be equally divided, also in the other cases, where, in the opinion of the referees they should be so treated. All arbitration allowances for inferior quality shall be stated in percentages and in multiples of $\frac{1}{4}$ per cent. (one quarter per cent), minimum $\frac{1}{2}$ per cent. (one half per cent).

III In the event of one of the parties refusing to appoint an arbitrator, or neglecting to do so for seven days after notice in writing of such an appointment by the other (such notice to be delivered personally or left at the usual place of business of the party so omitting to appoint), or in case the arbitrators shall not within seven days after their appointment agree to an award or appoint an umpire, or in case after the appointment of such arbitrators or umpire they or he or any of them shall die, or refuse to act, or become incapable of acting, and the party or parties with whom their or his appointment originally rested shall omit to appoint a substitute within three days after notice of such death or refusal, or incapacity, then upon application by either of the disputing parties, and provided the applicant at the same time pays to the Secretary of the Incorporated Oil Seed Association the sum of £2 2*s* 0*d* , the Executive Committee shall appoint an arbitrator or arbitrators, or umpire, who shall be members or a member of the Association, to fill the vacancy or vacancies so arising.

IV All awards by Arbitrators or an Umpire shall be in writing on an official form issued by the Secretary of the Association and the arbitrators or umpire shall have power to award the costs of and connected with the reference, and may assess the same at a fixed sum if they or he shall think fit

V. In case either party shall be dissatisfied with the award a right of appeal shall lie to the Committee of Appeal of the Incorporated Oil Seed Association provided it be claimed by notice given to the Secretary of the Association not later than 12 o'clock noon on the 14th day after the date of the award (Sundays and public holidays during that period not to count) and provided also that the Appellant at the same time pays to the Association as a fee for the appeal the sums following *viz* —If the appellant be a member or be a firm with one partner at least who is a member of the Association £21-0-0 and in any other case £26-5-0.

VI. The appeal shall be determined by a Board of Appeal consisting of four members of the Committee of Appeal of the Association in accordance with the Regulations of Association for the time being of the Incorporated Oil Seed Association, and the Rules of the Executive Committee for the time being in force. No member of the Committee of Appeal who has an interest in the matter of dispute or who has acted as arbitrator or umpire in the case and no member of the same firm or company to which either of the arbitrators or the umpire shall belong shall vote on the question of the appointment of members of the Board of Appeal or shall be appointed a member of the Board of Appeal.

VII. The parties to an arbitration or an appeal to the Committee of Appeal shall not be represented or appear by Counsel or Solicitor on the hearing of such arbitration or appeal unless in the sole discretion of the arbitrators, or umpire, as the case may be, or Board of Appeal, the case is of special importance or questions of law are likely to arise upon which the opinion of the High Court of Justice may be required.

VIII. The Board of Appeal shall confirm the award appealed from unless not less than three of the members of the Board of Appeal decide to vary such Award. The Board of Appeal may award the payment of the costs and expenses of and incidental to the appeal but the appeal fee shall follow the award unless three of the members of the Board of Appeal shall direct otherwise. The award of the Board of Appeal whether confirming or varying the original award shall be signed by two members of the Board of Appeal and countersigned by the Secretary of the Association and when so signed shall be deemed to be the award of the Board of Appeal and of the Committee of Appeal and shall be final and conclusive in all cases.

IX. No award by arbitrators or an umpire shall be questioned or invalidated on the ground that either of the arbitrators or the umpire is or was not qualified to act as provided in Rules 1 and 3 unless objection to his acting is made in writing before the hearing of such arbitration is begun and no award of a Board of Appeal shall be questioned or invalidated on the ground of any irregularity in the election of the Board of Appeal or of any of its Members or on the ground that any Member of the Board of Appeal was not eligible to serve unless objection is made in writing and established to the satisfaction of the Board of Appeal before the hearing of the Appeal is begun.

X. Any notice may be delivered personally or left at the place where the party to whom it is to be delivered is carrying on or (by reason of the provisions of the contract) is to be considered to be carrying on business.

APPENDIX IX.

List of Publications consulted in connection with the revision of the Handbook of Commercial Information for India.

Report on the Census of India, 1931.

Memorandum on Indian States, 1934

The Government of India Act, 1935.

Annual Reviews of the Trade of India.

Annual Statements of the Foreign Sea-borne Trade and Navigation of British India.

Statistical Abstracts for British India

Agricultural Statistics of India

Estimates of Area and Yield of principal crops in India.

Index Numbers of Indian prices (Quinquennial).

Wholesale prices of certain Staple Articles of Trade at selected stations in India (Quarterly)

Monthly Statistics of the production of certain selected Industries of India.

Monthly Statistics of Cotton Spinning and Weaving in Indian Mills

Monthly Survey of Business Conditions in India

Monthly Accounts relating to the Sea-borne Trade and Navigation of British India.

Accounts relating to the Coasting Trade and Navigation of British India.

Kathiawar Trade Statistics.

Trade at stations adjacent to Land Frontier Routes.

Raw Cotton Trade Statistics

Monthly Accounts relating to the Inland (Rail and River-borne) Trade of India.

The Indian Trade Journals.

International Year Book of Agricultural Statistics.

The Reports on the working of the Scheme of Preferences resulting from the Trade Agreement concluded at Ottawa between the Government of India and His Majesty's Government in the United Kingdom for fiscal years 1933-34 and 1934-35.

International Cotton Bulletins

Records of Geological Survey of India

The Indian Merchandise Marks Manual.

Report of the Indian Delegation to the Imperial Economic Conference, Ottawa, 1932

Report of Indian Tariff Board (Cotton Textile Industry Enquiry) 1927

Report of the Indian Tariff Board regarding the grant of protection to the Indian Cotton Textile Industry 1932.

Annual Statements of the Sea-borne Trade and Navigation of Burma.

Report on Cocoanut Enquiry in India by Dr. J. S. Patel.

Ceylon Trade Accounts.

Reports of the Hides Cess Enquiry Committee and Evidence Volume connected therewith.

Reports of the Indian Tariff Board on the Iron and Steel Industry, 1927 and 1934.

Report of the Royal Commission on Agriculture in India.

Indian Customs Tariff Guide.

Report of the Indian Tariff Board regarding the grant of protection to the Sericultural Industry, 1933.

Reports of the Director of Industries, Bengal and Madras Presidency on Cinchona cultivation.

Report of the Indian Tariff Board on the grant of protection to the Sugar Industry in India, 1931.

Review of the Sugar Industry in India in 1933-34 by Mr. R. C. Srivastava.

Indian Sea Customs Manual (1933 edition).

The Commercial Products of India by Sir George Watt.

Provincial Reports of the Departments of Agriculture.

Indian Central Cotton Committee Report, 1933-34.

Finance and Revenue Accounts of the Government of India.

Indian Tea Statistics.

Madras Fisheries Department Bulletin (No. 13).

Provincial Forest Administration Reports.

Indian Coal Statistics.

Annual Reports of the Chief Inspector of Mines

United Kingdom Trade Accounts

Burma Supplement to the Indian Sea Customs Manual

Annual Reports of the Government of India on the Traffic in Opium and other Dangerous Drugs.

Annual Memorandum of the Government of India on Excise (Opium) Administration in India (1931-32)

Annual Report on the operation of the Opium Department.

Government of India Note on production, consumption, import and export etc., of opium and other Dangerous Drugs in Indian States.

Annual Reports of the Northern India Salt Revenue Department.

Report of the Committee of the Indian Jute Mills Association for the year 1933.

Annual Administration Reports of the Madras Fisheries Department.

Report of the Indian Tariff Board on the Coal Industry, 1926.

Report of the Indian Coal Committee, 1925.

Indian Rubber Statistics.

Large Industrial Establishments in India

Indian Coffee Statistics.

Joint-stock Companies in British India and certain Indian States—Annual Report

Reports of the various Chambers of Commerce and Trade Associations.

Reports by the Railway Board on Indian Railways.

Report on Hemp Marketing in India by T. S. Sabins, 1931,

Annual Report of the Imperial Council of Agricultural Research, 1932-33.

INDEX

A

2 B

N

GIPD—9CD—20-8-37—7,000.